T0190464

The Springer Series on Challenges in Machine Learning

Series editors

Hugo Jair Escalante, Astrofisica Optica y Electronica, INAOE, Puebla, Mexico
Isabelle Guyon, ChaLearn, Berkeley, CA, USA
Sergio Escalera, University of Barcelona, Barcelona, Spain

The books of this innovative series collect papers written by successful competitions in machine learning. They also include analyses of the challenges, tutorial material, dataset descriptions, and pointers to data and software. Together with the websites of the challenge competitions, they offer a complete teaching toolkit and a valuable resource for engineers and scientists.

More information about this series at http://www.springer.com/series/15602

Sergio Escalera · Isabelle Guyon
Vassilis Athitsos
Editors

Gesture Recognition

 Springer

Editors
Sergio Escalera (iD)
Computer Vision Center
University of Barcelona
Barcelona
Spain

Isabelle Guyon
ChaLearn
Berkeley, CA
USA

Vassilis Athitsos
Department of Computer Science and
  Engineering
University of Texas at Arlington
Arlington, TX
USA

ISSN 2520-131X   ISSN 2520-1328   (electronic)
The Springer Series on Challenges in Machine Learning
ISBN 978-3-319-86059-6   ISBN 978-3-319-57021-1   (eBook)
DOI 10.1007/978-3-319-57021-1

Printed on acid-free paper

This Springer imprint is published by Springer Nature
The registered company is Springer International Publishing AG
The registered company address is: Gewerbestrasse 11, 6330 Cham, Switzerland

Foreword

A gesture is a form of non-verbal communication in which actions performed with the body communicates a particular message. Gestures are a fundamental aspect of human interaction, both interpersonally and in the context of human computer interaction. Gesture recognition technology is rapidly gaining popularity due to the availability of new non-invasive sensors such as Kinect, and the many driving applications in gaming, computer interaction technology, human robot interaction, security, commerce, assistive technologies and rehabilitation, sports, sign language interpreter, and gestures recognition for cars, appliances and the operating rooms of the future.

I was very pleased to be asked to write the foreword of this book, since I have been closely following the challenges and workshops on gesture recognition organized by the editors of this book. Organizing these challenges represents a significant effort from the editors, but they have created a unique dataset to explore a variety of interesting problems in machine learning, computer vision and gesture recognition. In 2011, when the first challenge was organized, there were not multi-modal and complex public databases available, and many times results were reported in proprietary dataset with varying size, difficulty and quality of labels. The organization of these public challenges that provide training/testing protocols, data and labels is fundamental to be able to analyze and compare in a fair manner gesture recognition algorithms. The book reviews some of the most promising techniques from the challenges 2011–2013 and 2014, along with several papers that broaden other aspects of gesture recognition.

A primary goal of gesture recognition algorithms is to create robust systems with the ability to identify and respond to different gestures of an individual. From a machine learning perspective detecting and recognizing a gesture from set of pre-defined gestures can be framed as a supervised event detection problem. Existing supervised methods will differ in the use of data, labels, features and models; however, there are a number of challenges that standard machine learning methods for time series analysis (e.g., DBN) have to address to build gesture recognition systems. These challenges include learning from few examples and noisy labels, dealing with the gesture's variability (e.g., duration, trajectory, appearance, shape) within and between subjects, incorporate geometric invariance (e.g., scale, rotation), learn optimal spatio-temporal representations, on-line temporal segmentation and real-time inference, robustness, and detecting the gesture with as little latency as possible. This book provides insight into all these challenges, and describes new problems and opportunities for gesture recognition, as well as describing state-of-the-art algorithms.

The first part of the book (Chaps. 1–9) reviews state of the art and covers articles that address diverse topics in gesture recognition with emphasis in machine learning methods. Three chapters focus on new machine learning methods for supervised gesture recognition. Chapter 2 presents a method to model video sequences as tensors and measure similarity between videos using product manifolds. Chapter 5 proposes a new DBN inspired by recent algorithms in language and text processing and Chap. 8 describes an appearance based method for affine invariant gesture recognition and its application to classification of sign language videos. The remaining of the chapters in the first part addresses different problems in gesture recognition. Chapter 4 proposes a method to select a set of gestures with low likelihood of false triggering. Chapter 6 describes original work on representing facial gestures by linearly combining a set of face spaces. This model is able to represent compound emotion categories. Chapter 7 presents a probabilistic method to learn models of recurring signs from multiple sign language video sequences containing the vocabulary of interest. Chapter 9 addresses the problem of parsing human poses from static images and recognizes the activities using hierarchical poselets. An important application of gesture recognition is sign language recognition, and Chap. 3 discusses sign language recognition using linguistic sub-units. All these articles give a complete picture of different researchers' efforts for this important and challenging problem.

The second part of the book consists of articles from authors participating in different challenges. Chapters 10–13 covers the methods from the participants in the 2011–2012 challenge on single user shot-learning gesture recognition with Kinect. All these methods propose different spatio-temporal descriptors (STDs) in combination with new classification schemes. Chapter 10 describes a real-time gesture recognition that combines a new STD with SVMs for on-line video segmentation and recognition. Chapter 11 encodes gestures as a Bag of Words from a sparse representation of a new STD, then it uses Dynamic Time Warping (DTW) to provide an effective method for temporal matching. Chapter 12 proposes two variants of STDs and DTW, in combination with a method to remove un-informative frames. Chapter 13 analyzes a multi-component network with motion, location, shape context and DTW that are combined for one-shot learning gesture recognition method. The book also describes some papers related to the 2013 challenge on user-independent task from continuously performed gesture using audio, skeletal, binary masks, RBG and depth information. Chapter 14 proposes a Bayesian co-boosting framework in combination with HMMs for multimodal gesture recognition. Chapter 15 presents a method for transfer learning which uses decision forests, and apply it to recognize gestures and characters. Chapter 16 presents a framework for multimodal gesture recognition that is based on a multiple hypotheses rescoring fusion scheme, including evaluation on ChaLearn multi-modal gesture recognition challenge 2013.

Chapter 17 describes an open-source C++ library for real-time gesture recognition. Chapter 18 discusses two template-based methods to learn from noisy annotations provided by crowdsourcing methods. This is a very important topic, since having access to well labeled data (i.e., consistent start/end of the gesture) is a key factor for the success of any machine learning gesture recognition method.

Finally, Chap. 19 discusses current deep learning methodologies for gesture recognition, including comparison of different architectures, fusion strategies, databases and challenges.

There has been depth research in systems for gesture recognition since the last four decades, and due to the advances in new sensors, computation and machine learning methods, I believe we are in a new age for gesture recognition. Looking forward, I can see several strands of emerging machine learning themes that are relatively unexplored such as early detection, recognition of subtle gestures, multiple instance learning type of methods to improve the quality of the labels, on-line temporal segmentation methods, and transfer learning methods for user-invariant gesture recognition. Last but not least, in the years to come we will see more and more new deep learning methods that can learn spatio-temporal representations in combination with dynamical models for temporal segmentation.

This book provides the most comprehensive and up to date review of vision-based methods for supervised gesture recognition methods that have been validated by several challenges, and touches on the most diverse topics in gesture recognition with an emphasis in machine learning methods. While the book discusses vision-based methods, many of the techniques are applicable to other sensors such as gloves, leap motion or inertial measurement units. This will surely become a "must have" book for any practitioner in gesture recognition.

Fernando de la Torre
Carnegie Mellon University, Pittsburgh, USA

Preface

In order to push research and analyze the gain of multimodal methods for gesture recognition, in the period 2011–2014, ChaLearn organized a series of challenges related to gesture recognition. Our first workshop at CVPR from our 2011 challenge emphasized mostly 2D video data meanwhile our second and third workshops at CVPR, ICPR, ICMI, ECCV conferences from our 2012, 2013, and 2014 challenges were focused on affordable 3D sensors for gesture recognition research, also including audio information. In ECCV 2014 and CVPR 2015 workshops we also promoted different aspects of looking at people, including pose recovery, activity recognition, and scene understanding where humans are present. In addition to best challenge results, many research papers devoted to gesture recognition were published and presented in our challenge workshops. Our workshops and competitions were sponsored mainly by Microsoft Research, Google, Facebook, AMAZON, NVIDIA, and Disney Research. Updates of our current and upcoming events can be found at http://gesture.chalearn.org/

In this book we present an up to date set of works related to the automatic analysis of gestures from still images and multi-modal RGB-Depth image sequences. It presents the most comprehensive and up to date review of vision-based methods for supervised gesture recognition methods that have been validated by several challenges. Several aspects of gesture recognition are reviewed, including data acquisition from different sources, feature extraction, learning, and recognition of gestures.

Chapter 1 of the book presents an up to date comprehensive analysis on Gesture recognition, defining a new taxonomy for the field. Then, the first part of the book (Chaps. 2–9) mainly focus on supervised machine learning methods for gesture recognition. The second part of the book (Chaps. 10–16) contains works related to the participants of ChaLearn challenges. Chapter 17 presents an open-source C++ library for real-time gesture recognition. Chapter 18 discusses two template-based methods to learn from noisy annotations provided by crowdsourcing methods. Finally, Chap. 19 reviews the most recent state of the art research involving deep learning architectures in order to deal with gesture and action recognition problems.

Barcelona, Spain   Sergio Escalera
Berkeley, USA   Isabelle Guyon
Arlington, USA   Vassilis Athitsos
2014

Contents

Chapter 1
Challenges in Multi-modal Gesture Recognition

Sergio Escalera⑩, **Vassilis Athitsos and Isabelle Guyon**

Abstract This paper surveys the state of the art on multimodal gesture recognition and introduces the JMLR special topic on gesture recognition 2011–2015. We began right at the start of the Kinect^{TM} revolution when inexpensive infrared cameras providing image depth recordings became available. We published papers using this technology and other more conventional methods, including regular video cameras, to record data, thus providing a good overview of uses of machine learning and computer vision using multimodal data in this area of application. Notably, we organized a series of challenges and made available several datasets we recorded for that purpose, including tens of thousands of videos, which are available to conduct further research. We also overview recent state of the art works on gesture recognition based on a proposed taxonomy for gesture recognition, discussing challenges and future lines of research.

Keywords Gesture recognition · Time series analysis · Multimodal data analysis · Computer vision · Pattern recognition · Wearable sensors · Infrared cameras · Kinect^{TM}

Editor: Zhuowen Tu.

S. Escalera (✉)
Computer Vision Center UAB and University of Barcelona, Barcelona, Spain
e-mail: sergio@maia.ub.es

V. Athitsos
University of Texas, Arlington, USA
e-mail: athitsos@uta.edu

I. Guyon
ChaLearn, Berkeley, CA, USA
e-mail: guyon@chalearn.org

1.1 Introduction

Gestures are naturally performed by humans. Gestures are produced as part of deliberate actions, signs or signals, or subconsciously revealing intentions or attitude. They may involve the motion of all parts of the body, but the arms and hands, which are essential for action and communication, are often the focus of studies. Facial expressions are also considered gestures and provide important cues in communication.

Gestures are present in most daily human actions or activities, and participate to human communication by either complementing speech or substituting themselves to spoken language in environments requiring silent communication (under water, noisy environments, secret communication, etc.) or for people with hearing disabilities. The importance of gestures in communication is rooted in primal behaviors: the gesture-first theory, supported by the analysis of mirror neurons in primates (Hewes 1973), indicated that the first steps of language phylogenetically were not speech, nor speech with gesture, but were gestures alone (McNeil 2012; Hewes 1973). See examples of primate communication by means of gestures in Fig. 1.1.

Given the indubitable importance of gestures in human activities, there has been huge interest by the Computer Vision and Machine Learning communities to analyze human gestures from visual data in order to offer new non-intrusive technological solutions. For completeness, in this paper we also review some gesture recognition systems with data acquired from wearable sensors, although the comprehensive review of papers focus on the analysis of different visual modalities.

Applications are countless, like Human Computer Interaction (HCI), Human Robot Interaction (HRI) (also named human machine interaction HMI), communication, entertainment, security, art, semiotics, commerce and sports, while having an important social impact in assistive technologies for the handicapped and the elderly. Some examples of applications are illustrated in Fig. 1.2.

In addition to the recent advances in human and gesture recognition from classical RGB visual data, the automatic analysis of human body from sensor data keeps making rapid progress with the constant improvement of (i) new published methods that constantly push the state-of-the-art and (ii) the recent availability of inexpensive

(a)   **(b)**   **(c)**   **(d)**

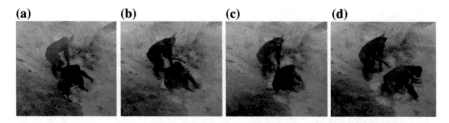

Fig. 1.1 Example of possible bonobo iconic gestures. **a** Start of swing gesture (or shove); **b** end of swing gesture (or shove); **c** start of iconic swing, other bonobo starts to move; **d** end of iconic swing, other moving. Image from McNeil (2012)

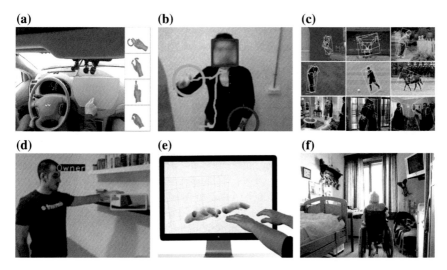

Fig. 1.2 Some applications of gesture recognition. **a** Gesture recognition for driver assistance, from Ohn-Bar and Trivedi (2014), **b** Sign Language Recognition, **c** action/gesture recognition for content retrieval and categorization, from Ma et al. (2013), **d** surveillance, **e** Human computer/robot/machine interaction, and **f** assistive technology for people with reduced autonomy

3D video sensors such as Kinect^{TM}, providing a complementary source of information, and thus allowing the computation of new discriminative feature vectors and improved recognition by means of fusion strategies. In Sect. 1.2 we review the state of the art in gesture recognition.

In order to push research and analyze the gain of multimodal methods for gesture recognition, in 2011 and 2012, ChaLearn organized a challenge on single user one-shot-learning gesture recognition with data recorded with Kinect^{TM} in which 85 teams competed. Starting from baseline methods making over 50% error (measured in Leveinshtein distance, a metric counting the number of substitutions, insertions and deletions, analogous to an error rate), the winners brought the error rate below 10%. While there was still some margin of improvement on such tasks to reach human performance (which is below 2% error), we were encouraged to make the task harder to push the state of the art in computer vision. In our second ChaLearn challenge on Multimodal Gesture Recognition in 2013, we proposed a user-independent task with data recorded with Kinect^{TM}, with a larger vocabulary and continuously performed gestures. Of 60 participating teams, the winner attained an error rate of 10% on this data set, in terms of Leveinshtein distance. In 2014, we used the same Multimodal Gesture Recognition dataset with the objective of performing gesture spotting. The winner of the competition, with a deep learning architecture, obtained an overlapping near 0.9. Lastly, in 2014 and 2015 we ran an action spotting challenge with a new dataset consisting of RGB sequences of actors performing different isolated and collaborative actions in outdoor environments. Future challenges we are planning include the analysis of gestures taking into account face and contextual information, involving many modalities in the recognition process. In this paper we also review other existing international challenges related to gesture recognition.

Our first workshop at CVPR from our 2011 challenge emphasized mostly 2D video data meanwhile our second and third workshops at CVPR, ICPR, ICMI, ECCV conferences from our 2012, 2013, and 2014 challenges were focused on affordable 3D sensors for gesture recognition research, also including audio information. In ECCV 2014 and CVPR 2015 workshops we also promoted different aspects of looking at people, including pose recovery, activity recognition, and scene understanding where humans are present. In addition to best challenge results, many research papers devoted to gesture recognition were published and presented in our challenge workshops. We also invited keynote speakers in diverse areas of pose and gesture research, including sign language recognition, body posture analysis, action and activity recognition, and facial expression or emotion recognition.

In this special topic on gesture recognition, extension of best challenge and workshop papers from previous events have been published. In addition, new description and learning strategies papers related to gesture recognition have been published. All of them will be shortly reviewed in the following sections.

The rest of the paper is organized as follows: Sect. 1.2 reviews the state of the art on gesture recognition, defining a taxonomy to describe existing works as well as available databases for gesture and action recognition. Section 1.3 describes the series of gesture and action recognition challenges organized by ChaLearn, describing the data, objectives, schedule, and achieved results by the participants. For completeness we also review other existing gesture challenge organizations. In Sect. 1.4 we review the published papers in this gesture recognition topic which are related to ChaLearn competitions. Section 1.5 describes special topic published papers related to gesture recognition which are not based on ChaLearn competitions. Finally, Sect. 1.6 discusses main observations about the published papers.

1.2   Related Work in Gesture Recognition

In this section we present a taxonomy for action/gesture recognition, we review most influential works in the field, and finally we review existing datasets for action/gesture recognition together with the performance obtained by state of the art methods.

1.2.1   Taxonomy for Gesture Recognition

Figure 1.3 is an attempt to create a taxonomy of the various components involved in conducting research in action/gesture recognition. We include various aspects relating to the problem setting, the data acquisition, the tools, the solutions, and the applications.

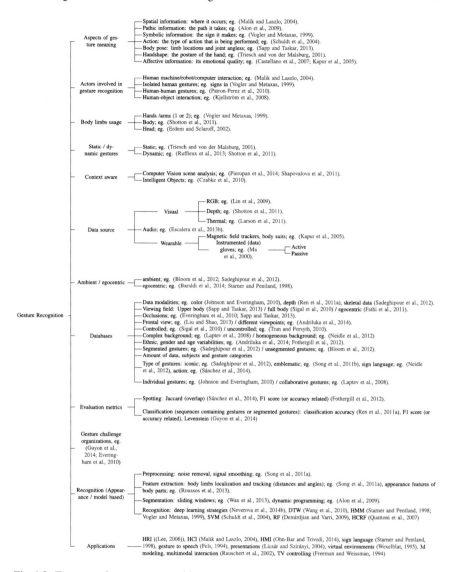

Fig. 1.3 Taxonomy for gesture recognition

First, regarding the problem setting, the interpretation of gestures critically depends on a number of factors, including the environment in which gestures are performed, their span in time and space, and the intentional meaning in terms of symbolic description and/or the subconscious meaning revealing affective/emotional states. The problem setting also involves different actors who may participate in the execution of gestures and actions: human(s) and/or machine(s) (robot, computer, etc.), performing with or without tools or interacting or not with objects. Additionally, independently of the considered modality, for some gestures/actions different parts of the body are involved. While many gesture recognition systems only focus on arms and hands, full body motion/configuration and facial expressions can also play a very important role. Another aspect of the problem setting involves whether recognized gestures are static or dynamic. For the first case, just considering features from an input frame or any other acquisition device describing spatial configuration of body limbs, a gesture can be recognized. In the second case, the trajectory and pose of body limbs provide the highest discriminative information for gesture recognition. In some settings, gestures are defined based not only on the pose and motion of the human, but also on the surrounding context, and more specifically on the objects that the human interacts with. For such settings, one approach for achieving context awareness is scene analysis, where information is extracted from the scene around the subject (e.g., Pieropan et al. 2014; Shapovalova et al. 2011). Another approach is to have the subject interact with intelligent objects. Such objects use embedded hardware and software to facilitate object recognition/localization, and in some cases to also monitor interactions between such objects and their environment (e.g., Czabke et al. 2010).

Second, the data are, of course, of very central importance, as in every machine learning application. The data sources may vary: when recognizing gestures, input data can come from different modalities, visual (RGB, 3D, or thermal, among others), audio, or wearable sensors (magnetic field trackers, instrumented (data) gloves, or body suits, among others). In the case of gloves, they can be active or passive. Active ones make use of a variety of sensors on a glove to measure the flexing of joints or the acceleration and communicates data to the host device using wired or wireless technology. Passive ones consist only of markers or colored gloves for finger detection by an external device such as a camera. Although most gestures are recognized by means of ambient intelligent systems, looking at the person from outside, some gesture recognition approaches are based on egocentric computing, using wearable sensors or wearable cameras that analyze, for instance, hand behaviors. Additionally, it is well-known that context provides rich information that can be useful to better infer the meaning of some gestures. Context information can be obtained by means of computer vision scene analysis, interaction with objects, but also via intelligent objects in the scene (objects with sensors that emit signals related to proximity and interaction). Some examples of acquisition devices are shown in Fig. 1.4.

Third, the field of gesture recognition has shaped up thanks to the adoption of standard methodology. In order to advance in the design of robust action/recognition approaches, several datasets with different complexity have been published, and several world challenges helped to push the research in the area. This required the definition of standard evaluation metrics to render methods comparable. Notably, when one wants to recognize actions/gestures from data, common steps involve pre-processing of the acquired data, feature extraction, segmentation of begin-end of gesture and its final gesture/action label classification. Many datasets include preprocessed and/or thoroughly annotated data.

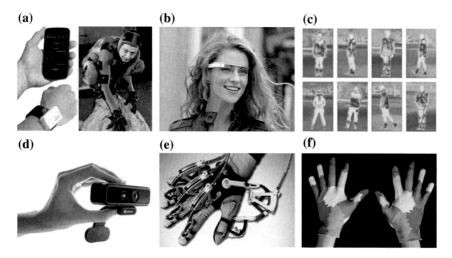

Fig. 1.4 Some examples of acquisition devices for gesture recognition. **a** *Left* mobile with GPS and accelerometer, *right* inertial sensor with accelerometer and gyroscope, **b** Google Glasses for egocentric computing, **c** thermal imagery for action recognition, **d** audio-RGB-depth device, **e** active glove, and **f** passive glove

Fourth, gesture recognition has offered many opportunities to algorithm developers to innovate. The approaches, which essentially can be categorized into appearance-based and model-based methods, are going to be reviewed in the next section. We will mention only the most influential works for action/gesture recognition illustrating various aspects of the problem setting, data acquisition, and methodology defined in our taxonomy. Note that although we defined a general taxonomy for gesture recognition, in this paper, we put special emphasis on computer vision and machine learning methods for action/gesture recognition.

Finally, our taxonomy would not be complete without the wide array of applications of gesture/action recognition, already mentioned in the introduction.

1.2.2 Overview of Gesture Recognition Methods

Different surveys have been published so far reviewing gesture recognition systems (LaViola 1999; Mitra and Acharya 2007; Chaudhary et al. 2011; Ibraheem and Khan 2012; Avci et al. 2010; Khan and Ibraheem 2012; Kausar and Javed 2011). In this section, we present an up-to-date review of most influential works in the field.

STATIC AND DYNAMIC

1.2.2.1   Recognizing Static Gestures and Hand Pose

In the case of static gestures, frequently hand shape is the important differentiating feature (Cui and Weng 2000; Freeman and Roth 1996; Kelly et al. 2010; Ren et al. 2011b; Triesch and von der Malsburg 2002), although the pose of the rest of the body can also be important, e.g., Yang et al. (2010), Van den Bergh et al. (2009). For static hand pose classification, some approaches rely on visual markers, such as a color glove with a specific color for each finger, e.g., Wang and Popović (2009). Other approaches can recognize the hand pose on unadorned hands. Appearance-based methods, like Moghaddam and Pentland (1995), Triesch and von der Malsburg (2002), Freeman and Roth (1996), Wu and Huang (2000), can be used for recognizing static hand postures observed from specific viewpoints.

Appearance and model based

Model-based methods for hand pose estimation (Oikonomidis et al. 2010, 2011; de La Gorce et al. 2011; Rehg and Kanade 1995) typically match visual observations to instances of a predefined hand model. Single frame pose estimation methods try to solve the hand pose estimation problem without relying on temporal information (Athitsos and Sclaroff 2003). Most recently, due to the advent of commercially available depth sensors, there is an increased interest in methods relying on depth data (Keskin et al. 2012; Mo and Neumann 2006; Oikonomidis et al. 2011; Pugeault and Bowden 2011; Lopes et al. 2014).

1.2.2.2   From Body Part Detection to Holistic Pattern Detection

Dynamic gestures are characterized by both the pose and the motion of the relevant body parts. Much effort has traditionally be put into detecting first **body parts** and then tracking their motion. In color videos, detecting hands can be quite challenging, although better performance can be achieved by placing additional constraints on the scene and the relative position of the subject and the hands with respect to the camera (Cui and Weng 2000; Isard and Blake 1998; Kolsch and Turk 2004; Ong and Bowden 2004; Stefanov et al. 2005; Stenger et al. 2003; Sudderth et al. 2004). Commonly-used visual cues for hand detection such as skin color, edges, motion, and background subtraction (Chen et al. 2003; Martin et al. 1998) may also fail to unambiguously locate the hands when the face, or other "hand-like" objects are moving in the background.

In Li and Kitani (2013) the authors propose a hand segmentation approach from egocentric RGB data by the combination of color and texture features. In Baraldi et al. (2014), dense features are extracted around regions selected by a new hand segmentation technique that integrates superpixel classification, temporal and spatial coherence. Bag of visual words and linear SVM are used for final representation and classification.

Depth cameras have become widely available in recent years, and hand detection (in tandem with complete body pose estimation) using such cameras (and also in combination with other visual modalities) can be performed sufficiently reliably for many applications (Shotton et al. 2011; Hernandez-Vela et al. 2012). The authors of Ren et al. (2013) propose a part-based hand gesture recognition system using Kinect^{TM} sensor. Finger-EarthMover's Distance (FEMD) metric is proposed to measure the dissimilarity between hand shapes. It matches the finger parts while not the whole hand based on hand segmentation and contour analysis. The method is tested on their own 10-gesture dataset.

Instead of estimating hand position and/or body pose before recognizing the gesture, an alternative is to customize the recognition module so that it does not require the exact knowledge of hand positions, but rather accepts as input a list of several candidate hand locations (Alon et al. 2009; Sato and Kobayashi 2002; Hernandez-Vela et al. 2013b).

Another approach is to use **global image/video features**. Such global features include motion energy images (Bobick and Davis 2001), thresholded intensity images and difference images (Dreuw et al. 2006), 3D shapes extracted by identifying areas of motion in each video frame (Gorelick et al. 2007) and histograms of pairwise distances of edge pixels (Nayak et al. 2005). Gestures can also be modelled as rigid 3D patterns (Ke et al. 2005), from which features can be extracted using 3D extensions of rectangle filters (Viola and Jones 2001). The work of Kong et al. (2015) uses pixel-level attributes in a hierarchical architecture of 3D kernel descriptors, and efficient match kernel is used to recognize gestures from depth data.

Along similar lines, Ali and Shah (2010) propose a set of kinematic features that are derived from the optical flow for human action recognition in videos: divergence, vorticity, symmetric and antisymmetric flow fields, second and third principal invariants of flow gradient and rate of strain tensor, and third principal invariant of rate of rotation tensor, which define spatiotemporal patterns. These kinematic features are computed by Principal Component Analysis (PCA). Then multiple instance learning (MIL) is applied for recognition in which each action video is represented by a bag of kinematic modes. The proposal is evaluated on the RGB Weizmann and KTH action data sets, showing comparable result to state of the art performances.

Much effort has also been put into **spatiotemporal invariant features**. In Yuan et al. (2011) the authors propose a RGB action recognition system based on a pattern matching approach, named naive Bayes mutual information maximization (NBMIM). Each action is characterized by a collection of spatiotemporal invariant features which are matched with an action class by measuring the mutual information between them. Based on this matching criterion, action detection is to localize a subvolume in the volumetric video space that has the maximum mutual information toward a specific action class. A novel spatiotemporal branch-and-bound (STBB) search algorithm is designed to efficiently find the optimal solution. Results show high recognition results on KTH, CMU, and MSR data sets, showing speed up inference in comparison with standard 3D branch-and-bound.

Another example is the paper of Derpanis et al. (2013) in which a compact local descriptor of video dynamics is proposed for action recognition in RGB data sequences. The descriptor is based on visual spacetime oriented energy measurements. An associated similarity measure is introduced that admits efficient exhaustive search for an action template, derived from a single exemplar video, across candidate video sequences. The method is speeded up by means of a GPU implementation. Method is evaluated on UCF and KTH data sets, showing comparable results to state of the art methods.

The work of Yang and Tian (2014b) presents a coding scheme to aggregate low-level descriptors into the super descriptor vector (SDV). In order to incorporate the spatio-temporal information, the super location vector (SLV) models the space-time locations of local interest points in a compact way, SDV and SLV are combined as the super sparse coding vector (SSCV) which jointly models the motion, appearance, and location cues. The approach is tested on HMDB51 and Youtube with higher performance in comparison to state of the art approaches.

1.2.2.3   Segmentation of Gestures and Gesture Spotting

Dynamic gesture recognition methods can be further categorized based on whether they make the assumption that gestures have already been segmented, so that the start frame and end frame of each gesture is known. Gesture spotting is the task of recognizing gestures in unsegmented video streams, that may contain an unknown number of gestures, as well as intervals were no gesture is being performed. Gesture spotting methods can be broadly classified into two general approaches: the direct approach, where temporal segmentation precedes recognition of the gesture class, and the indirect approach, where temporal segmentation is intertwined with recognition:

- **Direct methods** (also called heuristic segmentation) first compute low-level motion parameters such as velocity, acceleration, and trajectory curvature (Kang et al. 2004) or mid-level motion parameters such as human body activity (Kahol et al. 2004), and then look for abrupt changes (e.g., zero-crossings) in those parameters to identify candidate gesture boundaries.
- **Indirect methods** (also called recognition-based segmentation) detect gesture boundaries by finding, in the input sequence, intervals that give good recognition scores when matched with one of the gesture classes. Most indirect methods (Alon et al. 2009; Lee and Kim 1999; Oka 1998) are based on extensions of Dynamic Programming (DP) e.g., Dynamic Time Warping (DTW) (Darrell et al. 1996; Kruskal and Liberman 1983), Continuous Dynamic Programming (CDP) (Oka 1998), various forms of Hidden Markov Models (HMMs) (Brand et al. 1997; Chen et al. 2003; Stefanov et al. 2005; Lee and Kim 1999; Starner and Pentland 1998; Vogler and Metaxas 1999; Wilson and Bobick 1999), and most recently, Conditional Random Fields (Lafferty et al. 2001; Quattoni et al. 2007). Also hybrid probabilistic and dynamic programming approaches have been recently published (Hernandez-Vela et al. 2013a). In those methods, the gesture endpoint is detected by comparing the recognition likelihood score to a threshold. The threshold can be fixed or adaptively computed by a non-gesture garbage model (Lee and Kim 1999; Yang et al. 2009), equivalent to silence models in speech.

When attempting to recognize unsegmented gestures, a frequently encountered problem is the *subgesture problem*: false detection of gestures that are similar to parts of other longer gestures. Lee and Kim (1999) address this issue using heuristics to infer the user's completion intentions, such as moving the hand out of camera range or freezing the hand for a while. An alternative is proposed in Alon et al. (2009), where a learning algorithm explicitly identifies subgesture/supergesture relationships among gesture classes, from training data.

Another common approach for gesture spotting is to first extract features from each frame of the observed video, and then to provide a sliding window of those features to a recognition module, which performs the classification of the gesture (Corradini 2001; Cutler and Turk 1998; Darrell et al. 1996; Oka et al. 2002; Starner and Pentland 1998; Yang et al. 2002). Oftentimes, the extracted features describe the position and appearance of the gesturing hand or hands (Cutler and Turk 1998; Darrell et al. 1996; Starner and Pentland 1998; Yang et al. 2002). This approach can be integrated with recognition-based segmentation methods.

1.2.2.4 Action and Activity Recognition

The work of Li et al. (2010) presents an action graph to model explicitly the dynamics of 3D actions and a bag of 3D points to characterize a set of salient postures that correspond to the nodes in the action graph. The authors propose a projection based sampling scheme to sample the bag of 3D points from the depth maps. In Sminchisescu et al. (2006) it is proposed the first conditional/discriminative chain model for action recognition.

The work of Zanfir et al. (2013) propose the non-parametric Moving Pose (MP) framework for low-latency human action and activity recognition. The moving pose descriptor considers both pose information as well as differential quantities (speed and acceleration) of the human body joints within a short time window around the current frame. The descriptor is used with a modified kNN classifier that considers both the temporal location of a particular frame within the action sequence as well as the discrimination power of its moving pose descriptor compared to other frames in the training set. The method shows comparable results to state of the art methods on MSR-Action3D and MSR-DailyActivities3D data sets.

In Oreifej and Liu (2013), it is proposed a new descriptor for activity recognition from videos acquired by a depth sensor. The depth sequence is described using a histogram capturing the distribution of the surface normal orientation in the 4D space of time, depth, and spatial coordinates. To build the histogram, 4D projectors are created, which quantize the 4D space and represent the possible directions for the 4D normal. Projectors are initialized using the vertices of a regular polychoron. Projectors are refined using a discriminative density measure, such that additional projectors are induced in the directions where the 4D normals are more dense and discriminative. The proposed descriptor is tested on MSR Actions 3D, MSR Gesture 3D, and MSR Daily Activity 3D, slightly improving state of the art results.

In Wang et al. (2014), the authors propose to characterize the human actions with an "actionlet" ensemble model, which represents the interaction of a subset of human joints. Authors train an ensemble of SVM classifiers related to actionlet patterns, which includes 3D joint features, Local Occupancy Patterns, and Fourier Temporal Pyramid. Results on CMU MoCap, MSR-Action3D, MSR-DailyActivity3D, Cornell Activity, and Multiview 3D data sets show comparable and better performance than state of the art approaches.

The work of Yang and Tian (2014a) presents an approach for activity recognition in depth video sequences. Authors cluster hypersurface normals in a depth sequence to form the polynormal which is used to jointly characterize the local motion and shape information. In order to globally capture the spatial and temporal orders, an adaptive spatio-temporal pyramid is introduced to subdivide a depth video into a set of space-time grids. It is then proposed a scheme of aggregating the low-level polynormals into the super normal vector (SNV) which can be seen as a simplified version of the Fisher kernel representation. Authors validate the proposed approach on MSRAction3D, MSRDailyActivity3D, MSRGesture3D, and MSRActionPairs3D data sets slightly improving in all cases state of the art performances.

In Yu et al. (2014) the authors propose the orderlets to capture discriminative information for gesture recognition from depth maps. Orderlet features are discovered looking for frequent sets of skeleton joints that provide discriminative information. Adaboost is used for orderlets selection. Results on the ORGBD data set shows a recognition rate of 71.4% mean class average accuracy, improving by near 5% state of the art results on this data set, and near 20% improvement regarding frame level classification. However the results showed on the MSR-DailyActivity3D data set are inferior to the ones reported in Luo et al. (2014).

The work of Liang et al. (2014) presents a depth-based method for hand detection and pose recognition by segmentation of different hand parts. Authors based on RF for initial multipart hand segmentation. Then, a Superpixel-Markov Random Field (SMRF) parsing scheme is used to enforce the spatial smoothness and the label co-occurrence prior to remove the misclassified regions.

1.2.2.5 Approaches Using Non-video Modalities and Multimodal Approaches

In terms of multimodal approaches for gesture recognition, Luo et al. (2014) propose a sparse coding-based temporal pyramid matching approach (ScTPM) for feature representation using depth maps. The authors also propose the Center-Symmetric Motion Local Ternary Pattern (CS-Mltp) descriptor to capture spatial-temporal features from RGB videos. By fusing both RGB and Depth descriptors, the authors improve state of the art results on MSR-Action3D and MSR-DailyActivity3D data sets, with a 6 and 7% of improvement, respectively.

In Ionescu et al. (2014), it is presented the Human 3.6M data set, consisting of 3.6 Million accurate 3D Human poses, acquired by recording the performance of 5 female and 6 male subjects, under 4 different viewpoints, for training realistic human sensing systems and for evaluating the next generation of human pose estimation models and algorithms. Authors also provide a set of large scale statistical models and evaluation baselines for the dataset illustrating its diversity.

In Xiao et al. (2014) a wearable Immersion CyberGlove II is used to capture the hand posture and the vision-based Microsoft Kinect™ takes charge of capturing the head and arm posture. An effective and real-time human gesture recognition algorithm is also proposed.

In Liang et al. (2013) it is proposed to detect and segment different body parts using RGB and Depth data sequences. The method uses both temporal constraints and spatial features, and performs hand parsing and 3D fingertip localization for hand pose estimation. The hand parsing algorithm incorporates a spatial-temporal feature into a Bayesian inference framework to assign the correct label to each image pixel. The 3D fingertip localization algorithm adapts is based on geodesic extrema extraction to fingertip detection. The detected 3D fingertip locations are finally used for hand pose estimation with an inverse kinematics solver. The work of Joshi et al. (2015) use random forest for both segmenting and classifying gesture categories from data coming from different sensors.

Although many works base only on inertial data (Benbasat and Paradiso 2001; Berlemont et al. 2015), multimodal approaches are often considered in order to combine trajectory information will pose analysis based on visual data. The works of Liu et al. (2014) and Pardo et al. (2013) present approaches for gesture recognition based on the combination of depth and inertial data. In Liu et al. (2014) skeleton obtained from depth data and data from inertial sensors are train within HMM in order to perform hand gesture recognition. A similar approach is presented in Pardo et al. (2013), but also recognizing objects present in the scene and using DTW for recognition with the objective of performing ambient intelligent analysis to support people with reduced autonomy. In Gowing et al. (2014), it is presented a comparison of WIMU aWireless/Wearable Inertial Measurement Unit and Kinect™. However, comparison is performed independently, without considering a fusion strategy.

The work of Appenrodt et al. (2009) is one of the few that compare the performance of different segmentation approaches for gesture recognition comparing RGB, depth, and thermal modalities. They propose a simple segmentation approach of faces and one hand for recognizing letters and numbers for HCI. They obtained higher performance by the use of depth maps. Unfortunately no mutimodal fusion approaches are tested in order to analyze when each modality can complement the information provided by the rest of modalities.

The work of Escalera et al. (2013b) summarizes a 2013 challenge on multimodal gesture recognition, where in addition to RGB and depth data, audio can be used to identify the performed gestures.

Few works considered context information in order to improve gesture/action recognition systems. In Wilhelm (2012) it is proposed to adapt gesture recognition based on a dialogue manager as a partially observable Markov decision process (POMDP). In Caon et al. (2011) two Kinect™ devices and smart objects are used to estimate proximity and adapt the recognition prior of some gestures.

The recent emergence of deep learning systems in computer vision have also been applied to action/gesture recognition systems. In Neverova et al. (2014a), it is presented a deep learning based approach for hand pose estimation, targeting gesture recognition. The method integrates local and global structural information into the training objective. In Nagi et al. (2011), deep neural network (NN) combining convolution and max-pooling (MPCNN) is proposed for supervised feature learning and classification of RGB hand gestures given by humans to mobile robots using colored gloves. The hand contour is retrieved by color segmentation, then smoothed by morphological image processing which eliminates noisy edges. The system classifies 6 gesture classes with 96% accuracy, improving performance of several state of the art methods. The work of Duffner et al. (2014) presents an approach that classifies 3D gestures using jointly accelerometer and gyroscope signals from a mobile device using convolutional neural network with a specific structure involving a combination of 1D convolution. In Molchanov et al. (2015) convolutional deep neural networks are used to fuse data from multiple sensors (short-range radar, a color camera, and a depth camera) and to classify the gestures in a driver assistance scenario.

1.2.3 Sign Language Recognition

An important application of gesture recognition is sign language recognition. American Sign Language (ASL) is used by 500,000 to two million people in the U.S. (Lane et al. 1996; Schein 1989). Overall, national and local sign languages are used all over the world as the natural means of communication in deaf communities.

Several methods exist for recognizing isolated signs, as well as continuous signing. Some researchers have reported results on continuous signing with vocabularies of thousands of signs, using input from digital gloves, e.g., Yao et al. (2006). However, glove-based interfaces are typically expensive for adoption by the general public, as well as intrusive, since the user has to wear one or two gloves connected with wires to a computer.

Computer vision methods for sign language recognition offer hope for cheaper, non-intrusive interfaces compared to methods using digital gloves. Several such methods have been proposed (Bauer et al. 2000; Cui and Weng 2000; Dreuw et al. 2006; Kadir et al. 2004; Starner and Pentland 1998; Vogler and Metaxas 1999; Wang et al. 2010; Zieren and Kraiss 2005). However, computer vision methods typically report lower accuracies compared to methods using digital gloves, due to the difficulty of extracting accurate information about the articulated pose and motion of the signer.

An important constraint limiting the accuracy of computer vision methods is the availability of training data. Using more examples per sign typically improves accuracy (see, e.g., Kadir et al. 2004; Zieren and Kraiss 2005). However, existing datasets covering large vocabularies have only a limited number of examples per sign. As an example, the ASLLVD dataset (Athitsos et al. 2008) includes about 3,000 signs, but only two examples are available for most of the signs. Some interesting research has aimed at enabling automated construction of large datasets. For example, Cooper and Bowden (2009) aim at automatically generating large corpora by automatically segmenting signs from close-captioned sign language videos. As another example,

Farhadi et al. (2007) propose a method where sign models are learned using avatar-produced data, and then transfer learning is used to create models adapted for specific human signers.

The recent availability of depth cameras such as Kinect™ has changed the methodology and improved performance. Depth cameras provide valuable 3D information about the position and trajectory of hands in signing. Furthermore, detection and tracking of articulated human motion is significantly more accurate in depth video than in color video. Several approaches have been published in recent years that use depth cameras to improve accuracy in sign language recognition (Conly et al. 2015; Wang et al. 2015a; Zafrulla et al. 2011).

1.2.4 Data Sets for Gesture and Action Recognition

Tens of gesture recognition datasets have been made available to the research community over the last several years. A summary of available datasets is provided in Table 1.1. In that table, for each data set we mark some important attributes of the dataset, such as the type of gestures it contains, the data modalities it provides, the viewing field, background, amount of data, and so on. Regarding the "occlusions" attribute in that table, we should clarify that it only refers to occlusions of the subject by other objects (or subjects), and not to self occlusions. Self occlusions are quite common in gestures, and are observed in most datasets. We should also note that, regarding the complexity of the background, dynamic and/or cluttered backgrounds can make gesture recognition challenging in color images and video. At the same time, a complex background can be quite easy to segment if depth or skeletal information is available, as is the case in several datasets on Table 1.1.

In order to be able to fit Table 1.1 in a single page, we had to use abbreviations quite heavily. Table 1.2 defines the different acronyms and abbreviations used in Table 1.1.

The datasets we have created for our challenges have certain unique characteristics, that differentiate them from other existing datasets. The CDG2011 dataset (Guyon et al. 2014) has a quite diverse collection of gesture types, including static, pantomime, dance, signs, and activities. This is in contrast to other datasets, that typically focus on only one or maybe two gesture types. Furthermore, the CDG2011 dataset uses an evaluation protocol that emphasizes one-shot learning, whereas existing data sets typically have several training examples for each class. The CDG2013 dataset introduces audio data to the mix of color and depth that is available in some other data sets, such as Sadeghipour et al. (2012) and Bloom et al. (2012).

Table 1.1 Datasets

Dataset	Actors/objects	Body parts	Static/dynamic	Modalities	Viewing field	Occl.	Viewp. Var.	Controlled	Background	Variab.	Seg.	Amount	Subjects	Classes	Type	Indiv/collab.	Eval.
HUMANEVA (Sigal et al. 2010)	IH	F	SF	MC,ST	F	No	V	C	SF,C	E,G	SF	40000 F	5	CBP	BP	I	MPJPE
Human3.6M (Ionescu et al. 2014)	IH,O	F	SF	MC,D,ST	F	No	V	C	SF,C	G,AU,EU	SF	3.6M	11	CBP	BP	I	Multiple
LEEDS SPORTS (Johnson and Everingham 2010)	IH,O	F	SF	C	F	No	V	U	C,SF	AY,E,G	SF	2000 F	UI	CBP	BP	I	Fer.
Pascal VOC people (Everingham et al. 2010)	IH,HH,O	F	SF	C	F	Some	V	U	C,SF	A,E,G	SF	632 F	UI	CBP	BP	B	Pascal
UIUC People (Tran and Forsyth 2010)	IH,O	F	SF	C	F	No	V	U	C,SF	AY,E,G	SF	593 F	UI	CBP	BP	I	Fer.
Buffy (Ferrari et al. 2008)	IH,HH,O	U	SF	C	U	Some	V	U	C,SF	AY,G	SF	748 F	UM	CBP	BP	B	Fer.
Parse (Ramanan 2006)	IH,O	F	SF	C	F	No	V	U	C,SF	AY,E,G	SF	305 F	UI	CBP	BP	MI	Ram.
MPII Pose (Andriluka et al. 2014)	IH,O	F	SF	C	F	Yes	V	U	C,SF	A,E,G	SF	25000 F	UI	CBP	BP	MI	Fer.
FLIC Pose (Sapp and Taskar 2013)	IH,HH,O	U	SF	C	U	Some	V	U	C,SF	AY,E,G	SF	5003 F	UM	CBP	BP	MI	Sap.
H3D (Bourdev and Malik 2009)	IH,HH,O	U	SF	C	U	Some	V	U	C,SF	A,E,G	SF	520 F	US	CBP	BP	MI	Sap.
CDG2011 (Guyon et al. 2014)	IH	Mixed	Mixed	C,D	MU	Few	Fixed	C	ST,C	E,G	No	50000 G	20	CDG11	Mixed	I	L
CDG2013 (Escalera et al. 2013b)	IH	H	Dynamic	A,C,D,ST	U	No	F	C	ST,C	G	No	13858 G	27	20	E	I	L
3DIG (Sadeghipour et al. 2012)	IH	H	Dynamic	C,D,ST	U	No	F	C	ST,U	AY,E,G	Yes	1739 G	29	20	I	I	F
HuPBA8K+ (Sánchez et al. 2014)	IH,HH	F	Dynamic	C	F	Yes	Fixed	C	ST,U	G, AY	No	8000 F	14	1	A	B	L
HOHA (Laptev et al. 2008)	IH,HH,HO	F	Dynamic	C	F	Some	V	U	SD,C	AY,E,G	Yes	475 V	UM	8	A	B	CA
KTH (Schuldt et al. 2004)	IH	F	Dynamic	G	F	No	SV	C	ST,U	G	Yes	2391 A	25	6	A	I	CA

(continued)

Table 1.1 (continued)

Dataset	Actors/ objects	Body parts	Static/ dynamic	Modalities	Viewing field	Occl.	Viewp. Var.	Controlled	Background	Variab.	Seg.	Amount	Subjects	Classes	Type	Indiv/ collab.	Eval.
MSRC-12 (Fothergill et al. 2012)	IH	F	Dynamic	ST	F	No	F	C	N/A	A,E,G	No	719359 F	30	12	E,I	I	F
G3D (Bloom et al. 2012)	IH	F	Dynamic	C,D,ST	F	No	Fixed	C	ST,C	U	No	80000 F	10	20	A	I	F
ASLLVD (Neidle et al. 2012)	IH	H	Dynamic	MC	U	No	F	C	ST,U	G	Yes	9794 G	6	3314	S	I	RRC
UTA ASL (Conly et al. 2013)	IH	H	Dynamic	C,D	U	No	F	C	ST,U	E,A	Yes	1313 G	2	1113	S	I	RCC
ChAirGest (Ruffieux et al. 2013)	IH	H	Dynamic	ChAir	U	No	F	C	ST,C	U	No	1200 G	10	10	L,E	I	F,ATSR
SKIG (Liu and Shao 2013)	IH	H	Dynamic	C,D	A	No	F	C	ST,CU	U	Yes	1080 G	10	6	L,E	I	CA
6DMG (Chen et al. 2012)	IH	H	Dynamic	6DMG	H	No	F	C	N/A	G,A,U,EU	Yes	5600 G	28	20	I	I	CA
MSRGesture3D (Kurakin et al. 2012)	IH	H	Dynamic	B	H	No	Fixed	C	N/A	U	Yes	336 G	10	12	S	I	CA
NATOPS (Song et al. 2011)	IH	U	Dynamic	S,D,B	U	No	Fixed	C	ST,U	U	Yes	9600 G	20	24	E	I	CA
NTU Dataset (Ren et al. 2011a)	IH	H	Static	C,D	U	No	F	C	SF,C	G	SF	1000 G	10	10	HS	I	CA
Keck Gesture (Lin et al. 2009)	IH	H	Dynamic	C	F	No	F	C	ST,U	No	Yes	294 G	3	14	E	I	CA
Cambridge Gesture (Kim et al. 2007)	IH	H	Dynamic	C	H	No	F	C	ST,U	U	Yes	900 G	2	9	E	I	CA
(Triesch and von der Malsburg 2001)	IH	H	Static	G	H	No	Fixed	C	SF,CU	U	SF	717 G	24	10	HS	I	CA
Dataset	Modalities	Upper/	Occl.	Viewp.	Controlled	Background	Variab.	Seg.	Amount	Subjects	Classes	Type	Collab.	Eval.			

Occl. occlusions, *View. variab.* viewpoint variabilities, *Variab.* variabilities in gender, age, ethnicity, *Seg.* segmented, *Indiv/Collab.* individual or collaborative gestures, *Type* gesture type, *Eval.* evaluation

Table 1.2 Acronyms and abbreviations used in the table of datasets

Taxonomy attribute	Acronym/abbreviation	Meaning
Actors/objects	HH	Human–human interactions
Actors/objects	IH	Isolated human
Actors/objects	O	Humans with objects
Body parts	F	Full body
Body parts	H	Hands
Static/dynamic	SF	Subjects are in motion, but each frame is individually classified
Modalities	6DMG	WorldViz PPT-X4 (position + 3D orientation) + Wii Remote Plus (acceleration and angular speeds)
Modalities	A	Audio
Modalities	B	Binary segmentation mask
Modalities	C	RGB (color)
Modalities	ChAir	RGB, depth, skeletal, four inertial motion units
Modalities	D	Depth
Modalities	G	Grayscale
Modalities	MC	Multiple cameras
Modalities	S	Stereo images
Modalities	ST	Skeletal tracking
Viewing field	A	Arm and hand
Viewing field	E	Egocentric
Viewing field	F	Full body
Viewing field	MU	Upper body in most cases
Viewing field	U	Upper body
Occlusions		
Viewpoints	F	Frontal
Viewpoints	Fixed	Fixed viewpoint for each class
Viewpoints	SV	Fixed viewpoint for some classes, variable for other classes
Viewpoints	V	Variable viewpoint
Controlled/uncontrolled	C	Controlled
Controlled/uncontrolled	U	Uncontrolled
Background	CU	Some cluttered, some uncluttered
Background	C	Cluttered
Background	D	Dynamic

(continued)

Table 1.2 (continued)

Taxonomy attribute	Acronym/ abbreviation	Meaning
Background	SF	Each frame is individually classified, so background is seen only from a single frame
Background	SD	Static in some cases, dynamic in some cases
Background	ST	Static
Background	U	Uncluttered
Variabilities in gender/age/ethnicity	A	Variabilities in age
Variabilities in gender/age/ethnicity	AU	Unspecified whether there are variabilities in age
Variabilities in gender/age/ethnicity	AY	Mostly non-senior adults
Variabilities in gender/age/ethnicity	E	Variabilities in ethnicity
Variabilities in gender/age/ethnicity	EU	Unspecified whether there are variabilities in ethnicity
Variabilities in gender/age/ethnicity	G	variabilities in gender
Variabilities in gender/age/ethnicity	U	Unspecified
Segmented/unsegmented	SF	Each frame is individually classified
Amount of data	A	action samples
Amount of data	F	Frames
Amount of data	G	gesture samples
Amount of data	V	Video clips
Number of subjects	U1	Unspecified, but most subjects appear in only one sample
Number of subjects	UM	Unspecified, but most subjects appear in several samples
Number of subjects	US	Unspecified, but some subjects appear in more than one sample
Classes	CBP	Continuous space of body
Classes	CDG11	about 300, but broken into subsets of 8–12 classes
Gesture type	A	Action
Gesture type	BP	Body pose
Gesture type	D	Deictic
Gesture type	E	Emblematic
Gesture type	HS	Handshape
Gesture type	I	Iconic
Gesture type	S	Sign

(continued)

Table 1.2 (continued)

Taxonomy attribute	Acronym/ abbreviation	Meaning
Individual or collaborative	B	Both individual and collaborative
Individual or collaborative	C	Collaborative
Individual or collaborative	I	Individual
Individual or collaborative	MI	mostly individual
Evaluation criteria	ATSR	Defined in (Ruffieux et al. 2013), based on difference between detected and ground truth endpoints, normalized by duration of the gesture
Evaluation criteria	CA	Classification accuracy
Evaluation criteria	F	F-Score
Evaluation criteria	Fer.	Defined in (Ferrari et al. 2008), checks if detected endpoints are within distance of half length (of the body part in question) from the ground truth position
Evaluation criteria	L	Levenshtein distance
Evaluation criteria	MPJPE	Mean per-joint position error (measured as Euclidean distance)
Evaluation criteria	Pascal	At least 50% overlap of bounding boxes on all body parts
Evaluation criteria	Ram.	Defined in (Ramanan 2006), average negative log likelihood of correct pose
Evaluation criteria	RCC	Defined in (Wang et al. 2010), based on rank of the correct class for each test sign For any R, report percentage of test signs for which the correct class was in the top R classes
Evaluation criteria	Sap.	Defined in Sapp and Taskar (2013), Accuracy is based on (variable) threshold pixel distance between joint location and ground truth, scaled so that the torso length in the ground truth 100 pixels

1.3 Gesture Recognition Challenges

In this section we review the series of gesture and action recognition challenges organized by ChaLearn from 2011 to 2015, as well as other international challenges related to gesture recognition.

1.3.1 First ChaLearn Gesture Recognition Challenge (2011–2012): One Shot Learning

ChaLearn launched in 2012 a challenge with prizes donated by Microsoft using datasets described in Guyon et al. (2014). We organized two rounds in conjunction with the CVPR conference (Providence, Rhode Island, USA, June 2012) and the ICPR conference (Tsukuba, Japan, November 2012). Details on the challenge setting and results are found in Guyon et al. (2013). We briefly summarize the setting and results.

1.3.1.1 2011–2012 Challenge Protocol and Evaluation

The task of the challenge was to built a learning system capable of learning a gesture classification problem from a **single training example** per class, from dynamic video data complemented by a depth map obtained with Kinect^{TM}. The rationale behind this setting is that, in many computer interface applications to gesture recognition, users want to customize the interface to use their own gestures. Therefore they should be able to retrain the interface using a small vocabulary of their own gestures. We have also experimented with other use cases in gaming and teaching gesture vocabularies. Additionally, the problem of one-shot-learning is of intrinsic interest in machine learning and the solutions deviced could carry over to other applications. It is in a certain way an extreme case of transfer learning.

To implement this setting in the challenge, we collected a large dataset consisting of batches, each batch corresponding to the video recording of short sequences of gestures performed by the same person. The gestures in one batch pertained to a small vocabulary of gestures taken from a variety of application domains (sign language for the deaf, traffic signals, pantomimes, dance postures, etc.). During the development phase, the participants had access to hundreds of batches of diverse gesture vocabularies. This played the role of "source domain data" in the transfer learning task. The goal of the participants was to get ready to receive new batches from different gesture performers and different gesture vocabularies, playing the role of "transfer domain data". Their system would then need to learn from a single example of gesture performed by the particular performer, before being capable of recognizing the rest of the gestures in that batch. The full dataset is available from http://gesture.chalearn.org/data.

More specifically, each batch was split into a training set (of one example for each gesture) and a test set of short sequences of one to 5 gestures. Each batch contained gestures from a different small vocabulary of 8–12 gestures, for instance diving signals, signs of American Sign Language representing small animals, Italian gestures, etc. The test data labels were provided for the development data only (source domain data), so the participants could self-evaluate their systems and pre-train parts of it as is expected from transfer learning methods. The data also included 20 validation batches and 20 final evaluation batches as transfer domain data used by the organizers to evaluate the participants. In those batches, only the labels of the training gestures (one example each) was provided, the rest of the gesture sequences were unlabelled and the goal of the participants was to predict those labels. We used the Kaggle platform to manage submissions[1] The participants received immediate feedback on validation data on a on-line leaderboard. The final evaluation was carried out on the final evaluation data, and those results were only revealed after the challenge was over. The participants had a few days to train their systems and upload their predictions. Prior to the end of the development phase, the participants were invited to submit executable software for their best learning system to a software vault. This allowed the competition organizers to check their results and ensure the fairness of the competition.

To compare prediction labels for gesture sequences to the truth values, we used the generalized Levenshtein distances (each gesture counting as one token). The final evaluation score was computed as the sum of such distances for all test sequences, divided by the total number of gestures in the test batch. This score is analogous to an error rate. However, it can exceed one. Specifically, for each video, the participants provided an ordered list of labels R corresponding to the recognized gestures. We compared this list to the corresponding list of labels T in the prescribed list of gestures that the user had to play. These are the "true" gesture labels (provided that the users did not make mistakes). We computed the generalized Levenshtein distance $L(R, T)$, that is the minimum number of edit operations (substitution, insertion, or deletion) that one has to perform to go from R to T (or vice versa). The Levenhstein distance is also known as "edit distance". For example: $L([124], [32]) = 2$; $L([1], [2]) = 1$; $L([222], [2]) = 2$.

We provided code to browse though the data, a library of computer vision and machine learning techniques written in Matlab featuring examples drawn from the challenge datasets, and an end-to-end baseline system capable of processing challenge data and producing a sample submission. The competition pushed the state of the art considerably. The participants narrowed down the gap in performance between the baseline recognition system initially provided ($\simeq 60\%$ error) and human performance ($\simeq 2\%$ error) by reaching $\simeq 7\%$ error in the second round of the challenge. There remains still much room for improvement, particularly to recognize static postures and subtle finger positions.

---

[1]For round 1: http://www.kaggle.com/c/GestureChallenge. For round 2: http://www.kaggle.com/c/GestureChallenge2.

1.3.1.2 2011–2012 Challenge Data

The datasets are described in details in a companion paper (Guyon et al. 2014). Briefly, the data are organized in batches: development batches devel01–480, validation batches valid01–20, and final evaluation batches final01–20 (for round 1) and final21–40 (for round 2). For the development batches, we provided all the labels. To evaluate the performances on "one-shot-learning" tasks, the valid and final batches were provided with labels only for **one example of each gesture class** in each batch (training examples). The goal was to automatically predict the gesture labels for the remaining unlabelled gesture sequences (test examples).

Each batch includes 100 recorded gestures grouped in sequences of 1–5 gestures performed by the same user. The gestures are drawn from a small vocabulary of 8–12 unique gestures, which we call a "lexicon". For instance a gesture vocabulary may consist of the signs to referee volleyball games or the signs to represent small animals in the sign language for the deaf. We selected lexicons from nine categories corresponding to various settings or application domains (Fig. 1.5):

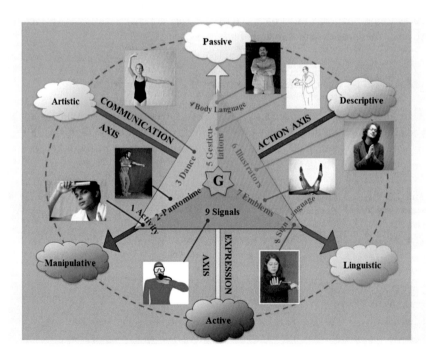

Fig. 1.5 Types of gestures. We created a classification of gesture types according to purpose defined by three complementary axes: communication, expression and action. We selected 85 gesture vocabularies, including Italian gestures, Indian Mudras, Sign language for the deaf, diving signals, pantomimes, and body language

1. **Body language** gestures (like scratching your head, crossing your arms).
2. **Gesticulations** performed to accompany speech.
3. **Illustrators** (like Italian gestures).
4. **Emblems** (like Indian Mudras).
5. **Signs** (from sign languages for the deaf).
6. **Signals** (like referee signals, diving signals, or Marshalling signals to guide machinery or vehicle).
7. **Actions** (like drinking or writing).
8. **Pantomimes** (gestures made to mimic actions).
9. **Dance postures**.

During the challenge, we did not disclose the identity of the lexicons and of the users.

1.3.1.3 2011–2012 Challenge Results

The results of the top ranking participants were checked by the organizers who reproduced their results using the code provided by the participants before they had access to the final evaluation data. All of them passed successfully the verification process. These results are shown in Tables 1.3 and 1.4.

1.3.1.4 2011–2012 Challenge, Summary of the Winner Methods

The results of the challenge are analyzed in details, based on papers published in this special topic and on descriptions provided by the top ranking participants in their fact sheets (Guyon et al. 2013). We briefly summarize notable methods below.

Table 1.3 Results of round 1. In round 1 the baseline method was a simple template matching method (see text). For comparison, we show the results on the final set number 2 not available in round 1

Team	Public score on validation set	Private score on final set #1	For comparison score on final set #2
Alfnie	0.1426	0.0996	0.0915
Pennect	0.1797	0.1652	0.1231
OneMillionMonkeys	0.2697	0.1685	0.1819
Immortals	0.2543	0.1846	0.1853
Zonga	0.2714	0.2303	0.2190
Balazs Godeny	0.2637	0.2314	0.2679
SkyNet	0.2825	0.2330	0.1841
XiaoZhuwWudi	0.2930	0.2564	0.2607
Baseline method 1	0.5976	0.6251	0.5646

Table 1.4   Results of round 2. In round 2, the baseline method was the "Principal Motion" method (see text)

Team	Public score on validation set	For comparison score on final set #1	Private score on final set #2
Alfnie	0.0951	0.0734	0.0710
Turtle Tamers	0.2001	0.1702	0.1098
Joewan	0.1669	0.1680	0.1448
Wayne Zhang	0.2814	0.2303	0.1846
Manavender	0.2310	0.2163	0.1608
HIT CS	0.1763	0.2825	0.2008
Vigilant	0.3090	0.2809	0.2235
Baseline method 2	0.3814	0.2997	0.3172

The winner of both rounds (Alfonso Nieto Castañon of Spain, a.k.a. alfnie) used a novel technique called "Motion Signature analyses", inspired by the neural mechanisms underlying information processing in the visual system. This is an unpublished method using a sliding window to perform simultaneously recognition and temporal segmentation, based solely on depth images. The method, described by the authors as a "Bayesian network", is similar to a Hidden Markov Model (HMM). It performs simultaneous recognition and segmentation using the Viterbi algorithm. The pre-processing steps include Wavelet filtering replacement of missing values and outlier detection. Notably, this method is one of the fastest despite the fact that he implemented it in Matlab (close to real time on a regular laptop). The author claims that it has linear complexity in image size, number of frames, and number of training examples.

The second best ranked participants (team Pennect of Universit of Pennsylvania, USA, in round 1 and team Turtle Tamers of Slovakia, in round 2) used very similar methods and performed similarly. The second team published their results in this special topic (Konecny and Hagara 2014). Both methods are based on an HMM-style model using HOG/HOF features to represent movie frames. They differ in that Pennect used RGB images only while Turtle Tamers used both RGB and depth. Another difference is that Pennect used HOG/HOF features at 3 different scales while Turtle Tamers created a bag of features using K-means clustering from only 40×40 resolution and 16 orientation bins. Pennect trained a one-versus-all linear classifier for each frame in every model and used the discriminant value as a local state score for the HMM while Turtle Tamers used a quadratic-chi kernel metric for comparing pairs of frames in the training and test movie. As preprocessing, Pennect uses mean subtraction and compensates for body translations while Turtle Tamers replaces the missing values by the median of neighboring values. Both teams claim a linear complexity in number of frames, number of training examples, and image size. They both provided Matlab software that processes all the batches of the final test set on a regular laptop in a few hours.

The next best ranked participants (who won **third place in round 2**), the Joewan team, who published in this special topic (Wan et al. 2013), used a slightly different approach. They relied on the motion segmentation method provided by the organizers to pre-segment videos. They then represented each video as a bag of 3D MOSIFT features (integrating RGB and depth data), and then used a nearest neighbor classifier. Their algorithm is super-quadratic in image size, linear in number of frames per video, and linear in number of training examples. The method is rather slow and takes over a day to process all the batches of the final test set on a regular laptop.

The third best ranked team in round 1 (OneMillionMonkeys) also used an HMM in which a state is created for each frame of the gesture exemplars. This data representation is based on edge detection in each frame. Edges are associated with several attributes including the X/Y coordinates, their orientation, their sharpness, their depth and location in an area of change. To provide a local state score to the HMM for test frames, OneMillionMonkeys calculated the joint probability of all the nearest neighbors in training frames using a Gaussian model. The system works exclusively from the depth images. The system is one of the slowest proposed. Its processing speed is linear in number of training examples but quadratic in image size and number of frames per video. The method is rather slow and takes over a day to process all the batches of the final test set on a regular laptop.

Methods robust against translation include those of Joewan (Wan et al. 2013) and Immortals/Manavender (this is the same author under two different pseudonyms for round 1 and round 2). The team Immortals/Manavender published their method in this special topic (Malgireddy et al. 2013). Their representations are based on a bag of visual words, inspired by techniques used in action recognition (Laptev 2005). Such representations are inherently shift invariant. The slight performance loss in translated data may be due to partial occlusions.

Although the team Zonga did not end up ranking among top ranking participants, the authors, who published their method in this special topic, proposed a very original method and ended up winning the best paper award. Notably, their outperformed all baseline methods early on in the challenge by applying their method without tuning it to the tasks of the challenge and remained at the top of the leaderboard for several weeks. The used a novel technique based on tensor geometry, which provides a data representation exhibiting desirable invariances and yields a very discriminating structure for action recognition.

ChaLearn also organized demonstration competitions of gesture recognition systems using Kinect™, in conjunction with those events. Novel data representations were proposed to tackle with success, in real time, the problem of hand and finger posture recognition. The demonstration competition winners showed systems capable of accurately tracking in real time hand postures in application for touch free exploration of 3D medical images for surgeons in the operating room, finger spelling (sign language for the deaf), virtual shopping, and game controlling. Combining the methods proposed in the demonstration competition tackling the problem of hand postures and those of the quantitative evaluation focusing on the dynamics of hand and arm movements is a promising direction of future research. For a long lasting impact, the challenge platform, the data and software repositories have been made available for further research.[2]

1.3.2 ChaLearn Multimodal Gesture Recognition Challenge 2013

The focus of this second challenge was on *multiple instance, user independent learning of gestures from multimodal data*, which means learning to recognize gestures from several instances for each category performed by different users, drawn from a vocabulary of 20 gesture categories (Escalera et al. 2013a, b). A gesture vocabulary is a set of unique gestures, generally related to a particular task. In this challenge we focus on the recognition of a vocabulary of 20 Italian cultural/anthropological signs (Escalera et al. 2013b), see Fig. 1.6 for one example of each Italian gesture.

1.3.2.1 2013 Challenge Data

In all the sequences, a single user is recorded in front of a Kinect^{TM}, performing natural communicative gestures and speaking in fluent Italian. The main characteristics of the dataset of gestures are:

- 13.858 gesture samples recorded with the Kinect^{TM} camera, including audio, skeletal model, user mask, RGB, and depth images.
- RGB video stream, 8-bit VGA resolution (640×480) with a Bayer color filter, and depth sensing video stream in VGA resolution (640×480) with 11-bit. Both are acquired in 20 fps on average.
- Audio data is captured using Kinect^{TM} 20 multiarray microphone.
- A total number of 27 users appear in the data set.
- The data set contains the following number of sequences, development: 393 (7.754 gestures), validation: 287 (3.362 gestures), and test: 276 (2.742 gestures), each sequence lasts between 1 and 2 min and contains between 8 and 20 gesture samples, around 1.800 frames. The total number of frames of the data set is 1.720.800.
- All the gesture samples belonging to 20 main gesture categories from an Italian gesture dictionary are annotated at frame level indicating the gesture label.
- 81% of the participants were Italian native speakers, while the remaining 19% of the users were not Italian, but Italian-speakers.
- All the audio that appears in the data is from the Italian dictionary. In addition, sequences may contain distractor words and gestures, which are not annotated since they do not belong to the main dictionary of 20 gestures.

---

[2]http://gesture.chalearn.org/.

(1) *Vattene*   (2) *Viene qui*   (3) *Perfetto*   (4) *E un furbo*   (5) *Che due palle*

(6) *Che vuoi*   (7)   *Vanno d'accordo*   (8) *Sei pazzo*   (9) *Cos hai combinato*   (10) *Nonme me friega niente*

(11) *Ok*   (12) *Cosa ti farei*   (13) *Basta*   (14) *Le vuoi prendere*   (15) *Non ce ne piu*

(16) *Ho fame*   (17) *Tanto tempo fa*   (18) *Buonissimo*   (19) *Si sono messi d'accordo*   (20) *Sono stufo*

Fig. 1.6 Data set gesture categories

Table 1.5 Easy and challenging aspects of the data

Easy
Fixed camera
Near frontal view acquisition
Within a sequence the same user
Gestures performed mostly by arms and hands
Camera framing upper body
Several available modalities: audio, skeletal model, user mask, depth, and RGB
Several instances of each gesture for training
Single person present in the visual field
Challenging
Within each sequence:
Continuous gestures without a resting pose
Many gesture instances are present
Distracter gestures out of the vocabulary may be present in terms of both gesture and audio
Between sequences:
High inter and intra-class variabilities of gestures in terms of both gesture and audio
Variations in background, clothing, skin color, lighting, temperature, resolution
Some parts of the body may be occluded
Different Italian dialects

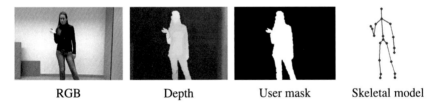

RGB   Depth   User mask   Skeletal model

Fig. 1.7 Different data modalities of the provided data set

This dataset, available at http://sunai.uoc.edu/chalearn, presents various features of interest as listed in Table 1.5. Examples of the provided visual modalities are shown in Fig. 1.7.

1.3.2.2 2013 Challenge Protocol and Evaluation

As in our previous 2011–2012 challenge, it consisted of two main components: a development phase (April 30th to Aug 1st) and a final evaluation phase (Aug 2nd to Aug 15th). The submission and evaluation of the challenge entries was via the

Kaggle platform.[3] The official participation rules were provided on the website of the challenge. In addition, publicity and news on the ChaLearn Multimodal Gesture Recognition Challenge were published in well-known online platforms, such as LinkedIn, Facebook, Google Groups and the ChaLearn website.

During the development phase, the participants were asked to build a system capable of learning from several gesture samples a vocabulary of 20 Italian sign gesture categories. To that end, the teams received the development data to train and self-evaluate their systems. In order to monitor their progress they could use the validation data for which the labels were not provided. The prediction results on validation data could be submitted online to get immediate feed-back. A real-time leaderboard showed to the participants their current standing based on their validation set predictions.

During the final phase, labels for validation data were published and the participants performed similar tasks as those performed in previous phase, using the validation data and training data sets in order to train their system with more gesture instances. The participants had only few days to train their systems and upload them. The organizers used the final evaluation data in order to generate the predictions and obtain the final score and rank for each team. At the end, the final evaluation data was revealed, and authors submitted their own predictions and fact sheets to the platform.

As an evaluation metric we also used the Levenshtein distance described in previous section. A public score appeared on the leaderboard during the development period and was based on the validation data. Subsequently, a private score for each team was computed on the final evaluation data released at the end of the development period, which was not revealed until the challenge was over. The private score was used to rank the participants and determine the prizes.

1.3.2.3   2013 Challenge Results

The challenge attracted high level of participation, with a total of 54 teams and near 300 total number of entries. This is a good level of participation for a computer vision challenge requiring very specialized skills. Finally, 17 teams successfully submitted their prediction in final test set, while providing also their code for verification and summarizing their method by means of a fact sheet questionnaire.

After verifying the codes and results of the participants, the final scores of the top rank participants on both validation and test sets were made public: these results are shown in Table 1.6, where winner results on the final test set are printed in bold. In the end, the final error rate on the test data set was around 12%.

---

[3]https://www.kaggle.com/c/multimodal-gesture-recognition.

Table 1.6 Top rank results on validation and test sets

TEAM	Validation score	Test score
IVA MM	0.20137	**0.12756**
WWEIGHT	0.46163	**0.15387**
ET	0.33611	**0.16813**
MmM	0.25996	0.17215
PPTK	0.15199	0.17325
LRS	0.18114	0.17727
MMDL	0.43992	0.24452
TELEPOINTS	0.48543	0.25841
CSI MM	0.32124	0.28911
SUMO	0.49137	0.31652
GURU	0.51844	0.37281
AURINKO	0.31529	0.63304
STEVENWUDI	1.43427	0.74415
JACKSPARROW	0.86050	0.79313
JOEWAN	0.13653	0.83772
MILAN KOVAC	0.87835	0.87463
IAMKHADER	0.93397	0.92069

Best scores are bolded

1.3.2.4 2013 Challenge Summary of the Winner Methods

Table 1.7 shows the summary of the strategies considered by each of the top ranked participants on the test set. Interestingly, the three top ranked participants agree in the modalities and segmentation strategy considered, although they differ in the final applied classifier. Next, we briefly describe in more detail the approach designed by the three winners of the challenge.

The first ranked team *IVA MM* on the test set used a feature vector based on audio and skeletal information, and applied late fusion to obtain final recognition results. A simple time-domain end-point detection algorithm based on joint coordinates is applied to segment continuous data sequences into candidate gesture intervals. A Gaussian Hidden Markov Model is trained with 39-dimension MFCC features and generates confidence scores for each gesture category. A Dynamic Time Warping based skeletal feature classifier is applied to provide complementary information. The confidence scores generated by the two classifiers are firstly normalized and then combined to produce a weighted sum. A single threshold approach is employed to classify meaningful gesture intervals from meaningless intervals caused by false detection of speech intervals.

The second ranked team *WWEIGHT* combined audio and skeletal information, using both joint spatial distribution and joint orientation. The method first searches

Table 1.7 Team methods and results. Early and late refer to early and late fusion of features/classifier outputs *HMM* Hidden Markov Models, *KNN* Nearest Neighbor, *RF* Random Forest, *Tree* Decision Trees, *ADA* Adaboost variants, *SVM* Support Vector Machines, *Fisher* Fisher Linear Discriminant Analysis, *GMM* Gaussian Mixture Models, *NN* Neural Networks, *DGM* Deep Boltzmann Machines, *LR* Logistic Regression, *DP* Dynamic Programming, *ELM* Extreme Learning Machines, *SK* skeleton

TEAM	Test score	Rank	Modalities	Segmentation	Fusion	Classifier
IVA MM	0.12756	1	Audio,SK	Audio	None	HMM,DP,KNN
WWEIGHT	0.15387	2	Audio,SK	Audio	Late	RF,KNN
ET	0.16813	3	Audio,SK	Audio	Late	Tree,RF,ADA
MmM	0.17215	4	Audio,RGB + Depth	Audio	Late	SVM,GMM,KNN
PPTK	0.17325	5	Skeleton,RGB, Depth	Sliding windows	Late	GMM,HMM
LRS	0.17727	6	Audio,SK, Depth	Sliding windows	Early	NN
MMDL	0.24452	7	Audio,SK	Sliding windows	Late	DGM+LR
TELEPOINTS	0.25841	8	Audio,SK,RGB	Audio,SK	Late	HMM,SVM
CSI MM	0.28911	9	Audio,SK	Audio	Early	HMM
SUMO	0.31652	10	Skeleton	Sliding windows	None	RF
GURU	0.37281	11	Audio,SK, Depth	DP	Late	DP,RF,HMM
AURINKO	0.63304	12	Skeleton,RGB	Skeleton	Late	ELM
STEVENWUDI	0.74415	13	Audio,SK	Sliding windows	Early	DNN,HMM
JACKSPARROW	0.79313	14	Skeleton	Sliding windows	None	NN
JOEWAN	0.83772	15	Skeleton	Sliding windows	None	KNN
MILAN KOVAC	0.87463	16	Skeleton	Sliding windows	None	NN
IAMKHADER	0.92069	17	Depth	Sliding windows	None	RF

for regions of time with high audio-energy to define 1.8-s-long windows of time that potentially contained a gesture. This had the effect that the development, validation, and test data were treated uniformly. Feature vectors are then defined using a log-spaced audio spectrogram and the joint positions and orientations above the hips. At each time sample the method subtracts the average 3D position of the left and right shoulders from each 3D joint position. Data is down-sampled onto a 5 Hz grid considering 1.8 s. There were 1593 features total (9 time samples × 177 features per time sample). Since some of the detected windows can contain distractor gestures, an extra 21st label is introduced, defining the 'not in the dictionary' gesture category. Python's scikit-learn was used to train two models: an ensemble of randomized decision trees (ExtraTreesClassifier, 100 trees, 40% of features) and a K-Nearest Neighbor model (7 neighbors, L1 distance). The posteriors from these models are

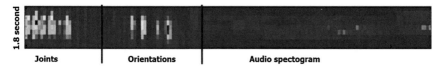

Fig. 1.8 ExtraTreesClassifier feature importance

averaged with equal weight. Finally, a heuristic is used (12 gestures maximum, no repeats) to convert posteriors to a prediction for the sequence of gestures.

Figure 1.8 shows the mean feature importance for the windows size of 1.8 s for the three sets of features: joint coordinates, joint orientations, and audio spectogram. One can note that features from the three sets are selected as discriminative by the classifier, although skeletal features becomes more useful for the ExtraTreesClassifier. Additionally, the most discriminative features are those in the middle of the windows size, since begin-end features are shared among different gestures (transitions) and thus are less discriminative for the classifier.

The third ranked team *ET* combined the output decisions of two designed approaches. In the first approach, they look for gesture intervals (unsupervised) using the audio files and extract these features from intervals (MFCC). Using these features, authors train a random forest and gradient boosting classifier. The second approach uses simple statistics (median, var, min, max) on the first 40 frames for each gesture to build the training samples. The prediction phase uses a sliding window. The authors create a weighted average of the output of these two models. The features considered were skeleton information and audio signal.

Finally, we extracted some statistics from the results of the three challenge winners in order to analyze common points and difficult aspects of the challenge. Figure 1.9 shows the recognition of the 276 test sequences by the winners. Black bin means that the complete list of ordered gestures was successfully recognized for those sequences. Once can see that there exists some kind of correlation among methods. Taking into account that consecutive sequences belong to the same user performing gestures, it means that some some gestures are easier to recognize than others. Since different users appear in the training and test sequences, it is sometimes difficult for the models to generalize to the style of new users, based on the gesture instances used for training.

Fig. 1.9 Recognition of test sequence by the three challenge winners. Black bin means that the complete list of ordered gestures has been successfully recognized

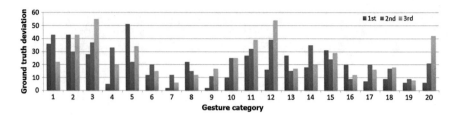

Fig. 1.10 Deviation of the number of gesture samples for each category by the three winners in relation to the GT data

We also investigated the difficulty of the problem by gesture category, within each of the 20 Italian gesture categories. Figure 1.10 shows for each winner method the deviation between the number of gesture instances recognized and the total number of gestures, for each category. This was computed for each sequence independently, and adding the deviation for all the sequences. In that case, a zero value means that the participant method recognized the same number of gesture instances for a category that was recorded in the ground truth data. Although we cannot guarantee with this measure that the order of recognized gesture matches with the ground truth, it gives us an idea of how difficult the gesture sequences were to segment into individual gestures. Additionally, the sum of total deviation for all the gestures for all the teams was 378, 469, and 504, which correlates with the final rank of the winners. The figure suggests a correlation between the performance of the three winners. In particular, categories 6, 7, 8, 9, 16, 17, 18, and 19 were the ones that achieved most accuracy for all the participants, meanwhile 1, 2, 3, 5, and 12 were the ones that introduced the highest recognition error. Note that the public data set provides accurate label annotations of end-begin of gestures, and thus, a more detailed recognition analysis could be performed applying a different recognition measurement to Leveinstein, such as Jaccard overlapping or sensitivity score estimation, which will also allow for confusion matrix estimation based on both inter and intra user and gesture category variability. This is left to future work.

1.3.3 ChaLearn Multimodal Gesture Spotting Challenge 2014

In ChaLearn LAP 2014 (Escalera et al. 2014) we focused on the user-independent automatic spotting of a vocabulary of 20 Italian cultural/anthropological signs in image sequences, see Fig. 1.6.

Table 1.8 Main characteristics of the *Montalbano* gesture dataset. SK: skeleton

Training seq.	Validation seq.	Test seq.	Sequence duration	FPS
393 (7,754 gestures)	287 (3,362 gestures)	276 (2,742 gestures)	1–2 min	20
Modalities	Num. of users	Gesture categories	Labeled sequences	Labeled frames
RGB, Depth, Mask, SK	27	20	13,858	1,720,800

1.3.3.1 2014 Gesture Challenge Data

This challenge was based on an Italian gesture data set, called *Montalbano gesture dataset*, an enhanced version of the ChaLearn 2013 multimodal gesture recognition challenge (Escalera et al. 2013a, b) with more ground-truth annotations. In all the sequences, a single user is recorded in front of a Kinect™, performing natural communicative gestures and speaking in fluent Italian. Examples of the different visual modalities are shown in Fig. 1.7.

The main characteristics of the data set are:

- Largest data set in the literature, with a large duration of each individual performance showing no resting poses and self-occlusions.
- There is no information about the number of gestures to spot within each sequence, and several distracter gestures (out of the vocabulary) are present.
- High intra-class variability of gesture samples and low inter-class variability for some gesture categories.

A list of data attributes for data set used in track 3 is described in Table 1.8.

1.3.3.2 2014 Gesture Challenge Protocol and Evaluation

The challenge was managed using the Microsoft Codalab platform.[4] We followed a development (February 9 to May 20 2014) and tests phases (May 20th to June 1st 2014) as in our previous challenges.

To evaluate the accuracy of action/interaction recognition, we use the Jaccard Index, For the n action, interaction, and gesture categories labelled for a RGB/RGBD sequence s, the Jaccard Index is defined as:

$$J_{s,n} = \frac{A_{s,n} \bigcap B_{s,n}}{A_{s,n} \bigcup B_{s,n}}, \tag{1.1}$$

---

[4]https://www.codalab.org/competitions/.

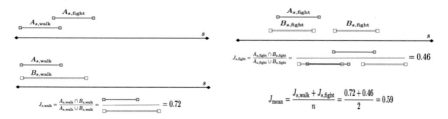

Fig. 1.11 Example of mean Jacquard Index calculation for gesture and action/interaction spotting

where $A_{s,n}$ is the ground truth of action/interaction/gesture n at sequence s, and $B_{s,n}$ is the prediction for such an action at sequence s. $A_{s,n}$ and $B_{s,n}$ are binary vectors where 1-values correspond to frames in which the n−th action is being performed. The participants were evaluated based on the mean Jaccard Index among all categories for all sequences, where motion categories are independent but not mutually exclusive (in a certain frame more than one action, interaction, gesture class can be active).

In the case of false positives (e.g. inferring an action, interaction or gesture not labelled in the ground truth), the Jaccard Index is 0 for that particular prediction, and it will not count in the mean Jaccard Index computation. In other words n is equal to the intersection of action/interaction/gesture categories appearing in the ground truth and in the predictions.

An example of the calculation for two actions is shown in Fig. 1.11. Note that in the case of recognition, the ground truth annotations of different categories can overlap (appear at the same time within the sequence). Also, although different actors appear within the sequence at the same time, actions/interactions/gestures are labelled in the corresponding periods of time (that may overlap), there is no need to identify the actors in the scene. The example in Fig. 1.11 shows the mean Jaccard Index calculation for different instances of actions categories in a sequence (single red lines denote ground truth annotations and double red lines denote predictions). In the top part of the image one can see the ground truth annotations for actions walk and fight at sequence s. In the center part of the image a prediction is evaluated obtaining a Jaccard Index of 0.72. In the bottom part of the image the same procedure is performed with the action fight and the obtained Jaccard Index is 0.46. Finally, the mean Jaccard Index is computed obtaining a value of 0.59 (Table 1.9).

1.3.3.3   2014 Gesture Challenge Results

Table 1.10 summarizes the methods of the 17 participants that contributed to the test set of track 3. Although DTW and HMM (and variants) were in the last edition of the ChaLearn Multimodal Gesture competition (Escalera et al. 2013a, b), random forest has been widely applied in this 2014 edition. Also, three participants used deep learning architectures.

Table 1.9 Top rows: action/interaction 2014 recognition results. *MHI* Motion History Image, *STIP* Spatio-Temporal interest points, *MBF* Multiscale Blob Features, *BoW* Bag of Visual Words, *RF* Random Forest. Bottom two rows: action/interaction 2015 recognition results. *IDT* Improved Dense Trajectories (Wang and Schmid 2013)

Team name	Accuracy	Rank	Features	Dimension reduction	Clustering	Classifier	Temporal coherence	Gesture representation
CUHK-SWJTU	**0.507173**	1	Improved trajectories (Wang and Schmid 2013)	PCA	–	SVM	Sliding windows	Fisher Vector
ADSC	**0.501164**	2	Improved trajectories (Wang and Schmid 2013)	–	–	SVM	Sliding windows	–
SBUVIS	**0.441405**	3	Improved trajectories (Wang and Schmid 2013)	–	–	SVM	Sliding windows	–
DonkeyBurger	0.342192	4	MHI, STIP	–	Kmeans	Sparse code	Sliding windows	–
UC-T2	0.121565	5	Improved trajectories (Wang and Schmid 2013)	PCA	–	Kmeans	Sliding windows	Fisher Vector
MindLAB	0.008383	6	MBF	–	Kmeans	RF	Sliding windows	BoW
MMLAB	**0.5385**	1	IDT	PCA	–	SVM	–	Fisher Vector
FIKIE	**0.5239**	2	IDT	PCA	–	HMM	Appearance + Kalman filter	–

Best scores are bolded

Table 1.10 Multimodal gesture recognition results. *SK* Skeleton, *DNN* Deep Neural Network, *RF* Random Forest, *2DMTM* 2D motion trail model, *RT* Regression Tree

Team	Accuracy	Rank	Modalities	Features	Fusion	Temp. segmentation	Dimension reduction	Gesture representation	Classifier
LIRIS	**0.849987**	1	SK, Depth, RGB	RAW, SK joints	Early	Joints motion	–	–	DNN
CraSPN	**0.833904**	2	SK, Depth, RGB	HOG, SK	Early	Sliding windows	–	BoW	Adaboost
JY	**0.826799**	3	SK, RGB	SK, HOG	Late	MRF	PCA	–	MRF, KNN
CUHK-SWJTU	0.791933	4	RGB	Improved trajectories (Wang and Schmid 2013)	–	Joints motion	PCA	Fisher Vector, VLAD	SVM
Lpigou	0.788804	5	Depth, RGB	RAW, SK joints	Early	Sliding windows	Max-pooling CNN	–	CNN
stevenwudi	0.787310	6	SK, depth	RAW	Late	Sliding windows	–	–	HMM, DNN
Ismar	0.746632	7	SK	SK	–	Sliding windows	–	–	RF
Quads	0.745449	8	SK	SK quads	–	Sliding windows	–	Fisher Vector	SVM
Telepoints	0.688778	9	SK, Depth, RGB	STIPS, SK	Late	Joints motion	–	–	SVM
TUM-fortiss	0.648979	10	SK, Depth, RGB	STIPS	Late	Joints motion	–	–	RF, SVM
CSU-SCM	0.597177	11	Skeleton, Depth, mask	HOG, Skeleton	Late	Sliding windows	–	2DMTM	SVM, HMM

(continued)

Table 1.10 (continued)

Team	Accuracy	Rank	Modalities	Features	Fusion	Temp. segmentation	Dimension reduction	Gesture representation	Classifier
iva.mm	0.556251	12	Skeleton, RGB, depth	Skeleton, HOG	Late	Sliding windows	–	BoW	SVM, HMM
Terrier	0.539025	13	Skeleton	Skeleton	–	Sliding windows	–	–	RF
Team Netherlands	0.430709	14	Skeleton, Depth, RGB	MHI	Early	DTW	Preserving projections	–	SVM, RT
VecsRel	0.408012	15	Skeleton, Depth, RGB	RAW, skeleton joints	Late	DTW	–	–	DNN
Samgest	0.391613	16	Skeleton, Depth, RGB, mask	Skeleton, blobs, moments	Late	Sliding windows	–	–	HMM
YNL	0.270600	17	Skeleton	Skeleton	–	Sliding windows	–	Fisher Vector	HMM, SVM

1.3.3.4 2014 Gesture Challenge Summary of the Winner Methods

Next, we describe the main characteristics of the three winning methods.

First place: The proposed method was based on a deep learning architecture that iteratively learned and integrated discriminative data representations from individual channels, modelling cross-modality correlations and short- and long-term temporal dependencies. This framework combined three data modalities: depth information, grayscale video and skeleton stream ("articulated pose"). Articulated pose served as an efficient representation of large-scale body motion of the upper body and arms, while depth and video streams contained complementary information about more subtle hand articulation. The articulated pose was formulated as a set of joint angles and normalized distances between upper-body joints, augmented with additional information reflecting speed and acceleration of each joint. For the depth and video streams, the authors did not rely on hand-crafted descriptors, but on discriminatively learning joint depth-intensity data representations with a set of convolutional neural layers. Iterative fusion of data channels was performed at output layers of the neural architecture. The idea of learning at multiple scales was also applied to the temporal dimension, such that a gesture was considered as an ordered set of characteristic motion impulses, or dynamic poses. Additional skeleton-based binary classifier was applied for accurate gesture localization. Fusing multiple modalities at several spatial and temporal scales led to a significant increase in recognition rates, allowing the model to compensate for errors of the individual classifiers as well as noise in the separate channels.

Second place: The approach combined a sliding-window gesture detector with multimodal features drawn from skeleton data, color imagery, and depth data produced by a first-generation Kinect^{TM} sensor. The gesture detector consisted of a set of boosted classifiers, each tuned to a specific gesture or gesture mode. Each classifier was trained independently on labeled training data, employing bootstrapping to collect hard examples. At run-time, the gesture classifiers were evaluated in a one-versus-all manner across a sliding window. Features were extracted at multiple temporal scales to enable recognition of variable-length gestures. Extracted features included descriptive statistics of normalized skeleton joint positions, rotations, and velocities, as well as HOG descriptors of the hands. The full set of gesture detectors was trained in under two hours on a single machine, and was extremely efficient at runtime, operating at 1700 fps using skeletal data.

Third place: The proposed method was based on four features: skeletal joint position feature, skeletal joint distance feature, and histogram of oriented gradients (HOG) features corresponding to left and right hands. Under the naïve Bayes assumption, likelihood functions were independently defined for every feature. Such likelihood functions were non-parametrically constructed from the training data by using kernel density estimation (KDE). For computational efficiency, k-nearest neighbor (kNN) approximation to the exact density estimator was proposed. Constructed likelihood functions were combined to the multimodal likelihood and this serves as a unary term for our pairwise Markov random field (MRF) model. For enhancing temporal coherence, a pairwise term was additionally incorporated to the MRF model. Final gesture labels were obtained via 1D MRF inference efficiently achieved by dynamic programming.

1.3.4 ChaLearn Action and Interaction Spotting Challenge 2014

The goal of this challenge was to perform automatic action and interaction spotting of people appearing in RGB data sequences.

1.3.4.1 2014 Action Challenge Data

We presented a novel fully limb labelled dataset, the Human Pose Recovery and Behavior Analysis *HuPBA* 8*k*+ dataset (Sánchez et al. 2014). This dataset is formed by more than 8000 frames where 14 limbs are labelled at pixel precision, thus providing 124, 761 annotated human limbs. The characteristics of the data set are:

- The images are obtained from 9 videos (RGB sequences) and a total of 14 different actors appear in the sequences. The image sequences have been recorded using a stationary camera with the same static background.
- Each video (RGB sequence) was recorded at 15 fps rate, and each RGB image was stored with resolution 480×360 in BMP file format.
- For each actor present in an image 14 limbs (if not occluded) were manually tagged: Head, Torso, R–L Upper-arm, R–L Lower-arm, R–L Hand, R–L Upper-leg, R–L Lower-leg, and R–L Foot.
- Limbs are manually labelled using binary masks and the minimum bounding box containing each subject is defined.
- The actors appear in a wide range of different poses and performing different actions/gestures which vary the visual appearance of human limbs. So there is a large variability of human poses, self-occlusions and many variations in clothing and skin color.
- Several actions and interactions categories are labelled at frame level.

A key frame example for each gesture/action category is shown in Fig. 1.12. The challenges the participants had to deal with for this new competition are:

- 235 action/interaction samples performed by 14 actors.
- Large difference in length about the performed actions and interactions. Several distracter actions out of the 11 categories are also present.
- 11 action categories, containing isolated and collaborative actions: Wave, Point, Clap, Crouch, Jump, Walk, Run, Shake Hands, Hug, Kiss, Fight. There is a high intra-class variability among action samples.

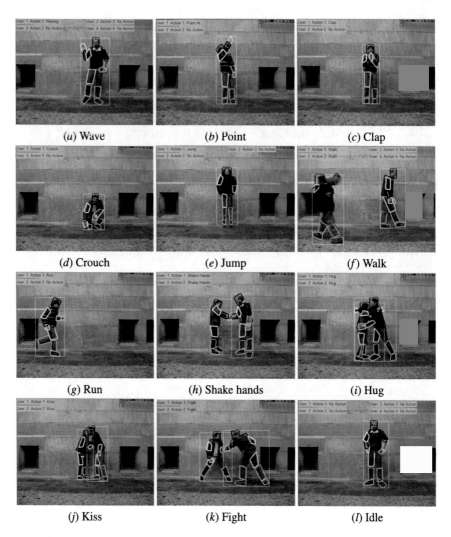

(*u*) Wave

(*b*) Point

(*c*) Clap

(*d*) Crouch

(*e*) Jump

(*f*) Walk

(*g*) Run

(*h*) Shake hands

(*i*) Hug

(*j*) Kiss

(*k*) Fight

(*l*) Idle

Fig. 1.12 Key frames of the *HuPBA* 8*K*+ dataset used in the tracks 1 and 2, showing actions (**a–g**), interactions (**h–k**) and the idle pose (**l**)

Table 1.11 summarizes the data set attributes for the case of action/interaction spotting.

1.3.4.2   2014 Action Challenge Protocol and Evaluation

To evaluate the accuracy of action/interaction recognition, we use the Jaccard Index as defined in Sect. 1.3.3.2.

Table 1.11 Action and interaction data characteristics

Training actions	Validation actions	Test actions	Sequence duration	FPS
150	90	95	$9 \times$ 1–2 min	15
Modalities	Num. of users	Action categories	Interaction categories	Labelled sequences
RGB	14	7	4	235

1.3.4.3 2014 Action Challenge Results

In this section we summarize the methods proposed by the participants and the winning methods. Six teams submitted their code and predictions for the test sets. Top rows of Table 1.9 summarizes the approaches of the participants who uploaded their models. One can see that most methods are based on similar approaches. In particular, alternative representations to classical BoW were considered, as Fisher Vector and VLAD (Jegou et al. 2012). Most methods perform sliding windows and SVM classification. In addition, to refine the tracking of interest points, 4 participants used improved trajectories (Wang and Schmid 2013).

1.3.4.4 2014 Action Challenge Summary of the Winner Methods

Next, we describe the main characteristics of the three winning methods.

First place: The method was composed of two parts: video representation and temporal segmentation. For the representation of video clip, the authors first extracted improved dense trajectories with HOG, HOF, MBHx, and MBHy descriptors. Then, for each kind of descriptor, the participants trained a GMM and used Fisher vector to transform these descriptors into a high dimensional super vector space. Finally, sum pooling was used to aggregate these codes in the whole video clip and normalize them with power L2 norm. For the temporal recognition, the authors resorted to a temporal sliding method along the time dimension. To speed up the processing of detection, the authors designed a temporal integration histogram of Fisher Vector, with which the pooled Fisher Vector was efficiently evaluated at any temporal window. For each sliding window, the authors used the pooled Fisher Vector as representation and fed it into the SVM classifier for action recognition.

Second place: a human action detection framework called "mixture of heterogeneous attribute analyzer" was proposed. This framework integrated heterogeneous attributes learned from various types of video features including static and dynamic, local and global features, to boost the action detection accuracy. The authors first detected a human from the input video by SVM-HOG detector and performed forward-backward tracking. Multiple local human tracks are linked into long trajectories by spatial-temporal graph based matching. Human key poses and local dense motion trajectories were then extracted within the tracked human bounding box sequences. Second, the authors proposed a mining method that learned discriminative attributes from three feature modalities: human trajectory, key pose and local motion trajectory features. The mining framework was based on the exemplar-SVM discriminative middle level feature detection approach. The learned discriminative attributes from the three types of visual features were then mixed in a max-margin learning algorithm which also explores the combined discriminative capability of heterogeneous feature modalities. The learned mixed analyzer was then applied to the input video sequence for action detection.

Third place: The framework for detecting actions in video is based on improved dense trajectories applied on a sliding windows fashion. Authors independently trained 11 one-versus-all kernel SVMs on the labelled training set for 11 different actions. The feature and feature descriptions used are improved dense trajectories, HOG, HOF, MBHx and MBHy. During training, for each action, a temporal sliding window is applied without overlapping. For every action, a segment was labelled 0 (negative) for a certain action only if there is no frame in this segment labelled 1. The feature coding method was bag-of-features. For a certain action, the features associated with those frames which are labelled 0 (negative) are not counted when we code the features of the action for the positive segments with bag-of-features. On the basis of the labelled segments and their features, a kernel SVM was trained for each action. During testing, non-overlap sliding window was applied for feature coding of the video. Every frame in a segment was consistently labelled as the output of SVM for each action. The kernel type, sliding window size and penalty of SVMs were selected during validation. When building the bag-of-features, the clustering method was K-means and the vocabulary size is 4000. For one trajectory feature in one frame, all the descriptors were connected to form one description vector. The bag-of-features were built upon this vector.

1.3.5   ChaLearn Action and Interaction Spotting Challenge 2015

The goal of this challenge was to perform automatic action and interaction spotting of people appearing in RGB data sequences. This corresponds to the second round of 2014 Action/Interaction challenge (Baró et al. 2015). Data, protocol, and evaluation were defined as explained in Sect. 1.3.4.

1.3.5.1   2015 Action Challenge Results

Results of the two top ranked participants are shown in bottom rows of Table 1.9. One can see that the methods of the participants are similar to the ones applied in the 2014 challenge for the same dataset (Top rows of Table 1.9). Results of this second competition round improved by 2% the results obtained in the first round of the challenge.

1.3.5.2   2015 Action Challenge Summary of the Winner Methods

First winner: This method is an improvement of the system proposed in Peng et al. (2015), which is composed of two parts: video representation and temporal segmentation. For the representation of video clip, the authors first extracted improved dense trajectories with HOG, HOF, MBHx, and MBHy descriptors. Then, for each kind of descriptor, the participants trained a GMM and used Fisher vector to transform these descriptors into a high dimensional super vector space. Finally, sum pooling was used to aggregate these codes in the whole video clip and normalize them with power L2 norm. For the temporal recognition, the authors resorted to a temporal sliding method along the time dimension. To speed up the processing of detection, the authors designed a temporal integration histogram of Fisher Vector, with which the pooled Fisher Vector was efficiently evaluated at any temporal window. For each sliding window, the authors used the pooled Fisher Vector as representation and fed it into the SVM classifier for action recognition. A summary of this method is shown in Fig. 1.13.

Second winner: The method implements an end-to-end generative approach from feature modelling to activity recognition. The system combines dense trajectories and Fisher Vectors with a temporally structured model for action recognition based on a

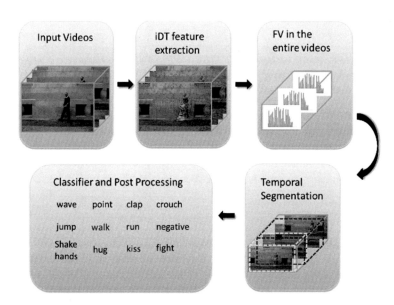

Fig. 1.13 Method summary for MMLAB team (Wang et al. 2015b)

(a)   **(b)**

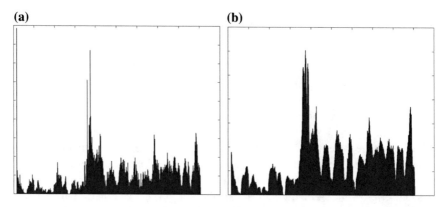

Fig. 1.14 Example of DT feature distribution for the first 200 frames of Seq01 for FKIE team, **a** shows the distribution of the original implementation, **b** shows the distribution of the modified version

simple grammar over action units. The authors modify the original dense trajectory implementation of Wang and Schmid (2013) to avoid the omission of neighborhood interest points once a trajectory is used (the improvement is shown in Fig. 1.14). They use an open source speech recognition engine for the parsing and segmentation of video sequences. Because a large data corpus is typically needed for training such systems, images were mirrored to artificially generate more training data. The final result is achieved by voting over the output of various parameter and grammar configurations.

1.3.6 Other International Competitions for Gesture and Action Recognition

In addition to the series of ChaLearn Looking at People challenges, different international challenges have also been performed in the field of action/gesture recognition. Some of them are reviewed below.

The ChAirGest challenge (Ruffieux et al. 2013) is a research oriented competition designed to compare multimodal gesture recognizers. The provided data came from one Kinect camera and 4 Inertial Motion Units (IMU) attached to the right arm and neck of the subject. The dataset contains 10 different gestures, started from 3 different resting postures and recorded in two different lighting conditions by 10 different subjects. Thus, the total dataset contains 1200 annotated gestures split in continuous video sequences containing a variable number of gestures. The goal of the challenge was to promote research on methods using multimodal data to spot and recognize gestures in the context of close human–computer interaction.

In 2015, OpenCV ran at CVPR different challenges,[5] one of them focusing on gesture recognition, using the ChaLearn gesture recognition data. The winner of the competition was also the work that won the ChaLearn challenge at ECCV 2014 (Neverova et al. 2014b).

Another recent action recognition competition is the THUMOS challenge (Gorban et al. 2015). Last round of the competition was ran at CVPR 2015. The last round of the challenge contained a forward-looking data set with over 430 hours of video data and 45 million frames (70% larger than THUMOS'14). All videos were collected from YouTube. Two tracks were performed: (1) Action Classification, for whole-clip action classification on 101 action classes, and (2) Temporal Action Localization, for action recognition and temporal localization on a subset of 20 action classes.

1.4 Summary of Special Topic Papers Not Related to the Challenges

In this special topic, in addition to the papers that described systems that participated in the ChaLearn gesture challenges, there are also several papers relating to broader aspects of gesture recognition, including topics such as sign language recognition, facial expression analysis, and facilitating development of real-world systems.

Three of these papers propose new methods for gesture and action recognition (Malgireddy et al. 2013; Fanello et al. 2013; Lui 2012), that were also evaluated on parts of the CDG2011 dataset (Guyon et al. 2014), used in the ChaLearn challenges held in 2011 and 2012. More specifically, Malgireddy et al. (2013) present an approach for detecting and recognizing activities and gestures. Hierarchical models are built to describe each activity as a combination of other, more simple activities. Each video is recursively divided into segments consisting of a fixed number of frames. The relationship between observed features and latent variables is modelled using a generative model that combines aspects of dynamic Bayesian networks and hierarchical Bayesian models. Fanello et al. (2013) describe a system for real-time action recognition using depth video. The paper proposes specific features that are well adapted to real-time constraints, based on histograms of oriented gradients and histograms of optical flow. Support vector machines trained on top of such features perform action segmentation and recognition. Lui (2012) propose a method for representing gestures as tensors. These tensors are treated as points on a product manifold. In particular, the product manifold is factorized into three manifolds, one capturing horizontal motion, one capturing vertical motion, and one capturing 2D appearance. The difference between gestures is measured using a geodesic distance on the product manifold.

---

[5]http://code.opencv.org/projects/opencv/wiki/VisionChallenge.

One paper Wang et al. (2012) studied an action recognition problem outside the scope of the ChaLearn contests, namely recognizing poses and actions from a single image. Hierarchical models are used for modelling body pose. Each model in this hierarchy covers a part of the human body that can range from the entire body to a specific rigid part. Different levels in this hierarchy correspond to different degrees of coarseness versus detail in the models at each level.

Three papers proposed novel methods within the area of sign language recognition (Cooper et al. 2012; Nayak et al. 2012; Roussos et al. 2013). Cooper et al. (2012) describe a method for sign language recognition using linguistic subunits that are learned automatically by the system. Different types of such subunits are considered, including subunits based on appearance and local motion of the hand, subunits based on combining tracked 2D hand trajectories and hand shape, and subunits based on tracked 3D hand trajectories. Nayak et al. (2012) address the problem of learning a model for a sign that occurs multiple times in a set of sentences. One benefit from such an approach is that it does not require the start and end frame of each sign as training data. Another benefit is that the method identifies the aspects of a sign that are least affected by movement epenthesis, i.e., by signs immediately preceding or following the sign in question. Roussos et al. (2013) present a method for classifying handshapes for the purpose of sign language recognition. Cropped hand images are converted to a normalized representation called "shape-appearance images", based on a PCA decomposition of skin pixel colors. Then, active appearance models are used to model the variation in shape and appearance of the hand.

One paper focused on the topic of facial expression analysis (Martinez and Du 2012). The paper proposes a model for describing how humans perceive facial expressions of emotion. The proposed model consists of multiple distinct continuous spaces. Emotions can be represented using linear combinations of these separate spaces. The paper also discusses how the proposed model can be used to design algorithms for facial expression recognition.

Another set of papers contributed methods that address different practical problems, that are important for building real-world gesture interfaces (Nguyen-Dinh et al. 2014; Gillian and Paradiso 2014; Kohlsdorf and Starner 2013). One such problem is obtaining manual annotations and ground truth for large amounts of training data. Obtaining such manual annotations can be time consuming, and can be an important bottleneck in building a real system. Crowdsourcing is a potential solution, but crowdsourced annotations often suffer from noise, in the form of discrepancies in how different humans annotate the same data. In Nguyen-Dinh et al. (2014), two template-matching methods are proposed, called SegmentedLCSS and WarpingLCSS, that explicitly deal with the noise present in crowdsourced annotations of gestures. These methods are designed for spotting gestures using wearable motion sensors. The methods quantize signals into strings of characters and then apply variations of the longest common subsequence algorithm (LCSS) to spot gestures.

In designing a real-world system, another important problem is rapid development. Gillian and Paradiso (2014) present a gesture recognition toolkit, a cross-platform open-source C++ library. The toolkit features a broad range of classification and regression algorithms and has extensive support for building real-time systems. This includes algorithms for signal processing, feature extraction and automatic gesture spotting.

Finally, choosing the gesture vocabulary can be an important implementation parameter. Kohlsdorf and Starner (2013) propose a method for choosing a vocabulary of gestures for a human–computer interface, so that gestures in that vocabulary have a low probability of being confused with each other. Candidate gestures for the interface can be suggested both by humans and by the system itself. The system compares examples of each gesture with a large repository of unlabelled sensor/motion data, to check how often such examples resemble typical session/motion patterns encountered in that specific application domain.

1.5 Summary of Special Topic Papers Related to 2011–2012 Challenges

Next we briefly review the contributions of the accepted papers for the special topic whose methods are applied on the data provided by 2011–2012 ChaLearn gesture recognition challenges. Interestingly, none of the methods proposed in these papers uses skeletal tracking. Instead, these methods use different features based on appearance and/or motion. Where the papers differ is in their choice of specific features, and also in the choice of gesture models that are built on top of the selected features.

Konecny and Hagara (2014) combine appearance (Histograms of Oriented Gradients) and motion descriptors (Histogram of Optical Flow) from RGB and depth images for parallel temporal segmentation and recognition. The Quadratic-Chi distance family is used to measure differences between histograms to capture cross-bin relationships. Authors also propose trimming videos by removing unimportant frames based on motion information. Finally, proposed descriptors with different Dynamic Time Warping variants are applied for final recognition.

In contrast to Konecny and Hagara (2014), which employes commonly used features, Wan et al. (2013) proposes a new multimodal descriptor, as well as a new sparse coding method. The multimodal descriptor is called 3D EMoSIFT, is invariant to scale and rotation, and has more compact and richer visual representations than other state-of-the-art descriptors. The proposed sparse coding method is named simulation orthogonal matching pursuit (SOMP), and is a variant of BoW. Using SOMP, each feature can be represented by some linear combination of a small number of codewords.

A different approach is taken in Jiang et al. (2015), which combines three different methods for classifying gestures. The first method uses an improved principal motion representation. In the second method, a particle-based descriptor and a weighted dynamic time warping are proposed for the location component classification. In the third method, the shape of the human subject is used, extracted from the frame in the gesture that exhibits the least motion. The explicit use of shape in this paper is in contrast to Konecny and Hagara (2014) and Wan et al. (2013), where shape information is implicitly coded in the extracted features.

In Goussies et al. (2014), the focus is on transfer learning. The proposed method did not do as well as the previous methods (Konecny and Hagara 2014; Wan et al. 2013; Jiang et al. 2015) on the CDG 2011 dataset, but nonetheless it contributes novel ideas for transfer learning, that can be useful when the number of training examples per class is limited. This is in contrast to the other papers related to the 2011–2012 challenges, that did not address transfer learning. The paper introduces two mechanisms into the decision forest framework, in order to transfer knowledge from the source tasks to a given target task. The first one is mixed information gain, which is a data-based regularizer. The second one is label propagation, which infers the manifold structure of the feature space. The proposed approach show improvements over traditional decision forests in the ChaLearn Gesture Challenge and on the MNIST dataset.

1.6 Summary of Special Issue Papers Related to 2013 Challenge

Next we briefly review the contributions of the accepted papers for the special issue whose methods are applied on the data provided by 2013 ChaLearn multimodal gesture recognition challenge. An important difference between this challenge and the previous ChaLearn challenges is the multimodal nature of the data. Thus, a key focus area for methods applied on this data is the problem of fusing information from multiple modalities.

Wu and Cheng (2014) propose a Bayesian Co-Boosting framework for multimodal gesture recognition. Inspired by boosting learning and co-training method, the system combines multiple collaboratively trained weak classifiers, Hidden Markov Models in this case, to construct the final strong classifier. During each iteration round, randomly a number of feature subsets are samples and weak classifiers parameters for each subset are estimated. The optimal weak classifier and its corresponding feature subset are retained for strong classifier construction. Authors also define an upper bound of training error and derive the update rule of instance's weight, which guarantees the error upper bound to be minimized through iterations. This methodology won the ChaLearn 2013 ICMI competition.

Pitsikalis et al. (2014) present a framework for multimodal gesture recognition that is based on a multiple hypotheses rescoring fusion scheme. Authors employ multiple modalities, i.e., visual cues, such as skeleton data, color and depth images, as well as audio, and extract feature descriptors of the hands movement, handshape, and audio spectral properties. Using a common hidden Markov model framework authors build single-stream gesture models based on which they can generate multiple single stream-based hypotheses for an unknown gesture sequence. By multimodally rescoring these hypotheses via constrained decoding and a weighted combination scheme, authors end up with a multimodally-selected best hypothesis. This is further refined by means of parallel fusion of the monomodal gesture models applied at a segmental level. The proposed methodology is tested on the ChaLearn 2013 ICMI competition data.

1.7 Discussion

We reviewed the gesture recognition topic, defining a taxonomy to characterize state of the art works on gesture recognition. We also reviewed the gesture and action recognition challenges organized by ChaLearn from 2011 to 2015, as well as other international competitions related to gesture recognition. Finally, we reviewed the papers submitted to the Special Topic on Gesture Recognition 2011–2014 we organized at Journal of Machine Learning Research.

Regarding the ChaLearn gesture recognition challenges, we began right at the start of the Kinect™ revolution when inexpensive infrared cameras providing image depth recordings became available. We published papers using this technology and other more conventional methods, including regular video cameras, to record data, thus providing a good overview of uses of machine learning and computer vision using multimodal data in this area of application. Notably, we organized a series of challenges and made available several datasets we recorded for that purpose, including tens of thousands of videos, which are available to conduct further research.[6]

Regarding the papers published in the gesture recognition special topic related to 2011–2012 challenges with the objective of performing one-shot learning, most of the authors proposed new multimodal descriptors taking benefit from both RGB and Depth cues in order to describe human body features, both static and dynamic ones. As the recognition strategies, common techniques used were variants of classical well-known Dynamic Time Warping and Hidden Markov Models. In particular, the most efficient techniques so far have used sequences of features processed by graphical models of the HMM/CRF family, similar to techniques used in speech recognition. Authors also considered a gesture candidate sliding window and motion-based video-cutting approaches. Last approach was frequently used since sign language videos included a resting pose. Also interesting novel classification strategies were proposed, such as multilayered decomposition, where different length gesture units are recognize at different levels (Jiang et al. 2015).

Regarding the papers published in the gesture recognition special topic related to 2013 and 2014 challenges with the objective of performing user independent multiple gesture recognition from large volumes of multimodal data (RGB, Depth and audio), different classifiers for gesture recognition were used by the participants. In 2013, the preferred one was Hidden Markov Models (used by the first ranked

---

[6]http://gesture.chalearn.org/.

team of the challenge), followed by Random Forest (used by the second and third winners). Although several state of the art learning and testing gesture techniques were applied at the last stage of the methods of the participants, still the feature vector descriptions are mainly based on MFCC audio features and skeleton joint information. The published paper of the winner to the special topic presents a novel coboosting strategy, where a set of HMM classifiers and collaboratively included in a boosting strategy considering random sets of features (Wu and Cheng 2014). In 2014, similar descriptors and classifiers were used, and in particular, three deep learning architectures were considered, including the method of the winner team (Neverova et al. 2014b).

In the case of the ChaLearn action/interaction challenges organized in 2014 and 2015 most methods were based on similar approaches. In particular, alternative representations to classical BoW were considered, as Fisher Vector and VLAD (Jegou et al. 2012). Most methods performed sliding windows and SVM classification. In addition, to refine the tracking of interest points, several participants used improved trajectories (Wang and Schmid 2013).

From the review of the gesture recognition topic, the achieved results in the performed challenges and the rest of papers published in the gesture recognition Special Topic, one can observe that still it is possible that progress will also be made in feature extraction by making better use of the multimodal development data for better transfer learning. For instance, we think that structural hand information around hand joint could be useful to discriminate among gesture categories that may share similar trajectories of hand/arms. Also recent approaches have shown that Random Forest and Deep Learning, such as considering Convolutional Neural Networks, are powerful alternatives to classical gesture recognition approaches, which still open the door for future the design of new gesture recognition classifiers.

In the case of action detection or spotting, most of the methods are still based on sliding-windows approaches, which makes recognition a time-consuming task. Thus, the research on methods that can generate gesture/action candidates from data in a different fashion are still an open issue.

Acknowledgements This work has been partially supported by ChaLearn Challenges in Machine Learning http://chalearn.org, the Human Pose Recovery and Behavior Analysis Group (HuPBA research group: http://www.maia.ub.es/~sergio/), the Pascal2 network of excellence, NSF grants 1128296, 1059235, 1055062, 1338118, 1035913, 0923494, and Spanish project TIN2013-43478-P. Our sponsors include Microsoft and Texas Instrument who donated prizes and provided technical support. The challenges were hosted by Kaggle.com and Coralab.org who are gratefully acknowledged. We thank our co-organizers of ChaLearn gesture and action recognition challenges: Miguel Reyes, Jordi Gonzalez, Xavier Baro, Jamie Shotton, Victor Ponce, Miguel Angel Bautista, and Hugo Jair Escalante.

References

S. Ali, M. Shah, Human action recognition in videos using kinematic features and multiple instance learning. IEEE Trans. Pattern Anal. Mach. Intell. **32**, 288–303 (2010)

J. Alon, V. Athitsos, Q. Yuan, S. Sclaroff, A unified framework for gesture recognition and spatiotemporal gesture segmentation. IEEE Trans. Pattern Anal. Mach. Intell. **31**(9), 1685–1699 (2009)

M. Andriluka, L. Pishchulin, P. Gehler, B. Schiele, Human pose estimation: new benchmark and state of the art analysis, in *CCVPR* (IEEE, 2014)

J. Appenrodt, A. Al-Hamadi, M. Elmezain, B. Michaelis, Data gathering for gesture recognition systems based on mono color-, stereo color- and thermal cameras, in *Proceedings of the 1st International Conference on Future Generation Information Technology, FGIT '09*, 2009, pp. 78–86. ISBN 978-3-642-10508-1

V. Athitsos, S. Sclaroff, Estimating hand pose from a cluttered image. IEEE Conf. Comput. Vis. Pattern Recognit. **2**, 432–439 (2003)

V. Athitsos, C. Neidle, S. Sclaroff, J. Nash, A. Stefan, Q. Yuan, A. Thangali, The American Sign Language lexicon video dataset, in *IEEE Workshop on Computer Vision and Pattern Recognition for Human Communicative Behavior Analysis (CVPR4HB)*, 2008

A. Avci, S. Bosch, M. Marin-Perianu, R. Marin-Perianu, P.J.M. Havinga, Activity recognition using inertial sensing for healthcare, wellbeing and sports applications: a survey, in *ARCS Workshops*, ed. M. Beigl, F.J. Cazorla-Almeida, 2010, pp. 167–176. ISBN 978-3-8007-3222-7

L. Baraldi, F. Paci, G. Serra, L. Benini, R. Cucchiara, Gesture recognition in ego-centric videos using dense trajectories and hand segmentation, in *Proceedings of the 10th IEEE Embedded Vision Workshop (EVW)*, Columbus, Ohio, June 2014

X. Baró, J. Gonzàlez, J. Fabian, M.A. Bautista, M. Oliu, H.J. Escalante, I. Guyon, S. Escalera, ChaLearn looking at people 2015 challenges: action spotting and cultural event recognition, in *ChaLearn Looking at People, Computer Vision and Pattern Recognition*, 2015

B. Bauer, H. Hienz, K.-F. Kraiss, Video-based continuous sign language recognition using statistical methods, in *International Conference on Pattern Recognition*, 2000, pp. 2463–2466

A.Y. Benbasat, J.A. Paradiso, Compact, configurable inertial gesture recognition, in *CHI '01: CHI '01 Extended Abstracts on Human factors in Computing Systems* (ACM Press, 2001), pp. 183–184. ISBN 1581133405

S. Berlemont, G. Lefebvre, S. Duffner, C. Garcia, Siamese neural network based similarity metric for inertial gesture classification and rejection, in *Automatic Face and Gesture Recognition*, 2015

V. Bloom, D. Makris, V. Argyriou, G3D: a gaming action dataset and real time action recognition evaluation framework, in *IEEE Computer Society Conference on Computer Vision and Pattern Recognition Workshops*, 2012, pp. 7–12

A.F. Bobick, J.W. Davis, The recognition of human movement using temporal templates. IEEE Trans. Pattern Anal. Mach. Intell. **23**(3), 257–267 (2001)

L. Bourdev, J. Malik, Poselets: body part detectors trained using 3d human pose annotations, in *ICCV* (IEEE, 2009), pp. 1365–1372

M. Brand, N. Oliver, A.P. Pentland, Coupled Hidden Markov Models for complex action recognition, in *IEEE Conference on Computer Vision and Pattern Recognition (CVPR)*, 1997, pp. 994–999

M. Caon, Y. Yong, J. Tscherrig, E. Mugellini, O. Abou Khaled, Context-aware 3D gesture interaction based on multiple Kinects, in *The First International Conference on Ambient Computing, Applications, Services and Technologies*, 2011, pp. 7–12. ISBN 978-1-61208-170-0

A. Chaudhary, J.L. Raheja, K. Das, S. Raheja, A survey on hand gesture recognition in context of soft computing. Adv. Comput. **133**, 46–55 (2011)

F.S. Chen, C.M. Fu, C.L. Huang, Hand gesture recognition using a real-time tracking method and Hidden Markov Models. Image Video Comput. **21**(8), 745–758 (2003)

M. Chen, G. AlRegib, B.-H. Juang, 6DMG: a new 6D motion gesture database, in *Multimedia Systems Conference*, 2012, pp. 83–88

C. Conly, P. Doliotis, P. Jangyodsuk, R. Alonzo, V. Athitsos, Toward a 3D body part detection video dataset and hand tracking benchmark, in *Pervasive Technologies Related to Assistive Environments (PETRA)*, 2013

C. Conly, Z. Zhang, V. Athitsos, An integrated RGB-D system for looking up the meaning of signs, in *Pervasive Technologies Related to Assistive Environments (PETRA)*, 2015

H. Cooper, R. Bowden, Learning signs from subtitles: a weakly supervised approach to sign language recognition, in *IEEE Conference on Computer Vision and Pattern Recognition (CVPR)*, 2009, pp. 2568–2574

H. Cooper, E.-J. Ong, N. Pugeault, R. Bowden, Sign language recognition using sub-units. J. Mach. Learn. Res. **13**(7), 2205–2231 (2012)

A. Corradini, Dynamic time warping for off-line recognition of a small gesture vocabulary, in *Recognition Analysis and Tracking of Faces and Gestures in Real-time Systems (RATFG-RTS)*, 2001, pp. 82–89

Y. Cui, J. Weng, Appearance-based hand sign recognition from intensity image sequences. Comput. Vis. Image Underst. **78**(2), 157–176 (2000)

R. Cutler, M. Turk, View-based interpretation of real-time optical flow for gesture recognition, in *Automatic Face and Gesture Recognition*, 1998, pp. 416–421

A. Czabke, J. Neuhauser, T.C. Lueth, Recognition of interactions with objects based on radio modules, in *International Conference on Pervasive Computing Technologies for Healthcare (PervasiveHealth)*, 2010

T.J. Darrell, I.A. Essa, A.P. Pentland, Task-specific gesture analysis in real-time using interpolated views. IEEE Trans. Pattern Anal. Mach. Intell. **18**(12), 1236–1242 (1996)

M. de La Gorce, D.J. Fleet, N. Paragios, Model-based 3D hand pose estimation from monocular video. IEEE Trans. Pattern Anal. Mach. Intell. **33**(9), 1793–1805 (2011)

K.G. Derpanis, M. Sizintsev, K.J. Cannons, R.P. Wildes, Action spotting and recognition based on a spatiotemporal orientation analysis. IEEE Trans. Pattern Anal. Mach. Intell. **35**(3), 527–540 (2013)

P. Dreuw, T. Deselaers, D. Keysers, H. Ney, Modeling image variability in appearance-based gesture recognition, in *ECCV Workshop on Statistical Methods in Multi-Image and Video Processing*, 2006, pp. 7–18

S. Duffner, S. Berlemont, G. Lefebvre, C. Garcia, 3D gesture classification with convolutional neural networks, in *The 39th International Conference on Acoustics, Speech and Signal Processing (ICASSP)*, 2014

S. Escalera, J. Gonzàlez, X. Baró, M. Reyes, I. Guyon, V. Athitsos, H.J. Escalante, L. Sigal, A. Argyros, C. Sminchisescu, R. Bowden, S. Sclaroff, Chalearn multi-modal gesture recognition 2013: grand challenge and workshop summary, in *15th ACM International Conference on Multimodal Interaction*, 2013a, pp. 365–368

S. Escalera, J. Gonzàlez, X. Baró, M. Reyes, O. Lopés, I. Guyon, V. Athitsos, H.J. Escalante, Multi-modal gesture recognition challenge 2013: Dataset and results, in *ChaLearn Multi-Modal Gesture Recognition Grand Challenge and Workshop, 15th ACM International Conference on Multimodal Interaction*, 2013b

S. Escalera, X. Baro, J. Gonzalez, M. Bautista, M. Madadi, M. Reyes, V. Ponce, H.J. Escalante, J. Shotton, I. Guyon, ChaLearn looking at people challenge 2014: dataset and results, in *ChaLearn Looking at People, European Conference on Computer Vision*, 2014

M. Everingham, L. Van Gool, C.K.I. Williams, J. Winn, A. Zisserman, The PASCAL visual object classes (VOC) challenge. IJCV **88**(2), 303–338 (2010)

S.R. Fanello, I. Gori, G. Metta, F. Odone, Keep it simple and sparse: real-time action recognition. J. Mach. Learn. Res. **14**(9), 2617–2640 (2013)

A. Farhadi, D.A. Forsyth, R. White, Transfer learning in sign language, in *IEEE Conference on Computer Vision and Pattern Recognition (CVPR)*, 2007

V. Ferrari, M. Marin-Jimenez, A. Zisserman, Progressive search space reduction for human pose estimation, in *CVPR*, 2008

S. Fothergill, H. Mentis, P. Kohli, S. Nowozin, Instructing people for training gestural interactive systems, in *SIGCHI Conference on Human Factors in Computing Systems*, 2012, pp. 1737–1746

W.T. Freeman, M. Roth, Computer vision for computer games, in *Automatic Face and Gesture Recognition*, 1996, pp. 100–105

N. Gillian, J.A. Paradiso, The gesture recognition toolkit. J. Mach. Learn. Res. **15**, 3483–3487 (2014)

A. Gorban, H. Idrees, Y.-G. Jiang, A. Roshan Zamir, I. Laptev, M. Shah, R. Sukthankar, THUMOS challenge: action recognition with a large number of classes (2015), http://www.thumos.info/

L. Gorelick, M. Blank, E. Shechtman, M. Irani, R. Basri, Actions as space-time shapes. IEEE Trans. Pattern Anal. Mach. Intell. **29**(12), 2247–2253 (2007)

N. Goussies, S. Ubalde, M. Mejail, Transfer learning decision forests for gesture recognition. J. Mach. Learn. Res. **15**, 3667–3690 (2014)

M. Gowing, A. Ahmadi, F. Destelle, D.S. Monaghan, N.E. O'Connor, K. Moran, *Kinect vs. Low-Cost Inertial Sensing for Gesture Recognition*. Lecture Notes in Computer Science, vol. 8325 (Springer, Berlin, 2014)

I. Guyon, V. Athitsos, P. Jangyodsuk, H.J. Escalante, B. Hamner, Results and analysis of the ChaLearn gesture challenge 2012, in *Advances in Depth Image Analysis and Applications*, ed. by X. Jiang, O.R.P. Bellon, D. Goldgof, T. Oishi, Lecture Notes in Computer Science, vol. 7854 (Springer, Berlin, 2013), pp. 186–204. ISBN 978-3-642-40302-6. doi:10.1007/978-3-642-40303-3_19

I. Guyon, V. Athitsos, P. Jangyodsuk, H.J. Escalante, The ChaLearn gesture dataset (CGD 2011). Mach. Vis. Appl. **25**, 1929–1951 (2014)

A. Hernandez-Vela, N. Zlateva, A. Marinov, M. Reyes, P. Radeva, D. Dimov, S. Escalera, Graph cuts optimization for multi-limb human segmentation in depth maps, in *IEEE Computer Vision and Pattern Recognition Conference*, 2012

A. Hernandez-Vela, M.A. Bautista, X. Perez-Sala, V. Ponce, S. Escalera, X. Baro, O. Pujol, C. Angulo, Probability-based dynamic time warping and bag-of-visual-and-depth-words for human gesture recognition in RGB-D. Pattern Recogn. Lett. (2013). doi:10.1016/j.patrec.2013.09.009

A. Hernandez-Vela, M. Reyes, V. Ponce, S. Escalera, Grabcut-based human segmentation in video sequences. Sensors **12**(1), 15376–15393 (2013b)

G. Hewes, Primate communication and the gestural origins of language. Curr. Antropol. **14**, 5–24 (1973)

N.A. Ibraheem, R.Z. Khan, Survey on various gesture recognition technologies and techniques. Int. J. Comput. Appl. **50**(7), 38 44 (2012)

C. Ionescu, D. Papava, V. Olaru, C. Sminchisescu, Human3.6M: Large scale datasets and predictive methods for 3D human sensing in natural environments. IEEE Trans. Pattern Anal. Mach. Intell. **36**(7), 1325–1339 (2014)

M. Isard, A. Blake, CONDENSATION—conditional density propagation for visual tracking. Int. J. Comput. Vis. **29**(1), 5–28 (1998)

H. Jegou, F. Perronnin, M. Douze, J. Sanchez, P. Perez, C. Schmid, Aggregating local image descriptors into compact codes. IEEE Trans. Pattern Anal. Mach. Intell. **34**(9), 1704–1716 (2012)

F. Jiang, S. Zhang, S. Wu, Y. Gao, D. Zhao, Multi-layered gesture recognition with Kinect. J. Mach. Learn. Res. **16**, 227–254 (2015)

S. Johnson, M. Everingham, Clustered pose and nonlinear appearance models for human pose estimation, in *BMVC*, 2010. doi:10.5244/C.24.12

A. Joshi, S. Sclaroff, M. Betke, C. Monnier, A random forest approach to segmenting and classifying gestures, in *Automatic Face and Gesture Recognition*, 2015

T. Kadir, R. Bowden, E. Ong, A. Zisserman, Minimal training, large lexicon, unconstrained sign language recognition, in *British Machine Vision Conference (BMVC)*, vol. 2, 2004, pp. 939–948

K. Kahol, P. Tripathi, S. Panchanathan, Automated gesture segmentation from dance sequences, in *Automatic Face and Gesture Recognition*, 2004, pp. 883–888

H. Kang, C.W. Lee, K. Jung, Recognition-based gesture spotting in video games. Pattern Recognit. Lett. **25**(15), 1701–1704 (2004)

S. Kausar, M.Y. Javed, A survey on sign language recognition, *Frontiers of Information Technology*, 2011, pp. 95–98

Y. Ke, R. Sukthankar, M. Hebert, Efficient visual event detection using volumetric features, in *IEEE International Conference on Computer Vision (ICCV)*, vol. 1, 2005, pp. 166–173

D. Kelly, J. McDonald, C. Markham, A person independent system for recognition of hand postures used in sign language. Pattern Recogn. Lett. **31**(11), 1359–1368 (2010)

C. Keskin, F. Kıraç, Y.E. Kara, L. Akarun, Hand pose estimation and hand shape classification using multi-layered randomized decision forests, in *European Conference on Computer Vision (ECCV)*, 2012, pp. 852–863

R.Z. Khan, N.A. Ibraheem, Survey on gesture recognition for hand image postures. Comput. Inf. Sci. **5**(3), 110–121 (2012)

T.-K. Kim, S.-F. Wong, R. Cipolla, Tensor canonical correlation analysis for action classification, in *IEEE Conference on Computer Vision and Pattern Recognition*, 2007

D.K.H. Kohlsdorf, T.E. Starner, MAGIC summoning: towards automatic suggesting and testing of gestures with low probability of false positives during use. J. Mach. Learn. Res. **14**(1), 209–242 (2013)

M. Kolsch, M. Turk, Fast 2D hand tracking with flocks of features and multi-cue integration, in *IEEE Workshop on Real-Time Vision for Human-Computer Interaction*, 2004, pp. 158–165

J. Konecny, M. Hagara, One-shot-learning gesture recognition using hog-hof features. J. Mach. Learn. Res. **15**, 2513–2532 (2014), http://jmlr.org/papers/v15/konecny14a.html

Y. Kong, B. Satarboroujeni, Y. Fu, Hierarchical 3D kernel descriptors for action recognition using depth sequences, in *Automatic Face and Gesture Recognition*, 2015

J.B. Kruskal, M. Liberman, The symmetric time warping algorithm: from continuous to discrete, in *Time Warps*, Addison-Wesley, 1983

A. Kurakin, Z. Zhang, Z. Liu, A real time system for dynamic hand gesture recognition with a depth sensor, in *European Signal Processing Conference, EUSIPCO*, 2012, pp. 1975–1979

J.D. Lafferty, A. McCallum, F.C.N. Pereira, Conditional random fields: probabilistic models for segmenting and labeling sequence data, in *International Conference on Machine Learning (ICML)*, 2001, pp. 282–289

H. Lane, R.J. Hoffmeister, B. Bahan, *A Journey into the Deaf-World* (DawnSign Press, San Diego, 1996)

I. Laptev, On space-time interest points, Int. J. Comput. Vis. **64**(2–3), 107–123, (2005). ISSN 0920-5691. doi:10.1007/s11263-005-1838-7

I. Laptev, M. Marszalek, C. Schmid, B. Rozenfeld, Learning realistic human actions from movies, in *CVPR*, 2008, pp. 1–8

J.J. LaViola Jr., A survey of hand posture and gesture recognition techniques and technology, Technical Report, Providence, RI, USA, 1999

H.K. Lee, J.H. Kim, An HMM-based threshold model approach for gesture recognition. IEEE Trans. Pattern Anal. Mach. Intell. **21**(10), 961–973 (1999)

C. Li, K.M. Kitani, Pixel-level hand detection for ego-centric videos, in *CVPR*, 2013

W. Li, Z. Zhang, Z. Liu, Action recognition based on a bag of 3D points, in *CVPR Workshops*, 2010, pp. 9–14

H. Liang, J. Yuan, D. Thalmann, Z. Zhang, Model-based hand pose estimation via spatial-temporal hand parsing and 3D fingertip localization. Vis. Comput. **29**(6–8), 837–848 (2013)

H. Liang, J. Yuan, D. Thalmann, Parsing the hand in depth images. IEEE Trans. Multimed. **16**(5), 1241–1253 (2014)

Z. Lin, Z. Jiang, L.S. Davis, Recognizing actions by shape-motion prototype trees, in *IEEE International Conference on Computer Vision, ICCV*, 2009, pp. 444–451

K. Liu, C. Chen, R. Jafari, N. Kehtarnavaz, Fusion of inertial and depth sensor data for robust hand gesture recognition. IEEE Sens. J. **14**(6), 1898–1903 (2014)

L. Liu, L. Shao, Learning discriminative representations from RGB-D video data, in *International Joint Conference on Artificial Intelligence (IJCAI)*, 2013, pp. 1493–1500

O. Lopes, M. Reyes, S. Escalera, J. Gonzàlez, Spherical blurred shape model for 3-D object and pose recognition: quantitative analysis and HCI applications in smart environments. IEEE T. Cybern. **44**(12), 2379–2390 (2014)

Y.M. Lui, Human gesture recognition on product manifolds. J. Mach. Learn. Res. **13**(11), 3297–3321 (2012)

J. Luo, W. Wang, H. Qi, Spatio-temporal feature extraction and representation for RGB-D human action recognition, in *PRL*, 2014

S. Ma, J. Zhang, N. Ikizler-Cinbis, S. Sclaroff, Action recognition and localization by hierarchical space-time segments, in *Proceedings of the IEEE International Conference on Computer Vision (ICCV)*, 2013

M.R. Malgireddy, I. Nwogu, V. Govindaraju, Language-motivated approaches to action recognition. J. Mach. Learn. Res. **14**, 2189–2212 (2013). http://jmlr.org/papers/v14/malgireddy13a.html

J. Martin, V. Devin, J.L. Crowley, Active hand tracking, in *Automatic Face and Gesture Recognition*, 1998, pp. 573–578

A. Martinez, S. Du, A model of the perception of facial expressions of emotion by humans: research overview and perspectives. J. Mach. Learn. Res. **13**(5), 1589–1608 (2012)

D. McNeil, How language began, gesture and speech in human evolution, (Cambridge editorial, 2012)

S. Mitra, T. Acharya, Gesture recognition: a survey. Trans. Syst. Man Cybern. Part C **37**(3), 311–324, 2007. ISSN 1094-6977

Z. Mo, U. Neumann, Real-time hand pose recognition using low-resolution depth images, in *IEEE Conference on Computer Vision and Pattern Recognition (CVPR)*, 2006, pp. 1499–1505

B. Moghaddam, A. Pentland, Probabilistic visual learning for object detection, Technical Report 326, MIT, June 1995

P. Molchanov, S. Gupta, K. Kim, K. Pulli, Multi-sensor system for driver's hand-gesture recognition, in *Automatic Face and Gesture Recognition*, 2015

J. Nagi, F. Ducatelle, G.A. Di Caro, D.C. Ciresan, U. Meier, A. Giusti, F. Nagi, J. Schmidhuber, L.M. Gambardella. Max-pooling convolutional neural networks for vision-based hand gesture recognition, in *ICSIPA* (IEEE, 2011), pp. 342–347. ISBN 978-1-4577-0243-3

S. Nayak, S. Sarkar, B. Loeding, Unsupervised modeling of signs embedded in continuous sentences, in *IEEE Workshop on Vision for Human-Computer Interaction*, 2005

S. Nayak, K. Duncan, S. Sarkar, B. Loeding, Finding recurrent patterns from continuous sign language sentences for automated extraction of signs. J. Mach. Learn. Res. **13**(9), 2589–2615 (2012)

C. Neidle, A. Thangali, S. Sclaroff, Challenges in development of the American Sign Language lexicon video dataset (ASLLVD) corpus, in *Workshop on the Representation and Processing of Sign Languages: Interactions Between Corpus and Lexicon*, 2012

N. Neverova, C. Wolf, G.W. Taylor, F. Nebout, Hand segmentation with structured convolutional learning, in *ACCV*, 2014a

N. Neverova, C. Wolf, G.W. Taylor, F. Nebout, Multi-scale deep learning for gesture detection and localization, in *ChaLearn Looking at People, European Conference on Computer Vision*, 2014b

L. Nguyen-Dinh, A. Calatroni, G. Troster, Robust online gesture recognition with crowdsourced annotations. J. Mach. Learn. Res. **15**, 3187–3220 (2014)

E. Ohn-Bar, M.M. Trivedi, Hand gesture recognition in real-time for automotive interfaces: a multi-modal vision-based approach and evaluations, in *IEEE Transactions on Intelligent Transportation Systems*, 2014

I. Oikonomidis, N. Kyriazis, A.A. Argyros, Markerless and efficient 26-DOF hand pose recovery, in *Asian Conference on Computer Vision (ACCV)*, 2010

I. Oikonomidis, N. Kyriazis, A.A. Argyros, Full DOF tracking of a hand interacting with an object by modeling occlusions and physical constraints, in *IEEE International Conference on Computer Vision (ICCV)*, 2011, pp. 2088–2095

K. Oka, Y. Sato, H. Koike, Real-time fingertip tracking and gesture recognition. IEEE Comput. Graphics Appl. **22**(6), 64–71 (2002)

R. Oka, Spotting method for classification of real world data. Comput. J. **41**(8), 559–565 (1998)

E.J. Ong, R. Bowden, A boosted classifier tree for hand shape detection, in *Face and Gesture Recognition*, 2004, pp. 889–894

O. Oreifej, Z. Liu, HON4D: histogram of oriented 4D normals for activity recognition from depth sequences, in *CVPR*, 2013, pp. 716–723

A. Pardo, A. Clapes, S. Escalera, O. Pujol, Actions in context: system for people with dementia, in *2nd International Workshop on Citizen Sensor Networks (Citisen2013) at the European Conference on Complex Systems (ECCS'13)*, 2013

X. Peng, L. Wang, Z. Cai, Y. Qiao, Action and gesture temporal spotting with super vector representation, in *Computer Vision—ECCV 2014 Workshops*, ed. by L. Agapito, M.M. Bronstein, C. Rother, *Lecture Notes in Computer Science*, vol. 8925 (Springer, Berlin, 2015), pp. 518–527. ISBN 978-3-319-16177-8. doi:10.1007/978-3-319-16178-5_36

A. Pieropan, G. Salvi, K.Pauwels, H. Kjellstrom, Audio-visual classification and detection of human manipulation actions, in *IEEE/RSJ International Conference on Intelligent Robots and Systems*, 2014

V. Pitsikalis, A. Katsamanis, S. Theodorakis, P. Maragos, Multimodal gesture recognition via multiple hypotheses rescoring. J. Mach. Learn. Res. (2014)

N. Pugeault, R. Bowden, Spelling it out: real-time ASL fingerspelling recognition, in *ICCV Workshops*, 2011, pp. 1114–1119

A. Quattoni, S.B. Wang, L.-P. Morency, M. Collins, T. Darrell, Hidden conditional random fields. IEEE Trans. Pattern Anal. Mach. Intell. **29**(10), 1848–1852 (2007)

D. Ramanan, Learning to parse images of articulated bodies, in *NIPS*, 2006, pp. 1129–1136

J.M. Rehg, T. Kanade, Model-based tracking of self-occluding articulated objects, in *IEEE International Conference on Computer Vision (ICCV)*, 1995, pp. 612–617

Z. Ren, J. Meng, J. Yuan, Z. Zhang, Robust hand gesture recognition with Kinect sensor, in *ACM International Conference on Multimedia*, 2011a, pp. 759–760

Z. Ren, J. Yuan, Z. Zhang, Robust hand gesture recognition based on finger-earth mover's distance with a commodity depth camera, in *ACM International Conference on Multimedia*, 2011b, pp. 1093–1096

Z. Ren, J. Yuan, J. Meng, Z. Zhang, Robust part-based hand gesture recognition using Kinect sensor. IEEE Trans. Multimed. **15**(5), 1110–1120 (2013)

A. Roussos, S. Theodorakis, V. Pitsikalis, P. Maragos, Dynamic affine-invariant shape-appearance handshape features and classification in sign language videos. J. Mach. Learn. Res. **14**(6), 1627–1663 (2013)

S. Ruffieux, D. Lalanne, E. Mugellini. ChAirGest: a challenge for multimodal mid-air gesture recognition for close HCI, in *Proceedings of the 15th ACM on International Conference on Multimodal Interaction*, 2013, pp. 483–488

A. Sadeghipour, L.-P. Morency, S. Kopp, Gesture-based object recognition using histograms of guiding strokes, in *British Machine Vision Conference*, 2012, pp. 44.1–44.11

D. Sánchez, M.A. Bautista, S. Escalera, HuPBA 8k+: dataset and ECOC-graphcut based segmentation of human limbs. *Neurocomputing*, 2014

B. Sapp, B. Taskar, Modec: multimodal decomposable models for human pose estimation, in *CVPR*, IEEE, 2013

Y. Sato, T. Kobayashi, Extension of Hidden Markov Models to deal with multiple candidates of observations and its application to mobile-robot-oriented gesture recognition, in *International Conference on Pattern Recognition (ICPR)*, vol, II, 2002, pp. 515–519

J.D. Schein, *At Home Among Strangers* (Gallaudet U. Press, Washington, DC, 1989)

C. Schuldt, I. Laptev, B. Caputo, Recognizing human actions: a local SVM approach, in *ICPR*, vol. 3, 2004, pp. 32–36

N. Shapovalova, W. Gong., M. Pedersoli, F.X. Roca, J. Gonzalez, On importance of interactions and context in human action recognition, in *Pattern Recognition and Image Analysis*, 2011, pp. 58–66

J. Shotton, A.W. Fitzgibbon, M. Cook, T. Sharp, M. Finocchio, R. Moore, A. Kipman, A. Blake, Real-time human pose recognition in parts from single depth images, in *IEEE Conference on Computer Vision and Pattern Recognition (CVPR)*, 2011, pp. 1297–1304

L. Sigal, A.O. Balan, M.J. Black, HumanEva: synchronized video and motion capture dataset and baseline algorithm for evaluation of articulated human motion. Int. J. Comput. Vis. **87**(1–2), 4–27 (2010)

C. Sminchisescu, A. Kanaujia, D. Metaxas, Conditional models for contextual human motion recognition. Comput. Vis. Image Underst. **104**, 210–220 (2006)

Y. Song, D. Demirdjian, R. Davis, Tracking body and hands for gesture recognition: NATOPS aircraft handling signals database, in *Automatic Face and Gesture Recognition*, 2011, pp. 500–506

T. Starner, A. Pentland, Real-time American Sign Language recognition using desk and wearable computer based video. IEEE Trans. Pattern Anal. Mach. Intell. **20**(12), 1371–1375 (1998)

N. Stefanov, A. Galata, R. Hubbold, Real-time hand tracking with variable-length Markov Models of behaviour, in *Real Time Vision for Human-Computer Interaction*, 2005

B. Stenger, A. Thayananthan, P.H.S. Torr, R. Cipolla, Filtering using a tree-based estimator, in *IEEE International Conference on Computer Vision (ICCV)*, 2003, pp. 1063–1070

E. Sudderth, M. Mandel, W. Freeman, A. Willsky, Distributed occlusion reasoning for tracking with nonparametric belief propagation, in *Neural Information Processing Systems (NIPS)*, 2004

D. Tran, D. Forsyth, Improved human parsing with a full relational model, in *ECCV* (IEEE, 2010), pp. 227–240

J. Triesch, C. von der Malsburg, A system for person-independent hand posture recognition against complex backgrounds. IEEE Trans. Pattern Anal. Mach. Intell. **23**(12), 1449–1453 (2001)

J. Triesch, C. von der Malsburg, Classification of hand postures against complex backgrounds using elastic graph matching. Image Vis. Comput. **20**(13–14), 937–943 (2002)

M. Van den Bergh, E. Koller-Meier, L. Van Gool, Real-time body pose recognition using 2D or 3D haarlets. Int. J. Comput. Vis. **83**(1), 72–84 (2009)

P. Viola, M. Jones, Rapid object detection using a boosted cascade of simple features, in *IEEE Conference on Computer Vision and Pattern Recognition (CVPR)*, vol. 1, 2001, pp. 511–518

C. Vogler, D Metaxas, Parallel Hidden Markov Models for American Sign Language recognition, In *IEEE International Conference on Computer Vision (ICCV)*, 1999, pp. 116–122

J. Wan, Q. Ruan, W. Li, S. Deng, One-shot learning gesture recognition from RGB-D data using bag of features. J. Mach. Learn. Res. **14**, 2549–2582 (2013). http://jmlr.org/papers/v14/wan13a.html

H. Wang, C. Schmid, Action recognition with improved trajectories, in *IEEE International Conference on Computer Vision*, 2013

H. Wang, A. Stefan, S. Moradi, V. Athitsos, C. Neidle, F. Kamangar, A system for large vocabulary sign search, in *Workshop on Sign, Gesture and Activity (SGA)*, 2010

H. Wang, X. Chai, Y. Zhou, X. Chen, Fast sign language recognition benefited from low rank approximation, in *Automatic Face and Gesture Recognition*, 2015a

J. Wang, Z. Liu, Y. Wu, J. Yuan, Learning actionlet ensemble for 3D human action recognition. IEEE Trans. Pattern Anal. Mach. Intell. **36**(5), 914–927 (2014)

R.Y. Wang, J. Popović, Real-time hand-tracking with a color glove. ACM Trans. Graph. **28**(3), 63:1–63:8 (2009)

Y. Wang, D. Tran, Z. Liao, D. Forsyth, Discriminative hierarchical part-based models for human parsing and action recognition. J. Mach. Learn. Res. **13**(10), 3075–3102 (2012)

Z. Wang, L. Wang, W. Du, Q. Yu, Action spotting system using Fisher vector, in *CVPR ChaLearn Looking at People Workshop 2015*, 2015

M. Wilhelm, A generic context aware gesture recognition framework for smart environments, in *PerCom Workshops*, 2012, pp. 536–537

A.D. Wilson, A.F. Bobick, Parametric Hidden Markov Models for gesture recognition. IEEE Trans. Pattern Anal. Mach. Intell. **21**(9), 884–900 (1999)

J. Wu, J. Cheng, Bayesian co-boosting for multi-modal gesture recognition. J. Mach. Learn. Res. **15**(1), 3013–3036 (2014)

Y. Wu, T.S. Huang, View-independent recognition of hand postures, in *IEEE Conference on Computer Vision and Pattern Recognition (CVPR)*, vol. 2, 2000, pp. 88–94

Y. Xiao, Z. Zhang, A. Beck, J. Yuan, D. Thalmann, Human-robot interaction by understanding upper body gestures. Presence **23**(2), 133–154 (2014)

H.D. Yang, S. Sclaroff, S.W. Lee, Sign language spotting with a threshold model based on conditional random fields. IEEE Trans. Pattern Anal. Mach. Intell. **31**(7), 1264–1277 (2009)

M.H. Yang, N. Ahuja, M. Tabb, Extraction of 2D motion trajectories and its application to hand gesture recognition. IEEE Trans. Pattern Anal. Mach. Intell. **24**(8), 1061–1074 (2002)

W. Yang, Y. Wang, G. Mori, Recognizing human actions from still images with latent poses, in *IEEE Conference on Computer Vision and Pattern Recognition (CVPR)*, 2010, pp. 2030–2037

X. Yang, Y. Tian, Super normal vector for activity recognition using depth sequences, in *CVPR*, 2014a

X. Yang, Y. Tian, Action recognition using super sparse coding vector with spatio-temporal awareness, in *ECCV*, 2014b

G. Yao, H. Yao, X. Liu, F. Jiang, Real time large vocabulary continuous sign language recognition based on OP/Viterbi algorithm, *International Conference on Pattern Recognition*, vol. 3, 2006, pp. 312–315

G. Yu, Z. Liu, J. Yuan, Discriminative orderlet mining for real-time recognition of human-object interaction, in *ACCV*, 2014

J. Yuan, Z. Liu, Y. Wu, Discriminative video pattern search for efficient action detection. IEEE Trans. Pattern Anal. Mach. Intell. **33**(9), 1728–1743 (2011)

Z. Zafrulla, H. Brashear, T. Starner, H. Hamilton, P. Presti, American Sign Language recognition with the Kinect, in *Proceedings of the 13th International Conference on Multimodal Interfaces, ICMI '11*, ACM, New York, NY, USA, 2011, pp. 279–286. ISBN 978-1-4503-0641-6. 10.1145/2070481.2070532. doi:10.1145/2070481.2070532

M. Zanfir, M. Leordeanu, C. Sminchisescu, The moving pose: An efficient 3D kinematics descriptor for low-latency action recognition and detection, in *ICCV*, 2013

J. Zieren, K.-F. Kraiss, Robust person-independent visual sign language recognition. Iberian Conf. Pattern Recognit. Image Anal. **1**, 520–528 (2005)

Chapter 2
Human Gesture Recognition on Product Manifolds

Yui Man Lui

Abstract Action videos are multidimensional data and can be naturally represented as data tensors. While tensor computing is widely used in computer vision, the geometry of tensor space is often ignored. The aim of this paper is to demonstrate the importance of the intrinsic geometry of tensor space which yields a very discriminating structure for action recognition. We characterize data tensors as points on a product manifold and model it statistically using least squares regression. To this aim, we factorize a data tensor relating to each order of the tensor using higher order singular value decomposition (HOSVD) and then impose each factorized element on a Grassmann manifold. Furthermore, we account for underlying geometry on manifolds and formulate least squares regression as a composite function. This gives a natural extension from Euclidean space to manifolds. Consequently, classification is performed using geodesic distance on a product manifold where each factor manifold is Grassmannian. Our method exploits appearance and motion without explicitly modeling the shapes and dynamics. We assess the proposed method using three gesture databases, namely the Cambridge hand-gesture, the UMD Keck body-gesture, and the CHALEARN gesture challenge data sets. Experimental results reveal that not only does the proposed method perform well on the standard benchmark data sets, but also it generalizes well on the one-shot-learning gesture challenge. Furthermore, it is based on a simple statistical model and the intrinsic geometry of tensor space.

Keywords Gesture recognition · Action recognition · Grassmann manifolds · Product manifolds · One-shot-learning · Kinect data

Editor: Isabelle Guyon and Vassilis Athitsos.

Y.M. Lui (✉)
School of Computer Science and Mathematics, University of Central Missouri,
Warrensburg, MO 64093, USA
e-mail: lui@ucmo.edu

© Springer International Publishing AG 2017
S. Escalera et al. (eds.), *Gesture Recognition*, The Springer Series
on Challenges in Machine Learning, DOI 10.1007/978-3-319-57021-1_2

2.1 Introduction

Human gestures/actions are the natural way for expressing intentions and can be instantly recognized by people. We use gestures to depict sign language to deaf people, convey messages in noisy environments, and interface with computer games. Having automated gesture-based communication would broaden the horizon of human-computer interaction and enrich our daily lives. In recent years, many gesture recognition algorithms have been proposed (Mitra and Acharya 2007; Wang et al. 2009; Bilinski and Bremond 2011). However, reliable gesture recognition remains a challenging area due in part to the complexity of human movements. To champion the recognition performance, models are often complicated, causing difficulty for generalization. Consequently, heavy-duty models may not have substantial gains in overall gesture recognition problems.

In this paper, we propose a new representation to gesture recognition based upon tensors and the geometry of product manifolds. Since human actions are expressed as a sequence of video frames, an action video may be characterized as a third order data tensor. The mathematical framework for working with high order tensors is multilinear algebra which is a useful tool for characterizing multiple factor interactions. Tensor computing has been successfully applied to many computer vision applications such as face recognition (Vasilescu and Terzopoulos 2002), visual tracking (Li et al. 2007), and action classification (Vasilescu 2002; Kim and Cipolla 2009). However, the geometrical aspect of data tensors remains unexamined. The goal of this paper is to demonstrate the importance of the intrinsic geometry of tensor space where it provides a very discriminating structure for action recognition.

Notably, several recent efforts (Lui 2012a) have been inspired by the characteristics of space and the associated construction of classifiers based upon the intrinsic geometry inherent in particular manifolds. Veeraraghavan et al. (2005) modeled human shapes from a shape manifold and expressed the dynamics of human silhouettes using an autoregressive (AR) model on the tangent space. Turaga and Chellappa (2009) extended this framework and represented the trajectories on a Grassmann manifold for activity classification. The use of tangent bundles on special manifolds was investigated by Lui (2012b) where a set of tangent spaces was exploited for action recognition. Age estimation was also studied using Grassmann manifolds (Turaga et al. 2010). The geodesic velocity from an average face to the given face was employed for age estimation where the space of landmarks was interpreted as a Grassmann manifold. Lui and Beveridge (2008) characterized tangent spaces of a registration manifold as elements on a Grassmann manifold for face recognition. The importance of the ordering on Stiefel manifolds was demonstrated by Lui et al. (2009) and an illumination model was applied to synthesize such elements for face recognition. These successes motivate the exploration of the underlying geometry of tensor space.

The method proposed in this paper characterizes action videos as data tensors and demonstrates their association with a product manifold. We focus attention on the intrinsic geometry of tensor space, and draw upon the fact that the geodesic on a product manifold is equivalent to the Cartesian product of geodesics from multiple factor manifolds. In other words, elements of a product manifold are the set of all elements inherited from factor manifolds. Thus, in our approach, action videos are factorized to three factor elements using higher order singular value decomposition (HOSVD) in which the factor elements give rise to three factor manifolds. We further extend the product manifold representation to least squares regression. In doing so, we consider the underlying geometry and formulate least squares regression as a composite function. As such, we ensure that both the domain values and the range values reside on a manifold through the regression process. This yields a natural extension from Euclidean space to manifolds. The least squares fitted elements from a training set can then be exploited for gesture recognition where the similarity is expressed in terms of the geodesic distance on a product manifold associated with fitted elements from factor manifolds.

We demonstrate the merits of our method on three gesture recognition problems including hand gestures, body gestures, and gestures collected from the Microsoft Kinect ^{TM} camera for the one-shot-learning CHALEARN gesture challenge. Our experimental results reveal that our method is competitive to the state-of-the-art methods and generalizes well to the one-shot-learning scheme, yet is based on a simple statistical model. The key contributions of the proposed work are summarized as follows:

- A new way of relating tensors on a product manifold to action recognition.
- A novel formulation for least squares regression on manifolds.
- The use of appearance and motion without explicitly modeling shapes or dynamics.
- A simple pixel-based representation (no silhouette or skeleton extraction).
- No extensive training and parameter tuning.
- No explicit assumption on action data.
- Competitive performance on gesture recognition.
- Applicable to other visual applications.

The rest of this paper is organized as follows: Related work is summarized in Sect. 2.2. Tensor algebra, orthogonal groups, and Grassmann manifolds are reviewed in Sect. 2.3. The formulation of the proposed product manifold is presented in Sect. 2.4 and is further elaborated with examples in Sect. 2.5. The statistical modeling on manifolds is introduced in Sect. 2.6. Section 2.7 reports our experimental results. Section 2.8 discusses the effect of using raw pixels for action recognition. Finally, we conclude this paper in Sect. 2.9.

2.2 Related Work

Many researchers have proposed a variety of techniques for action recognition in recent years. We highlight some of this work here, including bag-of-features models, autoregressive models, 3D Fourier transforms, tensor frameworks, and product spaces.

In the context of action recognition, bag-of-features models (Dollar et al. 2005; Wang et al. 2009; Bilinski and Bremond 2011) may be among the most popular methods wherein visual vocabularies are learned from feature descriptors and spatiotemporal features are typically represented by a normalized histogram. While encouraging results have been achieved, bag-of-features methods have heavy training loads prior to classification. In particular, feature detection and codebook generation can consume tremendous amounts of time if the number of training samples is large. Recently, Wang et al. (2009) have evaluated a number of feature descriptors and bag-of-features models for action recognition. This study concluded that different sampling strategies and feature descriptors were needed to achieve the best results on alternative action data sets. Similar conclusions were also found by Bilinski and Bremond (2011) where various sizes of codebooks are needed for different data sets in order to obtain peak performances.

Another school of thought for action classification is using an autoregressive (AR) model. Some of the earliest works involved dynamic texture recognition (Saisan et al. 2001) and human gait recognition (Bissacco et al. 2001). These works represented actions using AR models. The authors found that the most effective way to compare dynamics was by computing the Martin distance between AR models. Veeraraghavan et al. (2005) modeled human silhouettes based on Kendall's theory of shape (Kendall 1984) where shapes were expressed on a shape manifold. This method modeled the dynamics of human silhouettes using an AR model on the tangent space of the shape manifold. The sequences of human shapes were compared by computing the distance between the AR models. Turaga and Chellappa (2009) investigated statistical modeling with AR models for human activity analysis. In their work, trajectories were considered a sequence of subspaces represented by AR models on a Grassmann manifold. As such, the dynamics were learned and kernel density functions with Procrustes representation were applied to density estimation.

Three-dimensional Fourier transform has been demonstrated as a valuable tool in action classification. Weinland et al. (2006) employed Fourier magnitudes and cylindrical coordinates to represent motion templates. Consequently, the action matching was invariant to translations and rotations around the z-axis. Although this method was view invariant, the training videos needed to be acquired from multiple cameras. Rodriguez et al. (2008) synthesized a filter respond using the Clifford Fourier transform for action recognition. The feature representation was computed using spatiotemporal regularity flow from the xy-parallel component. The advantage of using Clifford algebra is the direct use of vector fields to Fourier transform.

Data tensors are the multidimensional generalizations to matrices. Vasilescu (2002) modeled the joint angle trajectories on human motion as a set of factorized matrices from a data tensor. Signatures corresponding to motion and identity were then extracted using PCA for person identification. Kim and Cipolla (2009) extended canonical correlation analysis to the tensor framework by developing a Tensor Canonical Correlation Algorithm (TCCA). This method factorized data tensors to a set of matrices and learned a set of projection matrices maximizing the canonical correlations. The inner product was employed to compute the similarity between two data tensors. The use of SIFT features with CCA was also considered for gesture recognition by Kim and Cipolla (2007). Recently, nonnegative tensor factorization has been exploited for action recognition by Krausz and Bauckhage (2010) where action videos were factorized using a gradient descent method and represented as the sum of rank-1 tensors associated with a weighting factor. As a result, the appearance was captured by the basis images and the dynamics was encoded with the weighting factor.

Product spaces have received attention in applications related to spatiotemporal interactions. Datta et al. (2009) modeled the motion manifold as a collection of local linear models. This method learned a selection of mappings to encode the motion manifold from a product space. Lin et al. (2009) proposed a probabilistic framework for action recognition using prototype trees. Shape and motion were explicitly learned and characterized via hierarchical K-means clustering. The joint likelihood framework was employed to model the joint shape-motion space. Li and Chellappa (2010) investigated the product space of spatial and temporal submanifolds for action alignment. Sequential importance sampling was then used to find the optimal alignment. Despite these efforts, the geometry of the product space has not been directly considered and the geodesic nature on the product manifold remains unexamined.

2.3   Mathematical Background

In this section, we briefly review the background mathematics used in this paper. Particularly, we focus on the elements of tensor algebra, orthogonal groups, Stiefel manifolds, and Grassmann manifolds.

2.3.1   Tensor Representation

Tensors provide a natural representation for high dimensional data. We consider a video as a third order data tensor $\in \mathbb{R}^{X \times Y \times T}$ where X, Y, and T are the image width, image height, and video length, respectively. High order data tensors can be regarded as a multilinear mapping over a set of vector spaces. Generally, useful information can be extracted using tensor decompositions. In particular, a Higher Order Singular Value Decomposition (HOSVD) (De Lathauwer et al. 2000) is considered in this paper because the data tensor can be factorized in a closed-form. A recent review paper on tensor decompositions can be found in Kolda and Bader (2009). Before we describe HOSVD, we illustrate a building block operation called matrix unfolding.

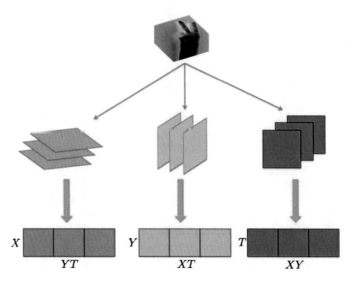

Fig. 2.1 An example of matrix unfolding for a third order tensor. The illustration is for a video action sequence with two spatial dimensions X and Y and a temporal dimension T

2.3.1.1 Matrix Unfolding

Let $\mathscr{A}$ be an order N data tensor $\in \mathbb{R}^{I_1 \times I_2 \times \cdots \times I_N}$. The data tensor $\mathscr{A}$ can be converted to a set of matrices via a matrix unfolding operation. Matrix unfolding maps a tensor $\mathscr{A}$ to a set of matrices $A_{(1)}, A_{(2)}, \ldots, A_{(N)}$, where $A_{(k)} \in \mathbb{R}^{I_k \times (I_1 \times \cdots \times I_{k-1} \times I_{k+1} \cdots \times I_N)}$ is a mode-k matrix of $\mathscr{A}$. An example of matrix unfolding of a third order, that is, $N = 3$, tensor is given in Fig. 2.1. As Fig. 2.1 shows, we can slice a third order tensor in three different ways along each axis and concatenate these slices into three different matrices $A_{(1)}$, $A_{(2)}$, and $A_{(3)}$ where the rows of an unfolded matrix are represented by a single variation of the tensor and the columns are composed by two variations of the tensor.

2.3.1.2 Higher Order Singular Value Decomposition

Just as a data matrix can be factorized using a singular value decomposition (SVD), a data tensor can also be factorized using higher order singular value decomposition (HOSVD), also known as multilinear SVD. HOSVD operates on the unfolded matrices $A_{(k)}$, and each unfolded matrix may be factored using SVD as follows:

$$A_{(k)} = U^{(k)} \Sigma^{(k)} V^{(k)^T} \tag{2.1}$$

where $\Sigma^{(k)}$ is a diagonal matrix, $U^{(k)}$ is an orthogonal matrix spanning the column space of $A_{(k)}$ associated with nonzero singular values, and $V^{(k)}$ is an orthogonal matrix spanning the row space of $A_{(k)}$ associated with nonzero singular values. Then, an N order tensor can be decomposed using HOSVD as follows:

$$\mathscr{A} = \mathscr{S} \times_1 U^{(1)} \times_2 U^{(2)} \cdots \times_n U^{(N)}$$

where $\mathscr{S} \in \mathbb{R}^{(I_1 \times I_2 \times \cdots \times I_N)}$ is a core tensor, $U^{(1)}$, $U^{(2)}$, ..., $U^{(N)}$ are orthogonal matrices spanning the column space described in (2.1), and $\times_k$ denotes mode-k multiplication. The core tensor signifies the interaction of mode matrices and is generally not diagonal when the tensor order is greater than two.

2.3.2 Orthogonal Groups

Matrix Lie groups arise in various kinds of non-Euclidean geometry (Belinfante and Kolman 1972). The General Linear Group[1] $\mathscr{GL}(n)$ is a set of nonsingular $n \times n$ matrices defined as:

$$\mathscr{GL}(n) = \{Y \in \mathbb{R}^{n \times n} : \det(Y) \neq 0\}.$$

The $\mathscr{GL}(n)$ is closed under a group operation, that is, matrix multiplication. This is because the product of two nonsingular matrices is a nonsingular matrix. Of practical importance here is the fact that elements of $\mathscr{GL}(n)$ are full rank and thus their row and column spaces span $\mathbb{R}^n$. A further subgroup of $\mathscr{GL}(n)$ is the orthogonal group denoted as:

$$\mathscr{O}(n) = \{Y \in \mathbb{R}^{n \times n} : Y^T Y = I\}.$$

It is known that the determinants of orthogonal matrices can be either $+1$ or -1 where the matrices with the determinant of 1 are rotation matrices and the matrices with the determinant of -1 are reflection matrices.

2.3.3 Stiefel Manifolds

The Stiefel manifold $\mathscr{V}_{n,p}$ is a set of $n \times p$ orthonormal matrices defined as:

$$\mathscr{V}_{n,p} = \{Y \in \mathbb{R}^{n \times p} : Y^T Y = I\}.$$

The Stiefel manifold $\mathscr{V}_{n,p}$ can be considered a quotient space of $\mathscr{O}(n)$ so we can identify an isotropy subgroup H of $\mathscr{O}(n)$ expressed as $\left\{ \begin{bmatrix} I_p & 0 \\ 0 & Q_{n-p} \end{bmatrix} : Q_{n-p} \in \mathscr{O}(n-p) \right\}$

---

[1] In this paper, we are only interested in the field of real number $\mathbb{R}$. Unitary groups may be considered in other contexts.

where the isotropy subgroup leaves the element unchanged. Thus, the Stiefel manifold can be expressed as $\mathcal{V}_{n,p} = \mathcal{O}(n) / \mathcal{O}(n - p)$. From a group theory point of view, $\mathcal{O}(n)$ is a Lie group and $\mathcal{O}(n - p)$ is its subgroup so that $\mathcal{O}(n) / \mathcal{O}(n - p)$ represents the orbit space. In other words, $\mathcal{V}_{n,p}$ is the quotient group of $\mathcal{O}(n)$ by $\mathcal{O}(n - p)$.

2.3.4 Grassmann Manifolds

When we impose a group action of $\mathcal{O}(n)$ onto the Stiefel manifold, this gives rise to the equivalence relation between orthogonal matrices so that the elements of Stiefel manifolds are rotation and reflection invariant. In other words, elements are considered being equivalent if there exists a $p \times p$ orthogonal matrix Q_p which maps one point into the other. This equivalence relation can be written as:

$$\lfloor Y \rfloor = \{Y Q_p : Q_p \in \mathcal{O}(n)\} \tag{2.2}$$

where $\lfloor Y \rfloor$ is an element on the Grassmann manifold. Therefore, the Grassmann manifold $\mathcal{G}_{n,p}$ is a set of p-dimensional linear subspaces of $\mathbb{R}^n$ and its isotropy subgroup composes all elements of $\left\{ \begin{bmatrix} Q_p & 0 \\ 0 & Q_{n-p} \end{bmatrix} : Q_p \in \mathcal{O}(p), \; Q_{n-p} \in \mathcal{O}(n - p) \right\}$. The quotient representation of Grassmann manifolds is expressed as $\mathcal{G}_{n,p} = \mathcal{O}(n) / (\mathcal{O}(p) \times \mathcal{O}(n - p)) = \mathcal{V}_{n,p} / \mathcal{O}(p)$. As such, the element of the Grassmann manifold represents the orbit of a Stiefel manifold under the group action of orthogonal groups. More details on the treatment of Grassmann manifolds can be found in Edelman et al. (1998) and Absil et al. (2008).

2.4   Elements of Product Manifolds

This section discusses the elements of product manifolds in the context of gesture recognition. We illustrate the essence of product manifolds and the factorization of action videos. Further, we describe the realization of geodesic distance on the product manifold and its use for action classification.

2.4.1   Product Manifolds

A product manifold can be recognized as a complex compound object in a high dimensional space composed by a set of lower dimensional objects. For example, the product of a line with elements y in $\mathbb{R}^1$ and a solid circle with elements x in $\mathbb{R}^2$ becomes a cylinder with elements (x, y) in $\mathbb{R}^3$ as shown in Fig. 2.2. Formally, this product topology can be expressed as:

Fig. 2.2 An example of a product manifold: a cylinder is a cross product of a circle and an interval

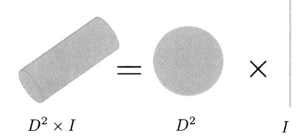

$$D^2 \times I \qquad\qquad D^2 \qquad\qquad I$$

$$I = \{y \in \mathbb{R} : |y| < 1\},$$
$$D^2 = \{x \in \mathbb{R}^2 : |x| < 1\},$$
$$D^2 \times I = \{(x, y) \in \mathbb{R}^2 \times \mathbb{R} : |x| < 1 \ \text{ and } \ |y| < 1\}$$

where D^2 and I are viewed as topological spaces.

The cylinder may be equally well interpreted as either a circle of intervals or an interval of circles. In general, a product manifold may be viewed as the cross section of lower dimensional objects. Formally, let $\mathcal{M}_1, \mathcal{M}_2, \dots , \mathcal{M}_q$ be a set of manifolds. The set $\mathcal{M}_1 \times \mathcal{M}_2 \times \cdots \times \mathcal{M}_q$ is called the product of the manifolds where the manifold topology is equivalent to the product topology. Hence, a product manifold is defined as:

$$\mathcal{M} = \mathcal{M}_1 \times \mathcal{M}_2 \times \cdots \times \mathcal{M}_q$$
$$= \{(x_1, x_2, \dots, x_q) : x_1 \in \mathcal{M}_1, x_2 \in \mathcal{M}_2, \dots, x_q \in \mathcal{M}_q\}$$

where $\times$ denotes the Cartesian product, $\mathcal{M}_k$ represents a factor manifold (a topological space), and x_k is an element in $\mathcal{M}_k$. Note that the dimension of a product manifold is the sum of all factor manifolds (Lee 2003).

The product manifold naturally expresses a compound topological space associated with a number of factor manifolds. For action video classification, third order data tensors are manifested as elements on three factor manifolds. As such, video data can be abstracted as points and classified on a product manifold.

2.4.2 Factorization in Product Spaces

As discussed in Sect. 2.3, HOSVD operates on the unfolded matrices (modes) via matrix unfolding in which the variation of each mode is captured by HOSVD. However, the traditional definition of HOSVD does not lead to a well-defined product manifold in the context of action recognition.

We observe that the column of every unfolded matrix $A_{(k)}$ is composed by multiple orders from the original data tensor $\mathcal{A} \in \mathbb{R}^{I_1 \times I_2 \times \cdots \times I_N}$. This fact can also be observed in Fig. 2.1. Let m be the dimension of the columns, $I_1 \times I_2 \times \cdots \times I_{k-1} \times I_{k+1} \cdots \times I_N$, and p be the dimension of the rows, I_k, for an unfolded matrix $A_{(k)}$. We can then assume that the dimension of the columns is greater than the dimension of the rows due to the nature of matrix unfolding for action videos, that is, $m > p$. This implies that the unfolded matrix $A_{(k)}$ only spans p dimensions.

Alternatively, one can factorize the data tensor using the right orthogonal matrices (Lui et al. 2010). From the context of action videos, the HOSVD can be expressed as:

$$\mathscr{A} = \hat{\mathscr{S}} \times_1 V^{(1)}_{\text{horizontal-motion}} \times_2 V^{(2)}_{\text{vertical-motion}} \times_3 V^{(3)}_{\text{appearance}}$$

where $\hat{\mathscr{S}}$ is a core tensor, $V^{(k)}$ are the orthogonal matrices spanning the row space with the first p rows associated with non-zero singular values from the unfolded matrices, respectively. Because we are performing action recognition on videos, the orthogonal matrices, $V^{(1)}_{\text{horizontal-motion}}$, $V^{(2)}_{\text{vertical-motion}}$, and $V^{(3)}_{\text{appearance}}$, correspond to horizontal motion, vertical motion, and appearance. Figure 2.3 shows some examples from the action decomposition.

From the factorization of HOSVD, each $V^{(k)}$ is a tall orthogonal matrix, thus it is an element on a Stiefel manifold. When we impose a group action of the orthogonal group, elements on the Stiefel manifold become rotation and reflection invariant. In other words, they are elements on the Grassmann manifold described in (2.2). As such, the action data are represented as the orbit of elements on the Stiefel manifold under the rotation and reflection actions with respect to appearance and dynamics. Section 2.5 will discuss how we benefit from imposing such a group action on the Stiefel manifold.

2.4.3 Geodesic Distance on Product Manifolds

The geodesic in a product manifold $\mathscr{M}$ is the product of geodesics in $\mathscr{M}_1, \mathscr{M}_2, \ldots, \mathscr{M}_q$ (Ma et al. 1998; Begelfor and Werman 2006). Hence, for any differentiable curve γ parametrized by t, we have $\gamma(t) = (\gamma_i(t), \gamma_j(t))$ where γ is the geodesic on the product manifold $\mathscr{M}$, and γ_i and γ_j are the geodesics on the factor manifold $\mathscr{M}_i$ and $\mathscr{M}_j$ respectively. From this observation, the geodesic distance on a product manifold may be expressed as a Cartesian product of canonical angles computed by factor manifolds.

Just as there are alternatives to induce a metric on a Grassmann manifold (Edelman et al. 1998) using canonical angles, the geodesic distance on a product manifold could also be defined in different ways. One possible choice is the chordal distance that approximates the geodesic via a projection embedding (Conway et al. 1996). Consequently, we define the geodesic distance on a product manifold as:

$$d_{\mathscr{M}}(\mathscr{A}, \mathscr{B}) = \| \sin \Theta \|_2 \tag{2.3}$$

where $\mathscr{A}$ and $\mathscr{B}$ are the N order data tensors, $\Theta = (\theta_1, \theta_2, \ldots, \theta_N)$, and $\theta_k \in \mathscr{G}_k$ is a set of canonical angles (Björck and Golub 1973) computed independently from each factor (Grassmann) manifold.

This development of geodesic distance on the product manifold can be related back to our cylinder example where a circle in $\mathbb{R}^2$ and a line in $\mathbb{R}^1$ form a cylinder in $\mathbb{R}^3$ where $\mathbb{R}^3$ is the product space. Recall that a Grassmann manifold is a set of p-dimensional linear subspaces. In analogous fashion, the product of a set of p_1, p_2, $\ldots$, p_N linear subspaces forms a set of product subspaces whose dimension is ($p_1 + p_2 + \cdots + p_N$). The product subspaces are the elements on a product manifold. This observation is consistent with the Θ in (2.3) where the number of canonical angles agrees with the dimension of product subspaces on the product manifold.

Note that canonical angles θ_k are measured between $V_{\mathscr{A}}^{(k)}$ and $V_{\mathscr{B}}^{(k)}$ where each is an orthogonal matrix spanning the row space associated with nonzero singular values from a mode-k unfolded matrix. As such, an N order tensor in $\mathbb{R}^{I_1 \times I_2 \times \cdots \times I_N}$ would span N row spaces in I_1, I_2, $\ldots$, I_N, respectively, and the dimension of a product manifold is the sum of each order of a data tensor, that is, ($\sum_{i=1}^{N} = I_1 + I_2 + \cdots + I_N$).

2.5 The Product Manifold Representation

The tensor representation on a product manifold models the variations in both space and time for action videos. Specifically, the product manifold captures the individual characteristics of spatial and temporal evolution through three factor manifolds. As such, one factor manifold is acquiring the change in time, resulting in the appearance (XY) component, while the other two capture the variations in horizontal and vertical directions, demonstrating the horizontal motion (YT) and vertical motion (XT). Putting all these representations together, geodesic distance on the product manifold measures the changes in both appearance and dynamics.

The aim of this section is to illustrate how the product manifold characterizes appearance and dynamics from action videos. To visualize the product manifold representation, let us consider the example given in Fig. 2.3 where the first row expresses the pairs of overlay appearance (XY) canonical variates, the second and third rows reveal the pairs of overlay horizontal motion (YT) and vertical motion (XT) canonical variates, and the bottom row gives the sum of canonical angles computed from the pairs of canonical variates. Note that the canonical variates are elements on Stiefel manifolds. In the first column, two distinct actions are factorized to canonical variates. We can see that all canonical variates exhibit very different characteristics in both appearance and motions. On the contrary, the second column shows the same action performed by different actors and the canonical variates are much more similar than the first column, resulting in smaller canonical angles overall.

One of the advantages of the product manifold representation is that actions do not need to be aligned in temporal space. To demonstrate this merit, we permute the frame order from action 3 denoted as action 4 and match it to action 1. Figure 2.4 shows the

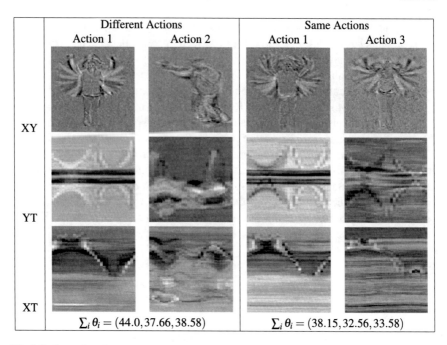

Fig. 2.3 Examples of appearance and motion changes where the *first row* is the overlay appearances, the *second* and *third rows* are the overlay horizontal motion and vertical motion, and the *bottom row* gives the sum of canonical angles computed from each factorization of the pairs of canonical variates

pairs of canonical variates between actions (1, 3) and actions (1, 4). We should first note that the appearance (XY) of action 3 and action 4 span the same space despite the visual differences resulting in the identical sum of canonical angles 38.15. This is because elements on the Grassmann manifold are rotation and reflection invariant from elements of the Stiefel manifold. This important concept is illustrated in Fig. 2.5 where the exchange matrix $\mathcal{O}(p)$ maps the appearance of action 4 to the appearance of action 3.

In the example given in Fig. 2.4, the most prominent change is related to the motion in vertical directions (XT) between action 3 and action 4. This arises from the fact that the change of motion mostly occurs in the vertical direction when we permute the order of the video frames from action 3. Consequently, the sum of canonical angles in XT varies from 33.58 to 38.16 which is less similar to action 1. When we identify a waving hand moving from top to bottom and from bottom to top, the vertical motion is the key feature. Otherwise, a simple cyclical search can compensate such variation. As a result, the product manifold representation is resilient to misregistration in the temporal space for appearance while keeping the dynamics intact.

Another intriguing attribute of the product manifold representation is its ability to capture the rate of motion, which is useful in identifying some particular actions. Figure 2.6 shows the pairs of canonical variates of two similar actions—walking and

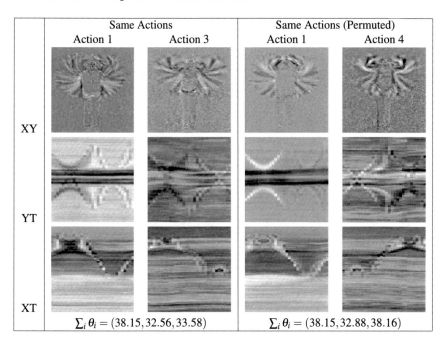

Fig. 2.4 Examples of appearance and motion changes where Action 4 is a permuted version of Action 3. The canonical angles for the appearance indicates that the action is not affected by the frame order

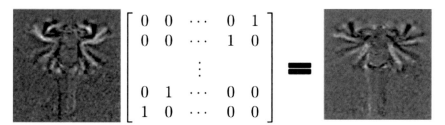

Fig. 2.5 The characterization of the Grassmann manifold where a point is mapped to another point on the Stiefel manifold via an exchanged matrix. The group action is $(X, Q) \longmapsto XQ$ where $X \in \mathscr{V}_{n,p}$ and $Q \in \mathscr{O}(p)$ so that elements on the Grassmann manifold are closed under the orthogonal matrix multiplication

running. First, we note that there is little information from the vertical motion since the movements of walking and running occur horizontally. The appearance differences between walking and running are not substantial, which is shown in the first column of Fig. 2.6. The key information between walking and running is embedded in the horizontal motion (YT). While the structure of horizontal motion between walking and running is similar exhibiting a line-like pattern, they have very distinct slopes shown in the horizontal motion column of Fig. 2.6. These slopes characterize the rate

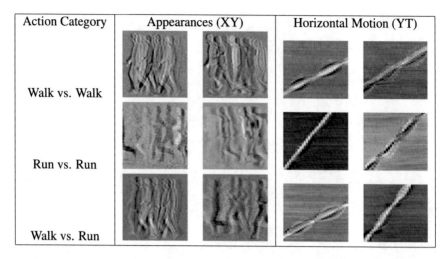

Action Category	Appearances (XY)	Horizontal Motion (YT)
Walk vs. Walk		
Run vs. Run		
Walk vs. Run		

Fig. 2.6 Illustration of capturing the rate of actions. The *first column* shows the change of appearance while the *second column* reveals the change of horizontal motion where the slopes exhibit the rate of motion

of motion and are the key factors in recognizing these types of actions. In particular, when walking and running are compared depicted in the third row of Fig. 2.6, the idiosyncratic aspect is captured by the rate of horizontal motion. In general, it is possible to see the rate of motion through both motion representations depending on the type of actions.

2.6 Statistical Modeling

Least squares regression is one of the fundamental techniques in statistical analysis. It is simple and often outperforms complicated models when the number of training samples is small (Hastie et al. 2001). Since video data do not reside in Euclidean space, we pay attention to the manifold structure. Here, we introduce a nonlinear regression framework in non-Euclidean space for gesture recognition. We formulate least squares regression as a composite function; as such, both domain and range values are constrained on a manifold through the regression process. The least squares fitted elements from a training set can then be exploited for gesture recognition.

2.6.1 Linear Least Squares Regression

Before we discuss the geometric extension, we will first review the standard form of least squares fitting. We consider a regression problem $y = A\beta$ where $y \in \mathbb{R}^n$ is the regression value, $A([a_1|a_2|\cdots|a_k]) \in \mathbb{R}^{n \times k}$ is the training set, and $\beta \in \mathbb{R}^k$ is the fitting parameter. The residual sum-of-squares can be written as:

$$R(\beta) = \| y - A\beta \|^2 \qquad (2.4)$$

and the fitting parameter β can be obtained by minimizing the residual sum-of-squares error from (2.4). Then, we have

$$\hat{\beta} = (A^T A)^{-1} A^T y.$$

The regressed pattern from the training set has the following form

$$\hat{y} = A\hat{\beta} = A(A^T A)^{-1} A^T y. \qquad (2.5)$$

The key advantage of least squares fitting is its simplicity and it intuitively measures the best fit of the data.

2.6.2 Least Squares Regression on Manifolds

Non-Euclidean geometry often arises in computer vision applications. We consider the nonlinear nature of space and introduce a geometric framework for least squares regression. First, we extend the linear least squares regression from (2.5) to a non-linear form by incorporating a kernel function shown in the following

$$A(A \star A)^{-1}(A \star y)$$

where $\star$ is a nonlinear similarity operator. Obviously, $\star$ is equal to $x^T y$ in the linear case. In this paper, we employ the RBF kernel given as:

$$x \star y = \exp\left(-\frac{\sum_k \theta_k}{\sigma}\right) \qquad (2.6)$$

where x and y are the elements on a factor manifold, θ_k is the canonical angle computed from the factor manifold, and σ is set to 2 in all our experiments. While other kernel functions can be considered, our goal is to demonstrate our geometric framework and choose a commonly used RBF kernel operator.

Considering the similarity measure given in (2.6), the regression model becomes three sub-regression estimators given by

$$\psi^{(k)}(y) = A^{(k)}(A^{(k)} \star A^{(k)})^{-1}(A^{(k)} \star y^{(k)}) \qquad (2.7)$$

where k denotes the mode of unfolding, $A^{(k)}$ is a set of orthogonal matrices factorized from HOSVD, and $y^{(k)}$ is an orthogonal matrix from the unfolded matrix.

To gain a better insight on the regression model, we explore the geometrical interpretation from (2.7). Given p training instances, the first element, $A^{(k)}$, is a set of factorized training samples residing on a manifold. Furthermore, $(A^{(k)} \star A^{(k)})^{-1}$ produces a $p \times p$ matrix from the training set and $(A^{(k)} \star y^{(k)})$ would create a $p \times 1$ vector. Therefore, the rest of the regression provides a weighting vector characterizing the training data on a factor manifold as:

$$w = (A^{(k)} \star A^{(k)})^{-1} (A^{(k)} \star y^{(k)})$$

where the weighting vector is in a vector space, that is, $w \in \mathcal{V}$.

Now, we have a set of factorized training samples, $A^{(k)}$, on a manifold and a weighting vector, w, in a vector space. To incorporate these two elements with the least squares fitting given in (2.7), we make a simple modification and reformulate the regression as follows

$$\Psi^{(k)}(y) = A^{(k)} \bullet (A^{(k)} \star A^{(k)})^{-1} (A^{(k)} \star y^{(k)}) \tag{2.8}$$

where $\bullet$ is an operator mapping points from a vector space back to a factor manifold. By introducing an additional operator, we ensure that both the domain values $y^{(k)}$ and the range values $\Psi^k(y)$ reside on a manifold. From a function composition point of view, the proposed regression technique can be viewed as a composition map $\mathcal{G} \circ \mathcal{H}$ where $\mathcal{H} : \mathcal{M} \longrightarrow \mathcal{V}$ and $\mathcal{G} : \mathcal{V} \longrightarrow \mathcal{M}$ where $\mathcal{M}$ is a manifold and $\mathcal{V}$ is a vector space.

One possible way to realize the composition map, $\mathcal{G} \circ \mathcal{H}$, is to employ the tangent space and modify the Karcher mean (Karcher 1977). The computation of Karcher mean considers the intrinsic geometry and iteratively minimizes the distance between the updated mean and all data samples via the tangent space. Since w is the weighting vector, it naturally produces the weight between training samples. All we need is to apply the weighting vector to weight the training samples on a factor manifold. This is equivalent to computing the weighted Karcher mean, which is an element of a manifold.

Algorithm 1: Weighted Karcher Mean Computation

---

1 Initialize a base point μ on a manifold
2 **while** *not converged* **do**
3   Apply the logarithmic map to the training samples Y_i to the base point μ
4   Compute the weighted average on the tangent space at the base point μ
5   Update the base point μ by applying the exponential map on the weighted average
6 **end**

So far, our geometric formulation on least squares regression is very general. To make it specific for gesture recognition, we impose rotation and reflection invariance to the factorized element $V^{(k)}$ such that they are elements on a Grassmann mani-

Fig. 2.7 An illustration of
logarithmic and exponential
maps where Y and μ are
points on a manifold, Δ is
the tangent vector, and $T_\mu \mathcal{M}$
is the tangent space at μ

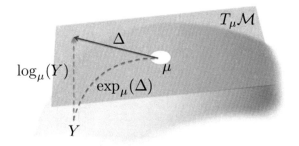

fold and the computation of the weighted Karcher mean can be realized. Here, we sketch the pseudo-code in Algorithm 1. As Algorithm 1 illustrates, the first step is to initialize a base point on a manifold. To do so, we compute the weighted average from the training samples in Euclidean space and project it back to the Grassmann manifold using QR factorization. Then, we iteratively update the base point on the Grassmann manifold. The update procedure involves the standard logarithmic map and the exponential map on Grassmann manifolds (Edelman et al. 1998) described as follows

$$\log_\mu(Y_i) = U_1 \Theta_1 V_1^T$$

where μ is the base point for the tangent space, Y_i is a training instance factorized from the Grassmann manifold, $\mu_\perp \mu_\perp^T Y_i (\mu^T Y_i)^{-1} = U_1 \Sigma_1 V_1^T$, $\Theta_1 = \arctan(\Sigma_1)$, and $\mu_\perp$ is the orthogonal complement to μ.

$$\exp_\mu(\Delta) = \mu V_2 \cos(\Sigma_2) + U_2 \sin(\Sigma_2)$$

where Δ is the weighted tangent vector at μ and $\Delta = U_2 \Sigma_2 V_2^T$. From a geometric point of view, the logarithmic operator maps a point on a manifold to a tangent space whereas the exponential map projects a point in the tangent space back to the manifold. A pictorial illustration is given in Fig. 2.7. In addition, the Karcher mean calculation exhibits fast convergence (Absil et al. 2004). Typically, convergence can be reached within 10 iterations in our experiments. A sample run is depicted in Fig. 2.8 where expeditious reduction of residuals occurs in the first few iterations.

To perform gesture recognition, a set of training videos is collected. All videos are normalized to a standard size. During the test phase, the category of a query video is determined by

$$j^* = \operatorname*{argmin}_j \mathscr{D}(Y, \Psi_j(Y))$$

where Y is a query video, Ψ_j is the regression instance for the class j given in (2.8), and $\mathscr{D}$ is a geodesic distance measure. Because the query gesture Y and the

Fig. 2.8 The residual values
of tangent vectors

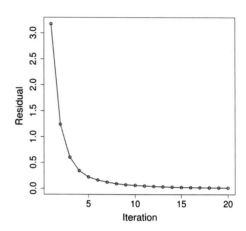

regression instance are realized as elements on a product manifold, we employ the
chordal distance given in (2.3) for gesture classification.

In summary, the least squares regression model applies HOSVD on a query
gesture Y and factorizes it to three sub-regression models ($\Psi_j^{(1)}$, $\Psi_j^{(2)}$, $\Psi_j^{(3)}$) on
three Grassmann manifolds where regressions are performed. The distance between
the regression output and query is then characterized on a product manifold; gesture recognition is achieved using the chordal distance. We note that our least
squares framework is applicable to many matrix manifolds as long as the logarithmic and exponential maps are well-defined. Furthermore, when the kernel operator is
$\star = x^T y$, $\log_x(y) = y$, and $\exp_x(\Delta) = x + \Delta$, the regression model in (2.8) becomes
the canonical least squares regression in Euclidean space.

When statistical models exhibit high variance, shrinkage techniques are often
applied (Hastie et al. 2001). We see that a simple regularization parameter turns least
squares regression into ridge regression. This observation can also be applied to our
non-Euclidean least squares regression framework.

2.7 Experimental Results

This section summarizes our empirical results and demonstrates the proficiency of
our framework on gesture recognition. To facilitate comparison, we first evaluate
our method using two publicly available gesture data sets namely Cambridge hand-
gesture (Kim and Cipolla 2009) and UMD Keck body-gesture (Lin et al. 2009).
We further extend our method to the one-shot-learning gesture challenge (Chalearn
2011). Our experiments reveal that not only does our method perform well on the
standard benchmark data sets, but also it generalizes well on the one-shot-learning
gesture challenge.

2.7.1 Cambridge Hand-Gesture Data Set

Our first experiment is conducted using the Cambridge hand-gesture data set which has 900 video sequences with nine different hand gestures (100 video sequences per gesture class). The gesture data are collected from five different illumination sets labeled as Set1, Set2, Set3, Set4, and Set5. Example gestures are shown in Fig. 2.9.

We follow the experimental protocol employed by Kim and Cipolla (2009) where Set5 is the target set, and Set1, Set2, Set3, and Set4 are the test sets. The target Set5 is further partitioned into a training set and validation set (90 video sequences in the training set and 90 video sequences in the validation set). We employ five random trials in selecting the training and validation videos in Set5. The recognition results are summarized in Table 2.1 where the classification rates are the average accuracy obtained from five trial runs followed by the standard deviation. As Table 2.1 shows, our method performs very well across all illumination sets obtaining 91.7% average classification rate.

Fig. 2.9 Hand gesture samples. Flat-leftward, flat-rightward, flat-contract, spread-leftward, spread-rightward, spread-contract, V-shape-leftward, V-shape-rightward, and V-shape-contract

Table 2.1 Recognition results on the Cambridge hand-gesture data set (five trial runs)

Method	Set1 (%)	Set2 (%)	Set3 (%)	Set4 (%)	Total (%)
Graph embedding (Yuan et al. 2010)	–	–	–	–	82
TCCA (Kim and Cipolla 2009)	81	81	78	86	82 ± 3.5
DCCA + SIFT (Kim and Cipolla 2007)	–	–	–	–	85 ± 2.8
RLPP (Harandi et al. 2012)	86	86	85	88	86.3 ± 1.3
TB$\{\mathscr{V}_{n,p}\}$ (Lui 2012b)	88	84	85	87	86 ± 3.0
PM 1-NN (Lui et al. 2010)	89	86	89	87	88 ± 2.1
Our method	93	89	91	94	91.7 ± 2.3

2.7.2   UMD Keck Body-Gesture Data Set

The UMD Keck body-gesture data set consists of 14 naval body gestures acquired from both static and dynamic backgrounds. In the static background, the subjects and the camera remain stationary whereas the subjects and the camera are moving in the dynamic environment during the performance of the gesture. There are 126 videos collected from the static scene and 168 videos taken from the dynamic environment. Example gestures are given in Fig. 2.10.

We follow the experimental protocol proposed by Lin et al. (2009) for both static and dynamic settings. The region of interest is tracked by a simple correlation filter. In the static background, the protocol is leave-one-subject-out (LOSO) cross-validation. As for the dynamic environment, the gestures acquired from the static scene are used for training while the gestures collected from the dynamic environment are the test videos. The recognition results for both static and dynamic backgrounds are reported in Table 2.2. We can see that our method is competitive to the current state-of-the-art methods in both protocols. One of the key advantages of our method is its direct use of raw pixels while the prototype-tree (Lin et al. 2009), MMI-2+SIFT (Qiu et al. 2011), and CC K-means (Jiang et al. 2012) methods operate on silhouette images which require image segmentation prior to classification. This makes our representation more generic.

Fig. 2.10 Body gesture samples. *First row* turn left, turn right, attention left, attention right, attention both, stop left, and stop right. *Second row* stop both, flap, start, go back, close distance, speed up, and come near

Table 2.2 Recognition results on the UMD Keck body-gesture data set

Method	Static setting (%)	Dynamic setting (%)
HOG3D (Bilinski and Bremond 2011)	–	53.6
Shape manifold (Abdelkadera et al. 2011)	82	–
MMI-2+SIFT (Qiu et al. 2011)	95	–
CC K-means (Jiang et al. 2012)	–	92.9
Prototype-tree (Lin et al. 2009)	95.2	91.1
TB{$\mathcal{V}_{n,p}$} (Lui 2012b)	92.1	91.1
PM 1-NN (Lui et al. 2010)	92.9	92.3
Our method	94.4	92.3

2.7.3   One-Shot-Learning Gesture Challenge

Microsoft Kinect™ has recently revolutionized gesture recognition by providing both RGB and depth images. To facilitate the adaptation to new gestures, CHALEARN (Guyon et al. 2012) has organized a one-shot-learning challenge for gesture recognition.

The key aspect of one-shot-learning is to perform machine learning on a single training example. As such, intra-class variability needs to be modeled from a single example or learned from different domains. While traditional machine learning techniques require a large amount of training data to model the statistical distribution, least squares regression appears to be more robust when the size of training samples is limited (Hastie et al. 2001). We employ our least squares regression framework and model the intra-class variability by synthesizing training examples from the original training instance. Consequently, we apply the same regression framework on the product manifold to the one-shot-learning gesture challenge.

One of the gesture variations is performing gesture positions. Our initial studies for frame alignment did not yield positive results due in part to the incidental features of the upper body. Since gesture positions are the key source of variations, we synthesize training examples for translational instances on both RGB and depth images. The synthesized examples are generated by shifting the entire action video horizontally and vertically. Specifically, we synthesize two vertically (up/down) and four horizontally (left/right) translated instances along with the original training example. As such, we have seven training instances for RGB and depth images, respectively. We stress that we do not apply any spatial segmentation or intensity normalization to video data; alignment is the only variation that we synthesize for one-shot-learning. Our experiments on the training batches indicate that there is about 2% gain by introducing the translational variations.

We assess the effectiveness of the proposed framework on the development data set for the one-shot-learning gesture challenge. The development data set consists of 20 batches of gestures. Each batch is made of 47 gesture videos and split into a training set and a test set. The training set includes a small set of vocabulary spanning from 8 to 15 gestures. Every test video contains 1–5 gestures. Detailed descriptions of the gesture data can be found in Guyon et al. (2012).

Since the number of gestures varies for test videos, we perform temporal segmentation to localize each gesture segment. It is supposed that the actor will return to the resting position before performing a new gesture. Thus, we employ the first frame as a template and compute the correlation coefficient with subsequent frames. We can then localize the gesture segments by identifying the peak locations from the correlations; the number of gestures is the number of peaks + 1. An illustration of temporal segmentation is given in Fig. 2.11 where the peak locations provide a good indication for the resting frames. Furthermore, we fix the spatial dimension to 32×32 and dynamically determine the number of frames by selecting 90% of the PCA energy from each training batch. Linear interpolation is then applied to normalize the video length.

Fig. 2.11 An illustration of temporal segmentation where the *dash lines* indicate the peak locations and the resting frames from the action sequence

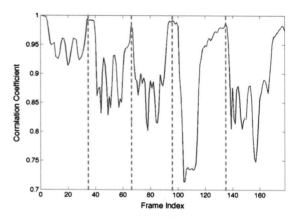

The recognition performance is evaluated using the Levenshtein distance (Levenshtein 1966), also known as edit distance. Table 2.3 shows the average errors over 20 batches. As Table 2.3 reveals, our method significantly outperforms the baseline algorithm (Chalearn 2011) and achieves 28.73% average Levenshtein distance per gesture on the development data set. Our method also ranks among the top algorithms in the gesture challenge (Guyon et al. 2012). This illustrates that our method can be effectively adopted for one-shot-learning from the traditional supervised learning paradigm.

While our method performs well on the one-shot-learning gesture challenge, it is not a complete system yet. There are three particular batches that cause difficulties for our algorithm. These batches are devel03, devel10, and devel19 where the example frames are shown in Fig. 2.12. These three batches share a common characteristic that the gesture is only distinguishable by identifying the hand positions. Since we do not have a hand detector, the gross motion dominates the whole action causing it to be confused with other similar gestures.

Another source of errors is made by the temporal segmentation. While the actor is supposed to return to the resting position before performing a new gesture, this rule has not always been observed. As a result, such variation introduces a mismatch between the template and subsequent frames resulting errors in partitioning the video sequence. The large error in devel03 is caused by the need for hand positions and temporal segmentation. Future work will focus on combining both appearance and motion for temporal segmentation.

Nevertheless, the experimental results from the Cambridge hand-gesture and the UMD Keck body-gesture data sets are encouraging. These findings illustrate that our method is effective in both hand gestures and body gestures. Once we have a reliable hand detector, we expect to further improve gesture recognition from a single training example. Currently, the processing time on 20 batches (2000 gestures) including both training and testing is about 2 hours with a non-optimized MATLAB implementation on a 2.5 GHz Intel Core i5 iMac.

Table 2.3 Recognition results on the development data for the one-shot-learning challenge where TeLev is the sum of the Levenshtein distance divided by the true number of gestures and TeLen is the average error made on the number of gestures

Batch	Baseline		Our method	
	TeLev (%)	TeLen (%)	TeLev (%)	TeLen (%)
devel01	53.33	12.22	13.33	4.44
devel02	68.89	16.67	35.56	14.44
devel03	77.17	5.43	71.74	20.65
devel04	52.22	30.00	10.00	2.22
devel05	43.48	10.87	9.78	7.61
devel06	66.67	17.78	37.78	14.44
devel07	81.32	19.78	18.68	3.30
devel08	58.43	12.36	8.99	5.62
devel09	38.46	9.89	13.19	1.10
devel10	75.82	21.98	50.55	1.10
devel11	67.39	18.48	35.87	2.17
devel12	52.81	5.62	22.47	4.49
devel13	50.00	17.05	9.09	2.27
devel14	73.91	22.83	28.26	3.26
devel15	50.00	8.70	21.74	0.00
devel16	57.47	17.24	31.03	6.90
devel17	66.30	32.61	30.43	4.35
devel18	70.00	28.89	40.00	11.11
devel19	71.43	15.38	49.45	3.30
devel20	70.33	36.26	35.16	12.09
Average	62.32	18.01	28.73	6.24

Fig. 2.12 Gesture samples on the one-shot-learning gesture challenge (devel03, devel10, and devel19)

2.8 Discussion

The proposed method is geometrically motivated. It decomposes a video tensor to three Stiefel manifolds via HOSVD where the orthogonal elements are imposed to Grassmannian spaces. As mentioned before, one of the key advantages of our method

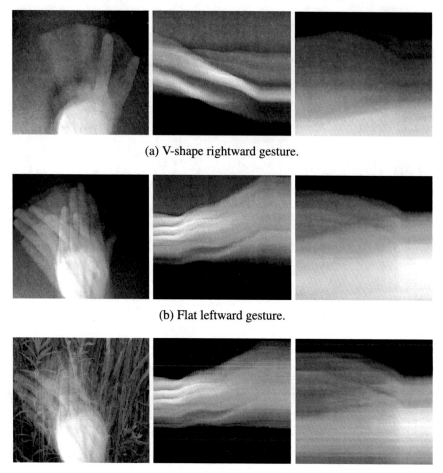

(a) V-shape rightward gesture.

(b) Flat leftward gesture.

(c) Superposed cluttered background on the flat leftward gesture.

Fig. 2.13 The effect of background clutter. Appearance, horizontal motion, and vertical motion are depicted in the first, second, and third columns, respectively

is its direct use of raw pixels. This gives rise to a practical and important question. *How robust can the raw pixel representation be against background clutter?*

To address this concern, we synthesize an illustrative example given in Fig. 2.13. The first, second, and third columns depict the appearance, horizontal motion, and vertical motion of the gesture, respectively. A V-shape rightward gesture and a flat leftward gesture are shown in the first row and second row. We superpose a cluttered background on every frame of the flat leftward gesture exhibited in the third row. While the appearances between the uniform flat gesture and the cluttered flat gesture emerge differently, the deterioration on the dynamics is quite minimal. As a result, the gesture performed with the background clutter can still be discriminated against other gestures. Numerically, the sum of the canonical angles between the uniform (second row) and the cluttered background (third row) gestures is (56.09, 7.99, 9.17) resulting in a geodesic distance of 5.91 on the product manifold. In contrast, the sum of the canonical angles between the V-shape (first row) and the flat (second row) gestures is (76.35, 23.66, 18.42) yielding a geodesic distance of 8.29. In addition, when the V-shape gesture (first row) matches against the cluttered flat gesture (third row), the sum of the canonical angles is (76.09, 23.75, 18.84) and the geodesic distance is 8.31. This finding reveals that the geodesic distance between the uniform and cluttered background gestures are quite similar against inter-class gestures, while the geodesic distance is significantly smaller for the intra-class gestures. Hence, raw pixels can be directly exploited in our representation.

As technology advances, we can now separate the foreground and background more easily using a Kinect^{TM} camera. We hypothesize that better recognition results may be obtained when the foreground gestures are extracted. On the other hand, our method can still perform gracefully when a cluttered background is present.

2.9 Conclusions

This paper promotes the importance of the underlying geometry of data tensors. We have presented a geometric framework for least squares regression and applied it to gesture recognition. We view action videos as third order tensors and impose them on a product manifold where each factor is Grassmannian. The realization of points on these Grassmannians is achieved by applying HOSVD to a tensor representation of the action video. A natural metric is inherited from the factor manifolds since the geodesic on the product manifold is given by the product of the geodesic on the Grassmann manifolds.

The proposed approach provides a useful metric and a regression model based on latent geometry for action recognition. To account for the underlying geometry, we formulate least squares regression as a composite function. This formulation provides a natural extension from Euclidean space to manifolds. Experimental results demonstrate that our method is effective and generalizes well to the one-shot-learning scheme.

For longer video sequences, micro-action detection is needed which may be modeled effectively using HMM. Future work will focus on developing more sophisticated models for gesture recognition and other regression techniques on matrix manifolds for visual applications.

References

M.F. Abdelkadera, W. Abd-Almageeda, A. Srivastavab, R. Chellappa, Gesture and action recognition via modeling trajectories on Riemannian manifolds. Comput. Vis. Image Underst. **115**(3), 439–455 (2011)

P.-A. Absil, R. Mahony, R. Sepulchre, Riemannian geometry of Grassmann manifolds with a view on algorithmic computation. Acta Appl. Math. **80**(2), 199–220 (2004)

P.-A. Absil, R. Mahony, R. Sepulchre, *Optimization Algorithms on Matrix Manifolds* (Princeton University Press, Princeton, 2008)

E. Begelfor, M. Werman, Affine invariance revisited, in *IEEE Conference on Computer Vision and Pattern Recognition, New York*, 2006

J.G.E. Belinfante, B. Kolman, *A Survey of Lie Groups and Lie Algebras with Applications and Computational Methods* (SIAM, Philadelphia, 1972)

P. Bilinski, F. Bremond, Evaluation of local descriptors for action recognition in videos, in *ICVS*, 2011

A. Bissacco, A. Chiuso, Y. Ma, S. Soatto, Recognition of human gaits, in *IEEE Conference on Computer Vision and Pattern Recognition, Hawaii*, 2001, pp. 270–277

Å. Björck, G.H. Golub, Numerical methods for computing angles between linear subspaces. Math. Comput. **27**, 579–594 (1973)

Chalearn, Chalearn gesture dataset (cgd 2011) (Chalearn, California, 2011)

J.H. Conway, R.H. Hardin, N.J.A. Sloane, Packing lines, planes, etc.: packings in Grassmannian spaces. Exp. Math. **5**(2), 139–159 (1996)

A. Datta, Y. Sheikh, T. Kanade, Modeling the product manifold of posture and motion, in *Workshop on Tracking Humans for the Evaluation of their Motion in Image Sequences (in conjunction with ICCV)*, 2009

L. De Lathauwer, B. De Moor, J. Vandewalle, A multilinear singular value decomposition. SIAM J. Matrix Anal. Appl. **21**(4), 1253–1278 (2000)

P. Dollar, V. Rabaud, G. Cottrell, S. Belongie. Behavior recognition via sparse spatio-temporal features, in *IEEE International Workshop on Visual Surveillance and Performance Evaluation of Tracking and Surveillance (in conjunction with ICCV)*, 2005

A. Edelman, R. Arias, S. Smith, The geometry of algorithms with orthogonality constraints. SIAM J. Matrix Anal. Appl. **20**(2), 303–353 (1998)

I. Guyon, V. Athitsos, P. Jangyodsuk, B. Hammer, H.J.E. Balderas, Chalearn gesture challenge: design and first results, in *CVPR Workshop on Gesture Recognition*, 2012

M.T. Harandi, C. Sanderson, A. Wiliem, B.C. Lovell, Kernel analysis over Riemannian manifolds for visual recognition of actions, pedestrians and textures, in *WACV*, 2012

T. Hastie, R. Tibshirani, J. Friedman, *The Elements of Statistical Learning: Data Mining, Inference, and Prediction* (Springer, New York, 2001)

Z. Jiang, Z. Lin, L. Davis, Class consistent k-means: application to face and action recognition. Comput. Vis. Image Underst. **116**(6), 730–741 (2012)

H. Karcher, Riemannian center of mass and mollifier smoothing. Commun. Pure Appl. Math. **30**(5), 509–541 (1977)

D. Kendall, Shape manifolds, procrustean metrics and complex projective spaces. Bull. Lond. Math. Soc. **16**, 81–121 (1984)

T-K. Kim, R. Cipolla, Gesture recognition under small sample size, in *Asian Conference on Computer Vision*, 2007

T.-K. Kim, R. Cipolla, Canonical correlation analysis of video volume tensors for action categorization and detection. IEEE Trans. Pattern Anal. Mach. Intell. **31**(8), 1415–1428 (2009)

T.G. Kolda, B.W. Bader, Tensor decompositions and applications. SIAM Rev. **51**(3), 455–500 (2009)

B. Krausz, C. Bauckhage, Action recognition in videos using nonnegative tensor factorization, in *International Conference on Pattern Recognition*, 2010

J. Lee, *Introduction to Smooth Manifolds* (Springer, New York, 2003)

V. Levenshtein, Binary codes capable of correcting deletions, insertions, and reversals. Sov. Phys. Dokl. **10**, 707–710 (1966)

R. Li, R. Chellappa, Group motion segmentation using a spatio-temporal driving force model, in *IEEE Conference on Computer Vision and Pattern Recognition*, 2010

X. Li, W. Hu, Z. Zhang, X. Zhang, G. Luo, Robust visual tracking based on incremental tensor subspace learning, in *IEEE International Conference on Computer Vision*, 2007

Z. Lin, Z. Jiang, L. Davis, Recognizing actions by shape-motion prototype trees, in *IEEE International Conference on Computer Vision*, 2009

Y.M. Lui, Advances in matrix manifolds for computer vision. Image Vis. Comput. **30**(6–7), 380–388 (2012a)

Y.M. Lui, Tangent bundles on special manifolds for action recognition. IEEE Trans. Circ. Syst. Video Technol. **22**(6), 930–942 (2012b)

Y.M. Lui, J.R. Beveridge, Grassmann registration manifolds for face recognition. in *European Conference on Computer Vision, Marseille, France*, 2008

Y.M. Lui, J.R. Beveridge, M. Kirby, Canonical Stiefel quotient and its application to generic face recognition in illumination spaces, in *IEEE International Conference on Biometrics: Theory, Applications and Systems, Washington, DC*, 2009

Y.M. Lui, J.R. Beveridge, M. Kirby, Action classification on product manifolds, in *IEEE Conference on Computer Vision and Pattern Recognition, San Francisco*, 2010

Y. Ma, J. Košecká, S. Sastry. Optimal motion from image sequences: a Riemannian viewpoint, Technical Report No. UCB/ERL M98/37, EECS Department, University of California, Berkeley, 1998

S. Mitra, T. Acharya, Gesture recognition: a survey. IEEE Trans. Syst. Man Cybern. Part C Appl. Rev. **37**, 311–324 (2007)

Q. Qiu, Z. Jiang, R. Chellappa, Sparse dictionary-based representation and recognition of action attributes, in *IEEE Conference on Computer Vision and Pattern Recognition*, 2011

M. Rodriguez, J. Ahmed, M. Shah, Action mach: a spatio-temporal maximum average correlation height filter for action recognition, in *IEEE Conference on Computer Vision and Pattern Recognition*, 2008

P. Saisan, G. Doretto, Y-N. Wu, S. Soatto, Dynamic texture recognition, in *IEEE Conference on Computer Vision and Pattern Recognition*, 2001

P. Turaga, R. Chellappa, Locally time-invariant models of human activities using trajectories on the Grassmannian, in *IEEE Conference on Computer Vision and Pattern Recognition*, 2009

P. Turaga, S. Biswas, R. Chellappa, The role of geometry for age estimation. in *IEEE International Conference Acoustics, Speech and Signal Processing*, 2010

M.A.O. Vasilescu, Human motion signatures: analysis, synthesis, recognition, in *International Conference on Pattern Recognition, Quebec City, Canada*, 2002, pp. 456–460

M.A.O. Vasilescu, D. Terzopoulos, Multilinear image analysis for facial recognition, in *International Conference on Pattern Recognition, Quebec City, Canada*, 2002, pp. 511–514

A. Veeraraghavan, A.K. Roy-Chowdhury, R. Chellappa, Matching shape sequences in video with applications in human movement analysis. IEEE Trans. Pattern Anal. Mach. Intell. **27**(12), 1896–1909 (2005)

H. Wang, M. Ullah, A Klaser, I. Laptev, C. Schmid, Evaulation of local spatio-temporal features for action recognition, in *British Machine Vision Conference*, 2009

D. Weinland, R. Ronfard, E. Boyer, Free viewpoint action recognition using motion history volumes. Comput. Vis. Image Underst. **104**, 249–257 (2006)

Y. Yuan, H. Zheng, Z. Li, D. Zhang, Video action recognition with spatio-temporal graph embedding and spline modeling, in *ICASSP*, 2010

Chapter 3
Sign Language Recognition Using Sub-units

Helen Cooper, Eng-Jon Ong, Nicolas Pugeault and Richard Bowden

Abstract This chapter discusses sign language recognition using linguistic sub-units. It presents three types of sub-units for consideration; those learnt from appearance data as well as those inferred from both 2D or 3D tracking data. These sub-units are then combined using a sign level classifier; here, two options are presented. The first uses Markov Models to encode the temporal changes between sub-units. The second makes use of Sequential Pattern Boosting to apply discriminative feature selection at the same time as encoding temporal information. This approach is more robust to noise and performs well in signer independent tests, improving results from the 54% achieved by the Markov Chains to 76%.

Keywords Sign language recognition · Sequential pattern boosting · Depth cameras · Sub-units · Signer independence · Data set

3.1 Introduction

This chapter presents several approaches to sub-unit based Sign language recognition (SLR) culminating in a real time Kinect™ demonstration system. SLR is a non-trivial task. Sign languages (SLs) are made up of thousands of different signs; each differing from the other by minor changes in motion, handshape, location or Non-manual

---

Editors: Isabelle Guyon and Vassilis Athitsos.

H. Cooper · E.-J. Ong · N. Pugeault · R. Bowden (✉)
Centre for Vision Speech and Signal Processing, University of Surrey,
Guildford GU2 9PY, UK
e-mail: R.Bowden@surrey.ac.uk

H. Cooper
e-mail: H.M.Cooper@surrey.ac.uk

E.-J. Ong
e-mail: E.Ong@surrey.ac.uk

N. Pugeault
e-mail: N.Pugeault@surrey.ac.uk

© Springer International Publishing AG 2017
S. Escalera et al. (eds.), *Gesture Recognition*, The Springer Series
on Challenges in Machine Learning, DOI 10.1007/978-3-319-57021-1_3

features (NMFs). While gesture recognition (GR) solutions often build a classifier per gesture, this approach soon becomes intractable when recognising large lexicons of signs, for even the relatively straightforward task of citation-form, dictionary look-up. Speech recognition was faced with the same problem; the emergent solution was to recognise the subcomponents (phonemes), then combine them into words using Hidden Markov Models (HMMs). Sub-unit based SLR uses a similar two stage recognition system, in the first stage, sign linguistic sub-units are identified. In the second stage, these sub-units are combined together to create a sign level classifier.

Linguists also describe SLs in terms of component sub-units; by using these sub-units, not only can larger sign lexicons be handled efficiently, allowing demonstration on databases of nearly 1000 signs, but they are also more robust to the natural variations of signs, which occur on both an inter and an intra signer basis. This makes them suited to real-time signer independent recognition as described later. This chapter will

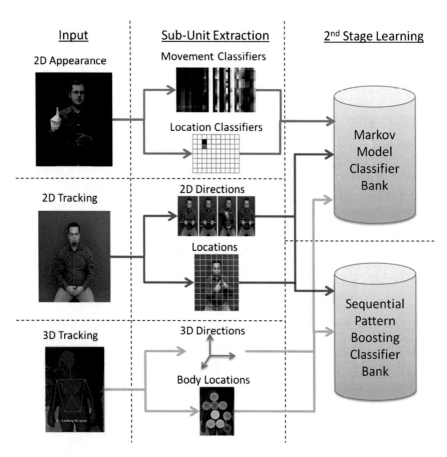

Fig. 3.1 Overview of the three types of sub-units extracted and the two different sign level classifiers used

focus on four main sub-unit categories based on *HandShape, Location, Motion* and *Hand-Arrangement*. There are several methods for labelling these sub-units and this work builds on both the Ha, Tab, Sig, Dez system from the BSL dictionary (British Deaf Association 1992) and The Hamburg Notation System (HamNoSys), which has continued to develop over recent years to allow more detailed description of signs from numerous SLs (Hanke and Schmaling 2004).

A comparison of sub-unit approaches is discussed, focussing on the advantages and disadvantages of each. Also presented is a newly released Kinect data set, containing multiple users performing signs in various environments. There are three different types of sub-units considered; those based on appearance data alone, those which use 2D tracking data with appearance based handshapes and those which use 3D tracking data produced by a Kinect™sensor. Each of these three sub-unit types is tested with a Markov model approach to combine sub-units into sign level classifiers. A further experiment is performed to investigate the discriminative learning power of Sequential Pattern (SP) Boosting for signer independent recognition. An overview is shown in Fig. 3.1.

3.2 Background

The concept of using sub-units for SLR is not novel. Kim and Waldron (1993) were among the first adopters, they worked on a limited vocabulary of 13–16 signs, using data gloves to get accurate input information. Using the work of Stokoe (1960) as a base, and their previous work in telecommunications (Waldron and Simon 1989), they noted the need to break signs into their component sub-units for efficiency. They continued this throughout the remainder of their work, where they used phonemic recognition modules for hand shape, orientation, position and movement recognition (Waldron and Kim 1994). They made note of the dependency of position, orientation and motion on one another and removed the motion aspect allowing the other sub-units to compensate (on a small vocabulary, a dynamic representation of position is equivalent to motion) (Waldron and Kim 1995).

The early work of Vogler and Metaxas (1997) borrowed heavily from the studies of sign language by Liddell and Johnson (1989), splitting signs into motion and pause sections. Their later work (Vogler and Metaxas 1999), used parallel HMMs on both hand shape and motion sub-units, similar to those proposed by the linguist Stokoe (1960). Kadir et al. (2004) took this further by combining head, hand and torso positions, as well as hand shape, to create a system based on hard coded sub-unit classifiers that could be trained on as little as a single example.

Alternative methods have looked at data driven approaches to defining sub-units. Yin et al. (2009) used an accelerometer glove to gather information about a sign, they then applied discriminative feature extraction and 'similar state tying' algorithms, to decide sub-unit level segmentation of the data. Whereas Kong and Ranganath (2008) and Han et al. (2009) looked at automatic segmentation of sign motion into sub-units, using discontinuities in the trajectory and acceleration to indicate where segments begin and end. These were then clustered into a code book of possible exemplar trajectories using either Dynamic Time Warping (DTW) distance measures Han et al. or Principal Component Analysis (PCA) Kong and Ranganath.

Traditional sign recognition systems use tracking and data driven approaches (Han et al. 2009; Yin et al. 2009). However, there is an increasing body of research that suggests using linguistically derived features can offer superior performance. Cooper and Bowden (2010) learnt linguistic sub-units from hand annotated data which they combined with Markov models to create sign level classifiers, while Pitsikalis et al. (2011) presented a method which incorporated phonetic transcriptions into sub-unit based statistical models. They used HamNoSys annotations combined with the Postures, Detentions, Transitions, Steady Shifts (PDTS) phonetic model to break the signs and annotations into labelled sub-units. These were used to construct statistical sub-unit models which they combined via HMMs.

The frequent requirement of tracked data means that the Kinect™ device has offered the sign recognition community a short-cut to real-time performance. In the relatively short time since its release, several proof of concept demonstrations have emerged. Ershaed et al. (2011) have focussed on Arabic sign language and have created a system which recognises isolated signs. They present a system working for 4 signs and recognise some close up handshape information (Ershaed et al. 2011). At ESIEA they have been using Fast Artificial Neural Networks to train a system which recognises two French signs (Wassner 2011). This small vocabulary is a proof of concept but it is unlikely to be scalable to larger lexicons. It is for this reason that many sign recognition approaches use variants of HMMs (Starner and Pentland 1997; Vogler and Metaxas 1999; Kadir et al. 2004; Cooper and Bowden 2007). One of the first videos to be uploaded to the web came from Zafrulla et al. (2011) and was an extension of their previous CopyCat game for deaf children (Zafrulla et al. 2010). The original system uses coloured gloves and accelerometers to track the hands. By tracking with a Kinect™, they use solely the upper part of the torso and normalise the skeleton according to arm length (Zafrulla et al. 2011). They have an internal data set containing 6 signs; 2 subject signs, 2 prepositions and 2 object signs. The signs are used in 4 sentences (subject, preposition, object) and they have recorded 20 examples of each. Their data set is currently single signer, making the system signer dependent, while they list under further work that signer independence would be desirable. By using a cross validated system they train HMMs (Via the Georgia Tech Gesture Toolkit Lyons et al. 2007) to recognise the signs. They perform 3 types of tests, those with full grammar constraints achieving 100%, those where the number of signs is known achieving 99.98% and those with no restrictions achieving 98.8%.

3.2.1 Linguistics

Sign language sub-units can be likened to speech phonemes, but while a spoken language such as English has only 40–50 phonemes (Shoup 1980), SLs have many more. For example, *The Dictionary of British Sign Language/English* (British

Deaf Association 1992) lists 57 'Dez' (*HandShape*), 36 'Tab' (*Location*), 8 'Ha' (*Hand-Arrangement*), 28 'Sig' (*Motion*) (plus 4 modifiers, for example, short and repeated) and there are two sets of 6 'ori' (*Orientation*), one for the fingers and one for the palm.

HamNoSys uses a more combinatorial approach to sub-units. For instance, it lists 12 basic handshapes which can be augmented using finger bending, thumb position and openeness characteristics to create a single *HandShape* sub-unit. These handshapes are then combined with palm and finger orientations to describe the final hand posture. *Motion* sub-units can be simple linear directions, known as 'Path Movements' these can also be modified by curves, wiggles or zigzags. *Motion* sub-units can also be modified by locations, for example, move from A to B with a curved motion or move down beside the nose.

In addition, whereas spoken phonemes are broadly sequential, sign sub-units are parallel, with some sequential elements added where required. This means that each of the 57 British Sign Language (BSL) *HandShape* options can (theoretically) be in any one of the 36 BSL *Orientation* combinations. In practice, due to the physical constraints of the human body, only a subset of comfortable combinations occur, yet this subset is still considerable.

An advantage of the parallel nature of sub-units, is that they can be recognised independently using different classifiers, then combined at the word level. The reason this is advantageous is that *Location* classifiers need to be spatially variant, since they describe where a sign happens. *Hand-Arrangement* should be spatially invariant but not rotationally variant, since they describe positional relationships between the hands. While *Motion* are a mixture of spatially, temporally, rotationally and scale variant sub-units since they describe types of motion which can be as generic as 'hands move apart' or more specific such as 'hand moves left'. Therefore each type of sub-unit can be recognised by classifiers incorporating the correct combination of invariances. This paper presents three methods for extracting sub-units; learnt appearance based (Sect. 3.3), hard coded 2D tracking based (Sect. 3.4) and hard coded 3D tracking based (Sect. 3.5).

3.3 Learning Appearance Based Sub-units

The work in this section learns a subset of each type of sub-unit using AdaBoost from hand labelled data. As has been previously discussed, not all types of sub-units can be detected using the same type of classifier. For *Location* sub-units, there needs to be correlation between where the motion is happening and where the person is; to this end spatial grid features centred around the face of the signer are employed. For *Motion* sub-units, the salient information is what type of motion is occurring, often regardless of its position, orientation or size. This is approached by extracting moment features and using Binary patterns (BPs) and additive classifiers based on their changes over time. *Hand-Arrangement* sub-units look at where the hands are in relation to each other, so these are only relevant for bi-manual signs. This is done using the same moment features as for *Motion* but this time over a single frame, as there is no temporal context required. All of these sub-unit level classifiers are learnt using AdaBoost (Freund and Schapire 1995). The features used in this section require segmentation of the hands and knowledge of where the face is. The Viola Jones face detector (Viola and Jones 2001) is used to locate the face. Skin segmentation could be used to segment the hands, but since sub-unit labels are required this work uses the data set from the work of Kadir et al. (2004) for which there is an in-house set of sub-unit labels for a portion of the data. This data set was created using a gloved signer and as such a colour segmentation algorithm is used in place of skin segmentation.

3.3.1 Location *Features*

In order that the sign can be localised in relation to the signer, a grid is applied to the image, dependent upon the position and scale of the face detection. Each cell in the grid is a quarter of the face size and the grid is 10 rectangles wide by 8 deep, as shown in Fig. 3.2a. These values are based on the signing space of the signer. However, in this case, the grid does not extend beyond the top of the signers head since the data set does not contain any signs which use that area. The segmented frame is quantised into this grid and a cell fires if over 50% of its pixels are made up of glove/skin. This is shown in Eq. 3.1 where R_{wc} is the weak classifier response and $\Lambda_{skin}(x, y)$ is the likelihood that a pixel contains skin. f is the face height and all the grid values are relative to this dimension.

$$R_{wc} = \begin{cases} 1 \text{ if } \frac{f^2}{8} < \sum_{i=x_1}^{x_2} \sum_{j=y_1}^{y_2} (\Lambda_{skin}(i, j) > 0), \\ 0 \text{ otherwise.} \end{cases}$$

Where x_1, y_1, x_2, y_2 are given by

 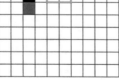 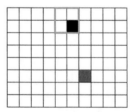

(*a*) The grid applied over the   (*b*) On Right Shoulder   (*c*) Lower Face/Chin
signer

Fig. 3.2 Grid features for two stage classification. **a** Shows an example of the grid produced from the face dimensions while *b* and *c* show grid features chosen by boosting for two of the 18 *Location* sub-units. The *highlighted box* shows the face location and the first and second features chosen, are shown in *black* and *grey* respectively

$$\forall G_x, \forall G_y \begin{cases} x_1 = G_x f, \\ x_2 = (G_x + 0.5)f, \\ y_1 = G_y f, \\ y_2 = (G_y + 0.5)f, \end{cases}$$

$$\text{given } G_x = \{-2.5, -2, -1.5 \dots 2\},$$
$$G_y = \{-4, -3.5, -3 \dots 0\}. \tag{3.1}$$

For each of the *Location* sub-units, a classifier was built via AdaBoost to combine cells which fire for each particular sub-unit, examples of these classifiers are shown in Fig. 3.2b, c. Note how the first cell to be picked by the boosting (shown in black) is the one directly related to the area indicated by the sub-unit label. The second cell chosen by boosting either adds to this location information, as in Fig. 3.2b, or comments on the stationary, non-dominant hand, as in Fig. 3.2c.

Some of the sub-units types contain values which are not mutually exclusive, this needs to be taken into account when labelling and using sub-unit data. The BSL dictionary (British Deaf Association 1992) lists several *Location* sub-units which overlap with each other, such as face and mouth or nose. Using boosting to train classifiers requires positive and negative examples. For best results, examples should not be contaminated, that is, the positive set should not contain negatives and the negative set should not contain positives. Trying to distinguish between an area and its sub-areas can prove futile, for example, the mouth is also on the face and therefore there are likely to be false negatives in the training set when training face against mouth. The second stage, sign-level classification does not require the sub-unit classifier responses to be mutually exclusive. As such a hierarchy can be created of *Location* areas and their sub-areas. This hierarchy is shown in Fig. 3.3; a classifier is trained for each node of the tree, using examples which belong to it, or its children, as positive data. Examples which do not belong to it, its parent or its child nodes provide negative data.

This eliminates false negatives from the data set and avoids confusion. In Fig. 3.3 the ringed nodes show the sub-units for which there exist examples. Exam-

Fig. 3.3 The three *Location* sub-unit trees used for classification. There are three separate trees, based around areas of the body which do not overlap. Areas on the leaves of the tree are sub-areas of their parent nodes. The *ringed* labels indicate that there are exact examples of that type in the data set

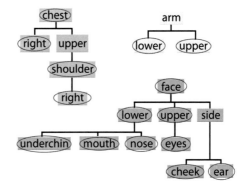

ples are labelled according to this hierarchy, for example, face, face_lower or face_lower_mouth which makes finding children and parents easier by using simple string comparisons.

3.3.2 Motion *and* Hand-Arrangement *Moment Feature Vectors*

For *Hand-Arrangement* and *Motion*, information regarding the arrangement and motion of the hands is required. Moments offer a way of encoding the shapes in an image; if vectors of moment values per frame are concatenated, then they can encode the change in shape of an image over time.

There are several different types of moments which can be calculated, each of them displaying different properties. Four types were chosen to form a feature vector, $\mathbf{m}$: spatial, m_{ab}, central, μ_{ab}, normalised central, $\bar{\mu}_{ab}$ and the Hu set of invariant moments (Hu 1962) $\mathcal{H}_1$–$\mathcal{H}_7$. The order of a moment is defined as $a + b$. This work uses all moments, central moments and normalised central moments up to the 3rd order, 10 per type, (00, 01, 10, 11, 20, 02, 12, 21, 30, 03). Finally, the Hu set of invariant moments are considered, there are 7 of these moments and they are created by combining the normalised central moments, see Hu (1962) for full details, they offer invariance to scale, translation, rotation and skew. This gives a 37 dimensional feature vector, with a wide range of different properties.

$$R_{wc} = \begin{cases} 1 \text{ if } \mathcal{T}_{wc} < \mathbf{M}_{i,t}, \\ 0 \text{ otherwise.} \end{cases}$$

$$(3.2)$$

Since spatial moments are not invariant to translation and scale, there needs to be a common point of origin and similar scale across examples. To this end, the spatial moments are treated in a similar way to the spatial features in Sect. 3.3.1, by centring and scaling the image about the face of the signer before computation. For training *Hand-Arrangement*, this vector is used to boost a set of thresholds for individual moments, $\mathbf{m}_i$ on a given frame t, Eq. 3.2. For *Motion*, temporal information needs to be included. Therefore the video clips are described by a stack of these vectors, $\mathbf{M}$, like a series of 2D arrays, as shown in Fig. 3.4a where the horizontal vectors of moments are concatenated vertically, the lighter the colour, the higher the value of the moment on that frame.

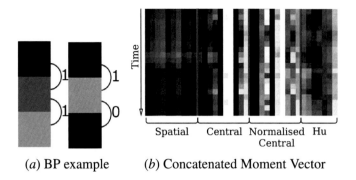

(a) BP example   *(b)* Concatenated Moment Vector

Fig. 3.4 Moment vectors and Binary Patterns for two stage classification. **a** A pictorial description of moment vectors (normalised along each moment type for a selection of examples), the lighter the colour the larger the moment value. **b** BP, working from *top* to *bottom* an increase in gradient is depicted by a 1 and a decrease or no change by a 0

3.3.3 Motion *Binary Patterns and Additive Classifiers*

As has been previously discussed, the *Motion* classifiers are looking for changes in the moments over time. By concatenating feature vectors temporally as shown in Fig. 3.4b, these spatio-temporal changes can be found. Component values can either increase, decrease or remain the same, from one frame to the next. If an increase is described as a 1 and a decrease or no change is described as a 0 then a BP can be used to encode a series of increases/decreases. A temporal vector is said to match the given BP if every '1' accompanies an increase between concurrent frames and every '0' a decrease/'no change'. This is shown in Eq. 3.3 where $\mathbf{M}_{i,t}$ is the value of the component, $\mathbf{M}_i$, at time t and $\mathbf{bp}_t$ is the value of the BP at frame t.

$$R_{wc} = || \max_{\forall t}(BP(\mathbf{M}_{i,t}))| - 1|,$$
$$BP(\mathbf{M}_{i,t}) = \mathbf{bp}_t - d(\mathbf{M}_{i,t}, \mathbf{M}_{i,t+1}),$$
$$d(\mathbf{M}_{i,t}, \mathbf{M}_{i,t+1}) = \begin{cases} 0 \text{ if } \mathbf{M}_{i,t} \leq \mathbf{M}_{i,t+1}, \\ 1 \text{ otherwise.} \end{cases} \tag{3.3}$$

See Fig. 3.5 for an example where feature vector A makes the weak classifier fire, whereas feature vector B fails, due to the ringed gradients being incompatible.

Discarding all magnitude information would possibly remove salient information. To retain this information, boosting is also given the option of using additive classifiers. These look at the average magnitude of a component over time. The weak classifiers are created by applying a threshold, $\mathscr{T}_{wc}$, to the summation of a given component, over several frames. This threshold is optimised across the training data

Fig. 3.5 An example of a BP being used to classify two examples. A comparison is made between the elements of the weak classifiers BP and the temporal vector of the component being assessed. If every '1' in the BP aligns with an increase in the component and every '0' aligns with a decrease or 'no change' then the component vector is said to match (e.g., case A). However if there are inconsistencies as ringed in case B then the weak classifier will not fire

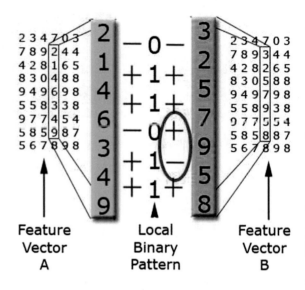

Feature Vector A   Local Binary Pattern   Feature Vector B

during the boosting phase. For an additive classifier of size T, over component $\mathbf{m}_i$, the response of the classifier, R_{wc}, can be described as in Eq. 3.4.

$$R_{wc} = \begin{cases} 1 \text{ if } \mathscr{T}_{wc} \leq \sum_{t=0}^{T} \mathbf{M}_{i,t}, \\ 0 \text{ otherwise.} \end{cases} \qquad (3.4)$$

Boosting is given all possible combinations of BPs, acting on each of the possible components. The BPs are limited in size, being between 2 and 5 changes (3–6 frames) long. The additive features are also applied to all the possible components, but the lengths permitted are between 1 and 26 frames, the longest mean length of *Motion* sub-units. Both sets of weak classifiers can be temporally offset from the beginning of an example, by any distance up to the maximum distance of 26 frames.

Examples of the classifiers learnt are shown in Fig. 3.6, additive classifiers are shown by boxes, increasing BPs are shown by pale lines and decreasing ones by dark lines. When looking at a sub-unit such as 'hands move apart' (Fig. 3.6a), the majority of the BP classifiers show increasing moments, which is what would be expected, as the eccentricity of the moments is likely to increase as the hands move apart. Conversely, for 'hands move together' (Fig. 3.6b), most of the BPs are decreasing.

Since some *Motion* sub-units occur more quickly than others, the boosted classifiers are not all constrained to being equal in temporal length. Instead, an optimal length is chosen over the training set for each individual sub-unit. Several different length classifiers are boosted starting at 6 frames long, increasing in steps of 2 and finishing at 26 frames long. Training classification results are then found for each

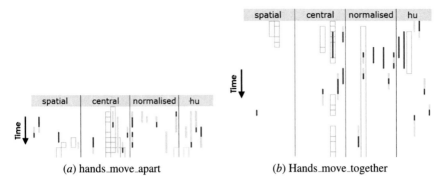

Fig. 3.6 Boosted temporal moments BP and additive *Motion* classifiers. The moment vectors are stacked one frame ahead of another. The *boxes* show where an additive classifier has been chosen, a *dark line* shows a decreasing moment value and a *pale line* an increasing value

sub-unit and the best length chosen to create a final set of classifiers, of various lengths suited to the sub-units being classified.

3.4 2D Tracking Based Sub-units

Unfortunately, since the learnt, appearance based, sub-units require expertly annotated data they are limited to data sets with this annotation. An alternative to appearance based features is given by tracking. While tracking errors can propagate to create sub-unit errors, the hand trajectories offer significant information which can aid recognition. With the advances of tracking systems and the real-time solution introduced by the Kinect™, tracking is fast becoming an option for real-time, robust recognition of sign language. This section works with hand and head trajectories, extracted from videos by the work outlined by Roussos et al. (2010). The tracking information is used to extract *Motion* and *Location* information. *Hand-Shape* information is extracted via Histograms of Gradients (HOGs) on hand image patches and learnt from labels using random forests. The labels are taken from the linguistic representations of Sign Gesture Mark-up Language (SiGML) (Elliott et al. 2001) or HamNoSys (Hanke and Schmaling 2004).[1]

---

[1]Note that conversion between the two forms is possible. However while HamNoSys is usually presented as a font for linguistic use, SiGML is more suited to automatic processing.

(*a*) Single handed   (*b*) Bimanual: Syn-   (*c*) Bimanual: Together/Apart
                   chronous

Fig. 3.7 Motions detected from tracking

3.4.1 Motion *Features*

In order to link the x, y co-ordinates obtained from the tracking to the abstract concepts used by sign linguists, rules are employed to extract HamNoSys based information from the trajectories. The approximate size of the head is used as a heuristic to discard ambient motion (that less than 0.25 the head size) and the type of motion occurring is derived directly from deterministic rules on the x and y co-ordinates of the hand position. The types of motions encoded are shown in Fig. 3.7, the single handed motions are available for both hands and the dual handed motions are orientation independent so as to match linguistic concepts.

3.4.2 Location *Features*

Similarly the x and y co-ordinates of the sign location need to be described relative to the signer rather than in absolute pixel positions. This is achieved via quantisation of the values into a codebook based on the signer's head position and scale in the image. For any given hand position (x_h, y_h) the quantised version (x'_h, y'_h) is achieved using the quantisation rules shown in Eq. 3.5, where (x_f, y_f) is the face position and (w_f, h_f) is the face size.

$$x' = (x_h - x_f)/w_f,$$
$$y' = (y_h - y_f)/h_f. \tag{3.5}$$

Due to the limited size of a natural signing space, this gives values in the range of $y' \in 0 \ldots 10$ and $x' \in \{0 \ldots 8\}$ which can be expressed as a binary feature vector of size 36, where the x and y positions of the hands are quantised independently.

Fig. 3.8 Example HOGs extracted from a frame

3.4.3   HandShape *Features*

While just the motion and location of the signs can be used for recognition of many examples, it has been shown that adding the handshape can give significant improvement (Kadir et al. 2004). HOG descriptors have proven efficient for sign language hand shape recognition (Buehler et al. 2009) and these are employed as the base feature unit. In each frame, the signer's dominant hand is segmented using the x,y position and a skin model. These image patches are rotated to their principal axis and scaled to a square, 256 pixels in size. Examples of these image patches are shown in Fig. 3.8 beside the frame from which they have been extracted. HOGs are calculated over these squares at a cell size of 32 pixels square with 9 orientation bins and with 2 × 2 overlapping blocks, these are also shown in Fig. 3.8. This gives a feature vector of 1764 histogram bins which describes the appearance of a hand.

3.4.4   HandShape *Classifiers*

This work focusses on just the 12 basic handshapes, building multi-modal classifiers to account for the different orientations. A list of these handshapes is shown in Fig. 3.9.

Unfortunately, linguists annotating sign do so only at the *sign* level while most sub-units occur for only *part* of a sign. Also, not only do handshapes change throughout the sign, they are made more difficult to recognise due to motion blur. Using the motion of the hands, the sign can be split into its component parts (as in Pitsikalis et al. 2011), that are then aligned with the sign annotations. These annotations are in HamNoSys and have been prepared by trained experts, they include the sign

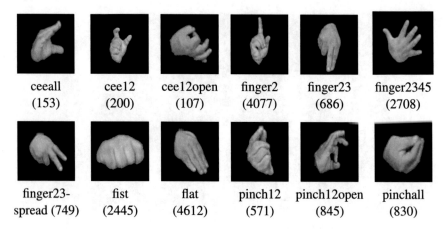

| ceeall
(153) | cee12
(200) | cee12open
(107) | finger2
(4077) | finger23
(686) | finger2345
(2708) |

| finger23-
spread (749) | fist
(2445) | flat
(4612) | pinch12
(571) | pinch12open
(845) | pinchall
(830) |

Fig. 3.9 The base handshapes (Number of occurrences in the data set)

(a)   **(b)**   **(c)**   **(d)**   **(e)**

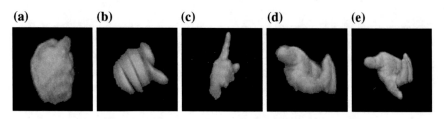

Fig. 3.10 A variety of examples for the HamNoSys/SiGML class 'finger2'

breakdown but not the temporal alignment. The frames most likely to contain a static handshape (i.e., those with limited or no motion) are extracted for training.

Note that, as shown in Fig. 3.10, a single SiGML class (in this case 'finger2') may contain examples which vary greatly in appearance, making visual classification an extremely difficult task.

The extracted hand shapes are classified using a multi-class random forest. Random forests were proposed by Amit and Geman (1997) and Breiman (2001). They have been shown to yield good performance on a variety of classification and regression problems, and can be trained efficiently in a parallel manner, allowing training on large feature vectors and data sets. In this system, the forest is trained from automatically extracted samples of all 12 handshapes in the data set, shown in Fig. 3.9. Since signs may have multiple handshapes or several instances of the same handshape, the total occurrences are greater than the number of signs, however they are not equally distributed between the handshape classes. The large disparities in the number of examples between classes (see Fig. 3.9) may bias the learning, therefore the training set is rebalanced before learning by selecting 1000 random samples for each class, forming a new balanced data set. The forest used consists of $N = 100$ multi-class decision trees T_i, each of which is trained on a random subset of the training data. Each tree node splits the feature space in two by applying a threshold on

Table 3.1 Confusion matrix of the handshape recognition, for all 12 classes

handshape	predictions											
flat	**0.35**	0.19	0.09	0.03	0.08	0.06	0.03	0.06	0.06	0.01	0.03	0.01
fist	0.03	**0.69**	0.02	0.04	0.11	0.05		0.02	0.03			0.02
finger2345	0.16	0.19	**0.36**	0.02	0.03	0.05		0.06	0.02	0.03	0.06	0.01
finger2	0.02	0.33	0.07	**0.31**	0.11	0.05	0.02	0.03	0.02		0.04	
pinchall	0.03	0.09	0.04	0.01	**0.65**	0.11	0.01	0.01				0.04
pinch12	0.02	0.20	0.01	0.02	0.13	**0.56**	0.01		0.01		0.01	0.02
finger23	0.05	0.17	0.04	0.02	0.05	0.04	**0.54**	0.01			0.07	0.01
pinch12op	0.03	0.12	0.07	0.01	0.15	0.04	0.01	**0.56**				0.01
cee12	0.01	0.05	0.01	0.03	0.04			0.01	**0.82**		0.01	
cee12open					0.01					**0.99**		
finger23sp	0.01	0.15	0.02		0.06	0.01	0.05	0.02			**0.65**	
ceeall	0.01	0.08	0.03		0.08	0.01	0.02	0.01			0.01	**0.77**

one dimension of the feature vector. This dimension (chosen from a random subset) and the threshold value are chosen to yield the largest reduction in entropy in the class distribution. This recursive partitioning of the data set continues until a node contains a subset of examples that belong to one single class, or if the tree reaches a maximal depth (set to 10). Each leaf is then labelled according to the mode of the contained samples. As a result, the forest yields a probability distribution over all classes, where the likelihood for each class is the proportion of trees that voted for this class. Formally, the confidence that feature vector x describes the handshape c is given by:

$$p[c] = \frac{1}{N} \sum_{i<N} \delta_c(T_i(x)),$$

where N is the number of trees in the forest, $T_i(x)$ is the leaf of the ith tree T_i into which x falls, and $\delta_c(a)$ is the Kronecker delta function ($\delta_c(a) = 1$ iff. $c = a$, $\delta_c(a) = 0$ otherwise).

The performance of this hand shape classification on the test set is recorded on Table 3.1, where each row corresponds to a shape, and each column corresponds to a predicted class (empty cells signify zero). Lower performance is achieved for classes that are more frequent in the data set. The more frequently a handshape occurs in the data set the more orientations it is likely to be used in. This in turn makes the appearance of the class highly variable; see, for example, Fig. 3.10 for the case of 'finger2'—the worst performing case. Also noted is the high confusion between 'finger2' and 'fist' most likely due to the similarity of these classes when the signer is pointing to themselves.

The handshape classifiers are evaluated for the right hand only during frames when it is not in motion. The sign recognition system is evaluated using two different encodings for the detected hand shapes. As will be described in Sect. 3.6, the next stage classifier requires inputs in the form of binary feature vectors. Two types of 12 bit binary feature vector can be produced from the classifier results. The first method applies a strict Winner Takes All (WTA) on the multi-class forest's response: the class with the highest probability is set to one, and the others to zero. For every non-motion frame, the vector contains a true value in the highest scoring class. The second method applies a fixed threshold ($\tau = 0.25$) on the confidences provided by the classifier for each of the 12 handshapes classes. Handshapes that have a confidence above threshold ($p[c] > \tau$) are set to one, and the others to zero. This soft approach carries the double advantage that a) the feature vector may encode the ambiguity between handshapes, which may itself carry information, and b) may contain only zeros if confidences in all classes are small.

3.5   3D Tracking Based Sub-units

With the availability of the Kinect™, real-time tracking in 3D is now a realistic option. Due to this, this final sub-unit section expands on the previous tracking sub-units to work in 3D. The tracking is obtained using the OpenNI framework (Ope 2010) with the PrimeSense tracker (Pri 2010). Two types of features are extracted, those encoding the *Motion* and *Location* of the sign being performed.

3.5.1   Motion *Features*

Again, the focus is on linear motion directions, as with the sub-units described in Sect. 3.4.1, but this time with the z axis included. Specifically, individual hand motions in the x plane (left and right), the y plane (up and down) and the z plane (towards and away from the signer). This is augmented by the bi-manual classifiers for 'hands move together', 'hands move apart' and 'hands move in sync', again, these are all now assessed in 3D. The approximate size of the head is used as a heuristic to discard ambient motion (that less than 0.25 the head size) and the type of motion occurring is derived directly from deterministic rules on the x, y, z co-ordinates of the hand position. The resulting feature vector is a binary representation of the found linguistic values. The list of 17 motion features extracted is shown in Table 3.2.

3.5.2   Location *Features*

Whereas previously, with 2D tracking, a coarse grid is applied, in this section the skeleton returned by the PrimeSense tracker can now be leveraged. This allows signer related locations to be described with higher confidence. As such, the location features are calculated using the distance of the dominant hand from skeletal joints. A feature will fire if the dominant hand is closer than $H^{head}/2$ of the joint in question. A list of the 9 joints considered is shown in Table 3.2 and displayed to scale in

Table 3.2 Table listing the locations and hand motions included in the feature vectors. The conditions for motion are shown with the label. Where x, y, z is the position of the hand, either left (L) or right (R), Δ indicates a change from one frame to the next and $\delta(L, R)$ is the Euclidean distance between the left and right hands. λ is the threshold value to reduce noise and increase generalisation, this is set to be a quarter the head height. F^R and F^L are the motion feature vectors relating to the right and left hand respectively

Locations	Motions		Bi-manual
	Right or left hand		
Head	Left	$\Delta x > \lambda$	In sync
Neck	Right	$\Delta x < -\lambda$	$|\delta(L, R)| < \lambda$
Torso	Up	$\Delta y > \lambda$	And
L shoulder	Down	$\Delta y < -\lambda$	$F^R = F^L$
L elbow	Towards	$\Delta z > \lambda$	Together
L hand	Away	$\Delta z < -\lambda$	$\Delta(\delta(L, R)) < -\lambda$
L hip	None	$\Delta L < \lambda$	Apart
R shoulder		$\Delta R < \lambda$	$\Delta(\delta(L, R)) > \lambda$
R hip			

Fig. 3.11. While displayed in 2D, the regions surrounding the joints are actually 3D spheres. When the dominant hand (in this image shown by the smaller red dot) moves into the region around a joint then that feature will fire. In the example shown, it would be difficult for two features to fire at once. When in motion, the left hand and elbow regions may overlap with other body regions meaning that more than one feature fires at a time.

3.6 Sign Level Classification

Each of the different sub-unit classifier sets is now combined with a sign-level classifier. The groups of binary feature vectors are each concatenated to create a single binary feature vector $F = (f_i)_{i=1}^{D}$ per frame, where $f_i \in \{0, 1\}$ and D is the number of dimensions in the feature vector. This feature vector is then used as the input to a sign level classifier for recognition. By using a binary approach, better generalisation is obtained. This requires far less training data than approaches which must generalise over both a continuous input space as well as the variability between signs (e.g., HMMs). Two sign level classification methods are investigated. Firstly, Markov models which use the feature vector as a whole and secondly Sequential Patten Boosting which performs discriminative feature selection.

Fig. 3.11 Body joints used
to extract sign locations

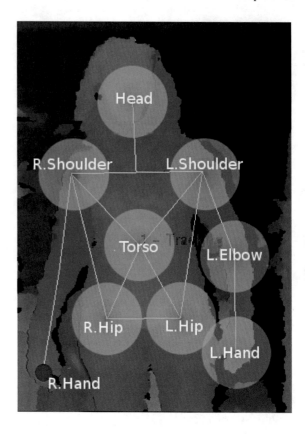

3.6.1 Markov Models

HMMs are a proven technology for time series analysis and recognition. While they
have been employed for sign recognition, they have issues due to the large training
requirements. Kadir et al. (2004) overcame these issues by instead using a simpler
Markov model when the feature space is discrete. The symbolic nature of linguistic
sub-units means that the discrete time series of events can be modelled without a
hidden layer. To this end a Markov chain is constructed for each sign in a lexicon.
An ergodic model is used and a Look Up Table (LUT) employed to maintain as
little of the chain as is required. Code entries not contained within the LUT are
assigned a nominal probability. This is done to avoid otherwise correct chains being
assigned zero probabilities if noise corrupts the input signal. The result is a sparse
state transition matrix, $P_\omega(F_t|F_{t-1})$, for each word ω giving a classification bank of
Markov chains. During creation of this transition matrix, secondary transitions can
be included, where $P_\omega(F_t|F_{t-2})$. This is similar to adding skip transitions to the left-
right hidden layer of a HMM which allows deletion errors in the incoming signal.
While it could be argued that the linguistic features constitute discrete emission prob-

abilities; the lack of a doubly stochastic process and the fact that the hidden states are determined directly from the observation sequence, separates this from traditional HMMs which cannot be used due to their high training requirements. During classification, the model bank is applied to incoming data in a similar fashion to HMMs. The objective is to calculate the chain which best describes the incoming data, that is, has the highest probability that it produced the observation F. Feature vectors are found in the LUT using an L1 distance on the binary vectors. The probability of a model matching the observation sequence is calculated as

$$P(\omega|s) = v_w \prod_{t=1}^{l} P_\omega(F_t|F_{t-1}),$$

where l is the length of the word in the test sequence and v_ω is the prior probability of a chain starting in any one of its states. In this work, without grammar, $\forall \omega, v_\omega = 1$.

3.6.2 SP Boosting

One limitation of Markov models is that they encode exact series of transitions over all features rather than relying only on discriminative features. This leads to reliance on user dependant feature combinations which if not replicated in test data, will result in poor recognition performance. Squential Patterns (SPs), on the other hand, compare the input data for relevant features and ignore the irrelevant features. A SP is a sequence of discriminative *itemsets* (i.e., feature subsets) that occur in positive examples and not negative examples (see Fig. 3.12). We define an itemset T as the dimensions of the feature vector $F = (f_i)_{i=1}^{D}$ that have the value of 1: $T \subset \{1, ..., D\}$ is a set of integers where $\forall t \in T, f_t = 1$. Following this, we define a SP $\mathbf{T}$ of length $|\mathbf{T}|$ as: $\mathbf{T} = (T_i)_{i=1}^{|\mathbf{T}|}$, where T_i is an itemset.

In order to use SPs for classification, we first define a method for detecting SPs in an input sequence of feature vectors. To this end, firstly let $\mathbf{T}$ be a SP we wish to detect. Suppose the given feature vector input sequence of $|\mathbf{F}|$ frames is $\mathbf{F} = (F_t)_{t=1}^{|\mathbf{F}|}$, where F_t is the binary feature vector defined in Sect. 3.6. We firstly convert $\mathbf{F}$ into the SP $\mathbf{I} = (I_t)_{t=1}^{|\mathbf{F}|}$, where I_t is the itemset of feature vector F_t. We say that the SP $\mathbf{T}$ is present in $\mathbf{I}$ if there exists a sequence $(\beta_i)_{i=1}^{|\mathbf{T}|}$, where $\beta_i < \beta_j$ when $i < j$ and $\forall i = \{1, ..., |\mathbf{T}|\}, T_i \subset I_{\beta_i}$. This relationship is denoted with the $\subset_S$ operator, that is, $\mathbf{T} \subset_S \mathbf{I}$. Conversely, if the sequence $(\beta_i)_{i=1}^{|\mathbf{T}|}$ does not exist, we denote it as $\mathbf{T} \not\subset_S \mathbf{I}$.

From this, we can then define a SP weak classifier as follows: Let $\mathbf{T}$ be a given SP and $\mathbf{I}$ be an itemset sequence derived from some input binary vector sequence F. A *SP weak classifier*, $h^{\mathbf{T}}(\mathbf{I})$, can be constructed as follows:

$$h^{\mathbf{T}}(\mathbf{I}) = \begin{cases} 1, & \text{if } \mathbf{T} \subset_S \mathbf{I}, \\ -1, & \text{if } \mathbf{T} \not\subset_S \mathbf{I}. \end{cases}$$

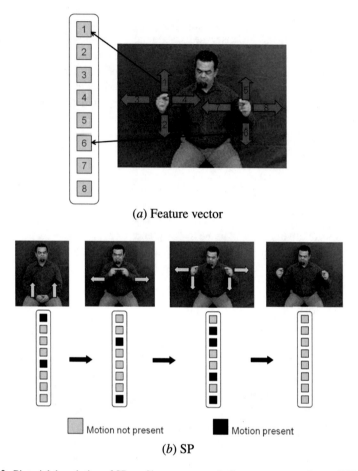

(a) Feature vector

(b) SP

Fig. 3.12 Pictorial description of SPs. **a** Shows an example feature vector made up of 2D motions of the hands. In this case the first element shows 'right hand moves up', the second 'right hand moves down' etc. **b** Shows a plausible pattern that might be found for the sign 'bridge'. In this sign the hands move up to meet each other, they move apart and then curve down as if drawing a hump-back bridge

A strong classifier can be constructed by linearly combining a number (S) of selected SP weak classifiers in the form of:

$$H(I) = \sum_{i=1}^{S} \alpha_i h_i^{\mathbf{T}_i}(I).$$

The weak classifiers h_i are selected iteratively based on example weights formed during training. In order to determine the optimal weak classifier at each Boosting iteration, the common approach is to exhaustively consider the entire set of candidate weak classifiers and finally select the best weak classifier (i.e., that with the lowest weighted error). However, finding SP weak classifiers corresponding to optimal SPs this way is not possible due to the immense size of the SP search space. To this end, the method of SP Boosting is employed (Ong and Bowden 2011). This method poses the learning of discriminative SPs as a tree based search problem. The search is made efficient by employing a set of pruning criteria to find the SPs that provide optimal discrimination between the positive and negative examples. The resulting tree-search method is integrated into a boosting framework; resulting in the SP-Boosting algorithm that combines a set of unique and optimal SPs for a given classification problem. For this work, classifiers are built in a one-versus-one manner and the results aggregated for each sign class.

3.7   Appearance Based Results

This section of work uses the same 164 sign data set as Kadir et al. (2004) and therefore a direct comparison can be made between their hard coded tracking based system and the learnt sub-unit approach using detection based sub-units. For this work, extra annotation was required as Kadir et al. (2004) used only sign boundaries. 7410 *Location* examples, 322 *Hand-Arrangement* examples and 578 *Motion* were hand labelled for training sub-unit classifiers. The data set consists of 1640 examples (ten of each sign). Signs were chosen randomly rather than picking specific examples which are known to be easy to separate. The sub-unit classifiers are built using only data from four of the ten examples of each sign and the word level classifier is then trained on five examples (including the four previously seen by the sub-unit classifiers) leaving five completely unseen examples for testing purposes. The second stage classifier is trained on the previously used four training examples plus one other, giving five training examples per sign. The results are acquired from the five unseen examples of each of the 164 signs. This is done for all six possible combinations of training/test data. Results are shown in Table 3.3 alongside the results from Kadir et al. (2004). The first three columns show the results of combining each type of appearance sub-unit with the second stage sign classifier. Unsurprisingly, none of the individual types contains sufficient information to be able to accurately separate the data. However, when combined, the appearance based classifiers learnt from the data are comparable to the hard coded classifiers used on perfectly tracked data. The performance drops by only 6.6 Percentage Points (pp), from 79.2 to 72.6% whilst giving the advantage of not needing the high quality tracking system.

Figure 3.13, visually demonstrates the sub-unit level classifiers being used with the second stage classifier. The output from the sub-unit classifiers are shown on the right hand side in a vector format on a frame by frame basis. It shows the repetition of features for the sign 'Box'. As can be seen there is a pattern in the vector which repeats each time the sign is made. It is this repetition which the second stage classifier is using to detect signs.

Table 3.3 Classification performance of the appearance based two-stage detector. Using the appearance based sub-unit classifiers. Kadir et al. (2004) results are included for comparison purposes

	Hand-arrangement	Location	Motion	Combined	(Kadir et al. 2004)
Minimum (%)	31.6	30.7	28.2	68.7	76.1
Maximum (%)	35.0	32.2	30.5	74.3	82.4
Std dev	0.9	0.4	0.6	1.5	2.1
Mean (%)	33.2	31.7	29.4	72.6	79.2

Fig. 3.13 Repetition of the appearance based sub-unit classifier vector. The band down the *right hand side* of the frame shows the sub-unit level classifier firing patterns for the last 288 frames, the vector for the most recent frame is at the bottom. The previous video during the 288 frames shows four repetitions of the sign 'Box'

3.8 2D Tracking Results

The data set used for these experiments contains 984 Greek Sign Language (GSL) signs with 5 examples of each performed by a single signer (for a total of 4920 samples). The handshape classifiers are learnt on data from the first 4 examples of each sign. The sign level classifiers are trained on the same 4 examples, the remaining sign of each type is reserved for testing.

Table 3.4 shows sign level classification results. It is apparent from these results, that out of the independent vectors, the location information is the strongest. This is due to the strong combination of a detailed location feature vector and the temporal information encoded by the Markov chain.

Table 3.4 Sign level classification results using 2D tracked features and the Markov Models. The first three rows show the results when using the features independently with the Markov chain (The handshapes used are non-mutually exclusive). The next three rows give the results of using all the different feature vectors. Including the improvement gained by allowing the handshapes to be non-mutually exclusive (thresh) versus the WTA option. The final method is the combination of the superior handshapes with the location, motion and the second order skips

Motion	25.1%
Location	60.5%
HandShape	3.4%
All: WTA	52.7%
All: thresh	68.4%
All + skips ($P(F_t|F_{t-2})$)	**71.4%**

Table 3.5 Comparison of recall results on the 2D tracking data using both Markov chains and SPs

	Markov chains		SPs	
	Top 1 (%)	Top 4 (%)	Top 1 (%)	Top 4 (%)
Recall	**71.4**	**82.3**	**74.1**	**89.2**

Shown also is the improvement afforded by using the handshape classifiers with a threshold vs a WTA implementation. By allowing the classifiers to return multiple possibilities more of the data about the handshape is captured. Conversely, when none of the classifiers is confident, a 'null' response is permitted which reduces the amount of noise. Using the non-mutually exclusive version of the handshapes in combination with the motion and location, the percentage of signs correctly returned is 68.4%. By including the 2nd order transitions whilst building the Markov chain there is a 3 pp boost to 71.4%.

This work was developed for use as a sign dictionary, within this context, when queried by a video search, the classification would not return a single response. Instead, like a search engine, it should return a ranked list of possible signs. Ideally the target sign would be close to the top of this list. To this end we show results for 2 possibilities; The percentage of signs which are correctly ranked as the first possible sign (Top 1) and the percentage which are ranked in the top 4 possible signs.

This approach is applied to the best sub-unit features above combined with either the Markov Chains or the SP trees. The results of these tests are shown in Table 3.5. When using the the same combination of sub-unit features as found to be optimal with the Markov Chains, the SP trees are able to improve on the results by nearly 3 pp, increasing the recognition rate from 71.4 to 74.1%. A further improvement is also found when expanding the search results list, within the top 4 signs the recall rate increases from 82.3 to 89.2%.

3.9 3D Tracking Results

While the Kinect™ work is intended for use as a live system, quantitative results can be obtained by the standard method of splitting pre-recorded data into training and test sets. The split between test and training data can be done in several ways. This work uses two versions, the first to show results on signer dependent data, as is often used, the second shows performance on unseen signers, a signer independent test.

3.9.1 Data Sets

Two data sets were captured for training; The first is a data set of 20 GSL signs, randomly chosen and containing both similar and dissimilar signs. This data includes six people performing each sign an average of seven times. The signs were all captured in the same environment with the Kinect™ and the signer in approximately the same place for each subject. The second data set is larger and more complex. It contains 40 Deutsche Gebärdensprache—German Sign Language (DGS) signs, chosen to provide a phonetically balanced subset of HamNoSys phonemes. There are 15 participants each performing all the signs 5 times. The data was captured using a mobile system giving varying view points.

3.9.2 GSL Results

Two variations of tests were performed; firstly the signer dependent version, where one example from each signer was reserved for testing and the remaining examples were used for training. This variation was cross-validated multiple times by selecting different combinations of train and test data. Of more interest for this application however, is signer independent performance. For this reason the second experiment involves reserving data from a subject for testing, then training on the remaining signers. This process is repeated across all signers in the data set. The results of both the Markov models and the Sequential Patten Boosting applied to the basic 3D features are shown in Table 3.6.

As is noted in Sect. 3.6.2, while the the Markov models perform well when they have training data which is close to the test data, they are less able to generalise. This is shown by the dependent results being high, average 92% within the top 4, compared to the average independent result which is 17 pp lower at 75%. It is even more noticeable when comparing the highest ranked sign only, which suffers from a drop of 25 pp, going from 79 to 54%. When looking at the individual results of the independent test it can be seen that there are obvious outliers in the data, specifically signer 3 (the only female in the data set), where the recognition rates are markedly lower. This is reflected in statistical analysis which gives high standard deviation

Table 3.6 Results across the 20 sign GSL data set

Test		Markov models		SP-boosting	
		Top 1 (%)	Top 4 (%)	Top 1 (%)	Top 4 (%)
Independent	1	56	80	72	91
	2	61	79	80	98
	3	30	45	67	89
	4	55	86	77	95
	5	58	75	78	98
	6	63	83	80	98
	Mean	**54**	**75**	**76**	**95**
	StdDev	12	15	5	4
Dependent mean		**79**	**92**	**92**	**99.90**

across the signers in both the top 1 and top 4 rankings when using the Markov Chains.

When the SP-Boosting is used, again the dependant case produces higher results, gaining nearly 100% when considering the top 4 ranked signs. However, due to the discriminative feature selection process employed; the user independent case does not show such marked degradation, dropping just 4.9 pp within the top 4 signs, going from 99.9 to 95%. When considering the top ranked sign the reduction is more significant at 16 pp, from 92 to 76%, but this is still a significant improvement on the more traditional Markov model. It can also be seen that the variability in results across signers is greatly reduced using SP-Boosting, whilst signer 3 is still the signer with the lowest percentage of signs recognised, the standard deviation across all signs has dropped to 5% for the first ranked signs and is again lower for the top 4 ranked signs.

3.9.3 DGS Results

The DGS data set offers a more challenging task as there is a wider range of signers and environments. Experiments were run in the same format using the same features as for the GSL data set. Table 3.7 shows the results of both the dependent and independent tests. As can be seen with the increased number of signs the percentage accuracy for the first returned result is lower than that of the GSL tests at 59.8% for dependent and 49.4% for independent. However the recall rates within the top 4 ranked signs (now only 10% of the data set) are still high at 91.9% for the dependent tests and 85.1% for the independent ones. Again the relatively low standard deviation of 5.2% shows that the SP-Boosting is picking the discriminative features which are able to generalise well to unseen signers.

Table 3.7 Subject independent (SI) and Subject dependent (SD) test results across 40 signs in the DGS data set

	Subject dependent		Subject independent	
	Top 1 (%)	Top 4 (%)	Top 1 (%)	Top 4 (%)
Min	56.7	90.5	39.9	74.9
Max	64.5	94.6	67.9	92.4
StdDev	1.9	1.0	8.5	5.2
Mean	**59.8**	**91.9**	**49.4**	**85.1**

Fig. 3.14 Aggregated confusion matrix of the first returned result for each subject independent test on the DGS data set

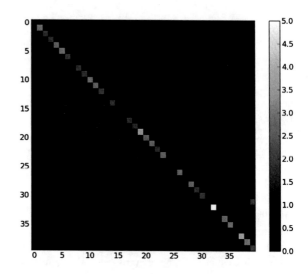

As can be seen in the confusion matrix (see Fig. 3.14), while most signs are well distinguished, there are some signs which routinely get confused with each other. A good example of this is the three signs 'already', 'Athens' and 'Greece' which share very similar hand motion and location but are distinguishable by handshape which is not currently modelled on this data set.

3.10   Discussion

Three different approaches to sub-unit feature extraction have been compared in this paper. The first based on appearance only, the latter two on tracking. The advantage of the first approach is that it doesn't depend on high quality tracking for good results. However, it would be easily confused via cluttered backgrounds or short sleeves (often a problem with sign language data sets). The other advantage of the appearance based classification is that it includes information not available by trajectories alone, thus encoding information about handshape within the moment based classifiers. While this may aid classification on small data sets it makes it more difficult to de-couple the handshape from the motion and location sub-units. This affects the generalisation ability of the classifiers due to the differences between signers.

Where 2D tracking is available, the results are superior in general to the appearance based results. This is shown in the work by Kadir et al. (2004), who achieve equivalent results on the same data using tracking trajectories when compared to the appearance based ones presented here. Unfortunately, it is not always possible to accurately track video data and this is why it is still valid to examine appearance based approaches. The 2D tracking *Location* sub-features presented here are based around a grid, while this is effective in localising the motion it is not as desirable as the HamNoSys derived features used in the improved 3D tracking features. The grid suffers from boundary noise as the hands move between cells. This noise causes problems when the features are used in the second stage of classification. With the 3D features this is less obvious due to them being relative to the signer in 3D and therefore the locations are not arbitrarily used by the signer in the same way as the grid is. For example if a signer puts their hands to their shoulders, this will cause multiple cells of the grid to fire and it may not be the same one each time. When using 3D, if the signer puts their hands to their shoulders then the shoulder feature fires. This move from an arbitrary grid to consciously decided body locations reduces boundary effect around significant areas in the signing space.

This in turn leads to the sign level classifiers. The Markov chains are very good at recognising signer dependent, repetitive motion, in these cases they are almost on a par with the SPs. However, they are much less capable of managing signer independent classification as they are unable to distinguish between the signer accents and the signs themselves and therefore over-fit the data. Instead the SPs look for the discriminative features between the examples, ignoring any signer specific features which might confuse the Markov Chains.

3.11 Conclusions

This work has presented three approaches to sub-unit based sign recognition. Tests were conducted using boosting to learn three types of sub-units based on appearance features, which are then combined with a second stage classifier to learn word level signs. These appearance based features offer an alternative to costly tracking.

The second approach uses a 2D tracking based set of sub-units combined with some appearance based handshape classifiers. The results show that a combination of these robust, generalising features from tracking and learnt handshape classifiers overcomes the high ambiguity and variability in the data set to achieve excellent recognition performance: achieving a recognition rate of 73% on a large data set of 984 signs.

The third and final approach translates these tracking based sub-units into 3D, this offers user independent, real-time recognition of isolated signs. Using this data a new learning method is introduced, combining the sub-units with SP-Boosting as a discriminative approach. Results are shown on two data sets with the recognition rate reaching 99.9% on a 20 sign multi-user data set and 85.1% on a more challenging and realistic subject independent, 40 sign test set. This demonstrates that true signer independence is possible when more discriminative learning methods are employed. In order to strengthen comparisons within the SLR field the data sets created within this work have been released for use within the community.

3.12 Future Work

The learnt sub-units show promise and, as shown by the work of Pitsikalis et al. (2011), there are several avenues which can be explored. However, for all of these directions, more linguistically annotated data is required across multiple signers to allow the classifiers to discriminate between the features which are signer specific and those which are independent. In addition, handshapes are a large part of sign, while the work on the multi-signer depth data set has given good results, handshapes should be included in future work using depth cameras. Finally, the recent creation of a larger, multi-signer data set has set the ground work in place for better quantitative analysis. Using this data in the same manner as the DGS40 data set should allow bench-marking of Kinect sign recognition approaches, both for signer dependent and independent recognition. Appearance only techniques can also be verified using the Kinect data set where appropriate as the RGB images are also available though they are not used in this paper. Though it should be noted that this is an especially challenging data set for appearance techniques due to the many varying backgrounds and subjects.

Acknowledgements The research leading to these results has received funding from the European Community's Seventh Framework Programme (FP7/2007–2013) under grant agreement number 231135 Dicta-Sign. The Dicta-Sign data sets used and additional SL resources are available via http://www.sign-lang.uni-hamburg.de/dicta-sign/portal/.

References

Y. Amit, D. Geman, Shape quantization and recognition with randomized trees. Neural Comput. **9**, 1545–1588 (1997)

L. Breiman, Random forests. Mach. Learn **45**, 5–32 (2001)

British Deaf Association, *Dictionary of British Sign Language/English*, (Faber and Faber Ltd, London, 1992)

P. Buehler, M. Everingham, A. Zisserman, Learning sign language by watching TV (using weakly aligned subtitles), in *Proceedings of the IEEE Computer Society Conference on Computer Vision and Pattern Recognition*, Miami, FL, USA, 20–26 June 2009, pp. 2961–2968

H. Cooper, R. Bowden, Large lexicon detection of sign language, in *Proceedings of the IEEE International Conference on Computer Vision: Workshop Human Computer Interaction*, Rio de Janario, Brazil, 16–19 October 2007, pp. 88–97 doi: 10.1007/978-3-540-75773-3_10

H. Cooper, R. Bowden, Sign language recognition using linguistically derived sub-units, in *Proceedings of the Language Resources and Evaluation Conference Workshop on the Representation and Processing of Sign Languages : Corpora and Sign Languages Technologies*, Valetta, Malta, 17–23 May 2010

R. Elliott, J. Glauert, J. Kennaway, K. Parsons, D5-2: SiGML Definition. *ViSiCAST Project working document*, 2001

H. Ershaed, I. Al-Alali, N. Khasawneh, M. Fraiwan, An arabic sign language computer interface using the xbox kinect, in *Annual Undergraduate Research Conference on Applied Computing*, May 2011

Y. Freund, R.E. Schapire, A decision-theoretic generalization of on-line learning and an application to boosting, in *Proceedings of the European Conference on Computational Learning Theory*, Springer, Barcelona, 13–15 March 1995, pp. 23–37. ISBN 3-540-59119-2

J.W. Han, G. Awad, A. Sutherland, Modelling and segmenting subunits for sign language recognition based on hand motion analysis. Pattern Recognit. Lett. **30**(6), 623–633 (2009)

T. Hanke, C. Schmaling. *Sign Language Notation System*, (Institute of German Sign Language and Communication of the Deaf, Hamburg, Germany, January 2004), http://www.sign-lang.uni-hamburg.de/projects/hamnosys.html

M.K. Hu, Visual pattern recognition by moment invariants. *IRE Transactions on Information Theory*, IT-8, pp. 179–187, February 1962

T. Kadir, R. Bowden, E.J. Ong, A. Zisserman, Minimal training, large lexicon, unconstrained sign language recognition, in *Proceedings of the BMVA British Machine Vision Conference*, vol. 2, Kingston, UK, 7–9 September 2004, pp. 939–948

S. Kim, M.B. Waldron, Adaptation of self organizing network for ASL recognition, in *Proceedings of the Annual International Conference of the IEEE Engineering in Engineering in Medicine and Biology Society*, San Diego, California, USA, 28–31 October 1993, pp. 254–254

W.W. Kong, S. Ranganath, Automatic hand trajectory segmentation and phoneme transcription for sign language, in *Proceedings of the IEEE International Conference on Automatic Face and Gesture Recognition*, Amsterdam, The Netherlands, 17–19, September 2008, pp. 1–6. doi: 10.1109/AFGR.2008.4813462

S.K. Liddell, R.E. Johnson, American sign language: the phonological base. Sign Lang. Stud. **64**, 195–278 (1989)

K. Lyons, H. Brashear, T.L. Westeyn, J.S. Kim, T. Starner, Gart: The gesture and activity recognition toolkit, in *Proceedings of the International Conference HCI*, July 2007, pp. 718–727

E.J. Ong, R. Bowden, Learning sequential patterns for lipreading, in *Proceedings of the BMVA British Machine Vision Conference* (Dundee, UK, August 29–September 10 2011)

OpenNI User Guide. OpenNI organization, November 2010. Accessed 20 Apr 2011 18:15

V. Pitsikalis, S. Theodorakis, C. Vogler, P. Maragos, Advances in phonetics-based sub-unit modeling for transcription alignment and sign language recognition, in *Proceedings of the International Conference IEEE Computer Society Conference on Computer Vision and Pattern Recognition-Workshop : Gesture Recognition*, Colorado Springs, CO, USA, 21–23 June 2011

Prime Sensor™NITE 1.3 Algorithms notes. PrimeSense Inc., 2010. Accesesed 20 Apr 2011 18:15

A. Roussos, S. Theodorakis, V. Pitsikalis, P. Maragos, Hand tracking and affine shape-appearance handshape sub-units in continuous sign language recognition, in *Proceedings of the International Conference European Conference on Computer VisionWorkshop : SGA*, Heraklion, Crete, 5–11 September 2010

J.E. Shoup, Phonological aspects of speech recognition. In Wayne A. Lea, editor, *Trends in Speech Recognition*, Prentice-Hall, Englewood Cliffs, NJ, 1980, pp. 125–138

T. Starner, A. Pentland, Real-time American sign language recognition from video using hidden Markov models. Comput. Imaging Vis. **9**, 227–244 (1997)

W.C. Stokoe, Sign language structure: an outline of the visual communication systems of the American Deaf. Stud. Linguist. **8**, 3–37 (1960)

P. Viola, M. Jones, Rapid object detection using a boosted cascade of simple features, *Proceedings of the IEEE Computer Society Conference on Computer Vision and Pattern Recognition*, vol. 1, Kauai, HI, USA, 2001, pp. 511–518

C. Vogler, D. Metaxas, Adapting hidden Markov models for ASL recognition by using three-dimensional computer vision methods, in *Proceedings of the IEEE International Conference on Systems, Man, and Cybernetics*, vol. 1, Orlando, FL, USA, 12–15 October 1997, pp. 156–161

C. Vogler, D. Metaxas, Parallel hidden Markov models for American sign language recognition, in *Proceedings of the IEEE International Conference on Computer Vision*, vol. 1, Corfu, Greece, 21–24 September 1999, pp. 116–122

M.B. Waldron, S. Kim, Increasing manual sign recognition vocabulary through relabelling, in *Proceedings of the IEEE International Conference on Neural Networks IEEE World Congress on Computational Intelligence*, vol. 5, Orlando, Florida, USA, June 27–July 2 1994, pp. 2885–2889. doi: 10.1109/ICNN.1994.374689

M.B. Waldron, S. Kim, Isolated ASL sign recognition system for deaf persons. IEEE Trans. Rehab. Eng. **3**(3), 261–271 (1995). doi:10.1109/86.413199

M.B. Waldron, D. Simon, Parsing method for signed telecommunication, in *Proceedings of the Annual International Conference of the IEEE Engineering in Engineering in Medicine and Biology Society: Images of the Twenty-First Century*, vol. 6, Seattle, Washington, USA, November 1989, pp. 1798–1799. doi: 10.1109/IEMBS.1989.96461

H. Wassner. kinect + reseau de neurone = reconnaissance de gestes, http://tinyurl.com/5wbteug, May 2011

P. Yin, T. Starner, H. Hamilton, I. Essa, J.M. Rehg, Learning the basic units in American sign language using discriminative segmental feature selection, in *Proceedings of the IEEE International Conference on Acoustics, Speech and Signal Processing*, Taipei, Taiwan, 19–24 April 2009, pp. 4757–4760. doi: 10.1109/ICASSP.2009.4960694

Z. Zafrulla, H. Brashear, P. Presti, H. Hamilton, T. Starner, Copycat-center for accessible technology in sign. http://tinyurl.com/3tksn6s, December 2010, http://www.youtube.com/watch?v=qFH5rSzmgFE&feature=related

Z. Zafrulla, H. Brashear, T. Starner, H. Hamilton, P. Presti, American sign language recognition with the kinect, in *Proceedings of the 13th International Conference on Multimodal Interfaces*, ICMI '11 (New York, NY, USA, 2011. ACM. ISBN 978-1-4503-0641-6), pp. 279–286. doi: 10.1145/2070481.2070532

Chapter 4
MAGIC Summoning: Towards Automatic Suggesting and Testing of Gestures with Low Probability of False Positives During Use

Daniel Kyu Hwa Kohlsdorf and Thad E. Starner

Abstract Gestures for interfaces should be short, pleasing, intuitive, and easily recognized by a computer. However, it is a challenge for interface designers to create gestures easily distinguishable from users' normal movements. Our tool MAGIC Summoning addresses this problem. Given a specific platform and task, we gather a large database of unlabeled sensor data captured in the environments in which the system will be used (an "Everyday Gesture Library" or EGL). The EGL is quantized and indexed via multi-dimensional Symbolic Aggregate approXimation (SAX) to enable quick searching. MAGIC exploits the SAX representation of the EGL to suggest gestures with a low likelihood of false triggering. Suggested gestures are ordered according to brevity and simplicity, freeing the interface designer to focus on the user experience. Once a gesture is selected, MAGIC can output synthetic examples of the gesture to train a chosen classifier (for example, with a hidden Markov model). If the interface designer suggests his own gesture and provides several examples, MAGIC estimates how accurately that gesture can be recognized and estimates its false positive rate by comparing it against the natural movements in the EGL. We demonstrate MAGIC's effectiveness in gesture selection and helpfulness in creating accurate gesture recognizers.

Keywords Gesture recognition · Gesture spotting · False positives · Continuous recognition

Editors: Isabelle Guyon and Vassilis Athitsos

D.K.H. Kohlsdorf (✉) · T.E. Starner
GVU & School of Interactive Computing, Georgia Institute of Technology,
Atlanta, GA 30332, USA
e-mail: dkohl@tzi.de

T.E. Starner
e-mail: thad@cc.gatech.edu

© Springer International Publishing AG 2017
S. Escalera et al. (eds.), *Gesture Recognition*, The Springer Series
on Challenges in Machine Learning, DOI 10.1007/978-3-319-57021-1_4

4.1 Introduction

The success of the Nintendo Wii, Microsoft Kinect, and Google's and Apple's mobile devices demonstrates the popularity of gesture-based interfaces. Gestural interfaces can be expressive, quick to access, and intuitive (Guimbretière and Winograd 2000; Pirhonen et al. 2002; Starner et al. 1998; Witt 2007). Yet gesture-based interfaces may trigger functionality incorrectly, confusing normal movement with a command. For example, the Apple IPod's "shake-to-shuffle" gesture, which is intended to signal when the user wants to skip a song and randomly select another, tends to trigger falsely while the user is walking (see Fig. 4.1a). Part of the difficulty is that the recognizer must constantly monitor an accelerometer to determine if the gesture is being performed. Some accelerometer or gyro-based interfaces constrain the problem by requiring the user to segment the gesture by pressing a button. For example, in Nintendo's Wii Bowling the player presses the "B" trigger when beginning to swing his arm and releases the trigger at the end of the swing to release the virtual bowling ball. Such a push-to-gesture approach is similar to the push-to-talk method that speech recognition researchers use to improve performance. Yet such mechanisms can slow interactions, confuse users, and limit the utility of gesture interaction. For example, the fast, easy-to-access nature of the shake-to-shuffle gesture would be impeded if the user needed to hold a button to perform the gesture. Ideally, such free-space "motion gestures" (Ashbrook 2009) should be short, pleasing to perform, intuitive, and easily recognized by a computer against a background of the user's normal movements.

Touchpad gesture shortcuts, which upon execution can start an affiliated application on a laptop or mobile phone (Ouyang and Li 2012), are another example of command gestures that must be differentiated from everyday motions. Fortunately, these gestures are naturally isolated in time from each other since most touchpad hardware does not even provide data to the operating system when no touches are being sensed. However, an interface designer must still create gesture commands that are not easily confused with normal click or drag and drop actions (see Fig. 4.1b).

Many "direct manipulation" (Hutchins et al. 1985) gestures such as pointing gestures and pinch-to-zoom gestures are used in modern interfaces. These gestures provide the user continuous feedback while the gesture is occurring, which allows the user to adjust to sensing errors or cancel the interaction quickly. However, representational gestures that are intended to trigger a discrete action are less common. We posit that their relative scarcity relates to the difficulty of discovering appropriate gestures for the task. Our previous studies have shown that designing command gestures that do not trigger accidentally during normal, everyday use is difficult for both human computer interaction (HCI) and pattern recognition experts (Ashbrook and Starner 2010). In addition, the current process to determine the viability of a gesture is challenging and expensive. Gestures are often found to be inappropriate only after the system has entered user testing. If a gesture is found to trigger accidentally during testing, the gesture set has to be changed appropriately, and the testing has to be repeated. Such an iterative design cycle can waste a month or more with each test. Thus, we posit the need for a tool to help designers quickly judge the

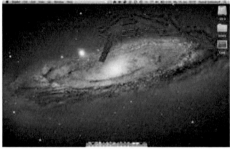

Fig. 4.1 *Top* a "shake-to-shuffle" gesture (*left*) can be confused with normal up-and-down movement while walking (*right*). *Bottom* a touchpad shortcut gesture (*left*) can be confused with normal cursor movement (*right*)

suitability of a gesture from a pattern recognition perspective while they focus on the user experience aspects of the gestural interface.

Several gesture design tools have been described in the HCI literature (Dannenberg and Amon 1989; Long 2001; Fails and Olsen 2003; Maynes-Aminzade et al. 2007; Dey et al. 2004), yet none address the issue of false positives. Similarly, most gesture recognition toolkits in the pattern recognition and related literature focus on isolated gestures (Wobbrock et al. 2007; Lyons et al. 2007) or the recognition of strings of gestures, such as for sign language (Westeyn et al. 2003). Rarely do such tools focus on gesture spotting (Yang et al. 2009) for which the critical metric is false positives per hour.

Ashbrook and Starner (2010) introduced the "Multiple Action Gesture Interface Creation" (MAGIC) Toolkit. A MAGIC user could specify gesture classes by providing examples of each gesture. MAGIC provided feedback on each example and each gesture class by visualizing intra- and inter-class distances and estimating the prototype recognizer's accuracy by classifying all provided gesture examples in isolation.

Unlike the above tools, MAGIC could predict whether a query gesture would tend to trigger falsely by comparing the gesture to a database of movements recorded in the everyday lives of users. Primarily designed as an HCI Tool, the system used a nearest neighbor method with a dynamic time warping (DTW) distance measure (Fu et al. 2008).

One shortcoming of this work was that the relative false positive rates predicted in user studies were not compared to the actual false positive rates of a gesture recognizer running in the field. Another shortcoming was the long time (up to 20 min) needed to search for potential hits in a database of everyday user movements (an "Everyday Gesture Library" or EGL) even while using approximations like scaling with matching (Fu et al. 2008). MAGIC was designed as an interactive tool, yet due to the delay in feedback, gesture interaction designers waited until all gestures were designed before testing them against the EGL. Often, when doing an EGL test in batch, the interface designers discovered that many of their gestures were poor choices. Designers "learned to fear the EGL." Faster feedback would allow designers to compare candidate gestures to the EGL as they perform each example, speeding the process and allowing more exploration of the space of acceptable gestures. Another result from previous studies is that users were frustrated by encountering too many false positives in the Everyday Gesture Library (Ashbrook and Starner 2010). In other words, many designed gestures are rejected since the number of predicted false positives is too high.

Here, we focus on the pattern recognition tasks needed to create MAGIC Summoning, a completely new, web-based MAGIC implementation designed to address the needs discovered from using the original. Section 4.2 introduces the basic operation of the tool. Section 4.3 describes an indexing method for the EGL using a multi-dimensional implementation of indexable Symbolic Aggregate approXimation (iSAX) that speeds EGL comparisons by an order of magnitude over the DTW implementation. While not as accurate as DTW or other methods such as HMMs, our system's speed allows interface designers to receive feedback after every gesture example input instead of waiting to test the gesture set in batch. We compare the iSAX approach to linear searches of the EGL with HMMs and DTW to show that our approach, while returning fewer matches, does predict the relative suitability of different gestures. Section 4.4.4 continues this comparison to show that the predictions made by MAGIC match observations made when the resulting gesture recognizers are tested in a real continuous gesture recognition setting. Sections 4.5 and 4.6 provide additional details. The first describes a method of using the EGL to create a null (garbage) class that improves the performance of a HMM classifier and a DTW classifier when compared to a typical thresholding method. The second demonstrates the stability of our method by examining its sensitivity to its parameters and provides a method capable of learning reasonable defaults for those parameters in an unsupervised manner. These sections expand significantly upon previous work published in Face and Gesture (Kohlsdorf et al. 2011), while the remaining sections represent unpublished concepts.

Section 4.7 may be of the most interest to many readers. This section describes how MAGIC Summoning suggests novel gestures that are predicted to have a low probability of false positives. While the capability may be surprising at first, the technique follows directly from the iSAX indexing scheme. In Sect. 4.7.2 we show that the suggested gestures have low false positive rates during a user study in a real life setting. In our tests, the space of gestures that are not represented in EGLs tends to be large. Thus, there are many potential gestures from which to choose. Section 4.7.3 describes our attempts at finding metrics that enable ordering of the suggested gestures with regard to brevity, simplicity, and "quality."

4.2 MAGIC Summoning Web-Based Toolkit

MAGIC Summoning is a web-based toolkit that helps users design motion-based gestural commands (as opposed to static poses) that are expected not to trigger falsely in everyday usage (Kohlsdorf 2011; Kohlsdorf et al. 2011). All MAGIC experiments described in this paper focus on creating **user-independent** recognizers. This choice reflects our interest in creating useful gesture interfaces and is also due to practicality; collecting large data sets for the EGL from a single user is time consuming and onerous. To ground the discussion with a practical problem, we focus on the challenge of designing gestures performed by moving an Android phone in one's hand. We assume a three-axis accelerometer, which is always included in modern Android phones. The goal is to create gestures (and an appropriate classifier) that, when recognized, trigger functions like "open mailbox" or "next song." Without a push-to-gesture trigger, such gestures are highly susceptible to false positives (Ashbrook 2009), which emphasizes the need for the MAGIC tool.

4.2.1 Creating Gesture Classes and Testing for Confusion Between Classes

MAGIC Summoning has two software components: a gesture recorder running on the Android device and the MAGIC web application. The first step in gesture creation is to start a new project in the web service. The interface designer specifies the set of gestures through collecting training data for each of the gestures using the recorder. In order to record a training example, the interaction designer opens the recorder on his smart phone and performs the gesture. The recorder automatically estimates when the gesture starts and when it ends using the method described by Ashbrook (2009). Specifically, the recorder tracks the variance of the accelerometer data in a sliding window. If the variance is above a user-defined threshold, recording starts. If it falls below the threshold, then recording ends.

After the example is recorded, the designer is asked to associate the example with an appropriate gesture label, and the recorder uploads the example to the web. The designer evaluates the gesture in the web application to determine how well it can be distinguished from other gestures. All gestures and their examples are listed

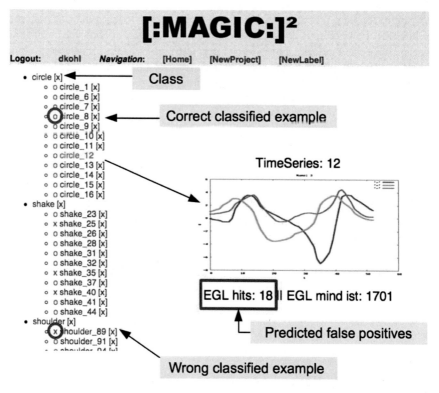

Fig. 4.2 Magic Summoning showing the gesture classes, their examples, and the number of EGL hits (lower numbers are better)

in MAGIC Summoning's sidebar (see Fig. 4.2). Examples marked with a red cross are misclassified given the current model, and instances marked with a green circle indicate correct classification. By default, MAGIC Summoning uses a one nearest neighbor classifier with dynamic time warping (NN-DTW) to classify gestures, although other classifiers such as a hidden Markov model (HMM) could be substituted. By clicking on an instance, the designer can see the raw sensor data plotted for that example as well as the predicted number of false positives in the EGL (the method used to calculated this number is explained in Sect. 4.3).

Clicking on a gesture in the sidebar opens a view with statistics about it. One statistic is the goodness of the gesture. The goodness is defined as the harmonic mean of precision and recall (Ashbrook 2009):

$$goodness = 2 * \frac{precision * recall}{precision + recall}.$$

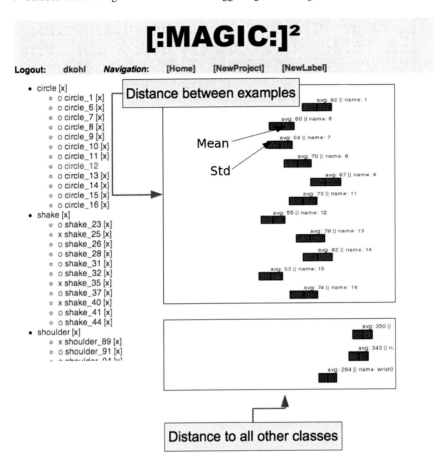

Fig. 4.3 Mean and standard deviation of the distance between each example in a class and of the class as a whole in relation to other classes

Similar to the original work by Ashbrook (2009), MAGIC Summoning provides users with information about the inter-class distance and the intra-class distance of the gesture. Both are visualized using a mean and standard deviation plot. In an intra-class distance plot we calculate the means and standard deviations of the distances from all examples in a class to all other examples in that class and visualize the result as a box plot (see Fig. 4.3). In an inter-class distance plot we calculate the means and standard deviations from one class to all the others in the training set. The distance between two classes is the mean distance of all examples of one class to all examples of another. These statistics and visualizations help designers find inconsistencies in the examples of a given gesture class as well as unintentional similarities between classes.

4.2.2 Android Phone Accelerometer Everyday Gesture Library

We collected a large EGL (>1.5 million seconds or 19 days total) using six participants' Android phones in Bremen, Germany. The age of the participants ranged from 20 to 30 years. We implemented a background process that wrote the three-axis accelerometer data to the phone's flash memory. Unfortunately, the sampling frequency varied as the models of Android phones we used return samples only when the change in the accelerometer reading exceeds a factory-defined threshold. The phones used are the Motorola Droid, the Samsung Galaxy, HTC Nexus One, the HTC Legend, and the HTC Desire. Other EGLs loadable in MAGIC include movements sensed with a Microsoft Kinect and gestures made on trackpads. We focus mostly on our EGL created with Android phones, but readers interested in experiments with other sensors can refer to Kohlsdorf (2011) for more information.

4.2.3 Testing for False Positives with the EGL

The original Macintosh-based MAGIC tool displayed a timeline that showed which candidate gesture matched the EGL and at which time. However, gesture designers did not care when or why a given gesture showed a given false positive in the EGL; they just wished to know how many "hits" occurred in the EGL so that they could accept or reject the gesture (Ashbrook 2009). Thus, we omitted the timeline for simplicity in the web-based application. In the following section we will describe our accelerated method for testing a gesture for potential false positives against the EGL. This method enables rapid iteration on different gesture sets by the interaction designer.

If a user is displeased by the results after testing, he can delete gestures suspected of high false positive rates or misclassification errors and design new gestures. When the user is satisfied with the gesture set, MAGIC Summoning can train a classifier based on hidden Markov models (HMMs) or the default NN-DTW method. The user can then download the trained recognizer. Note that we do not suggest using the iSAX method used to search the EGL as a gesture recognizer as we have tuned the method for speed, not accuracy.

4.3 False Positive Prediction

When testing a gesture set against the EGL, the original MAGIC calculates the DTW distance for every example of each candidate gesture, sliding a window through time across the EGL and allowing the window to grow or shrink to better match the example when a potential close match is discovered. If the resulting distance is above a certain user-defined threshold it counts as a false positive "hit." Ashbrook

Fig. 4.4 When finding start and stop points of a gesture or finding interesting regions in the EGL, we run a sliding window over the raw recorded time series and calculate the sample variance in that window when a new sample is inserted. If the variance is above a certain threshold, the gesture or interesting region starts. It stops when the variance falls below that threshold

and Starner (2010) assert that the sum of the hits predicts how well the gesture will perform in everyday life (an assertion supported by our experiments described later).

In optimizing the speed of the EGL comparison, Ashbrook (2009) observed that not all regions of the EGL need checking. Since we are interested in motion-based gestures instead of static poses, parts of the EGL with low variance in their signal need not be examined. Thus, we pre-process the EGL to find "interesting" regions where the average variance over all dimensions in the sensor data in a region defined by a sliding window over 10 samples exceeds a given threshold (see Fig. 4.4).[1] Eliminating regions from the EGL that can not possibly match candidate gestures significantly speeds EGL search. Note that a similar technique was described earlier to segment gestures when the interface designer is creating examples of candidate gestures. All experiments in this paper will use these techniques.

Searching the EGL parallelizes well, as each processor can be devoted to different regions of the EGL. However, even on a high-end, eight-core Macintosh workstation, searches were too slow for an interactive system. For a small, 5-h EGL with three-axis accelerometer data sampled at 40 Hz, each example required between 5 and 25 s to check. Thus, one gesture with 10 examples could require minutes to search in the EGL. This slowness causes interface designers to create gestures in batch and then check them against the EGL. Testing a set of eight gestures with all their examples could take up to 20 min, leading to a relatively long and frustrating development cycle for the designer (Ashbrook and Starner 2010). In the following sections, we describe a method to speed the EGL search using iSAX. We start with an overview of our method and our assumptions. We then provide the specific methods we used to adapt iSAX to our problem.

4.3.1 Overview of EGL Search Method and Assumptions

In MAGIC Summoning, we first segment the EGL into interesting regions as defined previously. Each region is divided into four even subregions to form a "word" of

---

[1] Word spotting algorithms in speech recognition perform similar checks, rejecting regions of "silence" before employing more computationally intensive comparisons.

length four. The region is then encoded into a string of symbols using the standard SAX quantization method. The string is entered into an iSAX tree representing the EGL. The iSAX tree is initialized with cardinality two but quickly grows as many regions hash to the same leaf on the suffix tree and the leaf needs to be split (Shieh and Keogh 2008). As each region is encoded into the iSAX tree, its location in the EGL is recorded in the leaf. Once the EGL is completely encoded into an iSAX tree, we can perform "approximate search" using a gesture example as a query (Shieh and Keogh 2008). The query is split into four regions and SAX-encoded in much the same way as the interesting regions of the EGL. An approximate search to determine the number of matches between the query and the EGL becomes a simple matter of matching the query string to the appropriate branch of the iSAX suffix tree and returning the number of strings contained in that branch.

One failing of this approach is that the interesting regions may be significantly larger or smaller than the candidate gestures. Regions significantly smaller than the command gestures are not of concern as they will never falsely match a command gesture in practice. We can eliminate such regions out-of-hand from the comparison. However, regions of movement that might match the query gesture may be hidden within longer regions in the EGL.

A key insight, which will be used repeatedly, is that we need not recover every region of the EGL that might cause a false match with the query. We are not intending iSAX to be used as a gesture recognizer. Instead, our goal is to allow the designer to compare the suitability of a gesture relative to other candidates quickly. As long as the movement occurs repeatedly in the EGL at isolated times as well as in longer regions, the iSAX method will report a number of "hits," which will be sufficient to warn the interaction designer of a problem.

A second insight is that users of gesture interfaces often pause before and after they perform a command gesture. Gesture recognizers exploit this behavior and use these pauses to help identify the command gesture. Movements that look like command gestures embedded in long regions of user motion are unlikely to be matched in practice by these recognizers. However, short everyday user motions that are similar to a command gesture are a particular worry for false positives. Thus, the iSAX encoding scheme of the EGL above seems suitable for our needs. However, if the goal of the interaction designer is to create gestures that can be chained together to issue a series of commands quickly, these longer regions in the EGL will need to be encoded more formally using constraints on how long a section can be encoded in each symbol. Such constraints can be derived from the length of expected command gestures (usually between 1 and 4 s in our experience), and the length of SAX word defined by the system.

A final insight is that a more precise comparison against the EGL can be made at the end of the gesture design process with the gesture recognizer that is output by MAGIC. During gesture design, all we require of the EGL search method is that it is fast enough to be interactive and that it provides an early warning when a given gesture may be susceptible to false triggering. Given the above operational scenario, we tune our iSAX implementation to provide fast feedback to the user. Details on the implementation follow below.

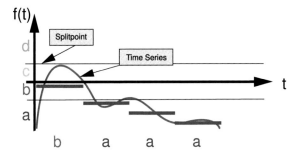

Fig. 4.5 SAX process used to convert a time series to a string. The raw data is segmented into a user-specified word length, in this case four. Then each segment is replaced by a symbol associated with that region on the y-axis, based on the average value. The resulting string is represented by the string of symbols with superscripts indicating the number of symbols used to quantize each region: $b^4 a^4 a^4 a^4$

4.3.2   SAX Encoding

SAX quantizes time series in both time and value and encodes them into a string of symbols (Lin et al. 2007). For example, the time series in Fig. 4.5 is divided into four equal portions (for a "word" length of four) and converted into a string using a four symbol vocabulary (a "cardinality" of four).

To be more precise, we first normalize the time series to have a zero mean and standard deviation of one. Assuming the original time series $T = t_1, \ldots, t_j, \ldots, t_n$ has n samples, we want to first quantize the time series into a shorter time series $\bar{T} = \bar{t}_1, \ldots, \bar{t}_i, \ldots \bar{t}_w$ of word length w. The ith element of $\bar{T}$ can be calculated by

$$\bar{t}_i = \frac{w}{n} \sum_{k=(\frac{n}{w}(i-1)+1)}^{\frac{n}{w}i} t_k.$$

Given the values in the compressed time series, we next convert them into symbols using a small alphabet of size (cardinality) a. Imagine the y-axis divided into an arbitrary number of regions bounded by $a - 1$ breakpoints. Each of these regions is assigned to a symbol from the alphabet. Since we wish each symbol in the vocabulary to be used approximately the same amount, we place a normal Gaussian curve centered at 0 on the y-axis and place the breakpoints such that the area under the Gaussian for each section is equal. By performing the SAX process on the EGL and each gesture example separately, we are able to compare the changes in the signals through time without concern regarding their offsets from zero or relative amplitudes.

One convenience of the SAX representation is that there exists a distance calculation between two strings, defined as MINDIST by Lin et al. (2007), that is a lower bound on the Euclidean distance between the original two time series. Thus, we can search the EGL for possible false positives with some measure of confidence.

Another convenience of the representation is that the cardinality of each separate region can be increased whenever more precision is needed. For example, suppose we increase the cardinality of the first region in Fig. 4.5 to eight (thus, the vocabulary would include letters a–h). The string might then be $d^8a^4a^4a^4$, as the region of the y-axis formerly covered by symbols a and b would now be covered by symbols a, b, c, and d. We can compare strings with regions of different cardinality by observing that we know that each time series is normalized before SAX encoding and that the regions are defined by a normal Gaussian centered at zero with all regions having an equal area under the Gaussian's curve. Thus, we still know the minimal distance possible between each region, and we can still use MINDIST to determine a lower bound on the Euclidean distance between the original two time series. This capability will be useful in our upcoming discussion on iSAX and its application to the EGL.

4.3.3 Multi-dimensional iSAX Indexing and EGL Search

iSAX is a tree-based method for time series indexing introduced in Shieh and Keogh (2008). For encoding the EGL, our goal is create an iSAX tree that can be traversed quickly when searching for a match to a SAX-encoded example of a gesture. Each leaf of the tree contains the number of occurrences of that string in the EGL as well as the position of each occurrence. To begin, assume we are searching an EGL represented by the simple iSAX tree in Fig. 4.6 with a query represented by $a^2a^2b^2b^2$ (for the sake of argument, assume we decided to represent the example gesture crudely, with regions of cardinality two). Immediately, we see that there is no branch of the tree with an a^2 in the first position, and we return no matches in the EGL. Now assume that we are searching the EGL for a query of $b^2b^2b^2b^2$. We find that there is a node of the EGL that contains that string, and that node has children (that is, the node is an "internal node"). Looking at the children in that branch, we see that we need to re-code the query gesture to have cardinality three in the first region. Re-coding reveals that the query gesture is better represented by the sequence $c^3b^2b^2b^2$, which matches one of the terminal leaves in the tree. The number of sequences from the EGL stored in that leaf is returned as the number of "hits" in the EGL.

Next we describe how to encode a one-dimensional EGL into an iSAX tree. First, we find all the "interesting" regions in the EGL using the variance method discussed earlier. We divide the regions evenly into four sections and encode them using SAX

Fig. 4.6 iSAX tree with three leaves. On the first level all symbols' cardinalities are equal. The node $b^2b^2b^2b^2$ is an internal node. For the children under this node, the cardinality of the first region is increased by one

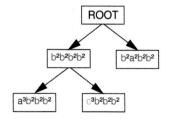

with cardinality two, allowing for sixteen possible strings. Note that each node in an iSAX tree holds a hash table mapping child nodes to an iSAX word. Thus, when inserting a region into the iSAX tree, we compare the region's SAX string to the hash table in the root node. If there is no match, we create a child node and enter it into the hash table using its SAX string. If the SAX string is found, we examine the node to see if it is a terminal leaf. Each leaf points to a file (called a "bucket") stored on disk holding all of the regions that have mapped to it. The leaf also contains the position of each of the regions in the EGL and a count of the number of regions contained in the leaf. If the number of regions in the bucket exceeds a user specified size (called the "bucket size"), it is deleted, and the cardinality of the iSAX word is increased at one position (picked by round robin). At the deleted node's position we insert a new internal node. All the time series of the deleted node are inserted into the new node but with a higher cardinality. Children of the internal node are created as needed, effectively splitting the previous leaf into several new leaves. When we encounter a internal node during the insertion of a region, we search the node's hash table for children that match and proceed normally, creating a new leaf node if no matching child exists.

Note that this method of creating the iSAX tree dynamically adjusts the size of the vocabulary to better distinguish similar regions in the EGL. Given a bigger vocabulary, the SAX word will fit more exactly to the region. In other words, this method of encoding devotes more bits to describing similar movements that are repeated often in the EGL. Thus, when a query gesture is compared to the EGL iSAX tree, MAGIC will quickly return with no or few hits (depending on the specified bucket size) if the query is very distinct from the EGL. If the query is similar to motions in the EGL, the search process will traverse deeper in the tree, examining finer and finer distinctions between the query and the regions contained in the EGL.

The above discussion assumed that the data was one-dimensional. For multi-dimensional data, such as is used in the experiments described below, we create n iSAX trees, one for each dimension of the recorded data. We index all dimensions separately and join those n trees under one new root node (see Fig. 4.7).

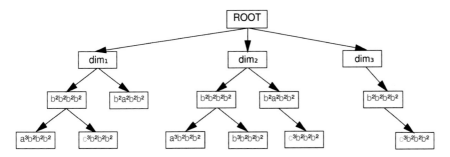

Fig. 4.7 A multi-dimensional iSAX tree. Under the root node there is a dimension layer. Each node in this layer is the root node for a one-dimensional iSAX tree. During search, we search all iSAX trees, one for each dimension

Table 4.1 Testing gestures for potential false positives against a database of pre-recorded device usage

Test preparation:
0) Collect a large data base of user movements in advance.
1) Find interesting regions by applying variance thresholding.
2) Build an n dimensional iSAX tree.

Gesture testing:
0) Find start and end point of gesture.
1) Search the iSAX tree in all n dimensions.
2) Return the number of time series in the minimum file.

We query the EGL iSAX tree (constructed from the EGL) in all n dimensions. The result of that search is n files, one for each dimension. The number of hits can then be calculated by counting the number of places where each hit from each dimension overlap for all dimensions. Comparing the timestamps can be costly, so we introduced an approximation based on the observation that there can never be more overlapping time series than the number in the dimension with the lowest number of matches. For example, consider the result of a search in three dimensions (x, y, z) where the number of hits in the EGL are $x = 4$, $y = 20$ and $z = 6$. There can never be more then four hits total if we require that hits must overlap in all dimensions. The overall EGL testing method is summarized in Table 4.1.

Upon reflection, the EGL search procedure described above raises several questions and possibilities. What are reasonable values for the bucket size, word size, and cardinalities used in encoding the EGL, and how sensitive is MAGIC to these parameters? This question will be examined in detail in Sect. 4.6. A nice side effect of EGL search is that we can use the matches found to train a class of gestures that a recognizer should ignore (a "garbage" or NULL class). Section 4.5 will explore this option. Searching for which SAX strings are not contained in the EGL tree can suggest which gestures are not made during everyday movement. In Sect. 4.7, we exploit this attribute to recommend gestures to the interaction designer. However, first we will provide evidence that searching the EGL does indeed predict the number of false positives during the usage of a gesture interface.

4.4 Experimental Verification

In the following section we describe two experiments that suggest that an iSAX search of the EGL is a viable means to predict false positives. Our first goal is to show that false positive prediction using iSAX is correlated with the previous method of searching the EGL linearly using dynamic time warping (Ashbrook 2009). We will also conduct an experiment in which we will show that the EGL is able to predict the relative number of false positives when using a gesture interface in everyday life.

We describe the data used for the experiments and our experimental method before presenting our findings.

4.4.1   EGLs and Gestures Used in Evaluations

We use three different data sets to serve as EGL databases. The first is our Android accelerometer data set as described earlier. Before indexing the recorded data, we extracted the interesting regions, applying a threshold of $th = 0.001$ (triggering at almost any movement) and a window size of $N = 10$ (0.25 s at 40 Hz). The average duration of the interesting regions is 11,696 ms. The second EGL is based on the Alkan database[2] of everyday movements collected with an iPhone (Hattori et al. 2011). The third data set is another collection of everyday movements collected on Android phones for a different project at Georgia Tech. These two latter EGLs were processed in the same manner as the first.

We collected a reference data set of gestures for evaluation purposes. We acted as interaction designers and designed four gestures by performing them while holding a smart phone. For each gesture we collected 10 examples, resulting in 40 examples total. The four gestures are: drawing a circle in the air, touching your shoulder, shaking the phone up and down, and hacking (a motion similar to swinging an ax). The average duration of the gestures is between 1 and 2 s.

4.4.2   Comparison Conditions: NN-DTW and HMMs

When comparing the dynamic time warping EGL search method to a search in iSAX index space we will use the following procedure. The DTW method compares each interesting region from the EGL to each gesture example (Ashbrook 2009). We calculate the dynamic time warping distance of a new gesture to all examples in the EGL and apply a threshold chosen empirically. All regions for which the distance is below this threshold for any example count as a false positive (in keeping with MAGIC's ability to output a one nearest neighbor classifier for live gesture recognition).

For yet another comparison, we use hidden Markov models to search the EGL for false positives. For the experiments in this paper, we use a six-state HMM (ignoring initial and end states) with one skip transition and one Gaussian output probability per state per dimension (see Fig. 4.8). We collect all the examples for our gesture set first and then train a HMM for each of the gestures. We classify each region in the EGL and apply a threshold based on maximum likelihood to determine if a region

---

[2] Alkan web site can be found at: http://alkan.jp/.

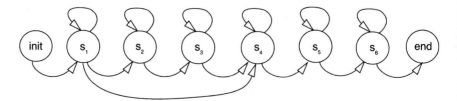

Fig. 4.8 The topology of the *left–right*, six-state HMM used in our experiments. The first state is the start state, and the eighth state is the end state. Each internal state transitions to itself and its successor. We include a skip transition to help recognize shorter gestures

in the EGL is close enough to the gesture to count as a false positive. We chose both the maximum likelihood threshold as well as the distance threshold so that classifier accuracy stayed high (93% for NN-DTW and 100% for HMM).

4.4.3 Comparison of iSAX to NN-DTW and HMM in Searching EGLs

We wish to compare our iSAX EGL search method to the more conventional NN-DTW and HMM techniques described above. When selecting between two candidate gestures, the interaction designer wishes to choose the one with a lower number of predicted false positives. Thus, if a first gesture has few hits when NN-DTW or HMMs are used and a second gesture has many hits, that same trend should be shown with iSAX. The absolute number of EGL hits does not matter, but there should be a strong correlation between the relative number of hits returned by iSAX and the other two techniques when run on the same set of gestures. We use the Pearson correlation coefficient as a metric to compare the techniques.

Regardless of the search method used, we store the number of hits in a vector. Each entry of that vector corresponds to the overall number of false positives for a given gesture. For iSAX and NN-DTW, the overall number of false positives for a gesture is calculated by searching the EGL for each example of that gesture and summing the resulting numbers of hits. For HMM models, thresholding on the log likelihood probability is used. For our set of four test gestures, testing returns three vectors (one for each method) of four elements (one for each gesture). We calculate the Pearson correlation coefficient between the iSAX vector and the NN-DTW vector and between the iSAX vector and the HMM vector.

To reassure ourselves that this technique produces a meaningful metric, we performed Monte Carlo simulation experiments. Indeed, the correlation of random vectors with four elements show low r values.

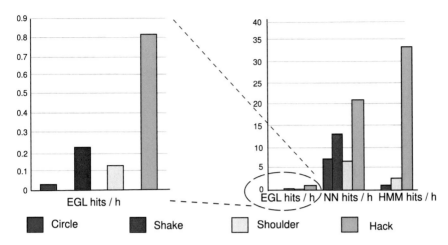

Fig. 4.9 *Left* the hits per hour in the EGL based on iSAX search. *Right* a comparison of the number of hits per hour returned by iSAX, NN-DTW, and HMMs from the EGL

First, we compare the search methods on the EGL from Bremen. We chose the iSAX parameters empirically:

word length: 4
base cardinality: 2
bucket: 6000.

Figure 4.9 compares the number of hits per hour returned by each method. The hits per hour metric reflects the number of matches found in the EGL divided by the original time required to record the EGL. One can see that our iSAX search approximation returns many fewer hits than NN-DTW or HMMs. However, the magnitude of the iSAX values correlate strongly with the NN-DTW ($r = 0.96$) and HMM ($r = 0.97$) results. Thus, a high number of hits returned by iSAX on the EGL (high compared to other gestures tested with iSAX) is a good indicator for when a gesture should be discarded. The remaining gestures are suitable candidates for user testing.

We also measured the time needed to complete the search for each method on a 2.0 GHz Intel Core Duo T2500 Macbook with 2 GB of RAM. The NN-DTW and HMM methods require more then 10 min to complete the search on all 40 gesture examples whereas iSAX search required 22 s, a 27X increase in speed. With such speed, each of the gesture examples could have been checked as it was entered by the interaction designer. In fact, the EGL search would require less than a second for each gesture example, which is less than the amount of time required to check a new example for confusion against all the other gesture examples with NN-DTW when creating a eight gesture interface (Ashbrook 2009). Thus, we have obtained our goal of maintaining interactivity during gesture design.

We were curious as to how much EGL data is needed to predict poor command gestures. We generated three random subsets of the EGL by picking 100, 200 and 500 interesting regions at random from the data set and comparing the correlation coefficient between iSAX and NN-DTW. The correlation between the results remained surprisingly high, even with an EGL containing only 100 regions:

- **n = 100:** $r = 0.89$
- **n = 200:** $r = 0.93$
- **n = 500:** $r = 0.93$.

As later experiments show, more data is better, but even a relatively small EGL can help the interaction designer avoid choosing troublesome gestures. We also compared iSAX versus NN-DTW in the Alkan and Georgia Tech EGLs, with similar results to the original Bremen EGL:

- **Alkan:** $r = 0.94$
- **Georgia Tech:** $r = 0.99$.

Our results suggest that the results of an iSAX search on the EGL correlate highly with those of the slower EGL search methods. Even though the absolute number of hits found by the iSAX method are significantly fewer than the other methods, the relative number of hits can be used to compare the desirability of one candidate gesture versus another.

4.4.4 Comparison of iSAX Predictions to HMM and NN-DTW Gesture Recognizer Use in Practice

Next, we examine whether our iSAX EGL search method is able to predict false positives in everyday life. In fact, this experiment is the first to verify that any EGL search is able to predict false positive rates of a gesture recognizer in practice.

We exported NN-DTW and HMM recognizers from MAGIC Summoning for the four gestures trained during the process described in the previous experiment. We integrated the HMM classifier into an interactive system. Next, we recruited four Android phone users who had not contributed to the EGLs nor the training of the gestures.

In order to understand how difficult it was to perform the gestures correctly, we asked the users to perform each gesture 10 times without feedback. The HMM classifier performed at 60% accuracy, which is not surprising given the gestures and testing procedure. Next we allowed the users to train with the HMM recognizer to become more familiar with how to perform the gestures so that they could be more easily recognized. This way of learning can be found in commercial systems like the Nintendo Wii, which uses avatars to help users learn control gestures. Not surprisingly, the four users' average accuracy with the HMM recognizer improved to 95% after training.

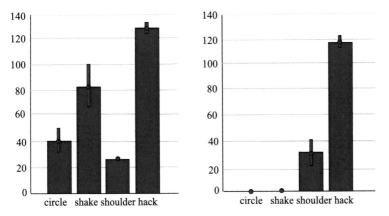

Fig. 4.10 The EGL hits per hour found during deployment. *Left* the EGL hits for NN-DTW search per gesture. *Right* the EGL hits for HMM search per gesture. The EGL hits for a gesture are the average hits over all four users. The bars correspond to one standard deviation

After the users completed their training, we installed a software application on their phones that notified the users when to perform one randomly selected gesture, once every hour. Otherwise, the users performed their normal activities, and the application records all the users' movements. We searched the recorded data for the intended gestures. The HMM classifier found 50–70% of the intentional gestures whereas NN-DTW search found all of them. However, the NN-DTW classifier had lower precision than the HMMs. Given that we specifically allowed gestures that were known to be poor (from EGL testing) and that the system did not provide feedback to the users, such poor performance is to be expected (and desired from the point of the experiment).

Figure 4.10 shows the false positive rates for each gesture and recognizer. We observed a high correlation ($r = 0.84$) between the relative false positive rates predicted by the iSAX search on the original EGL and the actual, tested NN-DTW performance on the users' data. The correlation was even higher ($r = 0.97$) for the HMM classifier. These results support our hypothesis that MAGIC Summoning can be used to predict gestures at risk of having many false positives when deployed in gesture recognizers in practice.

4.5 Improving Recognition Through a NULL Class Created from EGL Search

In the experiments in the previous section, we needed to specify a threshold to avoid false positives when distinguishing the four gestures from our four users' everyday motions. For NN-DTW, the threshold was a distance, while with HMMs it was a probability. Setting this threshold requires more pattern recognition experience than an interaction designer may possess, and often gestures are not separable from everyday movements with a simple threshold. Another option is to create a NULL (garbage) class, which attempts to capture all the motion not matching the gestures of interest. With this technique, the recognizer runs continually but does not return a result when the sensor data matches the NULL class.

Here, we use EGL data to train a NULL class automatically so that a user-defined threshold is not needed. Multi-dimensional iSAX search of the EGL returns time series similar to a query gesture. Thus, it is a simple matter to collect the EGL hits from all examples of all gestures in the gesture interface to train a NULL gesture (using either technique).

The following experiment is based on the data collected while our four users performed the four requested gestures during their daily activities. We adjusted the thresholds upward for the HMM and NN-DTW recognizers to avoid misclassifications in the EGL while still detecting the gestures from the training set. We also trained NULL classes for both recognizers. Figure 4.11 shows the results of all four recognizers running on the user study data. Using the EGL NULL class method resulted in a statistically significant improvement of both the NN-DTW ($p << 0.0001$) and HMM ($p < 0.05$) recognizers. Both avoided more false positives using the NULL class instead of a threshold. Gesture recognition accuracy and correlation to the iSAX EGL hits remained consistent with the experiment in the previous section. The results suggest that training a NULL class based on EGL hits can be a successful way to improve performance and reduce complexity for the interaction designer. Note that many variations of this technique are possible and might further improve results. For example, a different NULL class could be trained for each gesture.

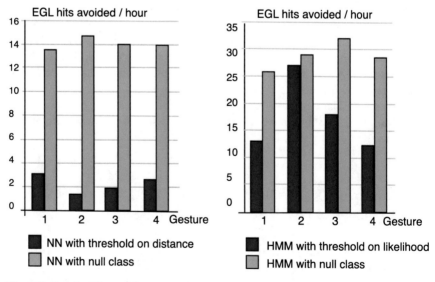

Fig. 4.11 *Left* the false positives per hour avoided using a NULL class for each gesture based on EGL hits versus the simple threshold. *Right* the false positives per hour avoided for HMMs using the NULL class versus the simple threshold

4.6 iSAX Parameter Sensitivity Experiments

In Sect. 4.4.4, iSAX was able to predict the relative performance of a gesture during continuous recognition. However, the process required setting several parameters: word length, bucket size, and initial cardinality. In addition, we compared the false positive predictions to that of the NN-DTW method, which itself required a distance threshold (when a NULL class is not used). How sensitive is our method to these parameters? We use the same four test gestures (circle, shake, shoulder, hack) and EGL as in our user study to explore this issue.

Observe that the cardinality of the sequences is automatically adjusted during the creation of the EGL iSAX tree, quickly changing from its initial minimal setting of two. Effectively, this parameter is not set by the user, and we can remove it from the following experiments on parameter sensitivity by holding it at a reasonable value. We choose a base cardinality of four ($card = 4$), given that this level of complexity was judged sufficient from observations in the original iSAX experiments (Shieh 2010; Shieh and Keogh 2008) and in our own work (Kohlsdorf et al. 2011).

In the experiments below, we compare the iSAX results, while varying the bucket size and word length, to the NN-DTW method using the correlation method described above. We also tried comparing the iSAX method to NN-DTW with different reasonable distance thresholds (3.3, 5, 10), but we found little change in the results. For example, the bottom of Fig. 4.12 shows graphs comparing iSAX word length to correlation with NN-DTW at each of the distance thresholds. The graphs are very similar, indicating that the comparison with NN-DTW is relatively stable with respect to the distance threshold used. Thus, we turn our attention to word length and bucket size.

In the first part of the experiment we test the correlation of the EGL searches using NN-DTW and iSAX trees constructed with different iSAX word lengths (4, 5, 6, …, 13) and bucket sizes (1000, 2000, …, 10000). Figure 4.12 plots the results. Changes in bucket size cause minor variations in correlation; however, word length has significant effects.

Since the performance of our method seems mostly dependent on one parameter, we propose an automatic parameter tuning method that does not require any data except a pre-recorded EGL. The central concept is to choose random regions from the EGL to serve as a gesture training set and to tune the iSAX parameters to that set using hill climbing.

We require the user to specify the number of gestures in the data set (N), how many examples we want to collect for each gesture (M), and a threshold on the dynamic time warping distance over which two time series are distinct. We pick N regions of motion ("interesting" regions) at random from the EGL to serve as "reference gestures." For those N reference gestures we extract M examples from the EGL where the DTW distance to the reference gesture is smaller than a threshold. Then we compute the false positives for this gesture set using the NN-DTW method. In order to find the appropriate word length we use hill climbing in the iSAX parameter space. At each step, we perform false positive prediction using iSAX and compare

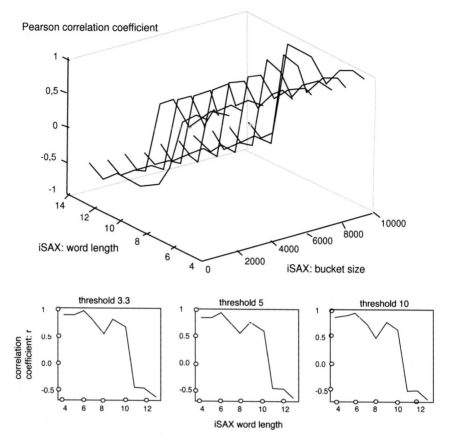

Fig. 4.12 *Top* correlation to NN-DTW versus iSAX word length versus iSAX bucket size. *Bottom* iSAX word length versus correlation to NN-DTW for distance thresholds of 3.3, 5, and 10, respectively

the results to the NN-DTW results using the Pearson correlation coefficient as an objective function.

We ran an experiment to test this hill-climbing technique, allowing the procedure to set the word length automatically and comparing the results to NN-DTW. We started the word length at 4 and increased it to 13. If the observed correlation at a given word length is followed by a smaller one when the next word length is tried, the algorithm stops and returns the last word length. As one can see in Fig. 4.12, after 3 iterations iSAX finds a local maximum. However, this sequential method is not optimal. For example, if the word length which maximizes the correlation is 9 and the local maximum at the word length 6 is smaller, we would stop too early. However, this problem can be solved by including simulated annealing or stochastic gradient descent in the future.

In this chapter, we showed that the iSAX EGL search relies on several parameters but that the parameters can be tuned automatically. Word length seems the primary parameter that needs to be tuned.

4.7   MAGIC Summoning: Suggesting Gestures with Low Probability of False Positives During Use

To this point, we have focused on efficient gesture testing. However, when using MAGIC to design gestures in previous studies, our participants wished to have MAGIC suggest potential gestures instead of creating their own. Often the gestures designed by the participants showed high false positive rates when tested against the EGL, leading to frustration. MAGIC users said they would rather select from a set of gestures that were "known good" than experiment blindly with constraints they did not understand (Ashbrook 2009).

In the next section, we describe a method for suggesting gestures based on a pre-recorded EGL. We then perform an experiment where we test suggested gestures for false positives during normal device usage by naive subjects. Finally, we examine different possible metrics to order the suggestions for easier selection by the designer. While we have mostly used accelerometers in our experiments to date, here we concentrate on capacitive trackpads, specifically those used on Apple's laptops. Data from inertial sensors are hard to visualize for an interaction designer without a inverse kinematic system to map the sensor readings into limb movement. While such systems are now feasible with adequate accuracy, we wished to avoid the additional complexity for these first experiments. Trackpads provide two dimensional data that are easy to visualize for an interaction designer, and trackpads are commonly used in everyday office work. In addition, industry has begun to include more complex command gestures in their trackpad-based products (Li 2010).

4.7.1   Synthesizing and Visualizing Gestures

We introduce a method for proposing gestures that do not collide with every day movements using four steps, briefly outlined here. First, we collect an EGL that is representative of the usage of the device or sensor. Next, we build an iSAX tree based on the EGL. We systematically enumerate the possible SAX strings and check for those which are NOT contained in the tree. Finally, we visualize these gestures and present them to the interaction designer. Once the designer selects a set of gestures for his interface, MAGIC Summoning can train a recognizer for the gestures using synthesized data.

4.7.1.1   Collecting an EGL

Collecting a representative EGL is often time-consuming and is best done by someone familiar both with the specific sensor involved and pattern recognition in general. Fortunately, the process is only necessary once for the device of interest and then can be used for different interface designers and tasks. Mostly, the EGL will be collected across multiple people to ensure that the resulting gestures can be user independent. Ideally, the EGL should be collected across every situation and physical context where the device might be used (for example, sitting at a desk or driving) to make sure that incidental motions are well represented. If the resulting gesture recognizer is intended to work across different devices (for example, across multiple version of Android phones), the EGL should be collected from a representative sample of those devices.

4.7.1.2   Representing the EGL and Generating Gestures

Next, we convert the EGL into a simplified iSAX tree structure. Unlike the work above, here we only care that a given string occurred in the EGL instead of how many times it occurred. Thus, we can use a simpler indexing method that will allow easier gesture building later. We convert interesting regions from the EGL to SAX words and build the set of all strings observed in the EGL. Since the sensor input is multivariate, we build the SAX word in each dimension and concatenate the words. Thus, for n dimensions and a word length of w, the indexing key grows to $n * w$. Given the cardinalities in the word, discovering gestures that are not represented in the EGL is a simple matter of combinatorics. We generate all possible gestures and store the gesture as a viable candidate if it is not contained in the EGL.

4.7.1.3   Visualizing Candidate Gestures and Training Gesture
                Recognizers

In order for the interface designer to select between the different candidate gestures, we must visualize them. Specifically, we need to convert the candidate gesture from a SAX string into a real valued time series. For each SAX symbol, we know that valid values are somewhere between the upper and lower breakpoint of the area assigned to the symbol. We choose a random point between these breakpoints for each symbol. We then use spline interpolation or re-sampling to fit a curve through the resulting values from each SAX symbol. We used an exponential moving average to smooth the resulting curve. The overall process is shown in Fig. 4.13. Note that by repeating this process we can generate a synthetic set of time series that could have generated the SAX word. This synthetic data is used to visualize acceptable versions of the trackpad gesture to the interaction designer. We will also use this synthetic data to train a recognizer for the gesture if it is selected (see below).

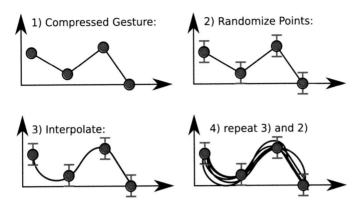

Fig. 4.13   Converting a SAX word to example gestures

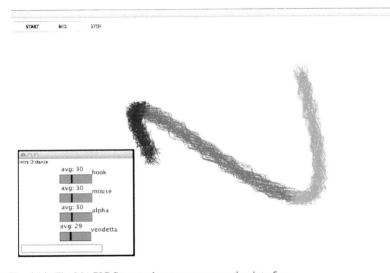

Fig. 4.14   The MAGIC Summoning gesture suggestion interface

Figure 4.14 shows MAGIC Summoning's user interface for gesture suggestion. In the center of the window we display a synthesized gesture. The color of the lines indicates the time course of the gesture as it is performed on the trackpad (from dark to light). Many synthetic examples of a given SAX word are drawn to give the interaction designer a sense of the possible shapes of the gesture. New suggestions are displayed periodically, effectively creating a movie of potential gestures. In our first implementation, gesture suggestions were selected randomly, keeping a list of previously viewed gestures so as to avoid repetition. If the interaction designer sees a desirable gesture, he stops the presentation with a key press.

If other gestures have already been selected by the user, the similarity of the currently displayed gesture to the already selected gestures is shown in a bar plot in a window at the bottom left. Based on these similarity scores, the user can retain the gesture or continue searching other suggestions. In this case, we decided to use the $1 Recognizer (Wobbrock et al. 2007) both for generating similarity scores and for gesture recognition. To train the gesture recognizer, we simply used the synthetic examples generated during the visualization process.

4.7.1.4 $1 Recognizer

Since the $1 Recognizer is widely used in HCI research (Belatar and Coldefy 2010; Dang and André 2010) but is not necessarily known to machine learning researchers, we give a quick overview here. The recognizer is optimized for single stroke gestures and can be considered instance-based learning. Each instance or template is re-sampled to be of equal length with all others and then rotated, scaled, and translated to a canonical form before being used. During recognition the query gesture is compared to all the stored templates using an angular distance metric. In continuous recognition we can apply a threshold on that distance, and the rest of the recognition process is similar to the dynamic time warping approach described earlier. The authors report recognition accuracies of 99%, which is comparable to DTW implementations on the same data sets. The method is simple, fast to compute, and understandable by pattern recognition novices. Thus, the algorithm is well-suited for experimentation by interface designers. With MAGIC Summoning, interaction designers do not need to collect any training data for the recognizer. The training data is produced synthetically from the EGL as described above. Note that we can use the $1 Recognizer as a distance measure for EGL search (albeit slowly compared to iSAX), which will be useful for comparison experiments below.

4.7.2 Testing Suggested Gestures and Recognizers in Practice

We collected an EGL consisting of ten participants using their personal Mac laptops for one week. Figure 4.15 visualizes the EGL. While indexing the EGL, we set the SAX word length to four. For a two dimensional touchpad, the length doubles to eight. Setting the cardinality to four leads to a total number of 65,536 (4^8) possible strings.

We observed 1222 unique strings in the collected EGL. The space is surprisingly sparse; there are 64,314 strings not found in the EGL, suggesting that there are a large number of gestures that could be made with a low probability of false positives.

We performed an experiment to evaluate if the proposed suggestion and selection process described in the previous section can produce gestures that show a low false positive rate in everyday life. In addition, we were concerned as to whether synthetic data would be sufficient to train a high accuracy recognizer for this domain. We acted as an interaction designer and selected six gestures using the visualization tool above (see Fig. 4.16). We preferred gestures that were simple and memorable.

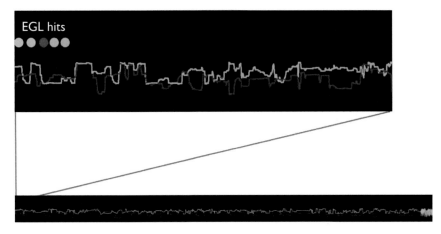

Fig. 4.15 *Bottom* the touch pad EGL. *Top* an excerpt from the EGL showing five false positives during testing of a gesture, indicated as *colored bubbles*

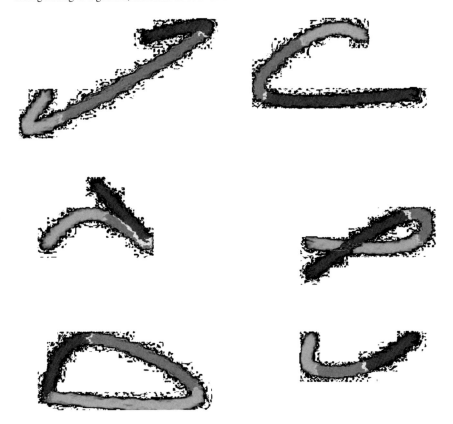

Fig. 4.16 The six gestures used in the study. Gestures are drawn from dark to light

Fig. 4.17 Seventy generated gestures with potential low false positive rates. Gestures ordered from left-to-right and from top-to-bottom with increasing entropy

Figure 4.17 demonstrates 70 other gestures suggested by the system that were not used. We trained a $1 Recognizer for each of the six gestures selected using synthetic data generated by MAGIC.

We designed a six user study with users who did not contribute to the EGL. As in the false positive prediction experiments from the previous section, we asked users to practice with the recognition system so that they could perform the gestures with confidence. Users were able to improve their performance from ≈46% to ≈90% quickly. Afterward, the users worked on their computers for 4 h while all touchpad movements were recorded. Every 10 min we sent a notification to the users asking them to perform one of the six gestures, resulting in four examples of each gesture for each participant. Thus, we collected 24 h of data and 144 gesture examples.

The gesture recognizer was able to recognize 98% of the performed gestures. Even though synthetic data was use to train the recognizer, these findings are similar to those of Wobbrock et al. (2007), who reported a 99% accuracy in their experiments. The false positive rates of the gestures are low except for one gesture (see Fig. 4.18). Thus, the experiment supports the hypothesis that MAGIC Summoning can suggest gestures and aid the interaction designer in creating a gesture system that results in low false positives. However, several questions remain. Can we order the suggestions so as to present the "best" gestures first? Also, the experiment as described has no control condition. What would have been the result if we had tried suggesting random gestures from the 64,314 available?

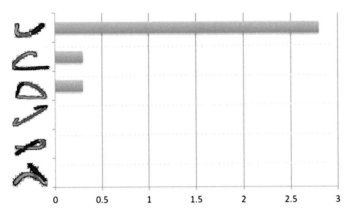

Fig. 4.18 Results of the trackpad gesture user study in false positives per hour. All but one of the gestures suggested by MAGIC Summoning show a low false positive rate

4.7.3   Ordering Gesture Suggestions

In this section we will explore possible ways of ordering gestures such that users can quickly find desirable gestures from the large number of possibilities. Our intuition is that users prefer simple gestures since they can be accessed quickly and are easy to memorize.

Our first approach is defining the complexity of a gesture as the entropy of its SAX word (Mitchell 1997):

$$H(word) = -\sum_{i=0}^{card} p(symbol_i) * log(symbol_i).$$

However, if we want to prefer simpler gestures, we should check to determine if false positive rates in real usage are correlated with simplicity. Otherwise, proposing simpler gestures first could be counterproductive. Intuitively, one would think that simpler gestures would trigger more often in everyday life. To investigate this question we trained the $1 Recognizer with 100 randomly chosen gestures and searched the EGL with it. For each gesture we calculated the entropy and compared the false positive rate to the entropy and found no correlation ($r^2 \approx 0.04$). Thus, there seems to be little additional risk to suggesting lower entropy gestures first.

The above heuristic seems logical for ordering suggestions. Low entropy gestures would seem to be simpler and easier to perform. To confirm this intuition we ran a small user study. We generated 100 gestures and sorted them using the above score. We examined the 20 best-ranked gestures and rejected ones that required significant overlap of the strokes (see Fig. 4.19) as the static visualization of the strokes could confuse subjects. For each of the 10 remaining gestures we asked six users to perform the gesture in the air, on the table or on their touchpad and asked them to assign a

Fig. 4.19 MAGIC
Summoning gestures with
significant overlap of the
strokes were rejected to
avoid user confusion

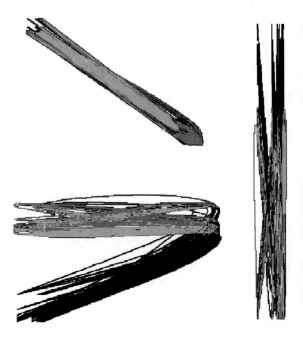

score of performability between 1 and 10. All participants received the same gestures. Interestingly, we were not able to find a correlation between the entropy of a gesture's SAX word and the users' ratings ($r^2 = 0.09$).

Given the above result, we desire gestures not in the EGL but that are known to be performable. With a trackpad, all suggested gestures should be physically possible, but in future work with inertial sensors the suggestions could become impossible without constraining the system in some manner.

We decided to prefer gesture suggestions where the substrings of the SAX word representing the candidate gesture are represented in the EGL, but the gesture string itself was not present. We will assume one dimension for ease of illustration. If a gesture ACBD is not in the EGL, but the subcomponents AC, CB, and BD or ACB and CBD were well represented in the EGL, we might conclude that ACBD is possible for the user to perform. In other words, we will prefer gestures where the most n-grams from the EGL are included in the suggested gesture's string. Intuitively, though, such a heuristic causes concern that such gestures might have a higher chance of false triggering.

To investigate this possibility, we extracted bi-grams and tri-grams from the EGL, created candidate gestures from them, and tried to find a correlation between the false positives in the EGL and the number of n-grams in the gesture's string. Note that this method of composition creates gestures with a variety of properties: ones common in the EGL, rare in the EGL, and not present in the EGL. A correlation would indicate an increased risk with this method of ordering the suggestions, but we did not find one, giving a modicum of assurance in the method:

Bi-grams $r^2 = 0.000676$
Tri-grams $r^2 = 0.000256$.

Beside low false positives, another criteria for a good gesture system is that there should be a low chance of confusion between gestures. If the user is creating a control system with six gestures and has already selected five of them, we should prefer suggestions that are distinct from the five gestures already chosen. We measure the distinguishably of a gesture using the Hamming distance (Hamming 1950) of the gesture's SAX word. Thus, when ordering gestures, we sort using a score defined as

$$score(word) = \frac{dist(word)}{(1 + entropy(word))}$$

where the distance of the word is the average Hamming distance to all other gestures in the gesture set. This metric provides a high distance to the other gestures and a low entropy. Note that we use $(1 + entropy(word))$ to avoid unreasonably high or infinite scores when the entropy value is near 0.

Given the results of the above experiments, we are now tuning MAGIC Summoning to generate gestures composed from parts of the EGL and to suggest gestures that are most dissimilar to each other. We intend to test this ordering system in our future work with suggesting gestures for use with inertial sensors.

4.7.4   How Selective are MAGIC Summoning's Suggestions?

In the above user study, we selected six gestures by hand from MAGIC Summoning's suggestions and tested the $1 Recognizer that MAGIC output for both accuracy and false triggering. However, there were many possible gestures that the system could have output instead. In this last section we will investigate if suggesting gestures based on our method is better generated ones by chance.

As we have seen previously, using iSAX results in fewer hits being identified in an EGL than those found by typical gesture recognizers (HMM, NN-DTW, $1 Recognizer, etc.). The sole reason to use iSAX is that it quickly returns whether or not a candidate gesture is worthwhile to investigate further. However, we do not need to generate gesture suggestions in real time. In fact, as soon as an EGL is collected, the same "overnight" process that generates the EGL's iSAX tree representation for prediction could track the gestures not represented in the EGL. Once these gestures are known, the recognizer of choice could be trained with synthetic data of the gesture, and the recognizer could be run on the EGL for a more precise estimate of the expected hits. The number of false positives returned should allow a finer discrimination between candidate gestures. In the following experiment, we use this new procedure to generate suggested gestures and test ones with the lowest number of false positives on the test data collected from subjects not represented in the EGL.

In this experiment, we generated 2000 random gestures from SAX strings not in the EGL. For each of the gestures we synthesized 40 examples and trained a $1

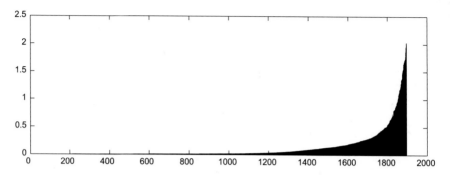

Fig. 4.20 Number of false positives identified in the EGL using the $1 Recognizer for each of 2000 gestures synthesized from SAX strings not represented in the EGL. Gestures with more than 2 hits per hour are not graphed to preserve scale

recognizer with them. We used this recognizer to test search the EGL in the classic way, that is testing each interesting region using the trained recognizer. We used a typical threshold ($th = 0.85$) for the $1 score. All results above that threshold count as a hit with the EGL. Figure 4.20 orders the gestures by least to most number of hits per hour in the EGL. Clearly the $1 Recognizer identifies many potential false positives, yet most of the gestures still have low rates.

Figure 4.21, top, shows another view of this data. Note that over 35% of the 2000 gestures have 0–0.0001 false positives/hour. Compare this rate to that of Fig. 4.21, bottom. This graph was generated using all the SAX strings represented in the EGL. Less than 12% of these gestures have such low false positive rates. Clearly, the SAX representation does have considerable predictive power on which suggested gestures are least likely to trigger falsely using the $1 Recognizer in the EGL. In fact, better than one in three of the gestures suggested by choosing SAX strings not in the EGL will be candidates for very low false positive rates with the synthetically trained $1 Recognizer.

The above observation suggests a relatively efficient method for creating gesture candidates for the interaction designer. First, randomly choose a unrepresented SAX string in the EGL. Train the desired recognizer using synthetic data. Run the recognizer on the EGL. If the rate of false positives per hour is less than 0.0001, keep the gesture. Otherwise, discard it. Generate as many gesture suggestions as is possible given time constraints. (Approximately 25 min is required to generate 100 gesture suggestions using a modern laptop, but such a process is highly parallelizable and can be run in batch before the interaction designer approaches the system.) Order the suggestions as described above and present them to the interaction designer for selection.

We conducted an experiment evaluating this algorithm. We split the collected EGL for touchpad gestures into two subsets. Each subset contains randomly chosen, distinct time series from the original EGL. The intersection between the subsets is empty. We used the first subset to generate 100 randomly chosen, distinct gestures candidates that show less then 0.0001 false positives per hour using the $1 Recognizer.

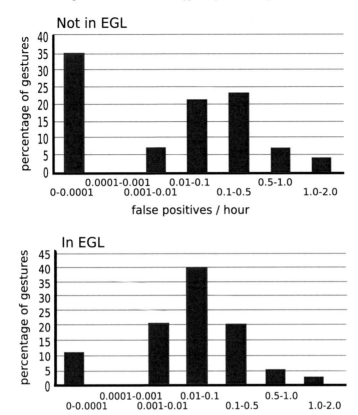

Fig. 4.21 Histogram demonstrating the percentages of the number of false positives per hour for gestures with SAX representations not in the EGL (*top*) and all gestures with SAX representations in the EGL (*bottom*)

We used these recognizers to then search the data in the second subset. On average we found the gestures to trigger 0.0022 times per hour, with a standard deviation of 0.003. These rates correspond to an average time between false triggerings of 455 h, or approximately one month assuming usage 16 h/day. Thus, this method of choosing gestures to suggest to an interaction designer seems desirable as well as practical.

4.8 Future Work

To date, the task for most gesture recognition systems has been to optimize accuracy given a set of gestures to be recognized. In this paper, we have reversed the problem, seeking to discover which gestures might be most suitable for recognition.

However, improved suggestion ordering is an area for improvement. Performability might be improved by modeling how gestures are produced (Cao and Zhai 2007) and prioritizing those gestures with least perceived effort. For domains where the coupling between sensor data and limb movement are not as apparent, such as accelerometer-based motion gestures, inverse kinematic models and 3D avatars seem appropriate both for prioritizing suggestions and for visualizing the gesture for the interaction designer. For situations with many degrees of freedom, such as whole body movement as tracked by the Microsoft Kinect©, the space of potential gestures may be extremely large. Physical and behavioral constraints might be applied to reduce the search space for the interaction designer. While MAGIC and MAGIC Summoning have been applied to multiple domains, we have only applied the gesture suggestion functions to trackpads. We are eager to investigate MAGIC Summoning's usefulness and usability in other domains.

4.9 Conclusion

We have described two pattern recognition tasks that can be used to help interaction designers create gesture interfaces: testing a user-defined gesture (and its classifier) against a previously captured database of typical usage sensor data to determine its tendency to trigger falsely and suggesting gestures automatically to the designer. We have shown that iSAX can be used to provide near immediate feedback to the user as to whether a gesture is inappropriate. While this method is approximate and recovers only a fraction of the total false positives in the EGL, MAGIC Summoning's results correlate strongly with those of HMMs, DTW, and the $1 Recognizer and can thus be used to provide guidance during training. We showed that MAGIC Summoning and the EGL could be used to create a null class of close false matches that increase the performance of the chosen classifier.

To suggest gestures to the interaction designer that may have low chance of triggering falsely, we exploited the SAX representation used to index the EGL. MAGIC Summoning generates all the strings not in the EGL, converts the SAX strings back into a gesture visualization, and suggests appropriate gestures to the designer. MAGIC Summoning also outputs classifiers for the gesture, trained on synthetic data generated from the SAX string. Using the task of finding command gestures for Mac trackpads, we showed that the gestures generated by MAGIC Summoning have generally low false positive rates when deployed and that the classifiers output by the system were adequate to the task of spotting the gesture.

Even if iSAX search of an EGL is not a perfect predictor for the false positives of a gesture in every day usage, we find that the approximations are sufficient to speed interface design significantly. MAGIC's methods are not intended to replace user testing with the final device. However, we believe that the tool will decrease the number of iterations needed to build a fast and stable gesture recognition interface.

Acknowledgements This material is based upon work supported, in part, by the National Science Foundation under Grant No. 0812281. We would also like to thank Google for their support of the most recent advances in this project. Thanks also to David Quigley for sharing his Android EGL data set and Daniel Ashbrook for his original MAGICal efforts and collaborations.

References

D. Ashbrook, *Enabling Mobile Microinteractions*, Ph.D. thesis, Georgia Institute of Technology, Atlanta, Georgia, 2009

D. Ashbrook, T. Starner. MAGIC: a motion gesture design tool, in *Proceedings of the ACM SIGCHI Conference on Human Factors in Computing Systems*, New York, 2010, pp. 2159–2168

M. Belatar, F. Coldefy. Sketched menus and iconic gestures, techniques designed in the context of shareable interfaces, in *Proceedings of the ACM International Conference on Interactive Tabletops and Surfaces*, New York, 2010, pp. 143–146

X. Cao, S. Zhai, Modeling human performance of pen stroke gestures, in *Proceedings of the ACM SIGCHI Conference on Human Factors in Computing Systems*, New York, 2007, pp. 1495–1504

C.T. Dang, E. André, Surface-poker: multimodality in tabletop games, in *Proceedings of the ACM International Conference on Interactive Tabletops and Surfaces*, New York, 2010, pp. 251–252

R. Dannenberg, D. Amon, A gesture based user interface prototyping system, in *Proceedings of the ACM Symposium on User Interface Software and Technology*, New York, 1989, pp. 127–132

A.K. Dey, R. Hamid, C. Beckmann, I. Li, D. Hsu, a CAPpella: programming by demonstration of context-aware applications, in *Proceedings of the ACM SIGCHI Conference on Human Factors in Computing Systems*, New York, 2004, pp. 33–40

J. Fails, D, Olsen, A design tool for camera-based interaction, in *Proceedings of the ACM SIGCHI Conference on Human Factors in Computing Systems*, New York, 2003, pp. 449–456

A.W.-C. Fu, E. Keogh, L.Y. Lau, C.A. Ratanamahatana, R.C.-W. Wong, Scaling and time warping in time series querying. Int. J. Very Large Data Bases **17**(4), 899–921 (2008)

F. Guimbretière, T. Winograd, Flowmenu: combining command, text, and data entry, in *Proceedings of the ACM Symposium on User Interface Software and Technology*, 2000, pp. 213–216

R. Hamming, Error detecting and error correcting codes. Bell Syst. Tech. J. **29**, 147–160 (1950)

Y. Hattori, S. Inoue, G. Hirakawa, A large scale gathering system for activity data with mobile sensors, in *Proceedings of the IEEE International Symposium on Wearable Computers*, Washington, DC, 2011, pp. 97–100

E.L. Hutchins, J.D. Hollan, D.A. Norman, Direct manipulation interfaces. Hum. Comput. Interact. **1**(4): 311–338 (1985). ISSN 0737-0024

D. Kohlsdorf, *Motion gesture: false positive prediction and prevention*, Master's thesis, University of Bremen, Bremen, 2011

D. Kohlsdorf, T. Starner, D. Ashbrook. MAGIC 2.0: a web tool for false positive prediction and prevention for gesture recognition systems, in *Proceedings of the International Conference on Automatic Face and Gesture Recognition*, Washington, DC, 2011, pp. 1–6

Y. Li, Gesture search: a tool for fast mobile data access, in *Proceedings of the ACM Symposium on User Interface Software and Technology*, New York, 2010, pp. 87–96

J. Lin, L. Wei, E. Keogh, Experiencing sax: a novel symbolic representation of time series. J. Data Min. Knowl. Discov. **15**(2), 107–144 (2007)

C. Long, *Quill: A Gesture Design Tool for Pen-based User Interfaces*, PhD thesis, University of California, Berkeley, California, 2001

K. Lyons, H. Brashear, T. Westeyn, J.S. Kim, T. Starner, GART: the gesture and activity recognition toolkit, in *Proceedings of the International Conference on Human-Computer Interaction: Intelligent Multimodal Interaction Environments*, Berlin, 2007, pp. 718–727

D. Maynes-Aminzade, T. Winograd, T. Igarashi. Eyepatch: prototyping camera-based interaction through examples, in *Proceedings of the ACM Symposium on User Interface Software and Technology*, New York, 2007, pp. 33–42

M.T. Mitchell, *Machine Learning* (McGraw Hill, New York, 1997)

T. Ouyang, Y. Li. Bootstrapping personal gesture shortcuts with the wisdom of the crowd and handwriting recognition, in *Proceedings of the ACM SIGCHI Conference on Human Factors in Computing Systems*, 2012, pp. 2895–2904

A. Pirhonen, S. Brewster, C. Holguin, Gestural and audio metaphors as a means of control for mobile devices, in *Proceedings of the ACM SIGCHI Conference on Human Factors in Computing Systems*, New York, 2002, pp. 291–298

J.-W. Shieh, *Time Series Retrievel: Indexing and Mapping Large Datasets*, Ph,D. thesis, University California, Riverside, 2010

J. Shieh, E. Keogh, iSAX: indexing and mining terabyte sized time series, in *Proceedings of the ACM SIGKDD International Conference on Knowledge Discovery and Data Mining*, New York, 2008, pp. 623–631

T. Starner, J. Weaver, A. Pentland, Real-time American sign language recognition using desk and wearable computer-based video. IEEE Trans. Pattern Anal. Mach. Intell. **20**(12), 1371–1375 (1998). December

T. Westeyn, H. Brashear, A. Atrash, T. Starner, Georgia tech gesture toolkit: supporting experiments in gesture recognition, in *Proceedings of the International Conference on Multimodal Interfaces*, New York, 2003, pp. 85–92

H. Witt, *Human-Computer Interfaces for Wearable Computers*, Ph.D. thesis, University Bremen, Bremen, 2007

J.O. Wobbrock, A.D. Wilson, Y. Li, Gestures without libraries, toolkits or training: a $1 recognizer for user interface prototypes, in *Proceedings of the ACM Symposium on User Interface Software and Technology*, pp. 159–168, New York, 2007

H.-D. Yang, S. Sclaroff, S.-W. Lee, Sign language spotting with a threshold model based on conditional random fields. IEEE Trans. Pattern Anal. Mach. Intell. **31**(7), 1264–1277 (2009)

Chapter 5
Language-Motivated Approaches to Action Recognition

Manavender R. Malgireddy, I. Nwogu and V. Govindaraju

Abstract We present language-motivated approaches to detecting, localizing and classifying activities and gestures in videos. In order to obtain statistical insight into the underlying patterns of motions in activities, we develop a dynamic, hierarchical Bayesian model which connects low-level visual features in videos with poses, motion patterns and classes of activities. This process is somewhat analogous to the method of detecting topics or categories from documents based on the word content of the documents, except that our documents are dynamic. The proposed generative model harnesses both the temporal ordering power of dynamic Bayesian networks such as hidden Markov models (HMMs) and the automatic clustering power of hierarchical Bayesian models such as the latent Dirichlet allocation (LDA) model. We also introduce a probabilistic framework for detecting and localizing pre-specified activities (or gestures) in a video sequence, analogous to the use of filler models for keyword detection in speech processing. We demonstrate the robustness of our classification model and our spotting framework by recognizing activities in unconstrained real-life video sequences and by spotting gestures via a one-shot-learning approach.

Keywords Dynamic hierarchical Bayesian networks · Topic models · Activity recognition · Gesture spotting · Generative models

Editors: Isabelle Guyon and Vassilis Athitsos.

M.R. Malgireddy (✉) · I. Nwogu · V. Govindaraju
Department of Computer Science and Engineering, University at Buffalo, SUNY,
Buffalo, NY 14260, USA
e-mail: mrm42@buffalo.edu

I. Nwogu
e-mail: inwogu@buffalo.edu

V. Govindaraju
e-mail: govind@buffalo.edu

© Springer International Publishing AG 2017
S. Escalera et al. (eds.), *Gesture Recognition*, The Springer Series
on Challenges in Machine Learning, DOI 10.1007/978-3-319-57021-1_5

155

5.1   Introduction

Vision-based activity recognition is currently a very active area of computer vision research, where the goal is to automatically recognize different activities from a video. In a simple case where a video contains only one activity, the goal is to classify that activity, whereas, in a more general case, the objective is to detect the start and end locations of different specific activities occurring in a video. The former, simpler case is known as *activity classification* and latter as *activity spotting*. The ability to recognize activities in videos, can be helpful in several applications, such as monitoring elderly persons; surveillance systems in airports and other important public areas to detect abnormal and suspicious activities; and content based video retrieval, amongst other uses.

There are several challenges in recognizing human activities from videos and these include videos taken with moving background such as trees and other objects; different lighting conditions (day time, indoor, outdoor, night time); different view points; occlusions; variations within each activity (different persons will have their own style of performing an activity); large number of activities; and limited quantities of labeled data amongst others.

Recent advances in applied machine learning, especially in natural language and text processing, have led to a new modeling paradigm where high-level problems can be modeled using combinations of lower-level segmental units. Such units can be learned from large data sets and represent the universal set of alphabets to fully describe a vocabulary. For example, in a high-level problem such as speech recognition, a phoneme is defined as the smallest segmental unit employed to form an utterance (speech vector). Similarly, in language based documents processing, words in the document often represent the smallest segmental unit while in image-based object identification, the bag-of-words (or bag-of-features) technique learns the set of small units required to segment and label the object parts in the image. These features can then be input to generative models based on hierarchical clustering paradigms, such as topic modeling methods, to represent different levels of abstractions.

Motivated by the successes of this modeling technique in solving general high-level problems, we define an activity as a sequence of contiguous sub-actions, where the sub-action is a discrete unit that can be identified in a action stream. For example, in a natural setting, when a person waves goodbye, the sub-actions involved could be (i) raising a hand from rest position to a vertical upright position; (ii) moving the arm from right to left; and (iii) moving the arm from left to right. The entire activity or gesture[1] therefore consists of the first sub-action occurring once and the second and third sub-actions occurring multiple times. Extracting the complete vocabulary of sub-actions in activities is a challenging problem since the exhaustive list of sub-actions involved in a set of given activities is not necessarily known beforehand. We therefore propose machine learning models and algorithms to (i) compose a compact, near-complete vocabulary of sub-actions in a given set of activities; (ii) recognize the

---

[1]When referring to activity spotting purposes, we use the term gestures instead of activities, only to be consistent with the terminology of the *ChaLearn Gesture Challenge*.

specific actions given a set of known activities; and (iii) efficiently learn a generative model to be used in recognizing or spotting a pre-specified action, given a set of activities.

We therefore hypothesize that the use of sub-actions in combination with the use of a generative model for representing activities will improve recognition accuracy and can also aid in activity spotting. We will perform experiments using various available publicly available benchmark data sets to evaluate our hypothesis.

5.2 Background and Related Work

Although extensive research has gone into the study of the classification of human activities in video, fewer attempts have been made to spot actions from an activity stream. A recent, more complete survey on activity recognition research is presented by Aggarwal and Ryoo (2011). We divide the related work in activity recognition into two main categories: activity classification and activity spotting.

5.2.1 Activity Classification

Approaches for activity classification can be grouped into three categories: (i) space-time approaches: a video is represented as a collection of space-time feature points and algorithms are designed to learn a model for each activity using these features; (ii) sequential approaches: features are extracted from video frames sequentially and a state-space model such as a hidden Markov model (HMM) is learned over the features; (iii) hierarchical approaches: an activity is modeled hierarchically, as combination of simpler low level activities. We will briefly describe each of these approaches along with the relevant literature, in sections below.

5.2.1.1 Space-Time Approaches

Space-time approaches represent a video as a collection of feature points and use these points for classification. A typical space-time approach for activity recognition involves the detection of interest points and the computation of various descriptors for each interest point. The collection of these descriptors (bag-of-words) is therefore the representation of a video. The descriptors of labeled training data are presented to a classifier during training. Hence, when an unlabeled, unseen video is presented, similar descriptors are extracted as mentioned above and presented to a classifier for labeling. Commonly used classifiers in the space-time approach to activity classification include support vector machines (SVM), K-nearest neighbor (KNN), etc.

Spatio-temporal interest points were initially introduced by Laptev and Lindeberg (2003) and since then, other interest-point-based detectors such as those based on spatio-temporal Hessian matrix (Willems et al. 2008) and Gabor filters (Bregonzio et al. 2009; Dollár et al. 2005) have been proposed. Various other descriptors such as those based on histogram-of-gradients (HoG) (Dalal and Triggs 2005) or histogram-of-flow (HoF) (Laptev et al. 2008), three-dimensional histogram-of-gradients (HoG3D) (Kläser et al. 2008), three-dimensional scale-invariant feature transform (3D-SIFT) (Scovanner et al. 2007) and local trinary patterns (Yeffet and Wolf 2009), have also been proposed to describe interest points. More recently, descriptors based on tracking interest points have been explored (Messing et al. 2009; Matikainen et al. 2009). These use standard Kanade-Lucas-Tomasi (KLT) feature trackers to track interest points over time.

In a recent paper by Wang et al. (2009), the authors performed an evaluation of local spatio-temporal features for action recognition and showed that dense sampling of feature points significantly improved classification results when compared to sparse interest points. Similar results were also shown for image classification (Nowak et al. 2006).

5.2.1.2 Sequential Approaches

Sequential approaches represent an activity as an ordered sequence of features, here the goal is to learn the order of specific activity using state-space models. HMMs and other dynamic Bayesian networks (DBNs) are popular state-space models used in activity recognition. If an activity is represented as a set of hidden states, each hidden state can produce a feature at each time frame, known as the observation. HMMs were first applied to activity recognition in 1992 by Yamato et al. (1992). They extracted features at each frame of a video by first binarizing the frame and dividing it into $(M \times N)$ meshes. The feature for each mesh was defined as the ratio of black pixels to the total number of pixels in the mesh and all the mesh features were concatenated to form a feature vector for the frame. An HMM was then learned for each activity using the standard Expectation-Maximization (EM) algorithm. The system was able to detect various tennis strokes such as forehand stroke, smash, and serve from one camera viewpoint. The major drawback of the conventional HMM was its inability to handle activities with multiple persons. A variant of HMM called coupled HMM (CHMM) was introduced by Oliver et al. (2000), which overcame this drawback by coupling HMMs, where each HMM in the CHMM modeled one person's activity. In their experiments they coupled two HMMs to model human-human interactions, but again this was somewhat limited in its applications. An approach to extend both HMM and CHMMs by explicitly modeling the duration of an activity using states was also proposed by Natarajan and Nevatia (2007). Each state in a coupled hidden semi-Markov model (CHSMMs) had its own duration and the sequence of these states defined the activity. Their experiments showed that CHSMM modeled an activity better than the CHMM.

5.2.1.3 Hierarchical Approaches

The main idea of hierarchical approaches is to perform recognition of higher-level activities by modeling them as a combination of other simpler activities. The major advantage of these approaches over sequential approaches is their ability to recognize activities with complex structures. In hierarchical approaches, multiple layers of state-based models such as HMMs and other DBNs are used to recognize higher level activities. In most cases, there are usually two layers. The bottom layer takes features as inputs and learns atomic actions called *sub-actions*. The results from this layer are fed into the second layer and used for the actual activity recognition. A layered hidden Markov model (LHMM) (Oliver et al. 2002) was used in an application for office awareness. The lower layer HMMs classified the video and audio data with a time granularity of less than 1 s while the higher layer learned typical office activities such as phone conversation, face-to-face conversation, presentation, etc. Each layer of the HMM was designed and trained separately with fully labeled data. Hierarchical HMMs (Nguyen et al. 2005) were used to recognize human activities such as person having "short-meal", "snacks" and "normal meal". They also used a 2-layer architecture where lower layer HMM modeled simpler behaviors such as moving from one location in a room to another and the higher layer HMM used the information from layer one as its features. The higher layer was then used to recognize activities. A method based on modeling temporal relationships among a set of different temporal events (Gong and Xiang 2003) was developed and used for a scene-level interpretation to recognize cargo loading and unloading events.

The main difference between the above mentioned methods and our proposed method, is that these approaches assume that the higher-level activities and atomic activities (sub-actions) are known a priori, hence, the parameters of the model can be learned directly based on this notion. While this approach might be suitable for a small number of activities, it does not hold true for real-word scenarios where there is often a large number of sub-actions along with many activities (such as is found in the HMDB data set which is described in more detail in Sect. 5.6.2). *For activity classification, we propose to first compute sub-actions by clustering dynamic features obtained from videos, and then learn a hierarchical generative model over these features, thus probabilistically learning the relations between sub-actions, that are necessary to recognize different activities including those in real-world scenarios.*

5.2.2 Activity Spotting

Only a few methods have been proposed for activity spotting. Among them is the work of Yuan et al. (2009), which represented a video as a 3D volume and activities-of-interest as sub-volumes. The task of activity spotting was therefore reduced to one of performing an optimal search for activities in the video. Another work in spotting by Derpanis et al. (2010) introduced a local descriptor of video dynamics based on visual spacetime oriented energy measures. Similar to the previous work, their input was also a video which was searched for a specific action. The limitation of these techniques is their inability to adapt to changes in view points, scale, appearance etc. Rather than being defined on the motion patterns involved in an activity, these methods performed template matching type techniques, which do not readily generalize to new environments exhibiting a known activity. Both methods reported their results on the KTH and CMU data sets (described in more detail in Sect. 5.6), where the environment in which the activities were being performed did not readily change.

5.3   A Language-Motivated Hierarchical Model for Classification

Our proposed language-motivated hierarchical approach aims to perform recognition of higher-level activities by modeling them as a combination of other simpler activities. The major advantage of this approach over the typical sequential approaches and other hierarchical approaches is its ability to recognize activities with complex structures. By employing a hierarchical approach, multiple layers of state-based dynamic models can be used to recognize higher level activities. The bottom layers take observed features as inputs in order to recognize atomic actions (sub-actions). The results from these lower layers are then fed to the upper layers and used to recognize the modular activity.

5.3.1   Hierarchical Activity Modeling Using Multi-class Markov Chain Latent Dirichlet Allocation (MCMCLDA)

We propose a supervised dynamic, hierarchical Bayesian model, the multi-class Markov chain latent Dirichlet allocation (MCMCLDA), which captures the temporal information of an activity by modeling it as sequence of motion patterns, based on the Markov assumption. We develop this generative learning framework in order to obtain statistical insight into the underlying motions patterns (sub-actions) involved in an activity. An important aspect of this model is that motion patterns are shared across activities. So although the model is generative in structure, it can act discriminatively as it specifically learns which motion patterns are present in each activity. The fact that motion patterns are shared across activities was validated empirically (Messing et al. 2009) on the University of Rochester activities data set. Our proposed generative model harnesses both the temporal ordering power of DBNs and the automatic clustering power of hierarchical Bayesian models. The model correlates these motion patterns over time in order to define the signatures for classes of activities. Figure 5.1 shows an overview of the implementation network although we do not display *poses*, since they have no direct meaningful physical manifestations.

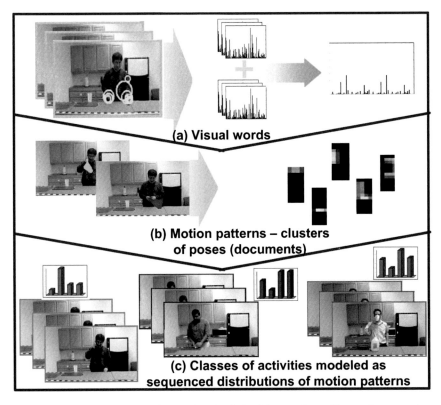

Fig. 5.1 Our general framework abstracts low-level visual features from videos and connects them to poses, motion patterns and classes of activity. **a** A video sequence is divided into short segments with a few frames only. In each segment, the space time interest points are computed. At the interest points, HoG and HoF are computed, concatenated and quantized to represent our low-level *visual words*. We discover and model a distribution over visual words which we refer to as *poses* (not shown in image). **b** Atomic motions are discovered and modeled as distributions over poses. We refer to these atomic motions as *motion patterns* or *sub-actions*. **c** Each video segment is modeled as a distribution over motion patterns. The time component is incorporated by modeling the transitions between the video segments, so that a complete video is modeled as a dynamic network of motion patterns. The distributions and transitions of underlying motion patterns in a video determine the final activity label assigned to that video

A given video is broken into motion segments comprising of either a combination of a fixed number of frames, or at the finest level, a single frame. Each motion segment can be represented as bag of vectorized descriptors (visual words) so that the input to the model (at time t) is the bag of visual words for motion segment t. Our model is similar in sprit to Hospedales et al. (2009), where the authors mine behaviors in video data from public scenes using an unsupervised framework. A major difference is that our MCMCLDA is a supervised version of their model in which motion-patterns/behaviors are shared across different classes, which makes it possible to handle a large number of different classes. If we assume that there exists only one class, then the motion-patterns are no longer shared, our model also becomes unsupervised and will thus be reduced to that of Hospedales et al. (2009).

We view MCMCLDA as a generative process and include a notation section before delving into the details of the LDA-type model:

m = any single video in the corpus,

z_t = motion pattern at time t (a video is assumed to be made up of motion patterns),

$y_{t,i}$ = the hidden variable representing a pose at motion pattern i, in time t (motion patterns are assumed to be made up of poses),

$x_{t,i}$ = the slices of the input video which we refer to as visual words and are the only observable variables,

ϕ_y = the visual word distribution for pose y,

θ_z = motion pattern specific pose distribution,

c_m is the class label for the video m (for one-shot learning, one activity is represented by one video ($N_m = 1$)),

ψ_j = jth class-specific transition matrix for the transition from one motion pattern to the next,

γ_c = the transition matrix distribution for a video,

α, β = the hyperparameters of the priors.

The complete generative model is given by:

$$\psi_j^z \sim Dir(\psi_j^z|\gamma_j),$$
$$\theta_z \sim Dir(\theta_z|\alpha),$$
$$\phi_y \sim Dir(\phi_y|\beta),$$
$$z_t \sim Mult(z_t|\psi_j^{z_{t-1}}),$$
$$y_{t,i} \sim Mult(y_{t,i}|\theta_{z_t}),$$
$$x_{t,i} \sim Mult(x_{t,i}|\phi_{y_{t,i}}),$$

where $Mult(\cdot)$ refers to a multinomial distribution.

Now, consider the Bayesian network of MCMCLDA shown in Fig. 5.2. This can be interpreted as follows: For each video m in the corpus, a motion pattern indicator z_t is drawn from $p(z_t|z_{t-1}, \psi_{c_m})$, denoted by $Mult(\psi_{c_m}^{z_{t-1}})$, where c_m is the class label for the video m. Then the corresponding pattern specific pose distribution θ_{z_t} is used to draw visual words for that segment. That is, for each visual word, a pose indicator $y_{t,i}$ is sampled according to pattern specific pose distribution θ_{z_t}, and then the corresponding pose-specific word distribution $\phi_{y_{t,i}}$ is used to draw a visual word. The poses ϕ_y, motion patterns θ_z and transition matrices ψ_j are sampled once for the entire corpus.

The joint distribution of all known and hidden variables given the hyperparameters for a video is:

$$p\left(\{x_t, y_t, z_t\}_1^T, \phi, \psi_j, \theta|\alpha, \beta, \gamma_j\right) = p(\phi|\beta)p(\theta|\alpha)p(\psi|\gamma_j)\prod_t\prod_i p(x_{t,i}|y_{t,i})p(y_{t,i}|z_t)p(z_t|z_{t-1}).$$

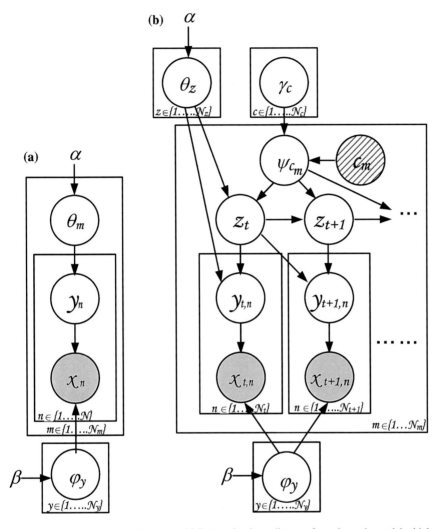

Fig. 5.2 *Left* plates diagram for standard LDA; *right* plates diagram for a dynamic model which extends LDA to learning the states from sequence data

5.3.2 Parameter Estimation and Inference of the MCMCLDA Model

As in the case with LDA, exact inference is intractable. We therefore use collapsed Gibbs sampler for approximate inference and learning. The update equation for pose from which the Gibbs sampler draws the hidden pose $y_{t,i}$ is obtained by integrating out the parameters θ, ϕ and noting that $x_{t,i} = x$ and $z_t = z$:

$$p\left(y_{t,i} = y | \mathbf{y}_{\neg(\mathbf{t},\mathbf{i})}, \mathbf{z}, \mathbf{x}\right) \propto \frac{n_{x,y}^{\neg(t,i)} + \beta}{\sum_{x=1}^{N_x} n_{x,y}^{\neg(t,i)} + N_x \beta} \left(n_{y,z}^{\neg(t,i)} + \alpha\right), \qquad (5.1)$$

where $n_{x,y}^{\neg(t,i)}$ denote the number of times that visual word x is observed with pose y excluding the token at (t, i) and $n_{y,z}^{\neg(t,i)}$ refers to the number of times that pose y is associated with motion pattern z excluding the token at (t, i). N_x is size of codebook and N_y is the number of poses.

The Gibbs sampler update for motion-pattern at time t is derived by taking into account that at time t, there can be many different poses associated to a single motion-pattern z_t and also the possible transition from z_{t-1} to z_{t+1}. The update equation for z_t can be expressed as:

$$p\left(z_t = z | \mathbf{y}, \mathbf{z}_{\neg t}\right) \propto p\left(y_t | z_t = z, z_{\neg t}, y_{\neg t}\right) p\left(z_t = z | z_{\neg t}^{c_m}, c_m\right). \qquad (5.2)$$

The likelihood term $p(y_t | z_t = z, z_{\neg t}, y_{\neg t})$ cannot be reduced to the simplified form as in LDA as the difference between $n_{y,z}^{\neg t}$ and $n_{y,z}$ is not one, since there will be multiple poses associated to the motion-pattern z_t. $n_{y,z}$ denotes the number of times pose y is associated with motion-pattern z and $n_{y,z}^{\neg t}$ refers to the number of times pose y is observed with motion-pattern z excluding the poses (multiple) at time t. Taking the above condition into account, the likelihood term can be obtained as below:

$$p\left(y_t | z_t = z, z_{\neg t}, y_{\neg t}\right) = \frac{\prod_y \Gamma(n_{y,z} + \alpha)}{\prod_y \Gamma(n_{y,z}^{\neg t} + \alpha)} \frac{\Gamma\left(\sum_y n_{y,z}^{\neg t} + N_y \alpha\right)}{\Gamma\left(\sum_y n_{y,z} + N_y \alpha\right)}.$$

Prior term $p(z_t = z | z_{\neg t}^{c_m}, c_m)$ is calculated as below depending on the values of z_{t-1}, z_t and z_{t+1}.

$$if \quad z_{t-1} \neq z :$$
$$= \frac{n_{z_{t-1},z,\neg t}^{(c_m)} + \gamma_{c_m}}{\sum_z n_{z_{t-1},z,\neg t}^{(c_m)} + N_z \gamma_{c_m}} \frac{n_{z,z_{t+1},\neg t}^{(c_m)} + \gamma_{c_m}}{\sum_{z_{t+1}} n_{z,z_{t+1},\neg t}^{(c_m)} + N_z \gamma_{c_m}},$$
$$if \quad z_{t-1} = z = z_{t+1} :$$
$$= \frac{n_{z_{t-1},z,\neg t}^{(c_m)} + 1 + \gamma_{c_m}}{\sum_z n_{z_{t-1},z,\neg t}^{(c_m)} + 1 + N_z \gamma_{c_m}} \frac{n_{z,z_{t+1},\neg t}^{(c_m)} + \gamma_{c_m}}{\sum_{z_{t+1}} n_{z,z_{t+1},\neg t}^{(c_m)} + N_z \gamma_{c_m}},$$
$$if \quad z_{t-1} = z \neq z_{t+1} :$$
$$= \frac{n_{z_{t-1},z,\neg t}^{(c_m)} + \gamma_{c_m}}{\sum_z n_{z_{t-1},z,\neg t}^{(c_m)} + N_z \gamma_{c_m}} \frac{n_{z,z_{t+1},\neg t}^{(c_m)} + \gamma_{c_m}}{\sum_{z_{t+1}} n_{z,z_{t+1},\neg t}^{(c_m)} + 1 + N_z \gamma_{c_m}}.$$

Here $n_{z_{t-1},z,\neg t}^{(c_m)}$ denotes the count from all the videos with the label c_m where motion-pattern z is followed by motion-pattern z_{t-1} excluding the token at t. $n_{z,z_{t+1},\neg t}^{(c_m)}$ denotes the count from all the videos with label c_m where motion-pattern z_{t+1} is followed by motion-pattern z_t excluding the token at t. N_z is the number of motion-patterns. The Gibbs sampling algorithm iterates between Eqs. 5.1 and 5.2 and finds the approximate posterior distribution. To obtain the resulting model parameters $\{\phi, \theta, \phi\}$ from the Gibbs sampler, we use the expectation of their distribution (Heinrich 2008), and collect N_s such samples of the model parameters.

For inference, we need to find the best motion-pattern sequence for a new video. The Gibbs sampler draws N_s samples of parameters during the learning phase. We assume that these are sufficient statistics for the model and that no further adaptation of parameters is necessary. We then adopt the Viterbi decoding algorithm to find the best motion-pattern sequence. We approximate the integral over ϕ, θ, ψ using the point estimates obtained during learning. To formulate the recursive equation for the Viterbi algorithm, we can define the quantity

$$\delta_t(i) = \max_{z_1,\dots,z_{t-1}} \int_{\phi,\theta,\psi_{c_m}} p\left(z_{1:(t-1)}, z_t = i, x_{1:t} | \phi, \theta, \psi_{c_m}\right),$$

$$\approx \max_{z_1,\dots,z_{t-1}} \left(\frac{1}{N_s} \sum_s p\left(z_{1:(t-1)}, z_t = i, x_{1:t} | \phi^s, \theta^s, \psi_{c_m}^s\right)\right),$$

that is $\delta_t(i)$ is the best score at time t, which accounts for first t motion-segments and ends in motion-pattern i. By induction we have

$$\delta_{t+1}(j) \approx \max_i \delta_t(i) \frac{1}{N_s} \sum_s p\left(z_{t+1} = j | z_t = i, \psi_{c_m}^s\right) p\left(x_{t+1} | z_{t+1} = j, \theta^s, \phi^s\right).$$

$$(5.3)$$

To find the best motion-pattern, we need to keep track of the arguments that maximized Eq. 5.3. For the classification task we calculate the likelihood $p^\star$ for each class and assign the label which has maximum value in:

$$p^\star = \max_{1 \le j \le N_z} \delta_T(j).$$

5.4 Experiments and Results Using MCMCLDA

In this section, we present our observations as well as the results of applying our proposed language-motivated hierarchical model to sub-action analysis as well as to activity classification, using both simulated data as well as a publicly available benchmark data set.

Fig. 5.3 Digital digits for
simulations

5.4.1 Study Performed on Simulated Digit Data

To flesh out the details of our proposed hierarchical classification model, we present a
study performed on simulated data. The ten simulated dynamic activity classes were
the writing of the ten digital digits, 0–9 as shown in Fig. 5.3. The word vocabulary
was made up of all the pixels in a 13×5 grid and the topics or poses represented the
distribution over the words. An activity class therefore consisted of the steps needed
to simulate the writing of each digit and the purpose of the simulation was to visually
observe the clusters of motion patterns involved in the activities.

5.4.1.1 Analysis of Results

A total of seven clusters were discovered and modeled, as shown in Fig. 5.4. These
represent the simulated strokes (or topics) involved in writing each digit. There were
fourteen motion patterns discovered, as shown in the two bottom rows of Fig. 5.4.
These are the probabilistic clusters of the stroke motions. An activity or digit written
was therefore classified based on the sequences of distributions of these motion
patterns over time.

5.4.2 Study Performed on the Daily Activities Data Set

The *Daily Activities data set* contains high resolution (1280×760 at 30 fps) videos,
with 10 different complex daily life activities such as *eating banana, answering
phone, drinking water, etc.*. Each activity was performed by five subjects three times,
yielding a total of 150 videos. The duration of each video varied between 10 and 60 s.

We generated visual words for the MCMCLDA model in a manner similar to
Laptev (2005), where the Harris3D detector (Laptev and Lindeberg 2003) was used to
extract space-time interest points at multiple scales. Each interest point was described
by the concatenation of HoF and HoG (Laptev 2005) descriptors. After the extraction
of these descriptors for all the training videos, we used the k-means clustering algorithm to form a codebook of descriptors (or visual words (VW)). Furthermore, we
vector-quantized each descriptor by calculating its membership with respect to the

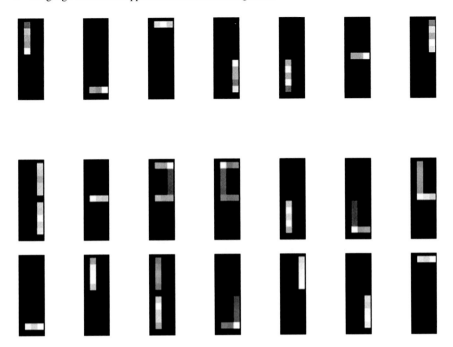

Fig. 5.4 The *top row* shows seven poses discovered from clustering words. The *middle* and *bottom rows* show the fourteen motion patterns discovered and modeled from the poses. A motion pattern captures one or more strokes in the order they are written

codebook. We used the original implementation available online[2] with the standard parameter settings to extract interest points and descriptors.

Due to the limitations of the distributed implementation of space-time interest points (Laptev et al. 2008), we reduced the video resolution to 320 × 180. In our experimental setup, we used 100 videos for training and 50 videos for testing exactly as pre-specified by the original publishers of this data set (Messing et al. 2009). Both the training and testing sets had a uniform distribution of samples for each activity. We learned our MCMCLDA model on the training videos, with a motion segment size of 15 frames. We ran a Gibbs sampler for a total of 6000 iterations, ignoring the first 5000 sweeps as burn-in, then took 10 samples at a lag of 100 sweeps. The hyperparameters were fixed initially with values ($\alpha = 5$, $\beta = 0.01$, $\gamma = 1$) and after burn-in, these values were empirically estimated using maximum-likelihood estimation (Heinrich 2008) as ($\alpha = 0.34$, $\beta = 0.001$ and $\gamma = \{0.04, 0.05, 0.16, 0.22, 0.006, 0.04, 0.13, 0.05, 0.14, 0.45\}$). We set the number of motion-patterns, poses and codebook size experimentally as $N_z = 100$, $N_y = 100$ and $N_x = 1000$.

---

[2]Implementation can be found at http://www.irisa.fr/vista/Equipe/People/Laptev/download.html# stip.

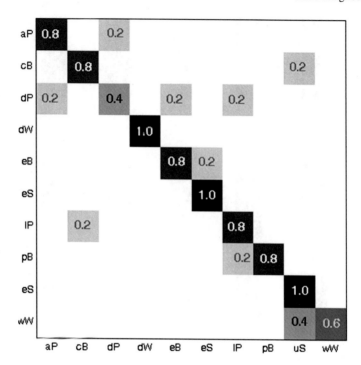

Fig. 5.5 Confusion matrix for analyzing the University of Rochester daily activities data set. Overall accuracy is 80.0%. Zeros are omitted for clarity. The labels and their corresponding meaning are: ap-answer phone; cB-chop banana; dP-dial phone; dW-drink water; eB-eat banana; eS-eat snack; lP-lookup in phonebook; pB-peel banana; uS-use silverware; wW-write on whiteboard

The confusion matrix computed from this experiment is given in Fig. 5.5 and a comparison with other activity recognition methods on the Daily Activities data set is given in Table 5.1. Because the data set was already pre-divided, the other recognition methods reported in Table 5.1 were trained and tested on the same sets of training and testing videos.

Qualitatively, Fig. 5.7 pictorially illustrates some examples of different activities having the same underlying shared motion patterns.

5.4.2.1 Analysis of Results

We present comparative results with other systems in Table 5.1. The results show that the approach based on computing a distribution mixture over motion orientations at each spatial location of the video sequence (Benabbas et al. 2010), slightly outperformed our hierarchical model. Interestingly, in our test, one activity, the *write on whiteboard (wW)* activity is quite confused with *use silverware (uS)* activity, significantly bringing down the overall accuracy. The confusion matrix for Benabbas et al.

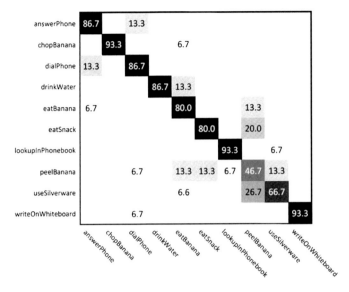

Fig. 5.6 Confusion matrix results from Benabbas et al. (2010) on the University of Rochester daily activities data set

(2010) is presented in Fig. 5.6 and it shows several of the classes being confused, no perfect recognition scores and also one of the class recognition rates being below

Table 5.1 The accuracy numbers reported in literature from applying different activity recognition techniques on the daily activities data set

Technique	Focus	Accuracy (%)
Latent velocity trajectory features (Messing et al. 2009)[a]	Motion feature enhancement	67
Naive-Bayes pairwise trajectory features (Matikainen et al. 2010)	Motion feature enhancement	70
Salient region tracking features (Bilen et al. 2011)	Motion feature enhancement	74
Video temporal cropping technique	Motion feature enhancement	80
Our supervised dynamic hierarchical model	Dynamic hierarchical modeling	80
Direction of motion features (Benabbas et al. 2010)	Motion feature enhancement	81

[a]The authors also reported velocity trajectory feature augmented with prior spatial layout information, resulting in an accuracy of 89%

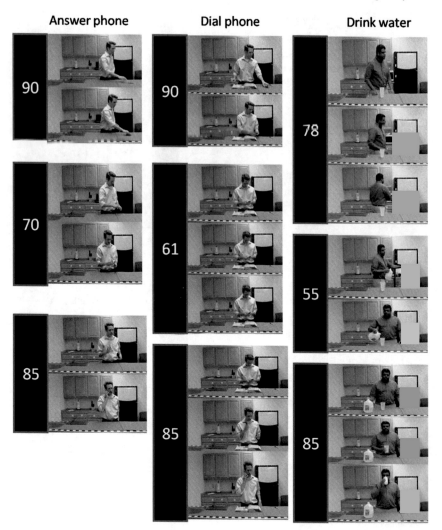

Fig. 5.7 Different activities showing shared underlying motion patterns. The shared motion patterns are 85 and 90, amidst other underlying motion patterns shown

50%. Being a generative model, the MCMCLDA model performs comparably to other discriminative models in a class labeling task.

Figure 5.7 pictorially illustrates some examples of different activities having the same underlying shared motion patterns. For example, the activity of answering the phone shares a common motion pattern (#85) with the activities of dialing the phone and drinking water. Semantically, we observe that this shared motion is related to the *lifting* sub-action.

5.5 A Language-Motivated Model for Gesture Recognition and Spotting

Few methods have been proposed for gesture spotting and among them include the work of Yuan et al. (2009), who represented a video as a 3D volume and activities-of-interest as sub-volumes. The task of gesture spotting was therefore reduced to performing an optimal search for gestures in the video. Another work in spotting was presented by Derpanis et al. (2010) who introduced a local descriptor of video dynamics based on visual space-time oriented energy measures. Similar to the previous work, their input was also a video in which a specific action was searched for. The limitation in these techniques is their inability to adapt to changes in view points, scale, appearance, etc. Rather than being defined on the motion patterns involved in an activity, these methods performed a type of 3D template matching on sequential data; such methods do not readily generalize to new environments exhibiting the known activity. *We therefore propose to develop a probabilistic framework for gesture spotting that can be learned with very little training data and can readily generalize to different environments.*

Justification: Although the proposed framework is a generative probabilistic model, it performs comparably to the state-of-the-art activity techniques which are typically discriminative in nature, as demonstrated in Tables 5.2 and 5.3. An additional benefit of the framework is its usefulness for gesture spotting based on learning from only one, or few training examples.

Background: In speech recognition, unconstrained keyword spotting refers to the identification of specific words uttered, when those words are not clearly separated from other words, and no grammar is enforced on the sentence containing them. Our proposed spotting framework uses the Viterbi decoding algorithm and is motivated by the *keyword-filler HMM for spotting keywords in continuous speech.* The current state of the art keyword filler HMM dates back to the seminal papers of Rohlicek et al. (1989) as well as Rose and Paul (1990), where the basic idea is to create one HMM of the keyword and a separate HMM of the filler or non keyword regions. These two models are then combined to form a composite filler HMM that is used to annotate speech parts using the Viterbi decoding scheme. Putative decisions arise when the Viterbi path crosses the keyword portion of the model. The ratio between the likelihood of the Viterbi path that passes through the keyword model and the

Table 5.2 Comparison of our proposed model and features for KTH data set	Method	Accuracy (%)
	(Laptev et al., 2008)	91.8
	(Yuan et al., 2009)	93.3
	(Wang et al., 2011)	94.2
	(Gilbert et al., 2011)	94.5
	(Kovashka and Grauman, 2010)	94.53
	Proposed mcHMM	94.67

Table 5.3 Comparison of our proposed model and features for the HMDB data set

Method	Accuracy (%)
Best results on 51 activities (original)	
(Kuehne et al. 2011)	23.18
Proposed mcHMM on 51 activities (original)	25.64
Best results on 10 activities (original)	
(Kuehne et al. 2011)	54.3
Proposed mcHMM on 10 activities (original)	57.67
Proposed mcHMM on 10 activities (stabilized)	66.67

likelihood of an alternate path that passes solely through the filler portion can be used to score the occurrence of keywords. In a similar manner, we compute the probabilistic signature for a gesture class, and using the filler model structure, we test for the presence of that gesture within a given video. For one-shot learning, the parameters of the single training video are considered to be sufficiently representative of the class.

5.5.1 Gesture Recognition Using a Multichannel Dynamic Bayesian Network

In a general sense, the spotting model can be interpreted as an HMM (whose random variables involve hidden states and observed input nodes) but unlike the classic HMM, this model has multiple input channels, where each channel is represented as a distribution over the visual words corresponding to that channel. In contrast to the classic HMM, our model can have multiple observations per state and channel, and we refer to this as the multiple channel HMM (mcHMM). Figure 5.8 shows a graphical representation of the mcHMM.

5.5.2 Parameter Estimation for the Gesture Recognition Model

To determine the probabilistic signature of an activity class, one mcHMM is trained for each activity. The generative process for mcHMM involves first sampling a state from an activity, based on the transition matrix for that activity; then a frame-feature comprising of the distribution of visual words is sampled according to a multinomial distribution for that state[3] and this is repeated for each frame. Similar to a classic HMM, the parameters for the mcHMM are therefore:

---

[3] States are modeled as multinomials since our input observables are discrete values.

Fig. 5.8 Plates model for mcHMM showing the relationship between activities or gestures, states and the two channels of observed visual words (VW)

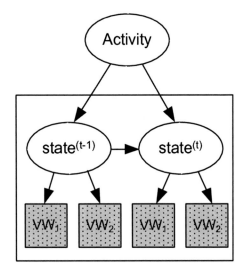

1. Initial state distribution $\pi = \{\pi_i\}$,
2. State transition probability distribution $A = \{a_{ij}\}$,
3. Observation densities for each state and descriptor $B = \{b_i^d\}$.

The joint probability distribution of observations (O) and hidden state sequence (Q) given the parameters of the multinomial representing a hidden state (λ) can be expressed as:

$$P(O, Q|\lambda) = \pi_{q_1} b_{q_1}(O_1) \prod_{t=2}^{T} a_{q_{t-1}q_t} \cdot b_{q_t}(O_t),$$

where $b_{q_t}(O_t)$ is modeled as follows:

$$b_{q_t}(O_t) = \prod_{d=1}^{D} b_q^d(O_t^d),$$
$$= \prod_{d=1}^{D} Mult(O_t^d|b_q^d),$$

and D is the number of descriptors.

EM is implemented to find the maximum likelihood estimates. The update equations for the model parameters are:

$$\hat{\pi} = \sum_{r=1}^{R} \gamma_1^r(i),$$

$$\hat{a}_{ij} = \frac{\sum_{r=1}^{R} \sum_{t=1}^{T} \eta_t^r(i, j)}{\sum_{r=1}^{R} \sum_{t=1}^{T} \gamma_t^r(i)},$$

$$\hat{b}_j^d(k) = \frac{\sum_{r=1}^{R} \sum_{t=1}^{T} \gamma_t^r(j) \cdot \frac{n_t^{d,k}}{n_t^{d,\cdot}}}{\sum_{r=1}^{R} \sum_{t=1}^{T} \gamma_t^r(j)},$$

where R is number of videos and $\gamma_1(i)$ is the expected number of times the activity being modeled started with state i;

$\eta_t^r(i, j)$ is the expected number of transitions from state i to state j and $\gamma_t^r(i)$ is the expected number of transitions from state i;

$n_t^{d,k}$ is the number of times that visual word k occurred in descriptor d at time t and $n_t^{d,\cdot\cdot}$ is the total number of visual words that occurred in descriptor d at time t.

5.5.3 Gesture Spotting via Inference on the Model

The gesture spotting problem is thus reduced to an inference problem where, given a new not-previously-seen test video, and the model parameters or probabilistic signatures of known activity classes, the goal is to establish which activity class distributions most likely generated the test video. This type of inference can be achieved using the Viterbi algorithm.

We constructed our spotting network such that there could be a maximum of five gestures in a video. This design choice was driven by our participation in the Chalearn competition where there was a maximum of five gestures in every test video. Each of these gesture classes was seen during training, hence, there were no random gestures inserted into the test video. This relaxed our network, compared to the original filler model in speech analysis, where there can exist classes that have not been previously seen. Figure 5.9 shows an example of the stacked mcHMMs involved the gesture spotting task. This toy example shown in the figure can spot

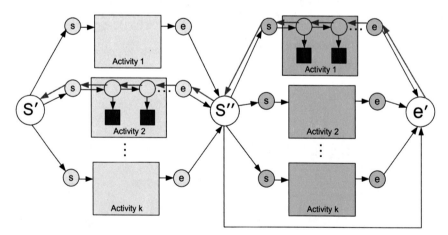

Fig. 5.9 Activity spotting by computing likelihoods via Viterbi decoding. The toy example shown assumes there are at most two activities in any test video, where the first activity is from the set of activities that start from s' and end at s'', followed by one from the set that start from s'' and end at e'. The image also shows an example of a putative decision path from e' to s', after the decoding is completed

gestures in a test video comprised of at most two gestures. This network has a non-emitting start state S'. This state does not have any observation density associated with it. From this state, we can enter any of K gestures, which is shown by having edges from S' to K mcHMMs. All the gestures are then connected to non-emitting state S'' which represents the end of first gesture. Similarly we can enter the second gesture from S'' and end at e' or directly go from S'' to e' which handles the case for a video having only one gesture. This can be easily extended to the case where there are at most five gestures.

The Viterbi decoding algorithm was implemented to traverse the stacked network and putative decisions arose when the Viterbi path crosses the keyword portion of the model. The ratio between the likelihood of the Viterbi path that passed through the keyword model and the likelihood of an alternate path that passes through the non-keyword portion was then used to score the occurrence of a keyword, where a keyword here referred to a gesture class. An empirically chosen threshold value was thus used to select the occurrence of a keyword in the video being decoded.

5.6 Experiments and Results Using mcHMM

In this section, we present our approach on generating visual words and our observations as well as the results of applying proposed mcHMM model to activity classification and gesture spotting, using publicly available benchmark data sets.

5.6.1 Generating Visual Words

An important step in generating visual words is the the need to extract interest points from frames sampled from the videos at 30 fps. Interest points were obtained from the KTH and HMDB data set by sampling dense points in every frame in the video and then tracking these points for the next L frames. These are known as dense trajectories. For each of these tracks, motion boundary histogram descriptors based on HoG and HoF descriptors were extracted. These features are similar to the ones used in dense trajectories (Wang et al. 2011), although rather than sampling interest points at every L frames or when the current point is lost before being tracked for L frames, we sampled at every frame. By so doing, we obtained a better representation for each frame, whereas the original work used the features to represent the whole video and was not frame-dependent.

Because the HMDB data set is comprised of real-life scenes which contain people and activities occurring at multiple scales, the frame-size in the video was reduced by a factor of two repeatedly, and motion boundary descriptors were extracted at multiple scales. In the Chalearn data set, since the videos were comprised of RGB-depth frames, we extracted interest points by (i) taking the difference between two consecutive depth frames and/or (ii) calculating the centroid of the depth foreground in

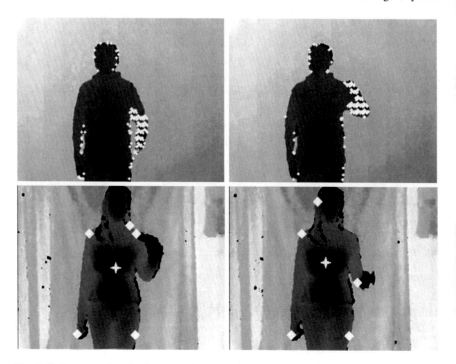

Fig. 5.10 Interest points for 2 consecutive video frames. *Top* Depth-subtraction interest points; *bottom* extrema interest points (with centroid)

every frame and computing the extrema points (from that centroid) in the depth fore-ground. The second process ensured that extrema points such as the hands, elbows, top-of-the-head, etc., were always included in the superset of interest points. The top and bottom image pairs in Fig. 5.10 show examples of consecutive depth frames from the Chalearn data set, with the interest points obtained via the two different methods, superimposed. Again, HoG and HoF descriptors were extracted at each interest point so that similar descriptors could be obtained in all the cases. We used a patch size of 32×32 and a bin size of 8 for HoG and 9 for HoF implementation.

The feature descriptors were then clustered to obtain visual words. In general, from the literature (Wang et al. 2011; Laptev et al. 2008), in order to limit complex-ity, researchers randomly select a finite number of samples (roughly in the order of 100,000) and cluster these to form visual words. This could prove reasonable when the number of samples is a few orders of magnitude greater than 100,000. But in dealing with densely sampled interest points at every frame, the amount of descrip-tors generated especially at multiple scales become significantly large. We therefore divided the construction of visual words for HMDB data set into a two step process where visual words were first constructed for each activity class separately, and then the visual words obtained for each class were used as the input samples to cluster the final visual words. For the smaller data sets such as KTH and Chalearn Gesture Data Set, we randomly sampled 100,000 points and clustered them to form the visual words.

5.6.2 Study Performed on the HMDB and KTH Data Sets

In order to compare our framework to the other current state-of-the-art methods, we performed activity classification on video sequences created from the KTH database (Schüldt et al. 2004); KTH is a relatively simplistic data set comprised of 2391 video clips used to train/test six human actions. Each action is performed several times by 25 subjects in various outdoor and indoor scenarios. We split the data into training set of 16 subjects and test set of 9 subjects, which is exactly the same setup used by the authors of the initial paper (Schüldt et al. 2004). Table 5.2 shows the comparison of accuracies obtained.

Similarly, we performed activity classification tests on Human Motion Database (HMDB) (Kuehne et al. 2011). HMDB is currently the most realistic database for human activity recognition comprising of 6766 video clips and 51 activities extracted from a wide range of sources like YouTube, Google videos, digitized movies and other videos available on the Internet. We follow the original experimental setup using three train-test splits (Kuehne et al. 2011). Each split has 70 video for training and 30 videos for testing for each class. All the videos in the data set are stabilized to remove the camera motion and the authors of the initial paper (Kuehne et al. 2011) report results on both original and stabilized videos for 51 activities. The authors also selected 10 common actions from HMDB data set that were similar to action categories in the UCF50 data set (University of Central Florida 2010) and compared the recognition performance. Table 5.3 summarizes the performance of proposed mcHMM method on 51 activities as well as 10 activities for both original and stabilized videos.

5.6.2.1 Analysis of Results

For both the case of simple actions as found in the KTH data set and the case of significantly more complex actions as found in the HMDB data set, the mcHMM model performs comparably with other methods, outperforming them in the activity recognition task. Our evaluation against state-of-the-art data sets suggest that performance is not significantly affected over a range of factors such as camera position and motion as well as occlusions. This suggests that the overall framework (combination of dense descriptors and a state-based probabilistic model) is fairly robust with respect to these low-level video degradations. At the time of this submission, although we outperformed the only currently reported accuracy results on the HMDB data set, as shown by the accuracy scores reported, the framework is still limited in its representative power to capture the complexity of human actions.

5.6.3 Study Performed on the ChaLearn Gesture Data Set

Lastly, we present our results of gesture spotting from the ChaLearn gesture data set (ChaLearn 2011). The ChaLearn data set consisted of video frames with RGB-Depth information. Since the task-at-hand was gesture spotting via one-shot learning, only one video per class was provided to train an activity (or gesture). The data set was divided into three parts: development, validation and final. In the first phase of the competition, participants initially developed their techniques against the development data set. Ground truth was not provided during the development phase. Once the participants had a working model, they then ran their techniques against the validation data set and uploaded their predicted results to the competition website, where they could receive feedback (scores based on edit distances) on the correctness of the technique. In the last phase of the competition, the final data set was released so that participants could test against it and upload their predicted results. Similarly, edit scores were used to measure the correctness of the results and the final rankings were published on the competition website.

We reported results using two methods (i) mcHMM (ii) mcHMM with LDA (Blei et al. 2003). For mcHMM method, we constructed visual words as described in Sect. 5.6.1 and represented each frame as two histograms of visual words. This representation was input to the model to learn parameters of the mcHMM model. In the augmented framework, mcHMM + LDA, the process of applying LDA to the input data can be viewed as a type of dimensionality reduction step since the number of topics are usually significantly smaller than the number of unique words. In our work, a frame is analogous to a document and visual words are analogous to words in a text document. Hence, in the combined method, we performed the additional step of using LDA to represent each frame as a histogram of topics. These reduced-dimension features were input to the mcHMM model. Gesture spotting was then performed by creating a spotting network made up of connected mcHMM models, one for each gesture learned, as explained in Sect. 5.5.3.

For the mcHMM model, we experimentally fixed the number of states to 10. The number of visual words was computed as the number of classes multiplied by a factor of 10, for example if the number of classes is 12, then number of visual words generated will be 120. The dimensionality of the input features to the mcHMM model was the number of visual words representing one training sample. For the augmented model the dimension of the features was reduced by a factor of 1.25, that is in the previous example, the length of feature vector would be reduced from 120 to 96. All the above parameters were experientially found using the development set. The same values were then used for the validation and final sets.

5.6.3.1   Analysis of Results

Table 5.4 shows the results of one-shot-learning on the ChaLearn data at the three different stages of the competition. We present results based on the two variants of our framework—the mcHMM model framework and the augmented mcHMM + LDA framework. Our results indicate that the framework augmented with LDA outperforms the unaugmented one, two out of three times. During implementation, the computational performance for the augmented framework was also significantly better than the unaugmented model due the reduced number of features needed for

Table 5.4 Results for ChaLearn gesture data set

Method	Data set	Edit distance
Proposed mcHMM	Development	0.26336
Proposed mcHMM + LDA	Development	0.2409
Baseline	Validation	0.59978
Proposed mcHMM	Validation	0.26036
Proposed mcHMM + LDA	Validation	0.23328
Top ranking participant	Validation	0.20287
Top ranking participant	Final	0.09956
Proposed mcHMM + LDA	Final	0.18465

training and for inference. It is also interesting to observe how the edit distances reduced from the development phase through the final phase, dropping by up to six percentage points, due to parameter tuning.

5.7   Conclusion and Future Work

In the course of this paper, we have investigated the use of motion patterns (representing sub-actions) exhibited during different complex human activities. Using a language-motivated approach we developed a dynamic Bayesian model which combined the temporal ordering power of dynamic Bayesian networks with the automatic clustering power of hierarchical Bayesian models such as the LDA word-topic clustering model. We also showed how to use the Gibbs samples for rapid Bayesian inference of video segment clip category. Being a generative model, we can detect abnormal activities based on low likelihood measures. This framework was validated by its comparable performance on tests performed on the daily activities data set, a naturalistic data set involving everyday activities in the home.

We also investigated the use of a multichannel HMM as a generative probabilistic model for single activities and it performed comparably to the state-of-the-art activity classification techniques which are typically discriminative in nature, on two extreme data sets—the simplistic KTH, and the very complex and realistic HMDB data sets. An additional benefit of this framework was its usefulness for gesture spotting based on learning from only one, or few training examples. We showed how the use of the generative dynamic Bayesian model naturally lent itself to the spotting task, during inference. The efficacy of this model was shown by the results obtained from participating in ChaLearn Gesture Challenge where an implementation of the model finished top-5 in the competition.

In the future, we will consider using the visual words learned from a set of training videos to automatically segment a test video. The use of auto-detected video segments could prove useful both in activity classification and gesture spotting. It will also be interesting to explore the use of different descriptors available in the literature, in order to find those best-suited for representing naturalistic videos.

Acknowledgements The authors wish to thank the associate editors and anonymous referees for all their advice about the structure, references, experimental illustration and interpretation of this manuscript. The work benefited significantly from our participation in the ChaLearn challenge as well as the accompanying workshops.

References

J.K. Aggarwal, M.S. Ryoo, Human activity analysis: a review. ACM Comput. Surv. **43**, 1–16 (2011)

Y. Benabbas, A. Lablack, N. Ihaddadene, C. Djeraba, Action recognition using direction models of motion, in *Proceedings of the 2010 International Conference on Pattern Recognition*, 2010, pp. 4295–4298

H. Bilen, V.P. Namboodiri, L. Van Gool, Action recognition: a region based approach, in *Proceedings of the 2011 IEEE Workshop on the Applications of Computer Vision*, 2011, pp. 294–300

David M. Blei, Andrew Y. Ng, Michael I. Jordan, Latent Dirichlet allocation. J. Mach. Learn. Res. **3**, 993–1022 (2003)

M. Bregonzio, S. Gong, T. Xiang, Recognising action as clouds of space-time interest points, in *Proceedings of the 2009 IEEE Conference on Computer Vision and Pattern Recognition*, 2009, pp. 1948–1955

ChaLearn. ChaLearn Gesture Dataset (CGD2011), ChaLearn, California, 2011. http://gesture.chalearn.org/2011-one-shot-learning

N. Dalal, B. Triggs, Histograms of oriented gradients for human detection, in *Proceedings of the 2005 IEEE Conference on Computer Vision and Pattern Recognition*, 2005, pp. 886–893

K.G. Derpanis, M. Sizintsev, K. Cannons, R.P. Wildes, Efficient action spotting based on a spacetime oriented structure representation, in *Proceedings of the 2010 IEEE Conference on Computer Vision and Pattern Recognition*, 2010, pp. 1990–1997

P. Dollár, V. Rabaud, G. Cottrell, S. Belongie, Behavior recognition via sparse spatio-temporal features, in *Proceedings of the 2005 IEEE Workshop on Visual Surveillance and Performance Evaluation of Tracking and Surveillance*, 2005, pp. 65–72

A. Gilbert, J. Illingworth, R. Bowden, Action recognition using mined hierarchical compound features. IEEE Trans. Pattern Anal. Mach. Intell. **33**(5), 883–897 (2011)

S. Gong, and T. Xiang, Recognition of group activities using dynamic probabilistic networks, in *Proceedings of the 2003 IEEE Conference on Computer Vision and Pattern Recognition*, vol. 2, 2003, pp. 742–749

G. Heinrich, Parameter estimation for text analysis. Technical report, University of Leipzig, 2008

T. Hospedales, S.G. Gong, T. Xiang, A Markov clustering topic model for mining behaviour in video, in *Proceedings of the 2009 International Conference on Computer Vision*, 2009, pp. 1165–1172

A. Kläser, M. Marszalek, C. Schmid, A spatio-temporal descriptor based on 3d-gradients, in *Proceedings of the 2008 British Machine Vision Conference* (2008)

A. Kovashka, K. Grauman, Learning a hierarchy of discriminative space-time neighborhood features for human action recognition, in *Proceedings of the 2010 IEEE Conference on Computer Vision and Pattern Recognition*, 2010, pp. 2046–2053

H. Kuehne, H. Jhuang, E. Garrote, T. Poggio, T. Serre, HMDB: a large video database for human motion recognition, in *Proceedings of the 2011 International Conference on Computer Vision* 2011

I. Laptev, On space-time interest points. Int. J. Comput. Vis. **64**, 107–123 (2005)

I. Laptev, T. Lindeberg, Space-time interest points, in *Proceedings of the 2003 International Conference on Computer Vision*, 2003, pp. 432–439

I. Laptev, M. Marszalek, C. Schmid, B. Rozenfeld, Learning realistic human actions from movies, in *Proceedings of the 2008 IEEE Conference on Computer Vision and Pattern Recognition*, 2008, pp. 1–8

P. Matikainen, M. Hebert, R. Sukthankar, Trajectons: Action recognition through the motion analysis of tracked features, in *Proceedings of the 2009 IEEE Workshop on Video-Oriented Object and Event Classification* (2009)

P. Matikainen, M. Hebert, R. Sukthankar, Representing pairwise spatial and temporal relations for action recognition, in *Proceedings of the 2010 European Conference on Computer Vision* 2010

R. Messing, C. Pal, H. Kautz, Activity recognition using the velocity histories of tracked keypoints, in *Proceedings of the 2009 International Conference on Computer Vision* 2009

P. Natarajan, R. Nevatia, Coupled hidden semi Markov models for activity recognition, in *Proceedings of the IEEE Workshop on Motion and Video Computing* 2007

N.T. Nguyen, D.Q. Phung, S. Venkatesh, Learning and detecting activities from movement trajectories using the hierarchical hidden Markov models, in *Proceedings of the 2005 IEEE Conference on Computer Vision and Pattern Recognition*, 2005, pp. 955–960

E. Nowak, F. Jurie, B. Triggs, Sampling strategies for bag-of-features image classification, in *Proceedings of the 2006 European Conference on Computer Vision*, 2006, pp. 490–503

N. Oliver, E. Horvitz, A. Garg, Layered representations for human activity recognition, in *Proceedings of the 2002 IEEE International Conference on Multimodal Interfaces*, 2002, pp. 3–8

Nuria M. Oliver, Barbara Rosario, Alex P. Pentland, A Bayesian computer vision system for modeling human interactions. IEEE Trans. Pattern Anal. Mach. Intell. **22**(8), 831–843 (2000)

J.R. Rohlicek, W. Russell, S. Roukos, H. Gish, Continuous hidden Markov modeling for speaker-independent word spotting, in *Proceedings of the 1989 International Conference on Acoustics, Speech, and Signal Processing*, 1989, pp. 627–630

R. Rose, D. Paul, A hidden Markov model based keyword recognition system, in *Proceedings of the 1990 International Conference on Acoustics, Speech, and Signal Processing* 1990

C. Schüldt, I. Laptev, B. Caputo, Recognizing human actions: a local svm approach, in *Proceedings of the 2004 International Conference on Pattern Recognition*, 2004, pp. 32–36

P. Scovanner, S. Ali, M. Shah, A 3-dimensional sift descriptor and its application to action recognition, in *Procedings of the ACM International Conference on Multimedia*, 2007, pp. 57–360

University of Central Florida. *University of Central Florida, Computer Vision Lab*, 2010. URL http://server.cs.ucf.edu/~vision/data/UCF50.rar

H. Wang, M.M. Ullah, A. Kläser, I. Laptev, C. Schmid, Evaluation of local spatio-temporal features for action recognition, in *Proceedings of the 2009 British Machine Vision Conference* 2009

H. Wang, A. Kläser, C. Schmid, L. Cheng-Lin, Action recognition by dense trajectories. in *Proceedings of the 2011 IEEE Conference on Computer Vision and Pattern Recognition*, 2011, pp. 3169–3176

G. Willems, T. Tuytelaars, L. Gool, An efficient dense and scale-invariant spatio-temporal interest point detector, in *Proceedings of the 2008 European Conference on Computer Vision*, 2008, pp. 650–663

J. Yamato, J. Ohya, K. Ishii, Recognizing human action in time-sequential images using hidden Markov model, in *Proceedings of the 1992 IEEE Conference on Computer Vision and Pattern Recognition*, 1992, pp. 379–385

L. Yeffet, L. Wolf, Local trinary patterns for human action recognition, in *Proceedings of the 2009 International Conference on Computer Vision* 2009

J. Yuan, Z. Liu, Y. Wu, Discriminative subvolume search for efficient action detection, in *Proceedings of the 2009 IEEE Conference on Computer Vision and Pattern Recognition* 2009

Chapter 6
A Model of the Perception of Facial Expressions of Emotion by Humans: Research Overview and Perspectives

Aleix M. Martinez and Shichuan Du

Abstract In cognitive science and neuroscience, there have been two leading models describing how humans perceive and classify facial expressions of emotion—the continuous and the categorical model. The continuous model defines each facial expression of emotion as a feature vector in a face space. This model explains, for example, how expressions of emotion can be seen at different intensities. In contrast, the categorical model consists of C classifiers, each tuned to a specific emotion category. This model explains, among other findings, why the images in a morphing sequence between a happy and a surprise face are perceived as either happy or surprise but not something in between. While the continuous model has a more difficult time justifying this latter finding, the categorical model is not as good when it comes to explaining how expressions are recognized at different intensities or modes. Most importantly, both models have problems explaining how one can recognize combinations of emotion categories such as happily surprised versus angrily surprised versus surprise. To resolve these issues, in the past several years, we have worked on a revised model that justifies the results reported in the cognitive science and neuroscience literature. This model consists of C distinct continuous spaces. Multiple (compound) emotion categories can be recognized by linearly combining these C face spaces. The dimensions of these spaces are shown to be mostly configural. According to this model, the major task for the classification of facial expressions of emotion is precise, detailed detection of facial landmarks rather than recognition. We provide an overview of the literature justifying the model, show how the resulting model can be employed to build algorithms for the recognition of facial expression of emotion, and propose research directions in machine learning and computer vision researchers to keep pushing the state of the art in these areas. We also discuss how the model can aid in studies of human perception, social interactions and disorders.

Editors: Isabelle Guyon and Vassilis Athitsos.

A.M. Martinez (✉) · S. Du
Department of Electrical and Computer Engineering, The Ohio State University,
2015 Neil Avenue, Columbus, OH 43210, USA
e-mail: aleix@ece.osu.edu

S. Du
e-mail: dus@ece.osu.edu

Keywords Vision · Face perception · Emotions · Computational modeling · Categorical perception · Face detection

6.1 Introduction

The face is an object of major importance in our daily lives. Faces tell us the identity of the person we are looking at and provide information on gender, attractiveness and age, among many others. Of primary interest is the production and recognition of facial expressions of emotion. Emotions play a fundamental role in human cognition (Damasio 1995) and are thus essential in studies of cognitive science, neuroscience and social psychology. Facial expressions of emotion could also play a pivotal role in human communication (Schmidt and Cohn 2001). And, sign languages use facial expressions to encode part of the grammar (Wilbur 2011). It has also been speculated that expressions of emotion were relevant in human evolution (Darwin 1872). Models of the perception of facial expressions of emotion are thus important for the advance of many scientific disciplines.

A first reason machine learning and computer vision researchers are interested in creating computational models of the perception of facial expressions of emotion is to aid studies in the above sciences (Martinez 2003). Furthermore, computational models of facial expressions of emotion are important for the development of artificial intelligence (Minsky 1988) and are essential in human-computer interaction (HCI) systems (Pentland 2000).

Yet, as much as we understand how facial expressions of emotion are produced, very little is known on how they are interpreted by the human visual system. Without proper models, the scientific studies summarized above as well as the design of intelligent agents and efficient HCI platforms will continue to elude us. A HCI system that can easily recognize expressions of no interest to the human user is of limited interest. A system that fails to recognize emotions readily identified by us is worse.

In the last several years, we have defined a computational model consistent with the cognitive science and neuroscience literature. The present paper presents an overview of this research and a perspective of future areas of interest. We also discuss how machine learning and computer vision should proceed to successfully emulate this capacity in computers and how these models can aid in studies of visual perception, social interactions and disorders such as schizophrenia and autism. In particular, we provide the following discussion.

- A model of human perception of facial expressions of emotion: We provide an overview of the cognitive science literature and define a computational model consistent with it.
- Dimensions of the computational space: Recent research has shown that human used mostly shape for the perception and recognition of facial expressions of emotion. In particular, we show that configural features are of much use in this

process. A configural feature is defined as a non-rotation invariant modeling of the distance between facial components; for example, the vertical distance between eyebrows and mouth.

- We argue that to overcome the current problems of face recognition algorithms (including identity and expressions), the area should make a shift toward a more shape-based modeling. Under this model, the major difficulty for the design of computer vision and machine learning systems is that of precise detection of the features, rather than classification. We provide a perspective on how to address these problems.

The rest of the paper is organized as follows. Section 6.2 reviews relevant research on the perception of facial expressions of emotion by humans. Section 6.3 defines a computational model consistent with the results reported in the previous section. Section 6.4 illustrates the importance of configural and shape features for the recognition of emotions in face images. Section 6.5 argues that the real problem in machine learning and computer vision is a detection one and emphasizes the importance of research in this domain before we can move forward with improved algorithms of face recognition. In Sect. 6.6, we summarize some of the implications of the proposed model. We conclude in Sect. 6.7.

6.2 Facial Expressions: From Production to Perception

The human face is an engineering marvel. Underneath our skin, a large number of muscles allow us to produce many configurations. The face muscles can be summarized as Action Unit (AU) (Ekman and Friesen 1976) defining positions characteristic of facial expressions of emotion. These face muscles are connected to the motor neurons in the cerebral cortex through the corticobulbar track. The top muscles are connected bilaterally, while the bottom ones are connected unilaterally to the opposite hemisphere. With proper training, one can learn to move most of the face muscles independently. Otherwise, facial expressions take on predetermined configurations.

There is debate on whether these predetermined configurations are innate or learned (nature vs. nurture) and whether the expressions of some emotions is universal (Izard 2009). By universal, we mean that people from different cultures produce similar muscle movements when expressing some emotions. Facial expressions typically classified as universal are joy, surprise, anger, sadness, disgust and fear (Darwin 1872; Ekman and Friesen 1976). Universality of emotions is controversial, since it assumes facial expressions of emotion are innate (rather than culturally bound). It also favors a categorical perception of facial expressions of emotion. That is, there is a finite set of predefined classes such as the six listed above. This is known as the *categorical model*.

In the categorical model, we have a set of C classifiers. Each classifier is specifically designed to recognize a single emotion label, such as surprise. Several psychophysical experiments suggest the perception of emotions by humans is categorical

(Ekman and Rosenberg 2005). Studies in neuroscience further suggest that distinct regions (or pathways) in the brain are used to recognize different expressions of emotion (Calder et al. 2001).

An alternative to the categorical model is the *continuous model* (Russell 2003; Rolls 1990). Here, each emotion is represented as a feature vector in a multidimensional space given by some characteristics common to all emotions. One such model is Russell's 2-dimensional circumplex model (Russell 1980), where the first basis measures pleasure-displeasure and the second arousal. This model can justify the perception of many expressions, whereas the categorical model needs to define a class (i.e., classifier) for every possible expression. It also allows for intensity in the perception of the emotion label. Whereas the categorical model would need to add an additional computation to achieve this goal (Martinez 2003), in the continuous model the intensity is intrinsically defined in its representation. Yet, morphs between expressions of emotions are generally classified to the closest class rather than to an intermediate category (Beale and Keil 1995). Perhaps more interestingly, the continuous model better explains the caricature effect (Rhodes et al. 1987; Calder et al. 1997), where the shape features of someone's face are exaggerated (e..g, making a long nose longer). This is because the farther the feature vector representing that expression is from the mean (or center of the face space), the easier it is to recognize it (Valentine 1991).

In neuroscience, the multidimensional (or continuous) view of emotions was best exploited under the limbic hypothesis (Calder et al. 2001). Under this model, there should be a neural mechanism responsible for the recognition of all facial expressions of emotion, which was assumed to take place in the limbic system. Recent results have however uncovered dissociated networks for the recognition of most emotions. This is not necessarily proof of a categorical model, but it strongly suggests that there are at least distinct groups of emotions, each following distinct interpretations.

Furthermore, humans are only very good at recognizing a number of facial expressions of emotion. The most readily recognized emotions are happiness and surprise. It has been shown that joy and surprise can be robustly identified extremely accurately at almost any resolution (Du and Martinez 2011). Figure 6.1 shows a happy expression at four different resolutions. The reader should not have any problem recognizing the emotion in display even at the lowest of resolutions. However, humans are not as good at recognizing anger and sadness and are even worse at fear and disgust.

A major question of interest is the following. Why are some facial configurations more easily recognizable than others? One possibility is that expressions such as joy and surprise involve larger face transformations than the others. This has recently proven not to be the case (Du and Martinez 2011). While surprise does have the largest deformation, this is followed by disgust and fear (which are poorly recognized). Learning why some expressions are so readily classified by our visual system should facilitate the definition of the form and dimensions of the computational model of facial expressions of emotion.

The search is on to resolve these two problems. First, we need to determine the *form* of the computational space (e.g., a continuous model defined by a multidimensional space). Second, we ought to define the *dimensions* of this model (e.g., the dimensions

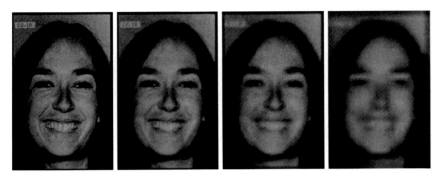

Fig. 6.1 Happy faces at four different resolutions. From *left* to *right* 240 by 160, 120 by 80, 60 by 40, and 30 by 20 pixels. All images have been resized to a common image size for visualization

of this multidimensional face space are given by configural features). In the following sections we overview the research we have conducted in the last several years leading to a solution to the above questions. We then discuss on the implications of this model. In particular, we provide a perspective on how machine learning and computer vision researcher should move forward if they are to define models based on the perception of facial expressions of emotion by humans.

6.3 A Model of the Perception of Facial Expressions of Emotion

In cognitive science and neuroscience researchers have been mostly concerned with models of the perception and classification of the six facial expressions of emotion listed above. Similarly, computer vision and machine learning algorithms generally employ a face space to represent these six emotions. Sample feature vectors or regions of this feature space are used to represent each of these six emotion labels. This approach has a major drawback—it can only detect one emotion from a single image. In machine learning, this is generally done by a winner-takes-all approach (Torre and Cohn 2011). This means that when a new category wants to be included, one generally needs to provide labeled samples of it to the learning algorithm.

Yet, everyday experience demonstrates that we can perceive more than one emotional category in a single image (Martinez 2011), even if we have no prior experience with it. For example, Fig. 6.2 shows images of faces expressing different surprises— happily surprised, angrily surprised, fearfully surprised, disgustedly surprised and the typically studied surprise.

If we were to use a continuous model, we would need to have a very large number of labels represented all over the space; including all possible types of surprises. This would require a very large training set, since each possible combination of labels would have to be learned. But this is the same problem a categorical model

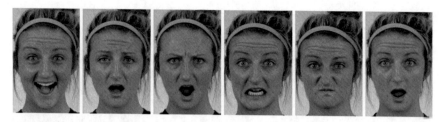

Fig. 6.2 Faces expressing different surprise. From *left* to *right* happily surprised, sadly surprised, angrily surprised, fearfully surprised, disgustedly surprised, and surprise

would face. In such a case, dozens if not hundreds of sample images for each possible category would be needed. Alternatively, Susskind et al. (2007) have shown that the appearance of a continuous model may be obtained from a set of classifiers defining a small number of categories.

If we define an independent computational (face) space for a small number of emotion labels, we will only need sample faces of those few facial expressions of emotion. This is indeed the approach we have taken. Details of this model are given next.

Key to this model is to note that we can define new categories as linear combinations of a small set of categories. Figure 6.3 illustrates this approach. In this figure, we show how we can obtain the above listed different surprises as a linear combination of known categories. For instance, happily surprised can be defined as expressing 40% joy plus 60% surprise, that is, expression = 0.4 happy + 0.6 surprise. A large number of such expressions exist that are a combination of the six emotion categories listed above and, hence, the above list of six categories is a potential set of basic emotion classes. Also, there is some evidence form cognitive science to suggest that these are important categories for humans (Izard 2009) Of course, one needs not base the model on this set of six emotions. This is an area that will undoubtedly attract lots of interest. A question of particular interest is to determine not only which basic categories to include in the model but how many. To this end both, cognitive studies with humans and computational extensions of the proposed model will be necessary, with the results of one area aiding the research of the other.

The approach described in the preceding paragraph would correspond to a categorical model. However, we now go one step further and define each of these face spaces as continuous feature spaces, Fig. 6.3. This allows for the perception of each emotion at different intensities, for example, less happy to exhilarant (Neth and Martinez 2010). Less happy would correspond to a feature vector (in the left most face space in the figure) closer to the mean (or origin of the feature space). Feature vectors farther from the mean would be perceived as happier. The proposed model also explains the caricature effect, because within each category the face space is continuous and exaggerating the expression will move the feature vector representing the expression further from the mean of that category.

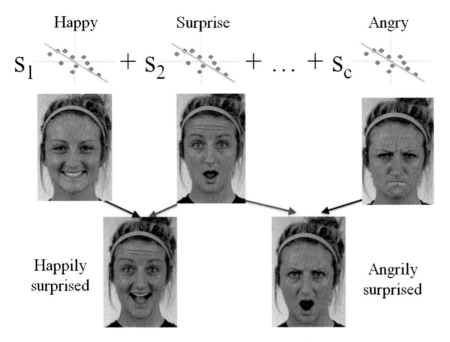

Fig. 6.3 This figure shows how to construct linear combinations of known categories. At the top of the figure, we have the known or learned categories (emotions). The coefficients s_i determine the contribution of each of these categories to the final perception of the emotion

Furthermore, the proposed model can define new terms, for example, "hatred" which is defined as having a small percentage of disgust and a larger percentage of anger; still linear. In essence, the intensity observed in this *continuous representation* defines the weight of the contribution of each basic category toward the final decision (classification). It also allows for the representation and recognition of a very large number of emotion categories without the need to have a categorical space for each or having to use many samples of each expression as in the continuous model.

The proposed model thus bridges the gap between the categorical and continuous ones and resolves most of the debate facing each of the models individually. To complete the definition of the model, we need to specify what defines each of the dimensions of the continuous spaces representing each category. We turn to this problem in the next section.

6.4   Dimensions of the Model

In the early years of computer vision, researchers derived several feature- and shape-based algorithms for the recognition of objects and faces (Kanade 1973; Marr 1976; Lowe 1983). In these methods, geometric, shape features and edges were extracted from an image and used to build a model of the face. This model was then fitted to the image. Good fits determined the class and position of the face.

Later, the so-called appearance-based approach, where faces are represented by their pixel-intensity maps or the response of some filters (e.g., Gabors), was studied (Sirovich and Kirby 1987). In this alternative texture-based approach, a metric is defined to detect and recognize faces in test images (Turk and Pentland 1991). Advances in pattern recognition and machine learning have made this the preferred approach in the last two decades (Brunelli and Poggio 1993).

Inspired by this success, many algorithms developed in computer vision for the recognition of expressions of emotion have also used the appearance-based model (Torre and Cohn 2011). The appearance-based approach has also gained momentum in the analysis of AUs from images of faces. The main advantage of the appearance-based model is that one does not need to predefine a feature or shape model as in the earlier approaches. Rather, the face model is inherently given by the training images.

The appearance-based approach does provide good results from near-frontal images of a reasonable quality, but it suffers from several major inherent problems. The main drawback is its sensitivity to image manipulation. Image size (scale), illumination changes and pose are all examples of this. Most of these problems are intrinsic to the definition of the approach since this cannot generalize well to conditions not included in the training set. One solution would be to enlarge the number of training images (Martinez 2002). However, learning from very large data sets (in the order of millions of samples) is, for the most part, unsolved (Lawrence 2005). Progress has been made in learning complex, non-linear decision boundaries, but most algorithms are unable to accommodate large amounts of data—either in space (memory) or time (computation).

This begs the question as to how the human visual system solves the problem. One could argue that, throughout evolution, the homo genus (and potentially before it) has been exposed to trillions of faces. This has facilitated the development of simple, yet robust algorithms. In computer vision and machine learning, we wish to define algorithms that take a shorter time to learn a similarly useful image representation. One option is to decipher the algorithm used by our visual system. Research in face recognition of identity suggests that the algorithm used by the human brain is not appearance-based (Wilbraham et al. 2008). Rather, it seems that, over time, the algorithm has identified a set of robust features that facilitate rapid categorization (Young et al. 1987; Hosie et al. 1988; Barlett and Searcy 1993).

This is also the case in the recognition of facial expressions of emotion (Neth and Martinez 2010). Figure 6.4 shows four examples. These images all bear a neutral expression, that is, an expression associated to no emotion category. Yet, human subjects perceive them as expressing sadness, anger, surprise and disgust. The most striking part of this illusion is that these faces do not and cannot express any emotion, since all relevant AUs are inactive. This effect is called over-generalization (Zebrowitz et al. 2010), since human perception is generalizing the learned features defining these face spaces over to images with a different label.

The images in Fig. 6.4 do have something in common though—they all include a configural transformation. What the human visual system has learned is that faces do not usually look like those in the image. Rather the relationship (distances) between brows, nose, mouth and the contour of the face is quite standard. They follow a Gaussian distribution with small variance (Neth and Martinez 2010). The images shown in this figure however bear uncanny distributions of the face components. In the sad-looking example, the distance between the brows and mouth is larger than normal (Neth and Martinez 2009) and the face is thinner than usual (Neth and Martinez 2010). This places this sample face, most likely, outside the 99% confidence interval of all Caucasian faces on these two measures. The angry-looking face has a much-shorter-than-average brow to mouth distance and a wide face. While the surprise-looking face has a large distance between eyes and brows and a thinner face. The disgust-looking face has a shorter distance between brows, eyes, nose and mouth. These effects are also clear in the schematic faces shown in the figure.

Yet, configural cues alone are not sufficient to create an impressive, lasting effect. Other shape changes are needed. For example, the curvature of the mouth in joy or the opening of the eyes—showing additional sclera—in surprise. Note how the surprise-looking face in Fig. 6.4 appears to also express disinterest or sleepiness. Wide-open eyes would remove these perceptions. But this can only be achieved with a shape change. Hence, our face spaces should include both, configural and shape features. It is important to note that configural features can be obtained from an appropriate representation of shape. Expressions such as fear and disgust seem to be mostly (if not solely) based on shape features, making recognition less accurate and more

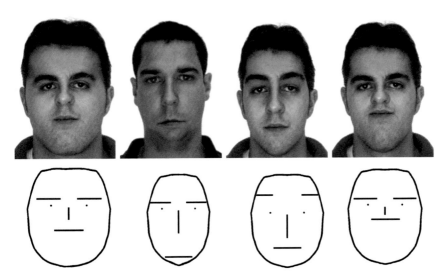

Fig. 6.4 The four face images and schematics shown above all correspond to neutral expressions (i.e., the sender does not intend to convey any emotion to the receiver). Yet, most human subjects interpret these faces as conveying anger, sadness, surprise and disgust. Note that although these faces look very different from one another, three of them are actually morphs from the same (original) image

(a)

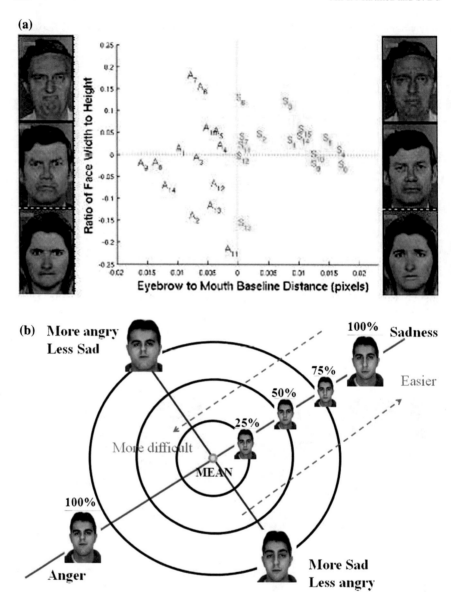

Fig. 6.5 a Shown here are the two most discriminant dimensions of the face shape vectors. We also plot the images of anger and sadness of Ekman and Friesen (1976). In *dashed* are simple linear boundaries separating angry and sad faces according to the model. The first dimension (distance between brows and mouth) successfully classifies 100% of the sample images. This continuous model is further illustrated in **b**. Note that, in the proposed computational model, the face space defining sadness corresponds to the *right-bottom quadrant*, while that of anger is given by the *left-top quadrant*. The *dashed arrows* in the figure reflect the fact that as we move away from the "mean" (or norm) face, recognition of that emotion become easier

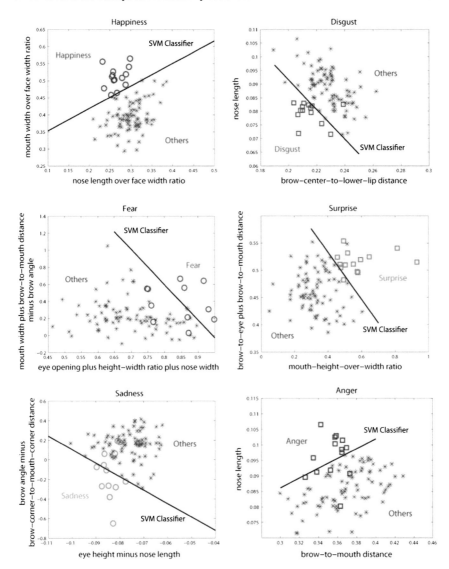

Fig. 6.6 Shown in the above are the six feature spaces defining each of the six basic emotion categories. A simple linear support vector machine (SVM) can achieve high classification accuracies; where we have used a one-versus-all strategy to construct each classifier and tested it using the leave-one-out strategy. Here, we only used two features (dimensions) for clarity of presentation. Higher accuracies are obtained if we include additional dimensions and training samples

susceptible to image manipulation. We have previously shown (Neth and Martinez 2010) that configural cues are amongst the most discriminant features in a classical (Procrustes) shape representation, which can be made invariant to 3D rotations of the face (Hamsici and Martinez 2009a).

Thus, each of the six categories of emotion (happy, sad, surprise, angry, fear and disgust) is represented in a shape space given by classical statistical shape analysis. First the face and the shape of the major facial components are automatically detected. This includes delineating the brows, eyes, nose, mouth and jaw line. The shape is then sample with d equally spaced landmark points. The mean (center of mass) of all the points is computed. The $2d$-dimensional shape feature vector is given by the x and y coordinates of the d shape landmarks subtracted by the mean and divided by its norm. This provides invariance to translation and scale. 3D rotation invariance can be achieved with the inclusion of a kernel as defined in Hamsici and Martinez (2009a). The dimensions of each emotion category can now be obtained with the use of an appropriate discriminant analysis method. We use the algorithm defined by Hamsici and Martinez (2008) because it minimizes the Bayes classification error.

As an example, the approach detailed in this section identifies the distance between the brows and mouth and the width of the face as the two most important shape features of anger and sadness. It is important to note that, if we reduce the computational spaces of anger and sadness to 2-dimensions, they are almost indistinguishable. Thus, it is possible that these two categories are in fact connected by a more general one. This goes back to our question of the number of basic categories used by the human visual system. The face space of anger and sadness is illustrated in Fig. 6.5, where we have also plotted the feature vectors of the face set of Ekman and Friesen (1976).

As in the above, we can use the shape space defined above to find the two most discriminant dimensions separating each of the six categories listed earlier. The resulting face spaces are shown in Fig. 6.6. In each space, a simple linear classifier in these spaces can successfully classify each emotion very accurately. To test this, we trained a linear support vector machine (Vapnik 1998) and use the leave-one-out test on the data set of images of Ekman and Friesen (1976). Happiness is correctly classified 99% of the time. Surprise and disgust 95% of the time. Sadness 90% and anger 94%. While fear is successfully classified at 92%. Of course, adding additional dimensions in the feature space and using nonlinear classifiers can readily achieve perfect classification (i.e., 100%). The important point from these results is to note that simple configural features can *linearly* discriminate most of the samples in each emotion. These features are very robust to image degradation and are thus ideal for recognition in challenging environments (e.g., low resolution)—a message to keep in mind for the development of machine learning and computer vision systems.

6.5 Precise Detection of Faces and Facial Features

As seen thus far, human perception is extremely tuned to small configural and shape changes. If we are to develop computer vision and machine learning systems that can emulate this capacity, the real problem to be addressed by the community is that of *precise detection of faces and facial features* (Ding and Martinez 2010). Classification is less important, since this is embedded in the detection process; that is, we want to precisely detect changes that are important to recognize emotions.

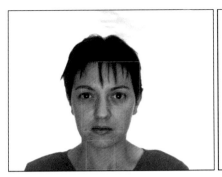

Fig. 6.7 Two example of imprecise detections of a face with a state of the art algorithm

Most computer vision algorithms defined to date provide, however, inaccurate detections. One classical approach to detection is template matching. In this approach, we first define a template (e.g., the face or the right eye or the left corner of the mouth or any other feature we wish to detect). This template is learned from a set of sample images; for example, estimating the distribution or manifold defining the appearance (pixel map) of the object (Yang et al. 2002). Detection of the object is based on a window search. That is, the learned template is compared to all possible windows in the image. If the template and the window are similar according to some metric, then the bounding box defining this window marks the location and size (scale) of the face. The major drawback of this approach is that it yields imprecise detections of the learned object, because a window of an non-centered face is more similar to the learned template than a window with background (say, a tree). An example of this result is shown in Fig. 6.7.

A solution to the above problem is to learn to discriminate between non-centered windows of the objects and well centered ones (Ding and Martinez 2010). In this alternative, a non-linear classifier (or some density estimator) is employed to discriminate the region of the feature space defining well-centered windows of the objects and non-centered ones. We call these non-centered windows the context of the object, in the sense that these windows provide the information typically found around the object but do not correspond to the actual face. This features versus context idea is illustrated in Fig. 6.8. This approach can be used to precisely detect faces, eyes, mouth, or any other facial feature where there is a textural discrimination between it and its surroundings. Figure 6.9 shows some sample results of accurate detection of faces and facial features with this approach.

The same features versus context idea can be applied to other detection and modeling algorithms, such as Active Appearance Models (AAM) (Cootes et al. 2001). AAM use a linear model—usually based on Principal Component Analysis (PCA)—to learn the relationship between the shape of an object (e.g., a face) and its texture. One obvious limitation is that the learned model is linear. A solution to this problem is to employ a kernel map. Kernel PCA is one option. Once we have introduced a kernel we can move one step further and use it to address additional issues of

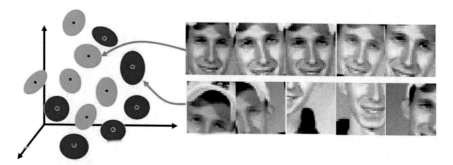

Fig. 6.8 The idea behind the features versus context approach is to learn to discriminate between the feature we wish to detect (e.g., a face, an eye, etc.) and poorly detected versions of it. This approach eliminates the classical overlapping of multiple detections around the object of interest at multiple scales. At the same time, it increases the accuracy of the detection because we are moving away from poor detections and toward precise ones

Fig. 6.9 Precise detections of faces and facial features using the algorithm of Ding and Martinez (2010)

interest. A first capability we may like to add to a AAM is the possibility to work with three-dimensions. The second could be to omit the least-squares iterative nature of the Procrustes alignment required in most statistical shape analysis methods such as AAM. An approach that successfully addresses these problem uses a set of kernels called Rotation Invariant Kernels (RIK) (Hamsici and Martinez 2009a). RIK add yet another important advantage to shape analysis: they provide rotation invariance. Thus, once the shape is been mapped to the RIK space, objects (e.g., faces) are invariant to translation, scale and rotation. These kernels are thus very attractive for the design of AAM algorithms (Hamsici and Martinez 2009b).

By now we know that humans are very sensitive to small changes. But we do not yet know how sensitive (or accurate). Of course, it is impossible to be pixel accurate when marking the boundaries of each facial feature, because edges blur over several pixels. This can be readily observed by zooming in the corner of an eye. To estimate the accuracy of human subjects, we performed the following experiment. First, we designed a system that allows users to zoom in at any specified location to facilitate delineation of each of the facial features manually. Second, we asked three people (herein referred to as judges) to manually delineate each of the facial components of close to 4, 000 images of faces. Third, we compared the markings of each of the three judges. The within-judge variability was (on average) 3.8 pixels, corresponding to a percentage of error of 1.2% in terms of the size of the face. This gives us an estimate of the accuracy of the manual detections. The average error of the algorithm of

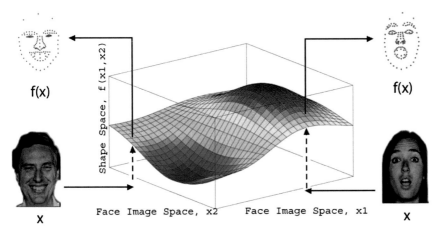

Fig. 6.10 Manifold learning is ideal for learning mappings between face (object) images and their shape description vectors

Ding and Martinez (2010) is 7.3 pixels (or 2.3%), very accurate but still far short of what humans can achieve. Thus, further research is needed to develop computer vision algorithms that can extract even more accurate detection of faces and its components.

Another problem is what happens when the resolution of the image diminishes. Humans are quite robust to these image manipulations (Du and Martinez 2011). One solution to this problem is to use manifold learning. In particular, we wish to define a non-linear mapping $f(.)$ between the image of a face and its shape. This is illustrated in Fig. 6.10. That is, given enough sample images and their shape feature vectors described in the preceding section, we need to find the function which relates the two. This can be done, for example, using kernel regression methods (Rivera and Martinez 2012). One of the advantages of this approach is that this function can be defined to detect shape from very low resolution images or even under occlusions. Occlusions can be "learned" by adding synthetic occlusions or missing data in the training samples but leaving the shape feature vector undisturbed (Martinez 2002). Example detections using this approach are shown in Fig. 6.11.

One can go one step further and recover the three-dimensional information when a video sequence is available (Gotardo and Martinez 2011a). Recent advances in non-rigid structure from motion allow us to recover very accurate reconstructions of both the shape and the motion even under occlusion. A recent approach resolves the nonlinearity of the problem using kernel mappings (Gotardo and Martinez 2011b).

Combining the two approaches to detection defined in this section should yield even more accurate results in low-resolution images and under occlusions or other image manipulations. We hope that more research will be devoted to this important topic in face recognition.

The approaches defined in this section are a good start, but much research is needed to make these systems comparable to human accuracies. We argue that research in

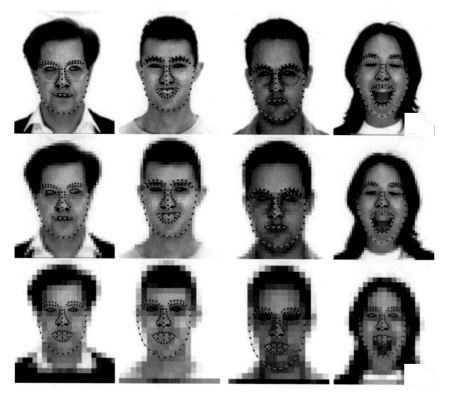

Fig. 6.11 Shape detection examples at different resolutions. Note how the shape estimation is almost as good regardless of the resolution of the image

machine learning should address these problems rather than the typical classification one. A first goal is to define algorithms that can detect face landmarks very accurately even at low resolutions. Kernel methods and regression approaches are surely good solutions as illustrated above. But more targeted approaches are needed to define truly successful computational models of the perception of facial expressions of emotion.

6.6 Discussion

In the real world, occlusions and unavoidable imprecise detections of the fiducial points, among others, are known to affect recognition (Torre and Cohn 2011; Martinez 2003). Additionally, some expressions are, by definition, ambiguous. Most importantly though seems to be the fact that people are not very good at recognizing facial expressions of emotion even under favorable condition (Du and Martinez 2011). Humans are very robust at detection joy and surprise from images of faces;

regardless of the image conditions or resolution. However, we are not as good at recognizing anger and sadness and are worst at fear and disgust.

The above results suggest that there could be three groups of expressions of emotion. The first group is intended for conveying emotions to observers. These expressions have evolved a facial construct (i.e., facial muscle positions) that is distinctive and readily detected by an observer at short or large distances. Example expressions in this group are happiness and surprise. A computer vision system—especially a HCI—should make sure these expressions are accurately and robustly recognized across image degradation. Therefore, we believe that work needs to be dedicated to make systems very robust when recognizing these emotions.

The second group of expressions (e.g., anger and sadness) is reasonably recognized at close proximity only. A computer vision system should recognize these expressions in good quality images, but can be expected to fail as the image degrades due to resolution or other image manipulations. An interesting open question is to determine why this is the case and what can be learned about human cognition from such a result.

The third and final group of emotions constitutes those at which humans are not very good recognizers. This includes expressions such as fear and disgust. Early work (especially in evolutionary psychology) had assumed that recognition of fear was primal because it served as a necessary survival mechanism (LeDoux 2000). Recent studies have demonstrated much the contrary. Fear is generally poorly recognized by healthy human subjects (Smith and Schyns 2009; Du and Martinez 2011). One hypothesis is that expressions in this group have evolved for other than communication reasons. For example, it has been proposed that fear opens sensory channels (i.e., breathing in and wide open eye), while disgust closes them (i.e., breathing out and closed eyes) (Susskind et al. 2008). Under this model, the receiver has learned to identify those face configurations to some extent, but without the involvement of the sender—modifying the expression to maximize transmission of information through a noisy environment—the recognition of these emotions has remained poor. Note that people can be trained to detect such changes quite reliably (Ekman and Rosenberg 2005), but this is not the case for the general population.

Another area that will require additional research is to exploit other types of facial expressions. Facial expressions are regularly used by people in a variety of setting. More research is needed to understand these. Moreover, it will be important to test the model in natural occurring environments. Collection and handling of this data poses several challenges, but the research described in these pages serves as a good starting point for such studies. In such cases, it may be necessary to go beyond a linear combination of basic categories. However, without empirical proof for the need of something more complex than linear combinations of basic emotion categories, such extensions are unlikely. The cognitive system has generally evolved the simplest possible algorithms for the analysis or processing of data. Strong evidence of more complex models would need to be collected to justify such extensions. One way to do this is by finding examples that cannot be parsed by the current model, suggesting a more complex structure is needed.

It is important to note that these results will have many applications in studies of agnosias and disorders. Of particular interest are studies of depression or anxiety disorders. Depression afflicts a large number of people in the developed countries. Models that can help us better understand its cognitive processes, behaviors and patterns could be of great importance for the design of coping mechanisms. Improvements may also be possible if it were to better understand how facial expressions of emotion affect these people. Other syndromes such as autism are also of great importance these days. More children than ever are being diagnosed with the disorder (CDC 2012; Prior 2003). We know that autistic children do not perceive facial expressions of emotion as others do (Jemel et al. 2006) (but see Castelli 2005). A modified computational model of the perception of facial expressions of emotion in autism could help design better teaching tools for this group and may bring us closer to understanding the syndrome.

There are indeed many great possibilities for machine learning researchers to help move these studies forward. Extending or modifying the modeled summarized in the present paper is one way. Developing machine learning algorithms to detect face landmark more accurately is another. Developing statistical tools that more accurately represent the underlying manifold or distribution of the data is yet another great way to move the state of the art forward.

6.7 Conclusions

In the present work we have summarized the development of a model of the perception of facial expressions of emotion by humans. A key idea in this model is to linearly combine a set of face spaces defining some basic emotion categories. The model is consistent with our current understanding of human perception and can be successfully exploited to achieve great recognition results for computer vision and HCI applications. We have shown how, to be consistent with the literature, the dimensions of these computational spaces need to encode configural and shape features.

We conclude that to move the state of the art forward, face recognition research has to focus on a topic that has received little attention in recent years—precise, detailed detection of faces and facial features. Although we have focused our study on the recognition of facial expressions of emotion, we believe that the results apply to most face recognition tasks. We have listed a variety of ways in which the machine learning community can get involved in this research project and briefly discussed applications in the study of human perception and the better understanding of disorders.

Acknowledgements This research was supported in part by the National Institutes of Health, Grants R01 EY 020834 and R21 DC 011081.

References

J.C. Barlett, J. Searcy, Inversion and configuration of faces. Cogn. Psychol. **25**(3), 281–316 (1993)

J.M. Beale, F.C. Keil, Categorical effects in the perception of faces. Cognition **57**, 217–239 (1995)

R. Brunelli, T. Poggio, Face recognition: features versus templates. IEEE Trans. Pattern Anal. Mach. Intell. **15**(10), 1042–1052 (1993)

A.J. Calder, A.W. Young, D. Rowland, D.I. Perrett, Computer-enhanced emotion in facial expressions. Proc. R. Soc. Lond. B **264**, 919–925 (1997)

A.J. Calder, A.D. Lawrence, A.W. Young, Neuropsychology of fear and loathing. Nat. Rev. Neurosci. **2**, 352–363 (2001)

F. Castelli, Understanding emotions from standardized facial expressions in autism and normal development. Autism **9**, 428–449 (2005)

CDC (Center for Disease Control and Prevention). Prevalence of autism spectrum disorders: autism and developmental disabilities monitoring network, 14 sites, united states, 2008. Morbidity and Mortality Weekly Report (MMWR), 61 (2012)

T.F. Cootes, G.J. Edwards, C.J. Taylor, Active appearance models. IEEE Trans. Pattern Anal. Mach. Intell. **23**(6), 681–685 (2001)

A.R. Damasio, *Descartes' Error: Emotion, Reason, and the Human Brain* (G. P. Putnam's Sons, New York, 1995)

C. Darwin, *The Expression of the Emotions in Man and Animal* (J. Murray, London, 1872)

L. Ding, A.M. Martinez, Features versus context: an approach for precise and detailed detection and delineation of faces and facial features. IEEE Trans. Pattern Anal. Mach. Intell. **32**, 2022–2038 (2010)

S. Du, A.M. Martinez, The resolution of facial expressions of emotion. J. Vis. **11**(13), 24 (2011)

P. Ekman, W.V. Friesen, *Pictures of Facial Affect* (Consulting Psychologists Press, Palo Alto, CA, 1976)

P. Ekman, E.L. Rosenberg, *What the Face Reveals: Basic and Applied Studies of Spontaneous Expression Using the Facial Action Coding System (FACS)*, 2nd edn. (Oxford University Press, New York, 2005)

P.F.U. Gotardo, A.M. Martinez, Computing smooth time-trajectories for camera and deformable shape in structure from motion with occlusion. IEEE Trans. Pattern Anal. Mach. Intell. **33**(10), 2051–2065 (2011a)

P.F.U. Gotardo, A.M. Martinez, Kernel non-rigid structure from motion, in *Proceedings of the IEEE International Conference on Computer Vision* (2011b)

O.C. Hamsici, A.M. Martinez. Bayes optimality in linear discriminant analysis. IEEE Trans. Pattern Anal. Mach. Intell. **30**, 647–657 (2008)

O.C. Hamsici, A.M. Martinez. Rotation invariant kernels and their application to shape analysis. IEEE Trans. Pattern Anal. Mach. Intell. **31**, 1985–1999 (2009a)

O.C. Hamsici, A.M. Martinez, Active appearance models with rotation invariant kernels, in *IEEE Proceedings of International Conference on Computer Vision* (2009b)

J.A. Hosie, H.D. Ellis, N.D. Haig, The effect of feature displacement on the perception of well-known faces. Perception **17**(4), 461–474 (1988)

C.E. Izard, Emotion theory and research: highlights, unanswered questions, and emerging issues. Annu. Rev. Psychol. **60**, 1–25 (2009)

B. Jemel, L. Mottron, M. Dawson, Impaired face processing in autism: fact or artifact? J. Autism Dev. Disord. **36**, 91–106 (2006)

T. Kanade, *Picture Processing System by Computer Complex and Recognition of Human Faces*, Ph.D. thesis, Kyoto University, November, 1973

N. Lawrence, Probabilistic non-linear principal component analysis with Gaussian process latent variable models. J. Mach. Learn. Res. **6**, 1783–1816 (2005)

J.E. LeDoux, Emotion circuits in the brain. Annu. Rev. Nuerosci. **23**, 155–184 (2000)

D. Lowe, Three-dimensional object recognition from single two-dimensional images. Artif. Intell. **31**(3), 355–395 (1983)

D. Marr, Early processing of visual information. Philos. Trans. R. Soc. Lond. **275**(942), 483–519 (1976)

A.M. Martinez, Recognizing imprecisely localized, partially occluded and expression variant faces from a single sample per class. IEEE Trans. Pattern Anal. Mach. Intell. **24**(6), 748–763 (2002)

A.M. Martinez, Matching expression variant faces. Vis. Res. **43**, 1047–1060 (2003)

A.M. Martinez, Deciphering the face, in *Proceedings of IEEE Conference on Computer Vision and Pattern Recognition, Workshop*, 2011

M. Minsky, *The Society of Mind* (Simon & Schuster, New York, 1988)

D. Neth, A.M. Martinez, Emotion perception in emotionless face images suggests a norm-based representation. J. Vis. **9**(1), 1–11 (2009)

D. Neth, A.M. Martinez, A computational shape-based model of anger and sadness justifies a configural representation of faces. Vis. Res. **50**, 1693–1711 (2010)

A. Pentland, Looking at people: sensing for ubiquitous and wearable computing. IEEE Trans. Pattern Anal. Mach. Intell. **22**(1), 107–119 (2000)

M. Prior, Is there an increase in the prevalence of autism spectrum disorders? J. Paediatr. Child Health **39**, 81–82 (2003)

G. Rhodes, S. Brennan, S. Carey, Identification and ratings of caricatures: implications for mental representations of faces. Cogn. Psychol. **19**, 473–497 (1987)

S. Rivera, A.M. Martinez, Learning shape manifolds. Pattern Recognit. **45**(4), 1792–1801 (2012)

E.T. Rolls, A theory of emotion, and its application to understanding the neural basis of emotion. Cogn. Emot. **4**, 161–190 (1990)

J.A. Russell, A circumplex model of affect. J. Pers. Social. Psych. **39**, 1161–1178 (1980)

J.A. Russell, Core affect and the psychological construction of emotion. Psychol. Rev. **110**, 145–172 (2003)

K.L. Schmidt, J.F. Cohn, Human facial expressions as adaptations: evolutionary questions in facial expression. Yearb. Phys. Anthropol. **44**, 3–24 (2001)

L. Sirovich, M. Kirby, Low-dimensional procedure for the characterization of human faces. J. Opt. Soc. Am. A **4**, 519–524 (1987)

F.W. Smith, P.G. Schyns, Smile through your fear and sadness: transmitting and identifying facial expression signals over a range of viewing distances. Psychol. Sci. **20**(10), 1202–1208 (2009)

J. Susskind, D. Lee, A. Cusi, R. Feinman, W. Grabski, A.K. Anderson, Expressing fear enhances sensory acquisition. Nat. Neurosci. **11**(7), 843–850 (2008)

J.M. Susskind, G. Littlewort, M.S. Bartlett, A.K. Anderson J. Movellanb, Human and computer recognition of facial expressions of emotion. Neuropsychologia **45**, 152–162 (2007)

F.D. Torre, J.F. Cohn, Facial expression analysis, in *Guide to Visual Analysis of Humans: Looking at People*, ed. by Th. B. Moeslund, A. Hilton, V. Kruger, L. Sigal (Springer, New York, 2011), pp. 377–410

M. Turk, A. Pentland, Eigenfaces for recognition. J. Cogn. Neurosci. **3**, 71–86 (1991)

T. Valentine, A unified account of the effects of distinctiveness, inversion, and race in face recognition. Q. J. Exp. Psychol. A **43**, 161–204 (1991)

V. Vapnik, *Statistical Learning Theory* (Wiley, New York, 1998)

D.A. Wilbraham, J.C. Christensen, A.M. Martinez, J.T. Todd, Can low level image differences account for the ability of human observers to discriminate facial identity? J. Vis. **8**(5), 1–12 (2008)

R.B. Wilbur, Nonmanuals, semantic operators, domain marking, and the solution to two outstanding puzzles in asl, in *Nonmanuals in Sign Languages* (John Benjamins, 2011)

M.-H. Yang, D. J. Kriegman, N. Ahuja, Detecting faces in images: a survey. IEEE Trans. Pattern Anal. Mach. Intell. **24**(1), 34–58 (2002)

A.W. Young, D. Hellawell, D.C. Hay, Configurational information in face perception. Perception **16**(6), 747–759 (1987)

L.A. Zebrowitz, M. Kikuchi, J.M. Fellous, Facial resemblance to emotions: group differences, impression effects, and race stereotypes. J. Pers. Soc. Psychol. **98**(2), 175–189 (2010)

Chapter 7
Finding Recurrent Patterns from Continuous Sign Language Sentences for Automated Extraction of Signs

Sunita Nayak, Kester Duncan, Sudeep Sarkar and Barbara Loeding

Abstract We present a probabilistic framework to automatically learn models of recurring signs from multiple sign language video sequences containing the vocabulary of interest. We extract the parts of the signs that are present in most occurrences of the sign in context and are robust to the variations produced by adjacent signs. Each sentence video is first transformed into a multidimensional time series representation, capturing the motion and shape aspects of the sign. Skin color blobs are extracted from frames of color video sequences, and a probabilistic relational distribution is formed for each frame using the contour and edge pixels from the skin blobs. Each sentence is represented as a trajectory in a low dimensional space called the space of relational distributions. Given these time series trajectories, we extract signemes from multiple sentences concurrently using iterated conditional modes (ICM). We show results by learning single signs from a collection of sentences with one common pervading sign, multiple signs from a collection of sentences with more than one common sign, and single signs from a mixed collection of sentences. The extracted signemes demonstrate that our approach is robust to some extent to the variations produced within a sign due to different contexts. We also show results whereby these learned sign models are used for spotting signs in test sequences.

Editors: Isabelle Guyon

S. Nayak (✉)
Taaz Inc., 4250 Executive Square, Suite 420, La Jolla, CA 92037, USA
e-mail: snayak@taaz.com

K. Duncan · S. Sarkar
Department of Computer Science & Engineering, University of South Florida,
Tampa, FL 33620, USA
e-mail: kkduncan@cse.usf.edu
S. Sarkar
e-mail: sarkar@cse.usf.edu

B. Loeding
Department of Special Education, University of South Florida, Lakeland,
FL 33803, USA
e-mail: barbara@usf.edu

Keywords Pattern extraction · Sign language recognition · Signeme extraction · Sign modeling · Iterated conditional modes

7.1 Introduction

Sign language research in the computer vision community has primarily focused on improving recognition rates of signs either by improving the motion representation and similarity measures (Yang et al. 2002; Al-Jarrah and Halawani 2001; Athitsos et al. 2004; Cui and Weng 2000; Wang et al. 2007; Bauer and Hienz 2000) or by adding linguistic clues during the recognition process (Bowden et al. 2004; Derpanis et al. 2004). Ong and Ranganath (2005) presented a review of the automated sign language research and also highlighted one important issue in continuous sign language recognition. While signing a sentence, there exists transitions of the hands between two consecutive signs that do not belong to either sign. This is called movement epenthesis (Liddell and Johnson 1989). This needs to be dealt with first before dealing with any other phonological issues in sign language (Ong and Ranganath 2005). Most of the existing work in sign language assumes that the training signs are already available and often signs used in the training set are the isolated signs with the boundaries chopped off, or manually selected frames from continuous sentences. The ability to recognize isolated signs does not guarantee the recognition of signs in continuous sentences. Unlike isolated signs, a sign in a continuous sentence is strongly affected by its context in the sentence. Figure 7.1 shows two sentences 'I BUY TICKET WHERE?' and 'YOU CAN BUY THIS FOR HER' with a common sign 'BUY' between them. The frames representing the sign 'BUY' and the neighboring signs are marked. The unmarked frames between the signs indicate the frames corresponding to movement epenthesis. It can be observed that the same sign 'BUY' is preceded and succeeded by movement epenthesis that depends on the end and start of the preceding and succeeding sign respectively. The movement epenthesis also affects how the sign is signed. This effect makes the automated extraction, modeling and recognition of signs from continuous sentences more difficult when compared to just plain gestures, isolated signs, or finger spelling.

In this paper, we address the problem of automatically extracting the part of a sign that is most common in all occurrences of the sign, and hence expected to be robust with respect to the variation of adjacent signs. These common parts can be used for spotting or recognition of signs in continuous sign language sentences. They can also be used by sign language experts for teaching or studying variations between instances of signs in continuous sign language sentences, or in automated sign language tutoring systems. Furthermore, they can be used even in the process of translating sign language videos directly to spoken words.

In a related work inspired by the success of the use of phonemes in speech recognition, the authors sought to extract common parts in different instances of a sign

(a) Continuous Sentence 'I BUY TICKET WHERE?'

(b) Continuous Sentence 'YOU CAN BUY THIS FOR HER'

Fig. 7.1 Movement epenthesis in sign language sentences. Frames corresponding to the common sign 'BUY' are marked in *red*. Signs adjacent to BUY are marked in *magenta*. Frames between marked frames represent movement epenthesis that is, the transition between signs. Note that the sign itself is also affected by having different signs preceding or following it

and thus arrive at a phoneme-analogue for signs (Bauer and Kraiss 2002). But unlike speech, sign language does not have a completely defined set of phonemes. Hence, we consider extracting commonalities at the sentence and sub-sentence level.

A different but a closely related problem is the extraction of common subsequences, also called motifs, from very long multiple gene sequences in biology (Bailey and Elkan 1995; Lawrence et al. 1993; Pevzner and Sze 2000; Rigoutsos and Floratos 1998). Lawrence et al. (1993) used a Gibbs sampling approach based on discrete matches or mismatches of subsequences that were strings of symbols of gene sequences. Bailey and Elkan (1995) used expectation maximization to find common subsequences in univariate biopolymer sequences. In biology, researchers deal with univariate discrete sequences, and hence their algorithms are not always directly applicable to other multivariate continuous domains in time series like speech or sign language. Some researchers tried to symbolize a continuous time series into discrete sequences and used existing algorithms from bioinformatics. For example, Chiu et al. (2003) symbolized the time series into a sequence of symbols using local approximations and used random projections to extract common subsequences in noisy data.

Tanaka et al. (2005) extended their work by performing principal component analysis on the multivariate time series data and projected them onto a single dimension and symbolized the data into discrete sequences. However, it is not always possible to get all the important information in the first principal component alone. Further extending his work, Duchene et al. (2007) find recurrent patterns from multivariate discrete data using time series random projections.

Due to the inherent continuous nature of many time series data like gesture and speech, new methods were developed that do not require approximating the data to a sequence of discrete symbols. Denton (2005) used a continuous random-walk noise model to cluster similar substrings. Nayak et al. (2005) and Minnen et al. (2007) use continuous multivariate sequences and dynamic time warping to find distances between the substrings. Oates (2002), Nayak et al. (2005, 2009a) are among the few works in finding recurrent patterns that address non-uniform sampling of time series. The recurrent pattern extraction approach proposed in this paper is based on multivariate continuous time series, uses dynamic time warping to find distances between substrings, and handles length variations of common patterns.

Following the success of Hidden Markov Models (HMMs) in speech recognition, they were used by sign language researchers (Vogler and Metaxas 1999; Starner and Pentland 1997; Bowden et al. 2004; Bauer and Hienz 2000; Starner et al. 1998) for representing and recognizing signs. However, HMMs require a large number of training data and unlike speech, data from native signers is not as easily available as speech data. Hence, non-HMM-based approaches have been used (Farhadi et al. 2007; Nayak et al. 2009a; Yang et al. 2010; Buehler et al. 2009; Nayak et al. 2009b; Oszust and Wysocki 2010; Han et al. 2009). In this paper, we use a continuous trajectory representation of signs in a multidimensional space and use dynamic time warping to match subsequences. The relative configuration of the two hands and face in each frame is represented by a relational distribution (Vega and Sarkar 2003; Nayak et al. 2005), which in itself is a probability density function. The motion dynamics of the signer is captured as changes in the relational distributions. It also allows us to interpolate motion, if required, for data sets with lower frame capture rates. It should also be noted that, unlike many of the previous works in sign language that perform tracking of the hands using 3D magnetic trackers or color gloves (Fang et al. 2004; Vogler and Metaxas 2001; Wang et al. 2002; Ma et al. 2000; Cooper and Bowden 2009), our representation does not require tracking and relies on skin segmentation.

We present a Bayesian framework to extract the common subsequences or signemes from all the given sentences simultaneously. Figure 7.2 depicts the overview of our approach. With this framework, we can extract the first most common sign, the second most common sign, the third most common sign and so on. We represent each sentence as a trajectory in a multi-dimensional space that implicitly captures the shape and motion in the video. Skin color blobs are extracted from frames of color video, and a relational distribution is formed for each frame using the edge pixels in the skin blobs. Each sentence is then represented as a trajectory in a low dimensional space called the space of relational distributions, which is arrived at by performing principal component analysis (PCA) on the relational distributions.

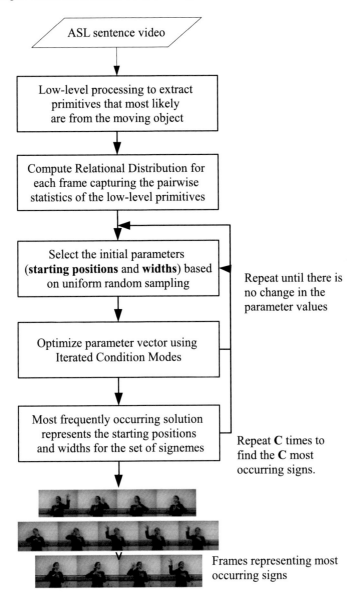

Fig. 7.2 Overview of our approach. Each of the *n* sentences is represented as a sequence in the Space of Relational Distributions, and common patterns are extracted using iterated conditional modes (ICM). The parameter set $\{a_1, w_1, \ldots, a_n, w_n\}$ is initialized using uniform random sampling and the conditional density corresponding to each sentence is updated in a sequential manner

There are other alternatives to PCA that are possible and discussed in Nayak et al. (2009b). The other choices do not change the nature of the signeme finding approach, they only affect the quality of the features. The starting locations $(a_1, \ldots, a_n)$ and widths $(w_1, \ldots w_n)$ of the candidate signemes in all the n sentences are together represented by a parameter vector. The starting locations are initialized with random starting locations, based on uniform random sampling from each sentence, and the initial width values are randomly selected from a given range of values. The parameter vector is updated sequentially by sampling the starting point and width of the possible signeme in each sentence from a joint conditional distribution that is based on the locations and widths of the target possible signeme in all other sentences. The process is iterated till the parameter values converge to a stable solution. Monte Carlo approaches like Gibbs sampling (Robert and Casella 2004; Gilks et al. 1998; Casella and George 1992), which is a special case of the Metropolis-Hastings algorithm (Chib and Greenberg 1995) can be used for global optimization while updating the parameter vector by performing importance sampling on the conditional probability distribution. However, this has a high burn-in period.

In this paper, we adopt a greedy approach based on the use of iterated conditional modes (ICM) (Besag 1986). ICM converges much faster than a Gibbs sampler, but is known to be largely dependent on the initialization. We overcome this limitation by performing ICM a number of times equal to the average length of the n sentences, with different initializations. The most frequently occurring solution from all the ICM runs is considered as the final solution.

The work in this paper builds on the work of Nayak et al. (2009a) and is different in multiple respects. We propose a system that is generalized to extract more than one common sign from a collection of sentences (first most common sign, second most common sign and so on), whereas in the previous work, only single signs were extracted. We also extract single signs from a mixed collection of sentences where there are more than one common sign in context. In addition to this, we present a more in-depth exposition of the underlying theory.

The contributions of this paper can be summarized as follows: (i) we present an unsupervised approach to automatically extract parts of signs that are robust to the variation of adjacent signs simultaneously from multiple sign language sentences, (ii) our approach does not consider all possible parameter combinations, instead samples each of them in a sequential manner until convergence, which saves a lot of computation, (iii) we show results on extracting signs from plain color videos of continuous sign language sentences without using any color gloves or magnetic trackers, and (iv) we show results whereby the learned signs are used for spotting signs in test sequences.

We organize the paper as follows. Section 7.2 presents a short review of relational distributions. In Sect. 7.3, we present the definition of signeme and then formulate the problem of finding signemes from a given set of sequences in a probabilistic framework. We describe how we solve it using iterated conditional modes. It is then followed by a description of our experiments and results in Sect. 7.4. Finally, Sect. 7.5 concludes the paper and discusses possible future work.

7.2 Relational Distributions

We use relational distributions to capture the global and relative configuration of the hands and the face in an image. Motion is then captured as the changes in the relational distributions. They were originally introduced by Vega and Sarkar (2003) for human gait recognition. They have also been used before for representing sign language sentences without the use of color gloves or magnetic trackers (Nayak et al. 2005, 2009b). We briefly review them here in this section.

How do we capture the global configuration of the object? We start with low-level primitives that are most likely to come from the articulated object. The exact nature of the low-level primitives can vary. Some common choices include edges, salient points, Gabor filter outputs and so on. We use edges in this work. We start from some level of segmentation of the object from the scene. These processes are fairly standard and have been used widely in gesture and sign recognition. They may involve color-based segmentation, skin-color segmentation, or background subtraction. In this work, we perform skin-color segmentation using histogram-based Bayesian classification (Phung et al. 2005). We use the contours of the skin blobs and Canny edges within the blobs as our low-level image primitives. The global configuration is captured by considering the relationships between these primitives.

We use the distance between two primitives in the vertical and horizontal directions (dx, dy) as relational attributes. Let vector $\mathbf{u} = \{dx, dy\}$ represent the vector of relational attributes. The joint probability function $P(\mathbf{u})$ then describes the distribution of primitives within an image and captures the shape of the pattern in the image. This probability is called a *relational distribution*. It captures the global configuration of the low-level primitives. Figure 7.3c illustrates how motion is captured using relational distributions. It shows the top view of the distributions. The region near to center represents points closer to each other, for example, the edge points within the face or within the hand, while farther from center represents the farther away points, for example, the relationship between edge points of a hand and the face. Notice the change in the relational distribution as the signer moves one of her hands. To be able to discriminate symmetrically opposite motion, we maintain the signs (or directions) of the horizontal and vertical distances between the edge pixels in each ordered pair. This leads to representing the probability distribution in a four quadrant system. Given that these relational distributions exhibit complicated shapes that are difficult to be modeled readily using a combination of simple shaped distributions such as Gaussian mixtures, we adopt non-parametric histogram-based representation. For better discrimination of the probabilities, we do not add counts to the center of the histogram which represents the distance of the edge pixels from itself or very close adjacent pixels. Each bin then counts the pairs of edge pixels between which the horizontal and vertical distances each lie in some fixed range that depends on the location of the bin in the histogram.

In our experiments, we found that an empirically-determined fixed histogram size of 51×51 was sufficient. The above range is then defined using linear mapping between the image size and the histogram size, for example, image size along the horizontal direction corresponds to half the histogram size in the horizontal direc-

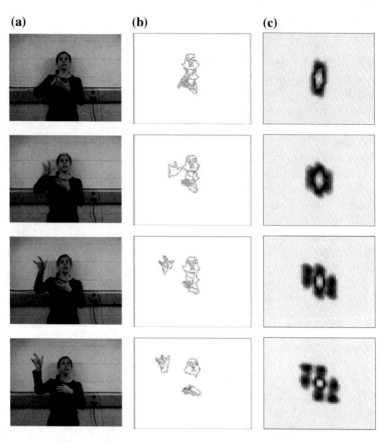

Fig. 7.3 Variations in relational distributions with motion. **a** Motion sequence. **b** Edge pixels from the skin color blobs. **c** Relational distributions constructed from the low level features (edge pixels) of the images in the motion sequence. The horizontal axis of the relational distribution represents the horizontal distance between the edge pixels and its vertical axis represents the vertical distance between edge pixels

tion. One could use histogram bin size optimization techniques for optimizing the histograms, but we do not address them in this paper. We then reduce the dimensionality of the relational distributions by performing PCA on the set of relational distributions from all the input sentences and retain the number of dimensions required to keep a certain percentage of energy, typically 95%. The new subspace arrived at is called the space of relational distributions (SoRD). Each video sequence is thus represented as a sequence of points in the SoRD space.

Note that the choice of the relational distribution is not a central requirement for the signeme learning process discussed in this paper. We use relational distributions to enable us to work with pure video data, without the use of markers or colored gloves. If magnetic markers or colored gloves are available then one could use their attributes to construct a different feature space and consider trajectories in them.

One advantage of our representation is that the face and head locations are implicitly taken into account in addition to the hands. In short, the first step of the process is to construct a time series representation in an appropriate feature space.

7.3 Problem Formulation

Sign language sentences are series of signs. Figure 7.4 illustrates the traces of the first versus second dimension in the feature space, of three sentences S_1, S_2 and S_3 with only one common sign, R, among them. The signeme represents the portion of the sign that is most similar across the sentences.

Table 7.1 defines the notations that will be used in this paper. We formulate the signeme extraction problem as finding the most recurring patterns among a set of n sentences $\{S_1, \ldots, S_n\}$, that have at least one common sign present in all the sentences.

The commonality concept underlying the definition of a signeme can be cast in terms of distances. Let $s_{a_i}^{w_i}$ represent a substring from the sequence S_i consisting of the points with indices $a_i, \ldots a_i + w_i - 1$, and $d(\mathbf{x}, \mathbf{y})$ denote the distance between two substrings $\mathbf{x}$ and $\mathbf{y}$ based on dynamic time warping. We define the set of signemes to be the set of substrings denoted by $\{s_{a_1}^{w_1}, \ldots, s_{a_n}^{w_n}\}$ that is most similar among all possible substrings from the given set of sentences. In the generalized case where C most common signs are sought, the set of signemes are defined as $\{s_{a_{11}}^{w_{11}}, s_{a_{12}}^{w_{11}}, \ldots, s_{a_{nC}}^{w_{nC}}\}$. In theory, C can extend to the number of words in the shortest sentence.

Let $\theta = \{a_1, w_1, \ldots a_n, w_n\}$ denote the parameter set representing a set of substrings, at least one from each of the n sentences, and θ_m denote the parameter set

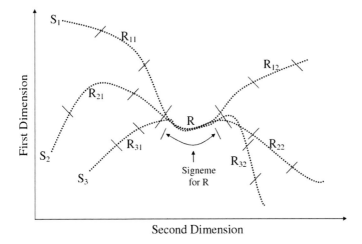

Fig. 7.4 Concept of signemes. First versus second dimensions of sentences S_1 with signs R_{11}, R, R_{12} in order, S_2 with signs R_{21}, R, R_{22} and S_3 with signs R_{31}, R, R_{32}. The common sign is R. The portion of R that is most similar across sentences is the signeme representative of R

Table 7.1 Notations

$\{S_1, \ldots, S_n\}$	Set of n sentences with at least one common sign present in all the sentences. The index within a sentence could represent time or arc length in configuration shape space
L_i	Length of sentence S_i
$s_{a_j}^{w_j}$	Subsequence of sentence S_j starting from index a_j to $a_j + w_j - 1$. We may sometimes use $s_{j,a}^{w}$ to make explicit the j-th index if it is not represented along with any other superscript or subscript of this term
A, B	Possible choices of width for signemes of a sign include all integers from A to B. The values of A and B are decided based on the dynamics involved in the sign
θ	Set of parameters $\{a_1, w_1, \ldots, a_n, w_n\}$ defining a set of substrings of the given sentences
$\theta_{(a_i)}$	Set of all parameters *excluding* the parameter a_i. We have similar interpretations for $\theta_{(w_i)}$ or $\theta_{(i)}$
$d(\mathbf{x}, \mathbf{y})$	Distance between the subsequences $\mathbf{x}$ and $\mathbf{y}$ based on a mapping found using dynamic time warping (DTW). This distance has to be calculated carefully so that it is not biased towards finding short subsequences only

representing the target set of signemes in the n sentences. We find θ_m using the probabilistic framework of Eq. 7.1.

$$\theta_m = \arg \max_{\theta} p(\theta) \tag{7.1}$$

Note that $p(\theta)$ is a probability over the space of all possible substrings. We define this probability to be a function of the inter-substring distances in Eq. 7.2:

$$p(\theta) = \frac{g(\theta)}{\sum_{\theta} g(\theta)}. \tag{7.2}$$

The term $g(\theta)$ is defined in Eq. 7.3 as follows:

$$g(\theta) = \exp \left(-\beta \sum_{i=1}^{n} \sum_{j=1}^{n} d(s_{a_i}^{w_i}, s_{a_j}^{w_j}) \right) \tag{7.3}$$

with β being a positive constant.

Note that $g(\theta)$ varies inversely with the summation of the pair-wise distances of all the subsequences given by θ. Also note that $p(\theta)$ is hard to compute or even sample from because it is computationally expensive to compute the denominator in Eq. 7.2, as it involves the summation over all possible parameter combinations. β acts as a scale parameter, which controls the slopes of the peaks in the probability space. It can also be looked upon as the smoothing parameter. If probability sampling algorithms like Gibbs sampling (Casella and George 1992) are used in later steps, then the rate of convergence would be determined by this parameter.

Let θ_i represent the parameters from the ith sentence, that is, $\{a_i, w_i\}$ and $\theta_{(i)}$ represent the rest of the parameters, $\{a_1, w_1 \ldots a_{i-1}, w_{i-1}, a_{i+1}, w_{i+1} \ldots a_n, w_n\}$. To make sampling easier, we construct a *conditional* density function of the parameters from each sentence, that is, θ_i, given the values of the rest of the parameters, that is, $\theta_{(i)}$. In other words, we construct a probability density function of the possible starting points and widths in each sentence, given the estimated starting points and widths of the common pattern in all other sentences, that is, $f(\theta_i|\theta_{(i)})$. Of course, this conditional density function has to be *derived* from the joint density function specified in Eq. 7.2. This is outlined in Eq. 7.4 as follows:

$$f(\theta_i|\theta_{(i)}) = \frac{p(\theta)}{p(\theta_{(i)})} = \frac{p(\theta)}{\sum_{\theta_i} p(\theta)} = \frac{g(\theta)}{\sum_{\theta_i} g(\theta)}. \tag{7.4}$$

Since the normalization to arrive at this conditional density function involves summation over one parameter, it is now easier to compute and sample from. The specific form for this conditional density function using the dynamic time warping (DTW) distances as described in Eq. 7.5 is

$$f(\theta_i|\theta_{(i)}) = \frac{\exp\left(-\beta \sum_{k=1}^{n} d(\mathbf{s}_{a_i}^{w_i}, \mathbf{s}_{a_k}^{w_k})\right)}{\sum_{\theta_i} \exp\left(-\beta \sum_{k=1}^{n} d(\mathbf{s}_{a_i}^{w_i}, \mathbf{s}_{a_k}^{w_k})\right)}. \tag{7.5}$$

Note that the distance terms that do not involve a_i and w_i, that is, do not involve the i-th sentence appear both in the numerator and the denominator and so cancel out. For notational convenience, this is sometimes represented using conditional g functions described below in Eq. 7.6 as:

$$f(\theta_i|\theta_{(i)}) = \frac{g(\theta_i|\theta_{(i)})}{\sum_{\theta_i} g(\theta_i|\theta_{(i)})}, \tag{7.6}$$

where $g(\theta_i|\theta_{(i)}) = \exp\left(-\beta \sum_{k=1}^{n} d(\mathbf{s}_{a_i}^{w_i}, \mathbf{s}_{a_k}^{w_k})\right)$.

7.3.1 Distance Measure

The distance function d in the above equations needs to be chosen carefully such that it is not biased towards the shorter subsequences. Here, we briefly describe how we compute the distance between two substrings using dynamic time warping. Let l_1 and l_2 represent the length of the two substrings and $e(i, j)$ represent the Euclidean distance between the ith data point from the first substring and the jth data point from the second substring. Let D represent the score matrix of size $(l_1 + 1) \times (l_2 + 1)$. The 0th row and 0th column of D are initialized to infinity, except $D(0, 0)$, which is initialized to 0. The rest of the score matrix, D, is completed using the following recursion of Eq. 7.7:

$$D(i, j) = e(i, j) + \min\{D(i-1, j), D(i-1, j-1), D(i, j-1)\}, \qquad (7.7)$$

where $1 \leq i \leq l_1$ and $1 \leq j \leq l_2$. The optimal warp path is then traced back from $D(l_1, l_2)$ to $D(0, 0)$. The distance measure between the two substrings is then given by $D(l_1, l_2)$ normalized by the length of the optimal warping path.

7.3.2 Parameter Estimation

In order to extract the common signs from a given set of sign language sentences, we need to compute θ_i for each of the sentences sequentially. Gibbs sampling (Casella and George 1992) is a Markov Chain Monte Carlo approach (Gilks et al. 1998) that allows us to sample the conditional probability density $f(\theta_i | \theta_{(i)})$ for all the sequences sequentially and then iterate the whole process until convergence. Gibbs sampling results in a global optimum, but its convergence is very slow. The burn-in period is typically thousands of iterations. Therefore, we perform the optimization using iterated conditional modes (ICM), first proposed by Besag (1986). ICM has much faster convergence, but it is also known to be heavily dependent on the initialization. We address this limitation by running the optimization multiple times with different initializations and choosing the most frequently occurring solution as the final solution.

Algorithm 1: Iterated Conditional Modes($\{a_1^0, w_1^0, \ldots, a_n^0, w_n^0\}$)

---

comment: Choose $\{a_1, w_1, \ldots, a_n, w_n\}$ that maximizes distribution $p(a_1, w_1, \ldots, a_n, w_n)$

comment: Initialization:

$\theta_0 \leftarrow \{a_1^0, w_1^0, \ldots, a_n^0, w_n^0\}$

repeat

    for $i \leftarrow 0$ **to** n

        comment: Jointly sample a_i, w_i. L_i is the length of sequence S_i

        for $w_i \leftarrow A$ **to** B

        do $\begin{cases} \textbf{for } a_i \leftarrow 0 \textbf{ to } L_i - w_i + 1 \\ \quad \textbf{do } g(a_i, w_i | \theta_{(a_i, w_i)}) \leftarrow \exp\left(-\beta \sum_{k=1}^{n} d(s_{a_i}^{w_i}, s_{a_k}^{w_k})\right) \end{cases}$

    do   **comment:** Normalize

        for $w_i \leftarrow A$ **to** B

        do $\begin{cases} \textbf{for } a_i \leftarrow 0 \textbf{ to } L_i - w_i + 1 \\ \quad \textbf{do } f(a_i, w_i | \theta_{(a_i, w_i)}) \leftarrow \frac{g(a_i, w_i | \theta_{(a_i, w_i)})}{\sum_{a_i, w_i} g(a_i, w_i | \theta_{(a_i, w_i)})} \end{cases}$

        $a_i, w_i \leftarrow \text{ARG MAX}\, (f(a_i, w_i | \theta_{(a_i, w_i)}))$

until CHANGE IN PARAMETERS($\{a_1, w_1, \ldots, a_n, w_n\}$) $== 0$

Algorithm 1 outlines the process of ICM to extract the common patterns or signemes from a set of sentences with a given initial parameter vector. We aim to select the set of parameters that maximizes the probability $p(\theta)$ or $p(a_1, w_1, \ldots, a_n, w_n)$. We do that by estimating each of the parameters $a_1, w_1, \ldots a_n, w_n$ in a sequential manner. Since we expect the starting location and width of a subsequence representing the common sign to be strongly correlated, we estimate a_i and w_i jointly. First we compute $g(\theta_i | \theta_{(i)})$ that is, $g(a_i, w_i | \theta_{(a_i, w_i)})$ from which we compute the conditional density functions $f(\theta_i | \theta_{(i)})$ that is, $f(a_i, w_i | \theta_{(a_i, w_i)})$. Note that it involves a summation over a_i and w_i only, which involves much less computation than that required for computing $p(\theta)$ which involves a summation over $a_1, w_1, \ldots a_n, w_n$. The values for a_i and w_i are updated with those that maximize the conditional density $f(\theta_i | \theta_{(i)})$. The process is carried out sequentially for $i = 1$ to n, and then repeated iteratively till the values of the parameter vector $\{a_1, w_1, a_2, w_2, \ldots a_n, w_n\}$ do not change any more.

Figure 7.5 depicts the sampling process for a single iteration, r. Note the conditional and sequential nature of sampling from various sentences within the single iteration. In Fig. 7.6, we show an example of how the conditional probability $f(\theta_{a_i, w_i} | \theta_{(a_i, w_i)})$ changes for the first six sentences from a given set of fourteen video sentences containing a common sign 'DEPART'. The vertical axis in the probabilities represents the starting locations and the horizontal axis represents the possible widths. The brighter regions represent a higher probability value. Note that the probabilities are spread out in the first iteration for each sentence and it slowly converges to a fixed starting location for each of them. They remain more spread out across the horizontal (width) axis because we vary the width only in a small range of A to B for each sign, that is decided based on the amount of motion present in the sign.

Figure 7.7 plots the typical convergence of the parameter values in a single ICM run. It plots the norm of difference between consecutive parameter vectors versus the parameter vector update count, which is incremented each time a parameter is sampled or selected from the probability distribution $f(\theta_i | \theta_{(i)})$. It shows that ICM converges in less than $56/14 = 4$ iterations. This, in turn, also indicates the local nature of the optimization achieved with ICM. The initialization is very important in this case. In the next subsection, we describe how we address this problem.

7.3.3 Sampling Starting Points for ICM

In order to address the local convergence nature of ICM, we adopt a uniform random sampling-based approach. We start by randomly assigning values to the parameter vector θ. The width w_i^0 is obtained by sampling a width value based on uniform random distribution from the set of all possible widths in a given range $[A, B]$. The value for a_i^0 is obtained by sampling a starting point based on uniform random distribution from the set of all possible starting points in the ith sequence, that is, from the set $\{1 \ldots (L_i - w_i^0 + 1)\}$.

Fig. 7.5 Sequential update of the parameter values using ICM. **a–c** Respectively show the parameter updates in the first sentence, the ith and the nth sentences. In the rth iteration, the parameters of the common sign in ith sentence are computed based on the parameter values of the previous $(l-1)$ sentences obtained in the same iteration, and those of the $(i+1)$th to nth sentences obtained in the previous, that is, the $(r-1)$th iteration

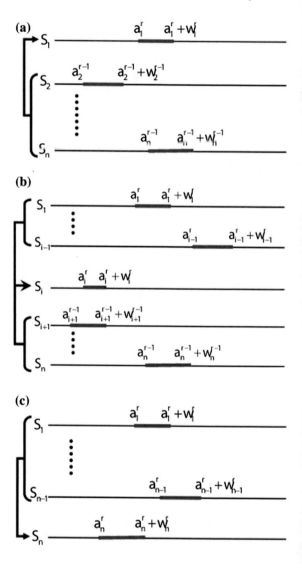

Different initial parameter vectors are obtained by independently sampling the sentences multiple times. ICM is run using each initial parameter vector generated and the most common solution is considered as the final solution. The uniform sampling of the frames in the sentences for selecting the starting locations ensures the whole parameter space is covered uniformly. The number of times we sample the initial parameter vector and run the ICM algorithm decides how densely we cover the whole parameter space. We run it the number of times equal to the average number

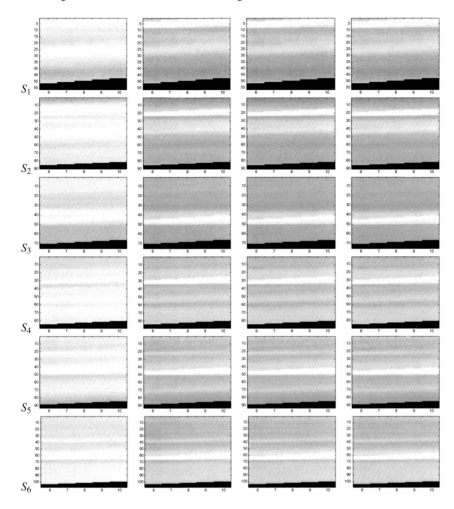

Fig. 7.6 Convergence of the conditional probability density $f(\theta_i|\theta_{(i)})$ for sentences $S_1 \ldots S_6$ from a given set of sentences $S_1 \ldots S_{14}$. The brighter regions represent a higher probability value. The vertical axis in the probabilities represents the starting locations and the horizontal axis represents the possible widths. Note that the probabilities are spread out in the first iteration and it slowly converges to a particular starting location. They are still spread across the horizontal (width) axis because we vary the width only in a small range that is decided based on the amount of motion present in the sign

of frames in each sentence from the given set of sentences for extracting the sign. One could choose to run a multiple of the average number of times as well, but we found the average number to be sufficient to show the stability of the solution in our experiments. Algorithm 2 presents the process as a pseudocode.

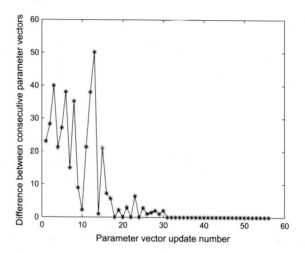

Fig. 7.7 Convergence of values of the parameter set. The above plot shows the norm of the difference between two consecutive parameter vectors representing the set of starting points and widths of the common subsequence in the given set of sequences. It shows the typical convergence with a given initialization vector. ICM is repeated with multiple initializations and the most frequently occurring solution is considered as the final solution

---

Algorithm 2: Extract Signemes($L_1, \ldots L_n, A, B$)

---

comment: Generate multiple initialization vectors and call ICM with each of them.

$N = \text{MEAN}(L_1, L_2, \ldots, L_n)$

for $j \leftarrow 1$ **to** N

$\text{do} \begin{cases} \textbf{for } i \leftarrow 1 \textbf{ to } n \\ \quad \text{do} \begin{cases} w_i^0 = \text{UNIFORM}(A \ldots B) \\ a_i^0 = \text{UNIFORM}(1 \ldots L_i - w_i^0 + 1) \end{cases} \\ \{a_1^j, w_1^j, \ldots, a_n^j, w_n^j\} = \text{ITERATED CONDITIONAL MODES}(a_1^0, w_1^0, \\ \ldots, a_n^0, w_n^0) \end{cases}$

for $i \leftarrow 1$ **to** n

$\text{do} \begin{cases} \textbf{comment: } \text{Assign most frequently occurring value as the final value.} \\ w_i = \text{MODE}(w_i^j) \\ a_i = \text{MODE}(a_i^j) \end{cases}$

For extracting the sign 'DEPART' from 14 sentences, we had 89 frames per sentence on an average. Hence we ran 89 different ICM runs for extracting the common subsequence representing 'DEPART'. Figure 7.8 shows the plots of histograms of start and end location of the sign in each of the 14 sentences from the 89 runs. It should be noted that in most of the sentences, more than 50% of the total number of runs result in the same solution.

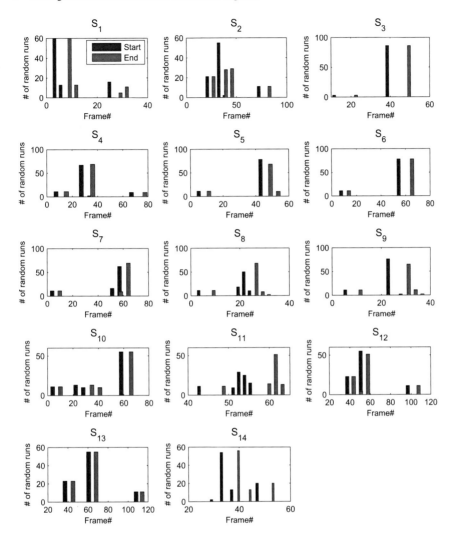

Fig. 7.8 Histograms showing the start and end locations of signs extracted from 14 different sentences using multiple ICM runs. The initial parameter vector for each ICM run was chosen independently using uniform random sampling. As it can be seen the start and end points found by most of the runs converge to the same solution (denoted by single high bars in most of sentences). The legend shown in the plot for the first sentence, S_1, holds for other sentences as well

7.4 Experiments and Results

In this section, we present visual and quantitative results of our approach for extracting signemes from video sequences representing sentences from American Sign Language. We first describe the data set used then present the results of the automatic common pattern extraction.

7.4.1   Data Set

Our data set consists of 155 American Sign Language (ASL) video sequences organized into 12 groups (collections) based on the vocabulary (word that pervades the sentences of the group). For instance, the 'DEPART' group is comprised of all the sentences containing the word 'DEPART', the 'PASSPORT' group is comprised of all the sentences containing the word 'PASSPORT' and so on. The breakdown of these 'pure' groups and the number of sentences (sequences) in each are as follows.

- DEPART - 14 sentences
- BAGGAGE - 14 sentences
- CANT - 14 sentences
- BUY - 11 sentences
- SECURITY - 16 sentences
- HAVE - 6 sentences
- MOVE - 11 sentences
- TIME - 14 sentences
- FUTURE - 12 sentences
- TABLE - 13 sentences
- PASSPORT - 14 sentences
- TICKET - 16 sentences

This data set was used to extract 12 common subsequences when we searched for the first most common sign, and 24 common subsequences when we searched for the second most common sign. We also organized the video sequences into 10 groups by combining two 'pure' groups of sentences as described above. This was used to investigate the power of our framework for selecting the common sequences in a 'mixed' collection. The breakdown of these 'mixed' groups and the number of sentences in each are as follows:

- DEPART (14 sentences) + BAGGAGE (14 sentences)
- CANT (14 sentences) + BUY (11 sentences)
- TIME (14 sentences) + TABLE (13 sentences)
- PASSPORT (14 sentences) + TICKET (16 sentences)
- SECURITY (16 sentences) + FUTURE (12 sentences)
- MOVE (11 sentences) + HAVE (6 sentences)
- BUY (11 sentences) + TABLE (13 sentences)
- DEPART (14 sentences) + FUTURE (12 sentences)
- BAGGAGE (14 sentences) + TICKET (16 sentences)
- SECURITY (16 sentences) + PASSPORT (14 sentences)

All of the signs were performed by the same signer with plain clothing and background. The video sequences were captured at 25 frames per second with a frame resolution of 490 × 370.

7.4.2 Common Pattern Extraction Results

In this section, we present the results of our method for extracting common patterns from sign language sentences. We first present results for extracting the single most common sign and multiple common signs from the 'pure' sentence groups, followed by results for the most common patterns from the 'mixed' groups.

7.4.2.1 Extracting the Most Common Pattern

We perform extraction of the most common patterns from the 'pure' sentence groups. We possess a priori knowledge of the most common word due to the organization of the sentence groups. However, our goal is to extract the most common sequences automatically. As an example, Fig. 7.9 depicts the result of extraction of the sign 'DEPART' from 14 video sequences. It plots the SoRD first dimension coefficients of the frames versus the frame number for each sentence. The highlighted portions represent the signeme. The odd columns show the ground truth and the even columns show the corresponding results. As can be seen, the extracted patterns and the corresponding ground truth patterns are quite similar, except for a few frames at the beginning and end of the some of the patterns. Note that since we deal with continuous video sequences, a difference of one or two frames between the ground truth and the extracted pattern is not considered a problem.

Figure 7.10a shows the scatter plot of the ground truth start positions versus the estimated start positions of the pattern extracted from each of the 155 sentences in the video data set. Figure 7.10b shows the corresponding scatter plot for the end position of the patterns in the sentences. As can be seen most of the points in the scatter plots lie along the diagonal. This indicates that very few of the extracted patterns are wrong. Incorrect results correspond to the points positioned far from the diagonal. Figures 7.11 and 7.12 show one instance of the signeme extracted from group of sentences.

7.4.2.2 Extracting Multiple Common Signs

In this section we present some visual results for the extraction of the two most common signs from the 'pure' groups of sentences. We focused on extracting only two signs because the shortest ASL sentence contained two signs. Figure 7.13 shows the results for the two most common signs extracted from the sentence 'BAGGAGE THERE NOT MINE THERE'. The extracted subsequences correspond to the ASL words 'BAGGAGE' and 'MINE'. Consequently, the word 'BAGGAGE' appears in all the 14 sentences of the group, whereas the word 'MINE' (or 'MY') shows up in 11 sentences coinciding with what was expected. Similarly, Fig. 7.14 shows the results for the two most common signs extracted from the sentence 'MY PASSPORT THERE STILL GOOD THERE'. The extracted subsequences correspond to the ASL

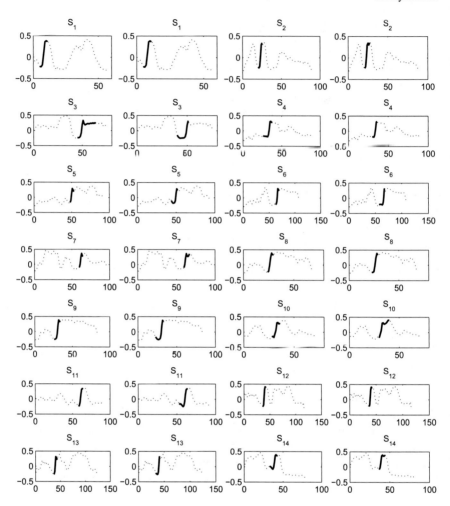

Fig. 7.9 The first dimension of the video sequences containing a common sign 'DEPART'. The sequences are indicated by the *dotted curves* and the *solid lines* on each of them indicate the common pattern or signeme. The odd columns represent the ground truth and the even columns show the results

words 'MY' and 'PASSPORT'. The word 'MY' appears in all the 11 sentences of the group, whereas the word 'PASSPORT' appears in all 14 sentences. These results are encouraging.

7.4.2.3 Extracting the Most Common Patterns from Mixed Sentences

We perform extraction of the most common patterns from the collection of 'mixed' sentences as outlined in Sect. 7.4.1. Figure 7.15a shows the scatter plot of the ground

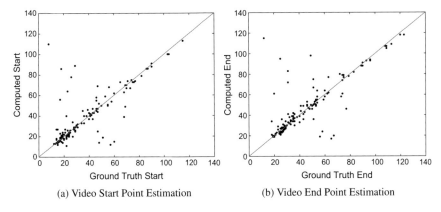

(a) Video Start Point Estimation   (b) Video End Point Estimation

Fig. 7.10 Extraction of the most common patterns or signemes from the 'pure' sentence groups. The closer the points are to the diagonal, the closer the result is to the ground truth

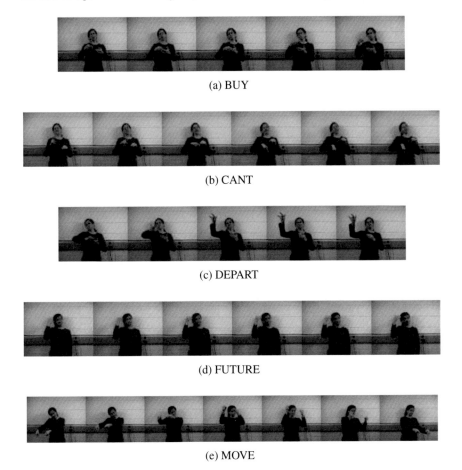

(a) BUY

(b) CANT

(c) DEPART

(d) FUTURE

(e) MOVE

Fig. 7.11 Signemes extracted from sentences

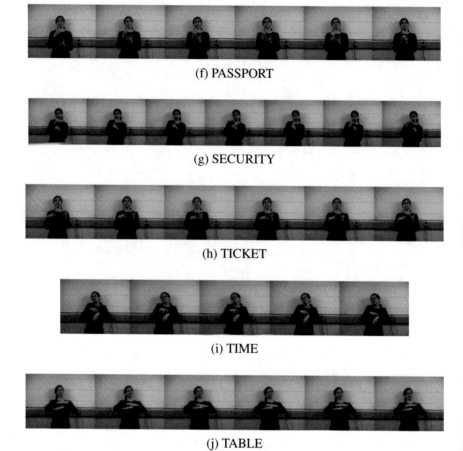

(f) PASSPORT

(g) SECURITY

(h) TICKET

(i) TIME

(j) TABLE

Fig. 7.12 Signemes extracted from sentences

truth start positions versus the estimated start positions of the pattern extracted from each of the sentences. Similarly, Fig. 7.15b shows the corresponding scatter plot for the end position of the patterns in the sentences. As can be seen, the points are more scattered as compared to the results shown in Fig. 7.10 where the sentences used were known to contain common words. However, this result is still encouraging. A large proportion of the extracted patterns are incorrect, but there are many relatively near the diagonal. This result demonstrates the robustness of our algorithm for finding similarities in the presence of great dissimilarity. We believe that the incorrect patterns extracted are due to the differences in the frame width ranges for the mixed sentence sets. For example, sentences containing the word 'MOVE' were combined with sentences containing the word 'HAVE'. The frame width range for the sign 'HAVE' is between 4 and 6 frames with 4 being the minimum width and 6 being the maximum width. On the other hand, the frame width range for the sign 'MOVE' is between

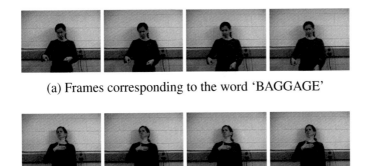

(a) Frames corresponding to the word 'BAGGAGE'

(b) Frames corresponding to the word 'MINE'

Fig. 7.13 Extraction of the two most common patterns or signemes from the sentence 'BAGGAGE THERE NOT MINE THERE'

(a) Frames corresponding to the word 'MY'

(b) Frames corresponding to the word 'PASSPORT'

Fig. 7.14 Extraction of the two most common patterns or signemes from the sentence 'MY PASSPORT THERE STILL GOOD THERE'

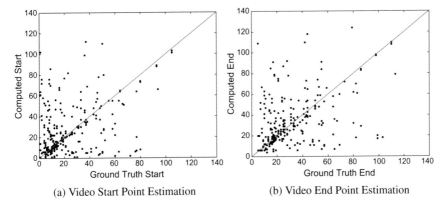

(a) Video Start Point Estimation

(b) Video End Point Estimation

Fig. 7.15 Extraction of the most common patterns or signemes from the 'mixed' sentence groups. The closer the points are to the diagonal, the closer the result is to the ground truth

19 and 27 frames. Combining these width ranges could be done using an average of the two or by selecting the minimum and maximum values between the two. However, these methods produced similar results. The correct combination of these range widths is a priority for future work.

7.4.3 Sign Localization

We used the extracted signemes to localize or spot signs in test sentences. The same process that is used for training sign models is used for sign localization. However, rather than randomly assigning initial parameter values, we use the parameters learned. We tested with 12 test sentences from the 'pure' group specified in Sect. 7.4.1 and their lengths varied from 4 to 12 signs. These test sentences were not used during training. The set of points representing the signeme were matched with the segments of the SoRD points from the test sentences to find the segment with the minimum matching score, which would represent the sign in the test sentence. The SoRD points of the signeme retrieved from the test sentence are mapped to their nearest frames and compared with the ground truth frame series representing the sign in the sentence. Localization performance is characterized as follows. Let a_1 and b_1 denote the start and end frame numbers of the underlying ground truth sign in the test sentence, and a_2 and b_2 denote the start and end frame numbers of the subsequence retrieved as the signeme for the test sentence. We calculate the precision and recall values of each test sentence as $\frac{m}{a_2-a_1+1}$ and $\frac{m}{b_2-a_2+1}$ respectively where m is the number of overlapping frames. Table 7.2 displays the results acquired. The 'Baggage', 'Cant', 'Have', and 'Table' test sequences were failure cases where there was no overlap between the extracted model frames and the localization frames (see Fig. 7.16). Notice that the localization results heavily depend on the extracted signeme models. For a visual representation of this information, we define the Start Offset, ΔS, and End Offset, ΔE, as $\Delta S = a_1 - a_2$ and $\Delta E = b_1 - b_2$. The plot of the Start Offset versus the End Offset is shown in Fig. 7.16. Ideally, both the offsets should be zero. The points for different signs are scattered in the four quadrants depending on the nature of the

Table 7.2 Localization performance

Test group	Precision	Recall
Buy	1.0	0.70
Depart	1.0	0.64
Future	0.71	0.756
Move	1.0	0.60
Passport	1.0	0.47
Security	0.57	0.67
Ticket	1.0	0.58
Time	0.63	1.0

Fig. 7.16 Start offset versus
end offset of localized signs

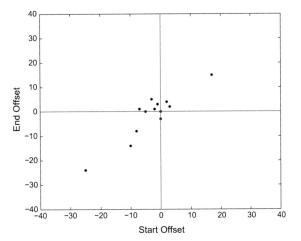

overlap between the ground truth sign and the retrieved signeme. Each point in the
plot corresponds to a separate test sign. Its distance from the origin indicates the
localizing quality of the signeme in its test sentence. The closer it is to the origin,
the better the quality.

7.5 Conclusion and Future Work

We presented a novel algorithm to extract signemes, that is, the common pattern
representing a sign, from multiple long video sequences of American Sign Language
(ASL). A signeme is a part of the sign that is robust to the variations of the adjacent
signs and the associated movement epenthesis. We first represent each sequence as
a series of points in a low dimensional space of relational distributions, and then use
a probabilistic framework to locate the signemes in each sequence concurrently. We
use iterative conditional modes (ICM) to sample the parameters, that is, the starting
location and width of the signemes in each sentence in a sequential manner. We show
results on ASL video sequences that do not involve using any magnetic trackers or
gloves for extracting the most common signs. The extracted signemes demonstrate
that our approach is robust to some extent to the variations produced within a sign
due to different contexts.

The approach in this paper can be used to speed up training set generation for
ASL algorithms by drastically reducing the manual aspect of the process. Rather
than manually demarcating signs in continuous sentences, which for our work took
an expert approximately 5 min, we would just need instances of sentences containing
the sign whose model is sought and based on our experiments this can be generated
in approximately 2 min. Another contribution of this work is an empirically derived
robust representation of the sign that is stable with respect to the variations due to

neighboring signs and sentence context. These stable representations could be useful for detection of signs and gestures in extended gesture sequences.

There are some ways we can advance the work in this paper. One issue is the precision of the features used for representing the video sequences. Relational distributions when used as fixed size histograms perform well for discriminating global motion. However, optimizing the bin size of the histograms to the required precision might improve the accuracy. Additionally, we plan to extend our work to address the challenge of handling the large variations encountered when automatically recognizing signemes across different signers. Also, the algorithm is dependent to a large extent on the distance measure and conventional dynamic time warping cannot deal with the amplitude variations in the signs, which are very common across signers. We plan to work on a variation of dynamic time warping that is robust to amplitude differences between various instances of signs.

Acknowledgements This work was supported in part by funds from University of South Florida's College of Engineering Interdisciplinary Scholarship Program and the National Science Foundation under ITR Grant IIS 0312993.

References

O. Al-Jarrah, A. Halawani, Recognition of gestures in Arabic Sign Language using neuro-fuzzy systems. Artif. Intell. **133**, 117–138 (2001)

V. Athitsos, J. Alon, S. Sclaroff, G. Kollios, Boostmap: a method for efficient approximate similarity rankings, in *IEEE Conference on Computer Vision and Pattern Recognition*, 2004, pp. 268–275

T. Bailey, C. Elkan, Unsupervised learning of multiple motifs in biopolymers using expectation maximization. Mach. Learn. **21**, 51–80 (1995)

B. Bauer, H. Hienz, Relevant features for video-based continuous sign language recognition, in *Automatic Face and Gesture Recognition*, 2000, pp. 440–445

B. Bauer, K.F. Kraiss, Video-based sign recognition using self-organizing subunits. Int. Conf. Pattern Recognit. **2**, 434–437 (2002)

J. Besag, On the statistical analysis of dirty pictures. J. R. Stat. Soc. **48**, 259–302 (1986)

R. Bowden, D. Windridge, T. Kadir, A. Zisserman, M. Brady, A linguistic feature vector for the visual interpretation of sign language. Eur. Conf. Comput. Vis. **1**, 390–401 (2004)

P. Buehler, A. Zisserman, M. Everingham, Learning sign language by watching tv (using weakly aligned subtitles), in *IEEE Conference on Computer Vision and Pattern Recognition*, June 2009, pp. 2961–2968

G. Casella, E.I. George, Explaining the Gibbs sampler. Am. Stat. **46**, 167–174 (1992)

S. Chib, E. Greenberg, Understanding the Metropolis-Hastings algorithm. Am. Stat. **49**, 327–335 (1995)

B. Chiu, E. Keogh, S. Lonardi, Probabilistic discovery of time series motifs, in *ACM SIGKDD International Conference on Knowledge Discovery and Data Mining*, 2003, pp. 493–498

H. Cooper, R. Bowden, Learning signs from subtitles: a weakly supervised approach to sign language recognition, in *IEEE Conference on Computer Vision and Pattern Recognition*, June 2009, pp. 2568–2574

Y. Cui, J. Weng, Appearance-based hand sign recognition from intensity image sequences. Comput. Vis. Image Underst. **78**, 157–176 (2000)

A. Denton, Kernel-density-based clustering of time series subsequences using a continuous random-walk noise model, in *International Conference on Data Mining*, 2005

K.G. Derpanis, R.R. Wildes, J.K. Tsotsos, Hand gesture recognition within a linguistics-based framework, in *European Conference on Computer Vision*, 2004, pp. 282–296

F. Duchene, C. Garbay, V. Rialle, Learning recurrent behaviors from heterogeneous multivariate time-series. Artif. Intell. Med. **39**(1), 25–47 (2007)

G. Fang, X. Gao, W. Gao, Y. Chen, A novel approach to automatically extracting basic units from Chinese Sign Language. Int. Conf. Pattern Recognit. **4**, 454–457 (2004)

A. Farhadi, D.A. Forsyth, R. White, Transfer learning in sign language, in *Computer Vision and, Pattern Recognition*, 2007, pp. 1–8

W.R. Gilks, S. Richardson, D.J. Spiegelhalter, *Markov chain Monte Carlo in practice*. Chapman and Hall, 1998

J. Han, G. Awad, A. Sutherland, Modelling and segmenting subunits for sign language recognition based on hand motion analysis. Pattern Recognit. Lett. **30**(6), 623–633 (2009)

C.E. Lawrence, S.F. Altschul, M.S. Boguski, J.S. Liu, A.F. Neuwald, J.C. Wootton, Detecting subtle sequence signals: a Gibbs sampling strategy for multiple alignment. Science **262**, 208–214 (1993)

S.K. Liddell, R.E. Johnson, American Sign Language: the phonological base. Sign Lang. Stud. 195–277 (1989)

J. Ma, W. Gao, C. Wang, J. Wu, A continuous Chinese Sign Language recognition system, in *International Conference on Automatic Face and Gesture Recognition*, 2000, pp. 428–433

D. Minnen, C.L. Isbell, I. Essa, T. Starner, Discovering multivariate motifs using subsequence density estimation and greedy mixture learning, in *Conference on Artificial Intelligence*, 2007

S. Nayak, S. Sarkar, B. Loeding, Unsupervised modeling of signs embedded in continuous sentences, in *IEEE Workshop on Vision for Human-Computer Interaction*, 2005

S. Nayak, S. Sarkar, B. Loeding, Automated extraction of signs from continuous sign language sentences using iterated conditional modes, in *IEEE Conference on Computer Vision and Pattern Recognition*, June 2009a, pp. 2583–2590

S. Nayak, S. Sarkar, B. Loeding, Distribution-based dimensionality reduction applied to articulated motion recognition. IEEE Trans. Pattern Anal. Mach. Intell. **31**(5), 795–810 (2009b)

T. Oates, PERUSE: an unsupervised algorithm for finding recurring patterns in time series, in *International Conference on Data Mining*, 2002, pp. 330–337

S.C.W. Ong, S. Ranganath, Automatic sign language analysis: a survey and the future beyond lexical meaning. IEEE Trans. Pattern Anal. Mach. Intell. **27**, 873–891 (2005)

M. Oszust, M. Wysocki, Determining subunits for sign language recognition by evolutionary cluster-based segmentation of time series, in *Artifical Intelligence and Soft Computing*, vol. 6114 of Lecture Notes in Computer Science (Springer, Berlin/Heidelberg, 2010), pp. 189–196

P.A. Pevzner, S.H. Sze, Combinatorial approaches to finding subtle signals in DNA sequences, in *International Conference on Intelligent Systems for Molecular Biology*, 2000, pp. 269–278

S.L. Phung, A. Bouzerdoum, D. Chai, Skin segmentation using color pixel classification: analysis and comparison. IEEE Trans. Pattern Anal. Mach. Intell. **27**, 148–154 (2005)

I. Rigoutsos, A. Floratos, Combinatorial pattern discovery in biological sequences: the Teiresias algorithm. Bioinformatics **14**, 55–67 (1998)

C.P. Robert, G. Casella, *Monte Carlo Statistical Methods* (Springer, New York, 2004)

T. Starner, A. Pentland, Real-time American Sign Language recognition from video using hidden Markov Models. Comput. Imaging Vis. **9**, 227–244 (1997)

T. Starner, J. Weaver, A. Pentland, Real-time American Sign Language recognition using desk and wearable computer based video. IEEE Trans. Pattern Anal. Mach. Intell. **20**(12), 1371–1375 (1998)

Y. Tanaka, K. Iwamoto, K. Uehara, Discovery of time-series motif from multidimensional data based on MDL principle. Mach. Learn. **58**(2–3), 269–300 (2005)

I.R. Vega, S. Sarkar, Statistical motion model based on the change of feature relationships: human gait-based recognition. IEEE Trans. Pattern Anal. Mach. Intell. **25**, 1323–1328 (2003)

C. Vogler, D. Metaxas, Parallel hidden Markov models for American sign language recognition. Int. Conf. Comput. Vis. **1**, 116–122 (1999)

C. Vogler, D. Metaxas, A framework of recognizing the simultaneous aspects of American Sign Language. Comput. Vis. Image Underst. **81**, 358–384 (2001)

C. Wang, W. Gao, S. Shan, An approach based on phonemes to large vocabulary Chinese Sign Language recognition, in *International Conference on Automatic Face and Gesture Recognition*, 2002, pp. 393–398

Q. Wang, X. Chen, L.G. Zhang, C. Wang, W. Gao, Viewpoint invariant sign language recognition. Comput. Vis. Image Underst. **108**, 87–97 (2007)

M.H. Yang, N. Ahuja, M. Tabb, Extraction of 2d motion trajectories and its application to hand gesture recognition. IEEE Trans. Pattern Anal. Mach. Intell. **24**, 1061–1074 (2002)

R. Yang, S. Sarkar, B. Loeding, Handling movement epenthesis and hand segmentation ambiguities in continuous sign language recognition using nested dynamic programming. IEEE Trans. Pattern Anal. Mach. Intell. **32**(3), 462–477 (2010)

Chapter 8
Dynamic Affine-Invariant Shape-Appearance Handshape Features and Classification in Sign Language Videos

Anastasios Roussos, Stavros Theodorakis, Vassilis Pitsikalis and Petros Maragos

Abstract We propose the novel approach of dynamic affine-invariant shape-appearance model (Aff-SAM) and employ it for handshape classification and sign recognition in sign language (SL) videos. Aff-SAM offers a compact and descriptive representation of hand configurations as well as regularized model-fitting, assisting hand tracking and extracting handshape features. We construct SA images representing the hand's shape and appearance *without* landmark points. We model the variation of the images by linear combinations of eigenimages followed by affine transformations, accounting for 3D hand pose changes and improving model's compactness. We also incorporate static and dynamic handshape priors, offering robustness in occlusions, which occur often in signing. The approach includes an *affine signer adaptation* component at the visual level, without requiring training from scratch a new singer-specific model. We rather employ a short development data set to adapt the models for a new signer. Experiments on the Boston-University-400 continuous SL corpus demonstrate improvements on handshape classification when compared to other feature extraction approaches. Supplementary evaluations of sign recognition experiments, are conducted on a multi-signer, 100-sign data set, from the Greek sign language lemmas corpus. These explore the fusion with movement cues as well as signer adaptation of Aff-SAM to multiple signers providing promising results.

Editors: Isabelle Guyon and Vassilis Athitsos

A. Roussos (✉)
Department of Computer Science, University of Exeter, Exeter EX4 4QF, UK
e-mail: troussos@imperial.ac.uk

A. Roussos
Department of Computing, Imperial College London, London SW7 2RH, UK

S. Theodorakis · V. Pitsikalis · P. Maragos
School of Electrical and Computer Engineering, National Technical University of Athens, Zografou Campus, 15773 Athens, Greece
e-mail: sth@cs.ntua.gr; sth@deeplab.ai

V. Pitsikalis
e-mail: vpitsik@cs.ntua.gr; vpitsik@deeplab.ai

P. Maragos
e-mail: maragos@cs.ntua.gr

S. Escalera et al. (eds.), *Gesture Recognition*, The Springer Series on Challenges in Machine Learning, DOI 10.1007/978-3-319-57021-1_8

Keywords Affine-invariant shape-appearance model · Landmarks-free shape representation · Static and dynamic priors · Feature extraction · Handshape classification

8.1 Introduction

Sign languages (SL), that is, languages that convey information via visual patterns, commonly serve as an alternative or complementary mode of human communication. The visual patterns of SL are formed mainly by handshapes and manual motion, as well as by non-manual patterns. The hand localization and tracking in a sign video as well as the derivation of features that reliably describe the configuration of the signer's hand are crucial for successful handshape classification. All the above are essential components for automatic sign language recognition systems or for gesture based human-computer interaction. Nevertheless, these tasks still pose several challenges, which are mainly due to the fast movement and the great variation of the hand's 3D shape and pose.

In this article, we propose a novel modeling of the shape and dynamics of the hands during signing that leads to efficient handshape features, employed to train statistical handshape models and finally for handshape classification and sign recognition. Based on 2D images acquired by a monocular camera, we employ a video processing approach that outputs reliable and accurate masks for the signer's hands and head. We construct *Shape-Appearance (SA) images* of the hand by combining (1) the hand's shape, as determined by its 2D hand mask, with (2) the hand's appearance, as determined by a normalized mapping of the colors inside the hand mask. The proposed modeling does not employ any landmark points and bypasses the point correspondence problem. In order to design a model of the variation of the SA images, which we call *Affine Shape-Appearance Model* (Aff-SAM), we modify the classic linear combination of eigenimages by incorporating *2D affine transformations*. These effectively account for various changes in the 3D hand pose and improve the model's compactness. After developing a procedure for the training of the Aff-SAM, we design a robust hand tracking system by adopting regularized model fitting that exploits prior information about the handshape and its dynamics. Furthermore, we propose to use as handshape features the Aff-SAM's eigenimage weights estimated by the fitting process.

The extracted features are fed into statistical classifiers based on Gaussian mixture models (GMM), via a supervised training scheme. The overall framework is evaluated and compared to other methods in extensive handshape classification experiments. The SL data are from the Boston University BU400 corpus (Neidle and Vogler 2012). The experiments are based on manual annotation of handshapes that contain 3D pose parameters and the American Sign Language (ASL) handshape configuration. Next, we define classes that account for varying dependency of the handshapes w.r.t. the orientation parameters. The experimental evaluation addresses first, in a qualitative analysis the feature spaces via a cluster quality index. Second, we evaluate via supervised training a variety of classification tasks accounting for dependency w.r.t. orientation/pose parameters, with/without occlusions. In all cases we also provide comparisons with other baseline approaches or more competitive ones. The experiments demonstrate improved feature quality indices as well as classification accuracies when compared with other approaches. Improvements in classification accuracy for the non-occlusion cases are on average of 35% over baseline methods and 3% over more competitive ones. Improvements by taking into account the occlusion cases are on average of 9.7% over the more competitive methods.

In addition to the above, we explore the impact of Aff-SAM features in a sign recognition task based on statistical data-driven subunits and hidden Markov models. These experiments are applied on data from the Greek Sign Language (GSL) lemmas corpus (DictaSign 2012), for two different signers, providing a test-bed for the fusion with movement-position cues, and as evaluation of the affine-adapted SA model to a new signer, for which there has been no Aff-SAM training. These experiments show that the proposed approach can be practically applied to multiple signers without requiring training from scratch for the Aff-SAM models.

8.2 Background and Related Work

The first step of a hand gesture analysis system is the localization of the hands. This is usually implemented using several types of visual features, as skin color, edge information, shape and motion. Color cues are applicable because of the characteristic colors of the human skin. Many methods, including the one presented here, use skin color segmentation for hand detection (Argyros and Lourakis 2004; Yang et al. 2002; Sherrah and Gong 2000). Some degree of robustness to illumination changes can be achieved by selecting color spaces, as the *HSV*, *YCbCr* or the *CIE-Lab*, that separate the chromaticity from the luminance components (Terrillon et al. 2000; Kakumanu et al. 2007). In our approach, we adopt the *CIE-Lab* color space, due to its property of being perceptually uniform. Cui and Weng (2000) and Huang and Jeng (2001) employ motion cues assuming the hand is the only moving object on a stationary background, and that the signer is relatively still.

The next visual processing step is the hand tracking. This is usually based on blobs (Starner et al. 1998; Tanibata et al. 2002; Argyros and Lourakis 2004), hand appearance (Huang and Jeng 2001), or hand boundary (Chen et al. 2003; Cui and Weng 2000). The frequent occlusions during signing make this problem quite challenging. In order to achieve robustness against occlusions and fast movements, Zieren et al. (2002), Sherrah and Gong (2000) and Buehler et al. (2009) apply probabilistic or heuristic reasoning for simultaneous assignment of labels to the possible hand/face regions. Our strategy for detecting and labeling the body-parts shares similarities with the above. Nevertheless, we have developed a more elaborate preprocessing of the skin mask, which is based on the mathematical morphology and helps us separate the masks of different body parts even in cases of overlaps.

Furthermore, a crucial issue to address in a SL recognition system is hand feature extraction, which is the focus of this paper. A commonly extracted positional feature is the 2D or 3D center-of-gravity of the hand blob (Starner et al. 1998; Bauer and Kraiss 2001; Tanibata et al. 2002; Cui and Weng 2000), as well as motion features (e.g., Yang et al. 2002; Chen et al. 2003). Several works use geometric measures related to the hand, such as shape moments (Hu 1962; Starner et al. 1998) or sizes and distances between fingers, palm, and back of the hand (Bauer and Kraiss 2001), though the latter employs color gloves. In other cases, the contour that surrounds the hand is used to extract translation, scale, and/or in-plane rotation invariant features, such as Fourier descriptors (Chen et al. 2003; Conseil et al. 2007).

Segmented hand images are usually normalized for size, in-plane orientation, and/or illumination and afterwards principal component analysis (PCA) is often applied for dimensionality reduction and descriptive representation of handshape (Sweeney and Downton 1996; Birk et al. 1997; Cui and Weng 2000; Wu and Huang 2000; Deng and Tsui 2002; Dreuw et al. 2008; Du and Piater 2010). Our model uses a similar framework but differs from these methods mainly in the following aspects. First, we employ a more general class of transforms to align the hand images, namely affine transforms that extend both similarity transforms, used, for example, by Birk et al. (1997) and translation-scale transforms as in the works of Cui and Weng (2000), Wu and Huang (2000) and Du and Piater (2010). In this way, we can effectively approximate a wider range of changes in the 3D hand pose. Second, the estimation of the optimum transforms is done simultaneously with the estimation of the PCA weights, instead of using a pipeline to make these two sets of estimations. Finally, unlike all the above methods, we incorporate combined static and dynamic priors, which make these estimations robust and allow us to adapt an existing model on a new signer.

Closely related to PCA approaches, active shape and active appearance models (Cootes and Taylor 2004; Matthews and Baker 2004) are employed for handshape feature extraction and recognition (Ahmad et al. 1997; Huang and Jeng 2001; Bowden and Sarhadi 2002; Fillbrandt et al. 2003). Our proposed shape-appearance model follows the same paradigm with these methods but differs: the modeled images are Shape-Appearance images and the image warps are not controlled by the shape landmarks but more simply by the 6 parameters of the affine transformation. In this way, it avoids shape representation through landmarks and the cumbersome manual annotation related to that.

Other more general purpose approaches have also been seen in the literature. A method earlier employed for action-type features is the histogram of oriented gradients (HOG): these descriptors are used for the handshapes of a signer (Buehler et al. 2009; Liwicki and Everingham 2009; Ong et al. 2012). Farhadi et al. (2007) employ the scale invariant feature transform (SIFT) descriptors. Finally, Thangali et al. (2011) take advantage of linguistic constraints and exploit them via a Bayesian network to improve handshape recognition accuracy. Apart from the methods that process 2D hand images, there are methods built on a 3D hand model, in order to estimate the finger joint angles and the 3D hand pose (Athitsos and Sclaroff 2002; Fillbrandt et al. 2003; Stenger et al. 2006; Ding and Martinez 2009; Agris et al.

2008). These methods have the advantage that they can potentially achieve view-independent tracking and feature extraction; however, their model fitting process might be computationally slow.

Finally, regarding our related work, Roussos et al. (2010b) have included a short description of an initial tracking system similar to the one we adopt here. A preliminary version of the Aff-SAM method was presented by Roussos et al. (2010a). This is substantially extended here in many aspects, the main of which are the following: (1) We incorporate dynamic and static handshape priors offering robustness in cases of occlusions (2) We develop an affine signer adaptation component, exploring the adaptation of Aff-SAM to multiple signers (3) Extensive handshape classification experiments are presented (4) Sign recognition experiments are conducted on a multi-signer database. In the sign recognition experiments of Sect. 8.8, we employ the handshape subunits construction presented by Roussos et al. (2010b). Finally, Theodorakis et al. (2011, 2012) present preliminary results on movement-handshape integration for continuous sign recognition.

8.3   Visual Front-End Preprocessing

The initial step of the visual processing is not the main focus of our method, nevertheless we describe it for completeness and reproducibility. The output of this subsystem at every frame is a set of skin region masks together with one or multiple *labels* assigned to every region, Fig. 8.1. These labels correspond to the *body-parts of interest* for sign language recognition: head (*H*), left hand (*L*) and right hand (*R*). The case that a mask has multiple labels reflects an *overlap* of the 2D regions of the corresponding body-parts, that is, there is an *occlusion* of some body-parts. Referring

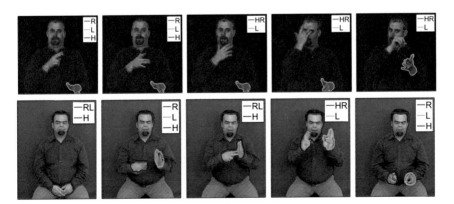

Fig. 8.1 Output of the initial hands and head tracking in two videos of two different signers, from different databases. Example frames with extracted skin region masks and assigned body-part labels *H* (head), *L* (left hand), *R* (right hand)

for example to the right hand, there are the following cases: (1) The system outputs a mask that contains the right hand only, therefore there is *no occlusion* related to that hand, and (2) The output mask includes the right hand as well as other body-part region(s), therefore there is an *occlusion*. As presented in Sect. 8.4, the framework of SA refines this tracking while extracting handshape features.

8.3.1 Probabilistic Skin Color Modeling

We are based on the color cue for body-parts detection. We consider a Gaussian model of the signer's skin color in the perceptually uniform color space *CIE-Lab*, after keeping the two chromaticity components a^*, b^*, to obtain robustness to illumination (Cai and Goshtasby 1999). We assume that the (a^*, b^*) values of skin pixels follow a bivariate Gaussian distribution $p_s(a^*, b^*)$, which is fitted using a training set of color samples (Fig. 8.2). These samples are automatically extracted from pixels of the signer's face, detected using a face detector (Viola and Jones 2003).

8.3.2 Morphological Processing of Skin Masks

In each frame, a first estimation of the skin mask S_0 is derived by thresholding at every pixel x the value $p_s(a^*(x), b^*(x))$ of the learned skin color distribution, see Figs. 8.2 and 8.3b. The corresponding threshold is determined so that a percentage of the training skin color samples are classified to skin. This percentage is set to

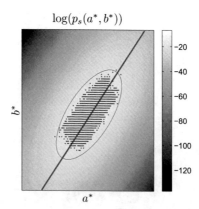

Fig. 8.2 Skin color modeling. Training samples in the a^*–b^* space and fitted pdf $p_s(a^*, b^*)$. The *ellipse* bounds the colors that are classified to skin, according to the thresholding of $p_s(a^*(x), b^*(x))$. The *straight line* corresponds to the first PCA eigendirection on the skin samples and determines the projection that defines the mapping $g(I)$ used in the Shape-Appearance images formation

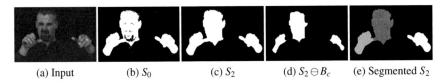

(a) Input   (b) S_0 (c) S_2 (d) $S_2 \ominus B_c$ (e) Segmented S_2

Fig. 8.3 Results of skin mask extraction and morphological segmentation. **a** Input. **b** Initial skin mask estimation S_0. **c** Final skin mask S_2 (morphological refinement). **d** Erosion $S_2 \ominus B_c$ of S_2 and separation of overlapped regions. **e** Segmentation of S_2 based on competitive reconstruction opening

99% to cope with training samples outliers. The skin mask S_0 may contain spurious regions or holes inside the head area due to parts with different color, as for instance eyes, mouth. For this, we regularize S_0 with tools from mathematical morphology (Soille 2004; Maragos 2005): First, we use the concept of *holes* $\mathcal{H}(S)$ of a binary image S, that is, the set of background components, not connected to the border of the image. In order to fill also some background regions that are not holes in the strict sense but are connected to the image border passing from a small "canal", we designed a filter that we call *generalized hole filling*. This filter yields a refined skin mask estimation $S_1 = S_0 \cup \mathcal{H}(S_0) \cup \{\mathcal{H}(S_0 \bullet B) \oplus B\}$ where B is a structuring element with size 5×5 pixels, and $\oplus$ and $\bullet$ denotes Minkowski dilation, closing respectively. The connected components (CCs) of relevant skin regions can be at most three (corresponding to the head and the two hands) and cannot have an area smaller than a threshold A_{min}, which corresponds to the smallest possible area of a hand region for the current signer and video acquisition conditions. Therefore, we apply an *area opening* with a varying threshold value: we find all CCs of S_1, compute their areas and finally discard all the components whose area is not on the top 3 or is less than A_{min}. This yields the final skin mask S_2, see Fig. 8.3c.

8.3.3 Morphological Segmentation of the Skin Masks

In the frames where S_2 contains three CCs, these yield an adequate segmentation. On the contrary, when S_2 contains less than three CCs, the skin regions of interest occlude each other. In such cases though, the occlusions are not always essential: different skin regions in S_2 may be connected via a thin connection, Fig. 8.3c. Therefore we further segment the skin masks of some frames by separating occluded skin regions with thin connections: If S_2 contains $N_{cc} < 3$ connected components, we find the CCs of $S_2 \ominus B_c$, Fig. 8.3d, for a structuring element B_c of small radius, for example, 3 pixels and discard those CCs whose area is smaller than A_{min}. A number of remaining CCs not greater than N_{cc} implies the absence of any thin connection, thus does not provide any occlusion separation. Otherwise, we use each one of these CCs as the seed of a different segment and expand it to cover S_2. For this we propose a *competitive reconstruction opening*, see Fig. 8.3e, described by the following iterative algorithm:

In every iteration (1) each evolving segment expands using its conditional dilation by the 3×3 cross, relative to S_2 (2) pixels belonging to more than one segment are excluded from all segments. This means that segments are expanded inside S_2 but their expansion stops wherever they meet other segments. The above two steps are repeated until all segments remain unchanged.

8.3.4 Body-Part Label Assignment

This algorithm yields (1) an assignment of one or multiple body-part labels, *head*, *left* and *right hand*, to all the segments and (2) an estimation of ellipses at segments with multiple labels (occluded). Note that these ellipses yield a rough estimate of the shapes of the occluded regions and contribute to the correct assignment of labels after each occlusion. A detailed presentation of this algorithm falls beyond the scope of this article. A brief description follows. *Non-occlusions*: For the hands' labels, given their values in the previous frames, we employ a prediction of the centroid position of each hand region taking into account three preceding frames and using a constant acceleration model. Then, we assign the labels based on minimum distances between the predicted positions and the segments' centroids. We also fit one ellipse on each segment since an ellipse can coarsely approximate the hand or head contour. *Occlusions*: Using the parameters of the body-part ellipses already computed from the three preceding frames, we employ similarly forward prediction for all ellipses parameters, assuming constant acceleration. We face non-disambiguated cases by obtaining an auxiliary centroid estimation of each body-part via template matching of the corresponding image region between consecutive frames. Then, we repeat the estimations backwards in time. Forward and backward predictions, are fused yielding a final estimation of the ellipses' parameters for the signer's head and hands. Figure 8.1 depicts the output of the initial tracking in sequences of frames with non-occlusion and occlusion cases. We observe that the system yields accurate skin extraction and labels assignment.

8.4 Affine Shape-Appearance Modeling

In this section, we describe the proposed framework of dynamic affine-invariant shape-appearance model which offers a descriptive representation of the hand configurations as well as a simultaneous hand tracking and feature extraction process.

8.4.1 Representation by Shape-Appearance Images

We aim to model all possible configurations of the dominant hand during signing, using directly the 2D hand images. These images exhibit a high diversity due to

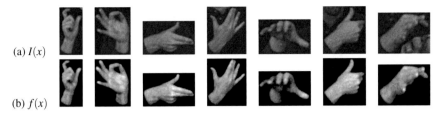

(a) $I(x)$

(b) $f(x)$

Fig. 8.4 Construction of Shape-Appearance images. **a** Cropped hand images $I(x)$. **b** Corresponding Shape-Appearance images $f(x)$. For the foreground of $f(x)$ we use the most descriptive feature of the skin chromaticity. The background has been replaced by a constant value that is out of the range of the foreground values

the variations on the configuration and 3D hand pose. Further, the set of the visible points of the hand is significantly varying. Therefore, it is more effective to represent the 2D handshape without using any landmarks. We thus represent the handshape by implicitly using its binary mask M, while incorporating also the *appearance* of the hand, that is, the color values inside this mask. These values depend on the hand texture and shading, and offer crucial 3D information.

If $I(x)$ is a cropped part of the current color frame around the hand mask M, then the hand is represented by the following *Shape-Appearance (SA) image* (see Fig. 8.4):

$$f(x) = \begin{cases} g(I(x)), & \text{if } x \in M \\ -c_b, & \text{otherwise} \end{cases},$$

where $g : \mathbb{R}^3 \to \mathbb{R}$ maps the color values of the skin pixels to a color parameter that is appropriate for the hand appearance representation. This mapping is more descriptive for hand representation than a common color-to-gray transform. In addition, g is normalized so that the mapped values $g(I)$ of skin colors I have zero mean and unit variance. $c_b > 1$ is a background constant that controls the balance between shape and appearance. As c_b gets larger, the appearance variation gets relatively less weighted and more emphasis is given to the shape part. In the experiments, we have used $c_b = 3$ (that is three times the standard deviation of the foreground values $g(I)$).

The mapping $g(I)$ is constructed as follows. First we transform each color value I to the *CIE-Lab* color space, then keep only the chromaticity components a^*, b^*. Finally, we output the normalized weight of the first principal eigendirection of the PCA on the skin samples, that is the major axis of the Gaussian $p_s(a^*, b^*)$, see Sect. 8.3.1 and Fig. 8.2c. The output $g(I)$ is the most descriptive value for the skin pixels' chromaticity. Furthermore, if considered together with the training of $p_s(a^*, b^*)$, the mapping $g(I)$ is invariant to global similarity transforms of the values (a^*, b^*). Therefore, the SA images are invariant not only to changes of the luminance component L but also to a wide set of global transforms of the chromaticity pair (a^*, b^*). As it will be described in Sect. 8.5, this facilitates the signer adaptation.

8.4.2 Modeling the Variation of Hand Shape-Appearance Images

Following Matthews and Baker (2004), the SA images of the hand, $f(x)$, are modeled by a linear combination of predefined variation images followed by an affine transformation:

$$f(W_p(\mathbf{x})) \approx A_0(x) + \sum_{i=1}^{N_c} \lambda_i A_i(x), \; x \in \Omega_M \; . \tag{8.1}$$

$A_0(x)$ is the mean image, $A_i(x)$ are N_c eigenimages that model the linear variation. These images can be considered as affine-transformation-free images. In addition, $\lambda = (\lambda_1 \ldots \lambda_{N_c})$ are the weights of the linear combination and W_p is an affine transformation with parameters $p = (p_1 \ldots p_6)$ that is defined as follows:

$$W_p(x, y) = \begin{pmatrix} 1 + p_1 & p_3 & p_5 \\ p_2 & 1 + p_4 & p_6 \end{pmatrix} \begin{pmatrix} x \\ y \\ 1 \end{pmatrix} .$$

The affine transformation models similarity transforms of the image as well as a significant range of changes in the 3D hand pose. It has a non-linear impact on the SA images and reduces the variation that is to be explained by the linear combination part, as compared to other appearance-based approaches that use linear models directly in the domain of the original images (e.g., Cui and Weng 2000). The linear combination of (8.1) models the changes in the configuration of the hand and the changes in the 3D orientation that cannot be modeled by the affine transform.

We will hereafter refer to the proposed model as *Shape-Appearance Model (SAM)*. A specific model of hand SA images is defined from the base image $A_0(x)$ and the eigenimages $A_i(x)$, which are statistically learned from training data. The vectors p and λ are the model parameters that fit the model to the hand SA image of every frame. These parameters are considered as features of hand pose and shape respectively.

8.4.3 Training of the SAM Linear Combination

In order to train the hand SA images model, we employ a representative set of hand-shape images from frames where the modeled hand is fully visible and non-occluded. Currently, this set is constructed by a random selection of approximately 500 such images. To exclude the variation that can be explained by the affine transformations of the model, we apply a semi-automatic affine alignment of the training SA images. For this, we use the framework of *procrustes analysis* (Cootes and Taylor 2004; Dryden and Mardia 1998), which is an iterative process that is repeatedly applying 1-1 alignments between pairs of training samples. In our case, the 1-1 alignments

Fig. 8.5 Semi-automatic affine alignment of a training set of Shape-Appearance images. (*Top row*) 6 out of 500 SA images of the training set. (*Bottom row*) Corresponding transformed images, after affine alignment of the training set. A video that demonstrates this affine alignment is available online (see text)

are affine alignments, implemented by applying the inverse-compositional (IC) algorithm (Gross et al. 2005) on pairs of SA images.

The IC algorithm result depends on the initialization of the affine warp, since the algorithm converges to a local optimum. Therefore, in each 1-1 alignment we test two different initializations: Using the binary masks M of foreground pixels of the two SA images, these initializations correspond to the two similarity transforms that make the two masks have the same centroid, area and orientation.[1] Among the two alignment results, the plausible one is kept, according to manual feedback from a user.

It must be stressed that the manual annotation of plausible alignment results is needed only during the training of the SA model, not during the fitting of the model. Also, compared to methods that use landmarks to model the shape (e.g., Cootes and Taylor 2004; Matthews and Baker 2004; Ahmad et al. 1997; Bowden and Sarhadi 2002), the amount of manual annotation during training is substantially decreased: The user here is not required to annotate points but just make a binary decision by choosing the plausible result of 1-1 alignments. Other related methods for aligning sets of images are described by Learned-Miller (2005) and Peng et al. (2010). However, the adopted Procrustes analysis framework facilitates the incorporation of the manual annotation in the alignment procedure. Figure 8.5 shows some results from the affine alignment of the training set. For more details, please refer to the following URL that contains a video demonstration of the training set alignment: http://cvsp. cs.ntua.gr/research/sign/aff_SAM. We observe that the alignment produces satisfactory results, despite the large variability of the images of the training set. Note that the resolution of the aligned images is 127×133 pixels.

Then, the images A_i of the linear combination of the SA model are statistically learned using principal component analysis (PCA) on the aligned training SA images. The number N_c of eigenimages kept is a basic parameter of the SA model. Using a larger N_c, the model can better discriminate different hand configurations. On the other hand, if N_c gets too large, the model may not generalize well, in the sense that it

---

[1] The existence of two such transforms is due to the modulo-π ambiguity of the orientation.

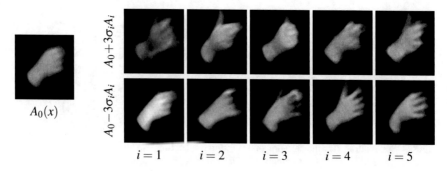

Fig. 8.6 Result of the PCA-based learning of the linear variation images of Eq. (8.1): mean image $A_0(x)$ and principal modes of variation that demonstrate the first 5 eigenimages. The top (*bottom*) row corresponds to deviating from A_0 in the direction of the corresponding eigenimage, with a weight of $3\sigma_i$ $(-3\sigma_i)$, where σ_i is the standard deviation of the corresponding component

will be consumed on explaining variation due to noise or indifferent information. In the setup of our experiments, we have practically concluded that the value $N_c = 35$ is quite effective. With this choice, the eigenimages kept explain 78% of the total variance of the aligned images.

Figure 8.6 demonstrates results of the application of PCA. Even though the modes of principal variation do not correspond to real handshapes, there is some intuition behind the influence of each eigenimage at the modeled hand SA image. For example, the first eigenimage A_1 has mainly to do with the foreground appearance: as its weight gets larger, the foreground intensities get darker and vice-versa. As another example, we see that by increasing the weight of the second eigenimage A_2, the thumb is extended. Note also that when we decrease the weight of A_4 all fingers extend and start detaching from each other.

8.4.4 Regularized SAM Fitting with Static and Dynamic Priors

After having built the shape-appearance model, we fit it in the frames of an input sign language video, in order to track the hand and extract handshape features. Precisely, we aim to find in every frame n the parameters $\lambda = \lambda[n]$ and $p = p[n]$ that generate a model-based synthesized image that is sufficiently "close" to the current input SA image $f(x)$. In parallel, to achieve robustness against occlusions, we exploit prior information about the handshape and its dynamics. Therefore, we minimize the following energy:

$$E(\lambda, p) = E_{rec}(\lambda, p) + w_S E_S(\lambda, p) + w_D E_D(\lambda, p) , \qquad (8.2)$$

where E_{rec} is a reconstruction error term. The terms $E_S(\lambda, p)$ and $E_D(\lambda, p)$ correspond to static and dynamic priors on the SAM parameters λ and p. The values w_S, w_D are positive weights that control the balance between the 3 terms.

The reconstruction error term E_{rec} is a mean square difference defined by:

$$E_{rec}(\lambda, p) = \frac{1}{N_M} \sum_x \left\{ A_0(x) + \sum_{i=1}^{N_c} \lambda_i A_i(x) - f(W_p(x)) \right\}^2 ,$$

where the above summation is done over all the N_M pixels x of the domain of the images $A_i(x)$.

The static priors term $E_S(\lambda, p)$ ensures that the solution stays relatively close to the parameters mean values λ_0, p_0:

$$E_S(\lambda, p) = \frac{1}{N_c} \|\lambda - \lambda_0\|_{\Sigma_\lambda}^2 + \frac{1}{N_p} \|p - p_0\|_{\Sigma_p}^2 ,$$

where N_c and N_p are the dimensions of λ and p respectively (since we model affine transforms, $N_p=6$). These numbers act as normalization constants, since they correspond to the expected values of the quadratic terms that they divide. Also, Σ_λ and Σ_p are the covariance matrices of λ and p respectively,[2] which are estimated during the training of the priors (Sect. 8.4.4.2). We denote by $\|y\|_A$, with A being a $N \times N$ symmetric positive-definite matrix and $y \in \mathbb{R}^N$, the following Mahalanobis distance from y to $\mathbf{0}$:

$$\|y\|_A \triangleq \sqrt{y^T A^{-1} y} .$$

Using such a distance, the term $E_S(\lambda, p)$ penalizes the deviation from the mean values but in a weighted way, according to the appropriate covariance matrices.

The dynamic priors term $E_D(\lambda, p)$ makes the solution stay close to the parameters estimations $\lambda^e = \lambda^e[n]$, $p^e = p^e[n]$ based on already fitted values on adjacent frames (for how these estimations are derived, see Sect. 8.4.4.1):

$$E_D(\lambda, p) = \frac{1}{N_c} \|\lambda - \lambda^e\|_{\Sigma_{\varepsilon_\lambda}}^2 + \frac{1}{N_p} \|p - p^e\|_{\Sigma_{\varepsilon_p}}^2 , \tag{8.3}$$

where $\Sigma_{\varepsilon_\lambda}$ and Σ_{ε_p} are the covariance matrices of the estimation errors of λ and p respectively, see Sect. 8.4.4.2 for the training of these quantities too. The numbers N_c and N_p act again as normalization constants. Similarly to $E_S(\lambda, p)$, the term $E_D(\lambda, p)$ penalizes the deviation from the predicted values in a weighted way, by taking into account the corresponding covariance matrices. Since the parameters λ are the weights of the eigenimages $A_i(x)$ derived from PCA, we assume that their mean $\lambda_0 = 0$ and their covariance matrix Σ_λ is diagonal, which means that each component of λ is independent from all the rest.

---

[2]We have assumed that the parameters λ and p are statistically independent.

It is worth mentioning that the energy-balancing weights w_S, w_D are not constant through time, but depend on whether the modeled hand in the current frame is occluded or not (this information is provided by the initial tracking preprocessing step of Sect. 8.3). In the occlusion cases, we are less confident than in the non-occlusion cases about the input SA image $f(x)$, which is involved in the term $E_{rec}(\lambda, p)$. Therefore, in these cases we obtain more robustness by increasing the weights w_S, w_D. In parallel, we decrease the relative weight of the dynamic priors term $\frac{w_D}{w_S+w_D}$, in order to prevent error accumulation that could be propagated in long occlusions via the predictions λ^e, p^e. After parameters tuning, we have concluded that the following choices are effective for the setting of our experiments: (1) $w_S = 0.07$, $w_D = 0.07$ for the non-occluded cases and (2) $w_S = 0.98$, $w_D = 0.42$ for the occluded cases.

An input video is split into much smaller temporal segments, so that the SAM fitting is *sequential* inside every segment as well *independent* from the fittings in all the rest segments: All the video segments of consecutive non-occluded and occluded frames are found and the middle frame of each segment is specified. For each non-occluded segment, we start from its middle frame and we get (1) a segment with forward direction by ending to the middle frame of the next occluded segment and (2) a segment with backward direction by ending after the middle frame of the previous occluded segment. With this splitting, we increase the confidence of the beginning of each sequential fitting, since in a non-occluded frame the fitting can be accurate even without dynamic priors. In the same time, we also get the most out of the dynamic priors, which are mainly useful in the occluded frames. Finally, this splitting strategy allows a high degree of parallelization.

8.4.4.1 Dynamical Models for Parameter Prediction

In order to extract the parameter estimations λ^e, p^e that are used in the dynamic prior term E_D (8.3), we use linear prediction models (Rabiner and Schafer 2007). At each frame n, a varying number $K = K(n)$ of already fitted frames is used for the parameter prediction. If the frame is far enough from the beginning of the current sequential fitting, K takes its maximum value, K_{max}. This maximum length of a prediction window is a parameter of our system (in our experiments, we used $K_{max} = 8$ frames). If on the other hand, the frame is close to the beginning of the corresponding segment, then K varies from 0 to K_{max}, depending on the number of frames of the segment that have been already fitted.

If $K = 0$, we are at the starting frame of the sequential fitting, therefore no prediction from other available frames can be made. In this case, which is degenerate for the linear prediction, we consider that the estimations are derived from the prior means $\lambda^e = \lambda_0$, $p^e = p_0$ and also that $\Sigma_{\varepsilon_\lambda} = \Sigma_\varepsilon$, $\Sigma_{\varepsilon_p} = \Sigma_p$, which results to $E_D(\lambda, p) = E_S(\lambda, p)$. In all the rest cases, we apply the framework that is described next.

Given the prediction window value K, the parameters λ are predicted using the following autoregressive model:

$$\lambda^e[n] = \sum_{\nu=1}^{K} A_\nu \, \lambda[n \mp \nu] ,$$

where the $-$ sign ($+$ sign) corresponds to the case of forward (backward) prediction. Also, A_ν are $N_c \times N_c$ weight matrices that are learned during training (see Sect. 8.4.4.2). Note that for every prediction direction and for every K, we use a different set of weight matrices A_ν that is derived from a separate training. This is done to optimize the prediction accuracy for the specific case of every prediction window. Since the components of λ are assumed independent to each other, it is reasonable to consider that all weight matrices A_ν are diagonal, which means that each component has an independent prediction model.

As far as the parameters p are concerned, they do not have zero mean and we cannot consider them as independent since, in contrast to λ, they are not derived from a PCA. Therefore, in order to apply the same framework as above, we consider the following re-parametrization:

$$\widetilde{p} = U_p^T (p - p_0) \Leftrightarrow p = p_0 + U_p \widetilde{p} ,$$

where the matrix U_p contains column-wise the eigenvectors of Σ_p. The new parameters $\widetilde{p}$ have zero mean and diagonal covariance matrix. Similarly to λ, the normalized parameters $\widetilde{p}$ are predicted using the following model:

$$\widetilde{p}^e[n] = \sum_{\nu=1}^{K} B_\nu \, \widetilde{p}[n \mp \nu] ,$$

where B_ν are the corresponding weight matrices which again are all considered diagonal.

8.4.4.2   Automatic Training of the Static and Dynamic Priors

In order to apply the regularized SAM fitting, we first learn the priors on the parameters λ and p and their dynamics. This is done by training subsequences of frames where the modeled hand is not occluded. This training does not require any manual annotation. We first apply a random selection of such subsequences from videos of the same signer. Currently, the randomly selected subsequences used in the experiments are 120 containing totally 2882 non-occluded frames and coming from 3 videos. In all the training subsequences, we fit the SAM in each frame independently by minimizing the energy in Eq. (8.2) with $w_S = w_D = 0$ (that is without prior terms). In this way, we extract fitted parameters λ, p for all the training frames. These are used to train the static and dynamic priors.

8.4.4.3 Static Priors

In this case, for both cases of λ and p, the extracted parameters from all the frames are used as samples of the same multivariate distribution, without any consideration of their successiveness in the training subsequences. In this way, we form the training sets T_λ and T_p that correspond to λ and p respectively. Concerning the parameter vector λ, we have assumed that its mean $\lambda_0 = 0$ and its covariance matrix Σ_λ is diagonal. Therefore, only the diagonal elements of Σ_λ, that is the variances $\sigma^2_{\lambda_i}$ of the components of λ, are to be specified. This could be done using the result of the PCA (Sect. 8.4.2), but we employ the training parameters of T_λ that come from the direct SAM fitting, since they are derived from a process that is closer to the regularized SAM fitting. Therefore, we estimate each $\sigma^2_{\lambda_i}$ from the empirical variance of the corresponding component λ_i in the training set T_λ. Concerning the parameters p, we estimate p_0 and Σ_p from the empirical mean and covariance matrix of the training set T_p.

8.4.4.4 Dynamic Priors

As already mentioned, for each prediction direction (forward, backward) and for each length K of the prediction window, we consider a different prediction model. The $(K + 1)$-plets[3] of samples for each one of these models are derived by sliding the appropriate window in the training sequences. In order to have as good accuracy as possible, we do not make any zero (or other) padding in unknown parameter values. Therefore, the samples are picked only when the window fits entirely inside the training sequence. Similarly to linear predictive analysis (Rabiner and Schafer 2007) and other tracking methods that use dynamics (e.g., Blake and Isard 1998) we learn the weight matrices A_ν, B_ν by minimizing the mean square estimation error over all the prediction-testing frames. Since we have assumed that A_ν and B_ν are diagonal, this optimization is done independently for each component of λ and $\widetilde{p}$, which is treated as 1D signal. The predictive weights for each component are thus derived from the solution of an ordinary least squares problem. The optimum values of the mean squared errors yield the diagonal elements of the prediction errors' covariance matrices $\Sigma_{\varepsilon_\lambda}$ and $\Sigma_{\varepsilon_{\widetilde{p}}}$, which are diagonal.

8.4.4.5 Implementation and Results of SAM Fitting

The energy $E(\lambda, p)$ (8.2) of the proposed regularized SAM fitting is a special case of the general objective function that is minimized by the *simultaneous inverse compositional with a prior* (SICP) algorithm of Baker et al. (2004). Therefore, in order to minimize $E(\lambda, p)$, we specialize this algorithm for the specific types of our prior terms. Details are given in the Appendix A. At each frame n of a video segment, the

---

[3]The $(K + 1)$-plets follow from the fact that we need K neighbouring samples + the current sample.

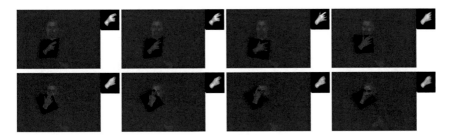

Fig. 8.7 Regularized Shape-Appearance Model fitting in a sign language video. In every input frame, we superimpose the model-based reconstruction of the hand in the frame domain, $A_0(W_p^{-1}(x)) + \sum \lambda_i A_i(W_p^{-1}(x))$. In the *upper-right corner*, we display the reconstruction in the model domain, $A_0(x) + \sum \lambda_i A_i(x)$, which determines the optimum weights λ. A demo video is available online (see text)

fitting algorithm is initialized as follows. If the current frame is not the starting frame of the sequential fitting (that is $K(n) \neq 0$), then the parameters λ, p are initialized from the predictions λ^e, p^e. Otherwise, if $K(n) = 0$, we test as initializations the two similarity transforms that, when applied to the SAM mean image A_0, make its mask have the same centroid, area and orientation as the mask of the current frame's SA image. We twice apply the SICP algorithm using these two initializations, and finally choose the initialization that yields the smallest regularized energy $E(\lambda, p)$.

Figure 8.7 demonstrates indicative results of the regularized fitting of the dominant hand's SAM in a sign language video. For more details, please refer to the following URL that contains a video of these results: http://cvsp.cs.ntua.gr/research/sign/aff_SAM. We observe that in non-occlusion cases, this regularized method is effective and accurately tracks the handshape. Further, in occlusion cases, even after a lot of occluded frames, the result is especially robust. Nevertheless, the accuracy of the extracted handshape is smaller in cases of occlusions, compared to the non-occlusion cases, since the prior terms keep the result closer to the SAM mean image A_0. In addition, extensive handshape classification experiments were performed in order to evaluate the extracted handshape features employing the proposed Aff-SAM method (see Sect. 8.7).

8.5 Signer Adaptation

We develop a method for adapting a trained Aff-SAM model to a new signer. This adaptation is facilitated by the characteristics of the Aff-SAM framework. Let us consider an Aff-SAM model trained to a signer, using the procedure described in Sect. 8.4.3. We aim to reliably adapt and fit the existing Aff-SAM model on videos from a *new signer*.

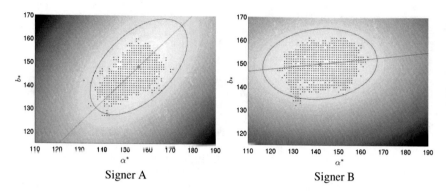

Signer A   Signer B

Fig. 8.8 Skin color modeling for the two signers of the GSL lemmas corpus, where we test the signer adaptation. Training samples in the a^*-b^* chromaticity space and fitted pdf's $p_s(a^*, b^*)$. In each case, the *straight line* defines the normalized mapping $g(I)$ used in the Shape-Appearance images formation

8.5.1 Skin Color and Normalization

The employed skin color modeling adapts on the characteristics of the skin color of a new signer. Figure 8.8 illustrates the skin color modeling for the two signers of the GSL lemmas corpus, where we test the adaptation. For each new signer, the color model is built from skin samples of a face tracker (Sects. 8.3.1, 8.4.1). Even though there is an intersection, the domain of colors classified as skin is different between the two. In addition, the mapping $g(I)$ of skin color values, used to create the SA images, is normalized according to the skin color distribution of each signer. The differences in the lines of projection reveal that the normalized mapping $g(I)$ is different in these two cases. This skin color adaptation makes the body-parts label extraction of the visual front-end preprocessing to behave robustly over different signers. In addition, the extracted SA images have the same range of values and are directly comparable across signers.

8.5.2 Hand Shape and Affine Transforms

Affine transforms can reliably compensate for the anatomical differences of the hands of different signers. Figure 8.9 demonstrates some examples. In each case, the right hands of the signers are in a similar configuration and viewpoint. We observe that there exist pairs of affine transformations that successfully align the handshapes of both signers to the common model domain. For instance, the affine transforms have the ability to stretch or shrink the hand images over the major hand axis. They thus automatically compensate for the fact that the second signer has thinner hands and longer fingers. In general, the class of affine transforms can effectively approximate the transformation needed to align the 2D hand shapes of different signers.

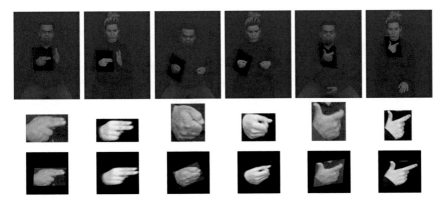

Fig. 8.9 Alignment of the hands of two different signers, using affine transformations. *First row* input frames with superimposed rectangles that visualize the affine transformations. *Second row* cropped images around the hand. *Third row* alignment of the cropped images in a common model domain, using the affine transformations

8.5.3   New Signer Fitting

To process a new signer the visual front-end is applied as in Sect. 8.3. Then, we only need to re-train the static and dynamic priors on the new signer. For this, we randomly select frames where the hand is not occluded. Then, for the purposes of this training, the existing SAM is fitted on them by minimizing the energy in Eq. (8.2) with $w_S = w_D = 0$, namely the reconstruction error term without prior terms. Since the SAM is trained on another signer, this fitting is not always successful, at this step. At that point, the user annotates the frames where this fitting has succeeded. This feedback is binary and is only needed during training and for a relatively small number of frames. For example, in the case of the GSL lemmas corpus, we sampled frames from approximately 1.2% of all corpus videos of this signer. In 15% of the sampled frames, this fitting with no priors was annotated as successful. Using the samples from these frames, we learn the static and dynamic priors of λ and p, as described in Sect. 8.4.4.2 for the new signer. The regularized SAM fitting is implemented as in Sect. 8.4.4.5.

Figure 8.10 demonstrates results of the SAM fitting, in the case of signer adaptation. The SAM eigenimages are learned using solely Signer A. The SAM is then fitted on the signer B, as above. For comparison, we also visualize the result of the SAM fitting to the signer A, for the same sign. Demo videos for these fittings also are included in the following URL: http://cvsp.cs.ntua.gr/research/sign/aff_SAM. We observe that, despite the anatomical differences of the two signers, the performance of the SAM fitting is satisfactory after the adaptation. In both signers, the fitting yields accurate shape estimation in non-occlusion cases.

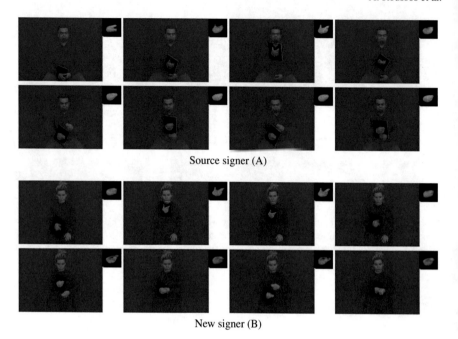

Source signer (A)

New signer (B)

Fig. 8.10 Regularized Shape-Appearance Model fitting on 2 signers. The SA model was trained on Signer A and adapted for Signer B. Demo videos are available online (see text)

8.6 Data Set and Handshape Annotation for Handshape Classification

The *SL Corpus BU400* (Neidle and Vogler 2012) is a continuous American sign language database. The background is uniform and the images have a resolution of 648×484 pixels, recorded at 60 frames per second. In the classification experiments we employ the front camera video, data from a single signer, and the story 'Accident'. We next describe the annotation parameters required to produce the ground-truth labels. These concern the pose and handshape configurations and are essential for the supervised classification experiments.

8.6.1 Handshape Parameters and Annotation

The parameters that need to be specified for the annotation of the data are the (pose-independent) handshape configuration and the 3D hand pose, that is the orientation of the hand in the 3D space. For the annotation of the handshape configurations we followed the *SignStream annotation conventions* (Neidle 2007). For the 3D hand pose we parametrized the 3D hand orientations inspired by the HamNoSys description

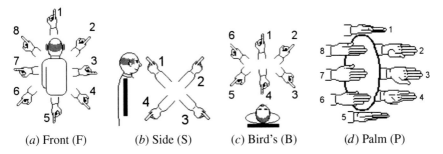

(*a*) Front (F)   (*b*) Side (S)   (*c*) Bird's (B)   (*d*) Palm (P)

Fig. 8.11 3D Hand Orientation parameters: **a–c** Extended Finger Direction Parameters: **a** Signer's front view (F), **b** side view (S), **c** birds' view (B); **d** palm orientation (P). Note that we have modified the corresponding figures of Hanke (2004) with numerical parameters

(Hanke 2004). The adopted annotation parameters are as follows: (1) *Handshape identity (HSId)* which defines the handshape configuration, that is, ('*A*', '*B*', '*I*', '*C*' etc.), see Table 8.1 for examples. (2) *3D Hand Orientation* (hand pose) consisting of the following parameters (see Fig. 8.11): (i) *Extended Finger Direction* parameters that define the orientation of the hand axis. These correspond to the hand orientation relatively to the three planes that are defined relatively to: the Signer's Front view (referred to as F), the Bird's view (B) and the Side view (S). (ii) *Palm Orientation* parameter (referred to as P) for a given extended finger direction. This parameter is defined w.r.t. the bird's view, as shown in Fig. 8.11d.

8.6.2 Data Selection and Classes

We select and annotate a set of occluded and non-occluded handshapes so that (1) they cover substantial handshape and pose variation as they are observed in the data and (2) they are quite frequent. More specifically we have employed three different data sets (DS): (1) *DS-1*: 1430 non-occluded handshape instances with 18 different HSIds. (2) *DS-1-extend*: 3000 non-occluded handshape instances with 24 different HSIds. (3) *DS-2*: 4962 occluded and non-occluded handshape instances with 42 different HSIds. Table 8.1 presents an indicative list of annotated handshape configurations and 3D hand orientation parameters.

8.7 Handshape Classification Experiments

In this section we present the experimental framework consisting of the statistical system for handshape classification. This is based (1) on the handshape features extracted as described in Sect. 8.4; (2) on the annotations as described in Sect. 8.6.1

Table 8.1 Samples of annotated handshape identities (HSId) and corresponding 3D hand orientation (pose) parameters for the D-HFSBP class dependency and the corresponding experiment; in this case each model is fully dependent on all of the orientation parameters. '# insts.' corresponds to the number of instances in the dataset. In each case, we show an example handshape image that is randomly selected among the corresponding handshape instances of the same class

HSId	1	1	4	4	5C	5	5	5	5	A	A	BL	BL	BL	BL
3D hand pose F	8	1	7	6	1	7	8	1	8	8	8	8	7	8	8
S	0	0	0	3	1	0	2	2	2	0	2	0	0	0	0
B	0	0	0	6	4	0	1	1	1	0	6	0	0	0	0
P	1	8	3	1	3	3	1	5	3	3	2	2	3	3	4
# insts.	14	24	10	12	27	38	14	19	14	14	31	10	15	23	30
Exmpls.															

HSId	BL	CUL	F	F	U	UL	V	Y	b1	c5	c5	c5	cS	cS	fO2
3D hand pose F	8	7	7	1	7	7	8	8	7	8	8	8	8	8	8
S	2	0	0	2	0	0	0	0	0	0	0	0	2	0	0
B	6	0	0	1	0	0	0	0	0	0	0	6	6	6	0
P	4	3	3	3	2	3	2	2	3	3	1	3	3	3	1
# insts.	20	13	23	13	10	60	16	16	10	17	18	10	34	10	12
Exmpls.															

as well as (3) on the data selection and classes (Sect. 8.6.2). Next, we describe the experimental protocol containing the main experimental variations of the data sets, of the class dependency, and of the feature extraction method.

8.7.1 Experimental Protocol and Other Approaches

The experiments are conducted by employing cross-validation by selecting five different random partitions of the dataset into train-test sets. We employ 60% of the data for training and 40% for testing. This partitioning samples data, among all realizations per handshape class in order to equalize class occurrence. The number of realizations per handshape class are on average 50, with a minimum and maximum number of realizations in the range of 10–300 depending on the experiment and the handshape class definition. We assign to each experiment's training set one GMM per handshape class; each has one mixture and diagonal covariance matrix. The GMMs are uniformly initialized and are afterwards trained employing Baum-Welch re-estimation (Young et al. 1999). Note that we are not employing other classifiers since we are interested in the evaluation of the handshape features and not the classifier. Moreover this framework fits with common hidden Markov model (HMM)-based SL recognition frameworks (Vogler and Metaxas 1999), as in Sect. 8.8.

8.7.1.1 Experimental Parameters

The experiments are characterized by the dataset employed, the class dependency and the feature extraction method as follows:

Data Set (DS): We have experimented employing three different data sets DS-1, DS-1-extend and DS-2 (Sect. 8.6.2 for details).

Class dependency (CD): The class dependency defines the orientation parameters in which our trained models are dependent to (Table 8.2). Take for instance the

Table 8.2 Class dependency on orientation parameters. One row for each model dependency w.r.t. the annotation parameters. The dependency or non-dependency state to a particular parameter for the handshape trained models is noted as 'D' or '*' respectively. For instance the D-HBP model is dependent on the HSId and Bird's view and Palm orientation parameters

Class	Annotation parameters				
Dependency label	HSId(H)	Front(F)	Side(S)	Bird's(B)	Palm(P)
D-HFSBP	D	D	D	D	D
D-HSBP	D	*	D	D	D
D-HBP	D	*	*	D	D
D-HP	D	*	*	*	D
D-H	D	*	*	*	*

orientation parameter 'Front' (F). There are two choices, either (1) construct hand-shape models independent to this parameter or (2) construct different handshape models for each value of the parameter. In other words, at one extent CD restricts the models generalization by making each handshape model specific to the annotation parameters, thus highly discriminable, see for instance in Table 8.2 the experiment corresponding to D-HFSBP. At the other extent CD extends the handshape models generalization w.r.t. to the annotation parameters, by letting the handshape models account for pose variability (that is depend only on the HSId; same HSId's with different pose parameters are tied), see for instance experiment corresponding to the case D-H (Table 8.2). The CD field takes the values shown in Table 8.2.

8.7.1.2 Feature Extraction Method

Apart from the proposed Aff-SAM method, the methods employed for handshape feature extraction are the following:

Direct Similarity Shape-Appearance Modeling (DS-SAM): Main differences of this method with Aff-SAM are as follows: *1)* we replace the affine transformations that are incorporated in the SA model (8.1) by simpler *similarity* transforms and *2)* we replace the regularized model fitting by direct estimation (*without* optimization) of the similarity transform parameters using the centroid, area and major axis orientation of the hand region followed by projection into the PCA subspace to find the eigenimage weights. Note that in the occlusion cases, this simplified fitting is done directly on the SA image of the region that contains the modeled hand as well as the other occluded body-part(s) (that is the other hand and/or the head), without using any static or dynamic priors as those of Sect. 8.4.4. This approach is similar to Birk et al. (1997) and is adapted to fit our framework.

Direct Translation Scale Shape-Appearance Modeling (DTS-SAM): The main differences of this method with Aff-SAM are the following: (1) we replace the affine transformations that are incorporated in the Shape-Appearance model (8.1) by sim-pler *translation-scale* transforms and (2) we replace the regularized model fitting by direct estimation of the translation and scale parameters using the square that tightly surrounds the hand mask, followed again by projection into the PCA subspace to find the eigenimage weights. In this simplified version too, the hand occlusion cases are treated by simply fitting the model to the Shape-Appearance image that contains the occlusion, without static or dynamic priors. This approach is similar to Cui and Weng (2000), Wu and Huang (2000) and Du and Piater (2010) and is adapted so as to fit our proposed framework.

Other tested methods from the literature contain the *Fourier Descriptors* (FD): These are derived from the Fourier coefficients of the contour that surrounds the hand, after appropriate normalizations for scale and rotation invariance (Chen et al. 2003; Conseil et al. 2007). For dimensionality reduction, we keep the descriptors that correspond to the first N_{FD} frequencies. We tested different values for the parameter N_{FD} and finally kept $N_{FD} = 50$ that yield the best performance. *Moments* (M): These consist of the seven Hu moment invariants of the hand region (Hu 1962).

These depend only on the central moment of the binary shape of the hand region and are invariant to similarity transforms of the hand region. *Region Based* (RB): These consist of the area, eccentricity, compactness and minor and major axis lengths of the hand region (Agris et al. 2008). Compared to the proposed Aff-SAM features we consider the rest five sets of features belonging to either *baseline features* or *more advanced features*. First, the baseline features contain the FD, M and RB approaches. Second, the more advanced features contain the DS-SAM and DTS-SAM methods which we have implemented as simplified versions of the proposed Aff-SAM. As it will be revealed by the evaluations, the more advanced features are more competitive than the baseline features and the comparisons with them are more challenging.

8.7.2   Feature Space Evaluation Results

Herein we evaluate the feature space of the Aff-SAM method. In order to approximately visualize it, we employ the weights λ_1, λ_2 of the two principal eigenimages of Aff-SAM. Figure 8.12(a) provides a visualization of the trained models per class,

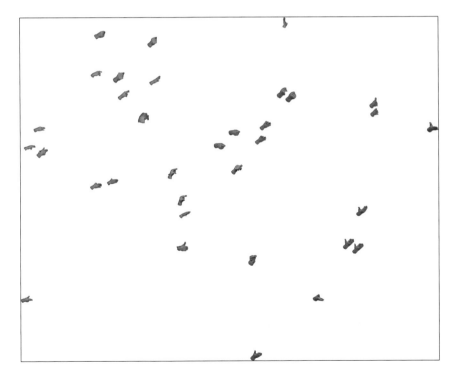

Fig. 8.12 Feature space for the Aff-SAM features and the D-HFSBP experiment case (see text). The trained models are visualized via projections on the $\lambda_1 - \lambda_2$ plane that is formed from the weights of the two principal Aff-SAM eigenimages. Cropped handshape images are placed at the models' centroids

for the experiment corresponding to D-HFSBP class dependency (that is each class is fully dependent on orientation parameters). It presents a single indicative cropped handshape image per class to add intuition on the presentation: these images correspond to the points in the feature space that are closest to the specific classes' centroids. We observe that similar handshape models share close positions in the space. The presented feature space is indicative and it seems clear when compared to feature spaces of other methods. To support this we compare the feature spaces with the Davies-Boulding index (DBi), which quantifies their quality. In brief, the DBi is the average over all n clusters, of the ratio of intra-cluster distances σ_i versus the inter-cluster distance $d_{i,j}$ of i, j clusters, as a measure of their separation: $DBi = \frac{1}{n} \sum_{i=1}^{n} \max_{i \neq j}(\frac{\sigma_i + \sigma_j}{d_{i,j}})$ (Davies and Bouldin 1979). Figure 8.13 presents the results. The reported indices are for varying CD field, that is the orientation parameters on which the handshape models are dependent or not (as discussed in Sect. 8.7.1) and are referred in Table 8.2. We observe that the DBi's for the Aff-SAM features are lower that is the classes are more compact and more separable, compared to the other cases. The closest DBi's are these of DS-SAM. In addition, the proposed features show stable performance over experiments w.r.t. class-dependency, indicating robustness to some amount of pose variation.

8.7.3　Results of Classification Experiments

We next show average classification accuracy results after 5-fold cross-validation for each experiment. together with the standard deviation of the accuracies. The experiments consist of (1) Class dependency and Feature variation for non-occlusion cases and (2) Class dependency and Feature variation for both occlusion and non-occlusion cases. Table 8.3 presents averages as well as comparisons with other features for

Fig. 8.13 Davies-Bouldin index (DBi) in logarithmic scale (y-axis) for multiple feature spaces and varying models class dependency to the orientation parameters. Lower values of DBi indicate better compactness and separability of classes

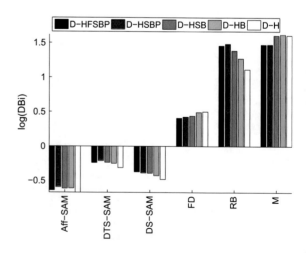

Table 8.3 Experiments overview with selected average overall results over different main feature extraction methods and experimental cases of DS and CD experiments, with occlusion or not (see Sect. 8.7.1). CD: class dependency. Occ.: indicates whether the dataset includes occlusion cases. # HSIds: the number of HSId employed, Avg.Acc.: average classification accuracy, Std.: standard deviation of the classification accuracy

Data Set	# HSIds	CD	Occ.	Feat. method	Avg. Acc.%	Std.
DS-1	18	Table. 8.2		Aff-SAM	**93.7**	1.5
			✗	DS-SAM	93.4	1.6
				DTS-SAM	89.2	1.9
DS-1-extend	24	'D-H'		Aff-SAM	**77.2**	1.6
			✗	DS-SAM	74	2.3
				DTS-SAM	67	1.4
DS-2	42	Table. 8.2		Aff-SAM	**74.9**	0.9
			✓	DS-SAM	66.1	1.1
				DTS-SAM	62.7	1.4

the three main experimental data sets discussed. The averages are over all cross-validation cases, and over the multiple experiments w.r.t. class dependency, where applicable. For instance, in the first block for the case 'DS-1', that is non-occluded data from the dataset DS-1, the average is taken over all cases of class dependency experiments as described in Table 8.2. For the 'DS-1-extend' case, the average is taken over the D-H class dependency experiment, since we want to increase the variability within each class.

8.7.3.1   Feature Comparisons for Non-occluded Cases

Next, follow comparisons by employing the referred feature extraction approaches, for two cases of data sets, while accounting for non-occluded cases.

8.7.3.2   Data Set DS-1

In Fig. 8.14 we compare the employed methods, while varying the models' dependency w.r.t. the annotation parameters (x axis). We employ the DS-1 data set, consisting of 18 handshape types from non-occlusion cases. The number of classes are shown in Table 8.4. In Fig. 8.14 we depict the performance over the different methods and models' dependency. At the one extent (that is 'D-HFBSP') we trained one GMM model for each different combination of the handshape configuration parameters (H, F, B, S, P). Thus, the trained models were dependent on the 3D handshape pose and so are the classes for the classification (34 different classes). In the other extent ('D-H') we trained one GMM model for each HSId thus the trained models

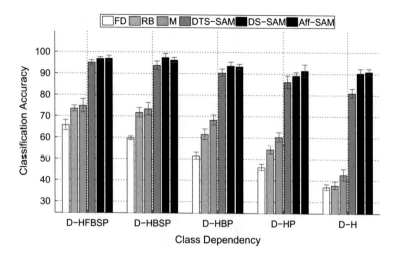

Fig. 8.14 Classification experiments for non-occlusion cases, dataset DS-1. Classification Accuracy for varying experiments (x-axis) that is the dependency of each class w.r.t. the annotation parameters [H, F, B, S, P] and the feature employed (legend). For the numbers of classes per experiment see Table 8.4

Table 8.4 Number of classes for each type of class dependency (classification experiments for Non-Occlusion cases)

Class dependency parameters	D-HFSBP	D-HSBP	D-HBP	D-HP	D-H
# Classes	34	33	33	31	18

were independent to the 3D handshape pose and so are the classes for the classification (18 different classes). Furthermore we observe that the proposed method outperforms the baseline methods (FD, RB, M) and DTS-SAM. However the classification performance of Aff-SAM and DS-SAM methods is quite close in some cases. This is due to the easy classification task (small number of HSIds and 3D pose variability and non-occlusion cases). The classification performance of the proposed method is slightly affected from the decrease of the dependency on the annotation parameters. This strengthens our previous observation that the proposed method can handle small pose variations. For a results' overview see Table 8.3 (DS-1 block). The averages are across all pose-dependency cases.

8.7.3.3   Data Set DS-1-extend

This is an extension of DS-1 and consists of 24 different HSIds with much more 3D handshape pose variability. We trained models independent to the 3D handshape pose. Thus, these experiments refer to the D-H case. Table 8.3 (DS-1-extend block) shows average results for the three competitive methods. We observe that Aff-SAM

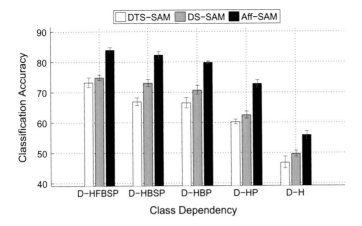

Fig. 8.15 Classification experiments for both occluded and non-occluded cases. Classification Accuracy by varying the dependency of each class w.r.t. to the annotation parameters [H,F,B,S,P] (x-axis) and the feature employed (legend). For the numbers of classes per experiment see Table 8.5

Table 8.5 Number of classes for each type of class dependency (classification experiments for Occlusion and Non-Occlusion cases)

Class dependency parameters	D-HFSBP	D-HSBP	D-HBP	D-HP	D-H
# Classes	100	88	83	72	42

outperforms both DS-SAM and DTS-SAM achieving average improvements of 3.2 and 10.2% respectively. This indicates the advancement of the Aff-SAM over the other two competitive methods (DS-SAM and DTS-SAM) in more difficult tasks. It also shows that, by incorporating more data with extended variability w.r.t. pose parameters, there is an increase in the average improvements.

8.7.3.4 Feature Comparisons for Occluded and Non-occluded Cases

In Fig. 8.15 we vary the models' dependency w.r.t. the annotation parameters similar to Sect. 8.7.3.1. However, DS-2 data set consists of 42 handshape HSIds for *both* occlusion and non-occlusion cases. For the number of classes per experiment see Table 8.5. Aff-SAM outperforms both DS-SAM and DST-SAM obtaining on average 10% performance increase in all cases (Fig. 8.15). This indicates that Aff-SAM handles handshape classification obtaining decent results even during occlusions. The performance for the other baseline methods is not shown since they cannot handle occlusions and the results are lower. The comparisons with the two more competitive methods show the differential gain due to the *claimed* contributions of the Aff-SAM. By making our models independent to 3D pose orientation, that is,-H, the classification performance decreases. This makes sense since by taking into consideration the occlusion cases the variability of the handshapes' 3D pose increases; as a consequence the classification task is more difficult. Moreover, the classification during occlusions may already include errors at the visual modeling level concerning the estimated occluded handshape. In this experiment, the range of 3D pose variations is larger than the amount handled by the affine transforms of the Aff-SAM.

8.8 Sign Recognition

Next, we evaluate the Aff-SAM approach, on automatic sign recognition experiments, while fusing with movement/position cues, as well as concerning its application on multiple signers. The experiments are applied on data from the GSL lexicon corpus (DictaSign 2012). By employing the presented framework for tracking and feature extraction (Sect. 8.3) we extract the Aff-SAM features (Sect. 8.4). These are then employed to construct data-driven subunits as in Roussos et al. (2010b) and Theodorakis et al. (2012), which are further statistically trained. The lexicon corpus contains data from two different signers, A and B. Given the Aff-SAM based models from signer A these are then adapted and fitted to another signer (B) as in Sect. 8.5 for which no Aff-SAM models have been trained. The features resulting as a product of the visual level adaptation, are employed next in the recognition experiment. For signer A, the features are extracted from the signer's own model. Note that, there are other aspects concerning signer adaptation during SL recognition, as for instance the manner of signing or the different pronunciations, which are not within the focus of this article.

GSL Lemmas: We employ 100 signs from the *GSL lemmas corpus*. These are articulated in isolation with five repetitions each, from two native signers (male and female). The videos have a uniform background and a resolution of 1440 × 1080 pixels, recorded at 25 fps.

8.8.1 Sub-unit Modeling and Sign Recognition

The SL recognition framework consists of the following: (1) First by employing the movement-position cue we construct dynamic/static SUs based on dynamic and static discrimination (Pitsikalis et al. 2010; Theodorakis et al. 2012). (2) Second we employ the handshape features and the sub-unit construction via clustering of the handshape features (Roussos et al. 2010b). (3) We then create one lexicon for each information cue, that is, movement-position and handshape. For the movement-position lexicon we recompose the constructed dynamic/static SUs, whereas for the Handshape lexicon we recompose the handshape subunits (HSU) to form each sign realization. (4) Next, for the training of the SUs we employ a GMM for the static and

Fig. 8.16 Sign recognition in GSL lemmas corpus employing 100 signs for each signer A and B, and multiple cues: Hanshape (HS), Movement-Position (MP) cue and MP+HS fusion between both via Parallel HMMs

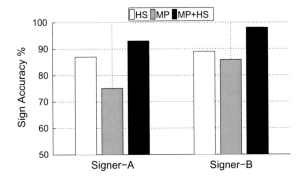

handshape subunits and an 5-state HMM for the dynamic subunits. Concerning the training, we employ four realizations for each sign for training and one for testing. (5) Finally, we fuse the movement-position and handshape cues via one possible late integration scheme, that is Parallel HMMs (PaHMMs) (Vogler and Metaxas 1999).

8.8.2 Sign Recognition Results

In Fig. 8.16 we present the sign recognition performance on the GSL lemmas corpus employing 100 signs from two signers, A and B, while varying the cues employed: movement-position (MP), handshape (HS) recognition performance and the fusion of both MP+HS cues via PaHMMs. For both signers A and B, handshape-based recognition outperforms the one of movement-position cue. This is expected, and indicates that handshape cue is crucial for sign recognition. Nevertheless, the main result we focus is the following: The sign recognition performance in Signer-B is similar to Signer-A, where the Aff-SAM model has been trained. Thus by applying the affine adaptation procedure and employing only a small development set, as presented in Sect. 8.5 we can extract reliable handshape features for multiple signers. As a result, when both cues are employed, and for both signers, the recognition performance increases, leading to a 15 and 7.5% absolute improvement w.r.t. the single cues respectively.

8.9 Conclusions

In this paper, we propose a new framework that incorporates dynamic affine-invariant Shape-Appearance modeling and feature extraction for handshape classification. The proposed framework leads to the extraction of effective features for hand config-urations. The main contributions of this work are the following: (1) We employ Shape-Appearance hand images for the representation of the hand configurations.

These images are modeled with a linear combination of eigenimages followed by an affine transformation, which effectively accounts for some 3D hand pose variations. (2) In order to achieve robustness w.r.t. occlusions, we employ a regularized fitting of the SAM that exploits prior information on the handshape and its dynamics. This process outputs an accurate tracking of the hand as well as descriptive handshape features. (3) We introduce an affine-adaptation for different signers than the signer that was used to train the model. (4) All the above features are integrated in a statistical handshape classification GMM and a sign recognition HMM-based system.

The overall visual feature extraction and classification framework is evaluated on classification experiments as well as on sign recognition experiments. These explore multiple tasks of gradual difficulty in relation to the orientation parameters, as well as both occlusion and non-occlusion cases. We compare with existing baseline features as well as with more competitive features, which are implemented as simplifications of the proposed SAM method. We investigate the quality of the feature spaces and evaluate the compactness-separation of the different features in which the proposed features show superiority. The Aff-SAM features yield improvements in classification accuracy too. For the non-occlusion cases, these are on average 35% over the baseline methods (FD, RB, M) and 3% over the most competitive SAM methods (DS-SAM, DST-SAM). Furthermore, when we also consider the occlusion cases, the improvements in classification accuracy are on average 9.7% over the most competitive SAM methods (DS-SAM, DST-SAM). Although DS-SAM yields similar performance in some cases, it under-performs in the more difficult and extended data set classification tasks. On the task of sign recognition for a 100-sign lexicon of GSL lemmas, the approach is evaluated via handshape subunits and also fused with movement-position cues, leading to promising results. Moreover, it is shown to have similar results, even if we do not train an explicit signer dependent Aff-SA model, given the introduction of the affine-signer adaptation component. In this way, the approach can be easily applicable to multiple signers.

To conclude with, given that handshape is among the main sign language phonetic parameters, we address issues that are indispensable for automatic sign language recognition. Even though the framework is applied on SL data, its application is extendable on other gesture-like data. The quantitative evaluation and the intuitive results presented show the perspective of the proposed framework for further research.

Acknowledgements This research work was supported by the EU under the research program Dictasign with Grant FP7-ICT-3-231135. A. Roussos was also supported by the ERC Starting Grant 204871-HUMANIS. This work was done while A. Roussos was with National Technical University of Athens, Greece and Queen Mary, University of London, UK; S. Theodorakis and V. Pitsikalis were both with the National Technical University of Athens; S. Theodorakis and V. Pitsikalis are now with deeplab.ai, Athens, GR.

Appendix A. Details about the Regularized Fitting Algorithm

We provide here details about the algorithm of the regularized fitting of the shape-appearance model. The total energy $E(\lambda, p)$ that is to be minimized can be written as (after a multiplication with N_M that does not affect the optimum parameters):

$$
\begin{aligned}
J(\lambda, p) = \sum_x \Bigg\{ A_0(x) &+ \sum_{i=1}^{N_c} \lambda_i A_i(x) - f(W_p(x)) \Bigg\}^2 + \\
&\frac{N_M}{N_c} \left(w_S \|\lambda - \lambda_0\|_{\Sigma_\lambda}^2 + w_D \|\lambda - \lambda^e\|_{\Sigma_{\varepsilon_\lambda}}^2 \right) + \\
&\frac{N_M}{N_p} \left(w_S \|p - p_0\|_{\Sigma_p}^2 + w_D \|p - p^e\|_{\Sigma_{\varepsilon_p}}^2 \right) .
\end{aligned}
\tag{8.4}
$$

If σ_{λ_i}, $\sigma_{\tilde{p}_i}$ are the standard deviations of the components of the parameters λ, $\tilde{p}$ respectively and $\sigma_{\varepsilon_{\lambda,i}}$, $\sigma_{\varepsilon_{\tilde{p},i}}$ are the standard deviations of the components of the parameters' prediction errors ε_λ, $\varepsilon_{\tilde{p}}$, then the corresponding covariance matrices Σ_λ, $\Sigma_{\tilde{p}}$, $\Sigma_{\varepsilon_\lambda}$, $\Sigma_{\varepsilon_{\tilde{p}}}$, which are diagonal, can be written as:

$$
\Sigma_\lambda = \mathrm{diag}(\sigma_{\lambda_1}^2, \ldots, \sigma_{\lambda_{N_c}}^2), \; \Sigma_{\tilde{p}} = \mathrm{diag}(\sigma_{\tilde{p}_1}^2, \ldots, \sigma_{\tilde{p}_{N_c}}^2),
$$
$$
\Sigma_{\varepsilon_\lambda} = \mathrm{diag}(\sigma_{\varepsilon_{\lambda,1}}^2, \ldots, \sigma_{\varepsilon_{\lambda,N_c}}^2), \; \Sigma_{\varepsilon_{\tilde{p}}} = \mathrm{diag}(\sigma_{\varepsilon_{\tilde{p},1}}^2, \ldots, \sigma_{\varepsilon_{\tilde{p},N_p}}^2).
$$

The squared norms of the prior terms in Eq. (8.4) are thus given by:

$$
\|\lambda - \lambda_0\|_{\Sigma_\lambda}^2 = \sum_{i=1}^{N_c} \left(\frac{\lambda_i}{\sigma_{\lambda_i}} \right)^2 ,
$$

$$
\|\lambda - \lambda^e\|_{\Sigma_{\varepsilon_\lambda}}^2 = \sum_{i=1}^{N_c} \left(\frac{\lambda_i - \lambda_i^e}{\sigma_{\varepsilon_{\lambda,i}}} \right)^2 ,
$$

$$
\|p - p_0\|_{\Sigma_p}^2 = (p - p_0)^T U_p \Sigma_{\tilde{p}}^{-1} U_p^T (p - p_0) = \|\tilde{p}\|_{\Sigma_{\tilde{p}}}^2 = \sum_{i=1}^{N_p} \left(\frac{\tilde{p}_i}{\sigma_{\tilde{p}_i}} \right)^2 ,
$$

$$
\|p - p^e\|_{\Sigma_{\varepsilon_p}}^2 = \|\tilde{p} - \tilde{p}^e\|_{\Sigma_{\varepsilon_{\tilde{p}}}}^2 = \sum_{i=1}^{N_p} \left(\frac{\tilde{p}_i - \tilde{p}_i^e}{\sigma_{\varepsilon_{\tilde{p},i}}} \right)^2 .
$$

Therefore, if we set:

$$
m_1 = \sqrt{w_S N_M / N_c}, \; m_2 = \sqrt{w_D N_M / N_c},
$$
$$
m_3 = \sqrt{w_S N_M / N_p}, \; m_4 = \sqrt{w_D N_M / N_p},
$$

the energy in Eq. (8.4) takes the form:

$$J(\lambda, p) = \sum_x \left\{ A_0(x) + \sum_{i=1}^{N_c} \lambda_i A_i(x) - f(W_p(x)) \right\}^2 + \sum_{i=1}^{N_G} G_i^2(\lambda, p) , \quad (8.5)$$

with $G_i(\lambda, p)$ being $N_G = 2N_c + 2N_p$ prior functions defined by:

$$G_i(\lambda, p) = \begin{cases} m_1 \frac{\lambda_i}{\sigma_{\lambda_i}}, & 1 \le i \le N_c \\ m_2 \frac{\lambda_j - \lambda_j^e}{\sigma_{\varepsilon_{\lambda,j}}}, j = i - N_c, & N_c + 1 \le i \le 2N_c \\ m_3 \frac{\tilde{p}_j}{\sigma_{\tilde{p}_j}}, j = i - 2N_c, & 2N_c + 1 \le i \le 2N_c + N_p \\ m_4 \frac{\tilde{p}_j - \tilde{p}_j^e}{\sigma_{\varepsilon_{\tilde{p},j}}}, j = i - 2N_c - N_p, & 2N_c + N_p + 1 \le i \le 2N_c + 2N_p \end{cases} .$$

$$(8.6)$$

Each component $\tilde{p}_j$, $j = 1, \ldots, N_p$, of the re-parametrization of p can be written as:

$$\tilde{p}_j = v_{\tilde{p}_j}^T (p - p_0) , \quad (8.7)$$

where $v_{\tilde{p}_j}$ is the j-th column of U_p, that is the eigenvector of the covariance matrix Σ_p that corresponds to the j-th principal component $\tilde{p}_j$.

In fact, the energy $J(\lambda, p)$, Eq. (8.5), for general prior functions $G_i(\lambda, p)$, has exactly the same form as the energy that is minimized by the algorithm of Baker et al. (2004). Next, we describe this algorithm and then we specialize it in the specific case of our framework.

A.1. Simultaneous Inverse Compositional Algorithm with a Prior

We briefly present here the algorithm *simultaneous inverse compositional with a prior* (SICP) (Baker et al. 2004). This is a *Gauss-Newton* algorithm that finds a local minimum of the energy $J(\lambda, p)$ (8.5) for general cases of prior functions $G_i(\lambda, p)$ and warps $W_p(x)$ that are controlled by some parameters p.

The algorithm starts from some initial estimates of λ and p. Afterwards, in every iteration, the previous estimates of λ and p are updated to λ' and p' as follows. It is considered that a vector $\Delta\lambda$ is added to λ:

$$\lambda' = \lambda + \Delta\lambda \quad (8.8)$$

and a warp with parameters Δp is applied to the synthesized image $A_0(x) + \sum \lambda_i A_i(x)$. As an approximation, the latter is taken as equivalent to updating the warp parameters from p to p' by composing $W_p(x)$ with the inverse of $W_{\Delta p}(x)$:

$$W_{p'} = W_p \circ W_{\Delta p}^{-1} . \tag{8.9}$$

From the above relation, given that p is constant, p' can be expressed as a $\mathbb{R}^{N_p} \to \mathbb{R}^{N_p}$ function of Δp, $p' = p'(\Delta p)$, with $p'(\Delta p = 0) = p$. Further, $p'(\Delta p)$ is approximated with a first order Taylor expansion around $\Delta p = 0$:

$$p'(\Delta p) = p + \frac{\partial p'}{\partial \Delta p} \Delta p . \tag{8.10}$$

where $\frac{\partial p'}{\partial \Delta p}$ is the Jacobian of the function $p'(\Delta p)$, which generally depends on Δp.

Based on the aforementioned type of updates of λ and p as well as the considered approximations, the values $\Delta \lambda$ and Δp are specified by minimizing the following energy:

$$F(\Delta \lambda, \Delta p) = \sum_x \left\{ A_0(W_{\Delta p}(x)) + \sum_{i=1}^{N_c} (\lambda_i + \Delta \lambda_i) A_i (W_{\Delta p}(x)) \right.$$
$$\left. - f(W_p(x)) \right\}^2 + \sum_{i=1}^{N_G} G_i^2 \left(\lambda + \Delta \lambda, \, p + \frac{\partial p'}{\partial \Delta p} \Delta p \right) ,$$

simultaneously with respect to $\Delta \lambda$ and Δp. By applying first order Taylor approximations on the two terms of the above energy $F(\lambda, p)$, one gets:

$$F(\Delta \lambda, \Delta p) \approx \sum_x \left\{ E_{sim}(x) + SD_{sim}(x) \begin{pmatrix} \Delta \lambda \\ \Delta p \end{pmatrix} \right\}^2 +$$
$$\sum_{i=1}^{N_G} \left\{ G_i(\lambda, p) + SD_{G_i} \begin{pmatrix} \Delta \lambda \\ \Delta p \end{pmatrix} \right\}^2 , \tag{8.11}$$

where $E_{sim}(x)$ is the image of reconstruction error evaluated at the model domain:

$$E_{sim}(x) = A_0(x) + \sum_{i=1}^{N_c} \lambda_i A_i(x) - f(W_p(x))$$

and $SD_{sim}(x)$ is a vector-valued "steepest descent" image with $N_c + N_p$ channels, each one of them corresponding to a specific component of the parameter vectors λ and p:

$$SD_{sim}(x) = \left[A_1(x), \, ..., \, A_{N_c}(x), \, \left(\nabla A_0(x) + \sum_{i=1}^{N_c} \lambda_i \nabla A_i(x) \right) \frac{\partial W_p(x)}{\partial p} \right], \tag{8.12}$$

where the gradients $\nabla A_i(x) = \left[\frac{\partial A_i}{\partial x_1}, \frac{\partial A_i}{\partial x_2} \right]$ are considered as row vector functions. Also SD_{G_i}, for each $i = 1, ..., N_G$, is a row vector with dimension $N_c + N_p$ that corresponds to the steepest descent direction of the prior term $G_i(\lambda, p)$:

$$SD_{G_i} = \left(\frac{\partial G_i}{\partial \lambda}, \frac{\partial G_i}{\partial p} \frac{\partial p'}{\partial \Delta p} \right). \tag{8.13}$$

The approximated energy $F(\lambda, p)$ (8.11) is quadratic with respect to both $\Delta\lambda$ and Δp, therefore the minimization can be done analytically and leads to the following solution:

$$\begin{pmatrix} \Delta\lambda \\ \Delta p \end{pmatrix} = -H^{-1} \left[\sum_x SD_{sim}^T(x) E_{sim}(x) + \sum_{i=1}^{N_G} SD_{G_i}^T G_i(\lambda, p) \right], \tag{8.14}$$

where H is the matrix (which approximates the Hessian of F):

$$H = \sum_x SD_{sim}^T(x) SD_{sim}(x) + \sum_{i=1}^{N_G} SD_{G_i}^T SD_{G_i}.$$

In conclusion, in every iteration of the SICP algorithm, the Eq. (8.14) is applied and the parameters λ and p are updated using Eqs. (8.8) and (8.10). This process terminates when a norm of the update vector $\begin{pmatrix} \Delta\lambda \\ \Delta p \end{pmatrix}$ falls below a relatively small threshold and then it is considered that the process has converged.

A.1.1. Combination with Levenberg-Marquardt Algorithm

In the algorithm described above, there is no guarantee that the original energy (8.5), that is the objective function before any approximation, decreases in every iteration; it might increase if the involved approximations are not accurate. Therefore, following Baker and Matthews (2002), we use a modification of this algorithm by combining it with the *Levenberg-Marquardt* algorithm: In Eq. (8.14) that specifies the updates, we replace the Hessian approximation H by $H + \delta \, \mathrm{diag}(H)$, where δ is a positive weight and $\mathrm{diag}(H)$ is the diagonal matrix that contains the diagonal elements of H. This corresponds to an interpolation between the updates given by the Gauss-Newton algorithm and weighted gradient descent. As δ increases, the algorithm has a behavior closer to gradient descent, which means that from the one hand is slower but from the other hand yields updates that are more reliable, in the sense that the energy will eventually decrease for sufficiently large δ.

In every iteration, we specify the appropriate weight δ as follows. Starting from setting δ to $1/10$ of its value in the previous iteration (or from $\delta = 0.01$ if this is the first iteration), we compute the updates $\Delta\lambda$ and Δp using the Hessian approximation $H +$

$\delta \operatorname{diag}(H)$ and then evaluate the original energy (8.5). If the energy has decreased we keep the updates and finish the iteration. If the energy has increased, we set $\delta \to 10\delta$ and try again. We repeat that step until the energy decreases.

A.2. Specialization in the Current Framework

In this section, we derive the SICP algorithm for the special case that concerns our method. This case arises when (1) the general warps $W_p(x)$ are specialized to affine transforms and (2) the general prior functions $G_i(\lambda, p)$ are given by Eq. (8.6).

A.2.1. The Case of Affine Transforms

In our framework, the general warps $W_p(x)$ of the SICP algorithm are specialized to affine transforms with parameters $p = (p_1 \cdots p_6)$ that are defined by:

$$W_p(x, y) = \begin{pmatrix} 1 + p_1 & p_3 & p_5 \\ p_2 & 1 + p_4 & p_6 \end{pmatrix} \begin{pmatrix} x \\ y \\ 1 \end{pmatrix}.$$

In this special case, which is analyzed also in Baker et al. (2004), the Jacobian $\frac{\partial W_p(x)}{\partial p}$ that is used in Eq. (8.12) is given by:

$$\frac{\partial W_p(x)}{\partial p} = \begin{pmatrix} x_1 & 0 & x_2 & 0 & 1 & 0 \\ 0 & x_1 & 0 & x_2 & 0 & 1 \end{pmatrix}.$$

The restriction to affine transforms implies also a special form for the Jacobian $\frac{\partial p'}{\partial \Delta p}$ that is used in Eq. (8.13). More precisely, as described in Baker et al. (2004), a first order Taylor approximation is first applied to the inverse warp $W_{\Delta p}^{-1}$ and yields $W_{\Delta p}^{-1} \approx W_{-\Delta p}$. Afterwards, based on Eq. (8.9) and the fact that the parameters of a composition $W_r = W_p \circ W_q$ of two affine transforms are given by:

$$r = \begin{pmatrix} p_1 + q_1 + p_1 q_1 + p_3 q_2 \\ p_2 + q_2 + p_2 q_1 + p_4 q_2 \\ p_3 + q_3 + p_1 q_3 + p_3 q_4 \\ p_4 + q_4 + p_2 q_3 + p_4 q_4 \\ p_5 + q_5 + p_1 q_5 + p_3 q_6 \\ p_6 + q_6 + p_2 q_5 + p_4 q_6 \end{pmatrix},$$

the function $p'(\Delta p)$ (8.10) is approximated as:

$$p'(\Delta p) = \begin{pmatrix} p_1 - \Delta p_1 - p_1 \Delta p_1 - p_3 \Delta p_2 \\ p_2 - \Delta p_2 - p_2 \Delta p_1 - p_4 \Delta p_2 \\ p_3 - \Delta p_3 - p_1 \Delta p_3 - p_3 \Delta p_4 \\ p_4 - \Delta p_4 - p_2 \Delta p_3 - p_4 \Delta p_4 \\ p_5 - \Delta p_5 - p_1 \Delta p_5 - p_3 \Delta p_6 \\ p_6 - \Delta p_6 - p_2 \Delta p_5 - p_4 \Delta p_6 \end{pmatrix}.$$

Therefore, its Jacobian is given by:

$$\frac{\partial p'}{\partial \Delta p} = - \begin{pmatrix} 1 + p_1 & p_3 & 0 & 0 & 0 & 0 \\ p_2 & 1 + p_4 & 0 & 0 & 0 & 0 \\ 0 & 0 & 1 + p_1 & p_3 & 0 & 0 \\ 0 & 0 & p_2 & 1 + p_4 & 0 & 0 \\ 0 & 0 & 0 & 0 & 1 + p_1 & p_3 \\ 0 & 0 & 0 & 0 & p_2 & 1 + p_4 \end{pmatrix}.$$

A.2.2. Specific Type of Prior Functions

Apart from the restriction to affine transforms, in the proposed framework of the regularized shape-appearance model fitting, we have derived the specific formulas of Eq. (8.6) for the prior functions $G_i(\lambda, p)$ of the energy $J(\lambda, p)$ in Eq. (8.5). Therefore, in our case, their partial derivatives, which are involved in the above described SICP algorithm (see Eq. (8.13)), are specialized as follows:

$$\frac{\partial G_i}{\partial p} \overset{(7)}{=} \begin{cases} 0, & 1 \le i \le 2N_c \\ \frac{m_3}{\sigma_{\tilde{p}_j}} v_{\tilde{p}_j}^T, \ j = i - 2N_c, & 2N_c + 1 \le i \le 2N_c + N_p \\ \frac{m_4}{\sigma_{\varepsilon \tilde{p}, j}} v_{\tilde{p}_j}^T, \ j = i - 2N_c - N_p, & 2N_c + N_p + 1 \le i \le 2N_c + 2N_p \end{cases},$$

$$\frac{\partial G_i}{\partial \lambda} = \begin{cases} \frac{m_1}{\sigma_{\lambda_i}} e_i^T, & 1 \le i \le N_c \\ \frac{m_2}{\sigma_{\varepsilon \lambda, j}} e_j^T, \ j = i - N_c, & N_c + 1 \le i \le 2N_c \\ 0, & 2N_c + 1 \le i \le 2N_c + 2N_p \end{cases},$$

where e_i, $1 \le i \le N_c$, is the ith column of the $N_c \times N_c$ identity matrix.

References

U. Agris, J. Zieren, U. Canzler, B. Bauer, K.F. Kraiss, Recent developments in visual sign language recognition. Univ. Access Inf. Soc. **6**, 323–362 (2008)

T. Ahmad, C.J. Taylor, T.F. Lanitis, A. Cootes, Tracking and recognising hand gestures, using statistical shape models. Image Vis. Comput. **15**(5), 345–352 (1997)

A. Argyros, M. Lourakis, Real time tracking of multiple skin-colored objects with a possibly moving camera, in *Proceedings of the European Conference on Computer Vision*, 2004

V. Athitsos, S. Sclaroff, An appearance-based framework for 3d hand shape classification and camera viewpoint estimation, in *Proceedings of the International Conference on Automatic Face and Gesture Recognition*, 2002, pp. 45–52

S. Baker, I. Matthews, Lucas-kanade 20 years on: a unifying framework: Part 1. Technical report, Carnegie Mellon University, 2002

S. Baker, R. Gross, I. Matthews, Lucas-kanade 20 years on: a unifying framework: Part 4, Technical report, Carnegie Mellon University, 2004

B. Bauer, K.F. Kraiss, Towards an automatic sign language recognition system using subunits, in *Proceedings of the International Gesture Workshop* vol. 2298, 2001, pp. 64–75

H. Birk, T.B. Moeslund, C.B. Madsen, Real-time recognition of hand alphabet gestures using principal component analysis, in *Proceedings of the Scandinavian Conference Image Analysis*, 1997

A. Blake, M. Isard, *Active Contours* (Springer, 1998)

R. Bowden, M. Sarhadi, A nonlinear model of shape and motion for tracking fingerspelt american sign language. Image Vis. Comput. **20**, 597–607 (2002)

P. Buehler, M. Everingham, A. Zisserman, Learning sign language by watching TV (using weakly aligned subtitles), in *Proceedings of the Conference on Computer Vision and Pattern Recognition*, 2009

J. Cai, A. Goshtasby, Detecting human faces in color images. Image Vis. Comput. **18**, 63–75 (1999)

F.-S. Chen, C.-M. Fu, C.-L. Huang, Hand gesture recognition using a real-time tracking method and hidden markov models. Image Vis. Comput. **21**(8), 745–758 (2003)

S. Conseil, S. Bourennane, L. Martin, Comparison of Fourier descriptors and Hu moments for hand posture recognition, in *Proceedings of the European Conference on Signal Processing*, 2007

T.F. Cootes, C.J. Taylor, Statistical models of appearance for computer vision. Technical report, University of Manchester, 2004

Y. Cui, J. Weng, Appearance-based hand sign recognition from intensity image sequences. Comput. Vis. Image Underst. **78**(2), 157–176 (2000)

D.L. Davies, D.W. Bouldin, A cluster separation measure. IEEE Trans. Pattern Anal. Mach. Intell. **1**, 224–227 (1979)

J.-W. Deng, H.T. Tsui, A novel two-layer PCA/MDA scheme for hand posture recognition. Proc. Int. Conf. Pattern Recognit. **1**, 283–286 (2002)

DictaSign, Greek sign language corpus, http://www.sign-lang.uni-hamburg.de/dicta-sign/portal, 2012

L. Ding, A.M. Martinez, Modelling and recognition of the linguistic components in american sign language. Image Vis. Comput. **27**(12), 1826–1844 (2009)

P. Dreuw, J. Forster, T. Deselaers, H. Ney, Efficient approximations to model-based joint tracking and recognition of continuous sign language, in *Proceedings of the International Conference on Automatic Face and Gesture Recognition*, 2008

I.L. Dryden, K.V. Mardia, *Statistical Shape Analysis* (Wiley, 1998)

W. Du, J. Piater, Hand modeling and tracking for video-based sign language recognition by robust principal component analysis, in *Proceedings of the ECCV Workshop on Sign, Gesture and Activity*, 2010

A. Farhadi, D. Forsyth, R. White, Transfer learning in sign language, in *Proceedings of the Conference on Computer Vision and Pattern Recognition* (IEEE, 2007), pp. 1–8

H. Fillbrandt, S. Akyol, K.-F. Kraiss, Extraction of 3D hand shape and posture from images sequences from sign language recognition, in *Proceedings of the International Workshop on Analysis and Modeling of Faces and Gestures*, 2003, pp. 181–186

R. Gross, I. Matthews, S. Baker, Generic vs. person specific active appearance models. Image Vis. Comput. **23**(12), 1080–1093 (2005)

T. Hanke, HamNoSys Representing sign language data in language resources and language processing contexts, in *Proceedings of the International Conference on Language Resources and Evaluation*, 2004

M.-K. Hu, Visual pattern recognition by moment invariants. IEEE Trans. Inf. Theory **8**(2), 179–187 (1962)

C.-L. Huang, S.-H. Jeng, A model-based hand gesture recognition system. Mach. Vis. Appl. **12**(5), 243–258 (2001)

P. Kakumanu, S. Makrogiannis, N. Bourbakis, A survey of skin-color modeling and detection methods. Pattern Recogn. **40**(3), 1106–1122 (2007)

E. Learned-Miller, Data driven image models through continuous joint alignment. IEEE Trans. Pattern Anal. Mach. Intell. **28**(2), 236–250 (2005)

S. Liwicki, M. Everingham, Automatic recognition of fingerspelled words in British sign language, in *Proceedings of the CVPR Workshop on Human Communicative Behavior Analysis*, 2009

P. Maragos, *Morphological Filtering for Image Enhancement and Feature Detection, The Image and Video Processing Handbook* (Elsevier, 2005)

I. Matthews, S. Baker, Active appearance models revisited. Int. J. Comput. Vis. **60**(2), 135–164 (2004)

C. Neidle, Signstream annotation: addendum to conventions used for the american sign language linguistic research project. Technical report, 2007

C. Neidle, C. Vogler, A new web interface to facilitate access to corpora: development of the ASLLRP data access interface, in *Proceedings of the International Conference on Language Resources and Evaluation*, 2012

E.J. Ong, H. Cooper, N. Pugeault, R. Bowden, Sign language recognition using sequential pattern trees, in *Proceedings of the Conference on Computer Vision and Pattern Recognition* (IEEE, 2012), pp. 2200–2207

Y. Peng, A. Ganesh, J. Wright, W. Xu, Y. Ma, RASL: Robust alignment by sparse and low-rank decomposition for linearly correlated images, in *Proceedings of the Conference on Computer Vision and Pattern Recognition*, 2010

V. Pitsikalis, S. Theodorakis, P. Maragos, Data-driven sub-units and modeling structure for continuous sign language recognition with multiple cues, in *LREC Workshop Repr. & Proc. SL*, Corpora and SL Technologies, 2010

L.R. Rabiner, R.W. Schafer, Introduction to digital speech processing. Found. Trends Signal Process. **1**(1–2), 1–194 (2007)

A. Roussos, S. Theodorakis, V. Pitsikalis, P. Maragos, Affine-invariant modeling of shape-appearance images applied on sign language handshape classification, in *Proceedings of the International Conference on Image Processing*, 2010a

A. Roussos, S. Theodorakis, V. Pitsikalis, P. Maragos, Hand tracking and affine shape-appearance handshape sub-units in continuous sign language recognition, in *Proceedings of the ECCV Workshop on Sign, Gesture and Activity*, 2010b

J. Sherrah, S. Gong, Resolving visual uncertainty and occlusion through probabilistic reasoning, in *Proceedings of the British Machine Vision Conference*, 2000, pp. 252–261

P. Soille, *Morphological Image Analysis: Principles and Applications* (Springer, 2004)

T. Starner, J. Weaver, A. Pentland, Real-time american sign language recognition using desk and wearable computer based video. IEEE Trans. Pattern Anal. Mach. Intell. **20**(12), 1371–1375 (1998). Dec

B. Stenger, A. Thayananthan, P.H.S. Torr, R. Cipolla, Model-based hand tracking using a hierarchical bayesian filter. IEEE Trans. Pattern Anal. Mach. Intell. **28**(9), 1372–1384 (2006). Sep

G.J. Sweeney, A.C. Downton, Towards appearance-based multi-channel gesture recognition, in *Proceedings of the International Gesture Workshop*, 1996, pp. 7–16

N. Tanibata, N. Shimada, Y. Shirai, Extraction of hand features for recognition of sign language words, in *Proceedings of the International Conference on Vision Interface*, 2002, pp. 391–398

J. Terrillon, M. Shirazi, H. Fukamachi, S. Akamatsu, Comparative performance of different skin chrominance models and chrominance spaces for the automatic detection of human faces in color images, in *Proceedings of the International Conference on Automatic Face and Gesture Recognition*, 2000, pp. 54–61

A. Thangali, J.P. Nash, S. Sclaroff, C. Neidle, Exploiting phonological constraints for handshape inference in asl video, in *Proceedings of the Conference on Computer Vision and Pattern Recognition* (IEEE, 2011) pp. 521–528

S. Theodorakis, V. Pitsikalis, P. Maragos, Advances in dynamic-static integration of movement and handshape cues for sign language recognition, in *Proceedings of the International Gesture Workshop*, 2011

S. Theodorakis, V. Pitsikalis, I. Rodomagoulakis, P. Maragos, Recognition with raw canonical phonetic movement and handshape subunits on videos of continuous sign language, in *Proceedings of the International Conference on Image Processing*, 2012

M. Viola, M.J. Jones, Fast multi-view face detection, in *Proceedings of the Conference on Computer Vision and Pattern Recognition*, 2003

C. Vogler, D. Metaxas, Parallel hidden markov models for american sign language recognition. Proc. Int. Conf. Comput. Vis. **1**, 116–122 (1999)

Y. Wu, T.S. Huang, View-independent recognition of hand postures. Proc. Conf. Comput. Vis. Pattern Recognit. **2**, 88–94 (2000)

M.-H. Yang, N. Ahuja, M. Tabb, Extraction of 2d motion trajectories and its application to hand gesture recognition. IEEE Trans. Pattern Anal. Mach. Intell. **24**(8), 1061–1074 (2002). Aug

S. Young, D. Kershaw, J. Odell, D. Ollason, V. Woodland, P. Valtchevand, *The HTK Book* (Entropic Ltd., 1999)

J. Zieren, N. Unger, S. Akyol, Hands tracking from frontal view for vision-based gesture recognition, in *Pattern Recognition*, LNCS, 2002, pp. 531–539

Chapter 9
Discriminative Hierarchical Part-Based Models for Human Parsing and Action Recognition

Yang Wang, Duan Tran, Zicheng Liao and David Forsyth

Abstract We consider the problem of parsing human poses and recognizing their actions in static images with part-based models. Most previous work in part-based models only considers rigid parts (e.g., torso, head, half limbs) guided by human anatomy. We argue that this representation of parts is not necessarily appropriate. In this paper, we introduce hierarchical poselets—a new representation for modeling the pose configuration of human bodies. Hierarchical poselets can be rigid parts, but they can also be parts that cover large portions of human bodies (e.g., torso + left arm). In the extreme case, they can be the whole bodies. The hierarchical poselets are organized in a hierarchical way via a structured model. Human parsing can be achieved by inferring the optimal labeling of this hierarchical model. The pose information captured by this hierarchical model can also be used as a intermediate representation for other high-level tasks. We demonstrate it in action recognition from static images.

Keywords Human parsing · Action recognition · Part-based models · Hierarchical poselets · Max-margin structured learning

Editors: Isabelle Guyon and Vassilis Athitsos.

Y. Wang (✉)
Department of Computer Science, University of Manitoba, Winnipeg,
MB R3T 2N2, Canada
e-mail: ywang@cs.umanitoba.ca

D. Tran · Z. Liao · D. Forsyth
Department of Computer Science, University of Illinois at Urbana-Champaign,
Urbana, IL 61801, USA
e-mail: ddtran2@uiuc.edu

Z. Liao
e-mail: liao17@uiuc.edu

D. Forsyth
e-mail: daf@uiuc.edu

© Springer International Publishing AG 2017
S. Escalera et al. (eds.), *Gesture Recognition*, The Springer Series
on Challenges in Machine Learning, DOI 10.1007/978-3-319-57021-1_9

273

9.1 Introduction

Modeling human bodies (or articulated objects in general) in images is a long-lasting problem in computer vision. Compared with rigid objects (e.g., faces and cars) which can be reasonably modeled using several prototypical templates, human bodies are much more difficult to model due to the wide variety of possible pose configurations.

A promising solution for dealing with the pose variations is to use part-based models. Part-based representations, such as cardboard people (Ju et al. 1996) or pictorial structure (Felzenszwalb and Huttenlocher 2005), provide an elegant framework for modeling articulated objects, such as human bodies. A part-based model represents the human body as a constellation of a set of rigid parts (e.g., torso, head, half limbs) constrained in some fashion. The typical constraints used are tree-structured kinematic constraints between adjacent body parts, for example, torso-upper half-limb connection, or upper-lower half-limb connection. Part-based models consist of two important components: (1) part appearances specifying what each body part should look like in the image; (2) configuration priors specifying how parts should be arranged relative to each other. Part-based models have been used extensively in various computer vision applications involving humans, such as human parsing (Felzenszwalb and Huttenlocher 2005; Ramanan 2006), kinematic tracking (Ramanan et al. 2005), action recognition (Yang et al. 2010) and human-object interaction (Yao and Fei-Fei 2010).

Considerable progress has been made to improve part-based models. For example, there has been a line of work on using better appearance models in part-based models. A representative example is the work by Ramanan (2006), who learns color histograms of parts from an initial edge-based model. Ferrari et al. (2008) and Eichner and Ferrari (2009) further improve the part appearance models by reducing the search space using various tricks, for example, the relative locations of part locations with respect to a person detection and the relationship between different part appearances (e.g., upper-arm and torso tend to have the same color), Andriluka et al. (2009) build better edge-based appearance models using the HOG descriptors (Dalal and Triggs 2005). Sapp et al. (2010b) develop efficient inference algorithm to allow the use of more expensive features. There is also work (Johnson and Everingham 2009; Mori et al. 2004; Mori 2005; Srinivasan and Shi 2007) on using segmentation as a pre-processing step to provide better spatial support for computing part appearances.

Another line of work is on improving configuration priors in part-based models. Most of them focus on developing representations and fast inference algorithms that by-pass the limitations of kinematic tree-structured spatial priors in standard pictorial structure models. Examples include common-factor models (Lan and Huttenlocher 2005), loopy graphs (Jiang and Martin 2008; Ren et al. 2005; Tian and Sclaroff 2010; Tran and Forsyth 2010), mixtures of trees (Wang and Mori 2008). There is also work on building spatial priors that adapt to testing examples (Sapp et al. 2010a).

Most of the previous work on part-based models use rigid parts that are anatomically meaningful, for example, torso, head, half limbs. Those rigid parts are usually represented as rectangles (e.g., Andriluka et al. 2009; Felzenszwalb and Huttenlocher

2005; Ramanan 2006; Ren et al. 2005; Sigal and Black 2006; Wang and Mori 2008) or parallel lines (e.g., Ren et al. 2005). However, as pointed out by some recent work (Bourdev and Malik 2009; Bourdev et al. 2010), rigid parts are not necessarily the best representation since rectangles and parallel lines are inherently difficult to detect in natural images.

In this paper, we introduce a presentation of parts inspired by the early work of Marr (1982). The work in Marr (1982) recursively represents objects as generalized cylinders in a coarse-to-fine hierarchical fashion. In this paper, we extend Marr's idea for two problems in the general area of "looking at people". The first problem is human parsing, also known as human pose estimation. The goal is to find the location of each body part (torso, head, limbs) of a person in a static image. We use a part-based approach for human parsing. The novelty of our work is that our notion of "parts" can range from basic rigid parts (e.g., torso, head, half-limb), to large pieces of bodies covering more than one rigid part (e.g., torso + left arm). In the extreme case, we have "parts" corresponding to the whole body. We propose a new representation called "hierarchical poselets" to capture this hierarchy of parts. We infer the human pose using this hierarchical representation.

The hierarchical poselet also provides rich information about body poses that can be used in other applications. To demonstrate this, we apply it to recognize human action in static images. In this application, we use hierarchical poselets to capture various pose information of the human body, this information is further used as some intermediate representation to infer the action of the person.

A preliminary version of this work appeared in Wang et al. (2011). We organize the rest of the paper as follows. Section 9.2 reviews previous work in human parsing and action recognition. Section 9.3 introduces hierarchical poselet, a new representation for modeling human body configurations. Section 9.4 describes how to use hierarchical poselets for human parsing. Section 9.5 develops variants of hierarchical poselets for recognizing human action in static images. We present experimental results on human parsing and action recognition in Sect. 9.6 and conclude in Sect. 9.7.

9.2   Previous Work

Finding and understanding people from images is a very active area in computer vision. In this section, we briefly review previous work in human parsing and action recognition that is most related to our work.

Human parsing Early work related to finding people from images is in the setting of detecting and tracking people with kinematic models in both 2D and 3D. Forsyth et al. (2006) provide an extensive survey of this line of work.

Recent work has examined the problem in static images. Some of these approaches are exemplar-based. For example, Toyama and Blake (2001) track people using 2D exemplars. Mori and Malik (2002) and Sullivan and Carlsson (2002) estimate human poses by matching pre-stored 2D templates with marked ground-truth 2D joint locations. Shakhnarovich et al. (2003) use local sensitive hashing to allow efficient matching when the number of exemplars is large.

Part-based models are becoming increasingly popular in human parsing. Early work includes the cardboard people (Ju et al. 1996) and the pictorial structure (Felzenszwalb and Huttenlocher 2005). Tree-structured models are commonly used due to its efficiency. But there are also methods that try to alleviate the limitation of tree-structured models, include common-factor models (Lan and Huttenlocher 2005), loopy graphs (Jiang and Martin 2008; Ren et al. 2005; Tian and Sclaroff 2010; Tran and Forsyth 2010), mixtures of trees (Wang and Mori 2008).

Many part-based models use discriminative learning to train the model parameters. Examples include the conditional random fields (Ramanan and Sminchisescu 2006; Ramanan 2006), max-margin learning (Kumar et al. 2009; Wang et al. 2011; Yang and Ramanan 2011) and boosting (Andriluka et al. 2009; Sapp et al. 2010b; Singh et al. 2010). Previous approaches have also explored various features, including image segments (superpixels) (Johnson and Everingham 2009; Mori et al. 2004; Mori 2005; Sapp et al. 2010a, b; Srinivasan and Shi 2007), color features (Ramanan 2006; Ferrari et al. 2008), gradient features (Andriluka et al. 2009; Johnson and Everingham 2010; Wang et al. 2011; Yang and Ramanan 2011).

Human action recognition Most of the previous work on human action recognition focuses on videos. Some work (Efros et al. 2003) uses global template for action recognition. A lot of recent work (Dollár et al. 2005; Laptev et al. 2008; Niebles et al. 2006) uses bag-of-words models. There is also work (Ke et al. 2007; Niebles and Fei-Fei 2007) using part-based models.

Compared with videos, human action recognition from static images is a relatively less-studied area. Wang et al. (2006) provide one of the earliest examples of action recognition in static images. Recently, template models (Ikizler-Cinbis et al. 2009), bag-of-words models (Delaitre et al. 2010), part-based models (Delaitre et al. 2010; Yang et al. 2010) have all been proposed for static-image action recognition. There is also a line of work on using contexts for action recognition in static images, including human-object context (Desai et al. 2010; Gupta et al. 2009; Yao and Fei-Fei 2010) and group context (Lan et al. 2010; Maji et al. 2011).

9.3 Hierarchical Poselets

Our pose representation is based on the concept of "poselet" introduced in Bourdev and Malik (2009). In a nutshell, poselets refer to pieces of human poses that are tightly clustered in both appearance and configuration spaces. Poselets have been shown to be effective at person detection (Bourdev and Malik 2009; Bourdev et al. 2010).

In this paper, we propose a new representation called *hierarchical poselets*. Hierarchical poselets extend the original poselets in several important directions to make them more appropriate for human parsing. We start by highlighting the important properties of our representation.

Beyond rigid "parts": Most of the previous work in part-based human modeling are based on the notion that the human body can be modeled as a set of rigid parts connected in some way. Almost all of them use a natural definition of parts (e.g., torso, head, upper/lower limbs) corresponding to body segments, and model those parts as rectangles, parallel lines, or other primitive shapes.

As pointed out by Bourdev and Malik (2009), this natural definition of "parts" fails to acknowledge the fact that rigid parts are not necessarily the most salient features for visual recognition. For example, rectangles and parallel lines can be found as limbs, but they can also be easily confused with windows, buildings, and other objects in the background. So it is inherently difficult to build reliable detectors for those parts. On the other hand, certain visual patterns covering large portions of human bodies, for example, "a torso with the left arm raising up" or "legs in lateral pose", are much more visually distinctive and easier to identify. This phenomenon was observed even prior to the work of poselet and was exploited to detect stylized human poses and build appearance models for kinematic tracking (Ramanan et al. 2005).

Multiscale hierarchy of "parts": Another important property of our representation is that we define "parts" at different levels of hierarchy to cover pieces of human poses at various granularity, ranging from the configuration of the whole body, to small rigid parts. In particular, we define 20 parts to represent the human pose and organize them in a hierarchy shown in Fig. 9.1. To avoid terminological confusion, we will use "part" to denote one of the 20 parts in Fig. 9.1 and use "primitive part" to denote rigid body parts (i.e., torso, head, half limbs) from now on.

In this paper, we choose the 20 parts and the hierarchical structure in Fig. 9.1 manually. Of course, it is possible to define parts corresponding to other combinations of body segments, for example, left part of the whole body. It may also be possible to learn the connectivity of parts automatically from data, for example, using structure learning methods similar to the Chow-Liu algorithm (Chow and Liu 1968). We would like to leave these issues as future work.

We use a procedure similar to Yang et al. (2010) to select poselets for each part. First, we cluster the joints on each part into several clusters based on their relative x

Fig. 9.1 An illustration of the hierarchical pose representation. The *black edges* indicate the connectivity among different parts

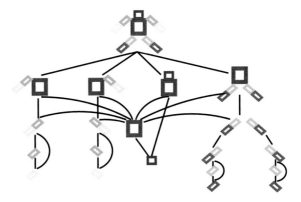

and y coordinates with respect to some reference joint of that part. For example, for the part "torso", we choose the middle-top joint as the reference and compute the relative coordinates of all the other joints on the torso with respect to this reference joint. The concatenation of all those coordinates will be the vector used for clustering. We run K-means clustering on the vectors collected from all training images and remove clusters that are too small. Similarly, we obtain the clusters for all the other parts. In the end, we obtain 5–20 clusters for each part. Based on the clustering, we crop the corresponding patches from the images and form a set of poselets for that part. Figure 9.2 shows examples of two different poselets for the part "legs".

Our focus is the new representation, so we use standard HOG descriptors (Dalal and Triggs 2005) to keep the feature engineering to the minimum. For each poselet, we construct HOG features from patches in the corresponding cluster and from random negative patches. Inspired by the success of multiscale HOG features (Felzenszwalb et al. 2010), we use different cell sizes when computing HOG features for different parts. For example, we use cells of 12×12 pixel regions for poselets of the whole body, and cells of 2×2 for poselets of the upper/lower arm. This is motivated by the fact that large body parts (e.g., whole body) are typically well-represented by coarse shape information, while small body parts (e.g., half limb) are better represented by more detailed information. We then train a linear SVM classifier for detecting the presence of each poselet. The learned SVM weights can be thought as a template for the poselet. Examples of several HOG templates for the "legs" poselets are shown as the last columns of Fig. 9.2. Examples of poselets and their corresponding HOG templates for other body parts are shown in Fig. 9.3.

A poselet of a primitive part contains two endpoints. For example, for a poselet of upper-left leg, one endpoint corresponds to the joint between torso and upper-left leg, the other one corresponds to the joint between upper/lower left leg. We record the mean location (with respect to the center of the poselet image patch) of each endpoint. This information will be used in human parsing when we need to infer the endpoints of a primitive part for a test image.

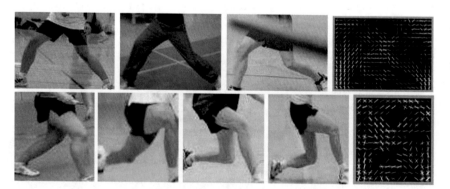

Fig. 9.2 Examples of two poselets for the part "legs". *Each row* corresponds to a poselet. We show several patches from the poselet cluster. The *last column* shows the HOG template of the poselet

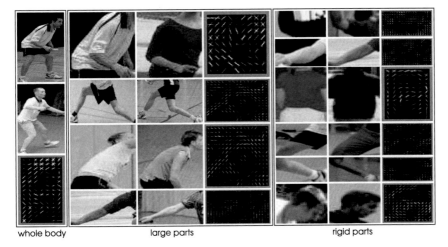

whole body   large parts   rigid parts

Fig. 9.3 Visualization of some poselets learned from different body parts on the UIUC people data set, including whole body, large parts (*top to bottom* torso+left arm, legs, torso+head, left arm), and rigid parts (*top to bottom* upper/lower left arm, torso, upper/lower left leg, head). For each poselet, we show two image patches from the corresponding cluster and the learned SVM HOG template

9.4 Human Parsing

In this section, we describe how to use hierarchical poselets in human parsing. We first develop an undirected graphical model to represent the configuration of the human pose (Sect. 9.4.1). We then develop the inference algorithm for finding the best pose configuration in the model (Sect. 9.4.2) and the algorithm for learning model parameters (Sect. 9.4.3) from training data.

9.4.1 Model Formulation

We denote the complete configuration of a human pose as $L = \{l_i\}_{i=1}^{K}$, where K is the total number of parts (i.e., $K = 20$ in our case). The configuration of each part l_i is parametrized by $l_i = (x_i, y_i, z_i)$. Here (x_i, y_i) defines the image location, and z_i is the index of the corresponding poselet for this part, that is, $z_i \in \{1, 2, ..., \mathscr{P}_i\}$, where $\mathscr{P}_i$ is the number of poselets for the i-th part. In this paper, we assume the scale of the person is fixed and do not search over multiple scales. It is straightforward to augment l_i with other information, for example, scale and foreshortening.

The complete pose L can be represented by a graph $\mathscr{G} = \{\mathscr{V}, \mathscr{E}\}$, where a vertex $i \in \mathscr{V}$ denotes a part and an edge $(i, j) \in \mathscr{E}$ captures the constraint between parts i and j. The structure of $\mathscr{G}$ is shown in Fig. 9.1. We define the score of labeling an image I with the pose L as:

$$F(L, I) = \sum_{i \in \mathcal{V}} \phi(l_i; I) + \sum_{(i,j) \in \mathcal{E}} \psi(l_i, l_j) \qquad (9.1)$$

The details of the potential functions in Eq. 9.1 are as follows.

Spatial prior $\psi(l_i, l_j)$ This potential function captures the compatibility of configurations of part i and part j. It is parametrized as:

$$\psi(l_i, l_j) = \alpha_{i;j;z_i;z_j}^{\top} \text{bin}(x_i - x_j, y_i - y_j)$$
$$= \sum_{a=1}^{\mathscr{P}_i} \sum_{b=1}^{\mathscr{P}_j} \mathbb{1}_a(z_i) \mathbb{1}_b(z_j) \alpha_{i;j;a;b}^{\top} \text{bin}(x_i - x_j, y_i - y_j)$$

Similar to Ramanan (2006), the function $\text{bin}(\cdot)$ is a vectorized count of spatial histogram bins. We use $\mathbb{1}_a(\cdot)$ to denote the function that takes 1 if its argument equals a, and 0 otherwise. Here $\alpha_{i;j;z_i;z_j}$ is a model parameter that favors certain relative spatial bins when poselets z_i and z_j are chosen for parts i and j, respectively. Overall, this potential function models the (relative) spatial arrangement and poselet assignment of a pair (i, j) of parts.

Local appearance $\phi(l_i; I)$ This potential function captures the compatibility of placing the poselet z_i at the location (x_i, y_i) of an image I. It is parametrized as:

$$\phi(l_i; I) = \beta_{i;z_i}^{\top} f(I(l_i)) = \sum_{a=1}^{\mathscr{P}_i} \beta_{i;a}^{\top} f(I(l_i)) \cdot \mathbb{1}_a(z_i)$$

where $\beta_{i;z_i}$ is a vector of model parameters corresponding to the poselet z_i and $f(I(l_i))$ is a feature vector corresponding to the image patch defined by l_i. We define $f(I(l_i))$ as a length $\mathscr{P}_i + 1$ vector as:

$$f(I(l_i)) = [f_1(I(l_i)), f_2(I(l_i)), ..., f_{\mathscr{P}_i}(I(l_i)), 1]$$

Each element $f_r(I(l_i))$ is the score of placing poselet z_r at image location (x_i, y_i). The constant 1 appended at the end of vector allows us to learn the model with a bias term. In other words, the score of placing the poselet z_i at image location (x_i, y_i) is a linear combination (with bias term) of the responses all the poselet templates at (x_i, y_i) for part i. We have found that this feature vector works better than the one used in Yang et al. (2010), which defines $f(I(l_i))$ as a scalar of a single poselet template response. This is because the poselet templates learned for a particular part are usually not independent of each other. So it helps to combine their responses as the local appearance model.

We summarize and highlight the important properties of our model and contextualize our research by comparing with related work.

Discriminative "parts" Our model is based on a new concept of "parts" which goes beyond the traditional rigid parts. Rigid parts are inherently difficult to detect. We instead consider parts covering a wide range of portions of human bodies. We use poselets to capture distinctive appearance patterns of various parts. These poselets have better discriminative powers than traditional rigid part detectors. For example, look at the examples in Figs. 9.2 and 9.3, the poselets capture various characteristic patterns for large parts, such as the "A"-shape for the legs in the first row of Fig. 9.2.

Coarse-to-fine granularity Different parts in our model are represented by features at varying levels of details (i.e., cell sizes in HOG descriptors). Conceptually, this multi-level granularity can be seen as providing an efficient coarse-to-fine search strategy. However, it is very different from the coarse-to-fine cascade pruning in Sapp et al. (2010b). The method in Sapp et al. (2010b) prunes the search space of small parts (e.g., right lower arm) at the coarse level using simple features and apply more sophisticated features in the pruned search space. However, we would like to argue that at the coarse level, one should not even consider small parts, since they are inherently difficult to detect or prune at this level. Instead, we should focus on large body parts since they are easy to find at the coarse level. The configurations of large pieces of human bodies will guide the search of smaller parts. For example, an upright torso with arms raising up (coarse-level information) is a very good indicator of where the arms (fine-level details) might be.

Structured hierarchical model A final important property of our model is that we combine information across different parts in a structured hierarchical way. The original work on poselets (Bourdev and Malik 2009; Bourdev et al. 2010) uses a simple Hough voting scheme for person detection, that is, each poselet votes for the center of the person, and the votes are combined together. This Hough voting might be appropriate for person detection, but it is not enough for human parsing which involves highly complex and structured outputs. Instead, we develop a structured model that organize information about different parts in a hierarchical fashion. Another work that uses hierarchical models for human parsing is the AND-OR graph in Zhu et al. (2008). But there are two important differences. First, the appearance models used in Zhu et al. (2008) are only defined on sub-parts of body segments. Their hierarchical model is only used to put all the small pieces together. As mentioned earlier, appearance models based on body segments are inherently unreliable. In contrast, we use appearance models associated with parts of varying sizes. Second, the OR-nodes in Zhu et al. (2008) are conceptually similar to poselets in our case. But the OR-nodes in Zhu et al. (2008) are defined manually, while our poselets are learned.

Our work on human parsing can be seen as bridging the gap between two popular schools of approaches for human parsing: part-based methods, and exemplar-based methods. Part-based methods, as explained above, model the human body as a collection of rigid parts. They use local part appearances to search for those parts in an image, and use configuration priors to put these pieces together in some plausible way. But since the configuration priors in these methods are typically defined as pairwise constraints between parts, these methods usually lack any notion that captures what a person should look like as a whole. In contrast, exemplar-based methods (Mori and Malik 2002; Shakhnarovich et al. 2003; Sullivan and Carlsson 2002) search for images with similar whole body configurations, and transfer the poses of those well-matched training images to a new image. The limitation of exemplar-based approaches is that they require good matching of the entire body. They cannot handle test images of which the legs are similar to some training images, while the arms are similar to other training images. Our work combines the benefits of both schools. On one hand, we capture the large-scale information of human pose via large parts. On the other hand, we have the flexibility to compose new poses from different parts.

9.4.2 Inference

Given an image I, the inference problem is to find the optimal pose labeling L^* that maximize the score $F(L, I)$, that is, $L^* = \arg\max_L F(L, I)$. We use the max-product version of belief propagation to solve this problem. We pick the vertex corresponding to part "whole body" as the root and pass messages upwards towards this root. The message from part i to its parent j is computed as:

$$m_i(l_j) = \max_{l_i}(u(l_j) + \psi(l_i, l_j)) \tag{9.2}$$

$$u(l_j) = \phi(l_j) + \sum_{k \in \text{kids}_j} m_k(l_j)$$

Afterwards, we pass messages downward from the root to other vertices in a similar fashion. This message passing scheme is repeated several times until it converges. If we temporarily ignore the poselet indices z_i and z_j and think of $l_i = (x_i, y_i)$, we can represent the messages as 2D images and pass messages using techniques similar to those in Ramanan (2006). The image $u(l_j)$ is obtained by summing together response images from its child parts $m_k(l_j)$ and its local response image $\phi(l_j)$. $\phi(l_j)$ can be computed in linear time by convolving the HOG feature map with the template of z_j. The maximization in Eq. 9.2 can also be calculated in time linear to the size of $u(l_j)$. In practice, we compute messages on each fixed (z_i, z_j) and enumerate all the possible assignments of (z_i, z_j) to obtain the final message. Note that since the graph structure is not a tree, this message passing scheme does not guarantee to find the globally optimal solution. But empirically, we have found this approximate inference scheme to be sufficient for our application.

The inference gives us the image locations and poselet indices of all the 20 parts (both primitive and non-primitive). To obtain the final parsing result, we need to compute the locations of the two endpoints for each primitive part. These can be obtained from the mean endpoint locations recorded for each primitive part poselet (see Sect. 9.3).

Figure 9.4 shows a graphical illustration of applying our model on a test image. For each part in the hierarchy, we show two sample patches and the SVM HOG template corresponding to the poselet chosen for that part.

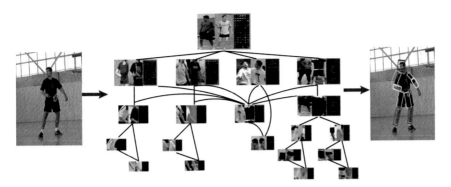

Fig. 9.4 A graphical illustration of applying our model on a test image. For each part (please refer to Fig. 9.1), we show the inferred poselet by visualizing two sample patches from the corresponding poselet cluster and the SVM HOG template

9.4.3   Learning

In order to describe the learning algorithm, we first write Eq. 9.1 as a linear function of a single parameter vector w which is a concatenation of all the model parameters, that is:

$$F(L, I) = w^\top \Phi(I, L), \quad \text{where}$$
$$w = [\alpha_{i;j;a;b}; \beta_{i;a}], \quad \forall i, j, a, b$$
$$\Phi(I, L) = [\mathbb{1}_a(z_i)\mathbb{1}_b(z_j)\text{bin}(x_i - x_j, y_i - y_j); f(I(l_i))\mathbb{1}_a(z_i)], \quad \forall i, j, a, b$$

The inference scheme in Sect. 9.4.2 solves $L^* = \arg\max_L w^\top \Phi(I, L)$. Given a set of training images in the form of $\{I^n, L^n\}_{n=1}^N$, we learn the model parameters w using a form of structural SVM (Tsochantaridis et al. 2005) as follows:

$$\min_{w, \xi} \frac{1}{2}||w||^2 + C \sum_n \xi^n, \quad \text{s.t. } \forall n, \ \forall L \tag{9.3}$$
$$w^\top \Phi(I^n, L^n) - w^\top \Phi(I^n, L) \geq \Delta(L, L^n) - \xi^n \tag{9.4}$$

Consider a training image I^n, the constraint in Eq. 9.4 enforces the score of the true label L^n to be larger than the score of any other hypothesis label L by some margin. The loss function $\Delta(L, L^n)$ measures how incorrect L is compared with L^n. Similar to regular SVMs, ξ_n are slack variables used to handle soft margins. This formulation is often called margin-rescaling in the SVM-struct literature (Tsochantaridis et al. 2005).

We use a loss function that decomposes into a sum of local losses defined on each part $\Delta(L, L^n) = \sum_{i=1}^K \Delta_i(L_i, L_i^n)$. If the i-th part is a primitive part, we define the local loss $\Delta_i(L_i, L_i^n)$ as:

$$\Delta_i(L_i, L_i^n) = \lambda \cdot \mathbb{1}(z_i \neq z_i^n) + d((x_i, y_i), (x_i^n, y_i^n)) \tag{9.5}$$

where $\mathbb{1}(\cdot)$ is an indicator function that takes 1 if its argument is true, and 0 otherwise. The intuition of Eq. 9.5 is as follows. If the hypothesized poselet z_i is the same as the ground-truth poselet z_i^n for the i-th part, the first term of Eq. 9.5 will be zero. Otherwise it will incur a loss λ (we choose $\lambda = 10$ in our experiments). The second term in Eq. 9.5, $d((x_i, y_i), (x_i^n, y_i^n))$, measures the distance (we use l_1 distance) between two image locations (x_i, y_i) and (x_i^n, y_i^n). If the hypothesized image location (x_i, y_i) is the same as the ground-truth image location (x_i^n, y_i^n) for the i-th part, no loss is added. Otherwise a loss proportional to the l_1 distance of these two locations will be incurred.

If the i-th part is not a primitive part, we simply set $\Delta(L_i, L_i^n)$ to be zero. This choice is based on the following observation. In our framework, non-primitive parts only serve as some intermediate representations that help us to search for and disambiguate small primitive parts. The final human parsing results are still obtained from configurations l_i of primitive parts. Even if a particular hypothesized L gets one of its non-primitive part labeling wrong, it should not be penalized as long as the labelings of primitive parts are correct.

The optimization problem in Eqs. (9.3, 9.4) is convex and can be solved using the cutting plane method implemented in the SVM-struct package (Joachims et al. 2008). However we opt to use a simpler stochastic subgradient descent method to allow greater flexibility in terms of implementation.

First, it is easy to show that Eqs. (9.3, 9.4) can be equivalently written as:

$$\min_{w} \frac{1}{2}||w||^2 + C \sum_n \mathscr{R}^n(L), \text{ where } \mathscr{R}^n(L) =$$

$$\max_L \left(\Delta(L, L^n) + w^\top \Phi(I^n, L) - w^\top \Phi(I^n, L^n) \right)$$

In order to do gradient descent, we need to calculate the subgradient $\partial_w \mathscr{R}^n(L)$ at a particular w. Let us define:

$$L^\star = \arg\max_L \left(\Delta(L, L^n) + w^\top \Phi(I^n, L) \right) \tag{9.6}$$

Equation 9.6 is called loss-augmented inference (Joachims et al. 2008). It can be shown that the subgradient $\partial_w \mathscr{R}^n(L)$ can be computed as $\partial_w \mathscr{R}(L) = \Phi(I^n, L^\star) - \Phi(I^n, L^n)$. Since the loss function $\Delta(L, L^n)$ can be decomposed into a sum over local losses on each individual part, the loss-augmented inference in Eq. 9.6 can be solved in a similar way to the inference problem in Sect. 9.4.2. The only difference is that the local appearance model $\phi(l_i; I)$ needs to be augmented with the local loss function $\Delta(L_i, L_i^n)$. Interested readers are referred to Joachims et al. (2008) for more details.

9.5 Action Recognition

The hierarchical poselet is a representation general enough to be used in many applications. In this section, we demonstrate it in human action recognition from static images.

Look at the images depicted in Fig. 9.5. We can easily perceive the actions of people in those images, even though only static images are given. So far most work in human action recognition has been focusing on recognition from videos. While videos certainly provide useful cues (e.g., motion) for action recognition, the examples in Fig. 9.5 clearly show that the information conveyed by static images is also an important component of action recognition. In this paper, we consider the problem of inferring human actions from static images. In particular, we are interested in exploiting the human pose as a source of information for action recognition.

Several approaches have been proposed to address the problem of static image action recognition in the literature. The first is a standard pattern classification approach, that is, learning a classifier based on certain image feature representations. For example, Ikizler-Cinbis et al. (2009) learn SVM classifiers based on HOG descriptors. The limitation with this approach is that it completely ignores the pose of a person. Another limitation is that SVM classifiers implicitly assume that images from the same action category can be represented by a canonical prototype (which are captured by the weights of the SVM classifier). However, the examples in Fig. 9.5 clearly show that humans can have very varied appearances when performing the same action, which are hard to characterize with a canonical prototype.

Another approach to static image action recognition is to explicitly recover the human pose, then use the pose as a feature representation for action recognition. For example, Ferrari et al. (2009) estimate the 2D human pose in TV shots. The estimated 2D poses can be used to extract features which in turn can be used to retrieve TV shots containing people with similar poses to a query. As point out in Yang et al.

dancing playing golf running   sitting   walking

athletics badminton baseball gymnastics parkour   soccer   tennis   volleyball

Fig. 9.5 Human actions in static images. We show some sample images and their annotations on the two data sets used in our experiments (see Sect. 9.6). Each image is annotated with the action category and joints on the human body. It is clear from these examples that static images convey a lot of information about human actions

(2010), the problem with this approach is that 2D human pose estimation is still a very challenging problem. The output of the state-of-the-art pose estimation system is typically not reliable enough to be directly used for action recognition.

The work in Yang et al. (2010) is the closest to ours. It uses a representation based on human pose for action recognition. But instead of explicitly recovering the precise pose configuration, it represents the human pose as a set of latent variables in the model. Their method does not require the predicted human pose to be exactly correct. Instead, it learns which components of the pose are useful for differentiating various actions.

The pose representation in Yang et al. (2010) is limited to four parts: upper body, left/right arm, and legs. Learning and inference in their model amounts to infer the best configurations of these four parts for a particular action. A limitation of this representation is that it does not contain pose information about larger (e.g., whole body) or smaller (e.g., half-limbs) parts. We believe that pose information useful for discerning actions can vary depending on different action categories. Some actions (e.g., *running*) have distinctive pose characteristics in terms of both the upper and lower bodies, while other actions (e.g., *pointing*) are characterized by only one arm. The challenge is how to represent the pose information at various levels of details for action recognition.

In this section, we use hierarchical poselets to capture richer pose information for action recognition. While a richer pose representation may offer more pose information (less bias), it must also be harder to estimate accurately (more variance). In this paper, we demonstrate that our rich pose representation (even with higher variance) is useful for action recognition.

9.5.1 Action-Specific Hierarchical Poselets

Since our goal is action recognition, we choose to use an action-specific variant of the hierarchical poselets. This is similar to the action-specific poselets used in Yang et al. (2010). The difference is that the action-specific poselets in Yang et al. (2010) are only defined in terms of four parts—left/right arms, upper-body, and legs. These four parts are organized in a star-like graphical model. In contrast, our pose representation captures a much wider range of information across various pieces of the human body. So ours is a much richer representation than Yang et al. (2010).

The training images are labeled with ground-truth action categories and joints on the human body (Fig. 9.5). We use the following procedure to select poselets for a specific part (e.g., *legs*) of a particular action category (e.g., *running*). We first collect training images of that action category (*running*). Then we cluster the joints on the part (*legs*) into several clusters based on their relative (x, y) coordinates with respect to some reference joint. Each cluster will correspond to a "running legs" poselet. We repeat this process for the part in other action categories. In the end, we obtain about 15–30 clusters for each part. Figures 9.6 and 9.7 show examples of poselets for "playing golf" and "running" actions, respectively.

Fig. 9.6 Examples of poselets for "playing golf". For each poselet, we visualize several patches from the corresponding cluster and the SVM HOG template. Notice the multi-scale nature of the poselets. These poselets cover various portions of the human bodies, including the whole body (*1st row*), both legs (*2nd row*), one arm (*3rd row*), respectively

Fig. 9.7 Examples of poselets for "running". For each poselet, we visualize several patches from the corresponding cluster and the SVM HOG template. Similar to Fig. 9.6, these poselets cover various portions of the human bodies

Similarly, we train a classifier based on HOG features (Dalal and Triggs 2005) to detect the presence of each poselet. Image patches in the corresponding poselet cluster are used as positive examples and random patches as negative examples for training the classifier. Similar to the model in Sect. 9.4, we use different cell sizes when constructing HOG features for different parts. Large cell sizes are used for poselets of large body parts (e.g., whole body and torso), while small cell sizes are used for small body parts (e.g., half limbs). Figures 9.6 and 9.7 show some examples of the learned SVM weights for some poselets.

9.5.2 Our Model

Let I be an image containing a person, $Y \in \mathcal{Y}$ be its action label where $\mathcal{Y}$ is the action label alphabet, L be the pose configuration of the person. The complete pose configuration is denoted as $L = \{l_i\}_{i=1}^{K}$ ($K = 20$ in our case), where $l_i = (x_i, y_i, z_i)$ represents the 2D image location and the index of the corresponding poselet cluster for the i-th part. The complete pose L can be represented by a graph $\mathcal{G} = \{\mathcal{V}, \mathcal{E}\}$ shown in Fig. 9.1. A vertex $i \in \mathcal{V}$ denotes the i-th part and an edge $(i, j) \in \mathcal{E}$ represents the spatial constraint between the i-th and the j-th parts. We define the following scoring function to measure the compatibility of the triple (I, L, Y):

$$F(I, L, Y) = \omega_Y(I) + \sum_{i \in \mathcal{V}} \phi_Y(I, l_i) + \sum_{i,j \in \mathcal{E}} \psi_Y(l_i, l_j) \tag{9.7}$$

Here we use the subscript to explicitly emphasize that these functions are specific for a particular action label Y. The details of the potential functions in Eq. 9.7 are as follows.

Root appearance $\omega_Y(I)$: This potential function models the compatibility of the action label Y and the global appearance of an image I. It is parametrized as:

$$\omega_Y(I) = \alpha_Y^\top \cdot f(I) \tag{9.8}$$

Here $f(I)$ is a feature vector extracted from the whole image I without considering the pose. In this paper, we use the HOG descriptor (Dalal and Triggs 2005) of I as the feature vector $f(I)$. The parameters α_Y can be interpreted as a HOG template for the action category Y. Note that if we only consider this potential function, the parameters $\{\alpha_Y\}_{Y \in \mathcal{Y}}$ can be obtained from the weights of a multi-class linear SVM trained with HOG descriptors $f(I)$ alone without considering the pose information.

Part appearance $\phi_Y(I, l_i)$: This potential function models the compatibility of the configuration l_i of the i-th part and the local image patch defined by $l_i = (x_i, y_i, z_i)$, under the assumption that the action label is Y. Since our goal is action recognition, we also enforce that the poselet z_i should comes from the action Y. In other words, if we define $\mathcal{Z}_i^Y$ as the set of poselet indices for the i-th part corresponding to the action category Y, this potential function is parametrized as:

$$\phi_Y(I, l_i) = \begin{cases} \beta_{i,Y}^\top \cdot f(I, l_i) & \text{if } z_i \in \mathcal{Z}_i^Y \\ -\infty & \text{otherwise.} \end{cases} \tag{9.9}$$

Here $f(I, l_i)$ is the score of placing the SVM HOG template z_i at location (x_i, y_i) in the image I.

Pairwise part constraint $\psi(l_i, l_j)$: This potential function models the compatibility of the configurations between the i-th and the j-th parts, under the assumption that the action label is Y. We parametrize this potential function using a vectorized counts of spatial histogram bins, similar to Ramanan (2006), Yang et al. (2010).

Again, we enforce poselets z_i and z_j to come from action Y as follows:

$$\psi_Y(l_i, l_j) = \begin{cases} \gamma_{i,Y}^\top \cdot \mathrm{bin}(l_i - l_j) & \text{if } z_i \in \mathcal{Z}_i^Y, z_j \in \mathcal{Z}_j^Y \\ -\infty & \text{otherwise} \end{cases} \tag{9.10}$$

Here $\mathrm{bin}(\cdot)$ is a vector all zeros with a single one for the occupied bin.

Note that if the potential functions and model parameters in Eqs. (9.7, 9.8, 9.9, 9.10) do not depend on the action label Y, the part appearance $\phi(\cdot)$ and pairwise part constraint $\psi(\cdot)$ exactly recover the human parsing model in Sect. 9.4.

9.5.3 Learning and Inference

We define the score of labeling an image I with the action label Y as follows:

$$H(I, Y) = \max_L F(I, L, Y) \tag{9.11}$$

Given the model parameters $\Theta = \{\alpha, \beta, \gamma\}$, Eq. 9.11 is a standard MAP inference problem in undirected graphical models. We can approximately solve it using message passing scheme similar to that in Sect. 9.4.2. The predicted action label Y^* is chosen as $Y^* = \arg\max_Y H(I, Y)$.

We adopt the latent SVM (Felzenszwalb et al. 2010) framework for learning the model parameters. First, it is easy to see that Eq. 9.7 can be written as a linear function of model parameters as $F(I, L, Y) = \Theta^\top \Phi(I, L, Y)$, where Θ is the concatenation of all the model parameters (i.e., α, β and γ) and $\Phi(I, L, Y)$ is the concatenation of the corresponding feature vectors. Given a set of training examples in the form of $\{I^n, L^n, Y^n\}_{n=1}^N$, the model parameters are learned by solving the following optimization problem:

$$\min_{\Theta, \xi} \frac{1}{2}||\Theta||^2 + C \sum_n \xi^n, \quad \text{s.t. } \forall n, \ \forall Y \tag{9.12}$$

$$H(I^n, Y^n) - H(I^n, Y) \geq \Delta(Y, Y^n) - \xi^n \tag{9.13}$$

It is easy to show that Eqs. (9.12, 9.13) can be equivalently written as:

$$\min_\Theta \frac{1}{2}||\Theta||^2 + C \sum_n \mathcal{R}^n, \quad \text{where} \tag{9.14}$$

$$\mathcal{R}^n = \max_{Y, L} \left(\Delta(Y, Y^n) + \Theta^\top \cdot \Phi(I^n, Y) \right) - \max_L \Theta^\top \cdot \Phi(I^n, L, Y^n)$$

The problem in Eq. 9.14 is not convex, but we can use simple stochastic subgradient descent to find a local optimum. Let us define:

$$(Y^*, L^*) = \arg\max_{Y,L}(\Delta(Y, Y^n) + \Theta^\top \cdot \Phi(I^n, L, Y))$$
$$L' = \arg\max_L(\Theta^\top \cdot \Phi(I^n, L, Y^n))$$

Then the gradient of Eq. 9.14 can be computed as:

$$\Theta + C \sum_n \left(\Phi(I^n, L^*, Y^*) - \Phi(I^n, L', Y^n) \right)$$

To initialize the parameter learning, we first learn a pose estimation model using the labeled (I^n, L^n) collected from training examples with class label Y. The parameters of these pose estimation models are used to initialize β_Y and γ_Y. The parameters α_Y are initialized from a linear SVM model based on HOG descriptors without considering the poses.

9.6 Experiments

In this section, we present our experimental results on human parsing (Sect. 9.6.1) and action recognition (Sect. 9.6.2).

9.6.1 Experiments on Human Parsing

There are several data sets popular in the human parsing community, for example, Buffy data set (Ferrari et al. 2008), PASCAL stickmen data set (Eichner and Ferrari 2009). But these data sets are not suitable for us for several reasons. First of all, they only contain upper-bodies, but we are interested in full-body parsing. Second, as pointed out in Tran and Forsyth (2010), there are very few pose variations in those data sets. In fact, previous work has exploited this property of these data sets by pruning search spaces using upper-body detection and segmentation (Ferrari et al. 2008), or by building appearance model using location priors (Eichner and Ferrari 2009). Third, the contrast of image frames of the Buffy data set is relatively low. This issue suggests that better performance can be achieved by engineering detectors to overcome the contrast difficulties. Please refer to the discussion in Tran and Forsyth (2010) for more details. In our work, we choose to use two data sets[1] containing very aggressive pose variations. The first one is the UIUC people data set introduced in Tran and Forsyth (2010). The second one is a new sport image data set we have collected from the Internet which has been used in Wang et al. (2011). Figure 9.8 shows scatter plots of different body parts of our data sets compared with the Buffy

---

[1]Both data sets can be downloaded from http://vision.cs.uiuc.edu/humanparse.

head + upper arm   head + lower arm

Buffy   UIUC people sport images   Buffy   UIUC people sport images

Fig. 9.8 Scatter plots of heads (*red*) and upper/lower arms (*blue* and *green*) with respect to fixed upper body position on three data sets

data set (Ferrari et al. 2008) using a visualization style similar to Tran and Forsyth (2010). It is clear that the two data sets used in this paper have much more variations.

9.6.1.1   UIUC People Data Set

The UIUC people data set (Tran and Forsyth 2010) contains 593 images (346 for training, 247 for testing). Most of them are images of people playing badminton. Some are images of people playing Frisbee, walking, jogging or standing. Sample images and their parsing results are shown in the first three rows of Fig. 9.9. We compare with two other state-of-the-art approaches that do full-body parsing (with published codes): the improved pictorial structure by Andriluka et al. (2009), and the iterative parsing method by Ramanan (2006). The results are also shown in Fig. 9.9.

To quantitatively evaluate different methods, we measure the percentage of correctly localized body parts. Following the convention proposed in Ferrari et al. (2008), a body part is considered correctly localized if the endpoints of its segment lies within

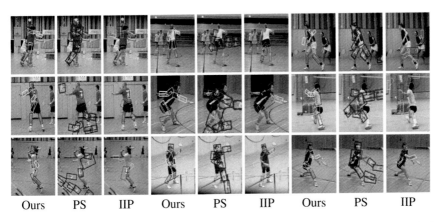

Ours   PS   IIP   Ours   PS   IIP   Ours   PS   IIP

Fig. 9.9 Examples of human body parsing on the UIUC people data set. We compare our method with the pictorial structure (PS) (Andriluka et al. 2009) and the iterative image parsing (IIP) (Ramanan 2006). Notice the large pose variations, cluttered background, self-occlusions, and many other challenging aspects of the data set

Table 9.1 Human parsing results by our method and two comparison methods (Ramanan 2006; Andriluka et al. 2009) on two data sets. The percentage of correctly localized parts is shown for each primitive part. If two numbers are shown in one cell, they indicate the left/right body parts. As a comparison, we also show the results of using only rigid parts (basic-level)

(a) UIUC people data set

Method	Torso	Upper leg		Lower leg		Upper arm		Forearm		Head
Ramanan (2006)	44.1	11.7	7.3	25.5	25.1	11.3	10.9	**25.9**	**25**	30.8
Andriluka et al. (2009)	70.9	37.3	35.6	23.1	22.7	22.3	30.0	9.7	10.5	59.1
Our method (basic-level)	79.4	53.8	53.4	47.8	39.7	17.8	21.1	11.7	16.6	65.2
Our method (full model)	**86.6**	**58.3**	**54.3**	**53.8**	**46.6**	**28.3**	**33.2**	23.1	17.4	**68.8**

(b) Sport image data set

Method	Torso	Upper leg		Lower leg		Upper arm		Forearm		Head
Ramanan (2006)	28.7	7.4	7.2	17.6	20.8	8.3	6.6	**20.2**	**21**	12.9
Andriluka et al. (2009)	71.5	44.2	43.1	30.7	31	**28**	**29.6**	17.3	15.3	**63.3**
Our method (basic-level)	73.3	45.0	47.6	40.4	39.9	19.4	27.0	13.3	9.9	47.5
Our method (full model)	**75.3**	**50.1**	**48.2**	**42.5**	**36.5**	23.3	27.1	12.2	10.2	47.5

50% of the ground-truth segment length from their true locations. The comparative results are shown in Table 9.1a. Our method outperforms other approaches in localizing most of body parts. We also show the result (3rd row, Table 9.1a) of using only the basic-level poselets corresponding to the rigid parts. It is clear that our full model using hierarchical poselets outperforms using rigid parts alone.

Detection and parsing: An interesting aspect of our approach is that it produces not only the configurations of primitive parts, but also the configurations of other larger body parts. These pieces of information can potentially be used for applications (e.g., gesture-based HCI) that do not require precise localizations of body segments. In Fig. 9.10, we visualize the configurations of four larger parts on some examples. Interestingly, the configuration of the whole body directly gives us a person detector. So our model can be seen as a principled way of unifying human pose estimation, person detection, and many other areas related to understanding humans. In the first row of Table 9.2, we show the results of person detection on the UIUC people data set by running our human parsing model, then picking the bounding box corresponding to the part "whole body" as the detection. We compare with the state-of-the-art person detectors in Felzenszwalb et al. (2010) and Andriluka et al. (2009). Since most images contain one person, we only consider the detection with the best score on an image for all the methods. We use the metric defined in the PASCAL VOC challenge to

Fig. 9.10 Examples of other information produced by our model. On each image, we show *bounding boxes* corresponding to the whole body, left arm, right arm and legs. The size of each bounding box is estimated from its corresponding poselet cluster

Table 9.2 Comparison of accuracies of person detection on both data sets. In our method, the configuration of the poselets corresponding to the whole body can be directly used for person detection

	Our method	Felzenszwalb et al. (2010)	Andriluka et al. (2009)
UIUC people	**66.8**	48.58	50.61
Sport image	**63.94**	45.61	59.94

measure the performance. A detection is considered correct if the intersection over union with respect to the ground truth bounding box is at least 50%. It is interesting to see that our method outperforms other approaches, even though it is not designed for person detection.

9.6.1.2   Sport Image Data Set

The UIUC people data set is attractive because it has very aggressive pose and spatial variations. But one limitation of that data set is that it mainly contains images of people playing badminton. One might ask what happens if the images are more diverse. To answer this question, we have collected a new sport image data set from more than 20 sport categories, including acrobatics, American football, croquet, cycling, hockey, figure skating, soccer, golf and horseback riding. There are in total 1299 images. We randomly choose 649 of them for training and the rest for testing. The last three rows of Fig. 9.9 show examples of human parsing results, together with results of Andriluka et al. (2009) and Ramanan (2006) on this data set. The quantitative comparison is shown in Table 9.1b. We can see that our approach outperforms the other two on the majority of body parts (Fig. 9.11).

Similarly, we perform person detection using the poselet corresponding to the whole body. The results are shown in the second row of Table 9.2. Again, our method outperforms other approaches.

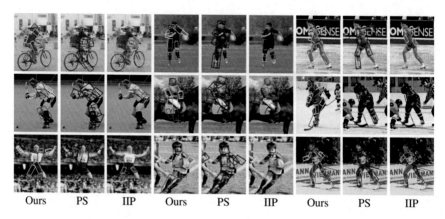

Ours   PS   IIP   Ours   PS   IIP   Ours   PS   IIP

Fig. 9.11 Examples of human body parsing on the sport image data set. We compare our method with the pictorial structure (PS) (Andriluka et al. 2009) and the iterative image parsing (IIP) (Ramanan 2006)

9.6.1.3   Kinematic Tracking

To further illustrate our method, we apply the model learned from the UIUC people data set for kinematic tracking by independently parsing the human figure in each frame. In Fig. 9.12, we show our results compared with applying the method in Ramanan (2006). It is clear from the results that kinematic tracking is still a very challenging problem. Both methods make mistakes. Interestingly, when our method makes mistakes (e.g., figures with blue arrows), the output still looks like a valid body configuration. But when the method in Ramanan (2006) makes mistakes (e.g., figures with red arrows), the errors can be very wild. We believe this can be explained by the very different representations used in these two methods. In Ramanan (2006), a human body is represented by the set of primitive parts. Kinematic constraints are used to enforce the connectivity of those parts. But these kinematic constraints have no idea what a person looks like as a whole. In the incorrect results of Ramanan (2006), all the primitive parts are perfectly connected. The problem is their connectivity does not form a reasonable human pose as a whole.

In contrast, our model uses representations that capture a spectrum of both large and small body parts. Even in situations where the small primitive parts are hard to detect, our method can still reason about the plausible pose configuration by pulling information from large pieces of the human bodies.

9.6.2   Experiments on Action Recognition

We test our approach on two publicly available data sets: the still images data set (Ikizler et al. 2008) and the Leeds sport data set (Johnson and Everingham 2010). Both data sets contain images of people with ground-truth pose annotations and action labels.

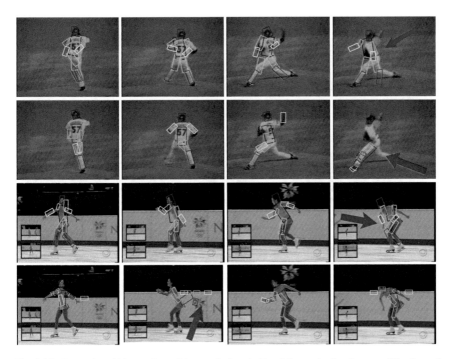

Fig. 9.12 Examples of kinematic tracking on the baseball and figure skating data sets. The *1st* and *3rd* rows are our results. The *2nd* and *4th* rows are results of Ramanan (2006). Notice how mistakes of our method (*blue arrows*) still look like valid human poses, while those of Ramanan (2006) (*red arrows*) can be wild

9.6.2.1   Still Image Data Set

We first demonstrate our model on the still image data set collected in Ikizler et al. (2008). This data set contains more than 2000 static images from five action categories: dancing, playing golf, running, sitting, and walking. Sample images are shown in the first two rows of Fig. 9.5. Yang et al. (2010) have annotated the pose with 14 joints on the human body on all the images in the data set. Following Yang et al. (2010), we choose 1/3 of the images from each category to form the training data, and the remaining ones as the test data.[2]

We compare our approach with two baseline method. The first baseline is a multi-class SVM based on HOG features. For the second baseline, we use mixtures of SVM models similar to that in Felzenszwalb et al. (2010). We set the number of mixtures for each class to be the number of whole-body poselets. From Table 9.3, we can see that our approach outperforms the baseline by a large margin. Our performance is

---

[2]A small number of images/annotations we obtained from the authors of Yang et al. (2010) are somehow corrupted due to some file-system failure. We have removed those images from the data set.

Table 9.3 Performance on the still image data set. We report both overall and average per-class accuracies

Method	Overall	Avg per-class
Our approach	**65.15**	**70.77**
Yang et al. (2010)[a]	63.49	68.37
SVM mixtures	62.8	64.05
Linear SVM	60.32	61.5

[a]The results are based on our own implementation

dancing   playing golf   running

sitting   walking

Fig. 9.13 Visualization of some inferred poselets on the still image data set. These test images have been correctly recognized by our model. For a test image, we show three poselets that have high responses. Each poselet is visualized by showing several patches from its cluster

also better than the reported results in Yang et al. (2010). However, the accuracy numbers are not directly comparable since the training/testing data sets and features are not completely identical. In order to do a fair comparison, we re-implemented the method in Yang et al. (2010) by only keeping the parts used in Yang et al. (2010). Our full model performs better.

In Fig. 9.13, we visualize several inferred poselets on some examples whose action categories are correctly classified. Each poselet is visualized by showing several patches from the corresponding poselet cluster.

9.6.2.2 Leeds Sport Data Set

The Leeds sport data set (Johnson and Everingham 2010) contains 2000 images from eight different sports: athletics, badminton, baseball, gymnastics, parkour, soccer, tennis, volleyball. Each image in the data set is labeled with 14 joints on the human

Table 9.4 Performance on the Leeds sport data set. We report both overall and average per-class accuracies

Method	Overall	Avg per-class
Our approach	**54.6**	**54.6**
SVM mixtures	52.7	49.13
Linear SVM	52.7	52.93

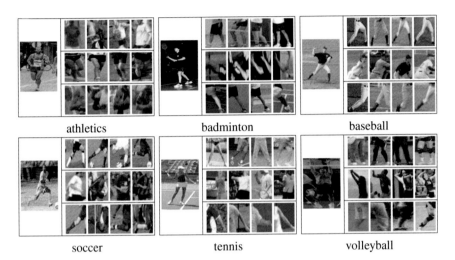

athletics   badminton   baseball

soccer   tennis   volleyball

Fig. 9.14 Visualization of some inferred poselets on the Leeds sport data set. These test images have been correctly recognized by our model. For a test image, we show three poselets that have high responses. Each poselet is visualized by showing several patches from its cluster

body. Sample images and the labeled joints are shown in the last four rows of Fig. 9.5. This data set is very challenging due to very aggressive pose variations.

We choose half of the images for training, and the other half for testing. The performance is shown in Table 9.4. Again, we compare with the HOG-based SVM and SVM mixtures as the baselines. We can see that our method still outperforms the baseline. Similarly, we visualize the inferred poselets on some examples in Fig. 9.14.

9.6.2.3   Unseen Actions

An interesting aspect of our model is that it outputs not only the predicted action label, but also some rich intermediate representation (i.e., action-specific hierarchical poselets) about the human pose. This information can potentially be exploited in various contexts. As an example, we apply the model learned from the still image data set to *describe* images from sports categories not available during training. In Fig. 9.15, we show examples of applying the model learned from the still image

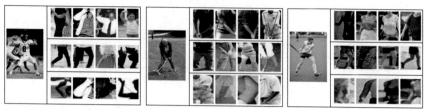

American football→dancing   croquet→playing golf   field hockey→running

Fig. 9.15 Visualization of inferred poses on unseen actions. Here the actions of the test images (*American football*, *croquet* and *field hockey*) are not available during training. Our model recognizes these examples as *dancing, playing golf, running*, respectively. Some of the results (e.g., *croquet→ golfing*) make intuitive sense. Others (e.g., *football→dancing*) might not be intuitive at first. But if we examine the poselets carefully, we can see that various pieces of the football player are very similar to those found in the dancing action

data set to images with unseen action categories. The action categories (*American football, croquet* and *field hockey*) for the examples in Fig. 9.15 are disjoint from the action categories of the still image data set. In this situation, our model obviously cannot correctly predict the action labels (since they are not available during training). Instead, it classifies those images using the action labels it has learned. For example, it classifies "American football" as "dancing", "croquet" as "playing golf", "field hockey" as "running". More importantly, our model outputs poselets for various parts which support its prediction. From these information, we can say a lot about "American football" even though the predicted action label is wrong. For example, we can say it is closer to "dancing" than "playing golf" because the pose of the football player in the image is similar to certain type of dancing legs, and certain type of dancing arms.

9.7 Conclusion and Future Work

We have presented hierarchical poselets, a new representation for modeling human poses. Different poselets in our representation capture human poses at various levels of granularity. Some poselets correspond to the rigid parts typically used in previous work. Others can correspond to large pieces of the human bodies. Poselets corresponding to different parts are organized in a structured hierarchical model. The advantage of this representation is that it infers the human pose by pulling information across various levels of details, ranging from the coarse shape of the whole body, to the fine-detailed information of small rigid parts. We have demonstrate the applications of this representation in human parsing and human action recognition from static images. Recently, similar ideas (Sun and Savarese 2011) have been applied in other applications, such as object detection.

As future work, we would like to explore how to automatically construct the parts and the hierarchy using data-driven methods. This will be important in order to extend hierarchical poselets to other objects (e.g., birds) that do not have obvious kinematic structures. We also like to apply the hierarchical poselet representation to other vision tasks, such as segmentation.

Acknowledgements This work was supported in part by NSF under IIS-0803603 and IIS-1029035, and by ONR under N00014-01-1-0890 and N00014-10-1-0934 as part of the MURI program. Yang Wang was also supported in part by an NSERC postdoc fellowship when the work was done. Any opinions, findings and conclusions or recommendations expressed in this material are those of the authors and do not necessarily reflect those of NSF, ONR, or NSERC.

References

M. Andriluka, S. Roth, B. Schiele, Pictorial structures revisited: people detection and articulated pose estimation, in *IEEE Computer Society Conference on Computer Vision and Pattern Recognition*, 2009

L. Bourdev, J. Malik, Poselets: body part detectors training using 3d human pose annotations, in *IEEE International Conference on Computer Vision*, 2009

L. Bourdev, S. Maji, T. Brox, J. Malik, Detecting people using mutually consistent poselet activations, in *European Conference on Computer Vision*, 2010

C.K. Chow, C.N. Liu, Approximating discrete probability distributions with dependence trees. IEEE Trans. Inf. Theory **14**(3), 462–467 (1968)

N. Dalal, B. Triggs, Histogram of oriented gradients for human detection, in *IEEE Computer Society Conference on Computer Vision and Pattern Recognition*, 2005

V. Delaitre, I. Laptev, J. Sivic, Recognizing human actions in still images: a study of bag-of-features and part-based representations, in *British Machine Vision Conference*, 2010

C. Desai, D. Ramanan, C. Fowlkes, Discriminative models for static human-object interactions, in *Workshop on Structured Models in Computer Vision*, 2010

P. Dollár, V. Rabaud, G. Cottrell, S. Belongie, Behavior recognition via sparse spatio-temporal features, in *ICCV'05 Workshop on Visual Surveillance and Performance Evaluation of Tracking and Surveillance*, 2005

A.A. Efros, A.C. Berg, G. Mori, J. Malik, Recognizing action at a distance, in *IEEE International Conference on Computer Vision*, 2003, pp. 726–733

M. Eichner, V. Ferrari, Better appearance models for pictorial structures, in *British Machine Vision Conference*, 2009

P.F. Felzenszwalb, D.P. Huttenlocher, Pictorial structures for object recognition. Int. J. Comput. Vis. **61**(1), 55–79 (2005)

P.F. Felzenszwalb, R.B. Girshick, D. McAllester, D. Ramanan, Object detection with discriminatively trained part based models. IEEE Trans. Pattern Anal. Mach. Intell. **32**(9), 1627–1645 (2010)

V. Ferrari, M. Marín-Jiménez, A. Zisserman, Progressive search space reduction for human pose estimation, in *IEEE Computer Society Conference on Computer Vision and Pattern Recognition*, 2008

V. Ferrari, M. Marín-Jiménez, A. Zisserman, Pose search: retrieving people using their pose, in *IEEE Computer Society Conference on Computer Vision and Pattern Recognition*, 2009

D.A. Forsyth, O. Arikan, L. Ikemoto, J. O'Brien, D. Ramanan, Computational studies of human motion: part 1, tracking and motion synthesis. Found. Trends Comput. Gr. Vis. **1**(2/3), 77–254 (2006)

A. Gupta, A. Kembhavi, L.S. Davis, Observing human-object interactions: using spatial and functional compatibility for recognition. IEEE Trans. Pattern Anal. Mach. Intell. **31**(10), 1775–1789 (2009)

N. Ikizler, R. Gokberk Cinbis, S. Pehlivan, P. Duygulu, Recognizing actions from still images, in *International Conference on Pattern Recognition*, 2008

N. Ikizler-Cinbis, R. Gokberk Cinbis, S. Sclaroff, Learning actions from the web, in *IEEE International Conference on Computer Vision*, 2009

H. Jiang, D.R. Martin, Globel pose estimation using non-tree models, in *IEEE Computer Society Conference on Computer Vision and Pattern Recognition*, 2008

T. Joachims, T. Finley, C.-N. Yu, Cutting-plane training of structural SVMs, in *Machine Learning*, 2008

S. Johnson, M. Everingham, Combining discriminative appearance and segmentation cues for articulated human pose estimation, in *International Workshop on Machine Learning for Vision-based Motion Analysis*, 2009

S. Johnson, M. Everingham, Clustered pose and nonlinear appearance models for human pose estimation, in *British Machine Vision Conference*, 2010

S.X. Ju, M.J. Black, Y. Yaccob, Cardboard people: a parameterized model of articulated image motion, in *International Conference on Automatic Face and Gesture Recognition*, 1996, pp. 38–44

Y. Ke, R. Sukthankar, M. Hebert, Event detection in crowded videos, in *IEEE International Conference on Computer Vision*, 2007

M.P. Kumar, A. Zisserman, P.H.S. Torr, Efficient discriminative learning of parts-based models, in *IEEE International Conference on Computer Vision*, 2009

T. Lan, Y. Wang, W. Yang, G. Mori, Beyond actions: discriminative models for contextual group activities, in *Advances in Neural Information Processing Systems* (MIT Press, 2010)

X. Lan, D.P. Huttenlocher, Beyond trees: common-factor models for 2d human pose recovery. IEEE Int. Conf. Comput. Vis. **1**, 470–477 (2005)

I. Laptev, M. Marszalek, C. Schmid, B. Rozenfeld, Learning realistic human actions from movies, in *IEEE Computer Society Conference on Computer Vision and Pattern Recognition*, 2008

S. Maji, L. Bourdev, J. Malik, Action recognition from a distributed representation of pose and appearance, in *IEEE Computer Society Conference on Computer Vision and Pattern Recognition*, 2011

D. Marr, *A Computational Investigation into the Human Representation and Processing of Visual Information* (W. H. Freeman, San Francisco, 1982)

G. Mori, Guiding model search using segmentation. IEEE Int. Conf. Comput. Vis. **2**, 1417–1423 (2005)

G. Mori, J. Malik, Estimating human body configurations using shape context matching. Eur. Conf. Comput. Vis. **3**, 666–680 (2002)

G. Mori, X. Ren, A. Efros, J. Malik, Recovering human body configuration: combining segmentation and recognition. IEEE Comput. Soc. Conf. Comput. Vis. Pattern Recognit. **2**, 326–333 (2004)

J.C. Niebles, L. Fei-Fei, A hierarchical model of shape and appearance for human action classification, in *IEEE Computer Society Conference on Computer Vision and Pattern Recognition*, 2007

J.C. Niebles, H. Wang, L. Fei-Fei, Unsupervised learning of human action categories using spatial-temporal words, in *British Machine Vision Conference*, vol. 3, 2006, pp. 1249–1258

D. Ramanan, Learning to parse images of articulated bodies. Adv. Neural Inf. Process. Syst. **19**, 1129–1136 (2006)

D. Ramanan, C. Sminchisescu, Training deformable models for localization. IEEE Comput. Soc. Conf. Comput. Vis. Pattern Recognit. **1**, 206–213 (2006)

D. Ramanan, D.A. Forsyth, A. Zisserman, Strike a pose: tracking people by finding stylized poses. IEEE Comput. Soc. Conf. Comput. Vis. Pattern Recognit. **1**, 271–278 (2005)

X. Ren, A. Berg, J. Malik, Recovering human body configurations using pairwise constraints between parts. IEEE Int. Conf. Comput. Vis. **1**, 824–831 (2005)

B. Sapp, C. Jordan, B. Taskar, Adaptive pose priors for pictorial structures, in *IEEE Computer Society Conference on Computer Vision and Pattern Recognition*, 2010a

B. Sapp, A. Toshev, B. Taskar, Cascaded models for articulated pose estimation, in *European Conference on Computer Vision*, 2010b

G. Shakhnarovich, P. Viola, T. Darrell, Fast pose estimation with parameter sensitive hashing. IEEE Int. Conf. Comput. Vis. **2**, 750–757 (2003)

L. Sigal, M.J. Black, Measure locally, reason globally: occlusion-sensitive articulated pose estimation. IEEE Comput. Soc. Conf. Comput. Vis. Pattern Recognit. **2**, 2041–2048 (2006)

V.K. Singh, R. Nevatia, C. Huang, Efficient inference with multiple heterogenous part detectors for human pose estimation, in *European Conference on Computer Vision*, 2010

P. Srinivasan, J. Shi, Bottom-up recognition and parsing of the human body, in *IEEE Computer Society Conference on Computer Vision and Pattern Recognition*, 2007

J. Sullivan, S. Carlsson, Recognizing and tracking human action, in *European Conference on Computer Vision LNCS 2352*, vol. 1, 2002, pp. 629–644

M. Sun, S. Savarese, Articulated part-base model for joint object detection and pose estimation, in *IEEE International Conference on Computer Vision*, 2011

T.-P. Tian, S. Sclaroff, Fast globally optimal 2d human detection with loopy graph models, in *IEEE Computer Society Conference on Computer Vision and Pattern Recognition*, 2010

K. Toyama, A. Blake, Probabilistic exemplar-based tracking in a metric space. IEEE Int. Conf. Comput. Vis. **2**, 50–57 (2001)

D. Tran, D. Forsyth, Improved human parsing with a full relational model, in *European Conference on Computer Vision*, 2010

I. Tsochantaridis, T. Joachims, T. Hofmann, Y. Altun, Large margin methods for structured and interdependent output variables. J. Mach. Learn. Res. **6**, 1453–1484 (2005)

Y. Wang, G. Mori, Multiple tree models for occlusion and spatial constraints in human pose estimation, in *European Conference on Computer Vision*, 2008

Y. Wang, H. Jiang, M.S. Drew, Z.-N. Li, G. Mori, Unsupervised discovery of action classes, in *IEEE Computer Society Conference on Computer Vision and Pattern Recognition*, 2006

Y. Wang, D. Tran, Z. Liao, Learning hierarchical poselets for human parsing, in *IEEE Computer Society Conference on Computer Vision and Pattern Recognition*, 2011

W. Yang, Y. Wang, G. Mori, Recognizing human actions from still images with latent poses, in *IEEE Computer Society Conference on Computer Vision and Pattern Recognition*, 2010

Y. Yang, D. Ramanan, Articulated pose estimation with flexible mixtures-of-parts, in *IEEE Computer Society Conference on Computer Vision and Pattern Recognition*, 2011

B. Yao, L. Fei-Fei, Modeling mutual context of object and human pose in human–object interaction activities, in *IEEE Computer Society Conference on Computer Vision and Pattern Recognition*, 2010

L. Zhu, Y. Chen, Y. Lu, C. Lin, A. Yuille, Max margin AND/OR graph learning for parsing the human body, in *IEEE Computer Society Conference on Computer Vision and Pattern Recognition*, 2008

Chapter 10
Keep It Simple and Sparse: Real-Time Action Recognition

Sean Ryan Fanello, Ilaria Gori, Giorgio Metta and Francesca Odone

Abstract Sparsity has been showed to be one of the most important properties for visual recognition purposes. In this paper we show that sparse representation plays a fundamental role in achieving one-shot learning and real-time recognition of actions. We start off from RGBD images, combine motion and appearance cues and extract state-of-the-art features in a computationally efficient way. The proposed method relies on descriptors based on 3D Histograms of Scene Flow (3DHOFs) and Global Histograms of Oriented Gradient (GHOGs); adaptive sparse coding is applied to capture high-level patterns from data. We then propose a simultaneous on-line video segmentation and recognition of actions using linear SVMs. The main contribution of the paper is an effective real-time system for one-shot action modeling and recognition; the paper highlights the effectiveness of sparse coding techniques to represent 3D actions. We obtain very good results on three different datasets: a benchmark dataset for one-shot action learning (the ChaLearn Gesture Dataset), an in-house dataset acquired by a Kinect sensor including complex actions and gestures differing by small details, and a dataset created for human-robot interaction purposes. Finally we demonstrate that our system is effective also in a human-robot interaction setting and propose a memory game, "All Gestures You Can", to be played against a humanoid robot.

Editors: Sergio Escalera, Isabelle Guyon and Vassilis Athitsos.

S.R. Fanello (✉) · I. Gori (✉) · G. Metta
iCub Facility, Istituto Italiano di Tecnologia, Via Morego 30, 16163 Genova, Italy
e-mail: sean.fanello@iit.it

I. Gori
e-mail: ilaria.gori@iit.it

G. Metta
e-mail: giorgio.metta@iit.it

F. Odone
Dipartimento di Informatica, Bioingegneria, Robotica e Ingegneria dei Sistemi,
Università degli Studi di Genova, Via Dodecaneso 35, 16146 Genova, Italy
e-mail: francesca.odone@unige.it

Keywords Real-time action recognition · Sparse representation · One-shot action learning · Human robot interaction

10.1 Introduction

Action recognition as a general problem is a very fertile research theme due to its strong applicability in several real world domains, ranging from video-surveillance to content-based video retrieval and video classification. This paper refers specifically to action recognition in the context of Human–Machine Interaction (HMI), and therefore it focuses on whole-body actions performed by a human who is standing at a short distance from the sensor.

Imagine a system capable of understanding when to turn the TV on, or when to switch the lights off on the basis of a gesture; the main requirement of such a system is an easy and fast learning and recognition procedure. Ideally, a single demonstration suffices to teach the system a new gesture. More importantly, gestures are powerful tools, through which languages can be built. In this regard, developing a system able to communicate with deaf people, or to understand paralyzed patients, would represent a great advance, with impact on the quality of life of impaired people. Nowadays these scenarios are likely as a result of the spread of imaging technologies providing real-time depth information at consumer's price (as for example the Kinect (Shotton et al. 2011) by Microsoft); these depth-based sensors are drastically changing the field of action recognition, enabling the achievement of high performance using fast algorithms.

Following this recent trend we propose a *complete system based on RGBD video sequences*, which models actions *from one example only*. Our main goal is to recognize actions in real-time with high accuracy; for this reason we design our system accounting for good performance as well as low computational complexity. The method we propose can be summarized as follows: after segmentation of the moving actor, we extract two types of features from each image, namely, Global Histograms of Oriented Gradient (GHOGs) to model the shape of the silhouette, and 3D Histograms of Flow (3DHOFs) to describe motion information. We then apply a sparse coding stage, which allows us to take care of noise and redundant information and produces a compact and stable representation of the image content. Subsequently, we summarize the action within adjacent frames by building feature vectors that describe the feature evolution over time. Finally, we train a Support Vector Machine (SVM) for each action class.

Our framework can segment and recognize actions accurately and in real-time, even though they are performed in different environments, at different speeds, or combined in sequences of multiple actions. Furthermore, thanks to the simultaneous appearance and motion description complemented by the sparse coding stage, the method provides a one-shot learning procedure. These functions are shown on three different experimental settings: a benchmark dataset for one-shot action learning (the ChaLearn Gesture Dataset), an in-house dataset acquired by a Kinect sensor including complex actions and gestures differing by small details, and an implementation of the method on a humanoid robot interacting with humans.

In order to demonstrate that our system can be efficiently engaged in real world scenarios, we developed a real-time memory game against a humanoid robot, called "All Gestures You Can" (Gori et al. 2012). Our objective in designing this interaction game is to stress the effectiveness of our gesture recognition system in complex and uncontrolled settings. Nevertheless, our long term goal is to consider more general contexts, which are beyond the game itself, such as rehabilitation and human assistance. Our game may be used also with children with memory impairment, for instance the Attention Deficit/Hyperactivity Disorder (ADHD) (Comoldi et al. 1999). These children cannot memorize items under different conditions, and have low performances during implicit and explicit memory tests (Burden and Mitchell 2005). Interestingly, Comoldi et al. (1999) shows that when ADHD children were assisted in the use of an appropriate strategy, they performed the memory task as well as controls. The game proposed in this paper could be therefore used to train memory skills to children with attention problems, using the robot as main assistant. The interaction with the robot may increase their motivation to maintain attention and help with the construction of a correct strategy.

The paper is organized as follows: in Sect. 10.2 we briefly review the state of the art. In Sect. 10.3 sparse representation is presented; Sect. 10.4 describes the complete modeling and recognition pipeline. Section 10.5 validates the approach in different scenarios; Sect. 10.6 shows a real application in the context of Human Robot Interaction (HRI). Finally, Sect. 10.7, presents future directions and possible improvements of the current implementation.

10.2   Related Work

The recent literature is rich of algorithms for gesture, action, and activity recognition—we refer the reader to Aggarwal and Ryoo (2011), Poppe (2010) for a complete survey of the topic. Even though many theoretically sound, good performing and original algorithms have been proposed, to the best of our knowledge, none of them fulfills at the same time *real-time*, *one-shot learning* and *high accuracy* requirements, although such requirements are all equally important in real world application scenarios.

Gesture recognition algorithms differ in many aspects. A first classification may be done with respect to the overall structure of the adopted framework, i.e. how the recognition problem is modeled. In particular, some approaches are based on machine learning techniques, where each action is described as a complex structure; in this class we find methods based on Hidden Markov Models (Malgireddy et al. 2012), Coupled Hidden Semi-Markov models (Natarajan and Nevatia 2007), action graphs (Li et al. 2010) or Conditional Markov Fields (Chatzis et al. 2013). Other methods are based on matching: the recognition of actions is carried out through a similarity match with all the available data, and the most similar datum dictates the estimated class (Seo and Milanfar 2012; Mahbub et al. 2011).

The two approaches are different in many ways. Machine learning methods tend to be more robust to intra-class variations, since they distill a model from different instances of the same gesture, while matching methods are more versatile and adapt more easily to one-shot learning, since they do not require a batch training procedure. From the point of view of data representation, the first class of methods usually extracts features from each frame, whereas matching-based methods try to summarize all information extracted from a video in a single feature vector. A recent and prototypical example of machine learning method can be found in Malgireddy et al. (2012), which proposes to extract local features (Histograms of Flow and Histograms of Oriented Gradient) on each frame and apply a bag-of-words step to obtain a global description of the frame. Each action is then modeled as a multi channel Hidden Markov Model (mcHMM). Although the presented algorithm leads to very good classification performance, it requires a computationally expensive offline learning phase that cannot be used in real-time for one-shot learning of new actions. Among the matching-based approaches, Seo and Milanfar (2012) is particularly interesting: the algorithm extract a new type of features, referred to as *3D LSKs*, from space-time regression kernels, particularly appropriate to identify the spatio-temporal geometric structure of the action; it then adopts the Matrix Cosine Similarity measure (Shneider and Borlund 2007) to perform a robust matching. Another recent method following the trend of matching-based action recognition algorithms is Mahbub et al. (2011); in this work the main features are standard deviation on depth (STD), Motion History Image (MHI) (Bobick and Davis 2001) and a 2D Fourier Transformation in order to map all information in the frequency domain. This procedure shows some benefits, for instance the invariance to camera shifts. For the matching step, a simple and standard correlation measure is employed. Considering this taxonomy, the work we propose falls within the machine learning approaches, but addresses specifically the problem of one-shot learning. To this end we leverage on the richness of the video signal used as a training example and on a dictionary learning approach to obtain an effective and distinctive representation of the action.

An alternative to classifying gesture recognition algorithms is based on the data representation of gesture models. In this respect there is a predominance of features computed on local areas of single frames (local features), but also holistic features are often used on the whole image or on a region of interest. Among the most known methods, it is worth mentioning the spatio-temporal interesting points (Laptev and Lindeberg 2003), spatio-temporal Hessian matrices (Willems et al. 2008), Gabor Filters (Bregonzio et al. 2009), Histograms of Flow (Fanello et al. 2010), Histograms of Oriented Gradient (Malgireddy et al. 2012), semi-local features (Wang et al. 2012), combination of multiple features (Laptev et al. 2008), Motion History Image (MHI) (Bobick and Davis 2001), Space–Time shapes Gorelick et al. (2007), Self-Similarity Matrices Efros et al. (2003). Also, due to the recent diffusion of real-time 3D vision technology, 3D features have been recently employed (Gori et al. 2012). For computational reasons as well as the necessity of specific invariance properties, we adopt global descriptors, computed on a region of interest obtained through motion segmentation. We do not rely on a single cue but rather combine motion and appearance similarly to Malgireddy et al. (2012).

The most similar works to this paper are in the field of HMI as for example Lui (2012) and Wu et al. (2012): they both exploit depth information and aim at one-shot learning trying to achieve low computational cost. The first method employs a nonlinear regression framework on manifolds: actions are represented as tensors decomposed via Higher Order Singular Value Decomposition. The underlying geometry of tensor space is used. The second one extracts Extended-MHI as features and uses Maximum Correlation Coefficient (Hirschfeld 1935) as classifier. Features from RBG and Depth streams are fused via a Multiview Spectral Embedding (MSE). Differently from these works, our approach aims specifically to obtain an accurate real-time recognition from one video example only.

We conclude the section with a reference to some works focusing on continuous action or activity recognition (Ali and Aggarwal 2001; Green and Guan 2004; Liao et al. 2006; Alon et al. 2009). In this case training and test videos contain many sequential gestures, therefore the temporal segmentation of videos becomes fundamental. Our work deals with continuous action recognition as well, indeed the proposed framework comprehends a novel and robust temporal segmentation algorithm.

10.3   Visual Recognition with Sparse Data

One-shot learning is a challenging requirement as the small quantity of training data makes the modeling phase extremely hard. For this reason, in one-shot learning settings a careful choice of the data representation is very important. In this work we rely on sparse coding to obtain a compact descriptor with a good discriminative power even if it is derived from very small datasets.

The main concept behind sparse coding is to approximate an input signal as a linear combination of a few components selected from a dictionary of basic elements, called atoms. We refer to *adaptive sparse coding* when the coding is driven by data. In this case, we require a *dictionary learning* stage, where the dictionary atoms are learnt (Olshausen and Fieldt 1997; Yang et al. 2009; Wang et al. 2010).

The motivations behind the use of image coding arise from biology: there is evidence that similar signal coding happens in the neurons of the primary visual cortex (V1), which produces sparse and overcomplete activations (Olshausen and Fieldt 1997). From the computational point of view the objective is to find an overcomplete model of images, unlike methods such as PCA, which aims at finding a number of components that is lower than the data dimensionality. Overcomplete representation techniques have become very popular in applications such as denoising, inpainting, super-resolution, segmentation (Elad and Aharon 2006; Mairal et al. 2008a, b) and object recognition (Yang et al. 2009). In this work we assess their effectiveness also for gesture recognition.

Let $\mathbf{X} = [\mathbf{x}_1, \ldots, \mathbf{x}_m] \in \mathbb{R}^{n \times m}$ be the matrix whose m columns $\mathbf{x}_i \in \mathbb{R}^n$ are the feature vectors. The goal of adaptive sparse coding is to learn a dictionary $\mathbf{D}$ (a $n \times d$ matrix, with d the dictionary size and n the feature vector size) and a code $\mathbf{U}$ (a $d \times m$

matrix) that minimize the reconstruction error:

$$\min_{\mathbf{D},\mathbf{U}} \|\mathbf{X} - \mathbf{D}\mathbf{U}\|_F^2 + \lambda \|\mathbf{U}\|_1, \tag{10.1}$$

where $\| \cdot \|_F$ is the Frobenius norm. As for the sparsity, it is known that the L_1-norm yields to sparse results while being robust to signals perturbations. Other penalties such as the L_0-norm could be employed, however the problem of finding a solution becomes NP-hard and there is no guarantee that greedy algorithms reach the optimal solution. Notice that fixing $\mathbf{U}$, the above optimization reduces to a least square problem, whilst, given $\mathbf{D}$, it is equivalent to linear regression with the sparsifying norm L_1. The latter problem is referred to as a feature selection problem with a known dictionary (Lee et al. 2007). One of the most efficient algorithms that converges to the optimal solution of the problem in Eq. 10.1 for a fixed $\mathbf{D}$, is the *feature-sign search* algorithm (Lee et al. 2007). This algorithm searches for the sign of the coefficients $\mathbf{U}$; indeed, considering only non-zero elements the problem is reduced to a standard unconstrained quadratic optimization problem (QP), which can be solved analytically. Moreover it performs a refinement of the signs if they are incorrect. For the complete procedure we refer the reader to Lee et al. (2007).

In the context of recognition tasks, it has been proved that a sparsification of the data representation improves the overall classification accuracy (see for instance Guyon and Elisseeff 2003; Viola and Jones 2004; Destrero et al. 2009 and references therein). In this case sparse coding is often cast into a *coding-pooling* scheme, which finds its root in the Bag of Words paradigm. In this scheme a *coding operator* is a function $f(\mathbf{x}_i) = \mathbf{u}_i$ that maps $\mathbf{x}_i$ to a new space $\mathbf{u}_i \in \mathbb{R}^k$; when $k > n$ the representation is called overcomplete. The action of coding is followed by a pooling stage, whose purpose is to aggregate multiple local descriptors in a single and global one. Common pooling operators are the max operator, the average operator, or the geometric L_p-norm pooling operator (Feng et al. 2011). More in general, a pooling operator takes the codes located in S regions — for instance cells of the spatial pyramid, as in Yang et al. (2009)—and builds a succinct representation. We define as Y_s the set of locations within the region s. Defining the pooling operator as g, the resultant feature can be rewritten as: $\mathbf{p}_{(s)} = g_{(i \in Y_s)}(\mathbf{u}_{(i)})$. After this stage, a region s of the image is encoded with a single feature vector. The final descriptor of the image is the concatenation of the descriptors $\mathbf{p}_s$ among all the regions. Notice that the effectiveness of pooling is subject to the coding stage. Indeed, if applied on non-coded descriptors, pooling would bring to a drastic loss of information.

10.4 Action Recognition System

In this section we describe the versatile real-time action recognition system we propose. The system, depicted in Fig. 10.1, consists of three layers, that can be summarized as follows:

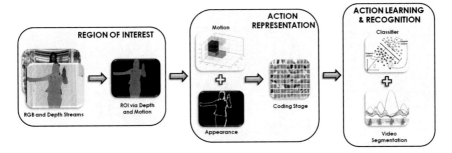

Fig. 10.1 Overview of the recognition system, where video segmentation and classification are performed simultaneously

- **Region Of Interest detection**: We detect a Region of Interest (ROI), where the human subject is actually performing the action. We use the combination of motion and depth to segment the subject from the background.
- **Action Representation**: Each ROI within a frame is mapped into a feature space with a combination of 3D Histogram of Flow (3DHOF) and Global Histogram of Oriented Gradient (GHOG) on the depth map. The resultant 3DHOF+GHOG descriptor is processed via a sparse coding step to compute a compact and meaningful representation of the performed action.
- **Action Learning**: Linear SVMs are used on frame buffers. A novel on-line video segmentation algorithm is proposed which allows isolating different actions while recognizing the action sequence.

10.4.1   Region of Interest Segmentation

The first step of each action recognition system is to identify correctly where in the image the action is occurring. Most of the algorithms in the literature involve background modeling techniques (Stauffer and Grimson 1999), or space-time image filtering in order to extract the interesting spatio-temporal locations of the action (Laptev and Lindeberg 2003). Other approaches require an a priori knowledge of the body pose (Lv and Nevatia 2007). This task is greatly simplified in our architecture, since in human-machine interaction we can safely assume the human to stand in front of the camera sensors and that there is no other motion in the scene. For each video in the dataset, we initially compute the frame differences within consecutive frames in a small buffer, obtaining the set P of pixels that are moving. Relying on this information, we compute the mean depth μ of the pixels belonging to P, which corresponds to the mean depth of the subject within the considered buffer. Thus, for the rest of the video sequence, we select the region of interest as $ROI(t) = \{p_{i,j}(t) : \mu - \epsilon \leq d(p_{i,j}(t)) \leq \mu + \epsilon\}$, where $d(p_{i,j}(t))$ is the depth of the pixel $p_{i,j}(t)$ at time t and ϵ is a tolerance value. In Fig. 10.2 examples of segmentation are

Fig. 10.2 Region of Interest detection. *Left* RGB video frames. *Center* depth frames. *Right* the detected ROI

shown. We determined empirically that this segmentation procedure achieves better performance with respect to classic thresholding algorithms such as Otsu's method (Otsu 1979).

10.4.2 Action Representation

Finding a suitable representation is the most crucial part of any recognition system. Ideally, an image representation should be both *discriminative* and *invariant* to image transformations. A discriminative descriptor should represent features belonging to the same class in a similar way, while it should show low similarity among data belonging to different classes. The invariance property, instead, ensures that image transformations such as rotation, translation, scaling do not affect the final representation. In practice, there is a trade-off between these two properties (Varma and Ray 2007): for instance, image patches are highly discriminative but not invariant, whereas image histograms are invariant but not discriminative, since different images could be associated to the same representation. When a lot of training data is provided, one could focus on a more discriminative and less invariant descriptor. In our specific case however, where only one training example is provided, invariance is a necessary condition in order to provide discriminant features; this aspect is greatly considered in our method.

From the neuroscience literature it is known that body parts are represented already in the early stages of human development (Mumme 2001) and that certainly adults have prior knowledge on the body appearance. Many suggests that motion alone can be used to recognize actions (Bisio et al. 2010). In artificial systems this developmental-scale experience is typically not available, although actions can still be represented from two main cues: motion and appearance (Giese and Poggio 2003). Although many variants of complex features describing human actions have been proposed, many of them imply computationally expensive routines. Differently, we rely on simple features in order to fulfill real-time requirements, and we show that they still have a good discriminative power. In particular we show that a combination of 3D Histograms of Flow (3DHOFs) and Global Histograms of Gradient (GHOGs) models satisfactorily human actions. When a large number of training examples is available, these two features should be able to describe a wide variety of actions, however in one-shot learning scenarios with noisy inputs, they are not sufficient. In this respect, a sparse representation, which keeps only relevant and robust components of the feature vector, greatly simplifies the learning phase making it equally effective.

10.4.2.1 3D Histogram of Flow

Whereas 2D motion vector estimation has been largely investigated and various fast and effective methods are available today (Papenberg et al. 2006; Horn and Shunk 1981), the scene flow computation (or 3D motion field estimation) is still an active research field due to the required additional binocular disparity estimation problem. The most promising works are the ones from Wedel et al. (2010), Huguet and Devernay (2007) and Cech et al. (2011); however these algorithms are computationally expensive and may require computation time in the range of 1.5 s per frame. This high computational cost is due to the fact that scene flow approaches try to estimate both the 2D motion field and disparity changes. Because of the real-time requirement, we opted for a simpler and faster method that produces a coarser estimation, but is effective for our purposes.

For each frame F_t we compute the 2D optical flow vectors $U(x, y, t)$ and $V(x, y, t)$ for the x and y components with respect to the previous frame F_{t-1}, via the Fanerbäck algorithm (Farnebäck 2003). Each pixel (x_{t-1}, y_{t-1}) belonging to the ROI of the frame F_{t-1} is reprojected in 3D space $(X_{t-1}, Y_{t-1}, Z_{t-1})$ where the Z_{t-1} coordinate is measured through the depth sensor and X_{t-1}, Y_{t-1} are computed by:

$$\begin{pmatrix} X_{t-1} \\ Y_{t-1} \end{pmatrix} = \begin{pmatrix} \dfrac{(x_{t-1} - x_0)Z_{t-1}}{f} \\ \dfrac{(y_{t-1} - y_0)Z_{t-1}}{f} \end{pmatrix},$$

where f is the focal length and $(x_0, y_0)^T$ is the principal point of the sensor. Similarly, we can reproject the final point (x_t, y_t) of the 2D vector representing the flow, obtaining another 3D vector $(X_t, Y_t, Z_t)^T$. For each pixel of the ROI, we can define the scene flow as the difference of the two 3D vectors in two successive frames F_{t-1} and F_t:

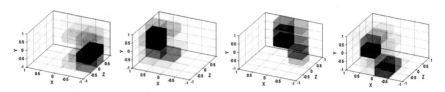

Fig. 10.3 The figure illustrates high level statistics obtained by the proposed scene flow description (3D-HOFs). Starting from the *left* we show the histogram of the scene flow directions at time t, for a moving hand going on the *Right*, *Left*, *Forward*, *Backward* respectively. Each cuboid represents one bin of the histogram, for visualization purposes we divided the 3D space in $n \times n \times n$ bins with $n = 4$. Filled cuboids represent high density areas

$$\mathbf{D} = (\dot{X}, \dot{Y}, \dot{Z})^T =$$
$$= (X_t - X_{t-1}, Y_t - Y_{t-1}, Z_t - Z_{t-1})^T.$$

Once the 3D flow for each pixel of the ROI at time t has been computed, we normalize it with respect to the $L2$-norm, so that the resulting descriptors $\mathbf{D_1}, \ldots, \mathbf{D_n}$ (n pixels of the ROI) are invariant to the overall speed of the action. In order to extract a compact representation we build a 3D Histogram of Flow (3DHOF) $\mathbf{z}(t)$ of the 3D motion vectors, where $\mathbf{z}(t) \in \mathbb{R}^{n_1}$ and $\sqrt[3]{n_1}$ is the quantization parameter of the space (i.e. the bin size). In addition we normalize each 3DHOF $\mathbf{z}(t)$ so that $\sum_j z_j(t) = 1$; hence we guarantee that these descriptors are invariant to the subject of interest's scale.

Figure 10.3 shows that the movements toward different directions reveal to be linearly separable, and the main directions are accurately represented: each cuboid represents one bin of the histogram, and the 3D space is divided in $n \times n \times n$ bins with $n = 4$. It is possible to notice how, in the *Right* direction for example, all the filled bins lay on the semi-space defined by $x < 0$. Similar observations apply all cases.

10.4.2.2 Global Histogram of Oriented Gradient

In specific contexts, motion information is not sufficient to discriminate actions, and information on the pose or appearance becomes crucial. One notable example is the American Sign Language (ASL), whose lexicon is based mostly on the shape of the hand. In these cases modeling the shape of a gesture as well as its dynamics is very important. Thus we extend the motion descriptor with a shape feature computed on the depth map. If we assume the subject to be in front of the camera, it is unlikely that the perspective transformation would distort his/her pose, shape or appearance, therefore we can approximately work with invariance to translation and scale. We are interested in characterizing shapes, and the gradient of the depth stream shows the highest responses on the contours, thus studying the orientation of the gradient is a suitable choice. The classical Histograms of Oriented Gradient (HOGs)

(Dalal and Triggs 2005) have been designed for detection purposes and do not show the above-mentioned invariance; indeed dividing the image in cells makes each sub-histogram dependent on the location and the dimension of the object. Furthermore, HOGs exhibit a high spatial complexity, as the classical HOG descriptor belongs to $\mathbb{R}^{(ncells \times nblocks \times n_2)}$. Since we aim at preserving such invariance as well as limiting the computational complexity, we employed a simpler descriptor, the Global Histogram of Oriented Gradient (GHOG). This appearance descriptor produces an overall description of the appearance of the ROI without splitting the image in cells. We compute the histogram of gradient orientations of the pixels on the entire ROI obtained from the depth map to generate another descriptor $\mathbf{h}(t) \in \mathbb{R}^{n_2}$, where n_2 is the number of bins. The scale invariance property is preserved normalizing the descriptor so that $\sum_j h_j(t) = 1$. Computing this descriptor on the depth map is fundamental in order to remove texture information; in fact, in this context, the only visual properties we are interested in are related to shape.

10.4.2.3 Sparse Coding

At this stage, each frame F_t is represented by two global descriptors: $\mathbf{z}(t) \in \mathbb{R}^{n_1}$ for the motion component and $\mathbf{h}(t) \in \mathbb{R}^{n_2}$ for the appearance component. Due to the high variability of human actions and to the simplicity of the descriptors, a feature selection stage is needed to catch the relevant information underlying the data and discarding the redundant ones such as background or body parts not involved in the action; to this aim we apply a sparse coding stage to our descriptor.

Given the set of the previously computed 3DHOFs $\mathbf{Z} = [\mathbf{z}(1), \dots, \mathbf{z}(K)]$, where K is the number of all the frames in the training data, our goal is to learn one motion dictionary $\mathbf{D_M}$ (a $n_1 \times d_1$ matrix, with d_1 the dictionary size and n_1 the motion vector size) and the codes $\mathbf{U_M}$ (a $d_1 \times K$ matrix) that minimize the Eq. 10.1, so that $\mathbf{z}(t) \sim \mathbf{D_M u_M}(t)$. In the same manner, we define the equal optimization problem for a dictionary $\mathbf{D_G}$ (a $n_2 \times d_2$ matrix) and the codes $\mathbf{U_G}$ (a $d_2 \times K$ matrix) for the set of GHOGs descriptors $\mathbf{H} = [\mathbf{h}(1), \dots, \mathbf{h}(K)]$. Therefore, after the Sparse Coding stage, we can describe a frame as a code $\mathbf{u}(i)$, which is the concatenation of the motion and appearance codes: $\mathbf{u}(i) = [\mathbf{u_M}(i), \mathbf{u_G}(i)]$.

Notice that we rely on global features, thus we do not need any pooling operator, which is usually employed to summarize local features into a single one.

10.4.3 Learning and Recognition

The goal of this phase is to learn a model of a given action from data. Since we are implementing a one-shot action recognition system, the available training data amounts to one training sequence for each action of interest. In order to model the temporal extent of an action we extract sets of sub-sequences from a sequence, each one containing T adjacent frames. In particular, instead of using single frame descriptors (described in Sect. 10.4.2), we move to a concatenation of frames: a set of T frames is represented as a sequence $[\mathbf{u}(1), \ldots, \mathbf{u}(T)]$ of codes. This representation allows us to perform simultaneously detection and classification of actions.

The learning algorithm we adopt is the Support Vector Machine (SVM) (Vapnik 1998). We employ linear SVMs, since they can be implemented with constant complexity during the test phase fulfilling real-time requirements (Fan et al. 2008). Additionally, recent advances in the object recognition field, such as Yang et al. (2009), showed that linear classifiers can effectively solve the classification problem if a preliminary sparse coding stage has previously been applied. Our experiments confirm these findings. Another advantage of linear SVMs is that they can be implemented with a linear complexity in training (Fan et al. 2008); given this property, we can provide a real-time one-shot learning procedure, extremely useful in real applications.

The remainder of the section describes in details the two phases of action learning and action recognition.

10.4.3.1 Action Learning

Given a video V_s of t_s frames, containing only one action A_s, we compute a set of descriptors $[\mathbf{u}(1), \ldots, \mathbf{u}(t_s)]$ as described in Sect. 10.4.2. Then, action learning is carried out on a set of data that are descriptions of a frame buffer $\mathbf{B}_T(t)$, where T is its length:

$$\mathbf{B}_T(t) = (\mathbf{u}(t - T), \ldots, \mathbf{u}(t - 1), \mathbf{u}(t))^T.$$

We use a one-versus-all strategy to train a binary linear SVM for each class A_s, so that at the end of the training phase we obtain a set of N linear SVM classifiers $f_1(\bar{\mathbf{B}}), \ldots, f_N(\bar{\mathbf{B}})$, where N is the number of actions. In particular, in this one-shot learning pipeline, the set of buffers

$$\mathbf{B_s} = [\mathbf{B}_T(t_0), \ldots, \mathbf{B}_T(t_s)]$$

computed from the single video V_s of the class A_s are used as positive examples for the action A_s. All the buffers belonging to A_j with $j \neq s$ are the negative examples. Although we use only one example for each class, we benefit from the chosen representation: indeed, descriptors are computed per frame, therefore one single video of length t_s provides a number of examples equal to $t_s - T$ where T is the buffer size. Given the training data $\{\mathbf{B}, \mathbf{y}\}$ where $\mathbf{B}$ is the set of positive and negative examples for the primitive A_s, $y_i = 1$ if the example is positive, $y_i = -1$ otherwise, the goal of SVM is to learn a linear function $(\mathbf{w}^T, b)$ such that a new test vector $\bar{\mathbf{B}}$ is predicted as:

$$y_{pred} = sign(f(\bar{\mathbf{B}})) = sign(\mathbf{w}^T\bar{\mathbf{B}} + b).$$

10.4.3.2   On-line Recognition: Video Segmentation

Given a test video V, which may contain one or more known actions, the goal is to predict the sequence of the performed actions. The video is analyzed using a sliding window $\mathbf{B}_T(t)$ of size T. We compute the output score $f_i(\mathbf{B}_T(t))$ of the $i = 1, \ldots, N$ SVM machines for each test buffer $\mathbf{B}_T(t)$ and we filter these scores with a low-pass filter W that attenuates noise. Therefore the new score at time t becomes:

$$H_i(\mathbf{B}_T(t)) = W \star f_i(\mathbf{B}_T(t)) \quad i = 1, \ldots, N, \qquad (10.2)$$

where the $\star$ is the convolution operator. Figure 10.4 depicts an example of these scores computed in real-time. As long as the scores evolve we need to predict (on-line) when an action ends and another one begins; this is achieved computing the standard deviation $\sigma(H)$ for a fixed t over all the scores H_i^t (Fig. 10.4, right chart). When an action ends we can expect all the SVM output scores to be similar, because no model should be predominant with respect to idle states; this brings to a local minimum in the function $\sigma(H)$. Therefore, each local minimum corresponds to the end of an action and the beginning of a new one. Let n be the number of local minima computed from the standard deviation function; there will be $n + 1$ actions, and in particular actions with the highest score before and after each break point will be recognized. We can easily find these minima in real-time: we calculate the mean value of the standard deviation over time using a sliding window. When the standard deviation trend is below the mean, all the SVMs scores predict similar values, hence it is likely that an action has just ended. In Fig. 10.5 the segmented and recognized actions are shown together with their scores.

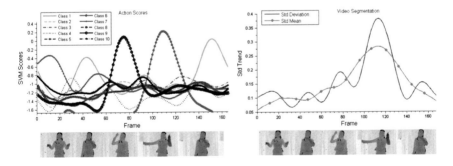

Fig. 10.4 The figure illustrates on the *left* the SVMs scores (Eq. 10.2) computed in real-time at each time step t over a sequence of 170 frames. On the *right* the standard deviation of the scores and its mean computed on a sliding window are depicted. The local minima of the standard deviation function are break points that define the end of an action and the beginning of another one. See Sect. 10.4.3.2 for details

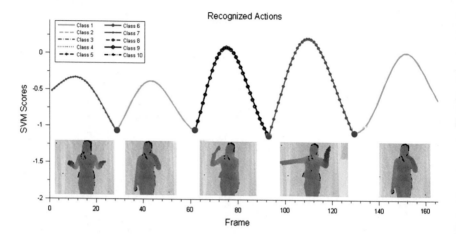

Fig. 10.5 The figure illustrates only the scores of the recognized actions via the method described in Sect. 10.4.3.2. *Blue dots* are the break points computed by the video segmentation algorithm that indicate the end of an action and the beginning of a new one

10.5 Experiments

In this section we evaluate the performance of our system in three different settings:

- **ChaLearn Gesture Dataset**. The first experiment has been conducted on a publicly available dataset, released by ChaLearn (CGD2011) (2011). The main goal of the experiment is to compare our method with other techniques.
- **Kinect Data**. In the second experiment we discuss how to improve the recognition rate using all the functionalities of a real Kinect sensor. Gestures with high level of detail are easily caught by the system.
- **Human-Robot Interaction**. For the last experiment we considered a real HMI scenario: we implement the system on a real robot, the iCub humanoid robot (Metta et al. 2008), showing the applicability of our algorithm also in human-robot interaction settings.

For the computation of the accuracy between a sequence of estimated actions and the ground truth sequence we use the normalized Levenshtein Distance (Levenshtein 1966), defined as:

$$TeLev = \frac{S + D + I}{M},$$

where each action is treated as a symbol in a sequence, S is the number of substitutions (misclassifications), D the number of deletions (false negatives), I the number of insertions (false positives) and M the length of the ground truth sequence. More specifically, this measure computes the minimum number of modifications that are required to transform a sequence of events in another one. It is widely used in speech recognition contexts, where each symbol represents an event. In action and gesture recognition, when sequences of gestures are to be evaluated, the Levenshtein Distance shows to be a particularly suitable metric, as it allows accounting not only for the single classifier accuracy, but also for the capability of the algorithm to accurately distinguish different gestures in a sequence (Minnen et al. 2006).

We empirically choose a quantization parameter for the 3DHOF, n_1 equal to 5, $n_2 = 64$ bins for the GHOG descriptor, and dictionary sizes d_1 and d_2 equal to 256 for both motion and appearance components. This led to a frame descriptor of size 189 for simple descriptors, which increases to 512 after the sparse coding processing. The whole system runs at 25 fps on 2.4 Ghz Core 2 Duo Processor.

10.5.1 ChaLearn Gesture Dataset

We firstly assess our method on the ChaLearn dataset for the One-Shot Gesture Recognition Challenge (Guyon et al. 2012), see Fig. 10.6. The dataset is organized in batches, where each batch includes 100 recorded gestures grouped in sequences of 1–5 gestures arbitrarily performed at different speeds. The gestures are drawn from a small vocabulary of 8–15 unique gestures called *lexicon*, which is defined within a batch. For each video both RGB and Depth streams are provided, but *only one example* is given for the training phase. In our experiments we do not use information on the body pose of the human. We consider the batches from *devel_01* to *devel_20*; each batch has 47 videos, where L (the lexicon size) videos are for training and the remaining are used as test data.

The main parameter of the system is the buffer size T, however in Fig. 10.6 it is possible to notice that the parameter offers stable performances with a buffer range of 1–20, so it does not represent a critical variable of our method. Furthermore, high performance for a wide buffer length range imply that our framework is able to handle different speeds implicitly. We compute the Levenshtein Distance as the average over all the batches, which is 25.11% for features processed with sparse coding, whereas simple 3DHOF+GHOG descriptors without sparse coding lead to a performance of

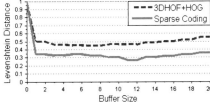

Fig. 10.6 On the *left* examples of 2 different batches from the ChaLearn Dataset (CGD2011) (2011). On the *right* the overall Levenshtein Distance computed in 20 batches with respect to the buffer size parameter is depicted for both 3DHOF+GHOG features and descriptors processed with sparse coding

43.32%. Notably, each batch has its own lexicon and some of them are composed of only gestures performed by hand or fingers; in these cases, if the GHOG is computed on the entire ROI, the greatest contribution of the histogram comes from the body shape, whilst finger actions (see Fig. 10.2, bottom row) represent a poor percentage of the final descriptor. If we consider batches where the lexicon is not composed of only hand/fingers gestures, the Levenshtein Distance reduces to 15%.

We compared our method with several approaches. First of all a Template Matching technique, where we used as descriptor the average of all depth frames for each action. The test video is split in slices estimated using the average size of actions. In the recognition phase we classify each slice of the video comparing it with all the templates. The overall Levenshtein Distance becomes 62.56%. For the second comparison we employ Dynamic Time Warping (DTW) method (Sakoe and Chiba 1978) with 3DHOF+GHOG features. We manually divided test videos in order to facilitate the recognition for DTW; nevertheless the global Levenshtein Distance is 49.41%. Finally we report the results presented in some recent works in the field, which exploit techniques based on manifolds (Lui 2012), Motion History Image (MHI) (Wu et al. 2012), Bag of Visual Words (BoVW) (Wu et al. 2012), 2D FFT-MHI (Mahbub et al. 2011) and Temporal Bayesian Model (TBM) with Latent Dirichlet Allocation (LDA) (Malgireddy et al. 2012).

Table 10.1 shows that most of the compared approaches are outperformed by our method except for Malgireddy et al. (2012); however the method proposed by Malgireddy et al. (2012) has a training computational complexity of $\mathcal{O}(n \times k^2)$ for each action class, where k is the number of HMM states and n the number of examples, while the testing computational complexity for a video frame is $\mathcal{O}(k^2)$. Thanks to the sparse representation, we are able to use linear SVMs, which reduce the training complexity with respect to the number of training examples to $\mathcal{O}(n \times d)$

Table 10.1 Levenshtein distance on the ChaLearn Gesture Dataset. For SVM classification we chose the appropriate buffer size for each batch according to the defined lexicon. TeLev is the Levenshtein Distance, TeLen is the average error (false positives + false negatives) made on the number of gestures (see text)

Method	TeLev (%)	TeLen
Sparse representation **(proposed)**	**25.11**	**5.02%**
3DHOF+GHOG	43.32	9.03%
Template matching	62.56	15.12%
DTW	49.41	Manual
Manifold LSR Lui (2012)	28.73	6.24%
MHI Wu et al. (2012)	30.01	NA
Extended-MHI Wu et al. (2012)	26.00	NA
BoVW Wu et al. (2012)	72.32	NA
2D FFT-MHI Mahbub et al. (2011)	37.46	NA
TBM+LDA Malgireddy et al. (2012)	24.09	NA

for each SVM, where d is the descriptor size. In our case d is a constant value fixed a priori, and does not influence the scalability of the problem. Therefore we may approximate the asymptotic behavior of the SVM in training to $\mathcal{O}(n)$. Similarly, in testing the complexity for each SVM is constant with respect to the number of training examples when considering a single frame, and it becomes $\mathcal{O}(N)$ for the computation of all the N class scores. This allows us to provide real-time training and testing procedures with the considered lexicons.

Furthermore our on-line video segmentation algorithm shows excellent results with respect to the temporal segmentation used in the compared frameworks; in fact it is worth noting that the proposed algorithm leads to an action detection error rate $TeLen = \frac{FP+FN}{M}$ equal to 5.02%, where FP and FN are false positives and false negatives respectively, and M is the number of all test gestures. Considering the final results of the ChaLearn Gesture Challenge (Round 1)[1], we placed 9th over 50 teams, but our method also fulfills real-time requirements for the entire pipeline, which was not a requirement of the challenge.

10.5.1.1 Motion Versus Appearance

In this section we evaluate the contribution of the frame descriptors. In general we notice that the combination of both motion and appearance descriptors leads to the best results when the lexicon is composed of actions where both motion and appearance are equally important. To show this, we considered the 20 development batches from the ChaLearn Gesture Dataset. For this experiment, we used only coded descriptors, since we have already experienced that they obtain higher performance. Using only the motion component, the Levenshtein Distance is equal to 62.89%, whereas a descriptor based only on the appearance leads to an error of 34.15%. The error obtained using only the 3DHOF descriptors was expected, due to the nature of the lexicons chosen: indeed in most gestures the motion component has little significance. Considering instead batch *devel_01*, where motion is an important component in the gesture vocabulary, we have that 3DHOF descriptors lead to a Levenshtein Distance equal to 29.48%, the GHOG descriptors to 21.12% and the combination is equal to 9.11%. Results are consistent with previous findings, but in this specific case the gap between the motion and the appearance components is not critical.

10.5.1.2 Linear Versus Non-linear Classifiers

In this section we compare the performances of linear and non linear SVM for the action recognition task. The main advantage of a linear kernel is the computational

---

[1]The leaderboard website is: https://www.kaggle.com.

time: non-linear SVMs have a worst case training computational complexity per class equal to $\mathcal{O}(n^3 \times d)$ against the $\mathcal{O}(n \times d)$ of linear SVMs, where n is the number of training examples, and d is the descriptor size. In testing, non linear SVMs show computational complexity of $\mathcal{O}(n \times d)$ per frame, since the number of support vectors grows linearly with n. Moreover, non-linear classifiers usually require additional kernel parameter estimation, which especially in one-shot learning scenarios is not trivial. Contrarily, linear SVMs take $\mathcal{O}(d)$ per frame. For this experiment we used coded features where both motion and appearance are employed. A non-linear SVM with RBF Kernel has been employed, where the kernel parameter and the SVM regularization term have been chosen empirically after 10 trials on a subset of the batches. The Levenshtein Distance among the 20 batches is 35.11%; this result confirms that linear classifiers are sufficient to obtain good results with low computational cost if an appropriate data representation, as the one offered by sparse coding, is adopted.

10.5.2 Kinect Dataset

In this section we assess the ability of our method to recognize more complex gestures captured by a Kinect for Xbox 360 sensor. In Sect. 10.5.1, we noted that the resolution of the proposed appearance descriptor is quite low and may not be ideal when actions differ by small details, especially on the hands, therefore a localization of the interesting parts to model would be effective. The simplest way to build in this specific information is to resort to a body part tracker; indeed, if a body tracker were available it would have been easy to extract descriptors from different limbs and then concatenate all the features to obtain the final frame representation. An excellent candidate to provide a reliable body tracker is Microsoft Kinect SDK, which implements the method in Shotton et al. (2011). This tool retrieves the 20 principal body joints position and pose of the user's current posture. Given these positions, we assign each 3D point of the ROI to its nearest joint, so that it is possible to correctly isolate the two hands and the body from the rest of the scene (see Fig. 10.7). Then, we slightly modify the approach, computing 3DHOF and GHOG descriptors on three different body parts (left/right hand and whole body shape); the final frame representation becomes the concatenation of all the part descriptors. As for the experiments we have acquired two different sets of data (see Fig. 10.7): in the first one the lexicon is composed of numbers performed with fingers, in the second one we replicate the lexicons *devel_3* of the ChaLearn Gesture Dataset, the one where we obtained the poorest performances. In Fig. 10.7 on the left the overall accuracy is shown; using sparse coding descriptors computed only on the body shape we obtain a Levenshtein Distance around 30%. By concatenating descriptors extracted from the hands the system achieves 10% for features enhanced with sparse coding and 20% for normal descriptors.

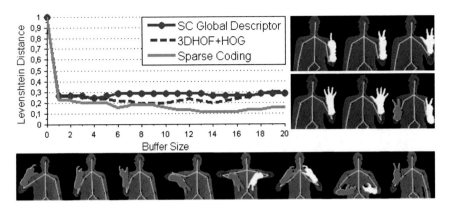

Fig. 10.7 On the *right* and *bottom* the two vocabularies used in Sect. 10.5.2; these gestures are difficult to model without a proper body tracker, indeed the most contribution for the GHOG comes from the body shape rather than the hand. On the *left* the Levenshtein Distance

We compared our method with two previously mentioned techniques: a Template Matching algorithm and an implementation of the Dynamic Time Warping approach (Sakoe and Chiba 1978). The resulted Levenshtein Distance is respectively 52.47 and 42.36%.

10.5.3   Human-Robot Interaction

The action recognition system has been implemented and tested on the iCub, a 53 degrees of freedom humanoid robot developed by the RobotCub Consortium (Metta et al. 2008). The robot is equipped with force sensors and gyroscopes, and it resembles a 3-years old child. It mounts two Dragonfly cameras, providing the basis for 3D vision, thus after an offline camera calibration procedure we can rely on a full stereo vision system; here the depth map is computed following Hirschmuller (2008). In this setting the action recognition system can be used for more general purposes such as Human-Robot-Interaction (HRI) or learning by imitation tasks. In particular our goal is to teach iCub how to perform simple manipulation tasks, such as move/grasp an object. In this sense, we are interested in recognizing actions related to the arm-hand movements of the robot. We define 8 actions, as shown in Fig. 10.8, bottom row, according to the robot manipulation capabilities. Each action is modeled using only the motion component (3DHOF), since we want the descriptor to be independent on the particular object shape used.

In Fig. 10.8 we show the accuracy based on the Levenshtein Distance; this measure has been calculated on more than 100 actions composed of sequences of 1–6 actions. Notably the error is less than 10%; these good results were expected due to the high

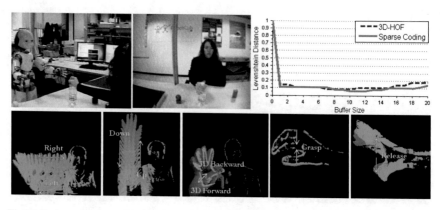

Fig. 10.8 Accuracy for actions sequences (see *bottom* row). We evaluated the performance on more than 100 actions composed of sequences of 1 to 6 actions

discriminative power of the 3DHOFs (Fig. 10.3) on the chosen lexicon, which leads to a linearly separable set.

10.6 All Gestures You Can: A Real Application

As pointed out in the previous sections, our approach was designed for real applications where real-time requirements need to be fulfilled. We developed and implemented a "game" against a humanoid robot, showing the effectiveness of our system in a real HRI setting: "All Gestures You Can" (Gori et al. 2012), a game aiming at improving memory skills, visual association and concentration. Our game takes inspiration from the classic "Simon" game; nevertheless, since the original version has been often defined as "visually boring", we developed a revisited version, based on gesture recognition, which involves a "less boring" opponent: the iCub (Metta et al. 2008). Both the human and the robot have to take turns and perform the longest possible sequence of gestures by adding one gesture at each turn: one player starts performing a gesture, the opponent has to recognize the gesture, imitate it and add another gesture to the sequence. The game is carried on until one of the two players loses: the human player can lose because of limited memory skills, whereas the robot can lose because the gesture recognition system fails. As described in the previous sections, the system has been designed for one-shot learning; however, Kinect does not provide information about finger configuration, therefore a direct mapping between human fingers and the iCub's ones is not immediate. Thus we set a predefined pool of 8 gestures (see Fig. 10.9, on the left). The typical game setting is shown in Fig. 10.10: the player stays in front of the robot while performing gestures that are recognized with Kinect. Importantly, hand gestures cannot be learned exploiting the Skeleton Data of Kinect: the body tracker detects the position of the hand and it is

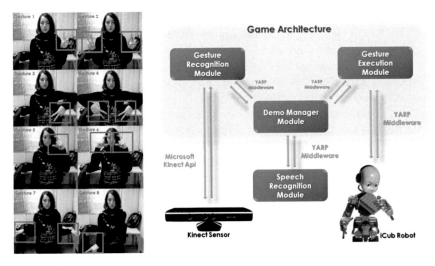

Fig. 10.9 On the *left* the hand gestures. The vision system has been trained using 8 different actors performing each gesture class for 3 times. On the right the game architecture. There are three main modules that take care of recognizing the action sequence, defining the game rules and making the robot gestures

Fig. 10.10 The first two turns of a match. *Left* the human player performs the first gesture of the sequence. *Center* iCub recognized the gesture and imitates it. *Right* iCub adds a new random gesture to the sequence

not enough to discriminate more complicate actions, – e.g. see gesture classes 1 and 5 or 2 and 6 in Fig. 10.9.

The system is simple and modularized as it is organized in three components (see Fig. 10.9) based on the iCub middleware, YARP (Metta et al. 2006), which manages the communication between sensors, processors, and modules. The efficiency of the proposed implementation is assured by its multithreading architecture, which also contributes to real-time performances. The software presented in this section is available in the iCub repository.[2]

---

[2]Code available at https://svn.code.sf.net/p/robotcub/code/trunk/iCub/contrib/src/demoGesture Recognition.

The proposed game has been played by more than 30 different players during the ChaLearn Kinect Demonstration Competition at CVPR 2012.[3] Most of them were completely naive without prior knowledge about the gestures. They were asked to play using a lexicon that had been trained specifically for the competition (Fig. 10.9). After 50 matches we had 75% of robot victories. This result indicates that the recognition system is robust also to different players performing variable gestures at various speeds. 15% of the matches have been won by humans and usually they finished during the first 3–4 turns of the game; this always occurred when players performed very different gestures with respect to the trained ones. A few players (10% of matches) succeeded in playing more than 8 turns, and they won due to recognition errors. "All Gestures You Can" ranked 2nd in the ChaLearn Kinect Demonstration Competition.

10.7 Discussion

This paper presented the design and implementation of a complete action recognition system to be used in real world applications such as HMI. We designed each step of the recognition pipeline to function in real-time while maximizing the overall accuracy. We showed how a sparse action representation could be effectively used for one-shot learning of actions in combination with conventional machine learning algorithms (i.e. SVM), even if the latter would normally require a larger set of training data. The comprehensive evaluation of the proposed approach showed that we achieve good trade-off between accuracy and computation time. The main strengths of our learning and recognition pipeline can be summarized as follows:

1. **One-Shot Learning**: One example is sufficient to teach an new action to the system; this is mainly due to the effective per-frame representation.
2. **Sparse Frame Representation**: Starting from a simple and computationally inexpensive description that combines global motion (3DHOF) and appearance (GHOG) information over a ROI, subsequently filtered through sparse coding, we obtained a sparse representation at each frame. We showed that these global descriptors are appropriate to model actions of the upper body of a person.
3. **On-line Video Segmentation**: We propose a new, effective, reliable and on-line video segmentation algorithm that achieved a 5% error rate on action detection on a set of 2000 actions grouped in sequences of 1–5 gestures. This segmentation procedure works concurrently with the recognition process, thus a sequence of actions is simultaneously segmented and recognized.
4. **Real-time Performances**: The proposed system can be used in real-time applications, as it does require neither a complex features processing nor a computationally expensive training and testing phases. From the computational point of view the proposed approach scales well even for large vocabularies of actions.

---

[3]The competition website is http://gesture.chalearn.org/.
A YouTube video of our game is available at http://youtu.be/U_JLoe_fT3I.

5. **Effectiveness in Real Scenarios**: Our method achieves good performances in a Human-Robot Interaction setting, where the RGBD images are obtained through binocular vision and disparity estimation. For testing purposes, we proposed a memory game, called "All Gestures You Can", where a person can challenge the iCub robot on action recognition and sequencing. The system ranked 2nd at the Kinect Demonstration Competition.[4]

We stress here the simplicity of the learning and recognition pipeline: each stage is easy to implement and fast to compute. It is shown to be adequate to solve the problem of gesture recognition; we obtained high-quality results while fulfilling real-time requirements. The approach is competitive against many of the state-of-the-art methods for action recognition.

We are currently working on a more precise appearance description at frame level still under the severe constraint of real-time performance; this would enable the use of more complex actions even when the body tracker is not available.

Acknowledgements This work was supported by the European FP7 ICT projects N. 270490 (EFAA) and N. 270273 (Xperience).

References

J.K. Aggarwal, M.S. Ryoo, Human activity analysis: A review. ACM Comput. Surv. **43**, 16 (2011)

A. Ali, J.K. Aggarwal, Segmentation and recognition of continuous human activity, in *IEEE Workshop on Detection and Recognition of Events in Video*, 2001

J. Alon, V. Athitsos, Q. Quan, S. Sclaroff, A unified framework for gesture recognition and spatiotemporal gesture segmentation. IEEE Trans. Pattern Anal. Mach. Intell. **31**(9), 1685–1699 (2009)

A. Bisio, N. Stucchi, M. Jacono, L. Fadiga, T. Pozzo, Automatic versus voluntary motor imitation: effect of visual context and stimulus velocity. PLoS ONE **5**(10), e13506 (2010)

A.F. Bobick, J.W. Davis, The recognition of human movement using temporal templates. IEEE Trans. Pattern Anal. Mach. Intell. **23**(3), 257–267 (2001)

M. Bregonzio, S. Gong, T. Xiang, Recognising action as clouds of space-time interest points, in *IEEE Conference on Computer Vision and Pattern Recognition*, 2009

M.J. Burden, D.B. Mitchell, Implicit memory development in school-aged children with attention deficit hyperactivity disorder (adhd): Conceptual priming deficit? Dev. Neurophysiol. **28**(3), 779–807 (2005)

J. Cech, J. Sanchez-Riera, R. Horaud, Scene flow estimation by growing correspondence seeds, in *IEEE Conference on Computer Vision and Pattern Recognition*, 2011

ChaLearn Gesture Dataset (CGD2011), http://gesture.chalearn.org/data, 2011

S.P. Chatzis, D.I. Kosmopoulos, P. Doliotis, A conditional random field-based model for joint sequence segmentation and classification. Pattern Recognit. **46**(6), 1569–1578 (2013)

C. Comoldi, A. Barbieri, C. Gaiani, S. Zocchi, Strategic memory deficits in attention deficit disorder with hyperactivity participants: the role of executive processes. Dev. Neurophysiol. **15**(1), 53–71 (1999)

N. Dalal, B. Triggs, Histograms of oriented gradients for human detection. IEEE Conf. Comput. Vis. Pattern Recognit. **1**, 886–893 (2005)

---

[4]The competition website is http://gesture.chalearn.org/.

A. Destrero, C. De Mol, F. Odone, A. Verri, A sparsity-enforcing method for learning face features. IEEE Trans. Image Process. **18**, 188–201 (2009)

A.A. Efros, A.C. Berg, G. Mori, J. Malik, Recognizing action at a distance. Int. Conf. Comput. Vis. **3**, 726–733 (2003)

M. Elad, M. Aharon, Image denoising via sparse and redundant representations over learned dictionaries. IEEE Trans. Image Process. **15**(12), 3736–3745 (2006)

R.E. Fan, K.-W. Chang, C.-J. Hsieh, X.-R. Wang, C.-J. Lin, Liblinear: a library for large linear classification. J. Mach. Learn. Res. **9**, 1871–1874 (2008)

S.R. Fanello, I. Gori, F. Pirri, Arm-hand behaviours modelling: from attention to imitation, in *International Symposium on Visual Computing*, 2010

G. Farnebäck, Two-frame motion estimation based on polynomial expansion, in *Scandinavian Conference on Image Analysis*, 2003

J. Feng, B. Ni, Q. Tian, S. Yan, Geometric lp-norm feature pooling for image classification, in *IEEE Conference on Computer Vision and Pattern Recognition*, 2011

M.A. Giese, T. Poggio, Neural mechanisms for the recognition of biological movements. Nat. Rev. Neurosci. **4**(3), 179–192 (2003)

L. Gorelick, M. Blank, E. Shechtman, M. Irani, R. Basri, Actions as space-time shapes. IEEE Trans. Pattern Anal. Mach. Intell. **29**, 1395–1402 (2007)

I. Gori, S.R. Fanello, F. Odone, G. Metta, All gestures you can: a memory game against a humanoid robot. *IEEE-RAS International Conference on Humanoid Robots*, 2012

R.D. Green, L. Guan, Continuous human activity recognition. Control Autom. Robotics Vision Conf. **1**, 706–711 (2004)

I. Guyon, V. Athitsos, P. Jangyodsuk, B. Hammer, H.J.E. Balderas, Chalearn gesture challenge: design and first results, in *Computer Vision and Pattern Recognition Workshops*, vol. 2 (Springer, Berlin, 2012), pp. 100–103

I. Guyon, A. Elisseeff, An introduction to variable and feature selection. Int. J. Mach. Learn. Res. **3**, 1157–1182 (2003)

H.O. Hirschfeld, A connection between correlation and contingency, in *Mathematical Proceedings of the Cambridge Philosophical Society*, vol. 31 (Cambridge University Press, Cambridge, 1935), pp. 520–524

H. Hirschmuller, Stereo processing by semiglobal matching and mutual information. IEEE Trans. Pattern Anal. Mach. Intell. **30**(2), 328–341 (2008)

B.K.P. Horn, B.G. Shunk, Determining optical flow. J. Artif. Intell. **17**, 185–203 (1981)

F. Huguet, F. Devernay, A variational method for scene flow estimation from stereo sequences, in *International Conference on Computer Vision*, 2007

I. Laptev, T. Lindeberg, Space-time interest points, in *IEEE International Conference on Computer Vision*, 2003

I. Laptev, M. Marszalek, C. Schmid, B. Rozenfeld, Learning realistic human actions from movies, in *IEEE Conference on Computer Vision and Pattern Recognition*, 2008

H. Lee, A. Battle, R. Raina, A.Y. Ng, Efficient sparse coding algorithms, in *Conference on Neural Information Processing Systems*, 2007

V. Levenshtein, Binary codes capable of correcting deletions, insertions, and reversals. Sov. Phys. Doklady **10**, 707–710 (1966)

W. Li, Z. Zhang, Z. Liu, Action recognition based on a bag of 3d points, in *Computer Vision and Pattern Recognition Workshops*, 2010

H.-Y.M. Liao, D.-Y. Chen, S.-W Shih, Continuous human action segmentation and recognition using a spatio-temporal probabilistic framework, in *IEEE International Symposium on Multimedia*, 2006

Y.M. Lui, A least squares regression framework on manifolds and its application to gesture recognition, in *Computer Vision and Pattern Recognition Workshops*, 2012

F. Lv, R. Nevatia. Single view human action recognition using key pose matching and viterbi path searching, in *IEEE Conference on Computer Vision and Pattern Recognition*, 2007

U. Mahbub, H. Imtiaz, T. Roy, S. Rahman, A.R. Ahad, Action Recognition from One Example. *Pattern Recognition Letters*, 2011

J. Mairal, F. Bach, J. Ponce, G. Sapiro, A. Zisserman, Discriminative learned dictionaries for local image analysis, in *IEEE Conference on Computer Vision and Pattern Recognition*, 2008a

J. Mairal, M. Elad, G. Sapiro. Sparse representation for color image restoration, in *IEEE Transactions on Image Processing*, 2008b, pp. 53–69

M.R. Malgireddy, I. Inwogu, V. Govindaraju, A temporal Bayesian model for classifying, detecting and localizing activities in video sequences, in *Computer Vision and Pattern Recognition Workshops*, 2012

G. Metta, G. Sandini, D. Vernon, L. Natale, F. Nori, The icub humanoid robot: an open platform for research in embodied cognition, in *Workshop on Performance Metrics for Intelligent Systems*, 2008

G. Metta, P. Fitzpatrick, L. Natale, YARP: yet another robot platform. Int. J. Adv. Robot. Syst. **3**(1), 8 (2006)

D. Minnen, T. Westeyn, T. Starner, Performance metrics and evaluation issues for continuous activity recognition, in *Performance Metrics for Intelligent Systems Workshop*, 2006

D.L. Mumme, Early social cognition: understanding others in the first months of life. J. Infant Child Dev., (2001)

P. Natarajan, R. Nevatia, Coupled hidden semi markov models for activity recognition, in *Workshop Motion and Video Computing*, 2007

B.A. Olshausen, D.J. Fieldt, Sparse coding with an overcomplete basis set: a strategy employed by v1. Vis. Res. **37**(23), 3311–3325 (1997)

N. Otsu, A threshold selection method from gray-level histograms. IEEE Trans. Syst. Man Cybern. **11**, 23–27 (1979)

N. Papenberg, A. Bruhn, T. Brox, J. Didas, J. Weickert, Highly accurate optic flow computation with theoretically justified warping. Int. J. Comput. Vis. **67**(2), 141–158 (2006)

R. Poppe, A survey on vision-based human action recognition. Image Vis. Comput. **28**, 976–990 (2010)

H. Sakoe, S. Chiba, Dynamic programming algorithm optimization for spoken word recognition, in *IEEE International Conference on Acoustics, Speech and Signal Processing*, 1978

H.J. Seo, P. Milanfar, A template matching approach of one-shot-learning gesture recognition, in *IEEE Transactions on Pattern Analysis and Machine Intelligence*, 2012

J.W. Shneider, P. Borlund, Matrix comparison, part 1: Motivation and important issues for measuring the resemblance between proximity measures or ordination results. J. Am. Soc. Info. Sci. Technol. **58**(11), 1586–1595 (2007)

J. Shotton, A. Fitzgibbon, M. Cook, T. Sharp, M. Finocchio, R. Moore, A. Kipman, A. Blake, Real-time human pose recognition in parts from a single depth image, in *IEEE Conference on Computer Vision and Pattern Recognition*, 2011

C. Stauffer, W.E.L. Grimson, Adaptive background mixture models for real-time tracking. IEEE Conf. Comput. Vis. Pattern Recognit. **2**, 246–252 (1999)

V. Vapnik, *Statistical learning theory* (Wiley, New York, 1998)

M. Varma, D. Ray, Learning the discriminative power-invariance trade-off, in *IEEE International Conference on Computer Vision*, 2007

P. Viola, M.J. Jones, Robust real-time face detection. Int. J. Comput. Vis. **57**, 137–154 (2004)

J. Wang, Z. Liu, J. Chorowski, Z. Chen, Y. Wu, Robust 3D Action Recognition with Random Occupancy Patterns, in *European Conference on Computer Vision*, 2012

J. Wang, J. Yang, K. Yu, F. Lv, T. Huang, Y. Gong, Locality-constrained linear coding for image classification, in *IEEE Conference on Computer Vision and Pattern Recognition*, 2010

A. Wedel, T. Brox, T. Vaudrey, C. Rabe, U. Franke, D. Cremers, Stereoscopic scene flow computation for 3D motion understanding. Int. J. Comput. Vis. **95**(1), 29–51 (2010)

G. Willems, T. Tuytelaars, L. Gool, An efficient dense and scale-invariant spatio-temporal interest point detector. Eur. Conf. Comput. Vis. **5303**, 650–663 (2008)

D. Wu, F. Zhu, L. Shao, One shot learning gesture recognition from rgbd images, in *Computer Vision and Pattern Recognition Workshops*, 2012

J. Yang, K. Yu, Y. Gong, T. Huang, Linear spatial pyramid matching using sparse coding for image classification, in *IEEE Conference on Computer Vision and Pattern Recognition*, 2009

Chapter 11
One-Shot Learning Gesture Recognition from RGB-D Data Using Bag of Features

Jun Wan, Qiuqi Ruan, Wei Li and Shuang Deng

Abstract For one-shot learning gesture recognition, two important challenges are: how to extract distinctive features and how to learn a discriminative model from only one training sample per gesture class. For feature extraction, a new spatio-temporal feature representation called 3D enhanced motion scale-invariant feature transform is proposed, which fuses RGB-D data. Compared with other features, the new feature set is invariant to scale and rotation, and has more compact and richer visual representations. For learning a discriminative model, all features extracted from training samples are clustered with the k-means algorithm to learn a visual codebook. Then, unlike the traditional bag of feature models using vector quantization (VQ) to map each feature into a certain visual codeword, a sparse coding method named simulation orthogonal matching pursuit (SOMP) is applied and thus each feature can be represented by some linear combination of a small number of codewords. Compared with VQ, SOMP leads to a much lower reconstruction error and achieves better performance. The proposed approach has been evaluated on ChaLearn gesture database and the result has been ranked amongst the top best performing techniques on ChaLearn gesture challenge (round 2).

Keywords Gesture recognition · Bag of features (BoF) model · One-shot learning · 3D enhanced motion scale invariant feature transform (3D EMoSIFT) · Simulation orthogonal matching pursuit (SOMP)

Editors: Isabelle Guyon and Vassilis Athitsos.

J. Wan (✉) · Q. Ruan · W. Li
Institute of Information Science, Beijing Jiaotong University, Beijing 100044, China
e-mail: jun.wan@ia.ac.cn

Q. Ruan
e-mail: qqruan@center.njtu.edu.cn

W. Li
e-mail: 08112050@bjtu.edu.cn

S. Deng
China Machinery TDI International Engineering Co., Ltd., Beijing 100083, China
e-mail: daisy_shuang@hotmail.com

© Springer International Publishing AG 2017
S. Escalera et al. (eds.), *Gesture Recognition*, The Springer Series
on Challenges in Machine Learning, DOI 10.1007/978-3-319-57021-1_11

11.1 Introduction

Human gestures frequently provide a natural and intuitive communication modality in daily life, and the techniques of gesture recognition can be widely applied in many areas, such as human computer interaction (HCI) (Pavlovic et al. 1997; Zhu et al. 2002), robot control (Malima et al. 2006; Shan et al. 2007), sign language recognition (Gao et al. 2004; T. Starner and Pentland 1998) and augmented reality (Reifinger et al. 2007). To model gesture signals and achieve acceptable recognition performance, the most common approaches are to use Hidden Markov Models (HMMs) or its variants (Kim et al. 2007) which are a powerful model that includes hidden state structure. Yamato et al. (1992) used image preprocessing operations (background subtraction, image blurring) to extract low-level features and used HMM to recognize tennis motions. Brand et al. (1997) suggested a coupled HMM that combined two HMMs with causal possibly asymmetric links to recognize gestures. Vogler (2003) presented a parallel HMM algorithm to model gesture components and can recognize continuous gestures in sentences. Then a more general probabilistic model named dynamic Bayesian network (DBN) is proposed. DBN includes HMMs and Kalman filters as special cases (Suk et al. 2010). Youtian et al. (2006) defined five classes of gestures for HCI and developed a DBN-based model which used local features (contour, moment, height) and global features (velocity, orientation, distance) as observations. Suk et al. (2010) proposed a DBN-based system to control media player or slide presentation. They used local features (location, velocity) by skin extraction and motion tracking to design the DBN inference.

However, both HMM and DBN models assume that observations given the motion class labels are conditional independent. This restriction makes it difficult or impossible to accommodate long-range dependencies among observations or multiple overlapping features of the observations (Sminchisescu et al. 2005). Therefore, Sminchisescu et al. (2005) proposed conditional random fields (CRF) which can avoid the independence assumption between observations and allow non-local dependencies between state and observations. Wang et al. (2006) then incorporated hidden state variables into the CRF model, namely, hidden conditional random field (HCRF). They used HCRF to recognize gesture recognition and proved that HCRF can get better performance. Later, the latent-dynamic conditional field (LDCRF) model (Morency et al. 2007) was proposed, which combines the strengths of CRFs and HCRFs by capturing both extrinsic dynamics and intrinsic sub-structure. The detailed comparisons are evaluated by Morency et al. (2007).

Another important approach is dynamic time warping (DTW) widely used in gesture recognition. Early DTW-based methods were applied to isolated gesture recognition (Corradini 2001; Lichtenauer et al. 2008). Then Ruiduo et al. (2007) proposed an enhanced Level-Building DTW method. This method can handle the movement epenthesis problem and simultaneously segment and match signs to continuous sign language sentences. Besides these methods, other approaches are also widely used for gesture recognition, such as linguistic sub-units (Cooper et al. 2012) and topology-preserving self-organizing networks (Flórez et al. 2002). Although the mentioned methods have delivered promising results, most of them assume that the local features (shape, velocity, orientation, position or trajectory) are detected well. However, the prior successes of hand detection and tracking are major challenging problems in complex surroundings. Moreover, as shown in Table 11.1, most of the mentioned methods need dozens or hundreds of training samples to achieve high recognition rates. For example, in Yamato et al. (1992), the authors used at least 50 samples for each class to train HMM and got the average recognition rate 96%. Besides, Yamato et al. (1992) suggested that the recognition rate will be unstable if the number of samples is small. When there is only one training sample per class, those methods are difficult to satisfy the requirement of high performance application systems.

In recent years, BoF-based methods derived from object categories (Fei-Fei and Perona 2005) and action recognition (Wang et al. 2009) have become an important branch for gesture recognition. Dardas and Georganas (2011) proposed a method for real-time hand gesture recognition based on standard BoF model, but they first needed to detect and track hands and that would be difficult in a clutter background. For example, when the hand and face are overlapped or the background is similar to skin color, hand detection may fail. Shen et al. (2012) extracted maximum stable extremal regions (MSER) features (Forssen and Lowe 2007) from the motion divergence fields which were calculated by optical flow (Lowe 2004), and learned a codebook using hierarchical k-means algorithm, then matched the test gesture sequence with the database using a term frequency-inverse document frequency (tf-idf) weighting scheme. These methods need dozens or hundreds of training samples. However, in this paper, we explore one-shot learning gesture recognition (Malgireddy et al. 2012), that is, using one training sample per each class. Some important challenging issues for one-shot learning gesture recognition are the following:

1. **How to extract distinctive features?** Different people have different speeds, trajectories and spatial positions to perform the same gesture. Even when a single person performs the gestures, the trajectories are not identical. Therefore, the extracted spatio-temporal features should be invariant to image-plane rotation, scale and spatial position. Simple descriptors, such as motion trajectories (Yang et al. 2002) and spatio-temporal gradients (Freeman and Roth 1995), may not meet the invariant conditions. Therefore, we propose a new spatio-temporal feature which is scale, image-plane rotation and space invariant and can capture more compact and richer visual representations. The new feature will be introduced in Sect. 11.3.1.

2. **How to select a suitable model?** Here, we select BoF-based model to recognize gestures because it reveals promising results for one-shot learning (Hernández-Vela et al. 2012) and has a number of attractive properties. First, in our BoF representation, we do not need the prior success of hand detection and tracking. Second, BoF is a modular system with three parts, namely, (i) spatio-temporal feature extraction, (ii) codebook learning and descriptor coding, (iii) classifier, each of which can be easily replaced with different methods. For instance, we can apply various methods,

Table 11.1 This table shows the training samples pre class needed in some traditional methods. "NA" means the training samples are not clearly mentioned

Paper/method	Kim et al. (2007)/HMM	Yamato et al. (1992)/HMM	Youtian et al. (2006)/DBN	Suk et al. (2010)/DBN	Sminchisescu et al. (2005)/CRF
Training samples per class	150	≥50	15	42	NA
Paper/method	Wang et al. (2006)/HCRF	Morency et al. (2007)/LDCRF	Corradini (2001)/DTW	Lichtenauer et al. (2008)/DTW	Ruiduo et al. (2007)/DTW
Training samples per class	≥45	≥269	45	≥60	NA

such as Cuboid (Dollár et al. 2005) or Harris3D (Laptev 2005) for the local spatio-temporal feature extraction while leaving the rest of the system unchanged.

In this paper, we focus on solving these two challenging issues and propose a new approach to achieve good performance for one-shot learning gesture recognition. Our experimental results reveal that our method is competitive to the state-of-the-art methods. The key contributions of the proposed method are summarized as follows: • A new framework derived from the BoF model is proposed. • A new spatio-temporal feature (3D EMoSIFT) is proposed. • The new feature is invariant to scale and rotation. • The new feature is not sensitive to slight motion. • Using SOMP instead of VQ in the coding stage. • Obtained high ranking results on ChaLearn gesture challenge.

The rest of paper is organized as follows: Sect. 11.2 reviews the background including BoF model and some local spatio-temporal features. In Sect. 11.3, we describe the proposed approach in detail. Section 11.4 presents the experimental results. In Sect. 11.5, we conclude the paper and discuss future work.

11.2   Background

In this section, we first introduce the traditional BoF framework for recognition and then review the local spatio-temporal features which are widely used in BoF model.

11.2.1   Traditional Bag of Feature (BoF) Model

Figure 11.1a illustrates the traditional BoF approach for gesture (or action) recognition. In the training part, after extracting local features from training videos, the visual codebook is learned with the k-means algorithm. Then each feature is mapped to a certain visual codeword through the clustering process and the video can be represented by the histogram of visual codewords. The histograms representing training videos are treated as input vectors for a support vector machine (SVM) (Chang and Lin 2011) to build a classifier. In the testing stage, the features are extracted from a new input video, and then those features are mapped into a histogram vector by the descriptor coding method (e.g., VQ) using the pre-trained codebook. Then, the histogram vector is finally fed into an SVM classifier to get the recognition result.

However, as shown in Fig. 11.1b, we list at least three differences between our model and the traditional BoF model. First, there is only one training sample per gesture class, while dozens or hundreds of training samples per class are provided in the traditional BoF model. Second, we use SOMP to replace VQ in the coding stage.

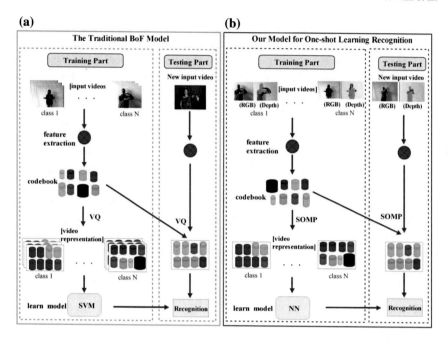

Fig. 11.1 **a** An overview of the traditional BoF model (the *left green rectangle*); **b** an overview of our model (the *right blue rectangle*)

That is because SOMP can get better performance. Third, in the recognition stage, we just use the simple nearest neighbor (NN) classifier instead of SVM to recognize gestures.

11.2.2 Spatio-Temporal Features

We describe some spatio-temporal features which represent the state-of-the-art techniques on object recognition tasks. Those features are commonly used to detect salient and stable local batches from videos.

The Cuboid detector depends on a set of linear filters for computing the response function of a video clip. The response function has the form of a 2D Gaussian smoothing function (applied in the spatial domain) and a quadrature pair of 1D Gabor filters (applied in the temporal direction). Then the keypoints are detected at the local maxima of the response function. The video batches extracted at each of the keypoints are converted to a descriptor. There are a number of ways to compute descriptors from video batches as discussed by Dollár et al. (2005). Among those, gradient-based descriptors such as histograms of oriented gradients (HOG) and concatenated gradient vectors are the most reliable ones. For more details about the Cuboid feature, please see Dollár et al. (2005).

The Harris3D detector (Laptev 2005) is an extension of the Harris corner detector (Harris and Stephens 1988). The author computes a spatio-temporal second-moment matrix at each video point using independent spatial and temporal scale values, a separable Gaussian smoothing function, and space-time gradients. The final locations of space-time interest points are given by the local positive spatio-temporal maxima. Then, at each keypoint, two types of descriptors are calculated, which are HOG and histograms of optical flow (HOF) descriptors.

The MoSIFT (Chen and Hauptmann 2009) is derived from scale invariant feature transform (SIFT) (Lowe 2004) and optical flow (Lucas et al. 1981). First, a pair of Gaussian pyramids are built from two successive frames, respectively. Then, optical flow pyramids are calculated by each layer of the pair of Gaussian pyramids. Next, a local extreme detected from difference of Gaussian pyramids (DoG) can only become an interest point if it has sufficient motion in the optical flow pyramid. Finally, as the process of the SIFT descriptor calculation, the MoSIFT descriptors are respectively computed from Gaussian pyramid and optical flow pyramid so that each MoSIFT descriptor now has 256 dimensions.

Ming et al. (2012) propose a new feature called 3D MoSIFT that is derived from MoSIFT. Compared with MoSIFT, 3D MoSIFT fuses the RGB data and depth information into the feature descriptors. First, Ming et al. (2012) adopt the same strategy using the RGB data to detect interest points. Then, for each interest point, 3D gradient space and 3D motion space are constructed by using RGB data and depth information. In 3D gradient (motion) space, they map 3D space into three 2D planes: xy plane, yz plane and xz plane. Next, for each plane, they used SIFT algorithm to calculate the descriptors. Therefore, each 3D MoSIFT descriptor has 768 dimensions.

11.3 The Proposed Approach for One-Shot Learning Gesture Recognition

We propose a new spatio-temporal feature called 3D EMoSIFT. The new feature is invariant to scale and image-plane rotation. Then we use kmeans algorithm to learn codebook and apply SOMP algorithm to achieve descriptor coding. Besides, we adopt a methodology based on DTW and motion energy for temporal segmentation. Below, we describe each stage in detail.

11.3.1 Spatio-Temporal Feature Extraction: 3D EMoSIFT

The first stage is to extract rich spatio-temporal representations from the video clips. To obtain such representations, there are many ways to select (Dollár et al. 2005; Laptev 2005; Chen and Hauptmann 2009). However, those approaches only rely on RGB data and do not consider the depth information, which may lead to acquire

(a)

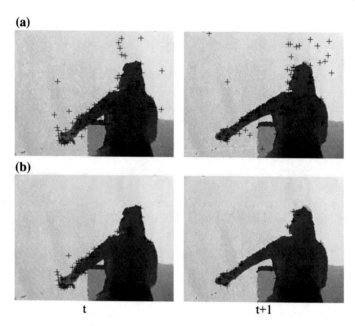

(b)

t   t+1

Fig. 11.2 Results of interest point detection (marked with the *red cross*) in two consecutive frames. **a** 3D MoSIFT; **b** 3D EMoSIFT. We can see that some redundant points are detected in some slight motion regions (i.e., background regions) which shows 3D MoSIFT is sensitive to slight movement. However, 3D EMoSIFT can detect interest points from the regions with large motion (i.e., hand and arm regions), which shows 3D EMoSIFT is not sensitive to slight motion

insufficient information. Although 3D MoSIFT can fuse the RGB-D data to calculate descriptors, it still cannot accurately detect interest points. For instance, as shown in Fig. 11.2a, 3D MoSIFT capture some redundant interest points when some slight motion happens (e.g., slight motion in the background), showing that 3D MoSIFT is sensitive to slight movement. Besides, 3D MoSIFT (Ming et al. 2012) is a little sketchy. To solve the mentioned problems, we propose a new spatio-temporal feature and give examples to explain how to extract the new feature step by step.

11.3.1.1 Feature Points Detection from RGB-D Data

Although the 3D MoSIFT feature has achieved good results in human activity recognition, it still cannot eliminate some influences from the slight motion as shown in Fig. 11.2a. Therefore, we fuse depth information to detect robust interest points. We know that SIFT algorithm (Lowe 2004) uses the Gaussian function as the scale-space kernel to produce a scale space of an input image. The whole scale space is divided into a sequence of octaves and each octave consists of a sequence of intervals, where each interval is a scaled image.

Building Gaussian Pyramid. Given a gesture sample including two videos (one for RGB video and the other for depth video),[1] a Gaussian pyramid for every grayscale frame (converted from RGB frame) and a depth Gaussian pyramid for every depth frame can be built via Eq. (11.1).

$$L_{i,j}^I(x, y) = G(x, y, k^j\sigma) * L_{i,0}^I(x, y), \ 0 \le i < n, 0 \le j < s + 3,$$
$$L_{i,j}^D(x, y) = G(x, y, k^j\sigma) * L_{i,0}^D(x, y), \ 0 \le i < n, 0 \le j < s + 3,$$
(11.1)

where (x, y) is the coordinate in an image; n is the number of octaves and s is the number of intervals; $L_{i,j}^I$ and $L_{i,j}^D$ denote the blurred image of the $(j + 1)$th image in the $(i + 1)$th octave; $L_{i,0}^I$ (or $L_{i,0}^D$) denotes the first grayscale (or depth) image in the $(i + 1)$th octave; For $i = 0$, $L_{0,0}^I$ (or $L_{0,0}^D$) is calculated from the original grayscale (depth) frame via bilinear interpolation and the size of $L_{0,0}^I$ is twice the size of the original frame; For $i > 1$, $L_{i,0}^I$ (or $L_{i,0}^D$) is down-sampled from $L_{i-1,s}^I$ (or $L_{i-1,s}^D$) by taking every second pixel in each row and column. In Fig. 11.3a, the blue arrow shows that the first image $L_{1,0}^I$ in the second octave is down-sampled from the third image $L_{0,2}^I$ in the first octave. $*$ is the convolution operation; $G(x, y, k^j\sigma) = \frac{1}{2\pi(k^j\sigma)^2}e^{-(x^2+y^2)/(2(k^j\sigma)^2)}$ is a Gaussian function with variable-scale value; σ is the initial smoothing parameter in Gaussian function and $k = 2^{1/s}$ (Lowe 2004). Then, the difference of Gaussian (DoG) images, Df, are calculated from the difference of two nearby scales in Eq. (11.2).

$$Df_{i,j} = L_{i,j+1}^I - L_{i,j}^I, \ 0 \le i < n, 0 \le j < s + 2.$$
(11.2)

We give an example to intuitively understand the Gaussian pyramid and DoG pyramid. Figure 11.3 shows two Gaussian pyramids $(L^{I_t}, L^{I_{t+1}})$ built from two consecutive grayscale frames and two depth Gaussian pyramids $(L^{D_t}, L^{D_{t+1}})$ built from the corresponding depth frames. In this example, the number of octaves is $n = 4$ and the number of intervals is $s = 2$; Therefore, for each frame, we can build five images for each octave. And we can see that larger $k^j\sigma$ results in a more blurred image (see the enlarged portion of the red rectangle in Fig. 11.3). Then, we use the Gaussian pyramid shown in Fig. 11.3a to build the DoG pyramid via Eq. (11.2), which is shown in Fig. 11.4.

Building Optical Flow Pyramid First, we briefly review the Lucas-Kanade method (Lucas et al. 1981) which is widely used in computer vision. The method assumes that the displacement of two consecutive frames is small and approximately constant within a neighborhood of the point ρ. The two consecutive frames are denoted by $F1$ and $F2$ at time t and $t + 1$, respectively. Then the optical flow vector (v^ρ) of the point ρ can be solved by the least squares principle (Lucas et al. 1981). Namely, it solves:

$$Av^\rho = b,$$

---

[1] The depth values are normalized to [0 255] in depth videos.

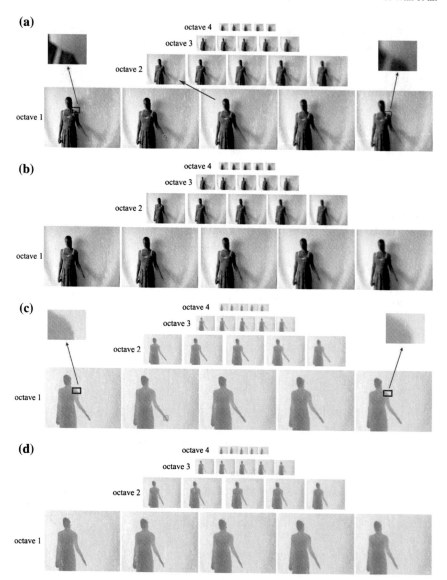

Fig. 11.3 Building Gaussian pyramids and depth Gaussian pyramids for two consecutive frames. **a** The Gaussian pyramid L^{I_t} at time t; **b** the Gaussian pyramid $L^{I_{t+1}}$ at time $t + 1$; **c** the depth Gaussian pyramid L^{D_t} at time t; **d** the depth Gaussian pyramid $L^{D_{t+1}}$ at time $t + 1$

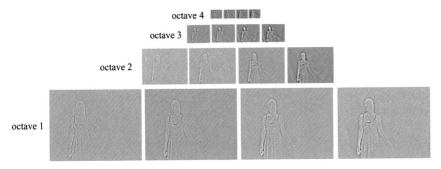

octave 4

octave 3

octave 2

octave 1

Fig. 11.4 Building the difference of Gaussian pyramid Df^{l_t} from Fig. 11.3a at time t

where $A=\begin{bmatrix} F1_x(q_1) & F1_y(q_1) \\ F1_x(q_2) & F1_y(q_2) \\ \cdot & \cdot \\ \cdot & \cdot \\ \cdot & \cdot \\ F1_x(q_n) & F1_y(q_n) \end{bmatrix}$, $v^{\rho}=\begin{bmatrix} v^{\rho}_x \\ v^{\rho}_y \end{bmatrix}$, and $b=\begin{bmatrix} -F1_t(q_1) \\ -F1_t(q_2) \\ \cdot \\ \cdot \\ \cdot \\ -F1_t(q_n) \end{bmatrix}$, $q_1, q_2, ..., q_n$ are

the pixels inside the window around the point ρ, $F1_x(q_i)$ and $F1_y(q_i)$ calculated by different operators (e.g., Scharr operator, Sobel operator) are the partial derivatives of the image $F1$ along the horizontal and vertical directions, and $F1_t(q_i) = F2(q_i) - F1(q_i)$ calculated by two consecutive frames is the partial derivatives along time. Besides, v^{ρ}_x (v^{ρ}_y) denotes the horizontal (vertical) velocity of the point ρ. So we can know the optical flow $V = [V_x \ V_y]^T$ of all the points in the image $F1$ via Eq. (11.3).

$$[V_x \ V_y]^T = \bigcup_{i=1}^{\zeta}[v^{\rho_i}_x \ v^{\rho_i}_y]^T, \tag{11.3}$$

where ζ is the number of points in the image $F1$, $v^{\rho_i}_x$ ($v^{\rho_i}_y$) denotes the horizontal (vertical) velocity of the point ρ_i, and V_x (V_y) denotes the horizontal (vertical) component of the estimated optical flow for all the points in an image. In order to facilitate the following description, we rewrite Eq. (11.3), so as to define $OpticalFlowKL(F1, F2)$, as follow:

$$[V_x \ V_y]^T = OpticalFlowKL(F1, F2) \overset{def}{=} \bigcup_{i=1}^{\zeta}[v^{\rho_i}_x \ v^{\rho_i}_y]^T.$$

Next, once two Gaussian pyramids (L^{l_t} and $L^{l_{t+1}}$) shown in Fig. 11.3a, b are obtained at time t and $t + 1$, respectively, we can calculate the optical flow at each interval of each octave via Eq. (11.4). That is say,

$$[V^{l_t}_{x,(i,j)} \ V^{l_t}_{y,(i,j)}]^T = OpticalFlowKL(L^{l_t}_{i,j}, L^{l_{t+1}}_{i,j}), \ 0 \le i < n, 0 \le j < s+3, \tag{11.4}$$

where $L_{i,j}^{I_t}$ denotes the blurred image of the $(j+1)$th interval in the $(i+1)$th octave at time t, n and s are defined the same as Eq. (11.1).

So the horizontal and vertical optical flow pyramids at time t are the union sets $\bigcup_{i,j} V_{x,(i,j)}^{I_t}$ and $\bigcup_{i,j} V_{y,(i,j)}^{I_t}$, respectively. For example, we use the Gaussian pyramids in Fig. 11.3a, b to compute the optical flow pyramid via Eq. (11.4). And the results are illustrated in Fig. 11.5a, b where we can see that the highlighted parts occur around the motion parts.

Local Extrema Detection Here, we describe three different methods (SIFT, 3D MoSIFT, 3D EMoSIFT) for interest point detection and show the similarities and differences among these methods.

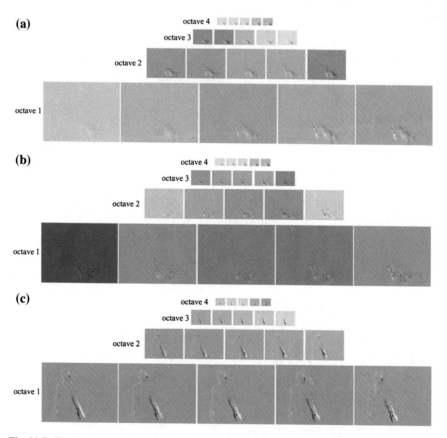

Fig. 11.5 The *horizontal* and *vertical optical* flow pyramids are calculated from Fig. 11.3a, b. **a** The horizontal component of the estimated optical flow pyramid $V_x^{I_t}$ at time t. **b** The vertical component of the estimated optical flow pyramid $V_y^{I_t}$ at time t. **c** The depth changing component $V_z^{D_t}$ at time t

(a) **(b)**

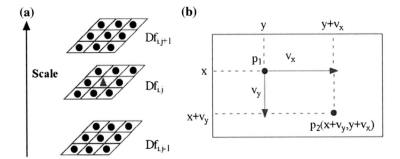

Fig. 11.6 **a** The SIFT algorithm for interest points detection. Maxima and minima of the DoG images are detected by comparing a pixel (marked with a *red triangle*) to its 26 neighbors in 3 × 3 regions at the current and adjacent scales (marked with *black circles*); **b** the point prediction via the optical flow vector

(1) *Local Extrema Detection: SIFT*

In order to detect the local maxima and minima in the DoG pyramid $Df_{i,j}^{I_t}$, each point is compared to its eight neighbors in the current image and nine neighbors in the above and below images of each octave, which is illustrated in Fig. 11.6a. A point is selected only if it is larger than all of these neighbors or smaller than all of them. In Fig. 11.4, the DoG pyramid $Df_{i,j}^{I_t}$ has four octaves and each octave has four images at time t. So we can find the local extrema points in the middle of two images at each octave, namely, $Df_{i,j}^{I_t}$, $\forall i \in [0, 3], j \in [1, 2]$. For example, in the first octave, we detect the local extrema points at the second image $Df_{0,1}^{I_t}$ (via comparing the point to his 8 neighbor points in the current image $Df_{0,1}^{I_t}$, 9 neighbor points in the image $Df_{0,0}^{I_t}$, and 9 neighbor points in the image $Df_{0,2}^{I_t}$) and the third image $Df_{0,2}^{I_t}$ (via comparing the point to his 8 neighbor points in the current image $Df_{0,2}^{I_t}$, 9 neighbor points in the image $Df_{0,1}^{I_t}$, and 9 neighbor points in the image $Df_{0,3}^{I_t}$). So we can detect the local extrema points in other octaves similar to the first octave. The detected points (marked with red points) are shown in Fig. 11.7a, which shows that many redundant points are detected in the background and torso regions.

(2) *Local Extrema Detection: 3D MoSIFT*[2]

3D MoSIFT first detect the local extrema like SIFT algorithm. Then those local extrema can only become interest points when those points have sufficient motion in the optical flow pyramid. That is to say, if a point is treated as an interest point, the velocity of this point should satisfy the following condition:

$$v_x \geq \beta_1 \times w, \ v_y \geq \beta_1 \times h, \tag{11.5}$$

where v_x (v_y) is the horizontal (vertical) velocity of a point from the horizontal (vertical) optical flow pyramid V_x (V_y); β_1 is a pre-defined threshold; w and h are the width and height of the blurred image in the scale space.

---

[2]MoSIFT and *3D MoSIFT* have the same strategy to detect interest points.

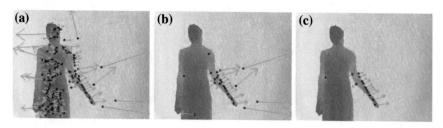

Fig. 11.7 After interest point detection, the SIFT-based descriptors are calculated by three methods: SIFT, 3D MoSIFT and 3D EMoSIFT. The detected points are marked with *red circles* and the *green arrows* show the direction of movements. The figure shows that SIFT and 3D MoSIFT detect many useless points in the background and torso regions while the result by 3D EMoSIFT is more accurate. **a** SIFT; **b** 3D MoSIFT; **c** 3D EMoSIFT

As shown in Fig. 11.5a, b, we can see that only the local extrema located in the highlighted parts of the optical flow pyramids ($V_x^{I_t}$ and $V_y^{I_t}$) will become interest points. Because only the points in the highlighted parts have large motions, which may satisfy the condition in Eq. (11.5). Other extrema will be eliminated, because they have no sufficient motion in the optical flow pyramids. The final results (marked with red points) are shown in Fig. 11.7b.[3] Comparing with SIFT algorithm, we can see that if the points are still, they will be filtered out via the conditions in Eq. (11.5). However, in Fig. 11.7b, some useless points (from the background and torso regions) are still detected, which indicate that 3D MoSIFT is sensitive to the slight motion.

(3) *Local Extrema Detection: 3D EMoSIFT*

To eliminate the effect of the slight motion, we introduce a new condition to filter out the detected points by the SIFT algorithm. According to the above mentioned description, we have obtained the pyramids L^{D_t}, $L^{D_{t+1}}$, $V_x^{I_t}$, $V_y^{I_t}$. For a given point p_1 from an image in different scale spaces at time t, we can easily know the horizontal and vertical velocities v_x, v_y by the corresponding image of the pyramids $V_x^{I_t}$, $V_y^{I_t}$. Then the predicted point p_2 at time $t + 1$ can be calculated by the point p_1 at time t according to Fig. 11.6b. Therefore, we can know the depth changing component at time t as:

$$V_{z,(i,j)}^{D_t}(p_1) = L_{i,j}^{D_{t+1}}(p_2) - L_{i,j}^{D_t}(p_1), \ 0 \le i < n, 0 \le j < s + 3. \quad (11.6)$$

Figure 11.5c shows the depth changing pyramid via Eq. (11.6). We can see that the highlighted parts accurately occur in the gesture motion region. Therefore, the local extrema shown in Fig. 11.7a by SIFT algorithm will become interest points when those points not only have sufficient motion which is satisfied with the condition of 3D MoSIFT in Eq. (11.5) but also have enough depth changing which is shown in the highlighted regions of Fig. 11.5c. That is say, the interest point detection must simultaneously satisfy the condition in Eq. (11.5) and a new condition defined as:

---

[3]Here, $\beta_1 = 0.005$ according to the reference (Ming et al. 2012).

$$v_z \geq \beta_2 \times \sqrt{w^2 + h^2}, \tag{11.7}$$

where v_z is the depth changing value of a point from the depth changing pyramid V_z; β_2 is a pre-defined threshold. The final results is shown in Fig. 11.7c.[4] We can see that 3D EMoSIFT can filter out the still points and the points with slight motion.

11.3.1.2 Feature Descriptors

The previous operations assigned an image location and scale to each interest point. That is say we can use the interest point to select the Gaussian images from different pyramids. Here, we give an example to illustrate how to compute the feature descriptor vector which is similar to the process in Ming et al. (2012). We assume that a detected point (marked with green dot) is found in DoG pyramid $Df_{0,1}^{I_t}$ at time t in Fig. 11.4, which indicates that the detected point locates at the second image of the first octave. Then the corresponding points (marked with green dot) in different pyramids are shown in Figs. 11.3 and 11.5 at time t. To calculate the feature descriptors, we first extract the local patches (Γ_1–Γ_5) around the detected point in five pyramids ($L^{I_t}, L^{D_t}, V_x^{I_t}, V_y^{I_t}$ and $V_z^{I_t}$), where Γ_1 is extracted from $L_{0,1}^{I_t}$, Γ_2 from $L_{0,1}^{D_t}$, Γ_3 from $V_{x,(0,1)}^{I_t}$, Γ_4 from $V_{y,(0,1)}^{I_t}$ and Γ_5 from $V_{z,(0,1)}^{D_t}$. These five patches are labeled as green rectangles in Figs. 11.3 and 11.5. The local patches Γ_1–Γ_5 are of the same size 16×16 pixels and are shown in Fig. 11.8. We first consider the appearance properties to construct the 3D gradient space via local patches Γ_1 and Γ_2. Then we use the rest of local patches (Γ_3, Γ_4 and Γ_5) to construct 3D motion space.

Feature Descriptors in 3D Gradient Space For a given point p with its coordinate (i, j), we can simply calculate its horizontal and vertical gradients from RGB-D data (Γ_1 and Γ_2) as follow:

$$I_x(i, j) = \Gamma_1(i, j + 1) - \Gamma_1(i, j),$$
$$I_y(i, j) = \Gamma_1(i + 1, j) - \Gamma_1(i, j),$$
$$D_z^x(i, j) = \Gamma_2(i, j + 1) - \Gamma_2(i, j),$$
$$D_z^y(i, j) = \Gamma_2(i + 1, j) - \Gamma_2(i, j),$$

where $I_x(i, j)$ and $I_y(i, j)$ are the horizontal and vertical gradients calculated from Γ_1; D_z^x and $D_z^y(i, j)$ are the horizontal and vertical gradients from Γ_2. We can calculate four gradients (I_x, I_y, D_z^x and D_z^y) for each point. Because the local patches (Γ_1 and Γ_2) are of size 16×16, there are 256 points and each point has four gradient values.

Then, as shown in Fig. 11.8a, for each point p, the 3D gradient space can be constructed by $I_x(i, j), I_y(i, j), D_z^x(i, j)$ and $D_z^y(i, j)$. Now we use the xy plane to illustrate how to calculate the feature descriptor in the 3D gradient space. For each point p with its coordinate (i, j), we compute the gradient magnitude, $mag(i, j) = \sqrt{I_x(i, j)^2 + I_y(i, j)^2}$, and orientation, $ori(i, j) = tan^{-1}(I_y(i, j)/I_x(i, j))$

---

[4] Here, $\beta_1 = \beta_2 = 0.005$.

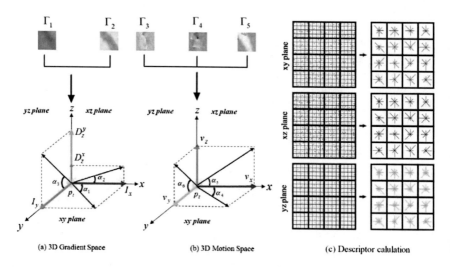

Fig. 11.8 Computing the feature descriptor in two parts: **a** 3D Gradient Space, **b** 3D Motion Space, **c** Feature descriptor calculation

in the xy plane. Then, in xy plane, we can generate a new patch Γ_{xy} which is the left image in the first row of Fig. 11.8c. The size of Γ_{xy} is 16×16. For each point with its coordinate (i, j) from Γ_{xy}, it has two values: the gradient magnitude $mag(i, j)$ and orientation $ori(i, j)$. Γ_{xy} can be divided into 16 (4×4) grids. For each grid with 4×4 points, we calculate its orientation histogram with 8 bins, which means the orientation is grouped into 8 directions which is represented by the right image in the first row of Fig. 11.8c. This leads to a descriptor vector with 128 ($4 \times 4 \times 8$) dimensions in xy plane. Here, each sample added to the histogram is weighed by its gradient magnitude and by a Gaussian weighting function (Lowe 2004). Similarly, we can calculate the descriptors in xz and yz planes. Therefore, the descriptor vector of the 3D gradient space has 384 (128×3) dimensions.

Feature Descriptors in 3D Motion Space For a given point p with coordinates $(i, j), \forall\, 0 \le i \le 15,\; 0 \le j \le 15$, we can easily know the velocities according to the local patches Γ_3, Γ_4, and Γ_5. That is say, $v_x(i, j) = \Gamma_3(i, j)$, $v_y(i, j) = \Gamma_4(i, j)$ and $v_z(i, j) = \Gamma_5(i, j)$.

Thus, we can construct the 3D motion space as shown in Fig. 11.8b. Similar to the descriptor calculation in 3D gradient space, we can compute the magnitude and orientation (using v_x, v_y, v_z) for the local patch around the detected points in three planes. The only difference is that v_z is the same in both xz and yz planes. Therefore, we obtain the descriptors with 384 dimensions in the 3D motion space. Finally, we integrate these two descriptor vectors into a long descriptor vector with 768 dimensions.

11.3.1.3 Overview the 3D EMoSIFT Features

In this section, we propose a new spatio-temporal feature called 3D EMoSIFT. Each 3D EMoSIFT feature descriptor has 768 dimensions. Since the 3D EMoSIFT feature is derived from SIFT algorithm, the features are invariant to scale and rotation. Besides, compared to other similar features (SIFT, MoSIFT, 3D MoSIFT), the new features can capture more compact motion patterns and are not sensitive to the slight motion (see the Fig. 11.7). For a given sample including an RGB video and a depth video, we can calculate feature descriptors between two consecutive frames. Then the sample can be represented by the set of all the feature descriptors extracted from the video clips. Algorithm 1 illustrates how to calculate the proposed features.

Now each sample is denoted by the set of descriptor vectors, and we want to use those vectors for BoF representation. To do that, we will create histograms counting how many times a descriptor vector (representing a feature) appears at interest points anywhere in the video clip representing the gesture. There is a need to first replace the descriptor vectors by codes to limit the number of features, otherwise there would be too many entries in the histogram and the representation would be too sparse. So, we will describe the means of creating a codebook in the next Sect. 11.3.2.

Algorithm 1: The algorithm for the 3D EMoSIFT feature

Input:

- A sample with two videos: $V_r = [I_1, I_2, ..., I_Q]$ (RGB data), $V_d = [D_1, D_2, ..., D_Q]$ (depth data)
- Number of frames : Q

Output:

- The set of feature descriptors : X

1: Initialization: $X = [\ ]$
2: **for** $i = 1$ to $Q - 1$ **do**
3:    Obtain the frames: I_i and I_{i+1} from V_r; D_i and D_{i+1} from V_d
4:    Build the Gaussian Pyramids: L^{I_i}, $L^{I_{i+1}}$, L^{D_i} and $L^{D_{i+1}}$ via Equation (11.1)
5:    Build the different of Gaussian (DoG) Pyramid: Df^{I_i} via Equation (11.2)
6:    Build the Optical Flow Pyramids: $V_x^{I_i}$ and $V_y^{I_i}$ via Equation (11.4)
7:    Build the depth changing Pyramid: $V_z^{D_i}$ via Equation (11.6)
8:    Find the set of interest points: $P = [p_1, ..., p_m]$ via Fig. 11.6(a), Equation (11.5) and (11.7)
9:    **for** $j = 1$ to m **do**
10:      Get the information of the interest point from the set P: p_i
11:      Compute feature descriptor from the local patch around p_i: $x \in \Re^{768}$ via Fig. 11.8
12:      $X = [X\ x]$
13:    **end for**
14: **end for**
15: Return X

11.3.2 Codebook Learning and Coding Descriptors

Suppose the matrix X is the set of all descriptor vectors for an entire video clip representing a gesture, and $X = [x_1, x_2, ..., x_N] \in \mathfrak{R}^{d \times N}$, where x_i denotes a description with d dimensions. A codebook B with M entries is denoted with $B = [b_1, b_2, ..., b_M] \in \mathfrak{R}^{d \times M}$. The coding methods map each descriptor into a M-dimensional code to generate the video representation. We first introduce how to learn a codebook B, then review VQ and introduce SOMP for code descriptors.

11.3.2.1 Codebook Learning

Let η denote the number of gesture classes (that means there are η training samples for one-shot learning), $\Omega = [X^1, X^2, ..., X^\eta]$, $\Omega \in \mathfrak{R}^{d \times L_{tr}}$ is the set of all the descriptor vectors extracted from all the training samples, $X^i \in \mathfrak{R}^{d \times N_i}$ with N_i descriptor vectors is the set extracted from the ith class, and $L_{tr} = \sum_{i=1}^{\eta} N_i$ is the number of features extracted from all the training samples. Then we learn the codebook $B \in \mathfrak{R}^{d \times M}$ ($M < \sum_{i=1}^{\eta} N_i$) with M entries by applying the k-means algorithm (Wang et al. (2010)) over all the descriptors Ω in our work. However, unlike traditional BoF models, we use a new parameter $\gamma \in (0, 1)$ instead of the codebook size M (The way we select γ will be discussed in Sect. 11.4.). γ is expressed as a fraction of L_{tr}. Therefore, the codebook size M can be calculated below:

$$M = L_{tr} \times \gamma. \tag{11.8}$$

11.3.2.2 Coding Descriptors by VQ

In the traditional VQ method, we can calculate the Euclidean distance between a given descriptor $x \in \mathfrak{R}^d$ and every codeword $b_i \in \mathfrak{R}^d$ of the codebook B and find the closest codeword. The VQ method can be formulated as:

$$\min_C \|X - BC\|_F^2, \ s.t. \|c_i\|_0 = 1, \|c_i\|_1 = 1, c_i \geqslant 0, \ \forall i, \tag{11.9}$$

where $\| \cdot \|_F$ is the Frobenius norm, $C = [c_1, c_2, ..., c_N] \in \mathfrak{R}^{M \times N}$ is the set of codes for X, $\| \cdot \|_0$ is the ℓ_0 norm that counts the number of nonzero elements, $\| \cdot \|_1$ is the ℓ_1 norm; The conditions $\|c_i\|_0 = 1$, $\|c_i\|_1 = 1$, $c_i \geqslant 0$, mean that only one element is equal to 1 and the others are zero in each code $c_i \in \mathfrak{R}^M$.

This formulation in Eq. (11.9) allows us to compare more easily with sparse coding (see the Sect. 11.3.2.3). In Eq. (11.9), the conditions may be too restrictive, which gives rise to usually a coarse reconstruction of X. Therefore, we use a sparse coding method instead of VQ.

11.3.2.3 Coding Descriptors by SOMP

Inspired by image classification (Yang et al. 2009) and robust face recognition (Wright et al. 2009) via sparse coding, we relax the restricted conditions in Equation (11.9) and suppose X has a sparse representation $C = [c_1, c_2, ..., c_N]$, $c_i \in \Re^M$ that means each c_i contains k ($k \ll M$) or fewer nonzero elements. Then, the problem can be stated as the following optimization problem:

$$\min_{C} \|X - BC\|_F^2, \ s.t. \|c_i\|_0 \leq k, \ \forall \ i. \tag{11.10}$$

Solving Equation (11.10) accurately is an NP-hard problem (Wright et al. 2009; Guo et al. 2013). Nevertheless, approximate solutions are provided by greedy algorithms or convex relaxation, such as SOMP (Tropp et al. 2006; Rakotomamonjy 2011). To the best of our knowledge, we are the first to use SOMP in BoF model for gesture recognition, especially for one-shot learning gesture recognition.

Then we give a brief introduction about the SOMP algorithm and analyze the computational complexity. SOMP is a greedy algorithm which is based on the idea of selecting an element of the codebook and building all signal approximations as the projection of the signal matrix X on the span of these selected codewords. This algorithm (Tropp et al. 2006; Rakotomamonjy 2011) is shown in Algorithm 2. Regarding the computational complexity, we note that the most demanding part of the SOMP is the correlation E computation which has the complexity $O(dMN)$. And the complexity of the linear system to be solved for obtaining C at each iteration is $O(|\Lambda|)$. So the complexity for k iterations is about $O(dkMN) + O(k|\Lambda|)$. Although the complexity of SOMP is more expensive than VQ which has $O(dMN)$ (Linde et al. 1980). SOMP has several merits which will be discussed later.

Algorithm 2: The SOMP algorithm

Input:

- A signal matrix (the feature set): $X = [x_1, x_2, ..., x_N] \in \Re^{d \times N}$
- A learned codebook: $B = [b_1, b_2, ..., b_M] \in \Re^{d \times M}$
- the sparsity: k

Output:

- The sparse representation: C

1: Initialization: the residual matrix $R_s = X$, the index set $\Lambda = [\ ]$;
2: **for** $i = 1$ to k **do**
3:   $E = B^T R_s$, where $E = \cup_{p,q}[e_{p,q}]$
4:   Find the index $\lambda = argmax_q \sum_p |e_{p,q}|$
5:   $\Lambda = [\Lambda \ \lambda]$
6:   $C = (B_\Lambda^T B_\Lambda)^{-1} B_\Lambda^T X$
7:   $R_s = X - BC$
8: **end for**
9: **return** C

When the codebook $B \in \mathfrak{R}^{D \times M}$ and a descriptor set $X \in \mathfrak{R}^{d \times N}$ are given, the set of codes $C \in \mathfrak{R}^{M \times N}$ can be calculated by the coding methods (VQ or SOMP). Then the mean reconstruction error (*MRE*) for X is defined as:

$$\varepsilon_{MRE} = \sum_{i=1}^{N} \varepsilon_i / N,$$

where $\varepsilon_i = \|x_i - Bc_i\|_2^2$ is the reconstruction error of the ith descriptor.

To compare the *MREs* for both the VQ and SOMP methods, a matrix $X \in \mathfrak{R}^{64 \times 2000}$ is randomly generated based on the standard normal distribution. Then the matrix X is split into two parts ($X_1 \in \mathfrak{R}^{64 \times 1000}$ and $X_2 \in \mathfrak{R}^{64 \times 1000}$). The matrix X_1 is used to build a codebook B by the k-means algorithm. Then we use X_2 to calculate the codes C_{VQ} and C_{SOMP} via Eqs. (11.9) and (11.10), respectively. Finally we calculate the *MREs* under varied cluster numbers and different sparsity values $k = \{5, 10, 15\}$. Figure 11.9 shows the results of both coding methods. We can see that the *MREs* of the SOMP method is much lower than the *MREs* of the VQ method.

Compared with the VQ method, SOMP has several advantages. First, the codebook B is usually overcomplete (i.e., $M > d$). Overcomplete codings smoothly interpolate between input vectors and are robust under input noise (Olshausen et al. 1997). Second, SOMP achieves a much lower reconstruction error. Although there is no direct relationship between lower reconstruction error and good recognition results, some authors (Yang et al. 2009; Wan et al. 2012) have shown that oftentimes better reconstruction leads to better performance. Third, the sparsity prior allows the learned representation to capture salient patterns of local descriptors. According to our experimental results in Sect. 11.4, although VQ can produce satisfactory accuracy, SOMP can achieve better performance.

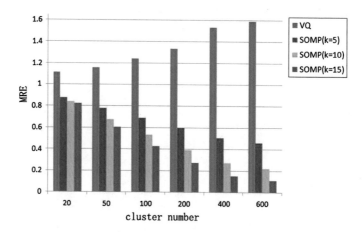

Fig. 11.9 Comparison *MREs* using both VQ and SOMP methods

11.3.3 Coefficient Histogram Calculation and Classification

The matrix X contains the descriptors obtained from a test sample and C contains their corresponding sparse representations over the learned codebook B. The sparse coefficients of the vector $c_i \in C$ present the contribution of all the entries in approximating the descriptor $x_i \in X$. The sparse coefficients associated with all the descriptors of the test sample thus collectively demonstrate the contribution of the entries toward the representation of that sample. Therefore, we use the coefficient histogram to denote the representation of each individual sample via Eq. (11.11).

$$h = \frac{1}{N} \sum_{i=1}^{N} c_i, \qquad (11.11)$$

where $c_i \in \Re^M$ is the ith descriptor of $C \in \Re^{M \times N}$, and N is the total number of descriptors extracted from a sample and $h \in \Re^M$.

Because we have only one sample per class for training, multi-class SVMs are not trivially applicable because they require in principle a large number of training examples. So we select the NN classification for gesture recognition.

In the above discussion, we assume that every video has one gesture but this assumption is not suitable for continuous gesture recognition system. Therefore, we first apply DTW to achieve temporal gesture segmentation, which splits the multiple gestures to be recognized. We use the sample code about DTW provided in ChaLearn gesture challenge website (http://gesture.chalearn.org/data/sample-code). The detailed description of how to use DTW in one-shot learning can be found in Guyon et al. (2013). We briefly introduce the process for temporal gesture segmentation by DTW so as to make this paper more self-contained.

11.3.4 Temporal Gesture Segmentation Based on DTW

Let $V = [I_1, ..., I_N]$ be a video with N frames, where I_i is the ith frame (grayscale image) in the video. A video is represented by a set of motion features obtained from difference images as follows. First, the difference image is computed by subtracting consecutive frames in a video, that is $E_i = I_{i+1} - I_i, i = 1, ..., N - 1$. The difference image is shown in Fig. 11.10b. Then a grid of equally spaced cells is defined over the difference image. The default size of the grid is 3×3 as shown in Fig. 11.10c. For each cell, we calculate the average value in the difference image, so a 3×3 matrix is generated. Finally, we flatten this matrix into a vector which is called motion feature. Therefore, a video V with N frames is represented by a matrix (the set of motion features) $f_V \in \Re^{9 \times (N-1)}$.

The reference sequence with κ training videos is denoted by $F_{tr} = [f_{V tr_1}, ..., f_{V tr_\kappa}]$, $f_{V tr}$ is the set of motion features of a training video. A test sequence is denoted by $F_{te} = f_{V te}$ (the set of motion features for the test video). We calculate the negative

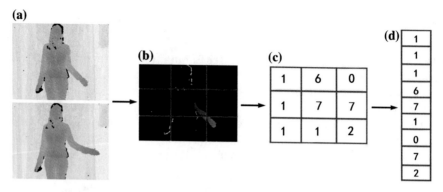

Fig. 11.10 An example for the calculation of motion feature vector

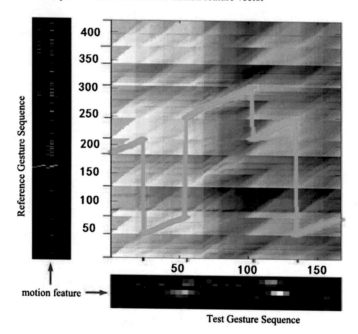

Fig. 11.11 Temporal gesture segmentation by DTW

Euclidean distance between each entry (a motion feature) from F_{tr} and each entry (a motion feature) from F_{te}. Then we calculate the DTW distance and apply the Viterbi algorithm Viterbi (1967) to find the temporal segmentation (an optimal warping path). In Fig. 11.11, the left gray image shows the set of motion features (F_{tr}) as the reference sequence calculated from training videos. A motion feature (F_{te}) as the test sequence is computed from a new input video. The optimal path is shown in the top right corner (the green line is the optimal path; the short red lines are the boundary of two neighboring gestures). We can see that the testing video is splitted into five gestures.

11.3.5 Overview of the Proposed Approach

In this section, we describe the proposed approach based on bag of 3D EMoSIFT features for one-shot learning gesture recognition in detail. In the recognition stage, it has five steps: temporal gesture segmentation by DTW, feature descriptor extraction using 3D EMoSIFT, coding descriptor via SOMP, coefficient histogram calculation and the recognition results via NN classifier. The overall process is summarized in Algorithm 3.

Algorithm 3: The proposed approach for one-shot learning gesture recognition

The condition for one-shot learning: given K training samples (RGB-D data) for K class (one sample per gesture class).

Input:

- Training samples (RGB-D data): $T_r = [t_{r1}, ..., t_{rK}]$
- A learned codebook: B (computed from training stage)
- Coefficient histograms of training samples: $H_r = [h_{r1}, h_{r2}, ..., h_{rK}]$ via Equation (11.11) (computed from training stage)
- A test sample (RGB-D data): t_e

Output:

- The recognition results: *class*

1: Initialization: *class* = [ ]
2: Temporal gesture segmentation: $[t_{e_1}, t_{e_2}, ..., t_{e_N}] = DTW(T_r, t_e), N \geq 1$
3: **for** $i = 1$ to N **do**
4:   Spatio-temporal feature extraction: $X_{t_e} = 3D\_EMoSIFT(t_{e_i})$
5:   For X_{t_e}, calculate its sparse representation C over the pre-trained codebook B
    $\min_C \|X_{t_e} - BC\|_F^2 \quad s.t. \quad \|c_j\|_0 \leq k, \ \forall j$
6:   Calculate the coefficient histogram h_{t_e} via Equation (11.11)
7:   Recognition: $tmp\_calss = nn\_classify(H_r, h_{t_e})$
8:   *class* = [*class tmp_calss*]
9: **end for**
10: **return** *class*

11.4 Experimental Results

This section summarizes our results and demonstrates the proposed method is well suitable for one-shot learning gesture recognition. We first discuss the parameters of the proposed method. We further extend our method to compare with other state-of-the-art methods. Our experiments reveal that the proposed method gives superior recognition performance than many existing approaches.

Fig. 11.12 Some samples from ChaLearn gesture database

11.4.1 Database

We evaluate the proposed method on development batches (*devel01–devel20*), validation batches (*valid01–valid20*) and final batches (*final21–final40*) which contain in total 6000 gestures. The sixty batches are from Chalearn gesture challenge. Each batch is made of 47 gesture videos and split into a training set and a test set. The training set includes a small set of vocabulary spanning from 8 to 15 gestures. Every test video contains 1–5 gestures. Detailed descriptions of the gesture data can be found in Guyon et al. (2012). All the samples are recorded with a Microsoft *Kinect*™ camera which provides both RGB and depth video clips. Some examples are shown in Fig. 11.12 where the first row is RGB images and the corresponding depth images are shown in the second row.

11.4.2 Metric of Evaluation

We adopt the metric of evaluation that was used by the challenge organizers (Guyon et al. 2012) to rank the entries. To evaluate performance, we use Levenshtein distance to calculate the score between the predicted labels and the truth labels. This distance between two strings is defined as the minimum number of operations (insertions, substitutions or deletions) needed to transform one string into the other. In our case, the strings contain the gesture labels detected in each sample. For all comparisons, we compute the mean Levenshtein distance (MLD) over all video clips and batches. MLD score is analogous to an error rate (although it can exceed 1).

11.4.3 Parameters Discussion

This part gives the discussion of the parameters of the proposed method. First, we analysis the parameters of 3D EMoSIFT. Then, two parameters from the BoF model are discussed.

11.4.3.1   Parameters of 3D EMoSIFT

There are five parameters for constructing 3D EMoSIFT features. Three parameters σ, n and s in Eq. (11.1) are derived from SIFT algorithm. We set $\sigma = 1.6$ and $s = 3$. Because Lowe (2004) suggest that when $\sigma = 1.6$ and $s = 3$, they can provide the optimal repeatability according to their experimental results. Besides, the number of octaves n can be calculated according to the original image size, such as $int(log_2(min(width, height)))$ Vedaldi and Fulkerson (2008).

The rest of parameters are β_1 in Eq. (11.5) and β_2 in Eq. (11.7). β_1 and β_2 determine the detection of interest points based on motion and depth change. When β_1 and β_2 are smaller, more interest points will be detected. We find that when $\beta_1 \in [0.003\ 0.008]$, $\beta_2 \in [0.003\ 0.008]$, the performances are very stable as shown in Fig. 11.13 where the results are calculated from two batches. We can see that MLD scores vary from 0.075 to 0.092 for *devel01* batch, from 0.089 to 0.134 for *devel02* batch. Therefore, $\beta_1 = \beta_2 = 0.005$ is used throughout this paper based on empirical results.

11.4.3.2   Parameters of the BoF Model

There are two parameters in the BoF model: γ in Eq. (11.8) and k in Eq. (11.10). Unlike traditional BoF models, we use a new parameter $\gamma \in (0, 1)$ to replace the codebook size M mentioned in Sect. 11.3.2. We first explain the reasons for choosing γ. Table 11.2 shows some information on different batches (*final21–final40*), such as the number of training samples and the number of features extracted from training samples. We can see that the number of features varies on different batches. If a given codebook size M is too large, it may cause over-clustering on some batches where the number of features is relatively fewer (e.g., *final25* and *final36*). Therefore, the over-clustering will effect the final MLD score. For instance, we evaluate seven different

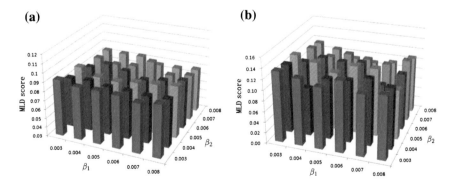

Fig. 11.13 Parameters: $\sigma = 1.6$, $s = 3$, $\gamma = 0.2$ and $k = 10$. The MLD scores are calculated with different values β_1, β_2. **a** On *devel01* batch; **b** on *devel02* batch

Table 11.2 This table shows some information for every batch. The last row reveals the average number. Although the average number of 3D EMoSIFT features has decreased by 28.15%, 3D EMoSIFT has a higher performance than 3D MoSIFT in our experimental results. Besides, compared 3D MoSIFT features, the process time of 3D EMoSIFT can be faster to build the cookbook

Batch names	Number of training samples:N_{tr}	Number of features (3D MoSIFT):$L1_{tr}$	Number of features (3D EMoSIFT):$L2_{tr}$	Decrease in ratio:$1 - \frac{L2_{tr}}{L1_{tr}}$ (%)
Final21	10	18116	13183	27.23
Final22	11	19034	15957	16.17
Final23	12	11168	7900	29.26
Final24	9	10544	7147	32.22
Final25	11	8547	6180	27.69
Final26	9	9852	7675	22.10
Final27	10	29999	20606	31.31
Final28	11	16156	10947	32.24
Final29	8	30782	22692	26.28
Final30	10	20357	14580	28.38
Final31	12	22149	17091	22.84
Final32	9	12717	10817	14.94
Final33	9	42273	29034	31.32
Final34	8	24099	16011	33.56
Final35	8	39409	27013	31.45
Final36	9	9206	6914	24.90
Final37	8	22142	14181	35.95
Final38	11	26160	18785	28.19
Final39	10	16543	11322	31.56
Final40	12	11800	10128	14.17
Average	9.85	20052.65	14408.15	**28.15**

codebook sizes: {800, 1000, 1500, 2000, 2500, 3000, 3500}. The corresponding results are shown in Table 11.3 where the best performance is 0.18242. Then we evaluate different values {0.1, 0.2, 0.3} for γ, and the results are shown in Table 11.4. We can see that even though $\gamma = 0.1$, the corresponding MLD score is 0.17415 which can easily beat the best performance in Table 11.3. Additionally, when $\gamma = 0.1$, the corresponding mean codebook size 1440 is much smaller than the given codebook size 3500 which is from the best result in Table 11.3.

The theory of sparse coding and the codebook learning are in a developing stage and the problems for selecting optimal parameters (e.g., γ, sparsity k) are still open issues (Guha and Ward 2012). In this paper, we use a simple strategy to decide these two parameters. At first, we keep $k = 10$ and set γ with different values (ranging from 0.1 to 0.5), then determine γ by the lowest MLD score. Figure 11.14a shows the results. It reveals when $\gamma = 0.5$, we can get a higher performance and the

Table 11.3 Parameters: $\beta_1 = \beta_2 = 0.005$, $\sigma = 1.6$, $s = 3$ and $k = 10$ (*final21–final40*). MLD scores with different codebook sizes M

Codebook size M	800	1000	1500	2000	2500	3000	3500
MLD score	0.21448	0.21504	0.19514	0.18961	0.18684	0.18574	**0.18242**

Table 11.4 Parameters: $\beta_1 = \beta_2 = 0.005$, $\sigma = 1.6$, $s = 3$ and $k = 10$ (*final21–final40*). MLD scores with different values for γ

γ	0.1	0.2	0.3
MLD score	0.17415	0.14753	0.14032
Mean codebook size	1440	2881	4322

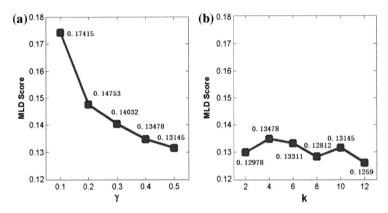

Fig. 11.14   a Parameters: $\beta_1 = \beta_2 = 0.005$, $\sigma = 1.6$, $s = 3$ and $k = 10$ (*final21–final40*). MLD scores with different values of γ; **b** Parameters: $\beta_1 = \beta_2 = 0.005$, $\sigma = 1.6$, $s = 3$ and $\gamma = 0.5$ (*final21–final40*). MLD scores with different values of sparsity k

corresponding MLD score is 0.13145. Then we set different values of k with $\gamma = 0.5$ and the results are shown in Fig. 11.14b. We can see that MLD scores remain stable. When $\gamma = 0.5$ and $k = 12$, the proposed method gets the lowest MLD score (the corresponding value is 0.1259).

11.4.4   Comparisons

In order to compare with other methods, we first use the standard BoF model to evaluate different spatio-temporal features. Then the performances of VQ and SOMP is given. Besides, we evaluate the performances of both the gradient-based and motion-based features. Finally, we compare the proposed approach with some popular sequence matching methods.

11.4.4.1 Comparison with Other Spatio-Temporal Features

In our experiments, we use the standard BoF model to evaluate different spatio-temporal features, which means VQ is used for coding descriptors. As shown in Fig. 11.14b, the results are relatively stable when sparsity k has different values. Therefore, we evaluate different values $\{0.1, 0.2, 0.3, 0.4, 0.5\}$ for γ and set $k = 10$. The results are shown in Table 11.5, where we can draw the following conclusions.

First, the results of 3D EMoSIFT and 3D MoSIFT consistently exceed traditional features (e.g., Cuboid, Harris3D and MoSIFT). More specifically, the least MLD scores (corresponding to the best recognition rate) for 3D EMoSIFT is 0.13311, compared to 0.14476 for 3D MoSIFT, 0.28064 for Cuboid, 0.18192 for Harris3D, and 0.335 for MoSIFT.

Second, from the previous works, we know that traditional features have achieved promising results (Dollár et al. 2005; Laptev 2005; Chen and Hauptmann 2009). However, those features may be not sufficient to capture the distinctive motion pattern only from RGB data because there is only one training sample per class.

Third, although 3D MoSIFT and 3D EMoSIFT are derived from the SIFT and MoSIFT features, MoSIFT still cannot achieve satisfactory outcomes. That is because the descriptors captured by MoSIFT are simply calculated from RGB data while 3D MoSIFT and 3D EMoSIFT construct $3D$ gradient and $3D$ motion space from the local patch around each interest point by fusing RGB-D data.

To show the distinctive views for both 3D MoSIFT and 3D EMoSIFT features, we record three gesture classes: clapping, pointing and waving. The samples are shown in Fig. 11.15, where the training samples are shown in the first three rows (of the first

Table 11.5 Parameters: $\beta_1 = \beta_2 = 0.005$, $\sigma = 1.6$, $s = 3$ and $k = 10$ (*final21–final40*). It shows MLD scores by different spatio-temporal features with different values of γ, where (R) means the features are extracted from RGB video, (R+D) means the features are extracted from the RGB and depth videos. The values shown in bold indicate superior performance, with MLD scores below 0.16

Methods\\γ	0.1	0.2	0.3	0.4	0.5
Cuboid(R)	0.36717	0.36495	0.34332	0.33111	0.31392
Cuboid(R+D)	0.33666	0.31559	0.30948	0.30782	0.28064
Harris3D hog(R)	0.30061	0.26012	0.25014	0.23516	0.23461
Harris3D hog(R + D)	0.24903	0.22795	0.22407	0.22795	0.22684
Harris3D hof(R)	0.34831	0.32668	0.31281	0.29895	0.29063
Harris3D hof(R + D)	0.32169	0.29174	0.28508	0.27898	0.27121
Harris3D hoghof(R)	0.24237	0.21963	0.20022	0.19468	0.18857
Harris3D hoghof(R + D)	0.20965	0.18802	0.18303	0.18747	0.18192
MoSIFT(R)	0.41653	0.39601	0.35885	0.36606	0.33500
MoSIFT(R + D)	0.44426	0.44260	0.43594	0.42318	0.40488
3D MoSIFT(R + D)	0.19135	0.16694	0.16195	**0.14476**	**0.14642**
3D EMoSIFT(R + D)	0.16528	**0.15419**	**0.14753**	**0.13977**	**0.13311**

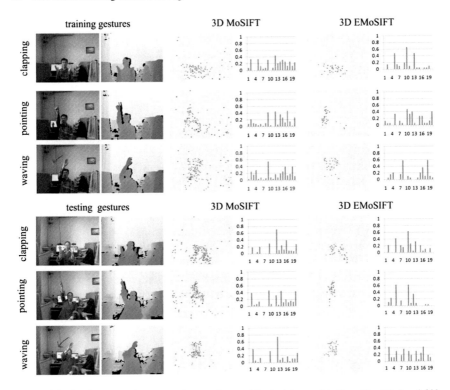

Fig. 11.15 The *first two columns* are the samples used for training and testing. The *third* and *fifth columns* reveal the spatial distribution of the visual words for the samples, which show 3D EMoSIFT is more compact. We superimpose the interest points in all frames into one image. Different visual words are represented by different *colors*. The *fourth* and *sixth columns* are shown the histograms for each sample. The histogram vector is ℓ_2 normalization. It shows each class has some dominating visual words. A compact feature encourages gestures from the same class to be described by similar histograms (or visual words), especially the dominating visual words. The histograms from the same class learned by 3D EMoSIFT are similar (i.e., clapping gesture)

two columns) and the testing samples are shown in the last three rows (of the first two columns). We first extract 3D MoSIFT and 3D EMoSIFT features from the six samples. Then we use 3D MoSIFT and 3D EMoSIFT features extracted from the three training samples to generate a codebook which has 20 visual words, respectively. Each descriptor is mapped into a certain visual word with VQ. The spatial distribution of visual words for each sample are shown in Fig. 11.15 where different visual words are represented by different colors. It shows that 3D EMoSIFT is more compact. A more compact feature leads to a better performance (see Table 11.5) and can effectively reduce the redundant features (see Table 11.2). Besides, a compact feature should encourage the signals from the same class to have similar representations. In other words, the signals from the same class are described by similar histograms (or visual words). From the Fig. 11.15, we can see that the samples from the same class have similar histograms (e.g., clapping gesture) when we use 3D EMoSIFT. However, 3D MoSIFT cannot get good similar histograms. From the above discussions, we see that 3D EMoSIFT is suitable for one-shot learning gesture recognition. Interestingly, 3D EMoSIFT is also more sparsity than 3D MoSIFT (see the histograms in Fig. 11.15).

11.4.4.2   Comparison Between VQ and SOMP

We then evaluate different coding methods (VQ, SOMP) on development (*devel01–devel20*) batches. Figure 11.16 shows the results. The minimum MLD by SOMP is 0.004 (see *devel13*), while 0.008 (see *devel01*) for VQ. And most of the performances by SOMP are much better than VQ. Later, we test 3D MoSIFT and 3D EMoSIFT features on *final21–final40* batches. MLD scores are given in Table 11.6. It can be seen that in most cases, SOMP leads the performance whenever 3D MoSIFT or 3D EMoSIFT is used. We also provide the results by 3D EMoSIFT for every batch in Fig. 11.17 which shows that SOMP is better than VQ in most cases. In a word, compared with VQ, SOMP not only has lower reconstruction errors (see

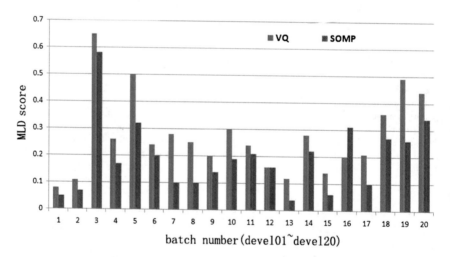

Fig. 11.16 Parameters: $\beta_1 = \beta_2 = 0.005, \sigma = 1.6, s = 3, k = 10$ and $\gamma = 0.3$ (*devel01–devel20*). The results with different coding methods (VQ, SOMP)

Table 11.6 Parameters: $\beta_1 = \beta_2 = 0.005$, $\sigma = 1.6$, $s = 3$, $k = 10$, and γ varies from 0.1 to 0.5 (*final21–final40*). MLD scores are calculated by different coding methods

Methods\γ	0.1	0.2	0.3	0.4	0.5
3D MoSIFT_VQ	0.19135	0.16694	0.16195	0.14476	0.14642
3D MoSIFT_SOMP	**0.18303**	**0.16251**	**0.15918**	0.15086	**0.14088**
3D EMoSIFT_VQ	0.16528	0.15419	0.14753	0.13977	0.13311
3D EMoSIFT_SOMP	0.17415	**0.14753**	**0.14032**	**0.13478**	**0.13145**

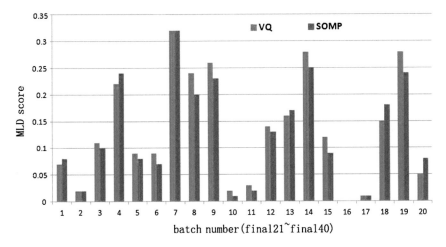

Fig. 11.17 Parameters: $\beta_1 = \beta_2 = 0.005$, $\sigma = 1.6$, $s = 3$, $k = 10$ and $\gamma = 0.3$ (*final21–final40*). The results with different coding methods (VQ, SOMP)

Fig. 11.9) but also achieves better performance. We note that 3D EMoSIFT does not work well on *devel03* batch as shown in Fig. 11.16. That is because there are static gestures (postures) on *devel03* batch, while 3D EMoSIFT can only capture distinctive features when the gestures are in motion.

11.4.4.3   Comparison Between Gradient-Based and Motion-Based Features

We know that 3D EMoSIFT feature includes two basic components, namely, gradient-based features and motion-based features. And each component is of size 384 dimensions. In this section, we separately evaluate these two components and determinate which component is more essential to gesture recognition. The results evaluated on development batches are separately shown in Fig. 11.18 where the integrated feature consists of the gradient-based and motion-based features. The average MLD scores are 0.1945 for the integrated feature, 0.216 for the gradient-based features, and 0.313 for the motion-based features. It can be seen that the performance of the gradient-based features, which are comparative to the results of the integrated feature, are much better than the performance of the motion-based features. In addition, our method outperforms two published papers on *devel01–devel20* batches, that is say, our method: 0.1945, Lui (2012): 0.2873, (Malgireddy et al. 2012): 0.2409.

As mentioned in Sect. 11.3.1, 3D EMoSIFT is constructed in two stages (interest point detection and descriptor calculation). So whenever the gradient-based or motion-based features are calculated, we should first detect the interest points. We randomly select a sample from Chalearn gesture database and test the average time with c++ programs and OpenCV library (Bradski 2000) on a standard personal com-

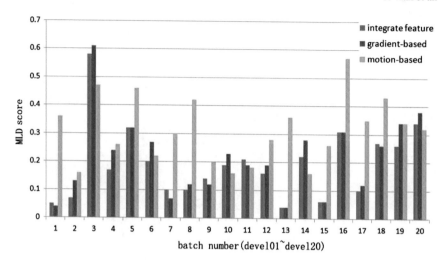

Fig. 11.18 Results for parameters: $\beta_1 = \beta_2 = 0.005$, $\sigma = 1.6$, $s = 3$, $k = 10$, and $\gamma = 0.3$ (*devel01–devel20*)

Table 11.7 The average computation time for different parts in 3D EMoSIFT feature

Interest point detection average time (ms/f)	Gradient-based descriptor average time (ms/f)	Motion-based descriptor average time (ms/f)
887	2.1	1.4

puter (CPU: 3.3GHz, RAM: 8GB). Table 11.7 shows that the main processing time occurs in the stage of interest point detection. The remaining parts for calculating the gradient-base and motion-based descriptor is small compared with the time for interest point detection. In our future work, we will focus on how to efficiently detect interest points.

11.4.4.4 Comparison with Other Methods

Here, we compare the proposed approach with some popular sequence matching methods such as HMM, DTW, CRF, HCRF and LDCRF, and also give the final results of top contestants. The results are reported in Table 11.8 where the principal motion method Escalante and Guyon (2012) is the baseline method and DTW is an optional method on Chalearn gesture challenge (round 2).

The top ranking results in the competition are from three teams (Alfine, Turtle Tamers and Joewan), which are provided in the technical report (Guyon et al. 2013). We use the code provided by Morency et al. (2007) to train the CRF-based classifiers, because this code was well developed and can be easily used. Every frame is represented by a vector of motion feature mentioned in Sect. 11.3.4. Those motion features extracted from training videos are used to train CRF-based models. For

Table 11.8 Results of different methods on Chalearn gesture data set

Method	Validation set(01–20)	Final set(21–40)	Team name
Motion signature analysis	0.0995	0.0710	Alfnie
HMM+HOGHOF	0.2084	0.1098	Turtle Tamers
BoF+3D MoSIFT	0.1824	0.1448	Joewan
Principle motion	0.3418	0.3172	–
DTW	0.4616	0.3899	–
CRF	0.6365	0.528	–
HCRF	0.64	0.6	–
LDCRF	0.608	0.5145	–
Our method	**0.1595**	**0.1259**	–

the CRF model, every class has a corresponding label (gesture label). CRF predicts a label for each frame in a video. During evaluation, the video label is predicted based on the most frequently occurring label per frame (Morency et al. 2007). For the HCRF (or LDCRF) model, we train a single HCRF (or LDCRF) model with different number of hidden states (from 2 to 6 states) and select the lowest MLD scores as the final results which are shown in Table 11.8. We can see that the proposed method is competitive to the state-of-the-art methods. Besides, the CRF-based methods get poor performances. That is because the simple motion features may be indistinguishable to represent the gesture pattern.

11.5 Conclusion

In this paper, we propose a unified framework based on bag of features for one-shot learning gesture recognition. The proposed method gives superior recognition performance than many existing approaches. A new feature, named 3D EMoSIFT, fuses RGB-D data to detect interest points and constructs 3D gradient and motion space to calculate SIFT descriptors. Compared with existing features such as Cuboid (Dollár et al. 2005), Harri3D (Laptev 2005), MoSIFT (Chen and Hauptmann 2009) and 3D MoSIFT (Ming et al. 2012), it gets competitive performance. Additionally, 3D EMoSIFT features are scale and rotation invariant and can capture more compact and richer video representations even though there is only one training sample for each gesture class. This paper also introduces SOMP to replace VQ in the descriptor coding stage. Then each feature can be represented by some linear combination of a small number of visual codewords. Compared with VQ, SOMP leads to a much lower reconstruction error and achieves better performance.

Although the proposed method has achieved promising results, there are several avenues which can be explored. At first, most of the existing local spatio-temporal features are extracted from a static background or a simple dynamic background. In our feature research, we will focus on extending 3D EMoSIFT to extract features from complex background, especially for one-shot learning gesture recognition. Next, to speed up processing time, we can achieve fast feature extraction on a Graphics Processing Unit (GPU) (Chen et al. 2003). Also, we will explore the techniques required to optimize the parameters, such as the codebook size and sparsity.

Acknowledgements We appreciate ChaLearn providing the gesture database (http://chalearn.org) whose directors are gratefully acknowledged. We would like to thank Isabelle Guyon, ChaLearn, Berkeley, California, who gives us insightful comments and suggestions to improve our manuscripts. And we are grateful to editors and anonymous reviewers whose instructive suggestions have improved the quality of this paper. Besides, thanks to acknowledge support for this project from National Natural Science Foundation (60973060, 61003114, 61172128), National 973 plans project (2012CB316304), the fundamental research funds for the central universities (2011JBM020, 2011JBM022) and the program for Innovative Research Team in University of Ministry of Education of China (IRT 201206).

References

G. Bradski, The OpenCV Library, *Dr. Dobb's Journal of Software Tools*, 2000

M. Brand, N. Oliver, A. Pentland. Coupled hidden markov models for complex action recognition, in *Proceedings of IEEE Conference on Computer Vision and Pattern Recognition*, 1997, pp 994–999

C.C. Chang, C.J. Lin. Libsvm: A library for support vector machines. ACM Trans. Intell. Syst. Technol., 2(3):27:1–27:27, 2011

F.S. Chen, C.M. Fu, C.L. Huang, Hand gesture recognition using a real-time tracking method and hidden markov models. Image Vis. Comput. **21**, 745–758 (2003)

M. Chen, A. Hauptmann. Mosift: Recognizing human actions in surveillance videos. *Technical Report*, 2009

H. Cooper, E.J. Ong, N. Pugeault, R. Bowden, Sign language recognition using sub-units. J. Mach. Learn. Res. **13**, 2205–2231 (2012)

A. Corradini. Dynamic time warping for off-line recognition of a small gesture vocabulary, in *IEEE ICCV Workshop on Recognition, Analysis, and Tracking of Faces and Gestures in Real-Time Systems*, 2001, pp. 82–89

N.H. Dardas, N.D. Georganas, Real-time hand gesture detection and recognition using bag-of-features and support vector machine techniques. IEEE Trans. Instrum. Meas. **60**(11), 3592–3607 (2011)

P. Dollár, V. Rabaud, G. Cottrell, and S. Belongie. Behavior recognition via sparse spatio-temporal features, in *Proceedings of IEEE International Workshop on Visual Surveillance and Performance Evaluation of Tracking and Surveillance*, 2005, pp. 65–72

H.J. Escalante, I. Guyon. Principal motion: Pca-based reconstruction of motion histograms. *Technical Memorandum*, 2012

L. Fei-Fei, P. Perona, A bayesian hierarchical model for learning natural scene categories. Proc. IEEE Conf. Comput. Vis. Pattern Recognit. **2**, 524–531 (2005)

F. Flórez, J.M. García, J. García, A. Hernández. Hand gesture recognition following the dynamics of a topology-preserving network, in *Proceedings of IEEE International Conference on Automatic Face and Gesture Recognition*, 2002, pp. 318–323

P.-E. Forssen, D.G. Lowe. Shape descriptors for maximally stable extremal regions, in *IEEE 11th International Conference on Computer Vision*, 2007, pp. 1–8

W.T. Freeman, M. Roth, Orientation histograms for hand gesture recognition. Proc. IEEE Int. Workshop Autom. Face Gesture Recognit. **12**, 296–301 (1995)

W. Gao, G. Fang, D. Zhao, Y. Chen, A chinese sign language recognition system based on sofm/srn/hmm. Pattern Recognit. **37**(12), 2389–2402 (2004)

T. Guha, R.K. Ward, Learning sparse representations for human action recognition. IEEE Trans. Pattern Anal. Mach. Intell. **34**(8), 1576–1588 (2012)

S. Guo, Z. Wang, Q. Ruan, Enhancing sparsity via ℓ_p ($0<p<1$) minimization for robust face recognition. Neurocomputing **99**, 592–602 (2013)

I. Guyon, V. Athitsos, P. Jangyodsuk, B. Hamner, and H.J. Escalante. Chalearn gesture challenge: Design and first results, in *IEEE Conference on Computer Vision and Pattern Recognition Workshops*, 2012, pp. 1–6

I. Guyon, V. Athitsos, P. Jangyodsuk, H.J. Escalante, B. Hamner. Results and analysis of the chalearn gesture challenge 2012. *Technical Report*, 2013

C. Harris and M. Stephens. A combined corner and edge detector, in *Proceedings of Alvey Vision Conference*, volume 15, p. 50, 1988

A. Hernández-Vela, M. A. Bautista, X. Perez-Sala, V. Ponce, X. Baró, O. Pujol, C. Angulo, S. Escalera. Bovdw: Bag-of-visual-and-depth-words for gesture recognition. *21st International Conference on Pattern Recognition (ICPR)*, 2012

D. Kim, J. Song, D. Kim, Simultaneous gesture segmentation and recognition based on forward spotting accumulative hmms. Pattern Recognit. **40**(11), 3012–3026 (2007)

I. Laptev, On space-time interest points. Int. J. Comput. Vis. **64**(2), 107–123 (2005)

J.F. Lichtenauer, E.A. Hendriks, M.J.T. Reinders, Sign language recognition by combining statistical dtw and independent classification. Pattern Anal. Mach. Intell. IEEE Trans. **30**(11), 2040–2046 (2008)

Y. Linde, A. Buzo, R. Gray, An algorithm for vector quantizer design. Commun. IEEE Trans. **28**(1), 84–95 (1980)

D.G. Lowe, Distinctive image features from scale-invariant keypoints. Int. J. Comput. Vis. **60**(2), 91–110 (2004)

B.D. Lucas, T. Kanade, et al. An iterative image registration technique with an application to stereo vision, in *Proceedings of the 7th International Joint Conference on Artificial Intelligence*, 1981

Y.M. Lui, Human gesture recognition on product manifolds. J. Mach. Learn. Res. **13**, 3297–3321 (2012)

M.R. Malgireddy, I. Inwogu, V. Govindaraju. A temporal bayesian model for classifying, detecting and localizing activities in video sequences, in *IEEE Conference on Computer Vision and Pattern Recognition Workshops*, 2012, pp. 43–48

A. Malima, E. Ozgur, M. Çetin. A fast algorithm for vision-based hand gesture recognition for robot control, in *Proceedings of IEEE Signal Processing and Communications Applications*, 2006, pp. 1–4

Y. Ming, Q. Ruan, A.G. Hauptmann. Activity recognition from rgb-d camera with 3d local spatio-temporal features, in *Proceedings of IEEE International Conference on Multimedia and Expo*, 2012 pp. 344–349

L.P. Morency, A. Quattoni, T. Darrell. Latent-dynamic discriminative models for continuous gesture recognition, in *Proceedings of IEEE Conference on Computer Vision and Pattern Recognition*, 2007, pp. 1–8

B.A. Olshausen, D.J. Field et al., Sparse coding with an overcomplete basis set: a strategy employed by vi? Vis. Res. **37**(23), 3311–3326 (1997)

V.I. Pavlovic, R. Sharma, T.S. Huang, Visual interpretation of hand gestures for human-computer interaction: a review. IEEE Trans. Pattern Anal. Mach. Intell. **19**, 677–695 (1997)

A. Rakotomamonjy, Surveying and comparing simultaneous sparse approximation (or group-lasso) algorithms. Signal Process. **91**(7), 1505–1526 (2011)

S. Reifinger, F. Wallhoff, M. Ablassmeier, T. Poitschke, and G. Rigoll. Static and dynamic hand-gesture recognition for augmented reality applications, in *Proceedings of the 12th International*

Conference on Human-computer Interaction: Intelligent Multimodal Interaction Environments, 2007, pp.728–737

Y. Ruiduo, S. Sarkar, and B. Loeding. Enhanced level building algorithm for the movement epenthesis problem in sign language recognition, in *Proceedings of IEEE Conference on Computer Vision and Pattern Recognition*, 2007, pp. 1–8

C. Shan, T. Tan, Y. Wei, Real-time hand tracking using a mean shift embedded particle filter. Pattern Recognit. **40**(7), 1958–1970 (2007)

X. Shen, G. Hua, L. Williams, Y. Wu, Dynamic hand gesture recognition: an exemplar-based approach from motion divergence fields. Image Vis. Comput. **30**(3), 227–235 (2012)

C. Sminchisescu, A. Kanaujia, Zhiguo Li, D. Metaxas. Conditional models for contextual human motion recognition, in *Tenth IEEE International Conference on Computer Vision*, volume 2, pp. 1808–1815, 2005

H.I. Suk, B.K. Sin, S.W. Lee, Hand gesture recognition based on dynamic bayesian network framework. Pattern Recognit. **43**(9), 3059–3072 (2010)

J. Weaver, T. Starner, A. Pentland, Real-time american sign language recognition using desk and wearable computer based video. IEEE Trans. Pattern Anal. Mach. Intell. **20**, 1371–1375 (1998)

J.A. Tropp, A.C. Gilbert, M.J. Strauss, Algorithms for simultaneous sparse approximation. part i: Greedy pursuit. Signal Process. **86**(3), 572–588 (2006)

A. Vedaldi, B. Fulkerson. VLFeat: An open and portable library of computer vision algorithms, http://www.vlfeat.org/, 2008

A.J. Viterbi, Error bounds for convolutional codes and an asymptotically optimum decoding algorithm. Inf. Theor. IEEE Trans. **13**(2), 260–269 (1967)

C. P. Vogler. *American Sign Language Recognition: Reducing the Complexity of the Task with Phoneme-based Modeling and Parallel Hidden Markov Models*. Ph.D. thesis, Doctoral dissertation, University of Pennsylvania, 2003

J. Wan, Q. Ruan, G. An, W. Li. Gesture recognition based on hidden markov model from sparse representative observations, in *IEEE 10th International Conference on Signal Processing (ICSP)*, 2012, pp. 1180–1183

H. Wang, M.M. Ullah, A. Klaser, I. Laptev, C. Schmid, et al. Evaluation of local spatio-temporal features for action recognition, in *Proceedings of British Machine Vision Conference*, 2009

J. Wang, J. Yang, K. Yu, F. Lv, T. Huang, Y. Gong. Locality-constrained linear coding for image classification, in *Proceedings of IEEE Conference on Computer Vision and Pattern Recognition*, 2010, pp. 3360–3367

S.B. Wang, A. Quattoni, L.P. Morency, D. Demirdjian, T. Darrell, Hidden conditional random fields for gesture recognition. Proc. IEEE Conf. Comput. Vis. Pattern Recognit. **2**, 1521–1527 (2006)

J. Wright, A.Y. Yang, A. Ganesh, S.S. Sastry, Yi Ma, Robust face recognition via sparse representation. IEEE Trans. Pattern Anal. Mach. Intell. **31**, 210–227 (2009)

J. Yamato, Jun Ohya, and K. Ishii. Recognizing human action in time-sequential images using hidden markov model, in *Proceedings of IEEE Conference on Computer Vision and Pattern Recognition*, 1992, pp. 379–385

J. Yang, K. Yu, Y. Gong, and T. Huang. Linear spatial pyramid matching using sparse coding for image classification, in *Proceedings of IEEE Conference on Computer Vision and Pattern Recognition*, 2009, pp. 1794–1801

M.H. Yang, N. Ahuja, M. Tabb, Extraction of 2d motion trajectories and its application to hand gesture recognition. IEEE Trans. Pattern Anal. Mach. Intell. **24**, 1061–1074 (2002)

D. Youtian, C. Feng, X. Wenli, Li. Yongbin. Recognizing interaction activities using dynamic bayesian network, in *18th International Conference on Pattern Recognition*, volume 1, pp. 618–621, 2006

Y. Zhu, G. Xu, D.J. Kriegman, A real-time approach to the spotting, representation, and recognition of hand gestures for human-computer interaction. Comput. Vis. Image Underst. **85**(3), 189–208 (2002)

Chapter 12
One-Shot-Learning Gesture Recognition Using HOG-HOF Features

Jakub Konečný and Michal Hagara

Abstract The purpose of this paper is to describe one-shot-learning gesture recognition systems developed on the *ChaLearn Gesture Dataset* (ChaLearn 2011). We use RGB and depth images and combine appearance (Histograms of Oriented Gradients) and motion descriptors (Histogram of Optical Flow) for parallel temporal segmentation and recognition. The Quadratic-Chi distance family is used to measure differences between histograms to capture cross-bin relationships. We also propose a new algorithm for trimming videos—to remove all the unimportant frames from videos. We present two methods that use a combination of HOG-HOF descriptors together with variants of a Dynamic Time Warping technique. Both methods outperform other published methods and help narrow the gap between human performance and algorithms on this task. The code is publicly available in the MLOSS repository.

Keywords Chalearn · Histogram of oriented gradients · Histogram of optical flow · Dynamic time warping

12.1 Introduction

Gesture recognition can be seen as a way for computers to understand human body language. Improving state-of-the-art algorithms for gesture recognition facilitates human-computer communication beyond primitive text user interfaces or GUIs (graphical user interfaces). With rapidly improving comprehension of human gestures we can start building NUIs (natural user interfaces) for controlling computers or

---

Editors: Isabelle Guyon, Vassilis Athitsos, and Sergio Escalera.

J. Konečný (✉) · M. Hagara
Korešpondenčný Matematický Seminár, Comenius University, Bratislava, Slovakia
e-mail: kubo.konecny@gmail.com

M. Hagara
e-mail: michal.hagara@gmail.com

J. Konečný
University of Edinburgh, Edinburgh, Scotland

robots. With the availability of such technologies, conventional input devices, such as a keyboard or mouse, could be replaced in situations in which they are inconvenient in future. Other applications of gesture recognition include sign language recognition, socially assistive robotics and game technology.

In this paper, we focus on the one-shot learning gesture recognition problem, in particular the *ChaLearn Gesture Dataset* (ChaLearn 2011). The data set was released jointly with a competition, where the goal was to develop a system capable of learning to recognize new categories of gestures from a single training example of each gesture. The large data set of hand and arm gestures was pre-recorded using an infrared sensor, Kinect^{TM}, providing both RGB and depth images (Guyon et al. 2012, 2013).

The purpose of this work is to describe methods developed during the *ChaLearn Gesture Challenge* by the Turtle Tamers team (authors of this paper). We finished in 2nd place in round 2 and were invited to present our solution at the International Conference on Pattern Recognition 2012, Tsukuba, Japan. The code has been made publicly available in the MLOSS repository.[1]

Since the goal of the challenge was to provide solid baseline methods for this data set, our methods were specifically tailored for this particular competition and data set. Hence, they lack a certain generality, and we discuss and suggest changes for more general settings later.

The rest of this work is organised as follows. Related work is summarized in Sect. 12.2. In Sect. 12.3 we describe the data set and the problem in detail. In Sect. 12.4 we focus on the preprocessing needed to overcome some of the problems in the data set. Section 12.5 covers feature representation, using Histogram of Oriented Gradients and Histogram of Optical Flow, as well as a method used to compare similarities between these representations. In Sect. 12.6 we describe the actual algorithms, and in Sect. 12.7 we briefly describe algorithms of other participants and compare their results with ours, as well as with other published works. In Sect. 12.8 we summarize our paper and suggest an area for future work.

12.2 Related Work

In this section we provide a brief literature review in the area of gesture and action recognition and motivate our choices of models.

One possible approach to the problem of gesture recognition consists of analyzing motion descriptors obtained from video. Ikizler and Forsyth (2007) use the output of Human Motion Capture systems in combination with Hidden Markov Models. Wu et al. (2012) use Extended Motion History Image as a motion descriptor and apply the method to the *ChaLearn Gesture Dataset*. They fuse dual modalities inherent in the Kinect sensor using Multiview Spectral Embedding (Xia et al. 2010) in a physically meaningful manner.

---

[1]The code is available at https://mloss.org/software/view/448.

A popular recent approach is to use Conditional Random Fields (CRF). Wang et al. (2006) introduce the discriminative hidden state approach, in which they combine the ability of CRFs to use long range dependencies and the ability of Hidden Markov Models to model latent structure. More recent work (Chatzis et al. 2012) describes joint segmentation and classification of sequences in the framework of CRFs. The method outperforms other popular related approaches with no sacrifices in terms of the imposed computational costs.

An evolution of Bag-of-Words (Lewis 1998), a method used in document analysis, where each document is represented using the apparition frequency of each word in a dictionary, is one of the most popular in Computer Vision. In the image domain, these words become visual elements of a certain visual vocabulary. First, each image is decomposed into a large set of patches, obtaining a numeric descriptor. This can be done, for example, using SIFT (Lowe 1999), or SURF (Bay et al. 2006). A set of N representative visual words are selected by means of a clustering process over the descriptors in all images. Once the visual vocabulary is defined, each image can be represented by a global histogram containing the frequencies of visual words. Finally, this histogram can be used as input for any classification technique. Extensions to image sequences have been proposed, the most popular being Space-Time Interest Points (Laptev 2005). Wang et al. (2009) have evaluated a number of feature descriptors and bag-of-features models for action recognition. This study concluded that different sampling strategies and feature descriptors were needed to achieve the best results on alternative action data sets. Recently an extension of these models to the RGB-D images, with a new depth descriptor was introduced by Hernandez-Vela et al. (2012).

The methods outlined above usually ignore particular spatial position of a descriptor. We wanted to exploit the specifics of the data set, particularly the fact that user position does not change within the same batch, thus also the important parts of the same gestures will occur roughly at the same place. We use a combination of appearance descriptor, Histogram of Oriented Gradients (Dalal and Triggs 2005) and local motion direction descriptor, Histogram of Optical Flow (Kanade and Lucas 1981). We adopted Quadratic-Chi distance (Pele and Werman 2010) to measure differences between these histograms. This approach only works well at high resolutions of descriptors. An alternative may be to use a non-linear support vector machine with a χ^2 kernel (Laptev et al. 2008). Another possible feature descriptor that includes spatio-temporal position of features could be HOG3D (Klaser and Marszalek 2008), which was applied to this specific data set by Fanello et al. (2013).

12.3   Data and Problem Setting

In this section, we discuss the easy and difficult aspects of the data set and state the goal of the competition.

The purpose of the *ChaLearn Gesture Challenge*[2] was to develop an automated system capable of learning to recognize new categories of gestures from a single training example of each gesture. A large data set of gestures was collected before the competition, which includes more than 50, 000 gestures recorded with the Kinect^{TM} sensor, providing both RGB and depth videos. The resolution of these videos is 240×320 pixels, at 10 frames per second. The gestures are grouped into more than 500 batches of 100 gestures, each batch including 47 sequences of 1–5 gestures drawn from small gesture vocabularies from 8 to 14 gestures. The gestures come from over 30 different gesture vocabularies, and were performed by 20 different users.

During the challenge, development batches devel01–480 were available, with truth labels of gestures provided. Batches valid01–20 and final01–40 were provided with labels for only one example of each gesture class in each batch (training set). These batches were used for evaluation purposes. The goal is to automatically predict the gesture labels for the unlabelled gesture sequences (test set). The gesture vocabularies were selected from nine categories corresponding to various settings or applications, such as body language gestures, signals or pantomimes.

Easy aspects of the data set include the use of a fixed camera and the availability of the depth data. Within each batch, there is a single user, only homogeneous recording conditions and a small vocabulary. In every sequence, different gestures are separated by the user returning to a resting position. Gestures are usually performed by hands and arms. In particular, we made use of the fact that the user is always at the same position within one batch.

The challenging aspects of the data are that within a single batch there is only one labelled example of each gesture. Between different batches there are variations in recording conditions, clothing, skin color and lightning. Some users are less skilled than others, thus there are some errors or omissions in performing the gestures. And in some batches, parts of the body may be occluded.

For the evaluation of results the Levenshtein distance was used, provided as the metric for the competition. That is the minimum number of edit operations (insertion, deletion or substitution) needed to be performed to go from one vector to another. For each unlabelled video, the distance $D(T, L)$ was computed, where T is the truth vector of labels, and L is our predicted vector of labels. This distance is also known as the "edit distance". For example, $D([1, 2], [1]) = 1$, $D([1, 2, 3], [2, 4]) = 2$, $D([1, 2, 3], [3, 2]) = 2$.

The overall score for a batch was computed as a sum of Levenshtein distances divided by the total number of gestures performed in the batch. This is similar to an error rate (but can exceed 1). We multiply the result by a factor of 100 to resemble the fail percentage. For simplicity, in the rest of this work, we call it the error rate.

---

[2]Details and website: http://gesture.chalearn.org/.

12.4 Preprocessing

In this section we describe how we overcame some of the challenges with the given data set as well as the solutions we propose. In Sect. 12.4.1 we focus on depth noise removal. Later we describe the need for trimming the videos—removing set of frames—and the method employed.

12.4.1 Depth Noise Removal

One of the problems with the given data set is the noise (or missing values) in the depth data. Whenever the Kinect sensor does not receive a response from a particular point, the sensor outputs a 0, resulting in the black areas shown in Fig. 12.1. This noise usually occurs along the edges of objects or, particularly in this data set, humans. The noise is also visible if the object is out of the range of the sensor (0.8–3.5 m).

The level of noise is usually the same within a single batch. However, there is a big difference in the noise level across different batches. If the level is not too high, it looks like 'salt and pepper' noise.

Later, in Sect. 12.5, we use Histograms of Oriented Gradients (HOGs), which work best with sharp edges, so we need a filter that preserves the edges. One of the best filters for removing this kind of noise is the median filter, and also has our desired property. Median filter replaces every pixel with the median of pixels in small area around itself. The effect of the median filter is shown in Fig. 12.2. We can see this filter does not erase big areas of noise, however, this is not a problem in our methods. As mentioned earlier, HOG features are sensitive to the edges, but these large areas usually occur along the edges, so the difference in computed features will not be significant.

Fig. 12.1 Examples of depth images with various levels of noise

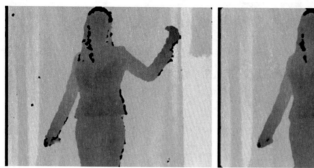

Fig. 12.2 Effect of median filter on depth image

12.4.2 Trimming

In most batches we can find videos with quite long parts, at the beginning or at the end of the video, where nothing important happens. Sometimes the user is not moving at all, sometimes trying to turn on/off the recorder.[3] Another problem occurring less often is in batches, where gestures are rather static. There is often variation in time the user stays in a particular gesture setting.[4] This is a problem for most possible approaches for tackling the one-shot-learning problem. A solution can be to remove frames from the beginning and end of the videos, as well as any part with too much inactivity.

One possible approach to removing parts of inactivity can be to watch the amount of motion in the video, and remove parts where nothing happens. This is the idea we employed.

A naive but effective way is to take the depth video and compute differences for every pixel between two consecutive frames. Taking depth videos allows us to ignore problems of texture of clothing or background. We then simply count the number of pixels whose change exceeds a given threshold, or we can simply sum the differences. After numerous experiments we ended up with Algorithm 1. Suppose we have a video, n frames long. First we remove the background[5] from individual frames and apply the median filter. Then we do not compute differences of consecutive frames, but rather between frames i and $i + 3$. This is to make the motion curve smoother and thus the method more robust. We also found that it was important to even out the amount of motion between, for instance, hand in front of body and hand in front of background. To that end, we set an upper boundary constraint on the difference at 15 (on a scale 0 to 255). Then we computed the actual motion as an average of differences between the chosen frames, as previously described, *above* particular frame, for example

---

[3] An example is batch devel12, video 23.

[4] An example is batch devel39, particularly video 18.

[5] Using an algorithm *bgremove* provided in sample code of the Challenge (ChaLearn 2011).

$$motion(2) \leftarrow (mot(1) + mot(2))/2,$$
$$motion(12) \leftarrow (mot(9) + mot(10) + mot(11) + mot(12))/4. \qquad (12.1)$$

In the *mot* variable we store the average change across all pixels. Then we scaled the motion to range [0, 1].

Algorithm 1 Trimming a video

$n \leftarrow length(video)$
$gap \leftarrow 3 \quad maxDiff \leftarrow 15 \quad threshold \leftarrow 0.1 \quad minTrim \leftarrow 5$
for $i = 1 \rightarrow n$ **do**
    $video(i) \leftarrow bgremove(video(i))$ ▷ Background removal
    $video(i) \leftarrow medfilt(video(i))$ ▷ Median filter
end for
for $i = 1 \rightarrow (n - gap)$ **do**
    $diff(i) \leftarrow abs(video(i) - video(i + gap))$
    $diff(i) \leftarrow min\{diff(i), maxDiff\}$
    $mot(i) \leftarrow mean(diff(i))$ ▷ Mean across all pixels
end for
$motion \leftarrow avgMotion(mot)$ ▷ As in Eq. 12.1
$motion \leftarrow scale(motion)$ ▷ Scale motion so its range is 0 to 1
$frames \leftarrow vector(1 : n)$
if $|beginSequence(motion < threshold)| \geq minTrim$ **then**
    $frames \leftarrow trimBegin(frames)$ ▷ Remove all frames
end if
if $|endSequence(motion < threshold)| \geq minTrim$ **then**
    $frames \leftarrow trimEnd(frames)$ ▷ Remove all frames
end if
for all $|sequence(motion < threshold)| > minTrim$ **do**
    $frames \leftarrow trimMiddle(sequence, frames)$ ▷ Remove all frames but $minTrim$
end for
return $video(frames)$

Once we have the motion in the expected range, we can start actually removing frames. At first, we remove sequences from the beginning and the end of the video with motion below a *threshold* (set to 0.1), under the condition that they are of length at least *minTrim* (set to 5) frames. Then we find all sequences in the middle of the video with motion below the *threshold* of length more than 5, and uniformly choose 5 frames to remain in the video. For example if we were to trim a sequence of length 13, only frames {1, 4, 7, 10, 13} would remain. Then we return the video with the remaining frames. Figure 12.3 illustrates the threshold and the motion computed by this algorithm on a particular video.

One possible modification of this algorithm is in the step in which we scale the motion to the range of [0, 1]. In this case, we simply subtract $min(motion)$, and divide by $(max(motion) - min(motion))$. However, especially in videos with 4 or 5 gestures, sometimes large outliers cause problems, because the threshold is too big. Since the motion curve tends to be relatively smooth, instead of choosing $max(motion)$ we could choose the value of the second highest local maximum.

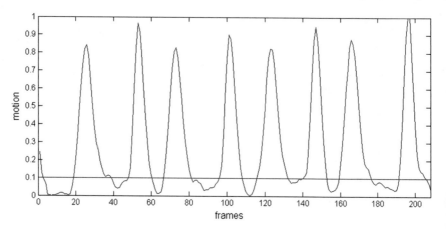

Fig. 12.3 Example of a motion graph, batch devel11, video 32

This scaling performs slightly better on long videos, but does not work well on short videos. Since, we do not know how many gestures to expect in advance, we used the simpler method.

It is not straightforward to generalize this approach to color videos, since there is no easy way to distinguish the background from the foreground. Additionally, the texture of clothing could cause big problems to this approach. This could be overcome by adding an algorithm that would subtract the background after seeing the whole video, but we have not tried this.

12.5 Feature Representation and Distance Measure

In this section, we briefly describe the tools we propose for extracting features. Gestures differ from each other, both in appearance and the amount of motion while performing a particular gesture. A good descriptor of the static part of a gesture is the Histogram of Oriented Gradients, proposed by Dalal and Triggs (2005). A good method for capturing the size and direction of motion is computing the Optical Flow using the Lucas-Kanade method (Kanade and Lucas 1981; Lucas 1984) and creating a histogram of flow. Motivation for these choices is explained in Sect. 12.2. Finally, we describe the Quadratic-Chi distance family proposed by Pele and Werman (2010) for measuring distances between histograms.

12.5.1 Histogram of Oriented Gradients

In this section we briefly describe the HOG features. The underlying idea is that the appearance and shape of a local object can often be characterized rather well

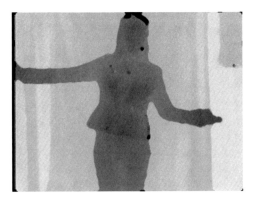

Fig. 12.4 Example visualisation of the HOG features

by the distribution of local intensity gradient (or edge) directions, even without precise knowledge of the corresponding gradient (or edge) positions. In practice this is implemented by dividing the image window into small spatial regions ("cells"), for each cell accumulating a local 1-D histogram of gradient directions (or edge orientations) over the pixels of the cell. It is also useful to contrast-normalize the local responses before using them. This can be done by accumulating a measure of local histogram "energy" over larger spatial regions ("blocks") and using the results to normalize all of the cells in the block.

We used a simple $[-1, 0, 1]$ gradient filter, applied in both directions and discretized the gradient orientations into 16 orientation bins between $0°$ and $180°$. We had cells of size 40×40 pixels and blocks of size 80×80 pixels, each containing 4 cells. The histogram in each cell is normalized with sum of Euclidean norms of histograms in the whole block. Each cell (except cells on the border) belongs to 4 blocks, thus for one cell we have 4 locally normalized histograms, the sum of which is used as the resulting histogram for the cell. Since this method cannot be used to normalize histograms of marginal cells, from 240×320 image we get only 4×6 spatial cells of 16 orientation bins each. Figure 12.4 provides a visual example of the HOG features at their actual resolution. The space covered is smaller than the original image, but that is not a problem, since the gestures from the data set are not performed on the border of the frames. Dalal and Triggs (2005) conclude, that fine-scale gradients, fine orientation binning, relatively coarse spatial cells, and high-quality local contrast normalization in overlapping descriptor blocks are all important for obtaining good performance.

As in Fig. 12.4, we computed the HOG features from depth images, since it captures only the edges we are interested in, and not textures of clothing and so on. We used the efficient implementation from Piotr's toolbox (Dollár 2017), function `hog(image, 40, 16)`.

12.5.2   Histogram of Optical Flow

In this section we describe the general optical flow principle and the Lucas-Kanade method (Kanade and Lucas 1981; Lucas 1984) for estimating the actual flow. For details we refer the reader to these works. Here we present only a brief description of the method.

The optical flow methods try to estimate the motion between two images, at times t and $t + \Delta t$ at every position (in our case two consecutive frames of video). In general, the optical flow equation is formulated as a single equation with two variables. All optical flow methods introduce additional conditions for estimating the flow. The Lucas-Kanade method assumes that the flow is essentially constant in a local neighbourhood of the pixel under consideration, and solves the equation for all the pixels in the neighbourhood. The solution is obtained using the least squares principle.

After obtaining the optical flow in every point of the image we divide the image (of 240×320 pixels) to a grid of 6×8 spatial cells. We then put each optical flow vector into one of 16 orientation bins in each spatial cell, and scale them so that they sum to 1 to get a histogram of $6 \times 8 \times 16$ fields. We also tried to scale in each spatial cell separately, and the difference of error rate in our methods on all development batches was less than 0.5. We computed the optical flow from color videos, converted to grayscale, again using efficient implementation of the Flow estimation from Piotr's toolbox (Dollár 2017), function `optFlowLk(image1, image2, [] , 4, 2, 9e-5);`

12.5.3   Measuring Distance of the Histograms

Our method relies on making comparisons between pairs of frames in two videos, which requires as a component, to measure differences between histograms. The relatively simple methods based on the sum of bin-to-bin distances suffer from the following limitation: If the number of bins is too small, the measure is not discriminative and if it is too large it is not robust. Distances, that take into account cross-bin relationships, can be both robust and discriminative. With the HOG and HOF feature at the resolution that we selected, simple bin-to-bin comparisons are not robust, as exemplified in Fig. 12.5. Thus we would like a measure that would look into surrounding orientation bins and, after experimenting, also to surrounding spatial cells. Thus we would also like a measure, that would reduce the effect of big differences, and also look into surrounding spatial cells. We adopted the following Quadratic-Chi distance family introduced by Pele and Werman (2010).

Let P and Q be two histograms. Let A be a non-negative symmetric bounded bin-similarity matrix, such that each diagonal element is bigger or equal to every other element in its row. Let $0 \leq m < 1$ be a normalization factor. A Quadratic-Chi histogram distance is defined as:

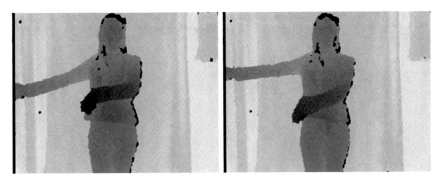

Fig. 12.5 Example of need for cross-bin similarities: the same moment in performance of the same gesture in two different videos. The *right hand* stays at the same place, the *left hand* is moving. This illustrates how the same element can result in different neighbouring orientation bins in HOG being big in different cases

$$QC_m^A(P, Q) = \sqrt{\sum_{i,j} \left(\frac{(P_i - Q_i)}{\left(\sum_c (P_c + Q_c) A_{ci}\right)^m} \right) \left(\frac{(P_j - Q_j)}{\left(\sum_c (P_c + Q_c) A_{cj}\right)^m} \right) A_{ij}},$$

where we define $\frac{0}{0} = 0$. The normalization factor m reduces the effect of big differences (the bigger it is, the bigger reduction; in our methods set to 0.5). While comparing the ith orientation bins of two histograms, we want to look into the matching orientation bins, to 4 surrounding orientation bins (2 left, 2 right), and into the same orientation bins within 8 surrounding spatial cells. MATLAB code for creating the matrix A which captures these properties is in Appendix B.

12.6 Recognition

In this section we describe the two methods we propose for one-shot-learning gesture recognition. We create a single model and look for the shortest path of a new video through the model in our first method. For the second method we create a separate model for every training video and using sliding frame window to look for similar parts of training videos.

12.6.1 Single Model—Dynamic Time Warping

In this method (we will call it *SM*) we use both Histograms of Oriented Gradients and Histograms of Optical Flow and perform temporal segmentation simultaneously with recognition.

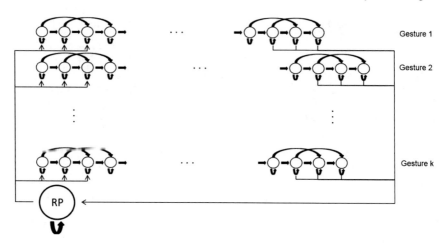

Fig. 12.6 Model for SM—Dynamic Time Warping. Each node represents a single frame of a train video. Each *row* (on the figure) represents single train video. We add a new node—RP, or Resting Position—representing state where the user is not performing any particular gesture. The *arrows indicate* possible transitions between states (nodes)

At first, we create a model illustrated in Fig. 12.6 for the whole batch in the following way: Every row in the figure represents a single training video. Every node represents a single frame of the video. In a node we store HOG and HOF features belonging to the particular frame. Recall that the HOF needs two consecutive frames. Thus if a video has f frames, the representation of this video has $f - 1$ nodes, ignoring the HOG of first frame. We add an arbitrary node, called Resting Position (RP), obtained as the average representation of first frames of each video.

Since we want to capture the variation in the speed of performing the gestures, we set the transitions in the following way. When being in a particular node n at time t, moving to time $t + 1$ we can either stay in the same node (slower performance), move to node $n + 1$ (the same speed of performance), or move to node $n + 2$ (faster performance). Experiments suggested allowing transition to node $n + 3$ is not needed with the trimming described in Sect. 12.4. It even made the whole method perform worse. From the node we call RP (Resting Position) we can move to the first three nodes of any video, and from the last three nodes of every video we can move to the RP.

When we have this model, we can start inferring the gestures present in a new video. First, we compute representations of all the frames in the new video. Then we compute similarities of every node of our model with every frame representation of the new video. We compute similarities of both matching HOGs and HOFs, using the Quadratic-Chi distance described in Sect. 12.5.3, and simply sum the distances. This makes sense since the empirical distribution functions of distances of HOGs and HOFs are similar. We can represent these distances as a matrix of size $N \times (f - 1)$, where N is the number of all nodes in the model, and f is the number of frames in the new video. Using the Viterbi algorithm we find the shortest path through this

Fig. 12.7 Example of flow
of states in model—devel01,
video number 11—true
labels are {9, 4, 4, 9}. The
gray levels represent the
shortest cumulative path
ending in a particular point

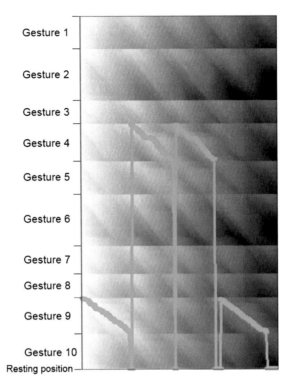

matrix (we constrain the algorithm to begin in RP or in any of the first three nodes
of any gesture). Every column is considered a time point, and in every time point
we are in one state (row of the matrix). Between neighbouring time points the states
can change only along the transitions in the model. This approach is also known as
Dynamic Time Warping, Berndt and Clifford (1994).

The result of the Viterbi algorithm is a path, a sequence of nodes which correspond
to states in which our new video was in time. From this path we can easily infer which
gestures were present (which rows in Fig. 12.6), and in what order. The flow of states
in time is displayed in Fig. 12.7 (the color represents the cumulative cost up to a
particular point—the darker the color, the larger the cumulative cost).

12.6.2   Multiple Models—Sliding Frame

The second method we propose is the MM. Here we used only the Histogram of
Oriented Gradients and perform temporal segmentation prior to recognition. We
created a similar model as in SM, but separately for every training video, illustrated
in Fig. 12.8. Again, every node represents HOG features of a single frame. Thus

Fig. 12.8 Model for every training video in MM. Every node represents a single frame of that video. The *arrows indicate* possible transitions between states (nodes)

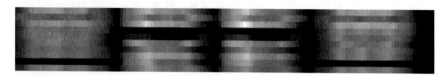

Fig. 12.9 Example of sliding frame matrix—devel01, video number 11

if we have k different gestures, we have k similar models. We do not need an RP node, since we will be looking for short sequences in these models similar to short sequences of frames of a new video. Again, the possible transitions between states in the models, capture variation in the speed of performing gestures.

MM differs from SM mainly in its approach to inferring the gestures that are present. First, we compute all the HOG representations of a new video and compute their similarities with all the nodes in k models. Then we employ the idea of a sliding frame. The idea is to take a small sequence of the new video and monitor the parts of the training videos that it resembles. First we select frames 1 to l (we set $l = 10$) and treat this similarly as in SM. We look for the shortest path through our first model without constraint on where to begin or end. We do the same with every model. This results in numerical values representing the resemblance of a small part of our new video with any part of every training video, and optionally also the number of nodes resembling it. Then we select frames 2 to $(l + 1)$, repeat the whole process, and move forward through the whole video.

Finally we obtain a matrix of size $k \times (f - l + 1)$, where k is the number of gestures and f is the number of frames in the new video. Every column represents a time instance and every row a gesture. An example of such a matrix is shown in Fig. 12.9. Humans can fairly easily learn to recognize where and which gestures are present, but this is a bit more challenging task for a computer. We tried to treat columns as feature vectors and feed it to SM and tried to build a Hidden Markov Model to infer gestures present. We also tried to include information of what nodes of a particular model were present for every time instant, so we can prefer gestures where most of the nodes were included. That was difficult to take into account, because the start and end of most videos are very similar (Resting Position). All the methods had problems identifying two identical gestures occurring after each other, and also two similar gestures occurring after each other. We did not find satisfactory solutions to these problems without deteriorating performance.

Neither of these methods manages to beat the naive approach. We resorted to first segment the video using an algorithm provided by the organizers in the sample code called *dtw_segment*. The algorithm is very fast and segments the videos very well. After segmenting, we simply summed along the rows in corresponding parts of the scores matrix and picked the minimum. An improvement was to perform a weighed sum that emphasizes the center of the video, since the important information is usually in the middle.

We used only HOG features in this method because every attempt to include HOF features resulted in considerably worse results. An explanation for this behaviour is we do not need to focus on the overall movement while looking only for short segments of videos, but it is more important to capture the static element. Thus the motion information is redundant in this setting.

12.7 Results

The performance of the two methods (SM & MM) on the data set is reported in this section. We also compare our results with those of other challenge participants as well as with other already published methods with experiments on this data set. Finally we summarize our contributions and suggest an area for future work.

12.7.1 Experimental Results

All our experiments were conducted on an Intel Core i7 3610QM processor, with 2 × 4 GB DDR3 1600 MHz memory. The running time of SM was approximately 115% of real-time (takes longer to process than to record), while MM was approximately 90% of real-time. However, none of our methods could be trivially converted to an online method, since we need to have the whole video in advance.

The performance of our methods on all available data sets is presented in Table 12.1. The results show that our preprocessing steps positively influence the final results. The MM works better on the first 20 development batches, but performs worse overall. All other published works provides results only on the first 20 batches—too few for any reliable conclusions. Therefore we suggest providing results on all the batches for bigger relevance.

As mentioned in Sect. 12.2, we chose our descriptors to exploit specific properties of the data set—the user stays at the same place, and thus the important parts of gestures occur roughly in the same position within the image. Hence it is not surprising that our model is not translation nor scale invariant. Guyon et al. (2013) created 20 translated and scaled data batches, and analyzed the robustness of methods of top ranking participants. In general, the bag-of-features models have this property, but they are usually rather slow. If we wanted to incorporate translation invariance, one method could be to extract body parts from the image (the algorithm is provided

Table 12.1 Overview of our results on data sets. The numbers are normalized Levenshtein distances described in Sect. 12.3

Batches	SM	MM
devel01–20	23.78	21.99
devel01–480	29.40	34.43
valid01–20	20.01	24.48
final01–20	17.02	23.08
final21–40	10.98	18.47
devel01–20 (without trimming)	26.24	22.82
devel01–20 (without medfilt)	24.70	23.92
devel01–20 (SM; only HOG)	24.53	
devel01–20 (MM; HOG and HOF)	28.73	

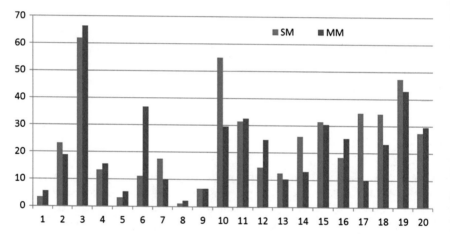

Fig. 12.10 Scores of our methods on first 20 development batches. The numbers on y-axis are normalized Levenshtein distances described in Sect. 12.3

within Kinect Development Toolkit[6]) and align the images so that the user is at the same position.

The results of our method on each of the first 20 batches is displayed in Fig. 12.10. Often our methods perform similarly, but one can spot significant differences in batches devel06 (SM—11.11, MM—36.67), devel10 (SM—54.95, MM—29.67) and devel17 (SM—34.78, MM—9.78). In batches devel10 and devel17, the gestures are only static and all occur in the same place in space. In this particular setting, the information about any motion (HOF) can be redundant. This could be a reason why MM performs better, since we do not include any motion descriptors in the representation. In devel06, the problem is, the gestures are performed very quickly,

---

[6]Available at http://www.microsoft.com/en-us/kinectforwindows/develop/.

Table 12.2 Comparison of results of methods from the competition as well as published methods. The numbers are normalized Levenshtein distances described in Sect. 12.3

Method/team	devel01–20	valid01–20	final01–20	final21–40
SM (ours)	23.78	20.01	17.02	10.98
MM (ours)	21.99	24.48	23.08	18.47
Alfnie	NA	9.51	7.34	7.10
Pennect	NA	17.97	16.52	12.31
Joewan	19.45	16.69	16.80	14.48
OneMillionMonkeys	NA	26.97	16.85	18.19
Mananender	26.34	23.32	21.64	19.25
Wu et al.	26.00	25.43	18.46	18.53
BoVDW	26.62	NA	NA	NA
Lui	28.73	NA	NA	NA
Fanello et al.	25.11	NA	NA	NA

thus the videos are often very short. This is a problem since the matrix in Fig. 12.9 has only a few columns, resulting in poor performance of MM.

The above analysis brings us to a new preprocessing step. Suppose we have many algorithms for solving this one-shot-learning task. If we knew in advance which algorithm was best at recognizing particular gestures, then we could boost the overall performance by selecting the 'best' algorithms in advance, after seeing the training videos. This is a problem we have unsuccessfully tried to solve, and which remains open for future work. If we always pick the better from our two methods, we would achieve score of 19.04 on the batches devel01–20.

The methods used by other challenge participants—alfnie, Pennect, Joewan (Wan et al. 2013), OneMillionMonkeys, Manavender (Malgireddy et al. 2012)—are summarized by Guyon et al. (2012, 2013). We briefly describe other published works applied on this data set. We provide a comparison of all of these methods in Table 12.2.

Wu et al. (2012) pre-segment videos and represent motions of users by Extended-Motion-History-Image and use a maximum correlation coefficient classifier. The Multi-view Spectral Embedding algorithm is used to fuse duo modalities in a physically meaningful manner.

Hernandez-Vela et al. (2012) present a Bag-of-Visual-and-Depth-Words (BoVDW) model for gesture recognition, that benefits from the multimodal fusion of visual and depth features. They combine HOG and HOF features with a new proposed depth descriptor.

Tensor representation of action videos is proposed by Lui (2012). The aim of his work is to demonstrate the importance of the intrinsic geometry of tensor space which yields a very discriminating structure for action recognition. The method is assessed using three gesture databases, including Chalearn gesture challenge data set.

Fanello et al. (2013) develop a real-time learning and recognition system for RGB-D images. The proposed method relies on descriptors based on 3D Histogram of Flow, Global Histogram of Oriented Gradient and adaptive sparse coding. The effectiveness of sparse coding techniques to represent 3D actions is highlighted in their work.

12.7.2 Contributions

Let us now summarize our contributions. As part of the competition we managed to create solid state-of-the-art methods for the new data set—the goal of the competition—which will serve as a reference point for future works. Although the crucial elements of our methods are not novel, they provide a new perspective on the possibilities of using well studied techniques, namely capturing the cross-bin relationships using the Quadratic-Chi distance. Further we present a novel algorithm for trimming videos, based only on depth data. As a preprocessing step we remove frames that bring little or no additional information, and thus make the method more robust. Experimental results show that this method does not only boost our performance, but also those of other published methods. Our detailed experiments with two very well performing methods suggest that different kinds of settings require different methods for the best performance. In particular, the possibility of choosing from more different types of models (like ours and bag-of-features) under different motion conditions remain unstudied and an open problem.

12.8 Discussion and Conclusions

In this paper we presented two methods for solving the one-shot-learning gesture recognition task introduced in the *ChaLearn Gesture Challenge* (ChaLearn 2011). We have significantly helped narrow the gap between human and machine performance (the baseline method achieved 50% error rate on final evaluation set, our method 11%, while the human error rate is under 2%). Our methods outperform other published methods and we suggest that other authors provide results on the whole data set for greater relevance of achieved results.

We combine static—Histograms of Oriented Gradients—and dynamic—Histogram of Optical Flow—descriptors in the first method, where we create one model and perform temporal segmentation simultaneously with recognition using Dynamic Time Warping. We use only static descriptors and use pre-segmentation as a preprocessing step in the second method, where we look for similar parts in the training videos using a sliding frame.

Our first method is similar to the one developed by team Pennect in the Challenge, and also performs similarly. They also used HOG features, but at different scales, and used a one-versus-all linear classifier, while we use the Quadratic-Chi distance

(Pele and Werman 2010) to measure distances between individual frames. The recognition was also parallel with temporal segmentation using a DTW model. Surprisingly, the Pennect team used only the color images.

Bag-of-features models provide comparable (Wan et al. 2013) or slightly worse results than ours (Hernandez-Vela et al. 2012). The advantage of these models is that they are scale and translation invariant - which is necessary for real-world applications like in gaming industry. On the other hand, these methods rely on presegmentation of videos to single gestures, and are considerably slower, hence are currently not applicable. An interesting property of these methods is their results seem to have lower variance—error rate at difficult data sets (for instance devel10) is smaller, but struggle to obtain strong recognition rate on easy data sets (devel08, devel09).

We present a novel video trimming technique, based on the amount of motion. Its motivation is to remove unimportant segments of videos and thus reduce the probability of confusing gestures. The method improves overall results of our methods (Table 12.1), and small improvement was confirmed by Wu et al. (2012)—2% and Wan et al. (2013)—0.5%.

Finally, we suggest an area for future work. Having more well working methods at our disposal, we can analyse their results on different types of gesture vocabularies, users and other settings. Overall performance could be boosted if we were able to decide which recognizer to use in advance. Especially, deeper analysis of the differences of results between Bag-of-words models and Dynamic Time Warping models is needed to obtain better description of their behaviour on different types of gesture recognition tasks.

Appendix A

In this appendix, we analyse the computational complexity of our methods.

Let us first describe the computational complexity of the building blocks of our algorithms. Let r, c be the resolution of our videos. For this data set we have $r = 240, c = 320$. Let P denote number of pixels ($P = rc$). Computing both HOG and HOF features requires performing a fixed number of iterations for every pixel. Creating histograms in spatial cells requires a fixed number of operations with respect to the size of these cells. Thus the complexity of computing HOG and HOF descriptors for one example requires $\mathcal{O}(P)$ operations. Let m be the number of pixels used in the median filter for every pixel. Since computing the median requires ordering, the complexity of filtering an image requires $\mathcal{O}(Pm \log m)$ operations. In total, for both SM and MM, the whole training on a batch of N frames in total requires $\mathcal{O}(NPm \log(m))$ operations.

Before evaluating a new video of F frames, we have to compute the representations of the frames, which is done in $\mathcal{O}(FPm \log m)$ operations. In both methods we then perform a Viterbi search. In MM this is divided into several searches, but the total complexity stays the same. The most time consuming part is computing the Quadratic-Chi distances (Sect. 12.5.3) between all FN pairs of frames from the new video and model. Computing the distance needs sum over elements over sparse $H \times H$ matrix (H being the size of the histograms used) described in Algorithm 2. The number of non-zero elements is linear in H. Thus, the overall complexity of evaluating a new video is $\mathcal{O}(NPm \log(m) + NFH)$.

To summarize, the running time of our methods is linear in the number of training frames, number of frames of a new video, number of pixels of a single frame, and size of histogram (number of spatial cell times number of orientation bins). Dependence on size of the filtering region for every pixel is linearithmic since it requires sorting.

Appendix B

In this Appendix, we provide MATLAB algorithm for creating similarity matrix used in the Quadratic-Chi distance described in Sect. 12.5.3. We have histograms of $h \times w$ spatial cells, and p orientation bins in each of the spatial bins. The size of the final matrix is $H \times H$, where $H = hwp$.

Algorithm 2 MATLAB code producing the similarity matrix

```
gauss = fspecial('gaussian', 3, 0.56);
B = diag(ones(1,h)) + 2*(diag(ones(1, h-1), 1) + diag(ones(1, h-1), -1));
C = diag(ones(1,w)) + 2*(diag(ones(1, w-1), 1) + diag(ones(1, w-1), -1));
D = kron(C, B); % Kronecker tensor product
D(D == 1) = gauss(5);
D(D == 2) = gauss(2);
D(D == 4) = gauss(1);
A = imfilter( eye(p), gauss, 'circular');
A = sparse(kron(D, A)); % The final similarity matrix
```

References

H. Bay, T. Tuytelaars, L. Van Gool, Surf: speeded up robust features, in *Computer Vision–ECCV 2006* (Springer, Berlin, 2006), pp. 404–417

D.J. Berndt, J. Clifford, Using dynamic time warping to find patterns in time series. KDD Workshop **10**, 359–370 (1994)

ChaLearn. ChaLearn Gesture Dataset (CGD2011), ChaLearn, California, (2011), http://gesture. chalearn.org/data

S.P. Chatzis, D.I. Kosmopoulos, P. Doliotis, A conditional random field-based model for joint sequence segmentation and classification. Pattern Recognit. **46**, 1569–1578 (2012)

N. Dalal, B. Triggs, Histograms of oriented gradients for human detection, in *IEEE Conference on Computer Vision and Pattern Recognition (CVPR)*, vol. 1 (IEEE, 2005), pp. 886–893

P. Dollár, Piotr's Image and Video Matlab Toolbox (PMT), http://vision.ucsd.edu/~pdollar/toolbox/doc/index.html

S.R. Fanello, I. Gori, G. Metta, F. Odone, *One-shot Learning for Real-time Action Recognition* (Springer, Berlin, 2013)

I. Guyon, V. Athitsos, P. Jangyodsuk, B. Hamner, H.J. Escalante, Chalearn gesture challenge: design and first results, in *IEEE Conference on Computer Vision and Pattern Recognition Workshops (CVPRW)* (IEEE, 2012), pp. 1–6

I. Guyon, V. Athitsos, P. Jangyodsuk, H.J. Escalante, B. Hamner, Results and analysis of the chalearn gesture challenge 2012 (2013)

A. Hernández-Vela, M.Á. Bautista, X. Perez-Sala, V. Ponce, X. Baró, O. Pujol, C. Angulo, S. Escalera, BoVDW: Bag-of-visual-and-depth-words for gesture recognition, in *International Conference on Pattern Recognition* (2012), pp. 449–452

N. Ikizler, D. Forsyth, Searching video for complex activities with finite state models, in *IEEE Conference on Computer Vision and Pattern Recognition (CVPR)* (IEEE, 2007), pp. 1–8

T. Kanade, B.D. Lucas, An iterative image registration technique with an application to stereo vision, in *Proceedings of the 7th International Joint Conference on Artificial Intelligence* (1981)

A. Klaser, M. Marszalek, A spatio-temporal descriptor based on 3d-gradients (2008)

I. Laptev, On space-time interest points. Int. J. Comput. Vis. **64**(2–3), 107–123 (2005)

I. Laptev, M. Marszalek, C. Schmid, B. Rozenfeld, Learning realistic human actions from movies, in *IEEE Conference on Computer Vision and Pattern Recognition (CVPR)* (IEEE, 2008), pp. 1–8

D.D. Lewis, Naive (bayes) at forty: the independence assumption in information retrieval, in *Machine Learning: ECML-98* (Springer, Berlin, 1998), pp. 4–15

D.G. Lowe, Object recognition from local scale-invariant features, in *The Proceedings of the Seventh IEEE International Conference on Computer Vision, 1999*, vol. 2 (IEEE, 1999), pp. 1150–1157

B.D. Lucas, *Generalized Image Matching by the Method of Differences*. Ph.D. thesis, Robotics Institute, Carnegie Mellon University, July 1984

Y.M. Lui, Human gesture recognition on product manifolds. J. Mach. Learn. Res. **13**, 3297–3321 (2012)

M.R. Malgireddy, I. Inwogu, V. Govindaraju. A temporal bayesian model for classifying, detecting and localizing activities in video sequences, in *IEEE Conference on Computer Vision and Pattern Recognition Workshops (CVPRW)* (IEEE, 2012), pp. 43–48

O. Pele, M. Werman, The quadratic-chi histogram distance family. Comput. Vis.-ECCV **2010**, 749–762 (2010)

J. Wan, Q. Ruan, W. Li, S. Deng, one-shot learning gesture recognition from RGB-D data using bag of features. J. Mach. Learn. Res. **14**, 2549–2582 (2013), http://jmlr.org/papers/v14/wan13a.html

H. Wang, M.M. Ullah, A. Klaser, I. Laptev, C. Schmid, et al., Evaluation of local spatio-temporal features for action recognition, in *BMVC 2009-British Machine Vision Conference* (2009)

S.B. Wang, A. Quattoni, L-P, Morency, D. Demirdjian, T. Darrell, Hidden conditional random fields for gesture recognition, in *IEEE Conference on Computer Vision and Pattern Recognition (CVPR)*, vol. 2 (IEEE, 2006), pp. 1521–1527

D. Wu, F. Zhu, L. Shao, One shot learning gesture recognition from RGBD images, in *IEEE Conference on Computer Vision and Pattern Recognition Workshops (CVPRW)* (IEEE, 2012), pp. 7–12

T. Xia, D. Tao, T. Mei, Y. Zhang, Multiview spectral embedding. IEEE Trans. Syst. Man Cybern. Part B: Cybern. **40**(6), 1438–1446 (2010)

Chapter 13
Multi-layered Gesture Recognition with Kinect

Feng Jiang, Shengping Zhang, Shen Wu, Yang Gao and Debin Zhao

Abstract This paper proposes a novel multi-layered gesture recognition method with Kinect. We explore the essential linguistic characters of gestures: the components concurrent character and the sequential organization character, in a multi-layered framework, which extracts features from both the segmented semantic units and the whole gesture sequence and then sequentially classifies the motion, location and shape components. In the first layer, an improved principle motion is applied to model the motion component. In the second layer, a particle-based descriptor and a weighted dynamic time warping are proposed for the location component classification. In the last layer, the spatial path warping is further proposed to classify the shape component represented by unclosed shape context. The proposed method can obtain relatively high performance for one-shot learning gesture recognition on the ChaLearn Gesture Dataset comprising more than 50,000 gesture sequences recorded with Kinect.

Keywords Gesture recognition · Kinect · Linguistic characters · Multi-layered classification · Principle motion · Dynamic time warping

Editors: Sergio Escalera, Isabelle Guyon and Vassilis Athitsos

F. Jiang (✉) · S. Zhang · S. Wu · Y. Gao · D. Zhao
School of Computer Science and Technology, Harbin Institute of Technology,
Harbin, China
e-mail: fjiang@hit.edu.cn

S. Zhang
e-mail: s.zhang@hit.edu.cn

S. Wu
e-mail: wu.shen.eltshan@gmail.com

Y. Gao
e-mail: lambyy.hit@gmail.com

D. Zhao
e-mail: dbzhao@hit.edu.cn

13.1 Introduction

Gestures, an unsaid body language, play very important roles in daily communication. They are considered as the most natural means of communication between humans and computers (Mitra and Acharya 2007). For the purpose of improving humans' interaction with computers, considerable work has been undertaken on gesture recognition, which has wide applications including sign language recognition (Vogler and Metaxas 1999; Cooper et al. 2012), socially assistive robotics (Baklouti et al. 2008), directional indication through pointing (Nickel and Stiefelhagen 2007) and so on (Wachs et al. 2011).

Based on the devices used to capture gestures, gesture recognition can be roughly categorized into two groups: wearable sensor-based methods and optical camera-based methods. The representative device in the first group is the data glove (Fang et al. 2004), which is capable of exactly capturing the motion parameters of the user's hands and therefore can achieve high recognition performance. However, these devices affect the naturalness of the user interaction. In addition, they are also expensive, which restricts their practical applications (Cooper et al. 2011). Different from the wearable devices, the second group of devices are optical cameras, which record a set of images overtime to capture gesture movements in a distance. The gesture recognition methods based on these devices recognize gestures by analyzing visual information extracted from the captured images. That is why they are also called vision-based methods. Although optical cameras are easy to use and also inexpensive, the quality of the captured images is sensitive to lighting conditions and cluttered backgrounds, thus it is very difficult to detect and track the hands robustly, which largely affects the gesture recognition performance.

Recently, the Kinect developed by Microsoft was widely used in both industry and research communities (Shotton et al. 2011). It can capture both RGB and depth images of gestures. With depth information, it is not difficult to detect and track the user's body robustly even in noisy and cluttered backgrounds. Due to the appealing performance and also reasonable cost, it has been widely used in several vision tasks such as face tracking (Cai et al. 2010), hand tracking (Oikonomidis et al. 2011), human action recognition (Wang et al. 2012) and gesture recognition (Doliotis et al. 2011; Ren et al. 2013). For example, one of the earliest methods for gesture recognition using Kinect is proposed in Doliotis et al. (2011), which first detects the hands using scene depth information and then employs Dynamic Time Warping for recognizing gestures. Ren et al. (2013) extracts the static finger shape features from depth images and measures the dissimilarity between shape features for classification. Although, Kinect facilitates us to detect and track the hands, exact segmentation of finger shapes is still very challenging since the fingers are very small and form many complex articulations.

Although postures and gestures are frequently considered as being identical, there are significant differences (Corradini 2002). A posture is a static pose, such as making a palm posture and holding it in a certain position, while a gesture is a dynamic process consisting of a sequence of the changing postures over a short duration.

Compared to postures, gestures contain much richer motion information, which is important for distinguishing different gestures especially those ambiguous ones. The main challenge of gesture recognition lies in the understanding of the unique characters of gestures. Exploring and utilizing these characters in gesture recognition are crucial for achieving desired performance. Two crucial linguistic models of gestures are the phonological model drawn from the component concurrent character (Stokoe 1960) and the movement-hold model drawn from the sequential organization character (Liddell and Johnson 1989). The component concurrent character indicates that complementary components, namely motion, location and shape components, simultaneously characterize a unique gesture. Therefore, an ideal gesture recognition method should have the ability of capturing, representing and recognizing these simultaneous components. On the other hand, the movement phases, i.e. the transition phases, are defined as periods during which some components, such as the shape component, are in transition; while the holding phases are defined as periods during which all components are static. The sequential organization character characterizes a gesture as a sequential arrangement of movement phases and holding phases. Both the movement phases and the holding phases are defined as semantic units. Instead of taking the entire gesture sequence as input, the movement-hold model inspires us to segment a gesture sequence into sequential semantic units and then extract specific features from them. For example, for the frames in a holding phase, shape information is more discriminative for classifying different gestures.

It should be noted that the component concurrent character and the sequential organization character demonstrate the essences of gestures from spatial and temporal aspects, respectively. The former indicates which kinds of features should be extracted. The later implies that utilizing the cycle of movement and hold phases in a gesture sequence can accurately represent and model the gesture. Considering these two complementary characters together provides us a way to improve gesture recognition. Therefore, we developed a multi-layered classification framework for gesture recognition. The architecture of the proposed framework is shown in Fig. 13.1, which contains three layers: the motion component classifier, the location component classifier, and the shape component classifier. Each of the three layers analyzes its corresponding component. The output of one layer limits the possible classification in the next layer and these classifiers complement each other for the final gesture classification. Such a multi-layered architecture assures achieving high recognition performance while being computationally inexpensive.

The main contributions of this paper are summarized as follows:

- The phonological model (Stokoe 1960) of gestures inspires us to propose a novel multi-layered gesture recognition framework, which sequentially classifies the motion, location and shape components and therefore achieves higher recognition accuracy while having low computational complexity.
- Inspired by the linguistic sequential organization of gestures (Liddell and Johnson 1989), the matching process between two gesture sequences is divided into two steps: their semantic units are matched first, and then the frames inside the semantic

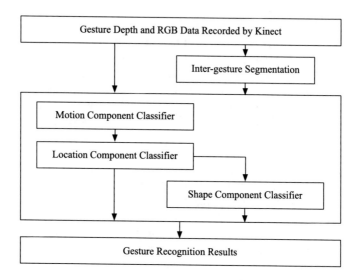

Fig. 13.1 Multi-layered gesture recognition architecture

units are further registered. A novel particle-based descriptor and a weighted dynamic time warping are proposed to classify the location component.

- The spatial path warping is proposed to classify the shape component represented by unclosed shape context, which is improved from the original shape context but the computation complexity is reduced from $O(n^3)$ to $O(n^2)$.

Our proposed method participated the one-shot learning CHALEARN gesture challenge and was top ranked (Guyon et al. 2013). The ChaLearn Gesture Dataset (CGD 2011) (Guyon et al. 2014) is designed for one-shot learning and comprises more than 50,000 gesture sequences recorded with Kinect. The remainder of the paper is organized as follows. Related work is reviewed in Sect. 13.2. The detailed descriptions of the proposed method are presented in Sect. 13.3. Extensive experimental results are reported in Sect. 13.4. Section 13.5 concludes the paper.

13.2 Related Work

Vision based gesture recognition methods encompasses two main categories: three dimensional (3D) model based methods and appearance based methods. The former computes a geometrical representation using the joint angles of a 3D articulated structure recovered from a gesture sequence, which provides a rich description that permits a wide range of gestures. However, computing a 3D model has high computational complexity (Oikonomidis et al. 2011). In contrast, appearance based methods extract appearance features from a gesture sequence and then construct a classifier to recognize different gestures, which have been widely used in vision based gesture recognition (Dardas 2012). The proposed multi-layered gesture recognition falls into the appearance based methods.

13.2.1 Feature Extraction and Classification

The well known features used for gesture recognition are color (Awad et al. 2006; Maraqa and Abu-Zaiter 2008), shapes (Ramamoorthy et al. 2003; Ong and Bowden 2004) and motion (Cutler and Turk 1998; Mahbub et al. 2013). In early work, color information is widely used to segment the hands of a user. To simplify the color based segmentation, the user is required to wear single or differently colored gloves (Kadir et al. 2004; Zhang et al. 2004). The skin color models are also used (Stergiopoulou and Papamarkos 2009; Maung 2009) where a typical restriction is wearing of long sleeved clothes. When it is difficult to exploit color information to segment the hands from an image (Wan et al. 2012b), motion information extracted from two consecutive frames is used for gesture recognition. Agrawal and Chaudhuri (2003) explores the correspondences between patches in adjacent frames and uses 2D motion histogram to model the motion information. Shao and Ji (2009) computes optical flow from each frame and then uses different combinations of the magnitude and direction of optical flow to compute a motion histogram. Zahedi et al. (2005) combines skin color features and different first- and second-order derivative features to recognize sign language. Wong et al. (2007) uses PCA on motion gradient images of a sequence to obtain features for a Bayesian classifier. To extract motion features, Cooper et al. (2011) extends haar-like features from spatial domain to spatio-temporal domain and proposes volumetric Haar-like features.

The features introduced above are usually extracted from RGB images captured by a traditional optical camera. Due to the nature of optical sensing, the quality of the captured images is sensitive to lighting conditions and cluttered backgrounds, thus the extracted features from RGB images are not robust. In contrast, depth information from a calibrated camera pair (Rauschert et al. 2002) or direct depth sensors such as LiDAR (Light Detection and Ranging) is more robust to noises and illumination changes. More importantly, depth information is useful for discovering the distance between the hands and body orthogonal to the image plane, which is an important cue for distinguishing some ambiguous gestures. Because the direct depth sensors are expensive, inexpensive depth cameras, e.g., Microsoft's Kinect, have been recently used in gesture recognition (Ershaed et al. 2011; Wu et al. 2012b). Although the skeleton information offered by Kinect is more effective in the expression of human actions than pure depth data, there are some cases that skeleton cannot be extracted correctly, such as interaction between human body and other objects. Actually, in the CHALERAN gesture challenge (Guyon et al. 2013), the skeleton information is not allowed to use. To extract more robust features from Kinect depth images for gesture recognition, Ren et al. (2013) proposes the part based finger shape features, which do not depend on the accurate segmentation of the hands. Wan et al. (2013, 2014b) extend SIFT to spatio-temporal domain and propose 3D EMoSIFT and 3D SMoSIFT to extract features from RGB and depth images, which are invariant to scale and rotation, and have more compact and richer visual representations. Wan et al. (2014a) proposes a discriminative dictionary learning method on 3D EMoSIFT features based on mutual information and then uses sparse reconstruction for classification. Based on 3D Histogram of Flow (3DHOF) and Global Histogram of Oriented Gradient (GHOG), Fanello et al. (2013) applies adaptive sparse coding to capture high-level feature patterns. Wu et al. (2012a) utilizes both RGB and depth information from Kinect and an extended-MHI representation is adopted as the motion descriptors.

The performance of a gesture recognition method is not only related to the used features but also to the adopted classifiers. Many classifiers can be used for gesture recognition, e.g., dynamic time warping (DTW) (Reyes et al. 2011; Lichtenauer et al. 2008; Sabinas et al. 2013), linear SVMs (Fanello et al. 2013), neuro-fuzzy inference system networks (Al-Jarrah and Halawani 2001), hyper rectangular composite NNs (Su 2000), and 3D Hopfield NN (Huang and Huang 1998). Due to the ability of modeling temporal signals, Hidden Markov Model (HMM) is possibly the most well known classifier for gesture recognition. Bauer and Kraiss (2002) proposes a 2D motion model and performes gesture recognition with HMM. Vogler (2003) presentes a parallel HMM algorithm to model gestures, which can recognize continuous gestures. Fang et al. (2004) proposes a self-organizing feature maps/hidden Markov model (SOFM/HMM) for gesture recognition in which SOFM is used as an implicit feature extractor for continuous HMM. Recently, Wan et al. (2012a) proposes ScHMM to deal with the gesture recognition where sparse coding is adopted to find succinct representations and Lagrange dual is applied to obtain a codebook.

13.2.2 One-Shot Learning Gesture Recognition and Gesture Characters

Although a large number of work has been done, gesture recognition is still very challenging and has been attracting increasing interests. One motivation is to overcome the well-known overfitting problem when training samples are insufficient. The other one is to further improve gesture recognition by developing novel features and classifiers.

In the case of training samples being insufficient, most of classification methods are very likely to overfit. Therefore, developing gesture recognition methods that use only a small training dataset is necessary. An extreme example is the one-shot learning that uses only one training sample per class for training. The proposed work in this paper is also for one-shot learning. In the literature, several previous work has been focused on one-shot learning. In Lui (2012a), gesture sequences are viewed as third-order tensors and decomposed to three Stiefel Manifolds and a natural metric is inherited from the factor manifolds. A geometric framework for least square regression is further presented and applied to gesture recognition. Mahbub et al. (2013)

proposes a space-time descriptor and applies Motion History Imaging (MHI) techniques to track the motion flow in consecutive frames. The Euclidean distance based classifiers is used for gesture recognition. Seo and Milanfar (2011) presents a novel action recognition method based on space-time locally adaptive regression kernels and the matrix cosine similarity measure. Malgireddy et al. (2012) presents an end-to-end temporal Bayesian framework for activity classification. A probabilistic dynamic signature is created for each activity class and activity recognition becomes a problem of finding the most likely distribution to generate the test video. Escalante et al. (2013) introduces principal motion components for one-shot learning gesture recognition. 2D maps of motion energy are obtained per each pair of consecutive frames in a video. Motion maps associated to a video are further processed to obtain a PCA model, which is used for gesture recognition with a reconstruction-error approach. More one-shot learning gesture recognition methods are summarized by Guyon et al. (2013).

The intrinsic difference between gesture recognition and other recognition problems is that gesture communication is highly complex and owns its unique characters. Therefore, it is crucial to develop specified features and classifiers for gesture recognition by exploring the unique characters of gestures as explained in Sect. 13.1. There are some efforts toward this direction and some work has modeled the component concurrent or sequential organization and achieved significant progress. To capture meaningful linguistic components of gestures, Vogler and Metaxas (1999) proposes PaHMMs which models the movement and shape of user's hands in independent channels and then put them together at the recognition stage. Chen and Koskela (2013) uses multiple Extreme Learning Machines (ELMs) (Huang et al. 2012) as classifiers for simultaneous components. The outputs from the multiple ELMs are then fused and aggregated to provide the final classification results. Chen and Koskela (2013) proposes a novel representation of human gestures and actions based on component concurrent character. They learn the parameters of a statistical distribution that describes the location, shape, and motion flow. Inspired by the sequential organization character of gestures, Wang et al. (2002) uses the segmented subsequences instead of the whole gesture sequence as the basic units that convey the specific semantic expression for the gesture and encode the gesture based on these units. It is successfully applied in large vocabulary sign gestures recognition.

To our best knowledge, there is no work in the literature modeling both the component concurrent character and the sequential organization character in gesture recognition, especially for one-shot learning gesture recognition. It should be noted that these two characters demonstrate the essences of gestures from spatial and temporal aspects, respectively. Therefore, the proposed method that exploits both these characters in a multi-layered framework is desirable to improve gesture recognition.

13.3 Multi-layered Gesture Recognition

The proposed multi-layered classification framework for one-shot learning gesture recognition contains three layers as shown in Fig. 13.1. In the first layer, an improved principle motion is applied to model the motion component. In the second layer, a particle based descriptor is proposed to extract dynamic gesture information and then a weighted dynamic time warping is proposed for the location component classification. In the last layer, we extract unclosed shape contour from the key frame of a gesture sequence. Spatial path warping is further proposed to recognize the shape component. Once the motion component classification at the first layer is accomplished, the original gesture candidates are divided into possible gesture candidates and impossible gesture candidates. The possible gesture candidates are then fed to the second layer which performs the location component classification. Compared with the original gesture candidates, classifying the possible gesture candidates is expected to reduce the computational complexity of the second layer distinctly. The possible gesture candidates are further reduced by the second layer. In the reduced possible gesture candidates, if the first two best matched candidates are difficult to be discriminated, i.e. the absolute difference of their matching scores is lower than a predefined threshold, then the reduced gesture candidates are forwarded to the third layer; otherwise the best matched gesture is output as the final recognition result.

In the remaining of this section, the illuminating cues are first observed in Sect. 13.3.1. Inter-gesture segmentation is then introduced in Sect. 13.3.2. The motion, location and shape component classifiers in each layer are finally introduced in Sects. 13.3.3, 13.3.4 and 13.3.5, respectively.

13.3.1 Gesture Meaning Expressions and Illuminating Cues

Although from the point of view of gesture linguistics, the basic components and how gestures convey meaning are given (Stokoe 1960), there is no reference to the importance and complementarity of the components in gesture communication. This section wants to draw some illuminating cues from observations. For this purpose, 10 undergraduate volunteers are invited to take part in the observations.

Five batches of data are randomly selected from the development data of CGD 2011. The pre-defined identification strategies are shown in Table 13.1. In each test, all the volunteers are asked to follow these identification strategies. For example, in Test 2, they are required to only use the motion cue and draw simple lines to record the motion direction of each gesture in the training set. Then the test gestures are shown to the volunteers to be identified using these drawn lines. The results are briefly summarized in Table 13.1.

From the observations above, the following illuminating cues can be drawn:

- During gesture recognition, gesture components in the order of importance are motion, location and shape.

Table 13.1 Observations on CGD 2011

Test	Avg. Acc. (%)	Identification strategy	Description
1	75.0	None	Memorizing all the training gestures, and identifying test gesture by recollection
2	90.3	Motion	Drawing lines to record motion direction of each training gesture
3	83.5	Shape	Drawing sketches to describe the hand shape of each training gesture
4	87.6	Location	Drawing sketches to describe the location of each training gesture
5	95.3	Motion and shape	Strategy 2 and 3
6	100.0	Motion and location and shape	Strategy 2, 3 and 4

- Understanding a gesture requires the observation of all these gesture components. None of these components can convey the complete gesture meanings independently. These gesture components complement each other.

13.3.2 Inter-gesture Segmentation Based on Movement Quantity

The inter-gesture segmentation is used to segment a multi-gesture sequence into several gesture sequences.[1] To perform the inter-gesture segmentation, we first measure the quantity of movement for each frame in a multi-gesture sequence and then threshold the quantity of movement to get candidate boundaries. Then, a sliding window is adopted to refine the candidate boundaries to produce the final boundaries of the segmented gesture sequences in a multi-gesture sequence.

13.3.2.1 Quantity of Movement

In a multi-gesture sequence, each frame has the relevant movement with respect to its adjacent frame and the first frame. These movements and their statistical information

---

[1] In this paper, we use the term "gesture sequence" to mean an image sequence that contains only one complete gesture and "multi-gesture sequence" to mean an image sequence which may contain one or multiple gesture sequences.

are useful for inter-gesture segmentation. For a multi-gesture depth sequence I, the Quantity of Movement (QOM) for frame t is defined as a two-dimensional vector

$$QOM(I, t) = [QOM_{Local}(I, t), QOM_{Global}(I, t)] , \tag{13.1}$$

where $QOM_{Local}(I, t)$ and $QOM_{Global}(I, t)$ measure the relative movement of frame t respective to its adjacent frame and the first frame, respectively. They can be computed as

$$QOM_{Local}(I, t) = \sum_{m,n} \sigma(I_t(m, n), I_{t-1}(m, n)) , \tag{13.2}$$

$$QOM_{Global}(I, t) = \sum_{m,n} \sigma(I_t(m, n), I_1(m, n)) , \tag{13.3}$$

where (m, n) is the pixel location and the indicator function $\sigma(x, y)$ is defined as

$$\sigma(x, y) = \begin{cases} 1 \ \text{if} |x - y| \geq Threshold_{QOM} \\ 0 \ \text{otherwise} \end{cases} , \tag{13.4}$$

where $Threshold_{QOM}$ is a predefined threshold, which is set to 60 empirically in this paper.

13.3.2.2 Inter-gesture Segmentation

We assume that there is a home pose between a gesture and another one in a multi-gesture sequence. The inter-gesture segmentation is facilitated by the statistical characteristics of QOM_{Global} of the beginning and ending phases of the gesture sequences in the training data. One advantage of using QOM_{Global} is that it does not need to segment the user from the background.

Firstly the average frame number L of all gestures in the training set is obtained. The mean and standard deviation of QOM_{Global} of the first and last $\lceil L/8 \rceil$ frames of each gesture sequence are computed. After that, a threshold $Threshold_{inter}$ is obtained as the sum of the mean and the doubled standard deviation. For a test multi-gesture sequence T which has t_s frames, the inter-gesture boundary candidate set is defined as

$$B_{inter}^{ca} = \{i | QOM_{Global}(T, i) \leq Threshold_{inter}, i \in \{1, \dots, t_s\}\} . \tag{13.5}$$

The boundary candidates are further refined through a sliding window of size $\lceil L/2 \rceil$, defined as $\{j + 1, j + 2, \dots, j + \lceil L/2 \rceil\}$ where j starts from 0 to $t_s - \lceil L/2 \rceil$. In each sliding window, only the candidate with the minimal QOM_{Global} is retained and other candidates are eliminated from B_{inter}^{ca}. After the sliding window stops,

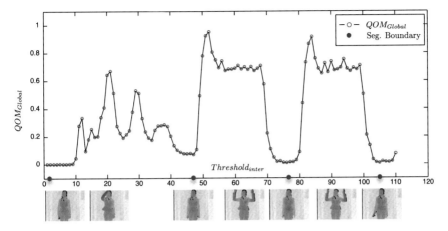

Fig. 13.2 An example of illustrating the inter-gesture segmentation results

the inter-gesture boundaries are obtained, which are exemplified as the blue dots in Fig. 13.2. The segmented gesture sequences will be used for motion, location, and shape component analysis and classification.

13.3.3 Motion Component Analysis and Classification

Owing to the relatively high importance of the motion component, it is analyzed and classified in the first layer. The principal motion (Escalante and Guyon 2012) is improved by using the overlapping block partitioning to reduce the errors of motion pattern mismatchings. Furthermore, our improved principal motion uses both the RGB and depth images. The gesture candidates outputted by the first layer is then fed to the second layer.

13.3.3.1 Principal Motion

Escalante and Guyon (2012) uses a set of histograms of motion energy information to represent a gesture sequence and implements a reconstruction based gesture recognition method based on principal components analysis (PCA). For a gesture sequence, motion energy images are calculated by subtracting consecutive frames. Thus, the gesture sequence with N frames is associated to $N - 1$ motion energy images. Next, a grid of equally spaced blocks is defined over each motion energy image as shown in Fig. 13.3c. For each motion energy image, the average motion energy in each of the patches of the grid is computed by averaging values of pixels within each patch. Then a 2D motion map for each motion energy image is obtained and each element of the map accounts for the average motion energy of the block centered on the

(a)   **(b)**   **(c)**   **(d)**

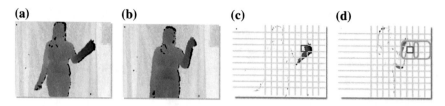

Fig. 13.3 An example of a gesture with large movements. **a, b** Two frames from a gesture. **c** The motion energy image of **a**. The grid of equally spaced bins adopted by the Principle Motion (Escalante and Guyon 2012). **d** The motion energy image of **b**. The overlapped grid used by our method where the overlapping neighborhood includes all 3 × 3 equally spaced neighbor bins

corresponding 2D location. The 2D map is then vectorized into an N_b-dimensional vector. Hence, an N frame gesture sequence is associated to a matrix Y of dimensions $(N - 1) \times N_b$. All gestures in the reference set with size V can be represented with matrices Y_v, $v \in \{1, \ldots, V\}$ and PCA is applied to each Y_v. Then the eigenvectors corresponding to the top c eigenvalues form a set W_v, $v = \{1, \ldots, V\}$.

In the recognition stage, each test gesture is processed as like training gestures and represented by a matrix S. Then, S is projected back to each of the V spaces induced by W_v, $v \in \{1, \ldots, V\}$. The V reconstructions of S are denoted by $R_1, \ldots, R_V$. The reconstruction error of each R_v is computed by

$$\varepsilon(v) = \frac{1}{n} \sum_{i=1}^{n} \sqrt{\sum_{j=1}^{m} (R_v(i,j) - S(i,j))^2} , \qquad (13.6)$$

where n and m are the number of rows and columns of S. Finally, the test gesture is recognized as the gesture with label obtained by $\arg\min_v \varepsilon(v)$.

13.3.3.2 Improved Principle Motion

Gestures with large movements are usually performed with significant deformation as shown in Fig. 13.3. In Escalante and Guyon (2012), motion information is represented by a histogram whose bins are related to spatial positions. Each bin is analyzed independently and the space interdependency among the neighboring bins is not further considered. The interdependency can be explored to improve the robustness of representing the gesture motion component, especially for the gestures with larger movement. To this end, an overlapping neighborhood partition is proposed. For example, if the size of bins is 20 × 20, the overlapping neighborhood contains 3 × 3 equally spaced neighboring bins in a 60 × 60 square region. The averaged motion energy in the square region is taken as the current bin's value as shown in Fig. 13.3.

The improved principle motion is applied to both the RGB and depth data. The RGB images are transformed into gray images before computing their motion energy images. For each reference gesture, the final V reconstruction errors are obtained by multiplying the reconstruction errors of the depth data and the gray data. These V reconstruction errors are further clustered by K-means to get two centers. The gesture labels associated to those reconstruction errors belonging to the center with smaller value are treated as the possible gesture candidates. The remaining gesture labels are treated as the impossible gesture candidates. Then the possible candidates are fed to the second layer.

We compare the performance of our improved principal motion model with the original principal motion model (Escalante and Guyon 2012) on the first 20 development batches of CGD 2011. Using the provided code (Guyon et al. 2014; Escalante and Guyon 2012) as baseline, the average Levenshtein distances (Levenshtein 1966) are 44.92 and 38.66% for the principal motion and the improved principal motion, respectively.

13.3.4 Location Component Analysis and Classification

Gesture location component refers to the positions of the arms and hands relative to the body. In the second layer, the sequential organization character of gestures is utilized in the gesture sequence alignment. According to the movement-hold model, each gesture sequence is segmented into semantic units, which convey the specific semantic meanings of the gesture. Accordingly, when aligning a reference gesture and a test gesture, the semantic units are aligned first, then the frames in each semantic unit are registered. A particle-based representation for the gesture location component is proposed to describe the location component of the aligned frames and a Weighted Dynamic Time Warping (WDTW) is proposed for the location component classification.

13.3.4.1 Intra-gesture Segmentation and Alignment

To measure the distance between location components of a reference gesture sequence $R = \{R_1, R_2 \ldots, R_{L_R}\}$ and a test gesture sequence $T = \{T_1, T_2 \ldots, T_{L_T}\}$, an alignment $\Gamma = \{(i_k, j_k)|k = 1, \ldots, K, i_k \in \{1, \ldots, L_R\}, j_k \in \{1, \ldots, L_T\}\}$ can be determined by the best path in the Dynamic Time Warping (DTW) grid and K is the path length. Then the dissimilarity between two gesture sequences can be obtained as the sum of the distances between the aligned frames.

The above alignment does not consider the sequential organization character of gestures. The movement-hold model proposed by Liddell and Johnson (1989) reveals sequential organization of gestures, which should be explored in the analysis and classification of gesture location component. $QOM_{Local}(I, t)$, described in Sect. 13.3.2.1, measures the movement between two consecutive frames. A large $QOM_{Local}(I, t)$ indicates that the t-th frame is in a movement phase, while a small $QOM_{Local}(I, t)$ indicates that the frame is in a hold phase. Among all the frames in a hold phase, the one with the minimal $QOM_{Local}(I, t)$ is the most representative frame and is marked

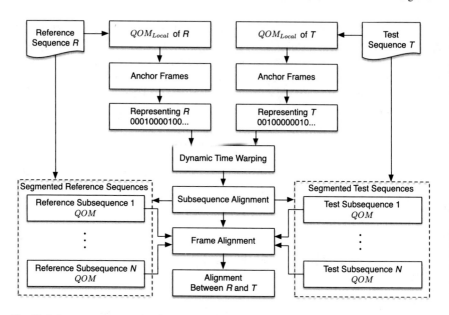

Fig. 13.4 Intra-gesture segmentation and the alignment between test and reference sequences

as an anchor frame. Considering the sequential organization character of gestures, the following requirement should be satisfied to compute Γ: each anchor frame in a test sequence must be aligned with one anchor frame in the reference sequence.

As shown in Fig. 13.4, the alignment between the test and reference sequences has two stages. In the first stage, DTW is applied to align the reference and test sequences. Each anchor frame is represented by "1" and the remaining frames are represented by "0". Then the associated best path $\widehat{\Gamma} = \{(\widehat{i}_k, \widehat{j}_k) | k = 1, \ldots, \widehat{K}\}$ in the DTW grid can be obtained. For each $(\widehat{i}_k, \widehat{j}_k)$, if both $\widehat{i}_k$ and $\widehat{j}_k$ are anchor frames, then $\widehat{i}_k$ and $\widehat{j}_k$ are the boundaries of the semantic units. According to the boundaries, the alignment between semantic units of the reference and test sequences is obtained. In the second stage, as shown in Fig. 13.4, each frame in a semantic unit is represented by $[QOM_{Local}, QOM_{Global}]$ and DTW is applied to align the semantic unit pairs separately. Then the final alignment Γ is obtained by concatenating the alignments of the semantic unit pairs.

13.3.4.2 Location Component Segmentation and Its Particle Representation

After the frames of the test and reference sequences are aligned, the next problem is how to represent the location information in a frame. Dynamic regions in each frame contain the most meaningful location information, which are illustrated in Fig. 13.5i.

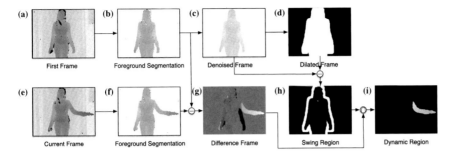

Fig. 13.5 Dynamic region segmentation

A simple thresholding-based foreground-background segmentation method is used to segment the user in a frame. The output of the segmentation is a mask frame that indicates which pixels are occupied by the user as shown in Fig. 13.5b. The mask frame is then denoised by a median filter to get a denoised frame as shown in Fig. 13.5c. The denoised frame is first binarized and then dilated with a flat disk-shaped structuring element with radius 10 as shown in Fig. 13.5d. The swing frame as shown in Fig. 13.5h is obtained by subtracting the binarized denoised frame from the dilated frame. The swing region (those white pixels in the swing frame) covers the slight swing of user's trunk and can be used to eliminate the influence of body swing. From frame t, define set Ξ as

$$\{(m, n)|F_1(m, n) - F_t(m, n) \geq Threshold_{QOM}\} , \qquad (13.7)$$

where F_1 and F_t are the user masks of the first frame and frame t, respectively. $Threshold_{QOM}$ is the same as in Sect. 13.3.2.1. For each connected region in Ξ, only if the number of pixels in this region exceeds N_p and the proportion overlapped with swing region is less than r, it is regarded as a dynamic region. Here $N_p = 500$ is a threshold used to remove the meaningless connected regions in the difference frame as shown in Fig. 13.5g. If a connected region has less than N_p pixels, we think this region should not be a good dynamic region for extracting location features, e.g., the small bright region on the right hand of the user in Fig. 13.5g. This parameter can be set intuitively. The parameter $r = 50\%$ is also a threshold used to complement with N_p to remove the meaningless connected regions in the difference frame. After using N_p to remove some connected regions, there may be a retained connected region which has more than N_p pixels but it may still not be a meaningful dynamic region for extracting position features if the connected region is caused by the body swing. Obviously we can exploit the swing region to remove such a region. To do this, we first compute the overlap rate between this region and the swing region. If the overlap rate is larger than r, it is reasonable to think this region is mainly produced by the body swing. Therefore, it should be further removed. As like N_p, this parameter is also very intuitive to set and is not very sensitive to the performance.

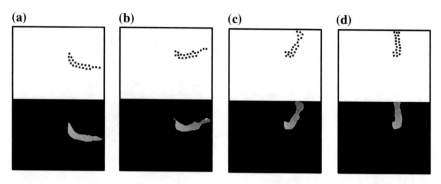

Fig. 13.6 Four examples of particle representation of the location component (the *black dots* are the particles projected onto X-Y plane)

To represent the dynamic region of frame t, a particle-based description is proposed to reduce the matching complexity. The dynamic region of frame t can be represented by a 3D distribution: $P_t(x, y, z)$ where x and y are coordinates of a pixel and $z = I_t(x, y)$ is the depth value of the pixel. In the form of non-parametric representation, $P_t(x, y, z)$ can be represented by a set of $\widehat{N}$ particles, $P_{Location}(I_t) = \{(x_n, y_n, z_n)|_{n=1}^{\widehat{N}}\}$. We use K-means to cluster all pixels inside the dynamic region into $\widehat{N}$ clusters. Note that for a pixel, both its spatial coordinates and depth value are used. Then the centers of clusters are used as the representative particles. In this paper, 20 representative particles are used for each frame, as shown in Fig. 13.6.

13.3.4.3 Location Component Classification

Assume the location component of two aligned frames can be represented as two particle sets, $P = \{P_1, P_2 \ldots P_{\widehat{N}}\}$ and $Q = \{Q_1, Q_2 \ldots Q_{\widehat{N}}\}$. The matching cost between particle P_i and Q_j, denoted by $C(P_i, Q_j)$, is computed as their Euclidean distance. The distance of the location component between these two aligned gesture frames is defined by the minimal distance between P and Q. Computing the minimal distance between two particle sets is indeed to find an assignment Π to minimize the cost summtion of all particle pairs

$$\Pi = \arg\min_{\Pi} \sum_{i=1}^{\widehat{N}} C(P_i, Q_{\Pi(i)}) . \tag{13.8}$$

This is a special case of the weighted bipartite graph matching and can be solved by the Edmonds method (Edmonds 1965). Edmonds method which finds an optimal assignment for a given cost matrix is an improved Hungarian method (Kuhn 1955) with time complexity $O(n^3)$ where n is the number of particles. Finally, the distance of the location component between two aligned gesture frames is obtained

$$dis(P, Q) = \sum_{i=1}^{\widehat{N}} C(P_i, Q_{\Pi(i)}) .$$ (13.9)

The distance between the reference sequence R and the test sequence T can be computed as the sum of all distance between the location components of the aligned frames in Γ

$$DIS_{Location}(R, T|\Gamma) = \sum_{k=1}^{K} dis(P_{Location}(R_{i_k}), P_{Location}(T_{j_k})) .$$ (13.10)

This measurement implicitly gives all the frames the same weights. However, in many cases gestures are distinguished by only a few frames. Therefore, rather than directly computing Eq. 13.10, we propose the Weighted DTW (WDTW) to compute the distance of location component between R and T as

$$WDIS_{Location}(R, T|\Gamma) = \sum_{k=1}^{K} W_{i_k}^R \times dis(P_{Location}(R_{i_k}), P_{Location}(T_{j_k})) ,$$ (13.11)

where $W^R = \{W_{i_k}^R | i_k \in \{1, \ldots, L_R\}\}$ is the weight vector. Different from the method of evaluating the phase difference between the test and reference sequences (Jeong et al. 2011) and the method of assigning different weights to features (Reyes et al. 2011), we assign different weights to the frames of the reference gesture sequence. For each reference gesture sequence, firstly we use the regular DTW to calculate and record the alignment Γ between the current reference gesture sequence and all the other reference gesture sequences. Secondly for each frame in the current reference gesture sequence, we accumulate its corresponding distances with the matched frames in the best path in the DTW. Then, the current frame is weighted by the average distance between itself and all the corresponding frames in the best path. The detailed procedure of computing the weight vector are summarized in Algorithm 1.

In the second layer, we first use K-means to cluster the input possible gesture candidates into two cluster centers according to the matching scores between the test gesture sequence and the possible gesture candidates. The candidates in the cluster with smaller matching score are discarded. In the remaining candidates, if the first two best matched candidates are difficult to be distinguished, i.e. the absolute difference of their normalized location component distances is lower than a predefined threshold ε, then these candidates are forwarded to the third layer; otherwise the best matched candidate is output as the final recognition result. Two factors influence the choice of the parameter ε. The first one is the number of the gesture candidates and the other one is the type of gestures. When the number of the gesture candidates is large or most of the gesture candidates are the shape dominant gestures, a high threshold is

Algorithm 1: Computing weight vector W^R for a reference R

Input: all the O reference gesture depth sequences: $I^1, I^2, \ldots, I^O$
Output: weight vector for R, $W^R = \{W_m^R | m \in \{1, \ldots, L_R\}\}$
1: **for** each $m \in [1, L_R]$ **do**
2:    $W_m^R = 0$
3:    $N_m^R = 0$
4: **end for**
5: **for** each $n \in [1, O]$ **do**
6:    Compute the alignment $\Gamma = \{(i_k, j_k)\}$ between R and I^n
7:    **for** each $m \in [1, L_R]$ **do**
8:       $W_m^R = W_m^R + \sum_{(i_k=m, j_k)\in\Gamma} dis(P_{Location}(R_{i_k}), P_{Location}(I_{j_k}^n))$
9:       $N_m^R = N_m^R + \sum_{(i_k, j_k)\in\Gamma} \delta(i_k = m)$
10:      **if** $n = O$ **then**
11:         $W_m^R = W_m^R / N_m^R$
12:      **end if**
13:   **end for**
14: **end for**

preferred. In our experiments, we empirically set its value with 0.05 by observing the matching scores between the test sample and each gesture candidates (Fig. 13.7).

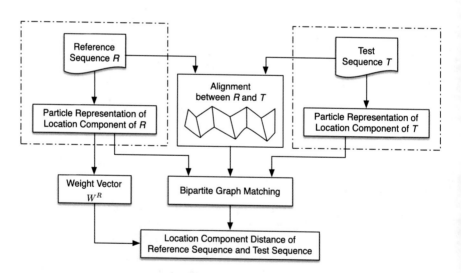

Fig. 13.7 Weighted dynamic time warping framework

13.3.5 Shape Component Analysis and Classification

The shape in a hold phase is more discriminative than the one in a movement phase. The key frame in a gesture sequence is defined as the frame which has the minimization QOM_{Local}. Shape component classifier classifies the shape features extracted from the key frame of a gesture sequence using the proposed Spatial Path Warping (SPW), which first extracts unclosed shape context (USC) features and then calculates the distance between the USCs of the key frames in the reference and the test gesture sequences. The test gesture sequence is classified as the gesture whose reference sequence has the smallest distance with the test gesture sequence.

13.3.5.1 Unclosed Shape Segmentation

The dynamic regions of a frame have been obtained in Sect. 13.3.4.2. In a key frame, the largest dynamic region D is used for shape segmentation. Although shapes are complex and do not have robust texture and structured appearance, in most cases shapes can be distinguished by their contours. The contour points of D are extracted by the Canny algorithm. The obtained contour point set is denoted by C_1 as shown in Fig. 13.8a. K-means is adopted to cluster the points in D into two clusters based on the image coordinates and depth of each point. If a user faces to the camera, the cluster with smaller average depth contains most of information for identifying the shape component. Canny algorithm is used again to extract contour points of the cluster with smaller average depth. The obtained closed contour point set is denoted by C_2 as shown in Fig. 13.8b. Furthermore, an unclosed contour point set can be obtained by $C_3 = C_2 \cap C_1$ as shown in Fig. 13.8c, which will be used to reduce the computational complexity of matching shapes.

13.3.5.2 Shape Representation and Classification

The contour of a shape consists of a 2-D point set $\mathbb{P} = \{p_1, p_2, \ldots, p_N\}$. Their relative positions are important for the shape recognition. From the statistical point of view,

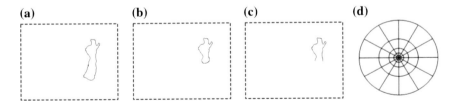

(a)   **(b)**   **(c)**   **(d)**

Fig. 13.8 Unclosed shape segmentation and context representation. **a** Is an example of point set C_1, **b** is an example of point set C_2 and **c** is an example of obtained point set C_3; **d** Is the log-polar space used to decide the ranges of K bins

Belongie et al. (2002) develops a strong shape contour descriptor, namely Shape Context (SC). For each point p_i in the contour, a histogram h_{p_i} is obtained as the shape context of the point whose k-th bin is calculated by

$$h_{p_i}(k) = \sharp\{(p_j - p_i) \in bin(k)|p_j \in \mathbb{P}, i \neq j, k \in \{1, \ldots, K\}\}, \qquad (13.12)$$

where $bin(k)$ defines the quantification range of the k-th bin. The log-polar space for bins is illustrated in Fig. 13.8d.

Assume $\mathbb{P}$ and $\mathbb{Q}$ are the point sets for the shape contours of two key frames, the matching cost $\Phi(p_i, q_j)$ between two points $p_i \in \mathbb{P}$ and $q_j \in \mathbb{Q}$ is defined as

$$\Phi(p_i, q_j) = \frac{1}{2} \sum_{k=1}^{K} \frac{[h_{p_i}(k) - h_{q_j}(k)]^2}{h_{p_i}(k) + h_{q_j}(k)}. \qquad (13.13)$$

Given the set of matching costs between all pairs of points $p_i \in \mathbb{P}$ and $q_j \in \mathbb{Q}$, computing the minimal distance between $\mathbb{P}$ and $\mathbb{Q}$ is to find a permutation Ψ to minimize the following sum

$$\Psi = \arg\min_{\Psi} \sum_i \Phi(p_i, q_{\Psi(i)}), \qquad (13.14)$$

which can also be solved by the Edmonds algorithm as like solving Eq. 13.8.

An unclosed contour contains valuable spatial information. Thus, a Spatial Path Warping algorithm (SPW) is proposed to compute the minimal distance between two unclosed contours. Compared with the Edmonds algorithm, the time complexity of the proposed SPW is reduced from $O(n^3)$ to $O(n^2)$ where n is the size of the point set of an unclosed shape contour. As shown in Fig. 13.8c, the points on an unclosed contour can be represented as a clockwise contour point sequence. SPW is used to obtain the optimal match between two given unclosed contour point sequences. For two unclosed contour point sequences $\{p'_1, \ldots, p'_n\}$, $\{q'_1, \ldots, q'_m\}$, a dynamic window is set to constrain the points that one point can match, which makes the matching more robust to local shape variation. We set the window size w with $\max(L_s, abs(n - m))$. In most cases, the window size is the absolute difference between the lengths of the two point sequences. In extreme cases, if two sequences have very close lengths, i.e., their absolute difference is less then L_s, we set the the window size with L_s. The details of proposed SPW are summarized in Algorithm 2.

Algorithm 2: Computing distance between two unclosed contour point sequences

Input: two unclosed contour point sequences $\{p'_1, \ldots, p'_n\}, \{q'_1, \ldots, q'_m\}$
Output: distance between these two point sequences $SPW[n, m]$.
1: Set $w = \max(L_s, abs(n - m))$
2: **for** each $i \in [0, n]$ **do**
3:      **for** each $j \in [0, m]$ **do**
4:          $SPW[i, j] = \infty$
5:      **end for**
6: **end for**
7: $SPW[0, 0] = 0$
8: **for** each $i \in [1, n]$ **do**
9:      **for** each $j \in [\max(1, i - w), \min(m, i + w)]$ **do**
10:         $SPW[i, j] = \Phi(p'_i, q'_j) + \min(SPW[i - 1, j], SPW[i, j - 1], SPW[i - 1, j - 1])$
11:     **end for**
12: **end for**

13.4 Experiments

In this section, extensive experiment results are presented to evaluate the proposed multi-layered gesture recognition method. All the experiments are performed in Matlab 7.12.0 on a Dell PC with Duo CPU E8400. The ChaLearn Gesture Dataset (CGD 2011) (Guyon et al. 2014) is used in all experiments, which is designed for one-shot learning. The CGD 2011 consists of 50,000 gestures (grouped in 500 batches, each batch including 47 sequences and each sequence containing 1–5 gestures drawn from one of 30 small gesture vocabularies of 8–15 gestures), with frame size 240 × 320, 10 frames/second, recorded by 20 different users.

The parameters used in the proposed method are listed in Table 13.2. Noted that the parameters c and N_b are set with the default values used in the sample code of the principal model.[2] The threshold for foreground and background segmentation is adaptively set to the maximal depth minus 100 for each batch data. For example, the maximal depth of the devel01 batch is 1964. Then the threshold for this batch is 1864. The number 100 is in fact a small bias from the maximal depth, which is empirically set in our experiments. We observed that slightly changing this number does not significantly affect the segmentation. Considering the tradeoff between the time complexity and recognition accuracy, in our experiments, we empirically set $\widehat{N}$ to 20, which achieves the desired recognition performance.

In our experiments, Levenshtein distance is used to evaluate the gesture recognition performance, which is also used in the CHALERAN gesture challenge. It is the minimum number of edit operations (substitution, insertion, or deletion) that have to be performed from one sequence to another (or vice versa). It is also known as "edit distance".

---

[2] Available at http://gesture.chalearn.org/data/sample-code.

Table 13.2 The parameters used in the proposed multi-layered gesture recognition and their descriptions

Parameter and description	Applied to	Value	From prior or not	Sensitive to performance	Training data used or not
N_p: Minimal number of pixels in a connected region	D	500	Y	N	Y
r: Maximal overlap rate between a connected region and the swing region	D	50%	N	N	N
ε: Threshold for the difference between the first two largest matches	D, E	0.05	Y	N	Y
L_s: Minimal length of the sliding window	E	5	N	N	N
$Threshold_{QOM}$	A, D, E	60	Y	Y	N
$Threshold_{inter}$	A	Adaptive	N	Y	Y
c: number of eigenvalues for each gesture	C	10	Y	N	N
N_b: number of bins for each motion energy image	C	192	Y	N	N
$\widehat{N}$: number of particles	D	20	Y	N	N
Threshold for foreground and background segmentation	D, E	Max depth—100	Y	N	Y

A Inter-gesture segmentation; **B** intra-gesture segmentation; **C** Motion component analysis and classification

D Location component analysis and classification; **E** Shape component analysis and classification; **Training data** CGD 2011

13.4.1 Performance of Our Method with Different layers

We evaluate the performance of the proposed method with different layers on the development (devel01–devel480) batches of CGD 2011 and Table 13.3 reports the results. If only the first layer is used for classification, the average Levenhstein distance is 37.53% with running time 0.54 s per gesture. If only the second layer is used for recognition, the average Levenhstein distance is 29.32% with running time 6.03 s per gesture. If only the third layer is used, the average Levenhstein distance is 39.12% with the running time 6.64 s per gesture. If the first two layers are used, the average Levenhstein distance is 24.36% with running time 2.79 s per gesture. If all three layers are used, the average normalized Levenhstein distance is 19.45% with running time 3.75 s per gesture.

From these comparison results, we can see that the proposed method achieves high recognition accuracy while having low computational complexity. The first

Table 13.3 Performance of using the first layer, the second layer, the third layer, first two layers and three layers on Chalearn gesture data set (devel01–devel480)

Methods	First layer for recognition	Second layer for recognition	Third layer for recognition	First two layers for recognition	Three layers for recognition
TeLev (%)	37.53	29.32	39.12	24.36	19.45
Recognition time per gesture (s)	0.54	6.03	6.64	2.79	3.75

layer can identify the gesture candidates at the speed of 80 fps (frames per second). The second layer has relatively high computational complexity. If we only use the second layer for classification, the average computing time is roughly 11 times of the first layer. Despite with relatively high computational cost, the second layer has stronger classification ability. Compared with using only the second layer, the computational complexity of using the first two layers in the proposed method is distinctly reduced and can achieve 16 fps. The reason is that although the second layer is relatively complex, the gesture candidates forwarded to it are significantly reduced by the first layer. When all three layers are used, the proposed method still achieve about 12 fps, which is faster than the video recording speed (10 fps) of CGD 2011.

13.4.2 Comparison with Recent Representative Methods

We compare the proposed method with other recent representative methods on the first 20 development data batches. Table 13.4 reports the performance of the proposed method on each batch and also the average performance on all 20 batches. The average performance of the proposed method and the compared methods are shown in Table 13.5.

For the comparison on each batch, the proposed method is compared with a manifold and nonlinear regression based method (Manifold LSR) (Lui 2012b), an extended motion-history-image and correlation coefficient based method (Extended-MHI) (Wu et al. 2012a), and a motion silhouettes based method (Motion History) (Mahbub et al. 2013). The comparison results are shown in Fig. 13.9.

In batches 13, 14, 17, 18, 19, the proposed method does not achieve the best performance. However, the proposed method achieves the best performance in the remaining 15 batches. In batches 3, 10 and 11, most of gestures consist of static shapes, which can be efficiently identified by the shape classifier in the third layer. Batches 1, 4, 7 and 8 consist of motion dominated gestures, which can be classified by the motion and location component classifiers in the first and second layers. In batches 18 and 19, the proposed method has relatively poor performance. As in batch 18, most of gestures have small motion, similar locations, and non-stationary

Table 13.4 Recognition performance of using the second layer, first two layers and three layers on first 20 development batches of CGD 2011 (TeLev is the average Levenshtein distance)

Batch	Second layer for recognition		First two layers for recognition		Three layers for recognition	
——	TeLev (%)	Recognize time per gesture (s)	TeLev (%)	Recognize time per gesture (s)	TeLev (%)	Recognize time per gesture (s)
1	7.24	6.78	0.11	3.40	1.11	3.59
2	41.21	11.38	44.21	7.10	34.35	10.00
3	62.98	8.86	69.20	2.99	39.95	5.61
4	4.51	5.98	3.93	2.10	6.93	2.30
5	11.68	10.96	2.62	3.05	4.77	3.31
6	44.64	5.59	39.94	2.69	23.51	3.42
7	12.44	3.59	8.51	1.70	8.51	1.79
8	5.56	4.94	0.00	2.14	5.71	2.94
9	10.56	5.10	6.44	2.50	6.44	3.01
10	44.21	5.88	29.13	3.24	16.52	3.95
11	42.75	6.46	36.36	3.98	28.93	6.31
12	8.56	5.16	1.06	2.00	7.06	2.34
13	16.24	3.68	12.93	1.20	12.93	1.99
14	44.69	2.50	40.13	0.90	27.98	2.35
15	15.78	4.61	4.21	1.09	6.21	2.19
16	36.54	8.35	36.27	4.21	23.41	6.94
17	36.25	9.10	29.55	5.10	26.32	5.39
18	62.4	1.99	69.21	0.81	53.55	1.60
19	54.31	5.07	51.32	2.84	47.61	3.02
20	17.74	2.58	10.61	1.40	10.61	2.01
Average	29.02	5.93	24.79	2.73	19.62	3.69

Table 13.5 Performance comparison on the 20 development data batches (TeLen is the average error made on the number of gestures)

Methods	Extend-MHI Wu et al. (2012a)	Manifold LSR Lui (2012a)	Sparse coding Fanello et al. (2013)	Temporal Bayesian Malgireddy et al. (2012)	Motion history Mahbub et al. (2013)	CSMMI+3D EMoSIFT Wan et al. (2014a)	Proposed
TeLev (%)	26.00	28.73	25.11	24.09	31.25	18.76	19.62
TeLen	#	6.24	5.02	#	18.01	#	5.91

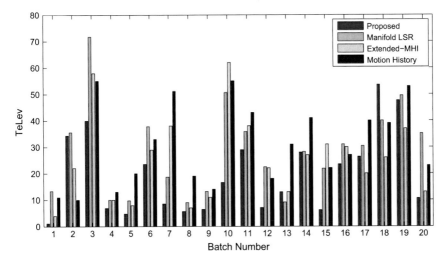

Fig. 13.9 Performance comparison on the 20 development batches in CGD 2011

hand shapes. These gestures may be difficult to be identified by the proposed method. In batch 19, the gestures have similar locations and hands coalescence, which is difficult to be identified by the second layer and the third layer classifiers in our method. Overall, the proposed method significantly outperforms other recent competitive methods.

The proposed method is further compared with DTW, continuous HMM (CHMM), semi-continuous HMM (SCHMM) and SOFM/HMM (Fang et al. 2004) on the development (devel01~devel480) batches of CGD 2011. All compared methods use one of three feature descriptors including dynamic region grid representation (DP), dynamic region particle representation (DG) and Dynamic Aligned Shape Descriptor (DS) (Fornés et al. 2010).

- **Dynamic region grid representation**. For the dynamic region of the current frame obtained in Sect. 13.3.4.2, a grid of equally spaced cells is defined and the default size of grid is 12×16. For each cell, the average value of depth in the square region is taken as the value of current bin. So a 12×16 matrix is generated, which is vectorized into the feature vector of the current frame.
- **Dynamic region particle representation**. The particles for the current frame obtained in Sect. 13.3.4.2 cannot directly be used as an input feature vector and they have to be reorganized. The 20 particles $\{(x_n, y_n, z_n)|_{n=1}^{20}\}$ are sorted according to $\|(x_n, y_n)\|^2$ and then the sorted particles are concatenated in order to get a 60-dimensional feature vector to represent the current frame.
- **Dynamic region D-Shape descriptor** (Fornés et al. 2010) Firstly, the location of some concentric circles is defined, and for each one, the locations of the equidistant voting points are computed. Secondly, these voting points will receive votes from the pixels of the shape of the dynamic region, depending on their distance to each

Table 13.6 Performance of different sequence matching methods on 480 development batches of CGD 2011

Method	Number of mixtures for each state	TeLev (%)			Recognition time per gesture (s)		
		DP	DG	DS	DP	DG	DS
DTW	#	38.23	41.19	33.16	2.67	2.51	2.60
CHMM	5	31.41	33.29	31.13	6.91	6.83	6.89
SCHMM	30	31.01	32.92	29.35	6.82	6.75	6.79
SOFM/HMM	5	28.27	30.31	27.20	6.77	6.71	6.74

DP dynamic region particle representation, **DG** dynamic region grid representation, **DS** dynamic region D-Shape descriptor

voting point. By locating isotropic equidistant points, the inner and external part of the shape could be described using the same number of voting points. In our experiment, we used 11 circles for the D-Shape descriptor. Once we have the voting points, the descriptor vector is computed.

Here, each type of HMM is a 3-state left-to-right model allowing possible skips. For CHMM and SCHMM, the covariance matrix is a diagonal matrix with all diagonal elements being 0.2. The comparison results are reported in Table 13.6.

Compared with these methods, the proposed method achieves the best performance. Noted that in all compared methods, SOFM/HMM classifier with the DS descriptor achieves the second best performance. As explained in Sect. 13.1, sequentially modeling motion, position and shape components is very important for improving the performance of gesture recognition. Except the proposed method, other compared methods do not utilize these components. On the other hand, statistical models like CHMM, SCHMM and SOFM/HMM need more training samples to estimate model parameters, which also affect their performance in the one-shot learning gesture recognition.

13.5 Conclusion

The challenges of gesture recognition lie in the understanding of the unique characters and cues of gestures. This paper proposed a novel multi-layered gesture recognition with Kinect, which is linguistically and perceptually inspired by the phonological model and the movement-hold model. Together with the illuminating cues drawn from observations, the component concurrent character and the sequential organization character of gestures are all utilized in the proposed method. In the first layer, an improved principle motion is applied to model the gesture motion component. In the second layer, a particle based descriptor is proposed to extract dynamic gesture information and then a weighted dynamic time warping is proposed to classify the location component. In the last layer, the spatial path warping is further proposed to classify the shape component represented by unclosed shape context, which is improved from the original shape context but needs lower matching time. The proposed method can obtain relatively high performance for one-shot learning gesture recognition. Our work indicates that the performance of gesture recognition can be significantly improved by exploring and utilizing the unique characters of gestures, which will inspire other researcher in this field to develop learning methods for gesture recognition along this direction.

Acknowledgements We would like to acknowledge the editors and reviewers, whose valuable comments greatly improved the manuscript. Specially, we would also like to thank Escalante and Guyon who kindly provided us the principal motion source code and Microsoft Asian who kindly provided two sets of Kinect devices. This work was supported in part by the Major State Basic Research Development Program of China (973 Program 2015CB351804) and the National Natural Science Foundation of China under Grant No. 61272386, 61100096 and 61300111.

References

T. Agrawal, S. Chaudhuri, Gesture recognition using motion histogram, in *Proceedings of the Indian National Conference of Communications*, 2003, pp. 438–442

O. Al-Jarrah, A. Halawani, Recognition of gestures in Arabic sign language using neuro-fuzzy systems. Artif. Intell. **133**(1), 117–138 (2001)

G. Awad, J. Han, A. Sutherland, A unified system for segmentation and tracking of face and hands in sign language recognition, in *Proceedings of the 18th International Conference on Pattern Recognition*, vol. 1, 2006, pp. 239–242

M. Baklouti, E. Monacelli, V. Guitteny, S. Couvet, Intelligent assistive exoskeleton with vision based interface, in *Proceedings of the 5th International Conference On Smart Homes and Health Telematics*, 2008, pp. 123–135

B. Bauer, K.-F. Kraiss, Video-based sign recognition using self-organizing subunits, in *Proceedings of the 16th International Conference on Pattern Recognition*, vol. 2, 2002, pp. 434–437

S. Belongie, J. Malik, J. Puzicha, Shape matching and object recognition using shape contexts. IEEE Trans. Pattern Anal. Mach. Intell. **24**(4), 509–522 (2002)

Q. Cai, D. Gallup, C. Zhang, Z. Zhang, 3D deformable face tracking with a commodity depth camera, in *Proceedings of the 11th European Conference on Computer Vision*, 2010, pp. 229–242

X. Chen, M. Koskela, Online RGB-D gesture recognition with extreme learning machines, in *Proceedings of the 15th ACM International Conference on Multimodal Interaction*, 2013, pp. 467–474

H. Cooper, B. Holt, R. Bowden, Sign language recognition, in *Visual Analysis of Humans*, 2011, pp. 539–562

H. Cooper, E.-J. Ong, N. Pugeault, R. Bowden, Sign language recognition using sub-units. J. Mach. Learn. Res. **13**, 2205–2231 (2012)

A. Corradini, Real-time gesture recognition by means of hybrid recognizers, in *Proceedings of International Gesture Workshop on Gesture and Sign Languages in Human-Computer Interaction*, 2002, pp. 34–47

R. Cutler, M. Turk, View-based interpretation of real-time optical flow for gesture recognition, in *Proceedings of the 10th IEEE International Conference and Workshops on Automatic Face and Gesture Recognition*, 1998, pp. 416–416

N. Dardas, *Real-time hand gesture detection and recognition for human computer interaction*, Ph.D. thesis, University of Ottawa, 2012

P. Doliotis, A. Stefan, C. Mcmurrough, D. Eckhard, V. Athitsos, Comparing gesture recognition accuracy using color and depth information, in *Proceedings of the 4th International Conference on PErvasive Technologies Related to Assistive Environments*, 2011, p. 20

J. Edmonds, Maximum matching and a polyhedron with 0, 1-vertices. J. Res. Natl. Bur. Stand. B **69**, 125–130 (1965)

H. Ershaed, I. Al-Alali, N. Khasawneh, M. Fraiwan, An Arabic sign language computer interface using the Xbox Kinect, in *Proceedings of the Annual Undergraduate Research Conference on Applied Computing*, vol. 1, 2011

H. Escalante, I. Guyon, Principal Motion, 2012, http://www.causality.inf.ethz.ch/Gesture/principal_motion.pdf

H.J. Escalante, I. Guyon, V. Athitsos, P. Jangyodsuk, J. Wan, Principal motion components for gesture recognition using a single-example, 2013, arXiv:1310.4822

S.R. Fanello, I. Gori, G. Metta, F. Odone, One-shot learning for real-time action recognition, in *Pattern Recognition and Image Analysis*, 2013, pp. 31–40

G. Fang, W. Gao, D. Zhao, Large vocabulary sign language recognition based on fuzzy decision trees. IEEE Trans. Syst. Man Cybern. A **34**(3), 305–314 (2004)

A. Fornés, S. Escalera, J. Lladós, E. Valveny, Symbol classification using dynamic aligned shape descriptor, in *Proceedings of the 20th International Conference on Pattern Recognition*, 2010, pp. 1957–1960

I. Guyon, V. Athitsos, P. Jangyodsuk, H.J. Escalante, B. Hamner, Results and analysis of the Chalearn gesture challenge 2012, in *Proceedings of International Workshop on Advances in Depth Image Analysis and Applications*, 2013, pp. 186–204

I. Guyon, V. Athitsos, P. Jangyodsuk, H.J. Escalante, The chalearn gesture dataset (CGD 2011). Mach. Vis. Appl. **25**(8), 1929–1951 (2014). doi:10.1007/s00138-014-0596-3

C.-L. Huang, W.-Y. Huang, Sign language recognition using model-based tracking and a 3D Hopfield neural network. Mach. Vis. Appl. **10**(5–6), 292–307 (1998)

G.-B. Huang, H. Zhou, X. Ding, R. Zhang, Extreme learning machine for regression and multiclass classification. IEEE Trans. Syst. Man Cybern. B **42**(2), 513–529 (2012)

V.I Levenshtein, Binary codes capable of correcting deletions, insertions and reversals, in *Soviet Physics Doklady*, vol. 10, 1966, p. 707

Y.-S. Jeong, M.K. Jeong, O.A. Omitaomu, Weighted dynamic time warping for time series classification. Pattern Recognit. **44**(9), 2231–2240 (2011)

T. Kadir, R. Bowden, E.J. Ong, A. Zisserman, Minimal training, large lexicon, unconstrained sign language recognition, in *Proceedings of the British Machine Vision Conference*, vol. 1, 2004, pp. 1–10

H.W. Kuhn, The Hungarian method for the assignment problem. Nav. Res. Logist. Q. **2**(1–2), 83–97 (1955)

J.F. Lichtenauer, E.A. Hendriks, M.J.T. Reinders, Sign language recognition by combining statistical DTW and independent classification. IEEE Trans. Pattern Anal. Mach. Intell. **30**(11), 2040–2046 (2008)

S.K. Liddell, R.E. Johnson, American sign language. Sign Lang. Stud. **64**, 195–278 (1989)

Y.M. Lui, Human gesture recognition on product manifolds. J. Mach. Learn. Res. **13**(1), 3297–3321 (2012a)

Y.M. Lui, A least squares regression framework on manifolds and its application to gesture recognition, in *Proceedings of the IEEE Computer Society Conference on Computer Vision and Pattern Recognition Workshops*, 2012b, pp. 13–18

U. Mahbub, T. Roy, M.S. Rahman, H. Imtiaz, One-shot-learning gesture recognition using motion history based gesture silhouettes, in *Proceedings of the International Conference on Industrial Application Engineering*, 2013, pp. 186–193

M.R. Malgireddy, I. Inwogu, V. Govindaraju, A temporal Bayesian model for classifying, detecting and localizing activities in video sequences, in *Proceedings of the IEEE Computer Society Conference on Computer Vision and Pattern Recognition Workshops*, 2012, pp. 43–48

M. Maraqa, R. Abu-Zaiter, Recognition of Arabic Sign Language (ArSL) using recurrent neural networks, in *Proceedings of the First International Conference on the Applications of Digital Information and Web Technologies*, 2008, pp. 478–481

T.H.H. Maung, Real-time hand tracking and gesture recognition system using neural networks. World Acad. Sci. Eng. Technol. **50**, 466–470 (2009)

S. Mitra, T. Acharya, Gesture recognition: a survey. IEEE Trans. Syst. Man Cybern. C **37**(3), 311–324 (2007)

S. Mu-Chun, A fuzzy rule-based approach to spatio-temporal hand gesture recognition. IEEE Trans. Syst. Man Cybern. C **30**(2), 276–281 (2000)

K. Nickel, R. Stiefelhagen, Visual recognition of pointing gestures for human-robot interaction. Image Vis. Comput. **25**(12), 1875–1884 (2007)

I. Oikonomidis, N. Kyriazis, A. Argyros, Efficient model-based 3D tracking of hand articulations using Kinect, in *Proceedings of the British Machine Vision Conference*, 2011, pp. 1–11

E.-J. Ong, R. Bowden, A boosted classifier tree for hand shape detection, in *Proceedings of the Sixth IEEE International Conference on Automatic Face and Gesture Recognition*, 2004, pp. 889–894

A. Ramamoorthy, N. Vaswani, S. Chaudhury, S. Banerjee, Recognition of dynamic hand gestures. Pattern Recognit. **36**(9), 2069–2081 (2003)

I. Rauschert, P. Agrawal, R. Sharma, S. Fuhrmann, I. Brewer, A. MacEachren, Designing a human-centered, multimodal GIS interface to support emergency management, in *Proceedings of the 10th ACM International Symposium on Advances in Geographic Information Systems*, 2002, pp. 119–124

Z. Ren, J. Yuan, J. Meng, Z. Zhang, Robust part-based hand gesture recognition using Kinect sensor. IEEE Trans. Multimed. **15**(5), 1110–1120 (2013)

M. Reyes, G. Dominguez, S. Escalera, Feature weighting in dynamic time warping for gesture recognition in depth data, in *Proceedings of the IEEE International Conference on Computer Vision Workshops*, 2011, pp. 1182–1188

Y. Sabinas, E.F. Morales, H.J. Escalante, A one-shot DTW-based method for early gesture recognition, in *Proceedings of 18th Iberoamerican Congress on Progress in Pattern Recognition, Image Analysis, Computer Vision, and Applications*, 2013, pp. 439–446

H.J. Seo, P. Milanfar, Action recognition from one example. IEEE Trans. Pattern Anal. Mach. Intell. **33**(5), 867–882 (2011)

L. Shao, L. Ji, Motion histogram analysis based key frame extraction for human action/activity representation, in *Proceedings of Canadian Conference on Computer and Robot Vision*, 2009, pp. 88–92

J. Shotton, A.W. Fitzgibbon, M. Cook, T. Sharp, M. Finocchio, R. Moore, A. Kipman, A. Blake, Real-time human pose recognition in parts from single depth images, in *Proceedings of the IEEE Conference on Computer Vision and Pattern Recognition*, 2011, pp. 1297–1304

E. Stergiopoulou, N. Papamarkos, Hand gesture recognition using a neural network shape fitting technique. Eng. Appl. Artif. Intell. **22**(8), 1141–1158 (2009)

W.C. Stokoe, Sign language structure: an outline of the visual communication systems of the American deaf. *Studies in Linguistics, Occasional Papers*, 8, 1960

C.P. Vogler, American Sign Language recognition: reducing the complexity of the task with phoneme-based modeling and parallel hidden Markov models, Ph.D. thesis, University of Pennsylvania, 2003

C. Vogler, D. Metaxas, Parallel hidden Markov models for American Sign Language recognition, in *Proceedings of the Seventh IEEE International Conference on Computer Vision*, vol. 1 1999, pp. 116–122

J. Wachs, M. Kolsch, H. Stem, Y. Edan, Vision-based hand-gesture applications. Commun. ACM **54**(2), 60–71 (2011)

J. Wan, Q. Ruan, G. An, W. Li, Gesture recognition based on hidden Markov model from sparse representative observations, in *Proceedings of the IEEE 11th International Conference on Signal Processing*, vol. 2 2012a, pp. 1180–1183

J. Wan, Q. Ruan, G. An, W. Li, Hand tracking and segmentation via graph cuts and dynamic model in sign language videos, in *Proceedings of IEEE 11th International Conference on Signal Processing*, vol. 2 (IEEE, Piscataway, 2012b), pp. 1135–1138

J. Wan, Q. Ruan, W. Li, S. Deng, One-shot learning gesture recognition from RGB-D data using bag of features. J. Mach. Learn. Res. **14**(1), 2549–2582 (2013)

J. Wan, V. Athitsos, P. Jangyodsuk, H.J. Escalante, Q. Ruan, I. Guyon, CSMMI: class-specific maximization of mutual information for action and gesture recognition. IEEE Trans. Image Process. **23**(7), 3152–3165 (2014a)

J. Wan, Q. Ruan, W. Li, G. An, R. Zhao, 3D SMoSIFT: three-dimensional sparse motion scale invariant feature transform for activity recognition from RGB-D videos. J. Electron. Imaging **23**(2), 023017 (2014b)

C. Wang, W. Gao, S. Shan, An approach based on phonemes to large vocabulary Chinese sign language recognition, in *Proceedings of the IEEE Conference on Automatic Face and Gesture Recognition*, 2002, pp. 411–416

J. Wang, Z. Liu, Y. Wu, J. Yuan, Mining actionlet ensemble for action recognition with depth cameras, in *Proceedings of the IEEE Conference on Computer Vision and Pattern Recognition*, 2012, pp. 1290–1297

S.-F. Wong, T.-K. Kim, R. Cipolla, Learning motion categories using both semantic and structural information, in *Proceedings of the IEEE Conference on Computer Vision and Pattern Recognition*, 2007, pp. 1–6

D. Wu, F. Zhu, L. Shao, One shot learning gesture recognition from RGBD images, in *Proceedings of the IEEE Computer Society Conference on Computer Vision and Pattern Recognition Workshops*, 2012a, pp. 7–12

S. Wu, F. Jiang, D. Zhao, S. Liu, W. Gao, Viewpoint-independent hand gesture recognition system, in *Proceedings of the IEEE Conference on Visual Communications and Image Processing*, 2012b, pp. 43–48

M. Zahedi, D. Keysers, H. Ney, Appearance-based recognition of words in american sign language, in *Proceedings of Second Iberian Conference on Pattern recognition and image analysis*, 2005, pp. 511–519

L.-G. Zhang, Y. Chen, G. Fang, X. Chen, W. Gao, A vision-based sign language recognition system using tied-mixture density HMM, in *Proceedings of the 6th International Conference on Multimodal Interfaces*, 2004, pp. 198–204

Chapter 14
Bayesian Co-Boosting for Multi-modal Gesture Recognition

Jiaxiang Wu and Jian Cheng

Abstract With the development of data acquisition equipments, more and more modalities become available for gesture recognition. However, there still exist two critical issues for multi-modal gesture recognition: how to select discriminative features for recognition and how to fuse features from different modalities. In this paper, we propose a novel Bayesian Co-Boosting framework for multi-modal gesture recognition. Inspired by boosting learning and co-training method, our proposed framework combines multiple collaboratively trained weak classifiers to construct the final strong classifier for the recognition task. During each iteration round, we randomly sample a number of feature subsets and estimate weak classifier's parameters for each subset. The optimal weak classifier and its corresponding feature subset are retained for strong classifier construction. Furthermore, we define an upper bound of training error and derive the update rule of instance's weight, which guarantees the error upper bound to be minimized through iterations. For demonstration, we present an implementation of our framework using hidden Markov models as weak classifiers. We perform extensive experiments using the ChaLearn MMGR and ChAirGest datasets, in which our approach achieves 97.63% and 96.53% accuracy respectively on each publicly available dataset.

Keywords Gesture recognition · Bayesian Co-Boosting · Hidden Markov model · Multi-modal fusion · Feature selection

Editor: Sergio Escalera.

J. Wu · J. Cheng (✉)
National Laboratory of Pattern Recognition, Institute of Automation,
Chinese Academy of Sciences, Beijing 100190, China
e-mail: jcheng@nlpr.ia.ac.cn

J. Wu
e-mail: jiaxiang.wu@nlpr.ia.ac.cn

© Springer International Publishing AG 2017
S. Escalera et al. (eds.), *Gesture Recognition*, The Springer Series
on Challenges in Machine Learning, DOI 10.1007/978-3-319-57021-1_14

417

14.1 Introduction

As one of the most natural and intuitive ways for human computer interaction, gesture recognition has been attracting more and more attention from academe and industry. With automatic gesture recognition techniques, one can use his/her hands to freely interact with computers. It has been widely applied to sign language recognition (Zafrulla et al. 2011; Oz and Leu 2011), robot control (Raheja et al. 2010), games (Roccetti et al. 2011), etc. In the early days, accelerometer-based approaches were especially popular for gesture recognition, due to their simpleness and accuracy in data acquirement (Mantyla et al. 2000; Chambers et al. 2002; Pylvänäinen 2005; Liu et al. 2009). As an extension to the accelerometer, the inertial measurement unit (IMU) can be adopted to collect more information, such as linear acceleration and angular acceleration. There are also several IMU-based gesture recognition methods proposed recently (Zhang et al. 2013; Yin and Davis 2013). Nevertheless, the requirement of wearing accelerometers or IMUs limits the applicability of the above approaches. Vision-based approaches, which do not need to wear any extra devices, offer an appealing approach to gesture recognition. However, vision-based approaches are vulnerable to illumination, self-occlusion, and variation of gesture. Moreover, visual feature representation is still an open problem.

As an alternative, depth-aware camera (e.g. Microsoft® Kinect™) can capture RGB image, depth image, and audio, which makes gesture recognition less sensitive to illumination changes, self-occlusion, and can offer strong information for background removal, object detection, and localization in 3D space. With the prevalence of depth-aware camera, the study of gesture recognition is extremely stimulated and multi-modal based approaches are becoming a hot topic. Recently, there are many research works to utilize multiple modalities acquired by depth-aware camera for gesture recognition (Wu et al. 2012; Lui 2012a; Malgireddy et al. 2012; Bayer and Silbermann 2013; Nandakumar et al. 2013; Chen and Koskela 2013). Since 2011, ChaLearn has organized a series of competitions based on the multi-modal gesture data captured by Kinect™. The tasks include one-shot-learning of gestures (Guyon et al. 2012) and continuous gesture spotting and recognition (Escalera et al. 2013). Many of participants achieved satisfactory performances on gesture recognition. However, for multi-modal based approaches, there still exist two critical issues for gesture recognition: how to select discriminative features for recognition, and how to fuse features from different modalities.

In the context of dynamic gesture recognition, an instance is represented by a time series sequence. Most of existing feature extraction methods for time series are mainly based on the self-defined criterion functions to evaluate each feature dimension's contribution (Kashyap 1978; Mörchen 2003; Yoon et al. 2005). For face detection, Viola and Jones (2001, 2004) constructed a strong classifier by selecting a small number of important features using AdaBoost. Foo et al. (2004) and Zhang et al. (2005) employed boosting learning for the single-modal gesture recognition task. However, boosting learning could be prone to be overfitting in practice when training data is rather small. As a late fusion strategy, co-training alternately uses the most confident unlabeled data instance(s) in one modality to assist the model training of another modality, to overcome the problem of insufficient training samples (Blum and Mitchell 1998). Furthermore, Yu et al. (2008, 2011) proposed a Bayesian undirected graphical model interpretation for co-training methods in the context of semi-supervised multi-view learning. These two publications clarified several fundamental assumptions underlying these models and can automatically estimate how much trust should be given to each view so as to accommodate noisy views.

Inspired by boosting and Bayesian co-training methods, we present a novel Bayesian Co-Boosting training framework to realize effectively the multi-modal fusion for gesture recognition task.[1] In our framework, weak classifiers are trained with weighted data instances through multiple iterations. In each iteration round, several feature subsets are randomly generated and weak classifiers are trained on different feature groups. Only the weak classifier, which achieves the minimal training error, together with the corresponding feature subset is retained. Instance's weight is updated according to the classification result given by the weak classifiers of two modalities, so that the difficult instances will gain more focus in the subsequent iterations. The strong classifier is constructed with all retained weak classifiers, and the classification decision is determined by the voting result of all weak classifiers. The weak classifier's voting weight is related to its prediction error on the training set.

The main contributions of this paper are concluded as follows:

1. The proposed framework is illuminated in a Bayesian perspective, and its error upper bound is minimized through iterations, which is guaranteed in theory.
2. Feature selection and multi-modal fusion are naturally embedded into the training process of weak classifiers in each Co-Boosting iteration round and bring significant improvement to the recognition performance.
3. A novel parameter estimation method is presented to address the training problem of hidden Markov model on the weighted dataset.

This paper is organized as follows. In Sect. 14.2, commonly used approaches for gesture recognition is reviewed. We describe our proposed approach and related theoretical derivation in Sect. 14.3. Section 14.4 presents the experimental result of our method, comparing with several state-of-the-art methods. Finally, we conclude our work in Sect. 14.5.

14.2 Related Work

Gesture recognition has been an important research topic in human computer interaction and computer vision field. There already exist a few published surveys in this area, such as Gavrila (1999), Mitra and Acharya (2007), Weinland et al. (2011),

---

[1]Our preliminary work of multi-modal fusion on ChaLearn MMGR challenge 2013 achieved the 1st prize on gesture recognition (Wu et al. 2013).

and Suarez and Murphy (2012). As concluded in these literatures, classifiers commonly used in gesture recognition include k-nearest neighbours (Malassiotis et al. 2002), hidden Markov model (Eickeler et al. 1998), finite state machine (Yeasin and Chaudhuri 2000), neural network (Yang and Ahuja 2001), and support vector machine (Biswas and Basu 2011).

Gesture recognition based on accelerometers has been investigated by many researchers (Mantyla et al. 2000; Chambers et al. 2002; Pylvänäinen 2005; Liu et al. 2009). As an extension to the accelerometer sensors, the applications of inertial measurement unit (IMU) have also been explored recently. Ruffieux et al. (2013) collected a benchmark dataset with Kinect™ and XSens IMU sensors for the development and evaluation of multi-modal gesture spotting and recognition algorithms. With this dataset, Yin and Davis (2013) presented a hand tracking method based on gesture salience, and concatenated hidden Markov models were applied to perform gesture spotting and recognition.

Considering the inconvenience of wearing accelerometers or IMUs while performing gestures, it is more natural to develop vision-based gesture recognition systems. Single or stereo camera is mostly widely used in research, but Kinect™ sensor has been attracting increasing interest, due to its ability to capture both color and depth images simultaneously. ChaLearn has organized several competitions focused on the Kinect™-based gesture recognition ever since 2011 (Guyon et al. 2012; Escalera et al. 2013).

Approaches based on hidden Markov model (HMM) are widely adopted in vision-based gesture recognition. Elmezain et al. (2008) applied HMM to recognize isolated and continuous gestures in real-time. Spatio-temporal trajectories were converted to orientation dynamic features and then quantized to one of the codewords. The quantized observation sequence was then used to inference the hidden gesture label. Gaus et al. (2013) compared the recognition performance given by both fixed state HMM and variable state HMM. In Nandakumar et al. (2013), gesture instances in the continuous data stream were segmented using both audio and hand joint information. Three modalities were used for classification: HMM classifier for MFCC[2] feature extracted from audio signal, and SVM (support vector machine) classifier for both RGB (STIP feature) and skeleton (covariance descriptor). Wu et al. (2013) performed automatic gesture detection based on the endpoint detection result in the audio data stream. HMM classifiers were then applied to both audio and skeleton features, and a late fusion strategy was employed to make the final classification decision.

In order to enhance the recognition performance of HMM-based approaches, ensemble learning, especially AdaBoost, has been embedded into the training process of hidden Markov models in a few researches. Adaptive boosting (Freund and Schapire 1995; Yoav and Robert 1997) is a training framework to generate multiple

---

[2]MFCC: Mel-Frequency Cepstral Coefficients (Zheng et al. 2001), a common used audio feature for speech recognition. The feature extraction process is as follows: (a) the signal segment is turned into frequency domain using Discrete Fourier Transform; (b) the short-term power spectrum is warped into the Mel-frequency; (c) the warped power spectrum is convolved with the triangular band-pass filter; (d) the MFCC feature is the Discrete Cosine Transform result of the convolved power spectrum.

weak classifiers with different training instances' weight distribution, and construct a strong classifier with these weak classifiers to achieve a better classification performance. Foo et al. (2004) proposed a novel AdaBoost-HMM classifier to boost the recognition of visual speech elements. Weak classifiers were trained using biased Baum-Welch algorithm under the AdaBoost framework to cover different groups of training instances. Their decisions on the unlabeled instance were combined following a novel probability synthesis rule to obtain the final decision. In Zhang et al. (2005), a similar approach was applied in the application of sign language recognition. However, both researches neglected the potential noisy dimensions in the feature space, which could cause the deterioration of recognition performance.

Besides HMM-based approaches, there are also many other methods proposed in the context of vision-based gesture recognition. In Lui et al. (2010) and Lui (2012b), action videos were factorized using higher order singular value decomposition (HOSVD) and the classification was performed based on the geodesic distance on the product manifold. Boyali and Kavakli (2012) proposed a variant version of sparse representation based classification (innovated by Wright et al. 2009; Wagner et al. 2009) for gesture recognition. For a more complete overview of commonly used approaches in gesture recognition, we recommend the survey papers mentioned at the beginning of this section.

14.3 Bayesian Co-Boosting with Hidden Markov Model

For multi-modal gesture recognition task, fusion of features from different modalities is one of the most vital problems. Many existing approaches use a simple weighted-based fusion strategy (Bayer and Silbermann 2013; Nandakumar et al. 2013). However, this weight coefficient usually needs to be empirically tuned, which is rather difficult if not impossible on large-scale dataset. As we mentioned before, Bayesian co-training (Yu et al. 2008, 2011) can automatically determine each view's confidence score, which inspired us to adopt a similar approach to fuse multiple modalities. Boosting learning can perform feature selection through training multiple weak classifiers, and can be used in gesture recognition to select optimal feature dimensions for the classification problem.

In this section, we introduce a novel Bayesian Co-Boosting training framework for combining multiple hidden Markov model classifiers for multi-modal gesture recognition. Based on the proposed Bayesian Co-Boosting framework, different modalities are naturally combined together and can provide complementary information for each other. We also analyze the minimization of the error upper bound so as to derive the update rule of instance's weight in Co-Boosting process.

14.3.1 Model Learning

In the task of multi-modal gesture recognition, two or more modalities (in this paper, we constraint the amount of modalities to be two) are simultaneously available for describing gesture instances. Based on the raw data of each modality, a time series sequence of feature vectors can be extracted according to certain feature extraction procedures. This time series sequence data is then used as the input to the pre-trained classifier for model training and evaluation.

The most straightforward approach to this problem is to separately train a classifier for each modality, and then combine their classification results in a late fusion style. However, this approach will bring the following issues. First, feature vectors may contain noisy data dimensions, which will lead to deterioration of classification performance. Second, one classifier for one modality may not be sufficient to achieve a satisfying classification accuracy level. Third, the fusion weights of different classifiers, which have significant impact on the final classification result, are difficult to be tuned manually.

In this paper, we propose an approach to solve all these problems together. Under the Co-Boosting framework, multiple weak classifiers of each modality are trained through a number of iterations. The final strong classifier is a linear combination of these weak classifiers, and each classifier's weight is determined by its prediction error on the training dataset. Figure 14.1 depicts the work flow of our proposed method, and Algorithm 1 describes the detailed procedures in the model training process.

The aim of our proposed Bayesian Co-Boosting framework is to generate a strong classifier for the multi-modal gesture recognition task. As we can see in Fig. 14.1, the resulting strong classifier $H(x_i)$ is the combination of multiple weak classifiers trained on V different modalities through T iterations. In each iteration round, M_v candidate weak classifiers are trained on the v-th modality using different feature

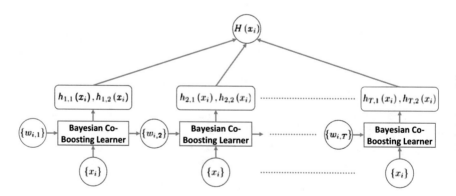

Fig. 14.1 Work flow of Bayesian Co-Boosting training framework.
x_i: training instance; $w_{i,t}$: training instance x_i's weight at the t-th iteration; $h_{t,v}(x_i)$: weak classifier learnt from modality v at the t-th iteration; $H(x_i)$: final strong classifier

dimension subsets, and the best candidate among them is selected as the optimal weak classifier $h_{t,v}^*(x_i)$. The optimal weak classifier is the one which achieves the minimal training error among all candidate weak classifiers for modality v. Then we use all these selected weak classifiers (one weak classifier per modality) obtained at this iteration round to update each training instance's weight.

In the rest of this section, we firstly introduce the training process of a single weak classifier with weighted instances. Secondly, we derive the update rule of the instance's weight to minimize the training error's upper bound from a Bayesian perspective. The construction of the strong classifier $H(x_i)$ is described at the end of this section.

Algorithm 1 Bayesian Co-Boosting Training Framework.[3]

Input: training instances $\{x_i\}$
Output: strong classifier $H(x_i)$
1: initialize data weight distribution $\{w_i\}$
2: **for** $t = 1, \ldots, T$ **do**
3:   **for** $v = 1, \ldots, V$ **do**
4:     **for** $m = 1, \ldots, M_v$ **do**
5:       randomly generate feature subset $\tilde{F}_{t,v,m} \subset F_v, |\tilde{F}_{t,v,m}| = \lambda_v \cdot |F_v|$
6:       generate training dataset $\{(\tilde{x}_i, w_i)\}$ with feature dimensions in $\tilde{F}_{t,v,m}$
7:       train candidate weak classifier $h_{t,v,m}(x_i)$ (refer to Algorithm 2)
8:       calculate classifier's training error $\varepsilon_{t,v,m}$
9:     **end for**
10:     select optimal candidate weak classifier $h_{t,v}^*(x_i)$ and feature subset $\tilde{F}_{t,v}^*$
11:     calculate weak classifier's voting weight $\alpha_{t,v}^*$
12:   **end for**
13:   update instances' weights $\{w_i\}$ (refer to Algorithm 3)
14: **end for**
15: construct strong classifier $H(x_i)$

14.3.1.1 Weak Classifier Training

As we concluded in Sect. 14.2, hidden Markov[3] model is one of the most commonly used classifiers in gesture recognition. Therefore, in this paper, we implement the Bayesian Co-Boosting training framework with HMM-based weak classifiers embedded. However, other weak classifiers can also be easily adopted in our framework.

Hidden Markov model is a statistical model based on Markov process, in which the generation of an observation sequence is modeled as the result of a series of unobserved state transitions (Rabiner 1989). In order to deal with continuous observation

---

[3] T: the number of Co-Boosting iteration rounds; V: the number of modalities; M_v: the number of candidate weak classifiers for modality v; F_v: all available feature dimensions for modality v; λ_v: the feature dimension selection ratio for modality v.

vectors, a multi-variate Gaussian distribution is adopted to determine the observation probability of each observation-state pair. To simplify the subsequent analysis, we define the following symbols:

$x_{i,1:T_i}$: observation sequence of length T_i, composed of feature vectors $x_{i,t}$.
$z_{i,1:T_i}$: state transition sequence; $z_{i,t} \in \{1, \ldots, K\}$, K is the number of states.
$\mathscr{D}$: the training dataset consists of N observation sequences $x_{i,1:T_i}$.
π_k: initial state probability, $\pi_k = P(z_{i,1} = k)$.
$A_{j,k}$: state transition probability, $A_{j,k} = P(z_{i,t+1} = k | z_{i,t} = j)$.
μ_k, Σ_k: mean vector and covariance matrix, $P(x_{i,t} | z_{i,t} = k) = \mathcal{N}(x_{i,t} | \mu_k, \Sigma_k)$.

For multiple-class classification problem in gesture recognition, a hidden Markov model is trained for each gesture class, with its parameters denoted as θ_c. The resulting classifier is denoted as

$$\hat{y}_i = \arg\max_c P(x_i | \theta_c)$$

where $x_i = x_{i,1:T_i}$ is the unlabeled gesture instance. $P(x_i | \theta_c)$ measures the probability for model θ_c generating observation sequence x_i and can be rewritten as

$$P(x_i | \theta_c) = \sum_{z_i} P(x_i, z_i | \theta_c)$$

where the full data probability $P(x_i, z_i | \theta_c)$ is given by

$$P(x_i, z_i | \theta_c) = P(z_i | \theta_c) P(x_i | z_i, \theta_c)$$
$$= \pi_{z_{i,1}} \prod_{t=1}^{T-1} A_{z_{i,t}, z_{i,t+1}} \prod_{t=1}^{T} \mathcal{N}(x_{i,t} | \mu_{z_{i,t}}, \Sigma_{z_{i,t}})$$

For the parameter estimation problem of HMM, commonly used Baum-Welch algorithm (a variation of EM algorithm) can only deal with unweighted training instances. In boosting learning, however, instances are assigned with different weights, which are adjusted at the end of each iteration round to guide the subsequent weak classifiers focus on more difficult instances. Hence, we need to extend the standard Baum-Welch algorithm (Murphy 2012) to accommodate the weighted instances' training problem in our approach. Our proposed parameter estimation method is also based on the EM algorithm.

Given the weighted training dataset $\{(x_i, w_i)\}$, parameter estimation problem is to find the optimal parameters that maximize the log likelihood of the observed data, which is defined as

$$\ell(\theta) = \sum_{i=1}^{N} w_i \log P(x_i | \theta) = \sum_{i=1}^{N} w_i \log \left[\sum_{z_i} P(x_i, z_i | \theta) \right]$$

But this is difficult to optimize, since the log cannot be pushed inside the sum. To get around this problem, we define the complete data log likelihood as

$$\ell_c(\theta) = \sum_{i=1}^{N} w_i \log P\left(x_i, z_i^* | \theta\right)$$

where z_i^* is the optimal state transition sequence, and is inferred with Viterbi algorithm.

Therefore, the expected complete data log likelihood for dataset $\mathscr{D}$ is given by

$$Q\left(\theta, \theta_{\text{old}}\right) = \mathscr{E}\left[\ell_c(\theta) | \mathscr{D}, \theta_{\text{old}}\right] \tag{14.1}$$

and the optimal parameters are estimated by maximizing this.

On the basis of the definition of $P\left(x_i, z_i | \theta_c\right)$, Eq. (14.1) can be rewritten as

$$
\begin{aligned}
Q\left(\theta, \theta_{\text{old}}\right) &= \mathscr{E}\left[\sum_{i=1}^{N} w_i \log P\left(x_i, z_i^* | \theta\right)\right] \\
&= \sum_{i=1}^{N} w_i \mathscr{E}\left[\log \prod_{z_i} P\left(x_i, z_i | \theta\right)^{\mathscr{I}\left(z_i^* = z_i\right)}\right] \\
&= \sum_{i=1}^{N} w_i \sum_{z_i} \mathscr{E}\left[\mathscr{I}\left(z_i^* = z_i\right)\right] \log P\left(x_i, z_i | \theta\right) \\
&= \sum_{i=1}^{N} \sum_{k=1}^{K} w_i P\left(z_{i,1}^* = k | x_i, \theta_{t-1}\right) \log \pi_k \\
&\quad + \sum_{i=1}^{N} \sum_{j=1}^{K} \sum_{k=1}^{K} \sum_{t=1}^{T_i-1} w_i P\left(z_{i,t}^* = j, z_{i,t+1}^* = k | x_i, \theta_{t-1}\right) \log A_{j,k} \\
&\quad + \sum_{i=1}^{N} \sum_{k=1}^{K} \sum_{t=1}^{T_i} w_i P\left(z_{i,t}^* = k | x_i, \theta_{t-1}\right) \log P\left(x_{i,t} | z_{i,t} = k\right)
\end{aligned}
$$

In the E step of EM algorithm, we firstly compute two groups of probabilities with forward-backward algorithm, as describe in Murphy (2012)

$$
\begin{aligned}
\gamma_{i,t}(k) &= P\left(z_{i,t} = k | x_i, \theta_{t-1}\right) \\
\xi_{i,t}(j,k) &= P\left(z_{i,t} = j, z_{i,t+1} = k | x_i, \theta_{t-1}\right)
\end{aligned} \tag{14.2}
$$

where $\gamma_{i,t}(k)$ indicates the probability of the hidden state at time t being state k, and $\xi_{i,t}(j,k)$ represents the probability of the hidden state being state j at time t and state k at time $(t+1)$. Based on these probabilities, we compute the following expectation items

$$\mathcal{E}\left[N_k^1\right] = \sum_{i=1}^{N} w_i \gamma_{i,1}(k)$$

$$\mathcal{E}\left[N_{j,k}\right] = \sum_{i=1}^{N} \sum_{t=1}^{T_i-1} w_i \xi_{i,t}(j,k)$$

$$\mathcal{E}[N_k] = \sum_{i=1}^{N} \sum_{t=1}^{T_i} w_i \gamma_{i,t}(k) \qquad (14.3)$$

$$\mathcal{E}[\bar{x}_k] = \sum_{i=1}^{N} \sum_{t=1}^{T_i} w_i \gamma_{i,t}(k) x_{i,t}$$

$$\mathcal{E}\left[\bar{x}_k \bar{x}_k^T\right] = \sum_{i=1}^{N} \sum_{t=1}^{T_i} w_i \gamma_{i,t}(k) x_{i,t} x_{i,t}^T$$

In the M step, parameters are updated so that $Q(\theta, \theta_{\text{old}})$ is maximized. Here, we only present the final update rule for each parameter, due to the limitation of space

$$\hat{\pi}_k = \frac{\mathcal{E}\left[N_k^1\right]}{\sum_{k'=1}^{K} \mathcal{E}\left[N_{k'}^1\right]}$$

$$\hat{A}_{j,k} = \frac{\mathcal{E}\left[N_{j,k}\right]}{\sum_{k'=1}^{K} \mathcal{E}\left[N_{j,k'}\right]}$$

$$\hat{\mu}_k = \frac{\mathcal{E}[\bar{x}_k]}{\mathcal{E}[N_k]} \qquad (14.4)$$

$$\hat{\Sigma}_k = \frac{\mathcal{E}\left[\bar{x}_k \bar{x}_k^T\right]}{\mathcal{E}[N_k]} - \hat{\mu}_k \hat{\mu}_k^T$$

The training procedure of weak classifier is demonstrated in Algorithm 2.

Algorithm 2 Weak Classifier Training

Input: weighted training instances $\{(x_i, w_i)\}$
Output: weak classifier $h(x_i)$
1: **for** $c = 1, \ldots, C$ **do**
2:   initialize model parameters θ_c
3:   **for** $t = 1, \ldots, T$ **do**
4:     initialize expectation items
5:     **for** $i = 1, \ldots, N$ **do**
6:       compute $\gamma_{i,t}(k)$, $\xi_{i,t}(j,k)$ according to Equation (14.2)
7:       update expectation items according to Equation (14.3)
8:     **end for**
9:     compute $\theta_c = \left\{\hat{\pi}_k, \hat{A}_{j,k}, \hat{\mu}_k, \hat{\Sigma}_k\right\}$ according to Equation (14.4)
10:   **end for**
11: **end for**
12: construct weak classifier $h(x_i) = \arg\max_c P(x_i|\theta_c)$

14.3.1.2 Instance's Weight Updating

In this sub-section, we define the training error for instances in each class, together with its upper bound to simplify the error minimization formulation. Based on this formulation, we derive the update rule for instance's weight in our proposed framework.

In the t-th iteration round of Bayesian Co-Boosting training process, the training error for class c is denoted by $E_{t,c}$, and the corresponding error upper bound is denoted by $B_{t,c}$.

We define the random variable $z_i \in \{1, \ldots, C\}$ to represent the hidden label for observation x_i. The binary prediction value for each candidate class of the strong classifier is determined by

$$H_{t,c}(x_i) = sgn\left(P_{t,c,i} > \bar{P}_{t,c,i}\right) = \begin{cases} +1, & P_{t,c,i} > \bar{P}_{t,c,i} \\ -1, & P_{t,c,i} \le \bar{P}_{t,c,i} \end{cases}$$

where

$$P_{t,c,i} = P\left(z_i = c | h_{1,1}(x_i), h_{1,2}(x_i), \ldots, h_{t,1}(x_i), h_{t,2}(x_i)\right)$$
$$\bar{P}_{t,c,i} = P\left(z_i \ne c | h_{1,1}(x_i), h_{1,2}(x_i), \ldots, h_{t,1}(x_i), h_{t,2}(x_i)\right)$$

and $h_{*,*}(x_i) \in \{1, \ldots, C\}$ represents the predicted class label of weak classifier.

The training error $E_{t,c}$ is defined as the sum of $0 - 1$ loss of classifier's binary predictions for the c-th class, which is

$$E_{t,c} = \sum_{i:y_i=c} \infty\left(H_{t,c}(x_i) \ne 1\right) + \sum_{i:y_i \ne c} \infty\left(H_{t,c}(x_i) = 1\right) \tag{14.5}$$

where function $\infty(\cdot)$ equals to 1 when the inner expression is true; otherwise, its value is 0.

The error upper bound $B_{t,c}$ is given by

$$B_{t,c} = \sum_{i=1}^{N} \left(\frac{\bar{P}_{t,c,i}}{P_{t,c,i}}\right)^{sgn(y_i=c)} = \sum_{i:y_i=c} \frac{\bar{P}_{t,c,i}}{P_{t,c,i}} + \sum_{i:y_i \ne c} \frac{P_{t,c,i}}{\bar{P}_{t,c,i}} \tag{14.6}$$

Theorem 1 $E_{t,c} \le B_{t,c}$ *always holds with definitions in Eqs. (14.5) and (14.6).*

Proof For each training instance x_i, we consider its training error $E_{t,c,i}$ and the corresponding upper bound $B_{t,c,i}$. It surely falls into one of the following conditions:

(1) $H_{t,c}(x_i) = 1$, $y_i = c$: Based on the definition of $H_{t,c}(x_i)$, we have $P_{t,i,c} > \bar{P}_{t,i,c}$. Since $E_{t,c,i} = 0$, $B_{t,c,i} = \bar{P}_{t,i,c}/P_{t,i,c} \in [0, 1)$, thus $E_{t,c,i} \le B_{t,c,i}$.
(2) $H_{t,c}(x_i) = 1$, $y_i \ne c$: Based on the definition of $H_{t,c}(x_i)$, we have $P_{t,i,c} > \bar{P}_{t,i,c}$. Since $E_{t,c,i} = 1$, $B_{t,c,i} = P_{t,i,c}/\bar{P}_{t,i,c} \in [1, +\infty)$, thus $E_{t,c,i} \le B_{t,c,i}$.
(3) $H_{t,c}(x_i) \ne 1$, $y_i = c$: Based on the definition of $H_{t,c}(x_i)$, we have $P_{t,i,c} \le \bar{P}_{t,i,c}$. Since $E_{t,c,i} = 1$, $B_{t,c,i} = \bar{P}_{t,i,c}/P_{t,i,c} \in [1, +\infty)$, thus $E_{t,c,i} \le B_{t,c,i}$.

(4) $H_{t,c}(x_i) \neq 1$, $y_i \neq c$: Based on the definition of $H_{t,c}(x_i)$, we have $P_{t,i,c} \leq \bar{P}_{t,i,c}$. Since $E_{t,c,i} = 0$, $B_{t,c,i} = P_{t,i,c}/\bar{P}_{t,i,c} \in [0, 1)$, thus $E_{t,c,i} \leq B_{t,c,i}$.

Therefore, $E_{t,c,i} \leq B_{t,c,i}$ holds for every instance x_i; hence, $E_{t,c} \leq B_{t,c}$ is proved. ∎

In the Co-Boosting training process, the weight of each training instance should reflect the difficulty for current weak classifiers to correctly classify it. Hence, instance's weight can be determined by

$$w_i = \frac{\bar{P}_{t,y_i,i}}{P_{t,y_i,i}} \tag{14.7}$$

Now we derive the update rule of training instance's weight so as to minimize the error upper bound $B_{t,c}$ through iterations, from a Bayesian perspective.

Based on the definition of $P_{t,c,i}$, we have

$$
\begin{aligned}
P_{t,c,i} &= P\left(z_i = c | h_{1,1}, h_{1,2}, \ldots, h_{t,1}, h_{t,2}\right) \\
&= \frac{P\left(z_i = c, h_{1,1}, h_{1,2}, \ldots, h_{t,1}, h_{t,2}\right)}{P\left(h_{1,1}, h_{1,2}, \ldots, h_{t,1}, h_{t,2}\right)} \\
&= \frac{P\left(z_i = c, h_{1,1}, h_{1,2}, \ldots, h_{t-1,1}, h_{t-1,2}\right)}{P\left(h_{1,1}, h_{1,2}, \ldots, h_{t-1,1}, h_{t-1,2}\right)} \cdot \frac{P\left(h_{t,1} | z_i = c\right) P\left(h_{t,2} | z_i = c\right)}{P\left(h_{t,1}, h_{t,2} | h_{1,1}, h_{1,2}, \ldots, h_{t-1,1}, h_{t-1,2}\right)} \\
&= P_{t-1,c,i} \cdot \frac{P\left(h_{t,1} | z_i = c\right) P\left(h_{t,2} | z_i = c\right)}{P\left(h_{t,1}, h_{t,2} | h_{1,1}, h_{1,2}, \ldots, h_{t-1,1}, h_{t-1,2}\right)}
\end{aligned}
$$

in which $h_{*,*} = h_{*,*}(x_i)$ is the predicted class label given by the weak classifier. Similarly, we can derive the update equation for $\bar{P}_{t,c,i}$

$$\bar{P}_{t,c,i} = \bar{P}_{t-1,c,i} \cdot \frac{P\left(h_{t,1} | z_i \neq c\right) P\left(h_{t,2} | z_i \neq c\right)}{P\left(h_{t,1}, h_{t,2} | h_{1,1}, h_{1,2}, \ldots, h_{t-1,1}, h_{t-1,2}\right)}$$

Therefore, the ratio between $\bar{P}_{t,c,i}$ and $P_{t,c,i}$ can be rewritten as

$$\frac{\bar{P}_{t,c,i}}{P_{t,c,i}} = \frac{\bar{P}_{t-1,c,i} \cdot P\left(h_{t,1} | z_i \neq c\right) P\left(h_{t,2} | z_i \neq c\right)}{P_{t-1,c,i} \cdot P\left(h_{t,1} | z_i = c\right) P\left(h_{t,2} | z_i = c\right)} \tag{14.8}$$

In order to simplify the following theoretical derivation, we define these symbols

$$
\begin{aligned}
P_{c,1} &= P\left(h_{t,1} = c | z_i = c\right), \quad P_{c,2} = P\left(h_{t,1} = c | z_i \neq c\right) \\
P_{c,3} &= P\left(h_{t,1} \neq c | z_i = c\right), \quad P_{c,4} = P\left(h_{t,1} \neq c | z_i \neq c\right) \\
Q_{c,1} &= P\left(h_{t,2} = c | z_i = c\right), \quad Q_{c,2} = P\left(h_{t,2} = c | z_i \neq c\right) \\
Q_{c,3} &= P\left(h_{t,2} \neq c | z_i = c\right), \quad Q_{c,4} = P\left(h_{t,2} \neq c | z_i \neq c\right)
\end{aligned}
\tag{14.9}
$$

For each instance x_i, considering whether its ground-truth label y_i and predicted label $h_{t,1}$, $h_{t,2}$ is equal to c or not, we can assign it into one of the following subsets

$$\mathcal{D}_1 = \{x_i | h_{t,1} = c, h_{t,2} = c, y_i = c\}, \ \mathcal{D}_2 = \{x_i | h_{t,1} = c, h_{t,2} = c, y_i \neq c\}$$
$$\mathcal{D}_3 = \{x_i | h_{t,1} = c, h_{t,2} \neq c, y_i = c\}, \ \mathcal{D}_4 = \{x_i | h_{t,1} = c, h_{t,2} \neq c, y_i \neq c\}$$
$$\mathcal{D}_5 = \{x_i | h_{t,1} \neq c, h_{t,2} = c, y_i = c\}, \ \mathcal{D}_6 = \{x_i | h_{t,1} \neq c, h_{t,2} = c, y_i \neq c\}$$
$$\mathcal{D}_7 = \{x_i | h_{t,1} \neq c, h_{t,2} \neq c, y_i = c\}, \ \mathcal{D}_8 = \{x_i | h_{t,1} \neq c, h_{t,2} \neq c, y_i \neq c\}$$

$$(14.10)$$

On the basis of the above data partitioning, $B_{t,c}$ can be expanded as

$$
\begin{aligned}
B_{t,c} &= \sum_{i:y_i=c} \frac{\bar{P}_{t,c,i}}{P_{t,c,i}} + \sum_{i:y_i \neq c} \frac{P_{t,c,i}}{\bar{P}_{t,c,i}} \\
&= \sum_{i:x_i \in \mathcal{D}_1} \frac{\bar{P}_{t-1,c,i} P_{c,2} Q_{c,2}}{P_{t-1,c,i} P_{c,1} Q_{c,1}} + \sum_{i:x_i \in \mathcal{D}_2} \frac{P_{t-1,c,i} P_{c,1} Q_{c,1}}{\bar{P}_{t-1,c,i} P_{c,2} Q_{c,2}} \\
&\quad + \sum_{i:x_i \in \mathcal{D}_3} \frac{\bar{P}_{t-1,c,i} P_{c,2} Q_{c,4}}{P_{t-1,c,i} P_{c,1} Q_{c,3}} + \sum_{i:x_i \in \mathcal{D}_4} \frac{P_{t-1,c,i} P_{c,1} Q_{c,3}}{\bar{P}_{t-1,c,i} P_{c,2} Q_{c,4}} \\
&\quad + \sum_{i:x_i \in \mathcal{D}_5} \frac{\bar{P}_{t-1,c,i} P_{c,4} Q_{c,2}}{P_{t-1,c,i} P_{c,3} Q_{c,1}} + \sum_{i:x_i \in \mathcal{D}_6} \frac{P_{t-1,c,i} P_{c,3} Q_{c,1}}{\bar{P}_{t-1,c,i} P_{c,4} Q_{c,2}} \\
&\quad + \sum_{i:x_i \in \mathcal{D}_7} \frac{\bar{P}_{t-1,c,i} P_{c,4} Q_{c,4}}{P_{t-1,c,i} P_{c,3} Q_{c,3}} + \sum_{i:x_i \in \mathcal{D}_8} \frac{P_{t-1,c,i} P_{c,3} Q_{c,3}}{\bar{P}_{t-1,c,i} P_{c,4} Q_{c,4}}
\end{aligned}
$$

To simplify the expression, we define

$$\alpha_1 = \frac{P_{c,1}}{P_{c,2}}, \alpha_2 = \frac{P_{c,3}}{P_{c,4}}, \alpha_3 = \frac{Q_{c,1}}{Q_{c,2}}, \alpha_4 = \frac{Q_{c,3}}{Q_{c,4}} \qquad (14.11)$$

$$S_1 = \sum_{i:x_i \in \mathcal{D}_1} \frac{\bar{P}_{t-1,c,i}}{P_{t-1,c,i}}, \ S_2 = \sum_{i:x_i \in \mathcal{D}_2} \frac{P_{t-1,c,i}}{\bar{P}_{t-1,c,i}}, \ S_3 = \sum_{i:x_i \in \mathcal{D}_3} \frac{\bar{P}_{t-1,c,i}}{P_{t-1,c,i}}, \ S_4 = \sum_{i:x_i \in \mathcal{D}_4} \frac{P_{t-1,c,i}}{\bar{P}_{t-1,c,i}}$$

$$S_5 = \sum_{i:x_i \in \mathcal{D}_5} \frac{\bar{P}_{t-1,c,i}}{P_{t-1,c,i}}, \ S_6 = \sum_{i:x_i \in \mathcal{D}_6} \frac{P_{t-1,c,i}}{\bar{P}_{t-1,c,i}}, \ S_7 = \sum_{i:x_i \in \mathcal{D}_7} \frac{\bar{P}_{t-1,c,i}}{P_{t-1,c,i}}, \ S_8 = \sum_{i:x_i \in \mathcal{D}_8} \frac{P_{t-1,c,i}}{\bar{P}_{t-1,c,i}}$$

$$(14.12)$$

where $\alpha_k, k = 1, \ldots 4$ are unknown variables and $S_k, k = 1, \ldots, 8$ can be computed with weak classifier's prediction. Then we rewrite $B_{t,c}$ as

$$
\begin{aligned}
B_{t,c} &= \frac{S_1}{\alpha_1 \alpha_3} + S_2 \cdot \alpha_1 \alpha_3 + \frac{S_3}{\alpha_1 \alpha_4} + S_4 \cdot \alpha_1 \alpha_4 \\
&\quad + \frac{S_5}{\alpha_2 \alpha_3} + S_6 \cdot \alpha_2 \alpha_3 + \frac{S_7}{\alpha_2 \alpha_4} + S_8 \cdot \alpha_2 \alpha_4
\end{aligned}
$$

The partial derivatives of $B_{t,c}$ for the unknown variables $\alpha_{1:4}$ are

$$\frac{\partial B_{t,c}}{\partial \alpha_1} = -\frac{S_1}{\alpha_1^2 \alpha_3} + S_2 \cdot \alpha_3 - \frac{S_3}{\alpha_1^2 \alpha_4} + S_4 \cdot \alpha_4$$

$$\frac{\partial B_{t,c}}{\partial \alpha_2} = -\frac{S_5}{\alpha_2^2 \alpha_3} + S_6 \cdot \alpha_3 - \frac{S_7}{\alpha_2^2 \alpha_4} + S_8 \cdot \alpha_4$$

$$\frac{\partial B_{t,c}}{\partial \alpha_3} = -\frac{S_1}{\alpha_1 \alpha_3^2} + S_2 \cdot \alpha_1 - \frac{S_5}{\alpha_2 \alpha_3^2} + S_6 \cdot \alpha_2 \qquad (14.13)$$

$$\frac{\partial B_{t,c}}{\partial \alpha_4} = -\frac{S_3}{\alpha_1 \alpha_4^2} + S_4 \cdot \alpha_1 - \frac{S_7}{\alpha_2 \alpha_4^2} + S_8 \cdot \alpha_2$$

The optimal values of α_k should ensure that all partial derivatives in Eq. (14.13) are equal to 0. Therefore, we obtain the following equations

$$\alpha_1 = \sqrt{\frac{S_1/\alpha_3 + S_3/\alpha_4}{S_2 \cdot \alpha_3 + S_4 \cdot \alpha_4}}, \alpha_2 = \sqrt{\frac{S_5/\alpha_3 + S_7/\alpha_4}{S_6 \cdot \alpha_3 + S_8 \cdot \alpha_4}}$$

$$\alpha_3 = \sqrt{\frac{S_1/\alpha_1 + S_5/\alpha_2}{S_2 \cdot \alpha_1 + S_6 \cdot \alpha_2}}, \alpha_4 = \sqrt{\frac{S_3/\alpha_1 + S_7/\alpha_2}{S_4 \cdot \alpha_1 + S_8 \cdot \alpha_2}} \qquad (14.14)$$

and α_k can be solved within a few iterations (less than 10 rounds for most conditions, according to our experimental results).

Based on the definitions in Eq. (14.9), it is obvious that

$$P_{c,1} + P_{c,3} = 1, \ P_{c,2} + P_{c,4} = 1$$
$$Q_{c,1} + Q_{c,3} = 1, \ Q_{c,2} + Q_{c,4} = 1 \qquad (14.15)$$

and these eight variables can be solved after all α_k are obtained.

Based on the above analysis for training error minimization, the detailed algorithm for multiple weak classifiers training is concluded in Algorithm 3.

Algorithm 3 Instance's Weight Updating

Input: training instances $\{x_i\}$
Input: instances' weight $\{w_{i,t-1}\}$
Input: weak classifiers $h_{t,1}(x_i)$, $h_{t,2}(x_i)$
Output: updated instances' weight $\{w_{i,t}\}$
1: **for** $c = 1, \ldots, C$ **do**
2:   assign instances into $\mathcal{D}_k$ according to Equation (14.10)
3:   compute S_k according to Equation (14.12)
4:   compute α_k according to Equation (14.14)
5:   compute $P_{c,k}$, $Q_{c,k}$ according to Equation (14.11) and (14.15)
6:   **for** instance x_i in the c-th class **do**
7:     compute $P_{t,c,i}$, $\bar{P}_{t,c,i}$ according to Equation (14.8)
8:     compute $w_{i,t}$ according to Equation (14.7)
9:   **end for**
10: **end for**

14.3.2 Class Label Inference

In our multi-modal gesture recognition system, the predicted class label of unclassi-fied instance is determined by the voting result of all weak classifiers.

For the optimal weak classifier $h_{t,v}^*(x_i)$ with training error $\varepsilon_{t,v}^*$, the classifier weight is defined as

$$\alpha_{t,v}^* = \log \frac{1 - \varepsilon_{t,v}^*}{\varepsilon_{t,v}^*}$$

where the training error is calculated by

$$\varepsilon_{t,v}^* = \sum_{c=1}^{C} \sum_{i:y_i=c} w_i \cdot \infty \left\{ h_{t,v}^*(x_i) \neq c \right\}$$

The final prediction of instance's class label is determined by

$$H(x_i) = \arg \max_c \sum_{t=1}^{T} \sum_{v=1}^{2} \alpha_{t,v}^* \infty \{ h_{t,v}^*(x_i) = c \}$$

14.4 Experimental Results

In this section, experiments are carried out on two multi-modal gesture recognition datasets, to prove the effectiveness of our proposed Bayesian Co-Boosting training framework. On the basis of comparative results of different training algorithms, the main contributing elements to our improvement on classification accuracy are also analyzed.

14.4.1 Baseline Methods Description

The training framework we propose in this paper is a general model, and some state-of-the-art methods can be considered as the special cases of our framework. The key parameters controlling the complexity of training process are T (number of iterations), V (number of modalities), and M_v (number of feature subset candi-dates). Various approaches can be obtained with different combinations of these three parameters.

If we set $T = 1$, then model is trained without boosting learning. Many approaches using a single HMM to model instances from one gesture class can be categorized into this case.

If we set $V = 1$, then the classifier is actually trained with only one feature modality. During iterations, feature selection procedure remains unchanged, but the update rule of instance's weight no longer applies. In this case, an instance's weight can be updated in a similar way as described in Viola and Jones (2004).

If we set $M_v = 1$ for each modality, the feature selection procedure is removed from training process. In this case, there is no need to generate feature subset, since it may cause unnecessary information loss. All feature dimensions are used during training.

Now we define 7 baseline approaches listed as follows, each of which is a special case of our framework. Through this comparison, we can discover which part of the framework is really contributing to the improvement in classification accuracy.

(1) M1: training a classifier with the 1st modality:
    Parameters setup: $T = 1$, $V = 1$, $M_1 = 1$.
    Classifier: $H(x_i) = \arg\max_c P(x_i|\theta_{1,c})$.
    x_i is the unlabeled instance, and $\theta_{1,c}$ are the parameters of hidden Markov model for instances in the c-th class, trained on the 1st modality.

(2) M2: training a classifier with the 2nd modality:
    Parameters setup: $T = 1$, $V = 1$, $M_2 = 1$.
    Classifier: $H(x_i) = \arg\max_c P(x_i|\theta_{2,c})$.
    x_i is the unlabeled instance, and $\theta_{2,c}$ are the parameters of hidden Markov model for instances in the c-th class, trained on the 2nd modality.

(3) M1+M2: training classifiers with the 1st and 2nd modality:
    Parameters setup: $T = 1$, $V = 2$, $M_1 = M_2 = 1$.
    Classifier: $H(x_i) = \arg\max_c [\alpha P(x_i|\theta_{1,c}) + (1 - \alpha) P(x_i|\theta_{2,c})]$.
    x_i is the unlabeled instance, and $\theta_{1,c}$ and $\theta_{2,c}$ are respectively the parameters of hidden Markov model for instances in the c-th class, trained on the 1st and 2nd modality.

(4) Boost.M1: training boosted classifiers with the 1st modality:
    Parameters setup: $T > 1$, $V = 1$, $M_1 = 1$.
    Classifier: $H(x_i) = \arg\max_c \sum_{t=1}^{T} \alpha_{t,1} \infty\{h_{t,1}(x_i) = c\}$.
    $h_{t,1}(x_i) = \arg\max_c P(x_i|\theta_{t,1,c})$ is the weak classifier learnt at the t-th boosting iteration, and $\alpha_{t,1}$ is the corresponding classifier's weight.

(5) Boost.M2: training boosted classifiers with the 2nd modality:
    Parameters setup: $T > 1$, $V = 1$, $M_2 = 1$.
    Classifier: $H(x_i) = \arg\max_c \sum_{t=1}^{T} \alpha_{t,2} \infty\{h_{t,2}(x_i) = c\}$.
    $h_{t,2}(x_i) = \arg\max_c P(x_i|\theta_{t,2,c})$ is the weak classifier learnt at the t-th boosting iteration, and $\alpha_{t,2}$ is the corresponding classifier's weight.

(6) Boost.Sel.M1: training boosted classifiers with selected features of the 1st modality:
    Parameters setup: $T > 1$, $V = 1$, $M_1 > 1$.
    Classifier: $H(x_i) = \arg\max_c \sum_{t=1}^{T} \alpha_{t,1} \infty\{h_{t,1}(x_i) = c\}$.
    $h_{t,1}(x_i) = \arg\max_c P(x_i|\theta_{t,1,c})$ is the weak classifier learnt at the t-th boosting iteration, and $\alpha_{t,1}$ is the corresponding classifier's weight. Unlike "Boost.M1", feature selection is performed in the training process of weak classifier $h_{t,1}(x_i)$.

(7) Boost.Sel.M2: training boosted classifiers with selected features of the 2nd modality:

Parameters setup: $T > 1$, $V = 1$, $M_2 > 1$.

Classifier: $H(x_i) = \arg\max_c \sum_{t=1}^{T} \alpha_{t,2} \infty \{h_{t,2}(x_i) = c\}$.

$h_{t,2}(x_i) = \arg\max_c P(x_i|\theta_{t,2,c})$ is the weak classifier learnt at the t-th boosting iteration, and $\alpha_{t,2}$ is the corresponding classifier's weight. Unlike "Boost.M2", feature selection is performed in the training process of weak classifier $h_{t,2}(x_i)$.

For convenience, we denote our proposed approach as "BayCoBoost". Its corresponding parameter setup is $T > 1$, $V = 2$, $M_1 > 1$, $M_2 > 1$.

"M1" and "M2" are two naive methods for single-modal gesture recognition, and many HMM-based recognizers can be categorized into one of these. "M1+M2" is the late fusion result of "M1" and "M2". Considering the weight coefficient α, we evaluate 11 candidate values from 0 to 1 with equal step length on the training set using cross validation, and select the optimal α which reaches the minimal error. The approach used in Wu et al. (2013) can be regarded as a variation of the "M1+M2" method.

In "Boost.M1" and "Boost.M2", boosting learning is applied to enhance the recognition performance. Multiple HMM-based weak classifiers are trained through iterations. Foo et al. (2004) and Zhang et al. (2005) respectively used this type of approach for the recognition of visual speech element and sign language. "Boost.Sel.M1" and "Boost.Sel.M2" are similar to them, but feature selection is embedded into the training process of each weak classifier. Finally, our proposed method "BayCoBoost" integrates both modalities under the Bayesian Co-Boosting framework.

14.4.2   Experiment 1: ChaLearn MMGR Dataset

In 2013, ChaLearn organized a challenge on multi-modal gesture recognition with motion data captured by the Kinect™ sensor. This challenge provides a benchmark dataset on the topic of multi-modal gesture recognition. Detailed information about this dataset can be found in Escalera et al. (2013).

This dataset contains 20 gesture categories, each of which is an Italian cultural or anthropological sign. Gestures in the dataset are performed with one or two hands by 27 users, along with the corresponding word/phase spoken out. Data modalities provided in this dataset include color image, depth image, skeletal model, user mask, and audio data.

The dataset has been divided into three subsets already, namely *Development*, *Validation*, and *Evaluation*. In our experiment, *Development* and *Validation* subsets are used respectively for model training and testing. Based on the labeled data, we can segment out 7, 205 gesture instances from *Development* subset and 3,280 instances from *Validation*. These two numbers are slightly smaller than the amount (7,754 and 3,362) announced in Escalera et al. (2013), since we filter out those gesture instances which contain invalid skeleton data (when Kinect™ fails to track the skeleton and outputs all-zero skeleton data).

Among all feature modalities offered in this dataset, we choose audio and skeleton feature to perform our proposed Bayesian Co-Boosting training process. We extract 39-dimension MFCC feature (Martin et al. 2001) from audio data stream and denote it as the first feature modality. The second modality is the 138-dimension skeleton feature extracted from 3D coordinates of 20 tracked joint points. The detailed extraction process of skeleton feature is described in the appendix.

In this experiment, parameters in Algorithm 1 are chosen as follows: $T = 20$, $V = 2$, $M_1 = 5$, and $M_2 = 10$. For MFCC feature, the size of feature subset is set to be 50% of all feature dimensions. The skeleton feature subset consists of 15% dimensions from the original feature space. Therefore, the number of feature dimensions used to train weak classifiers is respectively 20 for audio and 21 for skeleton. The number of iterations to estimate parameters of hidden Markov models for weak classifiers is set to 20. All these parameters are selected roughly using a grid search based on the cross validation result on the training subset.

We report the recognition accuracy of each gesture category in Fig. 14.2. Also, several statistics are computed to provide a quantitative comparison between different methods' average recognition performance across all categories, which are reported in Table 14.1. The recognition accuracy is defined as the ratio of the number of correctly classified gestures against the number of all existing gestures in each class.

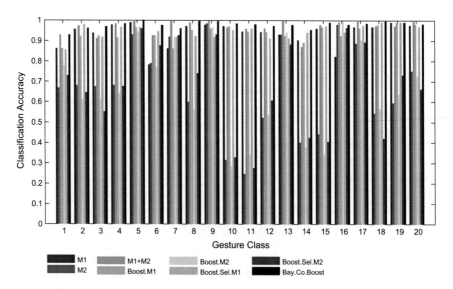

Fig. 14.2 Recognition accuracy of each gesture category on ChaLearn MMGR datasets

Table 14.1 Recognition accuracy on ChaLearn MMGR datasets

Method	Mean	Std	Conf	[Mean-Conf, Mean+Conf]
M1	0.9326	0.0584	0.0273	[0.9052, 0.9599]
M2	0.6749	0.2223	0.1040	[0.5709, 0.7790]
M1+M2	0.9666	0.0345	0.0162	[0.9504, 0.9827]
Boost.M1	0.9364	0.0366	0.0171	[0.9192, 0.9535]
Boost.M2	0.6705	0.2276	0.1065	[0.5640, 0.7770]
Boost.Sel.M1	0.9432	0.0334	0.0156	[0.9275, 0.9588]
Boost.Sel.M2	0.6793	0.2219	0.1038	[0.5754, 0.7831]
BayCoBoost	**0.9763**	**0.0173**	**0.0081**	**[0.9682, 0.9844]**

14.4.3   *Experiment 2: ChAirGest Dataset*

In Ruffieux et al. (2013), a multi-modal dataset was collected to provide a benchmark for the development and evaluation of gesture recognition methods. This dataset is captured with a Kinect™ sensor and four Xsens inertial motion units. Three data streams are provided by the Kinect™ sensor: color image, depth image, and 3D positions of upper-body joint points. Each Xsens IMU sensor can provide linear acceleration, angular acceleration, magnetometer, Euler orientation, orientation quaternion, and barometer data with a frequency of 50 Hz.

This dataset contains a vocabulary of 10 one-hand gestures commonly used in close human-computer interaction. Gestures are performed by 10 subjects, and each gesture is repeated 12 times, including 2 lighting conditions and 3 resting postures. The total number of gesture instances is 1200.

Similar to the previous experiment, two feature modalities are chosen to perform our Bayesian Co-Boosting training process. The first feature modality is based on the data captured by Xsens sensors. We use the raw data collected by four Xsens sensors as feature vector, which is of 68-dimension. Skeleton data captured by the Kinect™ is used as the second modality, and a 120-dimension feature vector is extracted per frame (see the appendix for details). The number of skeleton feature dimensions is smaller than the previous one, because the position of two joint points (hip-center and spine) cannot be tracked since all users were performing gestures while sitting.

The parameters in this experiment are almost identical with previous experiment. In Algorithm 1, parameters are: $T = 20$, $V = 2$, and $M_1 = M_2 = 10$. The feature selection ratio of Xsens and skeleton are respectively 20% and 15%. Under this setup, the feature dimension of Xsens data for weak classifier training is 14, and this number is 18 for skeleton feature. The number of iterations for weak classifier training is also set to 20. Similar to the previous experiment, these parameters are also determined by cross-validation.

Since no division of training and testing subset is specified in this dataset, we perform leave-one-out cross validation. In each round, gesture instances of one subject

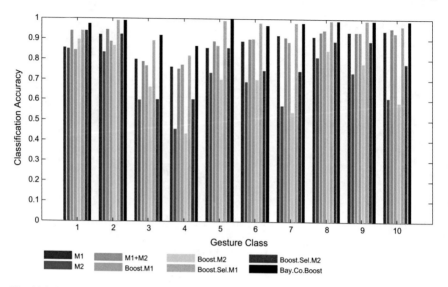

Fig. 14.3 Recognition accuracy of each gesture category on ChAirGest datasets

Table 14.2 Recognition accuracy on ChAirGest datasets

Method	Mean	Std	Conf	[Mean−Conf, Mean+Conf]
M1	0.8782	0.0598	0.0427	[0.8355, 0.9210]
M2	0.6884	0.1283	0.0918	[0.5966, 0.7801]
M1+M2	0.8940	0.0685	0.0490	[0.8450, 0.9430]
Boost.M1	0.8728	0.0623	0.0445	[0.8283, 0.9174]
Boost.M2	0.7003	0.1501	0.1074	[0.5929, 0.8077]
Boost.Sel.M1	0.9522	0.0564	0.0403	[0.9119, 0.9925]
Boost.Sel.M2	0.7958	0.1242	0.0889	[0.7070, 0.8847]
BayCoBoost	**0.9653**	**0.0420**	**0.0300**	**[0.9353, 0.9953]**

are used for model evaluation, and other instances are used to train the model. We compute the average recognition accuracy for each gesture class and report them in Fig. 14.3 and Table 14.2.

14.4.4 Result Analysis

From the above experimental results, it is obvious that our proposed Bayesian Co-Boosting training algorithm achieves the best recognition accuracy in both datasets. Our approach's recognition accuracy ranks first in 14 out of 20 classes on ChaLearn

MMGR dataset and 9 out of 10 classes on ChAirGest dataset. The average recognition accuracy of our method is also superior to any other baseline methods, as shown in Tables 14.1 and 14.2. This improvement of our method mainly benefits from two aspects: multi-modal fusion under Bayesian Co-Boosting framework, and boosting learning with feature selection.

The improvement brought by multi-modal fusion is inevitable, since different modalities surely can provide complementary information for each other. "M1+M2" implements late fusion using a weight coefficient α, which requires more training time to determine its optimal value through cross-validation. On the other hand, in our approach, each classifier's weight is determined during boosting process, which avoids extra parameter tuning and is more reasonable and explainable based on the above theoretical analysis.

Comparing the result of "M1", "M2", "Boost.M1", and "Boost.M2", we can see that boosting learning could not necessarily improve the recognition accuracy. This may due to the overfitting caused by the small amount of available training instances. The overfitting problem of boosting methods has been discussed in several literatures (Zhang and Yu 2005; Reyzin and Schapire 2006; Vezhnevets and Barinova 2007; Yao and Doretto 2010). Considering the high feature dimension of instances, the weak classifier may be too complex to be well trained on such few instances.

Based on the above observation, we tackle the overfitting problem from two aspects. Firstly, feature selection is used to reduce the number of feature dimensions while preserving enough discriminative information, which alleviates overfitting brought by the small size sample problem. Secondly, Bayesian Co-Boosting is employed to combine two weak classifiers together with collaborative training strategy, and each modality can provide complementary information for the other modality. Therefore, the amount of available training information for classifiers is actually increased to avoid overfitting problem to some extent.

As demonstrated in Tables 14.1 and 14.2, "Boost.Sel.M1" and "Boost.Sel.M2" outperform their corresponding training methods without feature selection. On this basis, after applying Co-Boosting method to fuse two modalities, our proposed "BayCoBoost" achieves superior recognition accuracy than all baseline methods.

As for the computation complexity, we compare the average classification time for each method. It takes around 0.31 s/0.11 s for our proposed "BayCoBoost" method to label an instance in ChaLearn MMGR and ChAirGest dataset, respectively. Although non-boosting methods can operate at higher speed (for "M1+M2", the time is about 0.037 s/0.013 s), we think it is worthy to spend more time since our method's performance is superior to these methods, especially for the second dataset. Another remarkable comparison is that by using feature selection strategy, "Boost.Sel.M1" and "Boost.Sel.M2" not only run twice as fast as "Boost.M1" and "Boost.M2", due to the lower classifier's complexity, but also outperform them in the classification performance. This also proves that the effectiveness of the feature selection strategy in our "BayCoBoost" method.

14.5 Conclusion

In this paper, a novel Bayesian Co-Boosting training framework for multi-modal gesture recognition is proposed. The merits of our work are three-fold: first, the collaborative training between multiple modalities provides complementary information for each modality; second, the boosting learning combines weak classifiers to construct a strong classifier of higher accuracy; third, the Bayesian perspective theoretically ensures that the training error of our method is minimized through iterations. Feature selection and multi-modal fusion are naturally embedded into the training process, which bring significant improvement to the recognition accuracy. Experimental results on two multi-modal gesture recognition datasets prove the effectiveness of our proposed approach. Moveover, our proposed framework can be easily extended to other related tasks in multi-modal scenarios, such as object detection and tracking.

Acknowledgements This work was supported in part by 973 Program (Grant No. 2010CB327905), National Natural Science Foundation of China (Grant Nos. 61332016, 61202325), and Key Project of Chinese Academy of Sciences (Grant No. KGZD-EW-103-5).

Appendix: Skeleton Feature Extraction

The Kinect™ sensor is able to provide 3D position information for 20 joint points of human body. We denote the original 3D coordinates of these joints as (x_i, y_i, z_i), $i = 1, \ldots, 20$.

In order to extract the skeleton feature which is invariant to user's position, orientation, and body size, we perform the following transformations:

1. Select one joint point as the origin of the normalized coordinate system.
   Translate all joint points to move the selected point to the origin.
2. Select three joint points to construct the reference plane.
   Rotate the reference plane so that it is orthogonal to the z-axis.
3. Calculate the distance sum of 19 directly connected joint pairs.
   Normalize all coordinates so that the sum is equal to 1.

After above transformations, we can obtain the normalized 3D coordinates (x_i^*, y_i^*, z_i^*), which are invariant to the user's position, orientation, and body size.

Since most gestures are performed with upper body, and the lower body's movement may interfere the recognition of gestures, we only select joint points in the upper body for feature extraction. The final feature vector consists of four parts:

1. Absolute 3D position of joint points.
2. Relative 3D position of joint points, defined on directly connected joint pairs.
3. First order difference in time of part 1 in the feature vector.
4. First order difference in time of part 2 in the feature vector.

References

I. Bayer, T. Silbermann. A multi modal approach to gesture recognition from audio and video data. in *Proceedings of the 15th ACM on International Conference on Multimodal Interaction*, 2013, pp. 461–466

K.K. Biswas, S.K. Basu. Gesture recognition using microsoft kinect. in *the 5th International Conference on Automation, Robotics and Applications*, 2011, pp. 100–103

A. Blum, T. Mitchell. Combining labeled and unlabeled data with co-training. in *Proceedings of the 11th Annual Conference on Computational Learning Theory*, 1998, pp. 92–100

A. Boyali, M. Kavakli. A robust gesture recognition algorithm based on sparse representation, random projections and compressed sensing. in *IEEE Conference on Industrial Electronics and Applications*, 2012, pp. 243–249

G.S. Chambers, S. Venkatesh, G.A.W. West, H.H. Bui. Hierarchical recognition of intentional human gestures for sports video annotation. in *Proceedings of the 16th International Conference on Pattern Recognition*, 2002, vol. 2, pp. 1082–1085

X. Chen, M. Koskela. Online rgb-d gesture recognition with extreme learning machines. in *Proceedings of the 15th ACM on International Conference on Multimodal Interaction*, 2013, pp. 467–474

S. Eickeler, A. Kosmala, G. Rigoll. Hidden markov model based continuous online gesture recognition. in *Proceedings of the 14th International Conference on Pattern Recognition*, 1998, vol. 2, pp. 1206–1208

M. Elmezain, A. Al-Hamadi, J. Appenrodt, B. Michaelis. A hidden markov model-based continuous gesture recognition system for hand motion trajectory. in *Proceedings of the 19th International Conference on Pattern Recognition*, 2008, pp. 1–4

S. Escalera, J. Gonzàlez, X. Baró, M. Reyes, O. Lopes, I. Guyon, V. Athitsos, H. Escalante. Multimodal gesture recognition challenge 2013: Dataset and results. in *Proceedings of the 15th ACM on International Conference on Multimodal Interaction*, 2013, pp. 445–452

F. Yoav, E.S. Robert, A decision-theoretic generalization of on-line learning and an application to boosting. J. Comput. Syst. Sci. **55**(1), 119–139 (1997)

S.W. Foo, Y. Lian, L. Dong, Recognition of visual speech elements using adaptively boosted hidden Markov models. IEEE Trans. Circuits Syst. Video Technol. **14**(5), 693–705 (2004)

Y. Freund, R.E. Schapire, A desicion-theoretic generalization of on-line learning and an application to boosting, *Computational Learning Theory* (Springer, Heidelberg, 1995), pp. 23–37

Y.F.A. Gaus, F. Wong, K. Teo, R. Chin, R.R. Porle, L.P. Yi, A. Chekima. Comparison study of hidden markov model gesture recognition using fixed state and variable state. in *IEEE International Conference on Signal and Image Processing Applications*, 2013, pp. 150–155

D.M. Gavrila, The visual analysis of human movement: a survey. Comput. Vis. Image Underst. **73**(1), 82–98 (1999)

I. Guyon, V. Athitsos, P. Jangyodsuk, B. Hamner, H.J. Escalante. Chalearn gesture challenge: design and first results. in *IEEE Computer Society Conference on Computer Vision and Pattern Recognition Workshops*, 2012, pp. 1–6

R.L. Kashyap, Optimal feature selection and decision rules in classification problems with time series. IEEE Trans. Inf. Theory **24**(3), 281–288 (1978)

J. Liu, L. Zhong, J. Wickramasuriya, V. Vasudevan, uWave: accelerometer-based personalized gesture recognition and its applications. Pervasive Mob. Comput. **5**(6), 657–675 (2009)

Y. M. Lui. A least squares regression framework on manifolds and its application to gesture recognition. in *IEEE Computer Society Conference on Computer Vision and Pattern Recognition Workshops*, 2012a, pp. 13–18

Y.M. Lui, Human gesture recognition on product manifolds. J. Mach. Learn. Res. **13**(1), 3297–3321 (2012b)

Y.M. Lui, J.R. Beveridge, M. Kirby. Action classification on product manifolds. in *IEEE Conference on Computer Vision and Pattern Recognition*, 2010, pp. 833–839

S. Malassiotis, N. Aifanti, M.G. Strintzis. A gesture recognition system using 3d data. in *Proceedings of the 1st International Symposium on 3D Data Processing Visualization and Transmission*, 2002, pp. 190–193

M.R. Malgireddy, I. Inwogu, V. Govindaraju. A temporal bayesian model for classifying, detecting and localizing activities in video sequences. in *IEEE Computer Society Conference on Computer Vision and Pattern Recognition Workshops*, 2012, pp. 43–48

V. Mantyla, J. Mantyjarvi, T. Seppanen, E. Tuulari, Hand gesture recognition of a mobile device user. IEEE Int. Conf. Multimed. Expo **1**, 281–284 (2000)

A. Martin, D. Charlet, L. Mauuary, Robust speech/non-speech detection using IDA applied to MFCC. Proc. IEEE Int. Conf. Acoust. Speech Signal Process. **1**, 237–240 (2001)

S. Mitra, T. Acharya, Gesture recognition: a survey. IEEE Trans. Syst. Man Cybern. Part C **37**(3), 311–324 (2007)

F. Mörchen. Time series feature extraction for data mining using DWT and DFT. Technical report, Philipps-University Marburg, 2003

K.P. Murphy. *Machine Learning: A Probabilistic Perspective*. MIT Press, 2012

K. Nandakumar, K.W. Wan, S.M.A. Chan, W.Z.T. Ng, J.G. Wang, W.Y. Yau. A multi-modal gesture recognition system using audio, video, and skeletal joint data. in *Proceedings of the 15th ACM on International Conference on Multimodal Interaction*, 2013, pp. 475–482

C. Oz, M.C. Leu, American sign language word recognition with a sensory glove using artificial neural networks. Eng. Appl. Artif. Intell. **24**(7), 1204–1213 (2011)

T. Pylvänäinen. Accelerometer based gesture recognition using continuous HMMS. in *Pattern Recognition and Image Analysis*, vol. 3522 of *Lecture Notes in Computer Science*, Springer, Heidelberg, 2005, pp. 639–646

L. Rabiner, A tutorial on hidden Markov models and selected applications in speech recognition. Proc. IEEE **77**(2), 257–286 (1989)

J.L. Raheja, R. Shyam, U. Kumar, P.B. Prasad. Real-time robotic hand control using hand gestures. in *the 2nd International Conference on Machine Learning and Computing*, 2010, pp. 12–16

L. Reyzin, R.E. Schapire. How boosting the margin can also boost classifier complexity. in *Proceedings of the 23rd International Conference on Machine Learning*, 2006, pp. 753–760

M. Roccetti, G. Marfia, A. Semeraro. A fast and robust gesture recognition system for exhibit gaming scenarios. in *Proceedings of the 4th International ICST Conference on Simulation Tools and Techniques*, 2011, pp. 343–350

S. Ruffieux, D. Lalanne, E. Mugellini. Chairgest—a challenge for multimodal mid-air gesture recognition for close HCI. in *Proceedings of the 15th ACM on International Conference on Multimodal Interaction*, 2013, pp. 483–488

J. Suarez, R.R. Murphy. Hand gesture recognition with depth images: a review. in *IEEE RO-MAN*, 2012, pp. 411–417

A. Vezhnevets, O. Barinova, Avoiding boosting overfitting by removing confusing samples, in *Proceedings of the 18th European Conference on Machine Learning*, vol. 4701 of Lecture Notes in Computer Science (Springer, Berlin Heidelberg, 2007), pp. 430–441

P. Viola, M. Jones. Robust real-time face detection. in *Proceedings of the 8th IEEE International Conference on Computer Vision*, 2001, vol. 2, pp. 747–747

P. Viola, M.J. Jones, Robust real-time face detection. Int. J. Comput. Vis. **57**(2), 137–154 (2004)

A. Wagner, J. Wright, A. Ganesh, Z. Zhou, Y. Ma. Towards a practical face recognition system: Robust registration and illumination by sparse representation. in *IEEE Conference on Computer Vision and Pattern Recognition*, 2009, pp. 597–604

D. Weinland, R. Ronfard, E. Boyer, A survey of vision-based methods for action representation, segmentation and recognition. Comput. Vis. Image Underst. **115**(2), 224–241 (2011)

J. Wright, A.Y. Yang, A. Ganesh, S.S. Sastry, Y. Ma, Robust face recognition via sparse representation. IEEE Trans. Pattern Anal. Mach. Intell. **31**(2), 210–227 (2009)

D. Wu, F. Zhu, L. Shao. One shot learning gesture recognition from rgbd images. in *IEEE Computer Society Conference on Computer Vision and Pattern Recognition Workshops*, 2012, pp. 7–12

J. Wu, J. Cheng, C. Zhao, H. Lu. Fusing multi-modal features for gesture recognition. in *Proceedings of the 15th ACM on International Conference on Multimodal Interaction*, 2013, pp. 453–460

M. Yang, N. Ahuja, Recognizing hand gestures using motion trajectories, in *Face Detection and Gesture Recognition for Human-Computer Interaction*, vol. 1 of The International Series in Video Computing (Springer, New York, 2001), pp. 53–81

Y. Yao, G. Doretto. Boosting for transfer learning with multiple sources. in *IEEE Conference on Computer Vision and Pattern Recognition*, 2010, pp. 1855–1862

M. Yeasin, S. Chaudhuri, Visual understanding of dynamic hand gestures. Pattern Recognit. **33**(11), 1805–1817 (2000)

Y. Yin, R. Davis. Gesture spotting and recognition using salience detection and concatenated hidden markov models. in *Proceedings of the 15th ACM on International Conference on Multimodal Interaction*, pp. 489–494, (2013)

H. Yoon, K. Yang, C. Shahabi, Feature subset selection and feature ranking for multivariate time series. IEEE Trans. Knowl. Data Eng. **17**(9), 1186–1198 (2005)

S. Yu, B. Krishnapuram, R. Rosales, H. Steck, RB. Rao. Bayesian co-training. in *Advances in Neural Information Processing Systems*, vol. 20, (MIT Press, Cambridge, 2008), pp. 1665–1672

S. Yu, B. Krishnapuram, R. Rosales, R.B. Rao, Bayesian co-training. J. Mach. Learn. Res. **12**, 2649–2680 (2011)

Z. Zafrulla, H. Brashear, T. Starner, H. Hamilton, P. Presti. American sign language recognition with the kinect. in *Proceedings of the 13th International Conference on Multimodal Interfaces*, 2011, pp. 279–286

L. Zhang, X. Chen, C. Wang, C. Chen, W. Gao. Recognition of sign language subwords based on boosted hidden markov models. in *Proceedings of the 7th International Conference on Multimodal Interfaces*, 2005, pp. 282–287

T. Zhang, B. Yu. Boosting with early stopping: convergence and consistency. *Ann. Stat.*, 2005, pp. 1538–1579

Y. Zhang, W. Liang, J. Tan, Y. Li, Z. Zeng. PCA & HMM based arm gesture recognition using inertial measurement unit. in *Proceedings of the 8th International Conference on Body Area Networks*, 2013, pp. 193–196

F. Zheng, G. Zhang, Z. Song, Comparison of different implementations of MFCC. J. Comput. Sci. Technol. **16**(6), 582–589 (2001)

Chapter 15
Transfer Learning Decision Forests for Gesture Recognition

Norberto A. Goussies, Sebastián Ubalde and Marta Mejail

Abstract Decision forests are an increasingly popular tool in computer vision problems. Their advantages include high computational efficiency, state-of-the-art accuracy and multi-class support. In this paper, we present a novel method for transfer learning which uses decision forests, and we apply it to recognize gestures and characters. We introduce two mechanisms into the decision forest framework in order to transfer knowledge from the source tasks to a given target task. The first one is mixed information gain, which is a data-based regularizer. The second one is label propagation, which infers the manifold structure of the feature space. We show that both of them are important to achieve higher accuracy. Our experiments demonstrate improvements over traditional decision forests in the ChaLearn Gesture Challenge and MNIST data set. They also compare favorably against other state-of-the-art classifiers.

Keywords Decision forests · Transfer learning · Gesture recognition

15.1 Introduction

Machine learning tools have achieved significant success in many computer vision tasks, including face detection (Viola and Jones 2004), object recognition (Felzenszwalb et al. 2010), character recognition (LeCun et al. 1998) and gesture recognition (Guyon et al. 2013). Those tasks are often posed as a classification problem, namely

Editors: Isabelle Guyon, Vassilis Athitsos, and Sergio Escalera

N.A. Goussies (✉) · S. Ubalde · M. Mejail
Facultad de Ciencias Exactas y Naturales, Departamento de Computación, Pabellón I,
Universidad de Buenos Aires, C1428EGA Buenos Aires, Argentina
e-mail: ngoussie@dc.uba.ar

S. Ubalde
e-mail: seubalde@dc.uba.ar

M. Mejail
e-mail: marta@dc.uba.ar

© Springer International Publishing AG 2017   443
S. Escalera et al. (eds.), *Gesture Recognition*, The Springer Series
on Challenges in Machine Learning, DOI 10.1007/978-3-319-57021-1_15

identifying to which of a set of categories a new observation belongs. Such classifiers are usually learned from scratch using a training data set collected for the task. A major advantage of using machine learning tools is that they tend to deal robustly with the complexities found in real data.

However, in many cases it is difficult to create new training data sets for each new computer vision task. Although the problem remains unsolved, some progress has already been made in certain computer vision tasks, such as object recognition (Fei-Fei et al. 2006) and action recognition (Seo and Milanfar 2011). The key insight is to try to replicate the ability of the human brain, which is capable of learning new concepts applying previously acquired knowledge.

Transfer learning aims at extracting the knowledge from one or more source tasks, and applying that knowledge to a target task. As opposed to multi-task learning, rather than simultaneously learning the source and target tasks, transfer learning focus more on learning the target task. The roles of the source and target tasks are not symmetric (Pan and Yang 2010). The goal is to exploit the knowledge extracted from the source tasks so as to improve the generalization of the classifier in the target task.

Many examples can be found in computer vision where transfer learning can be truly beneficial. One example is optical character recognition, which seeks to classify a given image into one of the characters of a given alphabet. Most methods have focused on recognizing characters from the English alphabet (LeCun et al. 1998). The recognition of characters from other alphabets, such as French, implies collecting a new training data set (Grosicki and Abed 2011). In that case, it would be helpful to transfer the classification knowledge into the new domain.

The need for transfer learning also arises in gesture recognition (Guyon et al. 2013), which aims at recognizing a gesture instance drawn from a gesture vocabulary. For example, a gesture vocabulary may consist of Italian gestures or referee signals. In this case, the classifier needs to predict the gesture of the vocabulary that corresponds to a given video. Again, it would be interesting to improve the performance of a system by exploiting the knowledge acquired from similar vocabularies.

In this paper, we present a novel method for transfer learning which extends the decision forests framework (Breiman 2001; Criminisi et al. 2012), and we apply it to transfer knowledge from multiple source tasks to a given target task. We introduce two mechanisms in order to transfer knowledge from the source tasks to the target task. The first one is mixed information gain, which is a data-based regularizer. The second one is label propagation, which infers the manifold structure of the feature space.

Decision forests have certain properties that make them particularly interesting for computer vision problems. First, decision forests are multi-class classifiers; therefore it is not necessary to train several binary classifiers for a multi-class problem. Second, they are fast both to train and test. Finally, they can be parallelized, which makes them ideal for GPU (Sharp 2008) and multi-core implementations.

The first key contribution is to revise the criterion for finding the parameters of each internal node of the decision forests in the transfer learning setting. The novel criterion exploits the knowledge from the source tasks and the target task to find the parameters for each internal node of the decision forests. The additional information penalizes split functions with a high information gain in the target task and a low information gain in the source tasks. We prove that the novel criterion is beneficial.

The second key contribution is to propagate labels through leaves in order to infer the manifold structure of the feature space. The aim of this step is to assign a predictive model to the leaves without training samples of the target task after the trees of the decision forest are grown. We create a fully connected graph, for each tree in the forest, where the nodes are the leaves of the tree and the weight of each edge takes into account the training data reaching the leaves. An implicit assumption of this step is that nearby leaves should have similar predictive models.

We extensively validate our approach in two challenging data sets. First, our experiments in the ChaLearn gesture challenge data set (Guyon et al. 2012) show that our method does not have a uniform margin of improvement over all the tasks. However, we demonstrate that when there are source tasks related to the target task, we obtain greater improvements. Second, our experiments in the MNIST data set (LeCun et al. 1998) show that greater improvements are obtained, compared to classification decision forests, when there are only a few training samples.

This paper is organized as follows. We summarize previous work on transfer learning in Sect. 15.2. Section 15.3 describes the novel transfer learning decision forest in, illustrates its performance on some artificial data sets, and proves some properties of the mixed information gain. In Sect. 15.4 we show how the transfer learning decision forests can be used to recognize gestures when there is only one training sample. We present our experiments on the ChaLearn data set and the MNIST data set in Sect. 15.5. Finally, Sect. 15.6 details our conclusions.

15.2   Related Work

In the following we will review transfer learning techniques which have been applied to computer vision problems. A recent survey (Pan and Yang 2010) provides a comprehensive overview of the developments for classification, regression and clustering. In recent years, the computer vision community has become increasingly interested in using transfer learning techniques, especially for object recognition (Levi et al. 2004; Sudderth et al. 2005; Fei-Fei et al. 2006; Bart and Ullman 2005; Torralba et al. 2007; Quattoni et al. 2008; Bergamo and Torresani 2010; Gopalan et al. 2011; Saenko et al. 2010; Tommasi et al. 2014).

A variety of methods have been proposed in the generative probabilistic setting (Fei-Fei et al. 2006; Sudderth et al. 2005). These models consider the relationships between different object parts during the training process. The key idea is to share some parameters or prior distributions between object categories, using the knowledge from known classes as a generic reference for newly learned models. The association of objects with distributions over parts can scale linearly (Sudderth et al. 2005), or exponentially (Fei-Fei et al. 2006).

Moreover, discriminative models have been extended to the transfer learning setting (Dai et al. 2007; Yao and Doretto 2010; Aytar and Zisserman 2011; Tommasi et al. 2014; Lim et al. 2011; Torralba et al. 2007). Transfer learning has been applied to the SVM framework, during the training process of the target detector the previously learned template is introduced as a regularizer into the cost function (Tommasi et al. 2014; Aytar and Zisserman 2011). Based on boosting (Freund and Schapire 1997) a framework that allows users to utilize a small amount of newly labeled data has been developed (Dai et al. 2007). Later, the framework has been extended for handling multiple sources (Yao and Doretto 2010).

More similar to our method, instance transfer approaches (Pan and Yang 2010) consider source and target data together during the training process. A loss function for borrowing examples from other classes in order to augment the training data of each class has been proposed by Lim et al. (2011). A method for learning new visual categories is described by Quattoni et al. (2008), using only a small subset of reference prototypes for a given set of tasks. As mentioned earlier, a boosting-based algorithm that allows knowledge to be effectively transferred from old to new data has been proposed by Dai et al. (2007) and extended later by Yao and Doretto (2010). The effectiveness of the novel algorithm is analyzed both theoretically and empirically. In this paper, we develop an instance transfer approach that exploits source and target data to find the parameters of each internal node of the decision forest.

Few researchers have addressed the problem of transfer learning using decision forests or trees. Leistner et al. (2009) extends random forests to semi-supervised learning. In order to incorporate unlabeled data a maximum margin approach is proposed, which is optimized using a deterministic annealing-style technique. Wang et al. (2008) proposed to treat each input attribute as extra task to bias each component decision tree in the ensemble. Pei et al. (2013) proposed a novel criterion for node splitting to avoid the rank deficiency in learning density forests for lipreading. The method proposed by won Lee and Giraud-Carrier (2007) learns a new task by traversing and transforming a decision tree previously learned for a related task. The transfer learning decision tree learns the target task from a partial decision tree model induced by ID3 (Quinlan 1986). In this paper, we follow a different approach, first we consider the source and target data when we build each tree of the decision forest. Second, decision forests reduce the variance of the classifier aggregating the results of multiple random decision trees.

Our approach shares some features with the work by Faddoul et al. (2012), who propose to transfer learning with boosted C4.5 decision trees. The main difference is that their method reduces the variance of the decision trees by means of boosting, which has been shown to be less robust against label noise when compared with decision forests (Breiman 2001; Leistner et al. 2009). In addition, we use label propagation to learn the manifold structure of the feature space, and assign predictive models only to the leaves of the trees.

There has been a growing interest in applying transfer learning techniques to gesture recognition. A method for transfer learning in the context of sign language is described by Farhadi et al. (2007). A set of labeled words in the source and target data is shared so as to build a word classifier for a new signer on a set of unlabeled target words. A transfer learning method for conditional random fields is implemented to exploit information in both labeled and unlabeled data to learn high-level features for gesture recognition by Liu et al. (2010). More recently, the ChaLearn Gesture Competition (Guyon et al. 2013) provided a benchmark of methods that apply transfer learning to gesture recognition. Several approaches submitted to the competition have been published (Malgireddy et al. 2013; Lui 2012; Wan et al. 2013).

15.3 Transfer Learning Decision Forests

We consider $N + 1$ classification tasks $T_0, \ldots, T_N$ over the instance space $\mathbb{R}^d$ and label sets $\mathcal{Y}_0, \ldots, \mathcal{Y}_N$. We are interested in solving the classification task T_0 using the knowledge of the other tasks in order to improve classification accuracy. Our transfer learning algorithm will take as input the training set $S = \{(\mathbf{x}_i, \mathbf{y}_i, j) | \mathbf{x}_i \in \mathbb{R}^d, \mathbf{y}_i \in \mathcal{Y}_j, j \in \{0, \ldots, N\}, 1 \leq i \leq M\}$. The projected sets $T_j S = \{(\mathbf{x}_i, \mathbf{y}_i) | \mathbf{x}_i \in \mathbb{R}^d, \mathbf{y}_i \in \mathcal{Y}_j, (\mathbf{x}_i, \mathbf{y}_i, j) \in S\}$ are the training sets for each task T_j. The empirical histogram for a training set S of a task T is defined as $\hat{p}_{TS}(\mathbf{y}) = \frac{1}{|TS|} \sum_{(\mathbf{x}', \mathbf{y}') \in TS} \delta_{\mathbf{y}'}(\mathbf{y})$ where $\delta_{\mathbf{y}'}(\mathbf{y})$ is the Kronecker delta and the empirical entropy is defined as $\mathcal{H}(TS) = -\sum_{\mathbf{y} \in \mathcal{Y}} \hat{p}_{TS}(\mathbf{y}) \log(\hat{p}_{TS}(\mathbf{y}))$, we will note $\hat{p}_S(\mathbf{y})$ or $\mathcal{H}(S)$ to make the notation simpler when it is convenient and unambiguous.

The goal is to find a decision forest $\mathcal{F} = \{F_1, \ldots, F_T\}$, defined as an ensemble of T decision trees F, which minimizes the classification error. A decision tree F is a strictly binary tree in which each node k represents a subset R_k in the instance space $\mathbb{R}^d$ and all the leaves ∂F form a partition $\mathcal{P}$ of $\mathbb{R}^d$. In addition, each leaf $k \in \partial F$ of a decision tree F has a predictive model associated with it: $p_F(\mathbf{y} | \mathbf{x} \in R_k)$. The internal nodes $k \in F^{\circ}$ of a decision tree have a linear split function: $h(\mathbf{x}, \boldsymbol{\theta}_k) = \mathbf{x} \cdot \boldsymbol{\theta}_k$, where $\boldsymbol{\theta}_k$ are the parameters of node k. The subset represented by the left child k_L of node k is defined as $R_{k_L} = R_k^L = \{\mathbf{x} \in \mathbb{R}^d | \mathbf{x} \in R_k \wedge h(\mathbf{x}, \boldsymbol{\theta}_k) < 0\}$ and, similarly, we define $R_{k_R} = R_k^R = \{\mathbf{x} \in \mathbb{R}^d | \mathbf{x} \in R_k \wedge h(\mathbf{x}, \boldsymbol{\theta}_k) \geq 0\}$ as the subset represented by the right child k_R. The training set reaching node k is defined as $S_k = \{(\mathbf{x}, \mathbf{y}, j) \in S | \mathbf{x} \in R_k\}$.

15.3.1 Training

The training algorithm of a decision forest $\mathcal{F}$ consists in training each of the trees $F \in \mathcal{F}$ independently, introducing a certain level of randomness in the training process in order to de-correlate individual tree predictions and improve generalization.

We grow each tree using an extension of the classical training algorithm (Criminisi et al. 2012). The algorithm follows a top-down approach, optimizing the parameters $\boldsymbol{\theta}$ of the root node in the beginning and recursively processing the child nodes. The recursion is stopped when all the items in the training set have the same labels, or the maximum depth D is reached, or the number of points reaching the node is below the minimum number of points allowed κ.

In this paper, we adapt the procedure for optimizing the parameters θ_k for each node $k \in F^\circ$ to the transfer learning setting (Pan and Yang 2010). The difference between the classification decision forest (Criminisi et al. 2012) and the transfer learning decision forest is the objective function. In the former, the information gain is used to find the best parameters, taking into account only one task. By contrast, in this paper we use the mixed information gain function as described in Sect. 15.3.1.1.

The partition $\mathcal{P}$ defined by the leaves ∂F after making a tree F grow might contain regions R with no training samples of the target task T_0. Therefore, we cannot define a predictive model for those regions. In order to overcome this issue we infer the labels from the regions that have training samples of task T_0, as described in Sect. 15.3.1.2.

15.3.1.1 Mixed Information Gain

We believe that valuable knowledge can be transferred from the source tasks $T_1, \ldots, T_N$ to the target task T_0, as it happens with humans. For example, it is simpler to learn a new sign language if another sign language has already been learned. In other words, there is latent information that can be understood as common sense.

In our formulation, this common sense information is included in the process of making each tree $F \in \mathcal{F}$ in the forest grow. The main idea is, therefore, to find parameters θ_k for each $k \in F^\circ$ in order to obtain a partition $\mathcal{P}$ of the feature space $\mathbb{R}^d$ such that, in each region $R \in \mathcal{P}$, the training samples of each task T have the same label. This aims at improving the generalization capabilities of each tree independently, since each region $R \in \mathcal{P}$ is found using more training samples, and is more general because it is encouraged to split the training samples of several tasks simultaneously.

Unfortunately, this is a very difficult problem. For this reason, we use a greedy heuristic which consist in recursively choosing for each internal node $k \in F^\circ$ the parameters θ_k of the split function $h(\mathbf{x}, \theta_k)$, which makes the training samples reaching the child nodes as "pure" as possible. The information gain achieved by splitting the training set TS_k reaching the internal node $k \in F^\circ$ of a task T using parameter θ_k is computed using the information gain function

$$\mathcal{I}(TS_k, \theta_k) = \mathcal{H}(TS_k) - \sum_{i \in \{L, R\}} \frac{|TS_k^i|}{|TS_k|} \mathcal{H}(TS_k^i)$$

where $TS_k^L = \{(\mathbf{x}, \mathbf{y}) | (\mathbf{x}, \mathbf{y}) \in TS_k \wedge h(\mathbf{x}, \theta_k) < 0\}$ and $TS_k^R = \{(\mathbf{x}, \mathbf{y}) | (\mathbf{x}, \mathbf{y}) \in TS_k \wedge h(\mathbf{x}, \theta_k) \geq 0\}$. In this paper, the parameters θ_k of each internal node $k \in F^\circ$ are found maximizing the information gain of all the tasks $T_0, \ldots, T_N$ simultaneously

$$\theta_k^* = \arg \max_{\theta_k \in T_k} (1 - \gamma)\mathcal{I}(T_0 S_k, \theta_k) + \gamma \sum_{n=1}^{N} p_{n,k} \mathcal{I}(T_n S_k, \theta_k) \tag{15.1}$$

where γ is a scalar parameter that weights the two terms, $\mathcal{T}_k \subset \mathbb{R}^d$ is a small subset of the instance space available when training the internal node $k \in F^\circ$, and $p_{n,k}$ is the fraction of samples of the source task T_n in the samples reaching the node k, $p_{n,k} = \frac{|T_n S_k|}{\sum_{j=1}^{N} |T_j S_k|}$.

The maximization of (15.1) is achieved using randomized node optimization (Criminisi et al. 2012). We perform an exhaustive search over subset $\mathcal{T}_k$ of the feature space parameters $\mathbb{R}^d$. The size of the subset is a training parameter noted as $\rho = |\mathcal{T}_k|$. The randomized node optimization is a key aspect of the decision forest model, since it helps to de-correlate individual tree predictions and to improve generalization.

The first term of the objective function in (15.1) is the information gain associated with the training samples reaching node k for the target task T_0. This term encourages the parameters $\boldsymbol{\theta}_k$ to find a split function $h(\mathbf{x}, \boldsymbol{\theta}_k)$ that decreases the entropy of the training set of the target task T_0 reaching the children nodes of k.

Additional information is introduced into the second term of the objective function in (15.1) for the purposes of increasing the generalization performance. This information encourages the parameters $\boldsymbol{\theta}_k$ to make the training samples of source tasks reaching the descendant nodes of k as pure as possible. The key idea is that this term penalizes split functions $h(\mathbf{x}, \boldsymbol{\theta}_k)$ with a high information gain in the target task T_0 and a low information gain in the source tasks $T_1, \ldots, T_N$. Those splits might have a high information gain in the target task T_0 only because the training set for task T_0 is limited, and if we choose them the generalization performance will decrease.

A key insight of our work is an alternative representation of the second term in (15.1). It is possible to consider all the source tasks $T_1, \ldots, T_N$ together concatenating the label sets $\mathcal{Y}_1, \ldots, \mathcal{Y}_N$, denoted by $\mathcal{Y}_{1\ldots N} = \oplus_{n=1}^{N} \mathcal{Y}_n$. The new task is noted as $T_{1\ldots N}$ and the training sample is noted as $T_{1\ldots N} S = \{(\mathbf{x}, \mathbf{y})|(\mathbf{x}, \mathbf{y}, j) \in S, j \in \{1, \ldots, N\}, \mathbf{y} \in \oplus_{n=1}^{N} \mathcal{Y}_n\}$. Using the generalized grouping rule of the entropy (Cover and Thomas 2006) an alternative expression for the second term in (15.1) is found

$$\mathcal{I}(T_{1\ldots N} S_k, \boldsymbol{\theta}_k) = \sum_{n=1}^{N} p_{n,k} \mathcal{I}(T_n S_k, \boldsymbol{\theta}_k).$$

This equation relates the information gain of several source tasks $T_1, \ldots, T_N$ to the information gain of another source task $T_{1\ldots N}$. An important consequence of this equation is that we can combine the training set of the simpler tasks $T_1, \ldots, T_N$ to obtain a larger training set for another source task $T_{1\ldots N}$. Therefore, increasing the number of training samples per source task or the number of source tasks has a similar effect.

This observation has previously been made in the multi-task learning literature (Faddoul et al. 2012). However, Faddoul et al. (2012) avoids the high variance of the decision trees by using the boosting framework, whereas we use a different approach, based on decision forest, for the same purpose.

We explain in more detail how the combination of the information gain of tasks $T_0, \ldots, T_N$ for finding the optimal parameters $\boldsymbol{\theta}_k$ improves the generalization properties of the decision forests. The parameters $\boldsymbol{\theta}_k$ are found using an empirical estimation

Fig. 15.1 Illustration of mixed information gain on a toy problem in which there are two tasks, each with two labels. The thickness of the *blue lines* indicates the mixed information gain of the split (all the splits have the same information gain). Task T_0 has *two green labels* ($\mathcal{Y}_0 = \{\times, *\}$) and task T_1 has *two red labels* ($\mathcal{Y}_1 = \{\bigcirc, \square\}$)

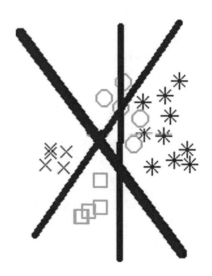

of the entropy $\mathcal{H}(S_k)$ of the training samples S_k reaching node k and its children. Consequently, errors in estimating entropy can result in very different trees. Tighter bounds for the expected entropy are found by increasing the number of training samples, as explained in Theorem 1.

Theorem 1 *Let P be a probability distribution on $\mathbb{R}^d \times \mathcal{Y}$ such that the marginal distribution over $\mathcal{Y}$ is a categorical distribution with parameters $p_1, \ldots, p_{|\mathcal{Y}|}$, and suppose $S_K = \{(\mathbf{x}_1, \mathbf{y}_1), \ldots, (\mathbf{x}_K, \mathbf{y}_K)\}$ is the set generated by sampling K times from $\mathbb{R}^d \times \mathcal{Y}$ according to P. Let $\mathcal{H}(P) = -\sum_{y=1}^{|\mathcal{Y}|} p_y \log(p_y)$ be the entropy of distribution P. Then $\mathbb{E}(\mathcal{H}(S_K)) + \sum_{y \in \mathcal{Y}} p_y \log\left(1 + \frac{1-p_y}{K p_y}\right) \leq \mathcal{H}(P) \leq \mathbb{E}(\mathcal{H}(S_K))$.*

This theorem is proved in the Appendix A.

Theorem 1 shows that the empirical entropy $\mathcal{H}(S_K)$ is closer to the entropy of the distribution P when the training set is larger, since when $K \to \infty, \log\left(1 + \frac{1-p_y}{K p_y}\right) \to 0$. Therefore, if we assume that the source tasks are related to the target task i.e., both have a similar distribution P, using Theorem 1 we can conclude that the mixed information gain (15.1) finds parameters $\boldsymbol{\theta}_k$ that achieve lower generalization errors than the traditional information gain $\mathcal{I}(T_0 S_k, \boldsymbol{\theta}_k)$.

To gain some insight into how the mixed information gain works, Fig. 15.1 considers a toy problem with two tasks, each with two labels. It is intuitively clear that the problem of estimating the information gain of a split with only a few training samples of the target task is that there are a lot of possible splits with the same empirical information gain but different generalization capabilities. Our goal is to discover which split to use, and we intend to choose the one with the best generalization capability. In Fig. 15.1 all the splits have the same information gain but different mixed information gain. When, in our formulation, we use the additional training samples from the source tasks to compute the information gain of a split, some of the splits

(a)   **(b)**

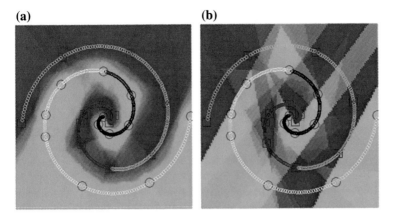

Fig. 15.2 *Left* Output classification of a transfer learning decision forest, tested on all points in a *rectangular* section of the feature space. The *color* associated with each test point is a linear combination of the *colors* (*red* and *green*) corresponding to the two labels (□, ○) in the target task. The training data for the target task is indicated with *big markers* and the training data for the source task is indicated with *small markers*. *Right* Output classification of a decision forest tested in the same feature space section as before but trained using only data for the target task

are penalized for having a low information gain in the source task and, thus, this allows us to find a split with increased generalization.

One of the major problems with decision trees is their high variance. A small change in the training data can often result in a very different series of splits. The major reason for this instability is the hierarchical nature of the process: the effect of an error in the top split is propagated down to all the splits below it (Hastie et al. 2003). Decision forests (Breiman 2001) build a large collection of de-correlated decision trees, and hence reduce the variance averaging the prediction of each of them. The mixed information gain is a complementary approach for reducing their variance which increases the generalization of each tree independently. It is important to note that the mixed information preserves the diversity of the forests, which is essential to improve the generalization error. The random nature of the random node optimization (Criminisi et al. 2012) used to optimize (15.1) allows us to keep a high diversity among the trees.

Figure 15.2a, b compare the output classification on all the points in a rectangular section of the feature space for a decision forest classifier and for our transfer learning decision forest classifier. Both decision forests were trained with the same maximum depth $D = 8$, and have the same number of trees $|\mathcal{F}| = 100$. The data set for the target and source task is organized in the shape of a two-arm spiral. We can see that the classification decision forests have serious generalization problems since, even when all the training data of the target task is correctly classified, the spiral structure is not predicted accurately. In contrast, the spiral structure is predicted by the transfer learning decision forests as shown in Fig. 15.2a.

15.3.1.2   Label Propagation

For each leaf $k \in \partial F$ of each tree $F \in \mathcal{F}$, we must have a predictive model $p_F(\mathbf{y}|\mathbf{x} \in R_k)$ that estimates the probability of label $\mathbf{y} \in \mathcal{Y}_0$ given a previously unseen test input $\mathbf{x} \in R_k \subseteq \mathbb{R}^d$. This poses a problem when we make each tree grow using the mixed information gain because we may end up with leaves $k \in \partial F$ that have no training samples of the target task T_0 to estimate the predictive model $p_F(\mathbf{y}|\mathbf{x} \in R_k)$. In this paper we use label propagation to assign a predictive model $p_F(\mathbf{y}|\mathbf{x} \in R_k)$ to those leaves.

We are given a set of leaves $\mathcal{U} \subseteq \partial F$ without training samples of the target task T_0 and a set of leaves $\mathcal{L} \subseteq \partial F$ with training samples of the target task T_0. The goal is to obtain a predictive model $p_F(\mathbf{y}|\mathbf{x} \in R_k)$ for the leaves $k \in \mathcal{U}$ avoiding the propagation of labels through low density regions but, at the same time, propagating labels between nearby leaves. We construct a complete graph $\mathcal{G} = (\mathcal{V}, \mathcal{E})$, where $\mathcal{V} = \partial F$ is the vertex set and $\mathcal{E}$ is the edge set with each edge $\mathbf{e}_{ij} \in \mathcal{E}$ representing the relationship between nodes $i, j \in \partial F$.

Edge $\mathbf{e}_{ij} \in \mathcal{E}$ is weighted taking into account the training samples of tasks $T_0, \ldots, T_N$. For each leaf $k \in \partial F$ we define the estimated mean μ_k and estimated covariance Σ_k using the training samples reaching the node

$$\mu_k = \frac{1}{|S_k|} \sum_{(\mathbf{x}, \mathbf{y}, j) \in S_k} \mathbf{x}$$

$$\Sigma_k = \sum_{(\mathbf{x}, \mathbf{y}, j) \in S_k} \sum_{(\mathbf{x}', \mathbf{y}', j') \in S_k} (\mathbf{x} - \mu_k)(\mathbf{x}' - \mu_k)^T.$$

We use the estimated mean μ_k and estimated covariance Σ_k to define the weight between two nodes $\mathbf{e}_{ij} \in \mathcal{E}$

$$\mathbf{e}_{ij} = \frac{1}{2} \left(d_{ij}^T \Sigma_i d_{ij} + d_{ij}^T \Sigma_j d_{ij} \right)$$

where $d_{ij} = \mu_i - \mu_j$ is the difference between the estimated mean of the leaves $i, j \in \partial F$. Weight $\mathbf{e}_{ij} \in \mathcal{E}$ is the symmetric Mahalanobis distance. We use it to discourage the propagation of labels through low density regions. For each node $k \in \mathcal{U}$ we find the shortest path in graph $\mathcal{G}$ to all the nodes in $\mathcal{L}$. Let $s_k^* \in \mathcal{L}$ be the node with the shortest path to node k. We assign the predictive model $p_F(\mathbf{y}|\mathbf{x} \in R_{s_k^*})$ to $p_F(\mathbf{y}|\mathbf{x} \in R_k)$.

Label propagation methods are usually at least quadratic $\mathcal{O}(n^2)$ in terms of the number of training samples, making them slow when a large number of training samples is available. We avoid this problem by propagating the predictive model of the leaves, instead of propagating the labels of the training samples.

We illustrate the behavior of label propagation in Fig. 15.3 using a 2D toy example. We consider the same two-arm spiral problem of Fig. 15.2 which has data that follow a complex structure. We show the predictive models for the regions of two randomly grown trees before and after propagating labels. We observe that the predictive models

(a)   **(b)**

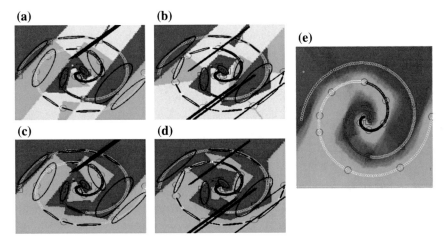

(e)

(c)   **(d)**

Fig. 15.3 Illustration of the label propagation procedure between regions, as before the training data for the target task is indicated with *big markers* and the training data for the source task is indicated with *small markers*. The ellipses in *black* are the isocontours of a Gaussian distribution learned by maximum likelihood for each region using the training samples in the region. **a, b** Show the predictive model for two different trees $F \in \mathcal{F}$ before propagating labels. The *color* associated with each region is a linear combination of the *colors* (*red* and *green*) corresponding to the two labels ($\square$, $\bigcirc$) in the target task. The regions in *yellow* are the ones without training data of the target task. **c, d** show the predictive model after the label propagation. **e** Output classification of the final transfer learning decision forest

are propagated following the intrinsic structure of the data, as a consequence of taking into account the training data of each region.

15.3.2   Testing

The predictive model of all the trees $F \in \mathcal{F}$ is combined to produce the final prediction of the forest

$$P_{\mathcal{F}}(\mathbf{y} = y | \mathbf{x}) = \frac{1}{|\mathcal{F}|} \sum_{F \in \mathcal{F}} P_F(\mathbf{y} = y | \mathbf{x}).$$

Let $l_F : \mathbb{R}^d \to \partial F$ be the function that, given a sample $\mathbf{x} \in \mathbb{R}^d$, returns the leaf such that $\mathbf{x} \in R_{l_F(\mathbf{x})}$. The prediction for a tree F is:

$$P_F(\mathbf{y} = y | \mathbf{x}) = P_F\left(\mathbf{y} = y | \mathbf{x} \in R_{l_F(\mathbf{x})}\right).$$

Finally, let $k \in \partial F$ be the leaf that is reached by sample $\mathbf{x} \in \mathbb{R}^d$. The class distribution for that leaf is:

$$P_F(\mathbf{y} = y | \mathbf{x} \in R_k) = \begin{cases} \hat{p}_{T_0 S_k}(y) & \text{if } T_0 S_k \neq \emptyset \\ \hat{p}_{T_0 S_{s_k^*}}(y) & \text{otherwise} \end{cases}.$$

Thus, $P_F(\mathbf{y} = y | \mathbf{x})$ is the empirical histogram of the training samples of the target task T_0 reaching node $l_F(\mathbf{x})$ if any. Otherwise, $P_F(\mathbf{y} = y | \mathbf{x})$ is the empirical histogram associated with the node that has the shortest path to $l_F(\mathbf{x})$.

15.4 Gesture Recognition

Gesture recognition is one of the open challenges in computer vision. There is a big number of potential applications for this problem, including surveillance, smart-homes, rehabilitation, entertainment, animation and human–robot interaction and sign language recognition just to mention a few. The task of gesture recognition is to determine the gesture label that best describes a gesture instance, even when performed by different people, from various viewpoints and in spite of large differences in manner and speed.

To reach that goal, many approaches combine vision and machine learning tools. Computer vision tools are employed to extract features that provide robustness to distracting cues and that, at the same time, are discriminative. Machine learning is used to learn a statistical model from those features, and to classify new examples using the models learned. This poses a problem in gesture recognition since it is difficult to collect big data sets to learn statistical models. Therefore, in this paper we perform experiments aimed at showing that our transfer learning decision forests are useful to mitigate this problem.

Recently, the ChaLearn competition (Guyon et al. 2012) provided a challenging data set to evaluate whether transfer learning algorithms can improve their classification performance using similar gesture vocabularies. The data set is organized into batches, with only one training example of each gesture in each batch. The goal is to automatically predict the gesture labels for the remaining gesture sequences (test examples). The gestures of each batch are drawn from a small vocabulary of 8–12 unique gestures, when we train a classifier to predict the labels of a target batch (or task) T_0 we use the training samples of T_0 and of the other batches $T_1, \ldots, T_N$.

Each batch of the ChaLearn competition includes 100 recorded gestures grouped in sequences of 1–5 gestures performed by the same user (Guyon et al. 2012). There is only one gesture in the training sequences, but there might be more than one gesture in the testing sequences. Therefore in order to use the method described in this section we need to temporally segment the testing sequences. To this end, we use the dynamic time warping (DTW) implementation given by the organizers.

In this section, we describe the features and the classifiers used to validate our approach, as well as their application to the ChaLearn competition (Guyon et al. 2012). First, Sect. 15.4.1 describes the features, and then, Sect. 15.4.2 describes the classifier.

15.4.1 Motion History Images

Given a depth video V where $V(x, y, t)$ is the depth of the pixel with coordinates (x, y) at the tth frame. We compute the motion history image (MHI) (Bobick and Davis 1996, 2001; Ahad et al. 2012) for each frame using the following function:

$$H_\tau(x, y, t) = \begin{cases} \tau & \text{if } |V(x, y, t) - V(x, y, t - 1)| \geq \xi \\ \max(0, H_\tau(x, y, t - 1) - 1) & \text{otherwise} \end{cases}$$

where τ defines the temporal extent of the MHI, and ξ is a threshold employed to perform the foreground/background segmentation at frame t. The result is a scalar-valued image for each frame of the original video V where pixels that have moved more recently are brighter. MHI H_τ represents the motion in an image sequence in a compact manner, the pixel intensity is a function of the temporal history of motion at that point. A common problem when computing MHI H_τ using the color channel is the presence of textured objects in the image sequence; here we use the depth video V to overcome this issue. This is a relevant problem in gesture recognition, because, as a result of the clothes texture, the MHI is noisy (Ahad et al. 2012).

An interesting property of the MHI is that it is sensitive to the direction of motion; hence it is well suited for discriminating between gestures with an opposite direction. An advantage of the MHI representation is that a range of times may be encoded in a single frame, and thus, the MHI spans the time scale of human gestures. After computing MHI H_τ we reduce the spatial resolution of each frame to $\omega_1 \times \omega_2$ pixels. Then, we flatten the MHI for each frame and obtain a feature $\mathbf{x}_m \in \mathbb{R}^{\omega_1 \omega_2}$.

Figure 15.4 contrasts the result of computing the MHI using the RGB channel with the one obtained using the depth channel. In the first row, we see that the clothes texture generates noise in the MHI computed using the RGB channel. In the

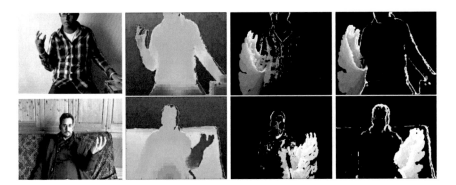

Fig. 15.4 Comparison of the MHI computed using the depth channel or the RGB channel for two different training videos of the ChaLearn competition. The first *two columns* show the RGB channel and the depth channel, whereas the *third* and *fourth columns* show the MHI computed using the RGB channel and the MHI computed using the depth channel, respectively

Table 15.1 Classification error in the test set of the *devel*11 batch for different combination of MHI parameters. In all the experiments we leave the the spatial resolution of each frame fixed to $\omega_1 \times \omega_2 = 16 \times 12$

$\tau \setminus \xi$	16 (%)	24 (%)	32 (%)	40 (%)
1	32.61 ± 0.14	32.61 ± 0.24	30.35 ± 0.22	29.26 ± 0.26
4	$\mathbf{30.43 \pm 0.17}$	31.52 ± 0.15	29.26 ± 0.15	28.17 ± 0.19
8	$\mathbf{30.43 \pm 0.13}$	$\mathbf{27.35 \pm 0.16}$	$\mathbf{28.09 \pm 0.14}$	$\mathbf{27.06 \pm 0.18}$
12	32.12 ± 0.23	32.61 ± 0.29	34.78 ± 0.31	29.35 ± 0.33
16	33.72 ± 0.28	32.61 ± 0.29	34.78 ± 0.25	30.43 ± 0.31

second row, the MHI of the RGB channel is noisy because of the shadow from the moving arm. Both problems are avoided using the depth channel for computing the MHI. The parameters to compute the MHI in all the cases were $\tau = 15$, and $\xi = 30$. Table 15.1 shows the classification error in the test set of the *devel*11 batch of the ChaLearn competition, after training a decision forest with the following parameters $D = 8$, $T = 50$.

15.4.2 Naive Bayes

A main research trend in gesture recognition is to train hidden Markov models (HMMs) and theirs variants (Bowden et al. 2004; Kurakin et al. 2012), in order to exploit the temporal relation of a gesture. A drawback of this approach is that many training samples are required to train the large number of parameters of an HMM. Additionally, recognition rates might not improve significantly (Li et al. 2008). This limitation has been recognized by Bowden et al. (2004) and a two-stage classifier was proposed to obtain one-shot learning.

Since in the ChaLearn competition (Guyon et al. 2012) there is only one labeled training sample of each gesture, we use the naive Bayes model which has a smaller number of parameters than HMM. We use transfer learning decision forests to predict the probability that each frame will be part of a given gesture. We combine the predictions of the transfer learning decision forests for each frame using the naive Bayes model. An advantage of the naive Bayes assumption is that it is not sensitive to irrelevant frames (the probabilities for all the labels will be quite similar).

Given a video V of an isolated gesture, we want to find its label $\mathbf{y} \in \mathcal{Y}_0$. Assuming that the class prior $p(\mathbf{y})$ is uniform we have:

$$\hat{\mathbf{y}} = \arg \max_{\mathbf{y} \in \mathcal{Y}_0} p(\mathbf{y}|V) = \arg \max_{\mathbf{y} \in \mathcal{Y}_0} p(V|\mathbf{y})$$

Let $\mathbf{x}_1, \ldots, \mathbf{x}_M$ denote the MHI for each frame of a video V with M frames. We assume the naive Bayes model i.e., that the features $\mathbf{x}_1, \ldots, \mathbf{x}_M$ are i.i.d. given the label $\mathbf{y}$, namely:

$$p(V|\mathbf{y}) = p(\mathbf{x}_1, \ldots, \mathbf{x}_M|\mathbf{y}) = \prod_{m=1}^{M} p(\mathbf{x}_m|\mathbf{y}) = \prod_{m=1}^{M} p(\mathbf{y}|\mathbf{x}_m)\frac{p(\mathbf{x}_m)}{p(\mathbf{y})} \qquad (15.2)$$

We compute the probability $p(\mathbf{y}|\mathbf{x}_m)$ using our proposed transfer learning decision forest $\mathcal{F}$. The data set for training the forest $\mathcal{F}$ consists of all the frames in each training video in the target task T_0 and source tasks $T_1, \ldots, T_N$. We propose to use the frames of the training videos in the source tasks to obtain a better classifier for each frame.

Taking the logarithm in (15.2) and ignoring the constant terms we obtain the following decision rule:

$$\hat{\mathbf{y}} = \arg\max_{\mathbf{y}\in\mathcal{Y}_0} p(\mathbf{y}|V) = \arg\max_{\mathbf{y}\in\mathcal{Y}_0} \sum_{m=1}^{M} \log\left(p_{\mathcal{F}}(\mathbf{y}|\mathbf{x}_m)\right)$$

Note that we use the same forest $\mathcal{F}$ for computing the label distribution of all the frames in video V. For this reason, given a frame $\mathbf{x}$, we expect distribution $p_{\mathcal{F}}(\mathbf{y}|\mathbf{x})$ to be multi-modal, which is an issue for several statistical methods. However, since the transfer learning decision forest has a predictive model for each leaf of its tree, it can deal with this type of distribution without major problems

Figure. 15.5 compares the classification error when predicting the label of a frame $p(\mathbf{y}|\mathbf{x})$ with the classification error when predicting the label of a video $p(\mathbf{y}|V)$, for different combinations of training parameters in the devel11 batch. We observe that the maximum depth D has a larger impact to predict the label of a video than the

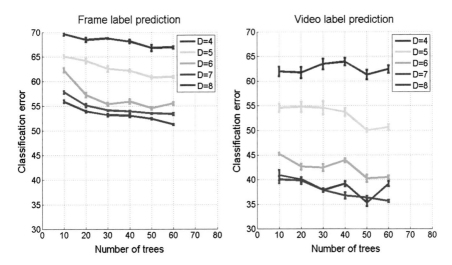

Fig. 15.5 Effect of the training parameters for the frame label classification error $p(\mathbf{y}|\mathbf{x})$ *(left)* and video label classification error $p(\mathbf{y}|V)$ *(right)* in the devel11 batch using the transfer learning decision forests

number of trees $|\mathcal{F}|$. Moreover, the classification error when predicting the label of a frame is greater than the classification error when predicting the label of a video. This means, as expected, that some frames are more discriminative than others, and that the misclassification of some frames is not a decisive factor for classifying a video correctly.

15.5 Experiments

In this section we present a series of experiments on the ChaLearn Gesture Challenge (Guyon et al. 2012) and MNIST data set (LeCun et al. 1998) to assess the performance of our proposed algorithm.

15.5.1 ChaLearn Gesture Challenge

Here, we evaluate the transfer learning decision forests on the ChaLearn Gesture Challenge. First, we compare the results obtained for different parameters of the transfer learning decision forests, and then we compare these results with the ones reported in related works. For the MHI computation in this section, we set the temporal extent $\tau = 8$, the threshold $\xi = 25$, and reduce the spatial resolution of each frame to $\omega_1 \times \omega_2 = 16 \times 12$ pixels.

15.5.1.1 Transfer Decision Learning Parameters

To obtain a general idea of the effect of the training parameters, Fig. 15.6 evaluates the classification error for different combinations of training parameters. We report the average classification error obtained in the *devel* batches. We use the temporal segmentation of the videos provided by the ChaLearn competition organizers. The experiments show that when the mixing coefficient γ is between 25 and 50%, the classification error is the smallest. This means that we obtain improvements when transferring knowledge from related tasks but, nevertheless, we still need to make the decision trees grow using information of the target task.

It is important to remark that when $\gamma = 0$ we are not using the training data of the source tasks and our mixed information gain simplifies to the usual information gain, thus, only the label propagation extension is being used. The classification error for the case $\gamma = 0$ indicates that we achieve an improvement using the label propagation alone. We obtain an additional improvement when γ is between 25 and 75%, therefore we can conclude that both extensions are important to reduce the classification error.

The maximum depth of the trees is a highly relevant parameter for the transfer learning decision forests, and has some influence for the classification decision

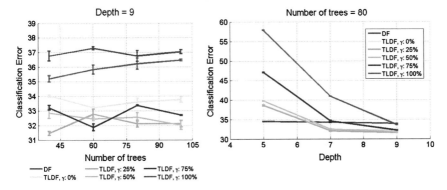

Fig. 15.6 Comparison of the classification error using different combination of training parameters

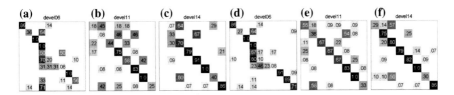

Fig. 15.7 Comparison of the confusion matrices obtained using the DF (**a–c**) and TLDF (**d–f**) classifiers on the *devel*06, *devel*11 and *devel*14 batches

forests. As expected, the greater the maximum depth, the smaller the classification error. It is interesting to observe that the difference in the classification error between different values of the mixing coefficients γ is reduced when the maximum depth is increased.

Figure 15.7 shows the confusion matrices for the classifiers of the transfer learning decision forests (TLDFs) and the decision forests (DFs) in the batches *devel*06, *devel*11 and *devel*14. To train the TLDFs, we set the number of trees $T = 50$, the maximum depth $D = 8$, the mixing coefficient $\gamma = 25\%$, and the size of the subset $|T| = 50$. In these batches the TLDFs classifier shows improvements over the DFs classifier. The improvement is not uniform for all the gestures of the batches, but only for some of them. This is because not all the gestures can benefit from the training data of the source tasks. Only the gestures that have, at least, one similar gesture in a source task show improvements.

The confusion matrix for the *devel*06 batch in Fig. 15.7 shows significant improvements in the classification of the last gesture. Figure 15.8 shows a representative image of that gesture and similar gestures in the *devel*13 and *devel*15 batches. The person in front of the camera moves the left hand to a fixed position and then shows a similar pattern of the fingers, for all these gestures. The frames of these gestures are usually found in the same leaf after training the decision forest.

Fig. 15.8 Similar gestures in different batches. The *first, second and third rows* show a gesture in the *devel06, devel13* and *devel15* batches respectively. The *first column* shows the RGB image for a representative frame of the video, the *second column* shows the corresponding depth image and the *last column* shows the MHI

15.5.1.2   Devel and Final Data

Table 15.2 compares our results for the development batches of the ChaLearn Challenge with the ones previously reported by Lui (2012) and Malgireddy et al. (2013), using the evaluation procedure of the ChaLearn competition (Guyon et al. 2012). To train the TLDFs, we set the number of trees $T = 50$, the maximum depth $D = 8$, the mixing coefficient $\gamma = 25\%$, and the size of the search space $|\mathcal{T}| = 50$. As shown in Table 15.2, for most batches, our transfer learning decision forests obtain improvements over the DFs, and for some batches, they obtain the smallest errors.

Table 15.3 compares our results for the final evaluation data with the final results of the ChaLearn competition (Guyon et al. 2013). The Joewan team proposed a novel feature which fuses RGB-D data and is invariant to scale and rotation (Wan et al. 2013). Most of the other teams have not described their approach in a publication.

Table 15.2 Comparison of reported results using the Levenshtein distance

	devel01 (%)	devel02 (%)	devel03 (%)	devel04 (%)	devel05 (%)	devel06 (%)	devel07 (%)	devel08 (%)	devel09 (%)	devel10 (%)
Principal motion	6.67	33.33	71.74	24.44	**2.17**	43.33	23.08	10.11	19.78	56.04
(Lui, 2012)	–	–	–	–	–	–	–	–	–	–
(Malgireddy et al., 2013)	13.33	35.56	71.74	**10.00**	9.78	**37.78**	18.68	**8.99**	**13.19**	**50.55**
DF	4.44	28.89	65.22	25.56	3.26	48.89	19.78	17.98	19.78	59.34
TLDF	**3.89**	**25.00**	**62.50**	13.89	4.89	45.00	**14.29**	10.11	15.38	60.99

	devel11 (%)	devel12 (%)	devel13 (%)	devel14 (%)	devel15 (%)	devel16 (%)	devel17 (%)	devel18 (%)	devel19 (%)	devel20 (%)	Avg. (%)
Principal motion	**29.35**	21.35	12.50	39.13	40.22	34.48	48.91	44.44	60.44	39.56	33.15
(Lui, 2012)	–	–	–	–	–	–	–	–	–	–	24.09
(Malgireddy et al., 2013)	35.87	22.47	**9.09**	28.26	**21.74**	31.03	**30.43**	40.00	**49.45**	**35.16**	28.73
DF	42.39	23.60	19.32	45.65	26.09	31.03	53.26	40.00	60.44	46.15	34.14
TLDF	39.13	**19.10**	25.00	**27.71**	31.52	**27.01**	45.11	**38.33**	54.95	67.22	31.55

Table 15.3 ChaLearn results of round 2

Team	Private score set on final set #1	For comparison score on final set #2
alfnie	0.0734	0.0710
Joewan	0.1680	0.1448
Turtle Tamers	0.1702	0.1098
Wayne Zhang	0.2303	0.1846
Manavender	0.2163	0.1608
HIT CS	0.2825	0.2008
Vigilant	0.2809	0.2235
Our Method	0.2834	0.2475
Baseline method 2	0.2997	0.3172

15.5.2   MNIST

The MNIST (LeCun et al. 1998) data set has been used to compare transfer learning results (Quadrianto et al. 2010; Faddoul et al. 2012). A small sample of the training set is used to simulate the situation when only a limited number of labeled examples is available. For each digit $0 \ldots 9$, we consider a binary task where label $+1$ means that the example belongs to the digit associated with the respective task, and label -1 means the opposite. We randomly choose 100 training samples for each task and test them on the 10,000 testing samples. The experiments are repeated ten times and the results are summarized in Table 15.4. We train the TLDFs with $D = 6$, $T = 40$, $\gamma = 50\%$, and we do not apply any preprocessing to the sample images. The experiments show that our approach achieves better results than state-of-the-art methods in terms of transfer learning.

To analyze the influence of the number of training samples, we compare the classification error of the TLDFs with the classification error of the DFs. Figure 15.9

Table 15.4 Comparison of the accuracies on the MNIST data set

	1/-1 (%)	2/-2 (%)	3/-3 (%)	4/-4 (%)	5/-5 (%)	6/-6 (%)
Adaboost (Faddoul et al. 2012)	91.77±1.89	83.14±2.35	82.96±1.24	83.98±1.41	78.42±0.69	88.95±1.60
MTL (Quadrianto et al. 2010)	96.80±1.91	69.95±2.68	74.18±5.54	71.76±5.47	57.26±2.72	80.54±4.53
MT-Adaboost (Faddoul et al. 2012)	96.80±0.56	86.87±0.68	87.68±1.04	**90.38±0.71**	84.25±0.73	92.88±0.90
Our approach	**97.23±0.44**	**96.74±0.31**	**93.29±0.96**	90.10±1.23	**92.79±1.62**	**97.35±0.45**
	7/-7 (%)	8/-8 (%)	9/-9 (%)	0/-0 (%)	Avg. (%)	
Adaboost (Faddoul et al. 2012)	87.11±0.90	77.51±1.90	81.84±1.85	93.66±1.29	84.93	
MTL (Quadrianto et al. 2010)	77.18±9.43	65.85±2.50	65.38±6.09	97.81±1.01	75.67	
MT-Adaboost (Faddoul et al. 2012)	92.81±0.57	85.28±1.73	**86.90±1.26**	97.14±0.42	90.10	
Our approach	**95.55±1.39**	**91.99±1.30**	84.76±1.67	**98.05±0.28**	**93.78**	

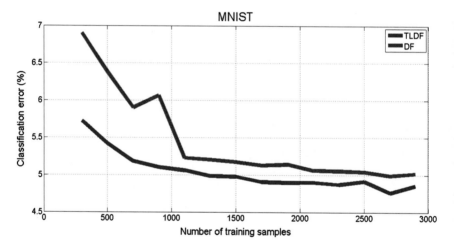

Fig. 15.9 This figure evaluates the classification error as a function of the number of training samples

plots the classification error as a function of the number of training samples for each classifier. As we did previously, we compute the classification error using the 10,000 test samples of the MNIST data set. We see that the classification error of the TLDF is smaller than that of the DF. In addition, it is interesting to note that the gap between both classifiers is larger when the number of training samples is smaller, thus suggesting that the TLDF is more suitable than DF for small training samples.

15.6 Conclusions

In this paper we have introduced a novel algorithm to transfer knowledge from multiple source tasks to a given target task. The result is a classifier that can exploit the knowledge from similar tasks to improve the predictive performance on the target task. Two extensions were made to the decision forest framework in order to extract knowledge from the source tasks. We showed that both extensions are important in order to obtain smaller classification errors. The major improvements are obtained when there are only a few training samples.

We have applied the algorithm to two important computer vision problems and the results show that the proposed algorithm outperforms decision forests (which are a state-of-the-art method). We believe that transfer learning algorithms will be an essential component of many computer vision problems.

Acknowledgements We would like to thank Zicheng Liu and Julio Jacobo-Berlles for their feedback and assistance.

Appendix A

We prove Theorem 1. First, we prove $\mathbb{E}(\mathcal{H}(S_K)) + \sum_{\mathbf{y} \in \mathcal{Y}} p_\mathbf{y} \log \left(1 + \frac{1 - p_\mathbf{y}}{K p_\mathbf{y}}\right) \leq \mathcal{H}(P)$

By definition of the empirical entropy and linearity of the expectation, we have:

$$\mathbb{E}(\mathcal{H}(S_K)) = -\mathbb{E}\left[\sum_{\mathbf{y} \in \mathcal{Y}} \hat{p}_{S_K}(\mathbf{y}) \log(\hat{p}_{S_K}(\mathbf{y}))\right] = -\sum_{\mathbf{y} \in \mathcal{Y}} \mathbb{E}\left[\hat{p}_{S_K}(\mathbf{y}) \log(\hat{p}_{S_K}(\mathbf{y}))\right]$$

Using the definitions of the empirical histogram $\hat{p}_{S_K}(\mathbf{y})$ and the expectation:

$$-\sum_{\mathbf{y} \in \mathcal{Y}} \mathbb{E}\left[\hat{p}_{S_K}(\mathbf{y}) \log(\hat{p}_{S_K}(\mathbf{y}))\right] = -\sum_{\mathbf{y} \in \mathcal{Y}} \sum_{j=0}^{K} P\left(\hat{p}_{S_K}(\mathbf{y}) = \frac{j}{K}\right) \frac{j}{K} \log \frac{j}{K}$$

Assuming that the samples are iid, then:

$$= -\sum_{\mathbf{y} \in \mathcal{Y}} \sum_{j=0}^{K} \binom{K}{j} p_\mathbf{y}^j (1 - p_\mathbf{y})^{K-j} \frac{j}{K} \log \frac{j}{K}$$

Note that, in this equation, $p_\mathbf{y}$ is the true probability of distribution P. After some algebraic manipulations, we obtain the following:

$$= -\sum_{\mathbf{y}\in\mathcal{Y}} p_{\mathbf{y}} \sum_{j=0}^{K-1} \binom{K-1}{j} p_{\mathbf{y}}^{j}(1-p_{\mathbf{y}})^{K-1-j} \log\frac{j+1}{K}$$

$$= -\sum_{\mathbf{y}\in\mathcal{Y}} p_{\mathbf{y}} \sum_{j=0}^{K-1} P\left(\hat{p}_{S_K}(\mathbf{y}) = \frac{j}{K}\right) \log\frac{j+1}{K}$$

Applying Jensen's inequality for the convex function $-\log(x)$, we obtain:

$$\geq -\sum_{\mathbf{y}\in\mathcal{Y}} p_{\mathbf{y}} \log\left(\sum_{j=0}^{K-1} P\left(\hat{p}_{S_K}(\mathbf{y}) = \frac{j}{K}\right)\frac{j+1}{K}\right)$$

$$= -\sum_{\mathbf{y}\in\mathcal{Y}} p_{\mathbf{y}} \log\frac{(K-1)p_{\mathbf{y}}+1}{K}$$

$$= -\sum_{\mathbf{y}\in\mathcal{Y}} p_{\mathbf{y}} \log\left(p_{\mathbf{y}} + \frac{1-p_{\mathbf{y}}}{K}\right)$$

$$= -\sum_{\mathbf{y}\in\mathcal{Y}} p_{\mathbf{y}} \log\left(p_{\mathbf{y}}\left(1 + \frac{1-p_{\mathbf{y}}}{Kp_{\mathbf{y}}}\right)\right)$$

$$= -\sum_{\mathbf{y}\in\mathcal{Y}} p_{\mathbf{y}} \log p_{\mathbf{y}} - \sum_{\mathbf{y}\in\mathcal{Y}} p_{\mathbf{y}} \log\left(1 + \frac{1-p_{\mathbf{y}}}{Kp_{\mathbf{y}}}\right)$$

$$= \mathcal{H}(P) - \sum_{\mathbf{y}\in\mathcal{Y}} p_{\mathbf{y}} \log\left(1 + \frac{1-p_{\mathbf{y}}}{Kp_{\mathbf{y}}}\right)$$

Now we prove $\mathcal{H}(P) \leq \mathbb{E}(\mathcal{H}(S_K))$.

By definition of the empirical entropy and linearity of the expectation, we have:

$$\mathbb{E}(\mathcal{H}(S_K)) = -\mathbb{E}\left[\sum_{\mathbf{y}\in\mathcal{Y}} \hat{p}_{S_K}(\mathbf{y}) \log(\hat{p}_{S_K}(\mathbf{y}))\right] = -\sum_{\mathbf{y}\in\mathcal{Y}} \mathbb{E}\left[\hat{p}_{S_K}(\mathbf{y}) \log(\hat{p}_{S_K}(\mathbf{y}))\right]$$

Applying Jensen's inequality for the convex function $x\log x$, we obtain the following:

$$\leq -\sum_{\mathbf{y}\in\mathcal{Y}} \mathbb{E}\left[\hat{p}_{S_K}(\mathbf{y})\right] \log(\mathbb{E}\left[\hat{p}_{S_K}(\mathbf{y})\right])$$

Since $\mathbb{E}\left[\hat{p}_{S_K}(\mathbf{y})\right] = p_{\mathbf{y}}$, we have:

$$= -\sum_{\mathbf{y}\in\mathcal{Y}} p_{\mathbf{y}} \log(p_{\mathbf{y}}) = \mathcal{H}(P)$$

References

M.A.R. Ahad, J.K. Tan, H. Kim, S. Ishikawa, Motion history image: its variants and applications. Mach. Vis. Appl. **23**(2), 255–281 (2012)

Y. Aytar, A. Zisserman, Tabula rasa: model transfer for object category detection, in *Proceedings of the IEEE Computer Vision and Pattern Recognition*, 2011

E. Bart, S. Ullman, Cross-generalization: learning novel classes from a single example by feature replacement, in *Proceedings of the IEEE Computer Vision and Pattern Recognition*, 2005

A. Bergamo, L. Torresani, Exploiting weakly-labeled web images to improve object classification: a domain adaptation approach, in *Proceedings of the Advances in Neural Information Processing Systems*, 2010, pp. 181–189

A. Bobick, J. Davis, An appearance-based representation of action, in *Proceedings of the International Conference on Pattern Recognition*, 1996, pp. 307–312

A. Bobick, J. Davis. The recognition of human movement using temporal templates. IEEE Trans. Pattern Anal. Mach., 2001

R. Bowden, D. Windridge, T. Kadir, A. Zisserman, J. M. Brady. A linguistic feature vector for the visual interpretation of sign language, in *Proceedings of the European Conference on Computer Vision*, 2004

L. Breiman, Random forests. Mach. Learn. **45**(1), 5–32 (2001)

T.M. Cover, J.A. Thomas, *Elements of Information Theory* (Wiley, Hoboken, 2006)

A. Criminisi, J. Shotton, E. Konukoglu, Decision forests: a unified framework for classification, regression, density estimation, manifold learning and semi-supervised learning. Found. Trends Comput. Graph. Vis. **7**(2–3), 81–227 (2012)

W. Dai, Q. Yang, G.R. Xue, Y. Yu, Boosting for transfer learning, in *Proceedings of the International Conference on Machine Learning*, New York, NY, USA, 2007, p. 193–200

J.B. Faddoul, B. Chidlovskii, R. Gilleron, F. Torre, Learning multiple tasks with boosted decision trees, in *Proceedings of the European Conference on Machine Learning and Knowledge Discovery in Databases*, 2012

A. Farhadi, D. Forsyth, R. White, Transfer learning in sign language, in *Proceedings of the IEEE Computer Vision and Pattern Recognition*, 2007, pp. 1–8

L. Fei-Fei, R. Fergus, P. Perona, One-shot learning of object categories. IEEE Trans. Pattern Anal. Mach. **28**(4), 594–611 (2006)

Pedro F. Felzenszwalb, Ross B. Girshick, David A. McAllester, Deva Ramanan, Object detection with discriminatively trained part-based models. IEEE Trans. Pattern Anal. Mach. **32**(9), 1627–1645 (2010)

Y. Freund, R.E. Schapire, A decision-theoretic generalization of on-line learning and an application to boosting. J. Comput. Syst. Sci. **55**(1), 119–139 (1997)

R. Gopalan, R. Li, R. Chellappa, Domain adaptation for object recognition: an unsupervised approach, in *Proceedings of the IEEE International Conference on Computer Vision*, 2011, pp. 999–1006

E. Grosicki, H.E. Abed, ICDAR 2011 - French handwriting recognition competition, in *Proceedings of the International Conference on Document Analysis and Recognition*, 2011, pp. 1459–1463

I. Guyon, V. Athitsos, P. Jangyodsuk, B. Hamner, H.J. Escalante, ChaLearn gesture challenge: design and first results, in *Workshop on Gesture Recognition and Kinect Demonstration Competition*, 2012

I. Guyon, V. Athitsos, P. Jangyodsuk, H.J. Escalante, B. Hamner, Results and analysis of the ChaLearn gesture challenge 2012, in *Advances in Depth Image Analysis and Applications*, vol. 7854 of *Lecture Notes in Computer Science* (Springer, New York, 2013), pp. 186–204

T. Hastie, R. Tibshirani, J.H. Friedman, *The Elements of Statistical Learning.* (Springer, New York, 2003)

A. Kurakin, Z. Zhang, Z. Liu, A real-time system for dynamic hand gesture recognition with a depth sensor, in *Proceedings of the European Signal Processing Conference*, 2012, pp. 1980–1984

Y. LeCun, L. Bottou, Y. Bengio, P. Haffner, Gradient-based learning applied to document recognition, in *Proceedings of the IEEE*, 1998, pp. 2278–2324

C. Leistner, A. Saffari, J. Santner, H. Bischof, Semi-supervised random forests, in *Proceedings of the IEEE International Conference on Computer Vision*, 2009, pp. 506–513

K. Levi, M. Fink, Y. Weiss. Learning from a small number of training examples by exploiting object categories, in *Proceedings of the IEEE Computer Vision and Pattern Recognition Workshop*, 2004, pp. 96–102

W. Li, Z. Zhang, Z. Liu, Graphical modeling and decoding of human actions, in *Proceedings of the IEEE International Workshop on Multimedia Signal Processing*, 2008, pp. 175–180

J.J. Lim, R. Salakhutdinov, A. Torralba, Transfer learning by borrowing examples for multiclass object detection, in *Proceedings of the Advances in Neural Information Processing Systems*, 2011

J. Liu, K. Yu, Y. Zhang, Y. Huang, Training conditional random fields using transfer learning for gesture recognition, in *Proceedings of the IEEE International Conference on Data Mining*, 2010, pp. 314–323

Y.M. Lui, Human gesture recognition on product manifolds. J. Mach. Learn. Res. **13**, 3297–3321 (2012)

M.R. Malgireddy, I. Nwogu, V. Govindaraju, Language-motivated approaches to action recognition. J. Mach. Learn. Res. **14**, 2189–2212 (2013)

S.J. Pan, Q. Yang, A survey on transfer learning. IEEE Trans. Knowl. Data Eng. **22**(10), 1345–1359, October 2010. ISSN 1041-4347

Y. Pei, T.-K. Kim, H. Zha, Unsupervised random forest manifold alignment for lipreading, in *Proceedings of the IEEE International Conference on Computer Vision*, 2013

N. Quadrianto, A.J Smola, T. Caetano, S.V.N. Vishwanathanand, J. Petterson, Multitask learning without label correspondences, in *Proceedings of the Advances in Neural Information Processing Systems*, 2010

A. Quattoni, M. Collins, T. Darrell, Transfer learning for image classification with sparse prototype representations, in *Proceedings of the IEEE Computer Vision and Pattern Recognition*, 2008, pp. 1–8

J.R. Quinlan, Induction of decision trees. Mach. Learn. **1**(1), 81–106 (1986)

K. Saenko, B. Kulis, M. Fritz, T. Darrell. Adapting visual category models to new domains, in *Proceedings of the European Conference on Computer Vision*, 2010, pp. 213–226

H.J. Seo, P. Milanfar, Action recognition from one example. IEEE Trans. Pattern Anal. Mach. **33**(5), 867–882 (2011)

T. Sharp, Implementing decision trees and forests on a GPU, in *Proceedings of the European Conference on Computer Vision*, 2008, pp. 595–608

E.B. Sudderth, A. Torralba, W.T. Freeman, A.S. Willsky, Learning hierarchical models of scenes, objects, and parts, in *Proceedings of the IEEE International Conference on Computer Vision*, 2005, pp. 1331–1338

T. Tommasi, F. Orabona, B. Caputo, Learning categories from few examples with multi model knowledge transfer. IEEE Trans. Pattern Anal. Mach. **36**(5), 928–941 (2014)

A. Torralba, K.P. Murphy, W.T. Freeman, Sharing visual features for multiclass and multiview object detection. IEEE Trans. Pattern Anal. Mach. **29**(5), 854–869 (2007)

P.A. Viola, M.J. Jones, Robust real-time face detection. Int. J. Comput. Vis. **57**(2), 137–154 (2004)

J. Wan, Q. Ruan, W. Li, S. Deng, One-shot learning gesture recognition from RGB-D data using bag of features. J. Mach. Learn. Res. **14**, 2549–2582 (2013)

Q. Wang, L. Zhang, M. Chi, J. Guo, MTForest: ensemble decision trees based on multi-task learning, in *Proceedings of the European Conference on Artificial Intelligence*, 2008, pp. 122–126

J. won Lee, C. Giraud-Carrier, Transfer learning in decision trees, in *Proceedings of the International Joint Conference on Neural Networks*, 2007

Y. Yao, G. Doretto, Boosting for transfer learning with multiple sources, in *Proceedings of the IEEE Computer Vision and Pattern Recognition*, 2010, pp. 1855–1862

Chapter 16
Multimodal Gesture Recognition via Multiple Hypotheses Rescoring

Vassilis Pitsikalis, Athanasios Katsamanis, Stavros Theodorakis and Petros Maragos

Abstract We present a new framework for multimodal gesture recognition that is based on a multiple hypotheses rescoring fusion scheme. We specifically deal with a demanding Kinect-based multimodal dataset, introduced in a recent gesture recognition challenge (CHALEARN 2013), where multiple subjects freely perform multimodal gestures. We employ multiple modalities, that is, visual cues, such as skeleton data, color and depth images, as well as audio, and we extract feature descriptors of the hands' movement, handshape, and audio spectral properties. Using a common hidden Markov model framework we build single-stream gesture models based on which we can generate multiple single stream-based hypotheses for an unknown gesture sequence. By multimodally rescoring these hypotheses via constrained decoding and a weighted combination scheme, we end up with a multimodally-selected best hypothesis. This is further refined by means of parallel fusion of the monomodal gesture models applied at a segmental level. In this setup, accurate gesture modeling is proven to be critical and is facilitated by an activity detection system that is also presented. The overall approach achieves 93.3% gesture recognition accuracy in the CHALEARN Kinect-based multimodal dataset, significantly outperforming all recently published approaches on the same challenging multimodal gesture recognition task, providing a relative error rate reduction of at least 47.6%.

Editors: Isabelle Guyon, Vassilis Athitsos and Sergio Escalera

V. Pitsikalis (✉) · A. Katsamanis · S. Theodorakis · P. Maragos
School of Electrical and Computer Engineering, National Technical University of Athens,
Zografou Campus, 15773 Athens, Greece
e-mail: vpitsik@cs.ntua.gr; vpitsik@deeplab.ai

A. Katsamanis
e-mail: nkatsam@cs.ntua.gr

S. Theodorakis
e-mail: sth@cs.ntua.gr; sth@deeplab.ai

P. Maragos
e-mail: maragos@cs.ntua.gr

Keywords Multimodal gesture recognition · HMMs · Speech recognition · Mulimodal fusion · Activity detection

16.1 Introduction

Human communication and interaction takes advantage of multiple sensory inputs in an impressive way. Despite receiving a significant flow of multimodal signals, especially in the audio and visual modalities, our cross-modal integration ability enables us to effectively perceive the world around us. Examples span a great deal of cases. Cross-modal illusions are indicative of lower perceptual multimodal interaction and plasticity (Shimojo and Shams 2001): for instance, when watching a video, a sound is perceived as coming from the speakers lips (the ventriloquism effect) while, in addition, speech perception may be affected by whether the lips are visible or not (the McGurk effect).

At a higher level, multimodal integration is also regarded important for language production and this is how the notion of multimodal gestures can be introduced. Several authors, as (McNeill 1992), support the position that hand gestures hold a major role, and together with speech they are considered to have a deep relationship and to form an integrated system (Bernardis and Gentilucci 2006) by interacting at multiple linguistic levels. This integration has been recently explored in terms of communication by means of language comprehension (Kelly et al. 2010). For instance, speakers pronounce words while executing hand gestures that may have redundant or complementary nature, and even blind speakers gesture while talking to blind listeners (Iverson and Goldin-Meadow 1998). From a developmental point of view, see references in the work of (Bernardis and Gentilucci 2006), hand movements occur in parallel during babbling of 6–8 month children, whereas word comprehension at the age of 8–10 months goes together with deictic gestures. All the above suffice to provide indicative evidence from various perspectives that hand gestures and speech seem to be interwoven.

In the area of human-computer interaction gesture has been gaining increasing attention (Turk 2014). This is attributed both to recent technological advances, such as the wide spread of depth sensors, and to groundbreaking research since the famous "put that there" (Bolt 1980). The natural feeling of gesture interaction can be significantly enhanced by the availability of multiple modalities. Static and dynamic gestures, the form of the hand, as well as speech, all together compose an appealing set of modalities that offers significant advantages (Oviatt and Cohen 2000).

In this context, we focus on the effective detection and recognition of multimodally expressed gestures as performed *freely* by multiple users. Multimodal gesture recognition (MGR) poses numerous challenging research issues, such as detection of meaningful information in audio and visual signals, extraction of appropriate features, building of effective classifiers, and multimodal combination of multiple information sources (Jaimes and Sebe 2007). The demanding dataset (Escalera et al. 2013b) used in our work has been recently acquired for the needs of the multimodal gesture recognition challenge (Escalera et al. 2013a). It comprises multimodal cultural-anthropological gestures of everyday life, in spontaneous realizations of both spoken and hand-gesture articulations by multiple subjects, intermixed with other random and irrelevant hand, body movements and spoken phrases.

A successful multimodal gesture recognition system is expected to exploit both speech and computer vision technologies. Speech technologies and automatic speech recognition (Rabiner and Juang 1993) have a long history of advancements and can be considered mature when compared to the research challenges found in corresponding computer vision tasks. The latter range from low-level tasks that deal with visual descriptor representations (Li and Allinson 2008), to more difficult ones, such as recognition of action (Laptev et al. 2008), of facial expressions, handshapes and gestures, and reach higher-level tasks such as sign language recognition (Agris et al. 2008). However, recently the incorporation of depth enabled sensors has assisted to partially overcome the burden of detection and tracking, opening the way for addressing more challenging problems. The study of *multiple modalities' fusion* is one such case, that is linked with subjects discussed above.

Despite the progress seen in either unimodal cases such as the fusion of multiple speech cues for speech recognition (e.g., Bourlard and Dupont 1997) or the multimodal case of audio-visual speech (Potamianos et al. 2004; Glotin et al. 2001; Papandreou et al. 2009), the integration of dissimilar cues in MGR poses several challenges; even when several cues are excluded such as facial ones, or the eye gaze. This is due to the complexity of the task that involves several intra-modality diverse cues, as the 3D hands' shape and pose. These require different representations and may occur both sequentially and in parallel, and at different time scales and/or rates. Most of the existing gesture-based systems have certain limitations, for instance, either by only allowing a reduced set of symbolic commands based on simple hand postures or 3D pointing (Jaimes and Sebe 2007), or by considering single-handed cases in controlled tasks. Such restrictions are indicative of the task's difficulty despite already existing work (Sharma et al. 2003) even before the appearance of depth sensors (Weimer and Ganapathy 1989).

The fusion of multiple information sources can be either early, late or intermediate, that is, either at the data/feature level, or at the stage of decisions after applying independent unimodal models, or in-between; for further details refer to relative reviews (Jaimes and Sebe 2007; Maragos et al. 2008). In the case of MGR late fusion is a typical choice since involved modalities may demonstrate synchronization in several ways (Habets et al. 2011) and possibly at higher linguistic levels. This is in contrast, for instance, to the case of combining lip movements with speech in audio-visual speech where early or state-synchronous fusion can be applied, with synchronization at the phoneme-level.

In this paper, we present a multimodal gesture recognition system that exploits the color, depth and audio signals captured by a Kinect sensor. The system first extracts features for the handshape configuration, the movement of the hands and the speech signal. Based on the extracted features and statistically trained models, single modality-based hypotheses are then generated for an unknown gesture sequence. The underlying single-modality modeling scheme is based on gesture-level hidden

Markov models (HMMs), as described in Sect. 16.3.1. These are accurately initialized by means of a model-based activity detection system for each modality, presented in Sect. 16.3.3. The generated hypotheses are re-evaluated using a statistical *multimodal multiple hypotheses fusion* scheme, presented in Sect. 16.3.2. The proposed scheme builds on previous work on N-best rescoring: N-best sentence hypotheses scoring was introduced for the integration of speech and natural language by Chow and Schwartz (1989) and has also been employed for the integration of different recognition systems based on the same modality, e.g., by Ostendorf et al. (1991), or for audio-visual speech recognition by Glotin et al. (2001). *Given* the best multimodally-selected hypothesis, and the implied gesture temporal boundaries in all information streams, a final *segmental parallel fusion* step is applied based on parallel HMMs (Vogler and Metaxas 2001). We show in Sect. 16.5 that the proposed overall MGR framework outperforms the approaches that participated in the recent demanding multimodal challenge (Escalera et al. 2013a), as published in the proceedings of the workshop, by reaching an accuracy of 93.3 and leading to a relative error rate (as Levenshtein distance) reduction of 47% over the first-ranked team.

16.2 Related Work

Despite earlier work in multimodal gesture recognition, it is considered an open field, related to speech recognition, computer vision, gesture recognition and human-computer interaction. As discussed in Sect. 16.1 it is a multilevel problem posing challenges on audio and visual processing, on multimodal stream modeling and fusion. Next, we first consider works related to the recent advances on multimodal recognition, including indicative works evaluated in the same CHALEARN challenge and recognition task by sharing the exact training/testing protocol and dataset. Then, we review issues related to basic components and tasks, such as visual detection and tracking, visual representations, temporal segmentation, statistical modeling and fusion.

There are several excellent reviews on multimodal interaction either from the computer vision or human-computer interaction aspect (Jaimes and Sebe 2007; Turk 2014). Since earlier pioneering works (Bolt 1980; Poddar et al. 1998) there has been an explosion of works in the area; this is also due to the introduction of everyday usage depth sensors (e.g., Ren et al. 2011). Such works span a variety of applications such as the recent case of gestures and accompanying speech integration for a problem in geometry (Miki et al. 2014), the integration of nonverbal auditory features with gestures for agreement recognition (Bousmalis et al. 2011), or within the aspect of social signal analysis (Ponce-López et al. 2013; Song et al. 2013) propose a probabilistic extension of first-order logic, integrating multimodal speech/visual data for recognizing complex events such as everyday kitchen activities.

The CHALEARN task is an indicative case of the effort recently placed in the field: Published approaches ranked in the first places of this gesture challenge, employ multimodal signals including audio, color, depth and skeletal information; for learning and recognition one finds approaches ranging from hidden Markov models (HMMs)/Gaussian mixture models (GMMs) to boosting, random forests, neural networks and support vector machines among others. Next, we refer to indicative approaches from therein (Escalera et al. 2013b). In Sect. 16.5 we refer to specific details for the top-ranked approaches that we compare with. Wu et al. (2013), the first-ranked team, are driven by the audio modality based on end-point detection, to detect the multimodal gestures; then they combine classifiers by calculating normalized confidence scores. Bayer and Thierry (2013) are also driven by the audio based on a hand-tuned detection algorithm, then they estimate class probabilities per gesture segment and compute their weighted average. Nandakumar et al. (2013) are driven by both audio HMM segmentation, and skeletal points. They discard segments not detected in both modalities while employing a temporal overlap coefficient to merge overlapping modalites' segments. Finally, they recognize the gesture with the highest combined score. Chen and Koskela (2013) employ the extreme learning machine, a class of single-hidden layer feed-forward neural network and apply both early and late fusion. In a late stage, they use the geometric mean to fuse the classification outputs. Finally, Neverova et al. (2013) propose a mutliple-scale learning approach that is applied on both temporal and spatial dimension while employing a recurrent neural network. Our contribution in the specific area of multimodal gestures recognition concerns the employment of a late fusion scheme based on multiple hypothesis rescoring. The proposed system, also employing multimodal activity detectors, all in a HMM statistical framework, demonstrates improved performance over the rest of the approaches that took part in the specific CHALEARN task.

From the visual processing aspect the first issue to be faced is *hand detection* and *tracking*. Regardless of the boost offered after the introduction of depth sensors there are unhandled cases as in the case of low quality video or resolution, in complex scene backgrounds with multiple users, and varying illumination conditions. Features employed are related to skin color, edge information, shape and motion for hand detection (Argyros and Lourakis 2004; Yang et al. 2002), and learning algorithms such as boosting (Ong and Bowden 2004). *Tracking* is based on blobs (Starner et al. 1998; Tanibata et al. 2002; Argyros and Lourakis 2004), hand appearance (Huang and Jeng 2001), or hand boundaries (Chen et al. 2003; Cui and Weng 2000), whereas modeling techiques include Kalman filtering (Binh et al. 2005), the condensation method (Isard and Blake 1998), or full upper body pose tracking (Shotton et al. 2013). Others directly employ global image features (Bobick and Davis 2001). Finally, Alon et al. (2009) employ a unified framework that performs spatial segmentation simultaneously with higher level tasks. In this work, similarly to other authors, see works presented by Escalera et al. (2013b), we take advantage of the kinect-provided skeleton tracking.

Visual feature extraction aims at the representation of the movement, the position and the shape of the hands. Representative measurements include the center-of-gravity of the hand blob (Bauer and Kraiss 2001), motion features (Yang et al. 2002), as well as features related with the hand's shape, such as shape moments (Starner et al. 1998) or sizes and distances within the hand (Vogler and Metaxas 2001). The contour of the hand is also used for invariant features, such as Fourier descriptors (Conseil et al. 2007). Handshape representations are extracted via principal component analysis (e.g., Du and Piater 2010), or with variants of active shape and appearance models (Roussos et al. 2013). Other approaches (e.g. Dalal and Triggs 2005 employ general purpose features as the Histogram of Oriented Gradients (HOG) (Buehler et al. 2009), or the scale invariant feature transform (Lowe 1999). Li and Allinson (2008) present a review on local features. In this work, we employ the 3D points of the articulators as extracted from the depth-based skeleton tracking and the HOG descriptors for the handshape cue.

Temporal detection or *segmentation* of meaningfull information concerns another important aspect of our approach. Often the segmentation problem is seen in terms of gesture spotting, that is, for the detection of the meaningful gestures, as adapted from the case of speech (Wilcox and Bush 1992) where all non-interesting patterns are modeled by a single filler model. Specifically, Lee and Kim (1999) employ in similar way an ergodic model termed as threshold model to set adaptive likelihood thresholds. Segmentation may be also seen in combination with recognition as by Alon et al. (2009) or Li and Allinson (2007) in the latter, start and end points of gestures are determined by zero crossing of likelihoods' difference between gesture/non-gestures. There has also been substantial related work in sign language tasks: Han et al. (2009) explicitly perform segmentation based on motion discontinuities, Kong and Ranganath (2010) segment trajectories via rule-based segmentation, whereas others apply systematic segmentation as part of the modeling of sub-sign components (sub-units) (Bauer and Kraiss 2001) the latter can be enhanced by an unsupervised segmentation component (Theodorakis et al. 2014) or by employing linguistic-phonetic information (Pitsikalis et al. 2011), leading to multiple subunit types. In our case, regardeless of the availability of ground truth temporal gesture annotations we employ independent monomodal model-based activity detectors that share a common HMM framework. These function independently of the ground truth annotations, and are next exploited at the statistical modeling stage.

Multimodal gesture recognition concerns multiple dynamically varying streams, requiring the handling of multiple variable time-duration diverse cues. Such requirements are met by approaches such as hidden Markov models that have been found to efficiently model temporal information. The corresponding framework further provides efficient algorithms, such as BaumWelch and Viterbi (Rabiner and Juang 1993), for evaluation, learning, and decoding. For instance, Nam and Wohn (1996) apply HMMs in gesture recognition, Lee and Kim (1999) in gesture spotting, whereas parametric HMMs (Wilson and Bobick 1999) are employed for gestures with systematic variation. At the same time parallel HMMs (Vogler and Metaxas 2001) accommodate multiple cues simultaneously. Extensions include conditional random fields (CRFs) or generalizations (Wang et al. 2006), while non-parametric methods are also present in MGR tasks (Celebi et al. 2013; Hernández-Vela et al. 2013). In this paper we build word-level HMMs, which fit our overall statistical framework, both for audio and visual modalities, while also employing parallel HMMs for late fusion.

16.3 Proposed Methodology

To better explain the proposed multimodal gesture recognition framework let us first describe a use case. Multimodal gestures are commonly used in various settings and cultures (Morris et al. 1979; Kendon 2004). Examples include the "Ok" gesture expressed by creating a circle using the thumb and forefinger and holding the other fingers straight and at the same time uttering "Okay" or "Perfect". Similarly, the gesture "Come here" involves the generation of the so-called beckoning sign which in Northern America is made by sticking out and moving repeatedly the index finger from the clenched palm, facing the gesturer, and uttering a phrase such as "Come here" or "Here". We specifically address automatic detection and recognition of a set of such spontaneously generated multimodal gestures even when these are intermixed with other irrelevant actions, which could be verbal, nonverbal or both. The gesturer may, for example, be walking in-between the gestures or talking to somebody else.

In this context, we focus only on gestures that are always multimodal, that is, they are not expressed only verbally or non-verbally, without implying however strictly synchronous realizations in all modalities or making any related assumptions apart from expecting consecutive multimodal gestures to be sufficiently well separated in time, namely a few milliseconds apart in all information streams. Further, no linguistic assumptions are made regarding the sequence of gestures, namely any gesture can follow any other.

Let $G = \{g_i\}, i = 1, \ldots, |G|$ be the set of multimodal gestures to be possibly detected and recognized in a recording and let $S = \{\mathbf{O}_i\}, i = 1, \ldots, |S|$ be the set of information streams that are concurrently observed for that purpose. In our experiments, the latter set comprises three streams, namely audio spectral features, the gesturer's skeleton and handshape features. Based on these observations the proposed system will generate a hypothesis for the sequence of gesture appearances in a specific recording/session, like the following:

$$\mathbf{h} = [bm, g_1, sil, g_5, \ldots, bm, sil, g_3].$$

The symbol sil essentially corresponds to inactivity in all modalities while bm represents any other activity, mono- or multimodal, that does not constitute any of the target multimodal gestures. This recognized sequence is generated by exploiting single stream-based gesture models via the proposed fusion algorithm that is summarized in Fig. 16.1 and described in detail in Sect. 16.3.2. For the sake of clarity, the single stream modeling framework is first presented in Sect. 16.3.1. Performance of the overall algorithm is found to depend on how accurately the single stream models

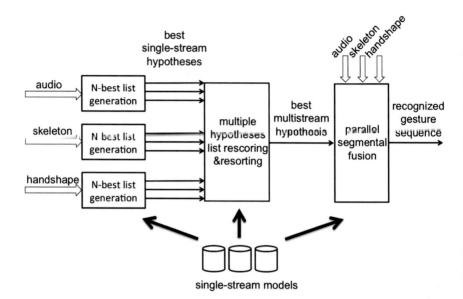

Fig. 16.1 Overview of the proposed multimodal fusion scheme for gesture recognition based on multiple hypotheses rescoring. Single-stream models are first used to generate possible hypotheses for the observed gesture sequence. The hypotheses are then rescored by all streams and the best one is selected. Finally, the observed sequence is segmented at the temporal boundaries suggested by the selected hypothesis and parallel fusion is applied to classify the resulting segments. Details are given in Sect. 16.3.2

represent each gesture. This representation accuracy can be significantly improved by the application of the multimodal activity detection scheme described in Sect. 16.3.3.

16.3.1   *Speech, Skeleton and Handshape Modeling*

The underlying single-stream modeling scheme is based on Hidden Markov Models (HMMs) and builds on the keyword-filler paradigm that was originally introduced for speech (Wilpon et al. 1990; Rose and Paul 1990) in applications like spoken document indexing and retrieval (Foote 1999) or speech surveillance (Rose 1992). The problem of recognizing a limited number of gestures in an observed sequence comprising other heterogeneous events as well, is seen as a keyword detection problem. The gestures to be recognized are the keywords and all the rest is ignored. Then, for every information stream, each gesture $g_i \in G$, or, in practice, its projection on that stream, is modeled by an HMM and there are two separate filler HMMs to represent either silence/inactivity (sil) or all other possible events (bm) appearing in that stream.

All these models are basically left-to-right HMMs with Gaussian mixture models (GMMs) representing the state-dependent observation probability distributions. They are initialized by an iterative procedure which sets the model parameters to the mean and covariance of the features in state-corresponding segments of the training instances and refines the segment boundaries via the Viterbi algorithm (Young et al. 2002). Training is performed using the Baum-Welch algorithm (Rabiner and Juang 1993), and mixture components are incrementally refined.

While this is the general training procedure followed, two alternative approaches are investigated, regarding the exact definition and the supervised training process of all involved models. These are described in the following. We experiment with both approaches and we show that increased modeling accuracy at the single-stream level leads to better results overall.

Training Without Activity Detection

Single-stream models can be initialized and trained based on coarse, multimodal temporal annotations of the gestures. These annotations are common for all streams and given that there is no absolute synchronization across modalities they may also include inactivity or other irrelevant events in the beginning or end of the target gestural expression. In this way the gesture models already include, by default, inactivity segments. As a consequence we do not train any separate inactivity (sil) model. At the same time, the background model (bm) is trained on all training instances of all the gestures, capturing in this way only generic gesture properties that are expected to characterize a non-target gesture. The advantage of this approach is that it may inherently capture cross-modal synchronicity relationships. For example, the waving hand motion may start before speech in the waving gesture and so there is probably some silence (or other events) to be expected before the utterance of a multimodal gesture (e.g. "Bye bye") which is modeled implicitly.

Training with Activity Detection

On the other hand, training of single-stream models can be performed completely independently using stream-specific temporal boundaries of the target expressions. In this direction, we applied an activity detection scheme, described in detail in Sect. 16.3.3. Based on that, it is possible to obtain tighter stream-specific boundaries for each gesture. Gesture models are now trained using these tighter boundaries, the sil model is trained on segments of inactivity (different for each modality) and the bm model is trained on segments of activity but outside the target areas. In this case, single-stream gesture models can be more accurate but any possible evidence regarding synchronicity across modalities is lost.

Algorithm 1 Multimodal Scoring and Resorting of Hypotheses

% N-best list rescoring
for all hypotheses **do**
   % Create a constrained grammar
   keep the sequence of gestures fixed
   allow introduction/deletion of *sil* and *bm* occurences between gestures
   for all modalities **do**
      by applying the constrained grammar and Viterbi decoding:
      1) find the best state sequence given the observations
      2) save corresponding score and temporal boundaries
   % Late fusion to rescore hypotheses
   final hypothesis score is a weighted sum of modality-based scores
the best hypothesis of the 1st-pass is the one with the maximum score

---

16.3.2 Multimodal Fusion of Speech, Skeleton and Handshape

Using the single-stream gesture models (see Sect. 16.3.1) and a gesture-loop grammar as shown in Fig. 16.2a we initially generate a list of N-best possible hypotheses for the unknown gesture sequence for each stream. Specifically, the Viterbi algorithm (Rabiner and Juang 1993) is used to directly estimate the best stream-based possible hypothesis $\hat{\mathbf{h}}_m$ for the unknown gesture sequence as follows:

$$\hat{\mathbf{h}}_m = \arg\max_{\mathbf{h}_m \in G} \log P(\mathbf{O}_m | \mathbf{h}_m, \lambda_m), \quad m = 1, \ldots, |S|$$

where $\mathbf{O}_m$ is the observation[1] sequence for modality m, λ_m is the corresponding set of models and G is the set of alternative hypotheses allowed by the gesture loop grammar. Instead of keeping just the best scoring sequence we apply essentially a variation of the Viterbi algorithm, namely the lattice N-best algorithm (Shwartz and Austin 1991), that apart from storing just the single best gesture at each node it also records additional best-scoring gestures together with their scores. Based on these records, a list of N-best hypotheses for the entire recording and for each modality can finally be estimated.

The N-best lists are generated independently for each stream and the final superset of the multimodally generated hypotheses may contain multiple instances of the same gesture sequence. By removing possible duplicates we end up with L hypotheses forming the set $H = \{\mathbf{h}_1, \ldots, \mathbf{h}_L\}$; $\mathbf{h}_i$ is a gesture sequence (possibly including *sil* and *bm* occurences as well). Our goal is to sort this set and identify the most likely hypothesis this time exploiting all modalities together.

---

[1]For the case of video data an observation corresponds to a single image frame; for the case of audio modality it corresponds to a 25 msec window.

Fig. 16.2 Finite-state-automaton (FSA) representations of finite state grammars: **a** an example gesture-loop grammar with 3 gestures plus inactivity and background labels. The "eps" transition represents an ϵ transition of the FSA, **b** an example hypothesis, **c** a hypothesis-dependent grammar allowing varying *sil* and *bm* occurences between gestures

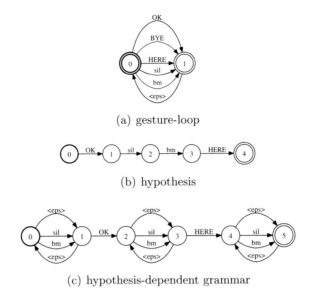

(a) gesture-loop

(b) hypothesis

(c) hypothesis-dependent grammar

Multimodal Scoring and Resorting of Hypotheses

Algorithm 2 Segmental Parallel Fusion

% Parallel scoring
for all modalities **do** segment observations based on given temporal boundaries
    for all resulting segments **do**
        estimate a score for each gesture given the segment observations
        temporally align modality segments
        for all aligned segments **do**
            estimate weighted sum of modality-based scores for all gestures
            select the best-scoring gesture (*sil* and *bm* included)

In this direction, and as summarized in Algorithm 1, we estimate a combined score for each possible gesture sequence as a weighted sum of modality-based scores:

$$v_i = \sum_{m \in S} w_m v_{m,i}^s, \quad i = 1 \ldots L, \qquad (16.1)$$

where the weights w_m are determined experimentally in a left-out validation set of multimodal recordings. The validation set is distinct from the final evaluation (test) set; more details on the selection of weights are provided in Sect. 16.5. The modality-based scores $v_{m,i}^s$ are standardized versions[2] of $v_{m,i}$ which are estimated by means of Viterbi decoding as follows:

---
[2]That is, transformed to have zero mean and a standard deviation of one.

$$v_{m,i} = \max_{\mathbf{h} \in G_{h_i}} \log P(\mathbf{O}_m | \mathbf{h}, \lambda_m), \quad i = 1, \ldots, L, \; m = 1, \ldots, |S| \qquad (16.2)$$

where $\mathbf{O}_m$ is the observation sequence for modality m and λ_m is the corresponding set of models. This actually solves a constrained recognition problem in which acceptable gesture sequences need to follow a specific hypothesis-dependent finite state grammar G_{h_i}. It is required that the search space of possible state sequences only includes sequences corresponding to the hypothesis $\mathbf{h}_i$ plus possible variations by keeping the appearances of target gestures unaltered and only allow sil and bm labels to be inserted, deleted and substituted with each other. An example of a hypothesis and the corresponding grammar is shown in Fig. 16.2b, c. In this way, the scoring scheme accounts for inactivity or non-targetted activity that is not necessarily multimodal, e.g., the gesturer is standing still but speaking or is walking silently. This is shown to lead to additional improvements when compared to a simple forced-alignment based approach.

It should be mentioned that hypothesis scoring via (16.2) can be skipped for the modalities based on which the particular hypothesis was originally generated. These scores are already available from the initial N-best list estimation described earlier.

The best hypothesis at this stage is the one with the maximum combined score as estimated by (16.1). Together with the corresponding temporal boundaries of the included gesture occurences, which can be different for the involved modalities, this hypothesized gesture sequence is passed on to the segmental parallel scoring stage. At this last stage, only local refinements are allowed by exploiting possible benefits of a segmental classification process.

Segmental Parallel Fusion

The segmental parallel fusion algorithm is summarized in Algorithm 2. Herein we exploit the modality-specific time boundaries for the most likely gesture sequence determined in the previous step, to reduce the recognition problem into a segmental classification one. First, we segment the audio, skeleton and handshape observation streams employing these boundaries. Given that in-between gestures, i.e., for sil or bm parts, there may not be one-to-one correspondence between segments of different observation streams these segments are first aligned with each other across modalities by performing an optimal symbolic string match using dynamic programming. Then, for every aligned segment t and each information stream m we compute the log probability:

$$LL^t_{m,j} = \max_{\mathbf{q} \in Q} \log P(\mathbf{O}^t_m, \mathbf{q} | \lambda_{m,j}), \quad j = 1, \ldots, |G| + 2,$$

where $\lambda_{m,j}$ are the parameters of the model for the gesture $g_j \in G \cup \{sil, bm\}$ and the stream $m \in S$; $\mathbf{q}$ is a possible state sequence. These segmental scores are linearly combined accross modalities to get a multimodal gestural score (left hand side) for each segment:

$$LL^t_j = \sum_{m \in S} w'_m LL^t_{m,j}, \qquad (16.3)$$

where w'_m, is the stream-weight for modality m set to optimize recognition performance in a validation dataset.[3] Finally, the gesture with the highest score is the recognized one for each segment t. This final stage is expected to give additional improvements and correct false alarms by seeking loosely overlapping multimodal evidence in support of each hypothesized gesture.

16.3.3 Multimodal Activity Detection

To achieve activity detection for each one of visual and audio modalities, we follow a common model-based framework. This is based on two complementary models of "activity" and "non-activity". In practice, these models, have different interpretations for the different modalities. This is first due to the nature of each modality, and second due to challenging data acquisition conditions. For the case of speech, the non-activity model may correspond to noisy conditions, e.g., keyboard typing or fan noise. For the case of the visual modality, the non-activity model refers to the rest cases in-between the articulation of gestures. However, these rests are not strictly defined, since the subject may not always perform a full rest and/or the hands may not stop moving. All cases of activity, in both the audio and the skeleton streams, such as out-of-vocabulary multimodal gestures and other spontaneous gestures are thought to be represented by the activity model. Each modality's activity detector is initialized by a modality-specific front-end, as described in the following.

For the case of speech, activity and non-activity models are initialized on activity and non-activity segments correspondingly. These are determined by taking advantage for initialization of a Voice Activity Detection (VAD) method recently proposed by Tan et al. (2010). This method is based on likelihood ratio tests (LRTs) and by treating the LRT's for the voice/unvoiced frames differently it gives improved results than conventional LRT-based and standard VADs. The activity and non-activity HMM models are further trained using an iterative procedure employing the Baum-Welch algorithm, better known as embedded re-estimation (Young et al. 2002). The final boundaries of the speech activity and non-activity segments are determined by application of the Viterbi algorithm.

For the visual modality, the goal is to detect activity concerning the dynamic gesture movements versus the rest cases. For this purpose, we first initialize our non-activity models on rest position segments which are determined on a recording basis. For these segments skeleton movement is characterized by low velocity and the skeleton is close to the rest position $\mathbf{x_r}$. To identify non-active segments, we need to estimate (a) the skeleton rest position (b) the hands velocity, and (c) the distance of the skeleton to that position. Hands' velocity is computed as $V(\mathbf{x}) = \|\dot{\mathbf{x}}\|$ where $\mathbf{x}(t)$ is the 3D hands' centroid coordinate vector and t is time. The rest position is estimated as

---

[3] The w'_m are different from the weights in (16.1). Their selection is similarly based on a separate validation set that is distinct from the final evaluation set; more details on the selection of weights are provided in Sect. 16.5.

the median skeleton position of all the segments for which hands' velocity V is below a certain threshold $V_{t_r} = 0.2 \cdot \bar{V}$, where $\bar{V}$ is the average velocity of all segments. The distance of the skeleton to the rest position is determined as: $D_r(\mathbf{x}) = \|\mathbf{x} - \mathbf{x_r}\|$. Initial non-activity segments t_{na} are the ones for which the following two criteria hold, namely $\mathbf{t_{na}} = \{t : D_r(\mathbf{x}) < D_{t_r} and\ V(\mathbf{x}) < V_{t_r}\}$. Taking as input these t_{na} segments we train a non-activity HMM model while an activity model is trained on all remaining segments using the skeleton feature vector as described in Sect. 16.5.1 Further, similar to the case of speech we re-train the HMM models using embedded re-estimation. The final boundaries of the visual activity and non-activity segments are determined by application of the Viterbi algorithm.

In Fig. 16.3, we illustrate an example of the activity detection for both audio and visual modalities for one utterance. In the first row, we depict the velocity of the hands (V), their distance with respect to the rest position (D_r) and the initial estimation of gesture non-activity (t_{na}) segments. We observe that in t_{na} segments both V and D_r

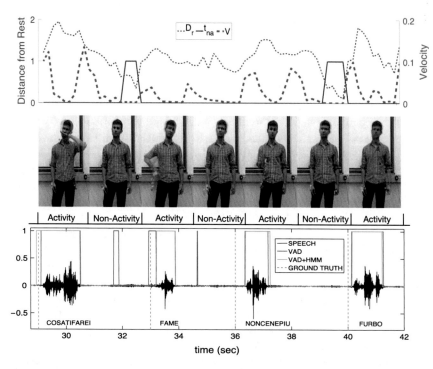

Fig. 16.3 Activity detection example for both audio and visual modalities for one utterance. *First row* the velocity of the hands (V), their distance with respect to the rest position (D_r) and the resulting initial estimation of gesture non-activity segments (t_{na}). *Second row* the estimated gesture activity depicted on the actual video images. *Third row*: The speech signal accompanied with the initial VAD, the VAD+HMM and the gesture-level temporal boundaries included in the gesture dataset (ground truth)

are lower than the predefined thresholds ($V_{t_r} = 0.6$, $D_{t_r} = 0.006$)[4] and correspond to non-activity. In the second row, we illustrate the actual video frames images. These are marked with the tracking of both hands and accompanied with the final model-based gesture activity detection. In the bottom, we show the speech signal, with the initial VAD boundaries, the refined HMM-based ones (VAD+HMM) and the gesture-level boundaries included in the dataset (ground truth). As observed the refined detection (VAD+HMM) is tighter and more precise compared to the initial VAD and the dataset annotations.

To sum up, after applying the activity detectors for both audio and visual modalities we merge the corresponding outputs with the gesture-level dataset annotations in order to obtain refined stream-specific boundaries that align to the actual activities. In this way, we compensate for the fact that the dataset annotations may contain non-activity at the start/end of each gesture.

16.4 Multimodal Gestures' Dataset

For our experiments we employ the ChaLearn multimodal gesture challenge dataset, introduced by Escalera et al. (2013b). Other similar datasets are described by Ruffieux et al. (2013, 2014). This dataset focuses on multiple instance, user independent learning of gestures from multi-modal data. It provides via Kinect RGB and depth images of face and body, user masks, skeleton information, joint orientation as well as concurrently recorded audio including the speech utterance accompanying/describing the gesture (see Fig. 16.4). The vocabulary contains 20 Italian cultural-anthropological gestures. The dataset contains three separate sets, namely for development, validation and final evaluation, including 39 users and 13,858 gesture-word instances in total. All instances have been manually transcribed and loosely end-pointed. The corresponding temporal boundaries are also provided; these temporal boundaries are employed during the training phase of our system.

There are several issues that render multimodal gesture recognition in this dataset quite challenging as described by Escalera et al. (2013b), such as the recording of continuous sequences, the presence of distracter gestures, the relatively large number of categories, the length of the gesture sequences, and the variety of users. Further, there is no single way to perform the included cultural gestures, e.g., "vieni qui" is performed with repeated movements of the hand towards the user, with a variable number of repetitions (see Fig. 16.5). Similarly, single-handed gestures may be performed with either the left or right hand. Finally, variations in background, lighting and resolution, occluded body parts and spoken dialects have also been introduced.

---

[4]These parameters are set after experimentation in a single video of the validation set, that was annotated in terms of activity.

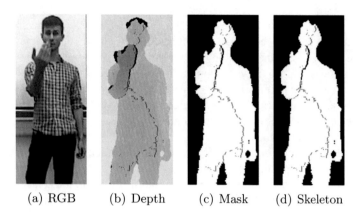

(a) RGB   (b) Depth   (c) Mask   (d) Skeleton

Fig. 16.4 Sample cues of the multimodal gesture challenge 2013 dataset

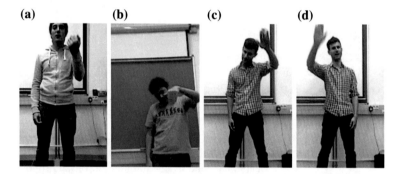

Fig. 16.5 **a, b** Arm position variation (low, high) for gesture 'vieni qui'; **c, d** Left and right handed instances of 'vattene'

16.5 Experiments

We first provide information on the multimodal statistical modeling that includes feature extraction and training. Then, we discuss the involved fusion parameters, the evaluation procedure, and finally, present results and comparisons.

16.5.1 Parameters, Evaluation, Structure

Herein, we describe first the employed feature representations, and training parameters for each modality, such as number of states and mixture components: as discussed in Sect. 16.3.1 we statistically train separate gesture HMMs per each information stream: skeleton, handshape and audio. Next, we describe the stream weight selection procedure, note the best stream weights, and present indicative results of the procedure. After presenting the evaluation metrics, we finally describe the overall rational of the experimental structure.

Multimodal Features, HMM and Fusion Parameters

The features employed for the *skeleton* cue include: the hands' and elbows' 3D position, the hands 3D velocity, the 3D direction of the hands' movement, and the 3D distance of hands' centroids. For the *handshape's* representation we employ the HOG feature descriptors. These are extracted on both hands' segmented images for both RGB and depth cues. We segment the hands by performing a threshold-based depth segmentation employing the hand's tracking information. For the *audio* modality we intend to efficiently capture the spectral properties of speech signals by estimating the Mel Frequency Cepstral Coefficients (MFCCs). Our frontend generates 39 acoustic features every 10 msec. Each feature vector comprises 13 MFCCs along with their first and second derivatives. All the above feature descriptors are well known in the related literature. The specific selections should not affect the conclusions as related to the main fusion contributions, since these build on the level of the likelihoods. Such an example would be the employment of other descriptors as for instance in the case of visual (e.g., Li and Allinson 2008) or speech related features (e.g., Hermansky 1990).

For all modalities, we train separate gesture, *sil* and *bm* models as described in Sect. 16.3.1. These models are trained either using the dataset annotations or based on the input provided by the activity detectors. The number of states, gaussian components per state, stream weights and the word insertion penalty in all modalities are determined experimentally based on the recognition performance on the validation set.[5] For skeleton, we train left-right HMMs with 12 states and 2 Gaussians per state. For handshape, the models correspondingly have 8 states and 3 Gaussians per state while speech gesture models have 22 states and 10 Gaussians per state.

The training time is on average 1 min per skeleton and handshape model and 90 min per audio model. The decoding time is on average 4xRT (RT refers to real-time).[6] A significant part of the decoding time is due to the generation of the N-best lists of hypotheses. In our experiments N is chosen to be equal to 200. We further observed that the audio-based hypotheses were always ranked higher than those from the other single-stream models. This motivated us to include only these hypotheses in the set we considered for rescoring.

Stream Weight Configuration

Herein, we describe the experimental procedure for the selection of the stream weights $w_m, w'_m, m \in S$ of (16.1) and (16.3), for the components of multimodal hypothesis rescoring (MHS) and segmental parallel fusion (SPF). The final weight value selection is based on the optimization of recognition performance in the *validation* dataset which is completely distinct from the final evaluation (test) dataset.

Specifically, the w_m's are first selected from a set of alternative combinations to optimize gesture accuracy at the output of the MHS component. The SPF weights

---

[5]Parameter ranges in the experiments for each modality are as follows. Audio: States 10–28, Gaussians: 2–32; Skeleton/Handshape: States 7–15, Gaussians: 2–10.

[6]For the measurements we employed an AMD Opteron(tm) Processor 6386 at 2.80 GHz with 32 GB RAM.

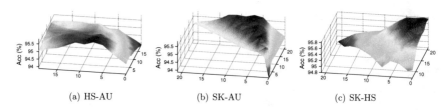

Fig. 16.6 Gesture recognition accuracy of the Multiple hypothesis rescoring component for various weight-pair combinations. From *left* to *right*, the handshape-audio, skeleton-audio, skeleton-handshape weight pairs are varied. The remaining weight is set to its optimal value, namely 63.6 for skeleton, 9.1 for handshape and 27.3 for audio

w'_m's are subsequently set to optimize the performance of the overall framework. The best weight combination for the multimodal hypothesis rescoring component is found to be $w^*_{SK,HS,AU} = [63.6, 9.1, 27.3]$, where SK, HS and AU correspond to skeleton, handshape and audio respectively.[7] This leads to the best possible accuracy of MHS in the validation set, namely 95.84%. Correspondingly, the best combination of weights for the segmental fusion component is [0.6, 0.6, 98.8]. Overall, the best achieved gesture recognition accuracy is 96.76% in the validation set.

In Figs. 16.6a–c we show the recognition accuracy of the MHS component for the various combinations of the w_m's. For visualization purposes we show accuracy when the weights vary in pairs and the remaining weight is set to its optimal value. For example, Fig. 16.6a shows recognition accuracy for various combinations of handshape and audio weights when the skeleton weight is equal to 63.6. Overall, we should comment that the skeleton's contribution appears to be the most significant in the rescoring phase. This is of course a first interpretation, since the list of original hypotheses is already audio-based only, and the audio contribution cannot be directly inferred. As a consequence these results should be seen under this viewpoint. In any case, given that audio-based recognition leads to 94.1% recognition accuracy (in the validation set) it appears that both skeleton and handshape contribute in properly reranking the hypotheses and improve performance (which is again confirmed by the results in the test set presented in the following sections).

Evaluation

The presented evaluation metrics include the Levensthein distance (LD)[8] which is employed in the CHALEARN publications (Escalera et al. 2013b) and the gesture recognition accuracy. The Levenshtein distance $LD(R, T)$, also known as "edit distance", is the minimum number of edit operations that one has to perform to go from symbol sequence R to T, or vice versa; edit operations include substitutions

---

[7]The weights take values in [0, 1] while their sum across the modalities adds to one; these values are then scaled by 100 for the sake of numerical presentation. For the w stream weights we sampled the [0, 1] with 12 samples for each modality, resulting to 1728 combinations. For the w' case, we sampled the [0, 1] space by employing 5, 5 and 21 samples for the gesture, handshape and speech modalities respectively, resulting on 525 combinations.

[8]Note that the Levensthein distance takes values in [0, 1] and is equivalent to the word error rate.

Table 16.1 Single modalities recognition accuracy %, including Audio (Aud.), Skeleton (Skel.), and Handshape (HS). AD refers to activity detection

AD	Single Modalities		
	Aud.	*Skel.*	*HS*
✗	78.4	47.6	13.3
✓	87.2	49.1	20.2

(S), insertions (I), or deletions (D). The overall score is the sum of the Levenshtein distances for all instances compared to the corresponding ground truth instances, divided by the total number of gestures. At the same time we report the standard word recognition accuracy $Acc = 1 - LD = \frac{N-S-D-I}{N}$, where N is the total number of instances of words.

Finally, we emphasize that all reported results have been generated by strictly following the original CHALEARN challenge protocol which means that they are directly comparable with the results reported by the challenge organizers and other participating teams (Escalera et al. 2013b; Wu et al. 2013; Bayer and Thierry 2013).

Structure of Experiments

For the evaluation of the proposed approach we examine the following experimental aspects:

1. First, we present results on the performance of the single modality results; for these the only parameter that we switch on/off is the activity detection, which can be applied on each separate modality; see Sect. 16.5.2 and Table 16.1.
2. Second, we examine the performance in the multimodal cases. This main axis of experiments has as its main reference Table 16.2 and concerns several aspects, as follows:

   (a) Focus on the basic components of the proposed approach.
   (b) Focus on two stream modality combinations; this serves for both the analysis of our approach, but also provides a more focused comparison with other methods that employ the specific pairs of modalities.
   (c) Finally, we provide several fusion based variation experiments, as competitive approaches.

3. Third, we show an indicative example from the actual data, together with its decoding results after applying the proposed approach, compared to the application of a couple of subcomponents.
4. Fourth, we specifically focus on comparisons within the gesture challenge competition. From the list of 17 teams/methods that submitted their results (54 teams participated in total) we review the top-ranked ones, and list their results for comparison. Moreover, we describe the components that each of the top-ranked participants employ, providing also focused comparisons to both our complete approach, and specific cases that match the employed modalities of the other methods. Some cases of our competitive variations can be seen as resembling cases of the other teams' approaches.

Table 16.2 Comparisons to first-ranked teams in the multimodal challenge recognition CHALEARN 2013, and to several variations of our approach

	Method/Exp. Code	Modality	Segm. Method	Classifier/ Modeling	Fusion	Acc. (%)	LD
Others	O1: 1st Rank[a]	SK, AU	AU:time-domain	HMM, DTW	Late:w-sum	87.24	0.1280
	O2: 2nd Rank[b]	SK, AU	AU:energy	RF, KNN	Late:posteriors	84.61	0.1540
	O3: 3rd Rank[c]	SK, AU	AU:detection	RF, Boosting	Late:w-average	82.90	0.1710
2 Streams	s2-A1	SK,AU	HMM	AD, HMM	Late:SPF	87.9	0.1210
	s2-B1	SK,AU	-	AD,HMM,GRAM	Late:MHS	92.8	0.0720
	s2-A2	HS,AU	HMM	AD, HMM	Late:SPF	87.7	0.1230
	s2-B2	HS,AU	-	AD,HMM,GRAM	Late:MHS	87.5	0.1250
3 Streams	C1	SK,AU,HS	HMM	AD, HMM	Late:SPF	88.5	0.1150
	D1	SK,AU,HS	-	HMM	Late:MHS	85.80	0.1420
	D2	SK,AU,HS	-	AD,HMM	Late:MHS	91.92	0.0808
	D3	SK,AU,HS	-	AD,HMM,GRAM	Late:MHS	93.06	0.0694
	E1	SK,AU,HS	HMM	HMM	Late:MHS+SPF	87.10	0.1290
	E2	SK,AU,HS	HMM	AD,HMM	Late:MHS+SPF	92.28	0.0772
	E3	SK,AU,HS	HMM	AD,HMM,GRAM	Late:MHS+SPF	93.33	0.0670

[a] Wu et al. (2013); [b] Escalera et al. (2013b); [c] Bayer and Thierry (2013)

16.5.2 Recognition Results: Single Modalities

In Table 16.1 we show the recognition results for each independent modality with and without the employment of activity detection (AD). Note that AD is employed for model training, as described in Sects. 16.3.1, 16.3.3, for each modality. In both cases the audio appears to be the dominant modality in terms of recognition performance. For all modalities, the model-based integration of the activity detectors during training appears to be crucial: they lead to refined temporal boundaries that better align to the actual single-stream activity. In this way we compensate for the fact that the dataset annotations may contain non-activity at the start/end of a gesture. By tightening these boundaries we achieve to model in more detail gesture articulation leading to more robustly trained HMMs. This is also projected on the recognition experiments: In all modalities the recognition performance increases, by 8.8%, 1.5% and 6.9% in absolute for the audio, the skeleton and the handshape streams respectively.

16.5.3 Recognition Results: Multimodal Fusion

For the evaluation of the proposed fusion scheme we focus on several of its basic components. For these we refer to the experiments with codes D1-3,[9] and E1-3 as shown in Table 16.2. These experiments correspond to the employment of all three modalities, while altering a single component each time, wherever this makes sense.

Main Components and Comparisons

First comes the *MHS component* (see D1-3), which rescores the multimodal hypotheses list employing all three information streams and linearly combining their scores. Comparing with Table 16.1 the MHS component results in improved performance compared to the monomodal cases, by leading to 38% relative Levenshtein distance reduction (LDR)[10] on average. This improvement is statistically significant, when employing the McNemar's test (Gillick and Cox 1989), with $p < 0.001$.[11]

Further, the employment of the activity detectors for each modality during training also affects the recognition performance after employing the MHS component, leading to a relative LDR of 38% which is statistically significant ($p < 0.001$); compare D1-D2, E1-E2.

For the N-best multimodal hypothesis rescoring we can either enforce each modality to rescore the exact hypothesis (forced alignment), or allow certain degrees of freedom by employing a *specific grammar* (GRAM) which allows insertions or deletions of either *bm* or *sil* models: By use of the aforementioned grammar *during*

---

[9]D1-3 notation refers to D1, D2 and D3 cases.

[10]All relative percentages, unless stated otherwise, refer to relative LD reduction (LDR). LDR is equivalent to the known relative word error rate reduction.

[11]Statistical significance tests are computed on the raw recognition values and not on the relative improvement scores.

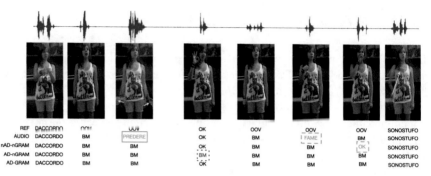

REF	DACCORDO	OOU	UUU	OK	OOV	OOV	OOV	SONOSTUFO
AUDIO	DACCORDO	BM	PREDERE	OK	BM	FAME	BM	SONOSTUFO
nAD-nGRAM	DACCORDO	BM	BM	OK	BM	BM	OK	SONOSTUFO
AD-nGRAM	DACCORDO	BM	BM	BM	BM	BM	BM	SONOSTUFO
AD-GRAM	DACCORDO	BM	BM	OK	BM	BM	BM	SONOSTUFO

Fig. 16.7 A gesture sequence decoding example. The audio signal is plotted in the *top row* the and visual modalities (*second row*) are illustrated via a sequence of images for a gesture sequence. Ground truth transcriptions are denoted by "REF". Decoding results are given for the single-audio modality (AUDIO) and the proposed fusion scheme employing or not the activity detection (AD) or the grammar (GRAM). In nAD-nGRAM we do not employ neither AD nor GRAM during rescoring, in AD-nGRAM we only employ AD but not GRAM and in AD-GRAM both AD and GRAM are employed. Errors are highlighted as: deletions, in blue color, and insertions in green. A background model (bm) models the out-of-vocabulary (OOV) gestures

rescoring (see D2–D3, E2–E3) we get an additional 14% of relative Levenshtein distance reduction, which is statistically significant ($p < 0.001$). This is due to the fact that the specific grammar accounts for activity or non-activity that does not necessarily occur simultaneously across all different modalities.

In addition, by employing the *SPF component* (E1-3) we further refine the gesture sequence hypothesis by fusing the single-stream models at the segmental level. By comparing corresponding pairs: D1-E1, D2-E2 and D3-E3, we observe that the application of the SPF component increases the recognition performance only slightly; this increase was not found to be statistically significant. The best recognition performance, that is, 93.33%, is obtained after employing the SPF component on top of MHS, together with AD and GRAM (see E3).

On the side, we additionally provide results that account for pairs of modalities; see s2-B1 (AU+SK) and s2-B2 (AU+HS), and for the case of the *MHS component*. These two stream pair results, are comparable with the corresponding 3-stream case of D1 (plus D2-3 for additional components). The rest of the results and pairs are discussed in Sect. 16.5.4, where comparisons with other approaches are presented.

Example from the Results

A decoding example is shown in Fig. 16.7. Herein we illustrate both audio and visual modalities for a word sequence accompanied with the ground truth gesture-level transcriptions (row: "REF"). In addition we show the decoding output employing the single-audio modality (AUDIO) and the proposed fusion scheme employing or not two of its basic components: activity detection (AD) and the above mentioned grammar (GRAM). In the row denoted by nAD-nGRAM we do not employ either AD or GRAM during rescoring, in the row AD-nGRAM we only employ AD but not G and in AD-GRAM both AD and grammar are used. As we observe there are several cases where the subject articulates an out-of-vocabulary (OOV) gesture. This indicates the difficulty of the task as these cases should be ignored. By focusing on the recognized word sequence that employs the single-audio modality we notice two insertions ('PREDERE' and 'FAME'). When employing either the nAD-nGRAM or AD-nGRAM the above word insertions are corrected as the visual modality is integrated and helps identifying that these segments correspond to OOV gestures. Finally, both nAD-nGRAM and AD-nGRAM lead to errors which our final proposed approach manages to deal with: nAD-nGRAM causes insertion of "OK", AD-nGRAM of a word deletion "BM". On the contrary, the proposed approach recognizes the whole sentence correctly.

16.5.4 Comparisons

Next, we first briefly describe the main components of the top-ranked approaches in CHALEARN. This description aims at allowing for focused and fair comparisons between (1) the first-ranked approaches, and (2) variations of our approach.

CHALEARN First-Ranked Approaches

The first-ranked team (IV AMM) (Wu et al. 2013; Escalera et al. 2013b) uses a feature vector based on audio and skeletal information. A simple time-domain endpoint detection algorithm based on joint coordinates is applied to segment continuous data sequences into candidate gesture intervals. A HMM is trained with 39-dimension MFCC features and generates confidence scores for each gesture category. A Dynamic Time Warping based skeletal feature classifier is applied to provide complementary information. The confidence scores generated by the two classifiers are firstly normalized and then combined to produce a weighted sum for late fusion. A single threshold approach is employed to classify meaningful gesture intervals from meaningless intervals caused by false detection of speech intervals.

The second-ranked team (WWEIGHT) (Escalera et al. 2013b) combines audio and skeletal information, using both joint spatial distribution and joint orientation. They first search for regions of time with high audio-energy to define time windows that potentially contained a gesture. Feature vectors are defined using a log-spaced audio spectrogram and the joint positions and orientations above the hips. At each time sample the method subtracts the average 3D position of the left and right shoulders from each 3D joint position. Data is down-sampled onto a 5 Hz grid. There were 1593 features total (9 time samples × 177 features per time sample). Since some of the detected windows contain distracter gestures, an extra 21st label is introduced, defining the "not in the dictionary" gesture category. For the training of the models they employed an ensemble of randomized decision trees, referred to as random forests (RF), (Escalera et al. 2013b), and a k-nearest neighbor (KNN) model. The posteriors from these models are averaged with equal weight. Finally, a heuristic is used (12 gestures maximum, no repeats) to convert posteriors to a prediction for the sequence of gestures.

Table 16.3 Our approach in comparison with the first 5 places of the Challenge. We include recognition accuracy (Acc.) %, Levenshtein distance (Lev. Dist., see also text) and relative Levenshtein distance reduction (LDR) (equivalent to the known relative error reduction) compared to the proposed approach (Our)

Rank	Approach	Lev. Dist.	Acc.%	LDR
–	Our	0.0667	93.33	–
1	iva. mm (Wu et al., 2013)	0.12756	87.244	+47.6
2	wweight	0.15387	84.613	+56.6
3	E.T. (Bayer and Thierry, 2013)	0.17105	82.895	+60.9
4	MmM	0.17215	82.785	+61.2
5	pptk	0.17325	82.675	+61.4

The third-ranked team (ET) (Bayer and Thierry 2013; Escalera et al. 2013b) combine the output decisions of two approaches. The features considered are based on the skeleton information and the audio signal. First, they look for gesture intervals (unsupervised) using the audio and extract features from these intervals (MFCC). Using these features, they train a random forest (RF) and a gradient boosting classifier. The second approach uses simple statistics (median, var, min, max) on the first 40 frames for each gesture to build the training samples. The prediction phase uses a sliding window. The authors late fuse the two models by creating a weighted average of the outputs.

Comparisons with Other Approaches and Variations

Herein we compare the recognition results of our proposed multimodal recognition and multiple hypotheses fusion framework with other approaches (Escalera et al. 2013b) which have been evaluated in the exact recognition task.[12]

First, let us briefly present an overview of the results (Table 16.3): Among the numerous groups and approaches that participated we list the first four ones as well as the one we submitted during the challenge, that is "pptk". As shown in Table 16.3 the proposed approach leads to superior performance with relative LD reduction of at least 47.6%. We note that our updated approach compared to the one submitted during the challenge leads to an improvement of 61.4%, measured in terms of relative LD reduction (LDR). Compared to the approach we submitted during the challenge, the currently proposed scheme: (1) employs activity detection to train single-stream models, (2) applies the SPF on top of the MHS step, (3) introduces the grammar-constrained decoding during hypothesis rescoring and further (4) incorporates both validation and training data for the final estimation of the model parameters.

---

[12]In all results presented we follow the same blind testing rules that hold in the challenge, in which we have participated (pptk team). In Table 16.3 we include for common reference the Levenshtein distance (LD) which was also used in the challenge results (Escalera et al. 2013b).

Now let us zoom into the details of the comparisons by viewing once again Table 16.2. In the first three rows, with side label "Others" (O1-3), we summarize the main components of each of the top-ranked approaches. These employ only the two modalities (SK+AU). The experiments with pairs of modalities s2-A1, s2-B1 can be directly compared with O1-3, since they all take advantage of the SK+AU modalities. Their differential concerns (1) the segmentation component, which is explicit for the O1-3; note that the segmentation of s2-A1 is implicit, as a by-product of the HMM recognition. (2) The modeling and recognition/classification component. (3) The fusion component. At the same time, s2-A1/s2-B1 refer to the employment of the proposed components, that is, either SPF or MHS. Specifically, s2-A1 and s2-B1 leads to at least 5 and 43.5% relative LD reduction respectively. Of course our complete system (see rest of variations) leads to even higher improvements.

Other comparisons to our proposed approach and variations are provided after comparing with the SPF-only case, by taking out the contribution of the rescoring component. In the case of all modalities, 3 stream case, (see C1) this is compared to the corresponding matching experiment E2; this (E2) only adds the MHS resulting to an improvement of 32.9% LDR. The GRAM component offers an improvement of 42% LDR (C1 vs. E3). Reduced versions compared to C1, with two-stream combinations can be found by comparing C1 with s2-A1 or s2-A2.

16.6 Conclusions

We have presented a complete framework for multimodal gesture recognition based on multiple hypotheses fusion, with application in automatic recognition of multi-modal gestures. In this we exploit multiple cues in the visual and audio modalities, namely movement, hands' shape and speech. After employing state-of-the-art feature respresentations, each modality is treated under a common statistical HMM frame-work: this includes model-based multimodal activity detection, HMM training of gesture-words, and information fusion. Fusion is performed by generating multiple unimodal hypotheses, which after constrained rescoring and weighted combination result in the multimodally best hypothesis. Then, segmental parallel fusion across all modalities refines the final result. On the way, we employ gesture/speech background (bm) and silence (sil) models, which are initialized during the activity detection stage. This procedure allows us to train our HMMs more accurately by getting tighter temporal segmentation boundaries.

The recognition task we dealt with contains parallel gestures and spoken words, articulated freely, containing multiple sources of multimodal variability, and with on purpose false alarms. The overall framework is evaluated in a demanding multimodal dataset (Escalera et al. 2013b) achieving 93.3% word accuracy. The results are compared with several approaches that participated in the related challenge (Escalera et al. 2013a), under the same blind testing conditions, leading to at least 47.6% relative Levenshtein distance reduction (equivalent to relative word error rate reduction) compared to the first-ranked team (Wu et al. 2013).

The power of the proposed fusion scheme stems from both its uniform across modalities probabilistic nature and its late character together with the multiple passes of monomodal decoding, fusion of the hypotheses, and then parallel fusion. Apart from the experimental evidence, these features render it appealing for extensions and exploitation in multiple directions: First, the method itself can be advanced by generalizing the approach towards an iterative fusion scheme, that gives feedback back to the training/refinement stage of the statistical models. Moreover in the current generative framework, we ignore statistical dependencies across cues/modalities. These could further be examined. Second, it can be advanced by incorporating in the computational modeling specific gesture theories, e.g., from linguistics, for the gesture per se or in its multimodal version; taxonomies of gestures, e.g., that describe deictic, motor, iconic and metaphoric cases. Such varieties of cases can be systematically studied with respect to their role. This could be achieved via automatic processing of multitudes of existing datasets, which elaborate more complex speech-gesture issues, leading to valuable analysis results. Then, apart from the linguistic role of gesture, its relation to other aspects, such as, psychological, behavioral socio-cultural, or communicative, to name but a few, could further be exploited. To conclude, given the potential of the proposed approach, the acute interdisciplinary interest in multimodal gesture calls for further exploration and advancements.

Acknowledgements This research work was supported by the European Union under the project "MOBOT" with grant FP7-ICT-2011-9 2.1 - 600796. The authors want to gratefully thank G. Pavlakos for his contribution in previous, earlier stages, of this work. This work was done while V. Pitsikalis and S. Theodorakis were both with the National Technical University of Athens; they are now with deeplab.ai, Athens, GR.

References

U. Agris, J. Zieren, U. Canzler, B. Bauer, K.-F. Kraiss, Recent developments in visual sign language recognition. Univers. Access Inf. Soc. **6**, 323–362 (2008)

J. Alon, V. Athitsos, O. Yuan, S. Sclaroff, A unified framework for gesture recognition and spatiotemporal gesture segmentation. IEEE Trans. Pattern Anal. Mach. Intell. **31**(9), 1685–1699 (2009)

A. Argyros, M. Lourakis, Real time tracking of multiple skin-colored objects with a possibly moving camera, in *Proceedings of the European Conference on Computer Vision*, 2004

B. Bauer, K.F. Kraiss, Towards an automatic sign language recognition system using subunits. in *Proceedings of International Gesture Workshop*, vol. 2298, 2001, pp. 64–75

I. Bayer, S. Thierry, A multi modal approach to gesture recognition from audio and video data, in *Proceedings of the 15th ACM International Conference on Multimodal Interaction* (ACM, 2013), pp. 461–466

P. Bernardis, M. Gentilucci, Speech and gesture share the same communication system. Neuropsychologia **44**(2), 178–190 (2006)

N.D. Binh, E. Shuichi, T. Ejima, Real-time hand tracking and gesture recognition system, in *Proceedings of International Conference on Graphics, Vision and Image Processing (GVIP)*, 2005, pp. 19–21

A.F. Bobick, J.W. Davis, The recognition of human movement using temporal templates. IEEE Trans. Pattern Anal. Mach. Intell. **23**(3), 257–267 (2001)

R. A. Bolt, "Put-that-there": voice and gesture at the graphics interface, in *Proceedings of the 7th Annual Conference on Computer Graphics and Interactive Techniques*, vol. 14 (ACM, 1980)

H. Bourlard, S. Dupont, Subband-based speech recognition, in *Proceedings of the International Conference on Acoustics, Speech and Signal Processings*, vol. 2 (IEEE, Piscataway, 1997), pp. 1251–1254

K. Bousmalis, L. Morency, M. Pantic, Modeling hidden dynamics of multimodal cues for spontaneous agreement and disagreement recognition, in *Proceedings of the International Conference on Automatic Face and Gesture Recognition* (IEEE, Piscataway, 2011), pp. 746–752

P. Buehler, M. Everingham, A. Zisserman, Learning sign language by watching TV (using weakly aligned subtitles), in *Proceedings of the International Conference on Computer Vision and Pattern Recognition*, 2009

S. Celebi, A.S. Aydin, T.T. Temiz, T. Arici, Gesture recognition using skeleton data with weighted dynamic time warping. Comput. Vis. Theory Appl. **1**, 620–625 (2013)

F.-S. Chen, C.-M. Fu, C.-L. Huang, Hand gesture recognition using a real-time tracking method and hidden markov models. Image Vis. Comput. **21**(8), 745–758 (2003)

X. Chen, M. Koskela, Online rgb-d gesture recognition with extreme learning machines, in *Proceedings of the 15th ACM International Conference on Multimodal Interaction* (ACM, 2013), pp. 467–474

Y. L. Chow, R. Schwartz, The n-best algorithm: An efficient procedure for finding top n sentence hypotheses, in *Proceedings of the Workshop on Speech and Natural Language* (Association for Computational Linguistics, 1989), pp. 199–202

S. Conseil, S. Bourennane, L. Martin, Comparison of Fourier descriptors and Hu moments for hand posture recognition, in *Proceedings of the European Conference on Signal Processing*, 2007

Y. Cui, J. Weng, Appearance-based hand sign recognition from intensity image sequences. Comput. Vis. Image Underst. **78**(2), 157–176 (2000)

N. Dalal, B. Triggs, Histogram of oriented gradients for human detection, in *Proceedins International Conference on Computer Vision and Pattern Recognition*, 2005

W. Du, J. Piater, Hand modeling and tracking for video-based sign language recognition by robust principal component analysis, in *Proceedings of the ECCV Workshop on Sign, Gesture and Activity*, September 2010

S. Escalera, J. Gonzàlez, X. Baró, M. Reyes, I. Guyon, V. Athitsos, H. Escalante, L. Sigal, A. Argyros, C. Sminchisescu, R. Bowden, S. Sclaroff, Chalearn multi-modal gesture recognition 2013: grand challenge and workshop summary, in *Proceedings of the 15th ACM on International Conference on Multimodal Interaction* (ACM, 2013a), pp. 365–368

S. Escalera, J. Gonzlez, X. Bar, M. Reyes, O. Lopes, I. Guyon, V. Athitsos, H.J. Escalante. Multimodal Gesture Recognition Challenge 2013: Dataset and Results, in *15th ACM International Conference on Multimodal Interaction (ICMI), ChaLearn Challenge and Workshop on Multimodal Gesture Recognition* (ACM, 2013b)

J. Foote, An overview of audio information retrieval. Multimedia Syst. 7(1):2–10 (1999), http://link.springer.com/article/10.1007/s005300050106

L. Gillick, S.J. Cox, Some statistical issues in the comparison of speech recognition algorithms, in *Proceedings of the International Conference on Acoustics, Speech and Signal Processing*, vol. 1, May 1989, pp. 532–535

H. Glotin, D. Vergyr, C. Neti, G. Potamianos, J. Luettin, Weighting schemes for audio-visual fusion in speech recognition, in *Proceedings of the International Conference on Acoustics, Speech and Signal Processing*, vol. 1 (IEEE, Piscataway, 2001), pp. 173–176

B. Habets, S. Kita, Z. Shao, A. Özyurek, P. Hagoort, The role of synchrony and ambiguity in speech-gesture integration during comprehension. J. Cogn. Neurosci. **23**(8), 1845–1854 (2011)

J. Han, G. Awad, A. Sutherland, Modelling and segmenting subunits for sign language recognition based on hand motion analysis. Pattern Recognit. Lett. **30**, 623–633 (2009)

H. Hermansky, Perceptual linear predictive (PLP) analysis of speech. J. Acoust. Soc. Am. **87**(4), 1738–1752 (1990)

A. Hernández-Vela, M.Á. Bautista, X. Perez-Sala, V. Ponce-López, S. Escalera, X. Baró, O. Pujol, C. Angulo, Probability-based dynamic time warping and bag-of-visual-and-depth-words for human gesture recognition in rgb-d. Pattern Recognit. Lett. (2013)

C.-L. Huang, S.-H. Jeng, A model-based hand gesture recognition system. Mach. Vis. Appl. **12**(5), 243–258 (2001)

M. Isard, A. Blake, Condensation-conditional density propagation for visual tracking. Int. J. Comput. Vis. **29**(1), 5–28 (1998)

J.M. Iverson, S. Goldin-Meadow, Why people gesture when they speak. Nature **396**(6708), 228 (1998)

A. Jaimes, N. Sebe, Multimodal human-computer interaction: a survey. Comput. Vis. Image Underst. **108**(1), 116–134 (2007)

S.D. Kelly, A. Özyürek, E. Maris, Two sides of the same coin speech and gesture mutually interact to enhance comprehension. Psychol. Sci. **21**(2), 260–267 (2010)

A. Kendon, *Gesture: Visible Action as Utterance* (Cambridge University Press, New York, 2004)

W. Kong, S. Ranganath, Sign language phoneme transcription with rule-based hand trajectory segmentation. J. Signal Process. Syst. **59**, 211–222 (2010)

I. Laptev, M. Marszalek, C. Schmid, B. Rozenfeld, Learning realistic human actions from movies, in *Proceedings of the International Conference on Computer Vision and Pattern Recognition* (IEEE, Piscataway, 2008), pp. 1–8

H.-K. Lee, J.-H. Kim, An HMM-based threshold model approach for gesture recognition. IEEE Trans. Pattern Anal. Mach. Intell. **21**(10), 961–973 (1999)

J. Li, N.M. Allinson, Simultaneous gesture segmentation and recognition based on forward spotting accumulative hmms. Pattern Recognit. **40**(11), 3012–3026 (2007)

J. Li, N.M. Allinson, A comprehensive review of current local features for computer vision. Neurocomputing **71**(10), 1771–1787 (2008)

D. G. Lowe, Object recognition from local scale-invariant features, in *Proceedings of the International Conference on Computer Vision*, 1999, pp. 1150–1157

P. Maragos, P. Gros, A. Katsamanis, G. Papandreou, Cross-modal integration for performance improving in multimedia: a review, in *Multimodal Processing and Interaction: Audio, Video, Text* ed. by P. Maragos, A. Potamianos, and P. Gros, chapter 1 (Springer, New York, 2008), pp. 3–48

D. McNeill, *Hand and Mind: What Gestures Reveal About Thought* (University of Chicago Press, Chicago, 1992)

M. Miki, N. Kitaoka, C. Miyajima, T. Nishino, K. Takeda, Improvement of multimodal gesture and speech recognition performance using time intervals between gestures and accompanying speech. EURASIP J. Audio Speech Music Process. **2014**(1), 17 (2014). doi:10.1186/1687-4722-2014-2

d Morris, p Collett, p Marsh, M. O'Shaughnessy, *Gestures: Their Origins and Distribution* (Stein and Day, New York, 1979)

Y. Nam, K. Wohn, Recognition of space-time hand-gestures using hidden Markov model, in *ACM Symposium on Virtual Reality Software and Technology*, 1996, pp. 51–58

K. Nandakumar, K. W. Wan, S. Chan, W. Ng, J. G. Wang, and W. Y. Yau. A multi-modal gesture recognition system using audio, video, and skeletal joint data. in *Proceedings of the 15th ACM Int'l Conf. on Multimodal Interaction* (ACM, 2013), pages 475–482

N. Neverova, C. Wolf, G. Paci, G. Sommavilla, G. Taylor, F. Nebout, A multi-scale approach to gesture detection and recognition, in *Proceedings of the IEEE International Conference on Computer Vision Workshop*, 2013, pp. 484–491

E.-J. Ong, R. Bowden, A boosted classifier tree for hand shape detection, in *Proceedings of the International Conference on Automation Face Gest Recognition* (IEEE, Piscataway, 2004), pp. 889–894

M. Ostendorf, A. Kannan, S. Austin, O. Kimball, R. M. Schwartz, J. R. Rohlicek, Integration of diverse recognition methodologies through reevaluation of N-best sentence hypotheses, in *HLT*, 1991

S. Oviatt, P. Cohen, Perceptual user interfaces: multimodal interfaces that process what comes naturally. Commun. ACM **43**(3), 45–53 (2000)

G. Papandreou, A. Katsamanis, V. Pitsikalis, P. Maragos, Adaptive multimodal fusion by uncertainty compensation with application to audiovisual speech recognition. IEEE Trans. Audio Speech Lang. Process. **17**(3), 423–435 (2009)

V. Pitsikalis, S. Theodorakis, C. Vogler, P. Maragos, Advances in phonetics-based sub-unit modeling for transcription alignment and sign language recognition, in *IEEE CVPR Workshop on Gesture Recognition*, 2011

I. Poddar, Y. Sethi, E. Ozyildiz, R. Sharma, Toward natural gesture/speech HCI: A case study of weather narration, in *Proceedings of the Workshop on Perceptual User Interfaces*, 1998

V. Ponce-López, S. Escalera, X. Baró, Multi-modal social signal analysis for predicting agreement in conversation settings, in *Proceedings of the 15th ACM International Conference on Multimodal Interaction* (ACM, 2013), pp. 495–502

G. Potamianos, C. Neti, J. Luettin, I. Matthews, Audio-visual automatic speech recognition: an overview. Issues Vis. Audio Vis Speech Process. **22**, 23 (2004)

L.R. Rabiner, B.H. Juang, *Fundamentals of Speech Recognition* (Prentice Hall, Upper Saddle River, 1993)

Z. Ren, J. Yuan, Z. Zhang, Robust hand gesture recognition based on finger-earth mover's distance with a commodity depth camera, in *Proceedings of the 19th ACM International Conference on Multimedia* (ACM, 2011), pp. 1093–1096

R. C. Rose, Discriminant wordspotting techniques for rejecting non-vocabulary utterances in unconstrained speech, in *Proceedings of the International Conference on Acoustics, Speech and Signal Processing*, vol. 2 (IEEE, Piscataway, 1992), pp. 105–108, http://ieeexplore.ieee.org/xpls/abs_all.jsp?arnumber=226109

R. C. Rose, D. B. Paul, A hidden Markov model based keyword recognition system, in *Proceedings of the International Conference on Acoustics, Speech and Signal Processing*, 1990, pp. 129–132, http://ieeexplore.ieee.org/xpls/abs_all.jsp?arnumber=115555

A. Roussos, S. Theodorakis, V. Pitsikalis, P. Maragos, Dynamic affine-invariant shape-appearance handshape features and classification in sign language videos. J. Mach. Learn. Res. **14**(1), 1627–1663 (2013)

S. Ruffieux, D. Lalanne, E. Mugellini, ChAirGest: a challenge for multimodal mid-air gesture recognition for close HCI, in *Proceedings of the 15th ACM International Conference on Multimodal Interaction, ICMI '13* (ACM, New York, NY, USA, 2013), pp. 483–488

S. Ruffieux, D. Lalanne, E. Mugellini, O. A. Khaled, A survey of datasets for human gesture recognition, in *Human-Computer Interaction. Advanced Interaction Modalities and Techniques* (Springer, 2014), pp. 337–348

R. Sharma, M. Yeasin, N. Krahnstoever, I. Rauschert, G. Cai, I. Brewer, A.M. MacEachren, K. Sengupta, Speech-gesture driven multimodal interfaces for crisis management. Proc. IEEE **91**(9), 1327–1354 (2003)

S. Shimojo, L. Shams, Sensory modalities are not separate modalities: plasticity and interactions. Curr. Opin. Neurobiol. **11**(4), 505–509 (2001)

J. Shotton, T. Sharp, A. Kipman, A. Fitzgibbon, M. Finocchio, A. Blake, M. Cook, R. Moore, Real-time human pose recognition in parts from single depth images. Commun. ACM **56**(1), 116–124 (2013)

R. Shwartz, S. Austin, A comparison of several approximate algorithms for finding multiple N-Best sentence hypotheses, in *Proceedings of the International Conference on Acoustics, Speech and Signal Processing*, 1991

Y. C. Song, H. Kautz, J. Allen, M. Swift, Y. Li, J. Luo, C. Zhang, A markov logic framework for recognizing complex events from multimodal data, in *Proceedings of the 15th ACM International Conference on Multimodal Interaction* (ACM, 2013), pp. 141–148

T. Starner, J. Weaver, A. Pentland, Real-time american sign language recognition using desk and wearable computer based video. IEEE Trans. Pattern Anal. Mach. Intell. **20**(12), 1371–1375 (1998)

L. N. Tan, B. J. Borgstrom, A. Alwan, Voice activity detection using harmonic frequency components in likelihood ratio test, in *Proceedings of the International Conference on Acoustics, Speech and Signal Processing* (IEEE, Piscataway, 2010), pp. 4466–4469

N. Tanibata, N. Shimada, Y. Shirai, Extraction of hand features for recognition of sign language words, in *Proceedings of the International Conference on Vision, Interface*, 2002, pp. 391–398

S. Theodorakis, V. Pitsikalis, P. Maragos, Dynamic-static unsupervised sequentiality, statistical subunits and lexicon for sign language recognition. Imave Vis. Comput. **32**(8), 533549 (2014)

M. Turk, Multimodal interaction: a review. Pattern. Recognit. Lett. **36**, 189–195 (2014)

C. Vogler, D. Metaxas, A framework for recognizing the simultaneous aspects of american sign language. Comput. Vis. Image Underst. **81**, 358 (2001)

S. B. Wang, A. Quattoni, L. Morency, D. Demirdjian, T. Darrell, Hidden conditional random fields for gesture recognition, in *Proceedings of the International Conference on Computer Vision and Pattern Recognition*, vol. 2 (IEEE, Piscataway, 2006), pp. 1521–1527

D. Weimer, S. Ganapathy, A synthetic visual environment with hand gesturing and voice input, in *ACM SIGCHI Bulletin*, vol. 20 (ACM, 1989), pp. 235–240

L. D Wilcox, M. Bush, Training and search algorithms for an interactive wordspotting system, in *Proceedings of the International Conference on Acoustics, Speech and Signal Processing*, vol. 2 (IEEE, Piscataway, 1992), pp. 97–100

J. Wilpon, L.R. Rabiner, C.-H. Lee, E.R. Goldman, Automatic recognition of keywords in unconstrained speech using hidden Markov models. IEEE Trans. Acoustics Speech Signal Process. **38**(11), 1870–1878 (1990)

A. Wilson, A. Bobick, Parametric hidden markov models for gesture recognition. IEEE Trans. Pattern Anal. Mach. Intell. **21**, 884–900 (1999)

J. Wu, J. Cheng, C. Zhao, H. Lu. Fusing multi-modal features for gesture recognition, in *Proceedings of the 15th ACM International Conference on Multimodal Interaction* (ACM, 2013), pp. 453–460

M.-H. Yang, N. Ahuja, M. Tabb, Extraction of 2d motion trajectories and its application to hand gesture recognition. IEEE Trans. Pattern Anal. Mach. Intell. **24**(8), 1061–1074 (2002)

S. Young, G. Evermann, T. Hain, D. Kershaw, G. Moore, J. Odell, D. Ollason, D. Povey, V. Valtchev, P. Woodland, *The HTK Book* (Entropic Cambridge Research Laboratory, Cambridge, 2002)

Chapter 17
The Gesture Recognition Toolkit

Nicholas Gillian and Joseph A. Paradiso

Abstract The Gesture Recognition Toolkit is a cross-platform open-source C++ library designed to make real-time machine learning and gesture recognition more accessible for non-specialists. Emphasis is placed on ease of use, with a consistent, minimalist design that promotes accessibility while supporting flexibility and customization for advanced users. The toolkit features a broad range of classification and regression algorithms and has extensive support for building real-time systems. This includes algorithms for signal processing, feature extraction and automatic gesture spotting.

Keywords Gesture recognition · Machine learning · C++ · Open source · Classification · Regression · Clustering · Gesture spotting · Feature extraction · Signal processing

17.1 Introduction

Gesture recognition is a powerful tool for human-computer interaction. It is increasingly redefining how we interact with our smartphones, wearable devices, televisions and gaming consoles. In addition to the increasing prevalence of gesture-based interactions in consumer devices, a diverse range of individuals are gaining access to affordable sensor technology and rapid-prototyping tools that facilitate non-specialists to build custom gesture-based applications. Commercial sensors such as the Microsoft Kinect or easy-to-use hardware platforms like Arduino

Editors: Isabelle Guyon, Vassilis Athitsos, Sergio Escalera.

N. Gillian (✉) · J.A. Paradiso
Media Lab, Responsive Environments Group,
Massachusetts Institute of Technology, Cambridge, MA 02139, USA
e-mail: nick@nickgillian.com

J.A. Paradiso
e-mail: joep@media.mit.edu

© Springer International Publishing AG 2017
S. Escalera et al. (eds.), *Gesture Recognition*, The Springer Series
on Challenges in Machine Learning, DOI 10.1007/978-3-319-57021-1_17

(Mellis et al. 2007), combined with prototyping environments, such as Processing[1] or Openframeworks,[2] are empowering professional developers, students, researchers, hobbyists, creative coders, interaction designers, musicians and artists to create novel-interactive systems that are playful, poignant, and expressive.

Nevertheless, while a diverse range of individuals now have access to powerful sensors and rapid-prototyping tools, performing *real-time* gesture recognition can pose a challenge, even to accomplished developers and engineers (Patel et al. 2010). This is despite the large number of sophisticated machine-learning applications currently available, such as WEKA (Hall et al. 2009), MATLAB and R (Team et al. 2010). Many of these applications are primarily designed for offline analysis of prerecorded datasets by domain experts, and require substantial effort to recognize real-time signals. There are accessible machine-learning libraries in Java Abeel et al. (2009) and Python (Pedregosa et al. 2011) that can be used to prototype real-time systems. However, many users need to build their systems in C++ due to the computational overhead of the sensor data and interactive visualizations and therefore benefit from C++ tools for real-time machine learning. While there are a number of powerful C++ libraries that can be adapted for gesture recognition (King 2009; Sonnenburg et al. 2010; Gashler 2011), these tools still require the user to develop the supporting infrastructure needed to build real-time systems and can have steep learning curves for non-specialists. This leaves C++ users with a sizable gulf of execution, specifically the gap between their goals and the actions needed to attain those goals with the system (Hutchins et al. 1985). This gap can significantly impede the process of building novel gesture-based interfaces for technologists, researchers, artists and beyond.

17.2   Gesture Recognition Toolkit

To address this issue, we have created the Gesture Recognition Toolkit (GRT), a cross platform open source C++ machine-learning library for real-time gesture recognition. The toolkit was developed with the following core design principles:

Accessibility: The GRT is a general-purpose tool for facilitating non-specialists to create their own machine-learning based systems. Emphasis is placed on ease of use, with a clear and consistent coding convention applied throughout the toolkit. The GRT provides a minimal code footprint for the user, reducing the need for arduous and error-prone boilerplate code to perform common functionality, such as passing data between algorithms or to preprocess datasets. This consistent, minimalist design significantly lowers the entry barrier for a new user because the same subset of core functions apply throughout the toolkit.

Flexibility: To support flexibility while maintaining consistency, the GRT uses an object-oriented modular architecture. This architecture is built around a set of

---

[1]Processing website: http://processing.org.

[2]Openframeworks website: http://www.openframeworks.cc.

core **modules** and a central **gesture-recognition pipeline**. The input to both the modules and pipeline consists of an N-dimensional double-precision vector, making the toolkit flexible to the type of input signal. The algorithms in each module can be used as stand-alone classes; alternatively a gesture-recognition pipeline can be used to chain modules together to create a more sophisticated gesture-recognition system. The GRT includes modules for preprocessing, feature extraction, clustering, classification, regression and post processing.

Choice: To date, there is no single machine-learning algorithm that can be used to recognize all gestures. It is therefore crucial for a user to be able to choose from, and quickly experiment with, a number of algorithms to see which might work best for their particular task. The GRT features a broad range of machine-learning algorithms such as AdaBoost, Decision Trees, Dynamic Time Warping, Hidden Markov Models, K-Nearest Neighbor, Linear and Logistic Regression, Naïve Bayes, Multilayer Perceptrons, Random Forests, Support Vector Machines[3] and more. In addition to supporting a broad range of algorithms, the toolkit's architecture facilities a user to seamlessly switch between different algorithms with minimal modifications to the user's code.

Supporting Infrastructure: Building sophisticated machine-learning based systems requires more than just a state-of-the-art classifier. In many real-world scenarios, the input to a classification algorithm must first be preprocessed and have salient features extracted. Preprocessing and feature extraction are important because they can significantly improve the predictive performance of a classifier, and also provide faster and more cost-effective predictors (Guyon and Elisseeff 2003). The GRT therefore supports a wide range of pre/post processing, feature extraction and feature selection algorithms, including popular preprocessing filters (e.g. Moving Average Filter), embedded feature extraction algorithms (e.g. AdaBoost), dimensionality reduction techniques (e.g. Principal Component Analysis), and unsupervised quantizers (e.g. K-Means Quantizer, Self-Organizing Map Quantizer). Accurate labeling of datasets is also critical for building robust machine-learning based systems. The toolkit therefore contains extensive support for recording, labeling and managing supervised and unsupervised datasets for classification, regression and timeseries analysis.[4]

Customizability: In addition to using the wide range of existing GRT algorithms, more advanced users commonly want to test or deploy their own algorithms when building novel recognition systems, such as using a custom feature-extraction algorithm. The GRT is therefore designed to facilitate users to easily incorporate their own algorithms within the toolkit's framework by inheriting from one of the GRT base classes. The toolkit leverages advanced object-orientated concepts, such as

---

[3]For Support Vector Machines, we provide an easy-to-use wrapper for LibSVM (Chang and Lin 2011). All other algorithms are custom implementations unless otherwise stated in the source documentation.

[4]A detailed description of the data structures can be found at http://www.nickgillian.com/wiki/pmwiki.php/GRT/Reference.

polymorphism and abstract base-class pointers, facilitating custom algorithms to be used alongside any of the existing GRT algorithms.

Real-time Support: The GRT supports common techniques for performing offline analysis on pre-recorded datasets, such as partitioning data into validation and test datasets, running cross validation and computing accuracy metrics. In addition to these offline techniques, the toolkit is designed to enable a user to seamlessly move from the offline analysis phase to the real-time recognition phase. One significant challenge involved in moving from offline analysis to real-time gesture recognition is automatically segmenting valid gestures from a continuous stream of data (Junker et al. 2008). This is a nontrivial task because the input data might consist of generic movements that are not valid gestures in the model. To support real-time gesture recognition, the GRT features algorithms that automatically perform gesture spotting. These algorithms, such as the Adaptive Naïve Bayes Classifier (Gillian et al. 2011a) and N-Dimensional Dynamic Time Warping (Gillian et al. 2011b), learn rejection thresholds from the training data, which are then used to automatically recognize valid gestures from a continuous stream of real-time data.

17.3   Code Example

The code example below demonstrates the core design principles of the GRT. This example shows how to setup a custom gesture-recognition system consisting of a moving-average filter preprocessing module, a fast Fourier transform and custom feature extraction modules, an AdaBoost classifier and a timeout-filter post processing module. The example also illustrates how to load some training data from a CSV file, train a classification model, and use this model to predict the class label of a new data sample.

```
    //Setup a custom recognition pipeline.
1:  GestureRecognitionPipeline pipeline;
2:  pipeline << MovingAverageFilter(5);
3:  pipeline << FFT(512);
4:  pipeline << MyCustomFeatureAlgorithm();
5:  pipeline << Adaboost(DecisionStump());
6:  pipeline << ClassLabelTimeoutFilter(1000);

    // Load some labeled data from a CSV file,
    // indicating the class label is the 1st column.
7:  ClassificationData trainingData;
8:  trainingData.load("TrainingData.csv", 0);

    // Train a classification model.
9:  bool success = pipeline.train(trainingData);

    // The following lines would be called each time
    // the user gets a new sample from the sensor.
10: vector< double > sample = //Data from sensor
11: bool success = pipeline.predict(sample);
```

```
12: UINT predictedClassLabel = pipeline.getPredictedClassLabel();
13: double maxLikelihood = pipeline.getMaximumLikelihood();
```

Lines 1 through 6 show how a GestureRecognitionPipeline can be used to link several modules together to build a more complex recognition system. Note that the customization of the recognition system is achieved with a minimal code footprint, as the pipeline will automatically connect the output of one module to next module's input; propagating signals through the entire pipeline at both the training, testing and real-time prediction phases. These six lines also illustrate the flexibility of the toolkit's modular design, and demonstrate how a user can easily experiment with different algorithms from existing modules, or insert a custom algorithm into the pipeline as illustrated on line 4. Line 10 demonstrates how real-time sensor data from a variety of devices can be incorporated; input can consist of something as simple as the three-dimensional data from an accelerometer connected to an Arduino, to more complex inputs, such as the high-dimensional skeleton data from a Kinect.

This example also demonstrates one of the key designs of the GRT that make it more accessible: clean and consistent coding through abstraction. For instance, lines 9 and 11 show respectively how a user can train a model and then predict the class label of a new sample using that model. These key functions are the same, regardless of which algorithms are used. This abstraction significantly reduces the learning curve for new users, because the same key functions are consistent across all the GRT algorithms.

17.4   Conclusion

The gesture recognition toolkit is open source under the MIT license and has been publicly available since 2012, receiving over 130K hits on the main website.[5] It has been downloaded several thousand times and has built up a community of over 300 users on the toolkit's forum. To support a diverse range of users, we have established a number of online resources, including detailed examples for each module[6] and a wide range of tutorials and references. Future work includes an interactive graphical user interface, in which a user can record and label training data; configure; train and test a gesture-recognition model; perform real-time prediction and then export their model and pipeline configuration so it can be loaded directly into the user's program, using the C++ API.

---

[5]Gesture Recognition Toolkit Website: http://www.nickgillian.com/grt.

[6]Gesture Recognition Toolkit Wiki: http://www.nickgillian.com/wiki.

References

T. Abeel, Y. Van de Peer, Y. Saeys, Java-ml: a machine learning library. J. Mach. Learn. Res. **10**, 931–934 (2009)

C.C. Chang, C.J. Lin, LIBSVM: a library for support vector machines. ACM Trans. Intell. Syst. Technol. **2**, 27:1–27:27 (2011)

M. Gashler, Waffles: a machine learning toolkit. J. Mach. Learn. Res. **12**, 2383–2387 (2011)

N. Gillian, R.B. Knapp, S. O'Modhrain, An adaptive classification algorithm for semiotic musical gestures, in *Proceedings of the 8th Sound and Music Computing Conference*, 2011a

N. Gillian, R.B. Knapp, S. O'Modhrain, Recognition of multivariate temporal musical gestures using n-dimensional dynamic time warping, in *Proceedings of the 2011 International Conference on New Interfaces for Musical Expression*, 2011b

I. Guyon, A. Elisseeff, An introduction to variable and feature selection. J. Mach. Learn. Res. **3**, 1157–1182 (2003)

M. Hall, E. Frank, G. Holmes, B. Pfahringer, P. Reutemann, I.H. Witten, The weka data mining software: an update. ACM SIGKDD Explor. Newsl. **11**(1), 10–18 (2009)

E.L. Hutchins, J.D. Hollan, D.A. Norman, Direct manipulation interfaces. Hum. Comput. Interact. **1**(4), 311–338 (1985)

H. Junker, O. Amft, P. Lukowicz, G. Tröster, Gesture spotting with body-worn inertial sensors to detect user activities. Pattern Recognit. **41**(6), 2010–2024 (2008)

D.E. King, Dlib-ml: a machine learning toolkit. J. Mach. Learn. Res. **10**, 1755–1758 (2009)

D. Mellis, M. Banzi, D. Cuartielles, T. Igoe, Arduino: an open electronics prototyping platform, in *alt. chi Section of the CHI 2007 Conference in San Jose*, 2007

K. Patel, N. Bancroft, S.M. Drucker, J. Fogarty, A.J. Ko, J. Landay, Gestalt: integrated support for implementation and analysis in machine learning, in *Proceedings of the 23rd Annual ACM Symposium on User Interface Software and Technology*, 2010

F. Pedregosa, G. Varoquaux, A. Gramfort, V. Michel, B. Thirion, O. Grisel, M. Blondel, P. Prettenhofer, R. Weiss, V. Dubourg et al., Scikit-learn: machine learning in python. J. Mach. Learn. Res. **12**, 2825–2830 (2011)

S. Sonnenburg, G. Rätsch, S. Henschel, C. Widmer, J. Behr, A. Zien, F. Bona, A. Binder, C. Gehl, V. Franc, The shogun machine learning toolbox. J. Mach. Learn. Res. **11**, 1799–1802 (2010)

R. Team et al., R: a language and environment for statistical computing, *R Foundation for Statistical Computing Vienna Austria*, 19 Jan 2010

Chapter 18
Robust Online Gesture Recognition
with Crowdsourced Annotations

Long-Van Nguyen-Dinh, Alberto Calatroni and Gerhard Tröster

Abstract Crowdsourcing is a promising way to reduce the effort of collecting annotations for training gesture recognition systems. Crowdsourced annotations suffer from "noise" such as mislabeling, or inaccurate identification of start and end time of gesture instances. In this paper we present SegmentedLCSS and WarpingLCSS, two template-matching methods offering robustness when trained with noisy crowdsourced annotations to spot gestures from wearable motion sensors. The methods quantize signals into strings of characters and then apply variations of the longest common subsequence algorithm (LCSS) to spot gestures. We compare the noise robustness of our methods against baselines which use dynamic time warping (DTW) and support vector machines (SVM). The experiments are performed on data sets with various gesture classes (10–17 classes) recorded from accelerometers on arms, with both real and synthetic crowdsourced annotations. WarpingLCSS has similar or better performance than baselines in absence of noisy annotations. In presence of 60% mislabeled instances, WarpingLCSS outperformed SVM by 22% F1-score and outperformed DTW-based methods by 36% F1-score on average. SegmentedLCSS yields similar performance as WarpingLCSS, however it performs one order of magnitude slower. Additionally, we show to use our methods to filter out the noise in the crowdsourced annotation before training a traditional classifier. The filtering increases the performance of SVM by 20% F1-score and of DTW-based methods by 8% F1-score on average in the noisy real crowdsourced annotations.

Keywords Gesture spotting · Crowdsourced annotation · Longest common subsequence · Template matching methods · Accelerometer sensors

---

Editors: Isabelle Guyon, Vassilis Athitsos and Sergio Escalera.

L.-V. Nguyen-Dinh (✉) · A. Calatroni · G. Tröster
Wearable Computing Lab, ETH Zürich, ETZ H 95, Gloriastrasse 35,
8092 Zürich, Switzerland
e-mail: longvan.nguyendinh@gmail.com

A. Calatroni
e-mail: alberto.calatroni@ife.ee.ethz.ch

G. Tröster
e-mail: troester@ife.ee.ethz.ch

© Springer International Publishing AG 2017
S. Escalera et al. (eds.), *Gesture Recognition*, The Springer Series
on Challenges in Machine Learning, DOI 10.1007/978-3-319-57021-1_18

18.1 Introduction

Wearable computing is gaining momentum through the availability of an increasing choice of devices, like smart watches, glasses and sensor-equipped garments. A core component to allow these devices to understand our context is online gesture recognition (*spotting*) in which types of gestures and their temporal boundaries must be recognized in the incoming streaming sensor data. This is carried out using machine learning approaches on different sensing modalities, like acceleration (Bao and Intille 2004) and video (Elmezain et al. 2009; Yoon et al. 2001).

Training a gesture recognition system requires an annotated training data set that is used to perform supervised learning (Bao and Intille 2004; Ravi et al. (2005); Aggarwal and Ryoo 2011; Chen et al. 2012). Specifically, the annotations comprise the start and end times (i.e., temporal boundaries) of gestures of interest and their corresponding labels. Reference data sets are usually annotated by a small number of experts to be as accurate as possible. However, the labeling process is extremely time-consuming: it may take up to 7–10 h to annotate gestures in a 30-min video (Roggen et al. 2010). Moreover, it is also costly to hire experts to annotate data corpora.

Crowdsourcing has been emerged recently to address these issues (Howe 2006; Doan et al. 2011). Crowdsourcing is defined as a model that outsources tasks which are traditionally performed by experts to a crowd of ordinary people. Thus, crowdsourcing is promising to reduce the cost and time of labeling. Recently, crowdsourcing has been exploited to get labeling for training data sets for gesture recognition (Nguyen-Dinh et al. 2013c). However, labels obtained from crowdsourcing are provided by low-commitment anonymous workers, thus they are commonly unreliable and noisy (Sheng et al. 2008). In gesture annotation from crowdsourcing, the challenge is to obtain labels matching ground truth, attaining both correct labels and correct temporal boundaries.

Using multiple annotators for the same annotation task by watching videos or audios is a popular strategy to get a good annotation from crowdsourcing (Yuen et al. 2011; Nguyen-Dinh et al. 2013c). However, multiple annotators may not be applicable in some cases, either due to the higher cost or because of some privacy concerns. This latter case occurs when the annotation involves some personal context information, including for example location or other sensitive data. Hence, the annotation is often provided and relied on the crowdsourced user for his recorded data. Moreover, it is very difficult to ask the anonymous low-commitment user to clean his annotation because it is time consuming and he may not remember exactly what he has done. In these cases, the large presence of noise in the training data annotation can degrade significantly the performance.

While other research is focusing on how to improve the quality of crowdsourced annotations, we here point out the need for algorithms that can cope with the kinds of annotation errors that will anyway remain. In this work, we show that our proposed template matching methods (TMMs) based on the longest common subsequence algorithm (known as LCSS or LCS in the literature) are suitable for online gesture recognition in a setting where training data are affected significantly by labeling noise. Additionally, the work targets the recognition of gestures based on acceleration data recorded from only one accelerometer mounted on the user's arm. The reason to just use one sensor is that this setting will be the most common one with smart watches in the close future. Recognizing gestures with just motion data from one sensor is challenging due to the ambiguities in the sensor data, especially with high percentage of *null* class (no gesture of interest).

18.1.1   *Contributions*

In this paper, we make the following contributions:

1. We discuss how gesture recognition systems can leverage crowdsourcing to collect annotated data. We address the challenges that arise and then propose a taxonomy of annotation noise which occur in a crowdsourcing setting. We also give analysis on annotation noise in the real crowdsourced annotated data set.
2. We propose SegmentedLCSS and WarpingLCSS as TMMs for online gesture recognition. These methods were first presented in our previous work (Nguyen-Dinh et al. 2012) and have been shown to perform well in clean annotated gesture data sets both in terms of computational complexity and accuracy. In this work, we show their robustness to the labeling noise from crowdsourcing.
3. We compare the robustness of our gesture recognition methods against three baselines using two variations of dynamic time warping and support vector machines. The algorithms are tested with annotations collected in real crowdsourcing scenarios as well as the synthetic crowdsourced annotations in three data sets recorded from accelerometers on arms. We also investigate the impact of different kinds of noises in crowdsourced annotation on the performance of the gesture recognition methods.
4. We investigate the property of LCSS of being able to select clean templates, which makes it suitable also as a filtering component to select good training examples despite noisy annotations. This filter can be used in combination with other classifiers. We show how inserting this filtering step improves the performance of SVMs and TMMs based on dynamic time warping.

The rest of the paper is organized as follows. In Sect. 18.2, we first review existing work in online gesture recognition and crowdsourcing. In Sect. 18.3, we discuss crowdsourcing in gesture recognition and propose a taxonomy of annotation noise in gesture labeling by crowdsourcing. Then, in Sect. 18.4, we present our proposed SegmentedLCSS and WarpingLCSS methods. The experiments are described in Sect. 18.5. We present quantitative results evaluating the robustness of our proposed methods against the baselines in Sect. 18.6. Finally, Sect. 18.7 concludes our work and gives some potential research directions.

18.2 Related Work

In this section we discuss related work in the fields of gesture recognition and crowdsourcing, pointing out the lack of an analysis of how noise present in typical crowdsourced annotations impacts gesture recognition algorithms.

18.2.1 Annotation Techniques

Supervised learning techniques require a set of annotated training samples to build gesture models. Therefore, many annotation techniques have been proposed to collect annotated data. There are *offline annotation* techniques which rely on video and audio recordings (Roggen et al. 2010), subject self-report of activities at the end of the day (Van Laerhoven et al. 2008). *Online annotation* (i.e., real-time) techniques perform the annotation during execution of the activities, like experience sampling (Froehlich et al. 2007) which prompts periodically to a user to ask information about his current activities, or direct annotation in which users responsibly provide a label before an activity begins and indicate when the activity ends (Rossi et al. 2012). There is a trade-off between accuracy of an annotation technique and the amount of time required for annotation (Stikic et al. 2011). For example, offline annotation on video recordings by experts can provide accurate annotations, however it is extremely time consuming (Roggen et al. 2010), and non-scalable to large number of users. In contrast, the self-report of the subject may require less time but the accuracy depends on the subject's ability to recall activities. Therefore, most of the existing works require video annotation by experts to obtain clean and correct annotated data sets (Roggen et al. 2010) or provide a course to teach subjects carefully how they should record and annotate their data correctly (Bao and Intille 2004).

18.2.2 Crowdsourcing

Crowdsourcing services, like Amazon Mechanical Turk (AMT)[1] and Crowdflower,[2] have emerged recently as a new cheap labor pool to distribute annotation tasks to a large number of workers (Yuen et al. 2011). Crowdsourcing tasks are performed by low-commitment anonymous workers, thus acquired data is commonly unreliable and noisy (Sheng et al. 2008). Therefore, the same task is often redundantly performed by multiple workers and majority voting is a popular decision making method used to identify the correct answers (Yuen et al. 2011). Moreover, in crowdsourcing, malicious workers often take advantage of the verification difficulty (the ground truth is unknown) and submit low-quality answers.

---

[1]The home page for AMT is http://www.mturk.com.
[2]The home page for Crowdflower is http://crowdflower.com.

Due to the error-prone nature of crowdsourcing, several strategies were proposed to estimate the quality of workers, in order to reject low-performing and malicious workers. Verifiable questions or pilot tasks for which the requester knows the correct answers is a common empirical strategy to screen workers from crowdsourcing (Kittur et al. 2008; Yuen et al. 2011). Another way to ensure quality is to check the agreement in annotations among workers to detect non-serious workers (Nguyen-Dinh et al. 2013c). Dawid and Skene (1979) proposed a theoretical model that used the redundancy in acquiring answers (i.e., the same task is completed by multiple workers) to measure the labeling quality of the workers. Recently, Raykar et al. (2010) proposed Bayesian versions of worker quality inference. Ipeirotis et al. (2010) improved the method by separating spammers who provide low-quality answers intentionally from biased workers who are careful but biased.

Recently, crowdsourcing has been exploited also in the field of activity recognition to collect annotated training data sets (Rossi et al. 2012; Nguyen-Dinh et al. 2013a, b, c; Lasecki et al. 2013). These works showed that crowdsourced data is erroneous, therefore, filtering strategies such as multiple labelers and outlier removal should be used to reduce labeling noise.

Although many strategies are used to reduce noise in crowdsourced data annotation, there is no guarantee to have a perfect annotation, especially when using multiple labelers can not be applied. Until now, the impact of the noisy annotations in crowdsourcing on the training of gesture recognition methods was not investigated. Furthermore, the nature of the noise that affects the annotations in a crowdsourcing scenario for gesture recognition has not been analyzed yet. These two latter topics are subject of the present paper.

18.2.3   Online Gesture Recognition Methods

Signals from body-worn sensors belong to the category of time series data. Suitable machine learning and pattern recognition techniques for online gesture recognition include Hidden Markov Models (HMM) (Lee and Kim 1999; Deng and Tsui 2000; Junker et al. 2008; Schlömer et al. 2008), template matching methods (TMM) using mostly dynamic time warping—in short DTW (Ko et al. 2005; Stiefmeier et al. 2008; Hartmann and Link 2010) and support vector machines (Ravi et al. (2005); He et al. 2008; Wu et al. 2009).

HMMs are not appealing since a large amount of training data is required to get results comparable to other TMMs and SVM. In Vogler and Metaxas (1999) for example, about 1300 instances for 22 classes (i.e., about 60 instances per class) are used to train the HMM, whereas TMMs can work with as little as one training instance per class. The issue of the amount of training data is mentioned also in Cooper et al. (2012), where the authors state, referring to HMMs: "While they have been employed for sign recognition, they have issues due to the large training requirements". In Alon et al. (2009), a variation of HMMs is selected but the parameters could not be learnt because of the scarcity of training data: "We fix the transition probabilities to simplify the learning task, because we do not have sufficient training data to learn more parameters". HMMs remain nevertheless an interesting approach for cases where a large data corpus is available, which is often the case in the field of video-based gesture or sign language recognition, see for example (Wilson and Bobick 1999; Lee and Kim 1999; Keskin et al. 2011).

Segmented DTW (Ko et al. 2005; Hartmann and Link 2010) performs online gesture recognition by first buffering the streaming signals into an observation window. A *test* segment is a sequence that is examined to classify whether it is an instance of a gesture class. The start and end boundaries of a test segment can vary inside the window. A DTW distance is computed between all templates which represents gesture classes and the test segment, and the class of the closest template is eventually selected as label for the test segment if the distance falls below a certain rejection threshold. As the sensor delivers a new reading, the window is shifted by one sample and the process is repeated. Segmented DTW is time consuming since DTW is recomputed to find the best boundaries for the test segment inside the window and it is also recomputed every time the window shifts by one sample. A *nonsegmented DTW* variation was proposed by Stiefmeier et al. (2008) to reuse the computation of previous readings, recognize gestures and determine their boundaries without segmenting the stream.

Along with DTW, the other commonly used similarity measure for matching two time series is *LCSS* (Fu 2011). In previous work (Nguyen-Dinh et al. 2012), we introduced two variations of LCSS-based template matching for online gesture spotting and recognition. We applied the methods to accelerometer data. These LCSS-based classifiers (SegmentedLCSS and WarpingLCSS) proved to outperform DTW-based TMMs, both in terms of computational complexity and accuracy (especially for data sets containing high variability in gesture execution as shown in Nguyen-Dinh et al. (2012)). Furthermore, our methods were designed with the goal of being robust in case of noisy annotations. The validation of this aspect is the main topic of the present article. The impact of the various kinds of noise occurring in crowdsourced annotations on TMMs has not been investigated in previous literature, to the best of our knowledge.

In sign language recognition literature, we find two other works proposing the use of LCSS as a classifier, applied to video data (Frolova et al. 2013; Stern et al. 2013). In both cases, the methods use a sliding window to set temporal boundaries of a gesture inside the window, similarly to our SegmentedLCSS. With our WarpingLCSS, this need of using a window is removed, reducing the computational complexity. It is interesting to note how Stern et al. (2013) states that "It can then be said that the MDSLCS algorithm can outperform the HMM classifier for both pre-cut and streaming gestures", which supports the idea of using TMMs instead of HMMs to make best use of the available training data. TMMs are competitive with HMMs also with respect to null-class rejection, meaning the ability to spot a gesture within a continuous stream.

Some algorithms present in the literature rely on k-means or spatio-temporal clustering to transform the raw signals into so-called "fenemes", or subunits (Bauer and Karl-Friedrich 2002; Fang et al. 2004), which allows to reduce the amount of training data, due to the fact that more gestures can contain the same feneme, so that a critical mass can be achieved in terms of amount of training data. We use a similar approach based on k-means clustering to find a quantization of the signals which gives good results.

A large body of literature focuses on a recognition performed on video data, for example for the recognition of sign language (see for example Wilson and Bobick 1999; Bowden et al. 2004; Alon et al. 2009; Keskin et al. 2011). However, gesture recognition from wearable sensors, e.g., one accelerometer at the wrist, would allow to scale up the recognition system to many users immediately because the system can be deployed easily wherever a user goes with the motion sensor mounted on hand. It does not need any other infrastructure like cameras, which do not follow us everywhere in practice. Of the video-based approaches, the one of Hao and Shibata (2009) captures the videos directly by a moving camera, which could be easily wearable. However, from the practical point of view, such an option has some limitations: first, such a device would be quite costly; second, processing signals from a camera is more computationally intensive than processing those from a motion sensor; third, capturing video data is much more intrusive due to privacy concerns.

18.2.4   Robustness Against Annotation Noise

The impact of noise in annotations on the performance of classifiers has been investigated in the literature (Angluin and Laird 1988; Amini and Gallinari 2005; Gayar et al. 2006; Lawrence and Schölkopf 2001; Stikic et al. 2011). The above cited studies do not concern template matching methods. Moreover, they conducted experiments on synthetic noisy data. Additionally, under "annotation noise", or "class noise", only the case of having wrong labels (i.e., labels are substituted as other classes) was considered. Noise in gestures annotation can nevertheless also mean having labelings with temporal boundaries differing from the ground truth, e.g., a gesture marked as starting earlier and ending later than the ground truth. These other kinds of noise were neglected until now, and they are investigated in this paper in both synthetic and real crowdsourced annotated data.

18.3   Crowdsourcing in Gesture Recognition

In this section we discuss how gesture recognition systems can leverage crowdsourcing. We outline the challenges that arise and provide a taxonomy of the annotation noises, i.e., the mistakes that affect crowdsourced annotations. We then measure these annotation noises in a real crowdsourced data set.

Gesture recognition systems can take advantages of crowdsourcing in three ways:

1. Crowdsourcing can be used to acquire annotations for an existing gesture data set by asking crowdsourced workers to watch video footage synchronized with the sensor data (Nguyen-Dinh et al. 2013c; Lasecki et al. 2013).
2. Berchtold et al. (2010) proposed a system that asks users to both record and annotate activities. This system can be deployed in a crowdsourcing manner. Users can sporadically select gestures they want to perform and record them with a device (e.g, smart watch, smart phone, etc.). This way, multiple annotated gestures provided by a large user base could contribute to a central repository which grows in time. The data set would capture the variability in gesture execution due to the different people contributing.
3. A more obtrusive crowdsourcing task would ask users to record and annotate as many activities and gestures as possible over a long time span (e.g., weeks). This type of crowdsourced data collection would be useful to gather data for long-term health care monitoring systems.

In any of the previous scenarios, the outcome would be an annotated training data set, with which algorithms can be trained. The benefit of the crowdsourcing setting is that a large data set can be collected quickly, if the crowdsourced user base is large enough.

18.3.1 Taxonomy of Sources of Annotation Noises

The major challenge in any of the settings outlined above is the quality of the labels obtained, which are unreliable for many reasons. We define the following taxonomy of annotation noises along with examples:

- Some gestures or activities can be understood differently with respect to when they actually start and end. The temporal boundaries of the gesture *drink* can be set from the time when the user picks up a glass to when he or she puts it back to the table. Another variation is that the gesture is annotated only when the person is actually drinking. Both annotations are valid, but this uncertainty of temporal boundaries has an impact on the algorithms that will be trained with the collected annotated data. However, even when we assume the definition of gesture boundary is given, the errors in gesture boundary still happen due to the carelessness of crowdsourced labelers. We call this form of noise *boundary jitter*. We define *boundary jitter* as the presence of a shift in the annotation boundaries, while the label matches the actual gesture (ground truth).
- Some instances of gestures can be wrongly annotated or missed altogether. This can occur for example if the video footage does not have enough resolution to spot subtle manipulative gestures, or more simply if the labeler does not annotate all gestures that are occurring. We use the term *label noise* to denote instances where gestures are associated to wrong labels or to no label at all.

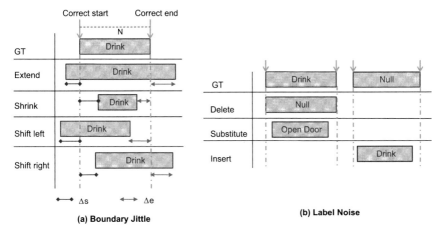

Fig. 18.1 Illustrations of boundary jitter and label noise in crowdsourcing annotation. GT stands for ground truth. The *blue dash-dotted lines* indicate the correct boundary of a gesture

We further categorize *boundary jitter* into four error types, namely *extend, shrink, shift left* and *shift right* according to how the temporal boundary of a gesture is shifted compared to the ground truth. Figure 18.1a illustrates the subclasses of *boundary jitter*.

- *Extend*: The starting boundary is set earlier and the ending boundary is set later. The information of the gesture instance is preserved, but noise is attached to the gesture instance in the form of samples which belong actually to another gesture class or to no class of interest at all (i.e., *null* class).
- *Shrink*: The starting boundary is set later and the ending boundary is set earlier. In this case, some information of the gesture instance is missed.
- *Shift left*: Both starting and ending boundaries are set earlier. In this case, some information of the gesture instance is missed and noise is added at the end of the gesture.
- *Shift right*: Both starting and ending boundaries are set later. In this case, some information of the gesture instance is missed and noise is added at the beginning of the gesture.

We also categorize *label noise* into three error types, namely *delete, substitute* and *insert*.

- *Delete*: A gesture instance is not annotated. It is automatically marked as *null* class.
- *Substitute*: A gesture instance is labeled as another gesture class.
- *Insert*: A gesture instance is labeled where no gesture of interest actually occurs.

Figure 18.1b illustrates the subclasses of *label noise*. The subclasses of *label noise* are similar to the definition of classification errors evaluated in performance metrics proposed by Ward et al. (2011). However, in this work, we consider those errors existing in annotations of training data set.

18.3.2 Annotation Noise Parameters

Along with the taxonomy provided in the previous section, we here list the parameters that quantify the amount of noise in the annotation. Given a gesture instance, let *start* and *end* be the start time and end time of the crowdsourced annotation. Let GT_start and GT_end be the corresponding ground truth boundaries. Let N denote the time length of the gesture ($N = |GT\_end - GT\_start|$). We define Δs as the time difference between the crowdsourced start time and the correct start time ($\Delta s = |start - GT\_start|$). Similarly, we define Δe as the time difference between the crowdsourced end time and the correct end time ($\Delta e = |end - GT\_end|$). Δs and Δe are illustrated in Fig. 18.1a for the different boundary jitter noises.

For *boundary jitter* and for the corresponding subclasses, we define a *jitter level* to quantify the proportion of time that is wrongly annotated in a gesture due to the jitter. The jitter level also indicates how much the boundaries stray from the correct annotation. These jitter parameters are calculated as follows:

$$
\begin{aligned}
\text{extend level} \quad &= \text{proportion of time noisy samples added} \\
&= \tfrac{\Delta s + \Delta e}{N}. \\
\text{shrink level} \quad &= \text{proportion of time good samples missed} \\
&= \tfrac{\Delta s + \Delta e}{N}. \\
\text{shift-left level} \quad &= \text{proportion of time noisy samples added and good samples missed} / 2 \\
&= \tfrac{\Delta s + \Delta e}{2 * N}. \\
\text{shift-right level} &= \text{proportion of time noisy samples added and good samples missed} / 2 \\
&= \tfrac{\Delta s + \Delta e}{2 * N}.
\end{aligned}
$$

18.3.3 Annotation Noise Statistics from A Real Crowdsourcing Experiment

To give a flavor of typical values encountered for the annotation noise levels, we report these levels measured in a real crowdsourcing experiment that we conducted in a previous study (Nguyen-Dinh et al. 2013c). In the crowdsourcing experiment we used video footage belonging to the Opportunity data set (Roggen et al. 2010), which contains gestures of normal daily routines (e.g., drink, open or close doors). We showed each short video to ten workers in Amazon Mechanical Turk (AMT), described the task and collected their annotations. The AMT labelers must annotate the start, end boundaries and the label of all occurrences of gestures of interest in the videos. We applied two strategies to detect and filter non-serious labelers and erroneous labeling (Nguyen-Dinh et al. 2013c). Individual filtering checks the correctness in the answers of each labeler for qualification questions whose answers are known in advance. Collaborative filtering checks the agreement in annotations among workers to detect non-serious labelers. Specifically, the labeler X who has a

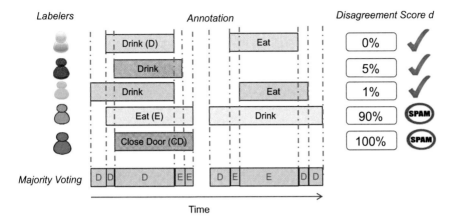

Fig. 18.2 An illustration of the collaborative filtering technique to calculate the disagreement score of each labeler against the majority. The last two labelers are spammers and then their annotations will be removed

disagreement score $d(X) = \frac{\text{Annotation times of X disagree with majority}}{\text{Total annotation times of X}} > threshold$ is a spammer. We chose a threshold = 0.3, it means if the disagreement score $d \geq 0.3$ (i.e., less than 70% of annotation of a labeler agrees with the majority), the labeler is a spammer and his annotations are removed. The collaborative filtering is illustrated in Fig. 18.2. After filtering, the majority voting among qualified annotations is performed to generate a final crowdsourced gesture annotation. A more detail on the crowdsourcing experiment is given in Nguyen-Dinh et al. (2013c).

Each video footage of the Opportunity data set was already examined and annotated carefully by one expert (Roggen et al. 2010) and the expert's annotations are used as a ground truth to evaluate our crowdsourced annotation. Here we report the sample-based accuracy (i.e., fraction of correctly labeled samples compared to expert's annotation) for a one-labeler annotation scenario where only one crowdsourced labeler is selected, and for a multiple-labeler scenario where the filterings and majority voting are applied for the ten workers. For a one-labeler annotation, the sample-based accuracy gets as low as 55%. In the multiple-labeler annotation, the accuracy reaches 80%. A breakdown of the types of annotation mistakes, according to the taxonomy introduced in Sect. 18.3.1, is shown in Fig. 18.3a. The values for *label noise* and for the *boundary jitter* are shown for one and for multiple labelers. In the scenario of only one labeler, about 52% of the instances are affected by *label noises*, comprising mostly *substitute* and *delete* errors. In the multiple-labeler scenario, *label noise* decreases to 18%. In Fig. 18.3b, we give the average, the min and the max values of jitter level of boundary jitters for one and for multiple labelers. On average, jitter levels ranges from 27 to 60%. However, there are good annotated instances with very low jitter levels (only 2%).

It can be seen that requesting multiple labelers for an annotation task can reduce labeling errors. However, the result from a one-labeler annotation represents for the scenarios where multiple labelers cannot be applied. Our experiment belongs to

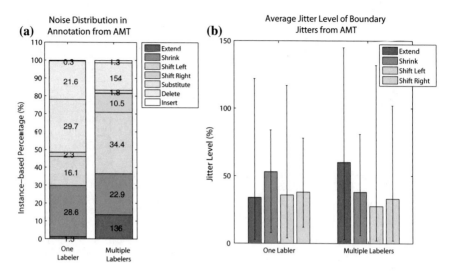

Fig. 18.3 Analysis of crowdsourcing annotation from AMT. *Blue lines* in the figure a separate boundary jitter part and label noise part. *Black lines* in the figure b show the minimum and maximum level of jitter in each type of noise

the first crowdsourcing category described at the beginning of the present section, i.e., crowdsourcing labeling of data which were previously recorded. The amount and distribution of annotation noises will change depending on the crowdsourcing scenario and on the kind of gesture data, but there is no reason to think that some scenarios will achieve much lower noise levels. On the contrary, in real-time annotation (i.e., providing labels while recording data) , it is more likely that the level of noise increases: more gestures could be forgotten and others would be labeled only after they really occurred, leading to imprecise time boundaries. We therefore argue that annotation noise is a fact that cannot be completely removed and that calls the attention of robust methods when designing gesture recognition systems which use noisy crowdsourced annotations.

In the next sections we present our SegmentedLCSS and WarpingLCSS TMMs which are designed with the aim of being robust to annotation noise for gesture recognition.

18.4 SegmentedLCSS and WarpingLCSS Gesture Recognition Methods

In this section, we describe in details our proposed methods, Segmented LCSS and WarpingLCSS for online gesture recognition using signals obtained from body-worn sensors.

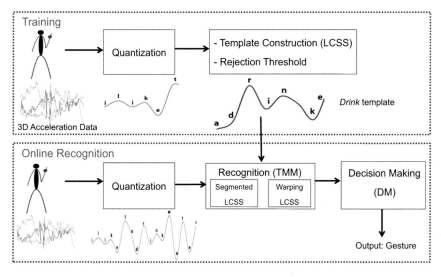

Fig. 18.4 Data processing flow of the proposed LCSS-based template matching methods for gesture recognition

The methods proposed to recognize gestures are based on template matching (TM). The training phase uses a set of labeled signals to train the gesture recognition algorithm. In the training phase, the sensor signals are quantized and converted into sequences of symbols (strings); furthermore, one template is created for each gesture of interest. When deploying the recognition algorithm, the quantization scheme is again applied to the streaming signals. The strings obtained are then compared with the learned templates by either using the longest common subsequence (LCSS) algorithm in segmented windows (SegmentedLCSS) or using our faster variant of LCSS (namely WarpingLCSS). Figure 18.4 shows the data flow through different processing components in the training phase and the recognition phase of our proposed system.

The rationale using LCSS is that it gives a measure of similarity between templates and signals to be recognized. Moreover, LCSS is robust to the high variability in gesture execution as shown in our previous work (Nguyen-Dinh et al. 2012) because LCSS can ignore the dissimilarity and accumulate the similarity between two gesture instances.

In the following, we first briefly review LCSS, then we describe the different processing components of the recognition system in Fig. 18.4.

18.4.1   The Longest Common Subsequence Algorithm (LCSS)

Let s_A and s_B be two strings comprising l_A and l_B symbols respectively. Let $s(i)$ denote the i-th symbol within a string s. For each pair of positions $0 \leq i \leq l_A$ and

$0 \le j \le l_B$ within the strings, we call $LCSS_{(A,B)}(i, j)$ the length of the longest symbol subsequence in common between the first i symbols of s_A and the first j symbols of s_B. The LCSS between the complete strings is then denoted as $L_{(A,B)}$ or, when the strings are clear from the context, just with L.

$$L_{(A,B)}(i, j) = \begin{cases} 0 & \text{, if } i = 0 \text{ or } j = 0 \\[2mm] L_{(A,B)}(i - 1, j - 1) + 1 & \text{, if } s_A(i) = s_B(j) \\[2mm] \max \begin{cases} L_{(A,B)}(i - 1, j) \\ L_{(A,B)}(i, j - 1) \end{cases} & \text{, otherwise.} \end{cases} \tag{18.1}$$

Let Ω_A and Ω_B be the sets of indices corresponding to the longest subsequences of s_A and s_B that are matching. The sets $\Omega_A = \omega_A^{(0)} \dots \omega_A^{(L-1)}$ and $\Omega_B = \omega_B^{(0)} \dots \omega_B^{(L-1)}$ contain then $L_{(A,B)}$ indices. $L_{(A,B)}$ and the corresponding matching subsequences, hence the sets Ω_A and Ω_B, can be found using dynamic programming (see Cormen et al. 2001).

18.4.2   Training Phase: Quantization Step

Let n denote the number of signal channels provided by the body-worn sensors (e.g., $n = 3$ for one triaxial accelerometer). Let N be the number of available samples. Let x_i be the time series corresponding to the i-th signal channel, with $1 \le i \le n$ and $x_i(t)$ be the value of the time series x_i at time t, with $1 \le t \le N$. Let the n-dimensional vector $\mathbf{x}(t) = [x_1(t) \dots x_n(t)]$ denote one sample from all channels at time t.

The quantization step converts the vectors $\mathbf{x}(t)$ into a sequence of symbols (string) $\mathbf{s}(t)$. This is done by performing k-means clustering on the set of n-dimensional vectors $\mathbf{x}(t)$, $\forall t, 1 \le t \le N$. The choice of k is performed through cross-validation or empirically. For the gesture data sets used in this paper, $k = 20$ provided a good tradeoff between complexity (k-means' complexity scales linearly with k) and performance. The output of k-means is a set of k n-dimensional cluster centers, $\zeta_0 \dots \zeta_{k-1}$, to which k symbols $\alpha_0 \dots \alpha_{k-1}$ are assigned. The quantization procedure then operates on each sample $\mathbf{x}(t)$ to obtain the symbols $s(t)$ as follows:

$$s(t) = \alpha_i | i = \operatorname*{argmin}_i \|\mathbf{x}(t) - \zeta_i\|_2 \ .$$

Let us denote with $d(\alpha_l, \alpha_m)$ the distance between two symbols, given by the correspondent distance between their assigned cluster centers, normalized to fall in the interval $[0, 1]$.

$$d(\alpha_i, \alpha_j) = \frac{\|\zeta_i - \zeta_j\|_2}{max_{i,j}\|\zeta_i - \zeta_j\|_2} \ . \tag{18.2}$$

18.4.3   Training Phase: Template Construction

For each labeled gesture in the training data set, a corresponding string is derived used the quantization described in Sect. 18.4.2. Denote with $s_i^{(c)}$ the i-th string belonging to class c. The template $\bar{s}^{(c)}$ that represents a gesture class c is then chosen as the string that has the highest average LCSS to all other strings of the same class.

$$\bar{s}^{(c)} = \underset{s_i^{(c)}}{\mathrm{argmax}} \sum_{j \neq i} L_{(s_i^{(c)}, s_j^{(c)})}.$$

18.4.4   Training Phase: Calculation of Rejection Thresholds

In order to be able to reject signals not belonging to a gesture class upon deployment, a threshold needs to be calculated in the training phase. We define one rejection threshold ϵ_c for each class c. Let $\mu^{(c)}$ and and $\sigma^{(c)}$ be the mean and the standard deviation, respectively, of LCSS values between the template of a class c and any string belonging to the same class. We calculate the rejection threshold to be below $\mu^{(c)}$ by some standard deviations.

$$\epsilon_c = \mu^{(c)} - h * \sigma(c),$$

with h = 0, 1, 2, . . .

The rationale is that the good instances belonging to a class should have the similarity with the template around the mean value. ϵ_c is also chosen to be robust with the existence of noisy training instances in gesture class. In our experiments, $h = 1$ provided a good performance.

18.4.5   Recognition Phase: Quantization Step

In the online recognition, streaming data from a body-worn sensor are quantized to the k-means centroids (i.e., symbols) identified during training, then come to template matching module (TM) which uses either Segmented LCSS or WarpingLCSS to recognize gestures.

18.4.6   Recognition Phase: SegmentedLCSS

In the SegmentedLCSS approach, the sensor readings $\mathbf{x}(t)$ are first quantized into a string s through the quantization step described in Sect. 18.4.5. For each gesture

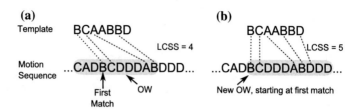

Fig. 18.5 The SegmentedLCSS recognition process. The *shaded* part represents the observation window OW_c. For each class c, the LCSS is computed between the gesture template $\bar{s}^{(c)}$ and the quantized signal in the window. If the LCSS exceeds the rejection threshold, the samples between the first and the last matching symbols are assigned to class c. The next observation window will start at the first matched point of the previous calculation as illustrated in **b**

class c, the string s is then segmented into a sliding observation window OW_c. The length of OW_c is chosen as the length of the template $\bar{s}^{(c)}$. A substring of s in OW_c is denoted as s_{OW}^c. Each substring is compared to the template $\bar{s}^{(c)}$ for class c.

The LCSS algorithm is used to calculate $L_{(s_{OW}^c, \bar{s}^{(c)})}$ and the set Ω_s of reference indices of the symbols of s_{OW}^c in the string s matching with symbols in the template. Because the LCSS algorithm can find matching points, the boundaries of the detected gesture can be decided easily. Specifically, if $L_{(s_{OW}^c, \bar{s}^{(c)})} \geq \epsilon_c$, the symbols ranging from $s(\omega_s^{(0)})$ and $s^c(\omega_s^{(L-1)})$ are marked as belonging to class c.

In order to reduce the computational complexity, the next observation window is started at the index $\omega_s^{(0)}$ of the first matching symbol of the previous observation window. In case the set Ω_s is empty, the next observation window is shifted quickly by the window length. Figure 18.5 illustrates the SegmentedLCSS.

18.4.6.1 Computational Complexity of SegmentedLCSS

Let T_c denote the length of a gesture template of class c ($|OW_c| = T_c$). The worst case computational complexity of SegmentedLCSS occurs when new observation windows are shifted by just one sample compared to the preceding ones. In this case, for each class c, the time complexity of SegmentedLCSS is $\mathcal{O}(T_c^2)$. The overall time complexity is then $\mathcal{O}(C * \overline{T}^2)$, where C is the number of classes and $\overline{T}$ stands for the average template length across the classes. The memory usage in SegmentedLCSS is at most $\mathcal{O}(T^2)$, where T is the length of the longest template.

18.4.7 Recognition Phase: WarpingLCSS

In the SegmentedLCSS, the LCSS must be recomputed every time the observation window shifts, in order to find the beginning and end of each gesture. WarpingLCSS is our variant of LCSS that can find the gesture boundaries without the need of sliding windows, thereby reducing the computational complexity.

In WarpingLCSS, after each new sample of $\mathbf{x}(t)$ is available, the string s is updated by appending the symbol obtained through the quantization of the sample and the LCSS value is recomputed accordingly, relying on the previous values.

Given the gesture template for class c, $\bar{s}^{(c)}$, the WarpingLCSS score $W_{(\bar{s}^{(c)},s)}(i, j)$ between the first i symbols of the template $\bar{s}^{(c)}$ and the first j symbols of the string s is obtained through a modified version of Eq. 18.1 as follows.

$$W_{(\bar{s}^{(c)},s)}(i, j) = \begin{cases} 0 & , \text{if } i = 0 \text{ or } j = 0 \\[2mm] W_{(\bar{s}^{(c)},s)}(i - 1, j - 1) + 1 & , \text{if } \bar{s}^{(c)}(i) = s(j) \\[2mm] \max \begin{cases} W_{(\bar{s}^{(c)},s)}(i - 1, j - 1) - p * d(\bar{s}^{(c)}(i), s(j)) \\ W_{(\bar{s}^{(c)},s)}(i - 1, j) - p * d(\bar{s}^{(c)}(i), \bar{s}^{(c)}(i - 1)) \\ W_{(\bar{s}^{(c)},s)}(i, j - 1) - p * d(s(j), s(j - 1)) \\ \qquad , \text{otherwise,} \end{cases} \end{cases}$$

(18.3)

where p is a penalty parameter of the dissimilarity and $d(\cdot, \cdot)$ is the distance between two symbols as defined in Eq. 18.2. The rationale of the WarpingLCSS is the following: if the WarpingLCSS algorithm encounters the same symbol in a template and in the current string, W is increased by a reward of 1. Otherwise, W is decreased by a penalty which depends on the parameter p and on the distance between the symbols. Furthermore, if the string s is "warped", that is, it contains contiguous repetitions of a symbol due to a slower execution of a gesture, the penalty is counted only once.

The algorithm starts with an empty string s and $W(0, 0) = 0$. As new symbols are appended, W is updated according to Eq. 18.3. If a gesture of a class is performed, it symbols matching the corresponding template are found and W grows, until reaching a local maximum and eventually decreasing again, as soon as the gesture is over. A gesture of class c is recognized for each local maximum of W that also exceeds the rejection threshold ϵ_c. The end point of the gesture is set to the local maximum itself. The start point is found by tracing back the matching path. The LCSS between the template and the matched gesture is accumulated during the trace-back process if necessary (i.e., when a gesture is spotted as belonging to multiple classes) to make a decision (discussed in next section).

When gestures differ from those encoded by the stored templates, W drops significantly due to the penalty terms. The value of the penalty parameter p depends on the application and can be chosen by cross-validation to maximize the recognition accuracy.

Figure 18.6 illustrates an example of behavior of W. Figure 18.7 shows a close-up of W where a gesture was matched to a template. It also shows how the WarpingLCSS detects the temporal boundaries of matched gestures.

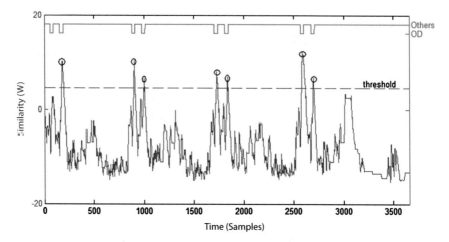

Fig. 18.6 WarpingLCSS between a template of the gesture "open door" (OD) and a streaming string s, $p = 3$. The value W is updated for each new sample. The *line* on the *top* shows the ground truth. The *small circles* show gesture detection at spotting time

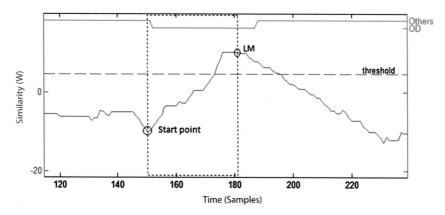

Fig. 18.7 Close-up of the first detected "open door" gesture (OD) in the string s (see Fig. 18.6). The local maximum (LM) marks the end of the gesture, while the start is traced back through the matching symbols

18.4.7.1 Computational Complexity of WarpingLCSS

WarpingLCSS only needs to update the value of W for each new sample. Thus, the time complexity of WarpingLCSS is $\mathcal{O}(T)$. WarpingLCSS has a linear complexity in T compared to SegmentedLCSS, whose complexity grows quadratically in T. The WarpingLCSS maintains at most $\mathcal{O}(T^2)$ memory for the need to trace back the starting boundary of detected gestures.

18.4.8 Decision Making and Solving Conflicts

The incoming streaming string is concurrently "compared" with templates of all concerned gesture classes in TM module. If a gesture is spotted as belonging to multiple classes (i.e., boundaries of spotted instances are overlapping), the decision making module (DM) will resolve conflicts (as discussed below) by deciding which class is the best match. If a gesture is classified into only one gesture class, the DM will output the class. Otherwise, if no gesture class is spotted, the DM will output *null*.

Resolving spotting conflicts: We define the normalized similarity between two strings A and B as NormSim(A,B) $= LCSS(A, B)/max(\|A\|, \|B\|)$, with $\|A\|$ and $\|B\|$ are the lengths of the strings A and B, respectively. The NormSim between the template and the matched gesture is output to the decision making module (DM). The class with highest NormSim is chosen as the best match. This process is the same for both SegmentedLCSS and WarpingLCSS.

18.5 Experiments

To analyze the effect of annotation noise in terms of performance of gesture recognition algorithms, we compare our SegmentedLCSS and WarpingLCSS TMMs against state-of-the-art recognition methods to assess their robustness. We first present three gesture data sets used to evaluate the recognition systems. We then describe how synthetic crowdsourced annotations are obtained. Finally, we discuss baseline methods and evaluation metrics.

18.5.1 Description of Data Sets

We used three data sets including various gestures which have been labeled manually by experts. The experts' annotation is the ground truth of the data sets. The data sets used also include *null* class, data which do not correspond to any of the gestures of interest. The list of gestures of these data sets are shown in Table 18.1. In each data set, we use a 3D accelerometer at a subject' dominant (right) lower arm for the evaluations (30Hz sampling rate). Following, we describe briefly each data set.[3]

---

[3] Skoda and Opportunity data sets can be downloaded from http://www.wearable.ethz.ch/resources/Dataset.

Table 18.1 Gestures in Opportunity, Skoda, and HCI data sets

HCI Gestures					Opportunity Gestures		
					Null	clean Table	open Drawer 1-2-3
Circle	Triangle	Square	Infinity	Slider	close Drawer 1-2-3	open Door 1-2	close Door 1-2
Their Speculars				Null	open Fridge	close Fridge	open Dishwasher
					close Dishwasher	drink Cup	toggle Switch

Skoda Gestures			
write on notepad	check gaps on the front door	open hood	close hood
open left front door	close left front door	close both left door	check trunk gaps
check steering wheel	open and close trunk	Null	

18.5.1.1 Skoda

The Skoda data set (Zappi et al. 2008) contains 10 manipulative gestures performed in a car maintenance scenario by one subject. The *null* class takes 23%. Each gesture class has about 70 instances. This data set is characterized as low variant in execution because the subject performed carefully each manipulative gesture in the same manner.

18.5.1.2 HCI

The HCI data set (Banos et al. 2012) contains 10 gestures executed by a single person. The gestures are geometric shapes executed with the arm in the vertical plane. This data set has a low variability in the execution of gestures and well-defined labeling. The *null* class takes 57% and each gesture class has about 50 instances.

18.5.1.3 Opportunity

The Opportunity data set (Roggen et al. 2010) is a rich multi-modal data set collected in a naturalistic environment akin to an apartment, where users execute 16 daily gestures. The data set is characterized by a predominance of *null* class (37%) and a large variability in the execution of the daily activities. Each gesture class has 20 instances excepts "Drink Cup" and "Toggle Switch" each having 40 instances. Note that in Opportunity data set, there are three drawers at different heights which makes the recognition more challenging.

18.5.2   Experiments on Synthesized Crowdsourced Annotation

To analyze how much noise in annotation the gesture recognition methods can tolerate, we conduct experiments with synthesized annotations. We modify clean annotations from the three data sets described above by emulating *label noise* and *boundary jitter* as discussed in the taxonomy in Sect. 18.3.1. In order to evaluate the effect of the different types of noise, we run simulations for each type of noise separately.

18.5.2.1   Label Noise Simulation

In the *label noise* simulation, we assume the label boundaries are perfect. Let α be the label noise percentage in each class. This means that α percent of the instances are selected and their labels are randomly flipped to other classes (including *null class*). Consequently, each gesture class will have $(1 - \alpha)$ percent of clean instances.

18.5.2.2   Boundary Jitter Simulation

We run different simulations for different error types in boundary jitter. We assume that all gesture instances get affected from boundary jitter. Let β be the *jitter level* defined in Sect. 18.3.2. In the *extend* simulation, each gesture instance will have an *extend level* of β, with boundaries extended at both ends equally ($\beta/2$ per side). Similarly, in the *shrink* simulation, each gesture instance will be shrunk at both ends equally by $\beta/2$. In the *shift left* and *shift right* simulations, each gesture instance is shifted to the left or to the right respectively by β compared to the correct starting point.

We assume that all gesture instances have the same jitter level β. This assumption is not realistic however it can show how much jitter level in the training data set the spotting methods can tolerate given the same style of annotation (for example, a labeler always extends all his annotation 20% level). For a more realistic scenario where jitter levels vary from one instance to another instance, the experiment on the real crowdsourced annotation is presented in Sect. 18.6.2.

18.5.3   Evaluation with Baseline Methods

To investigate the effect of noisy crowdsourced data sets on gesture recognition, we compare the performance of recognition methods trained with ground truth annotations against those trained with crowdsourced annotations. With crowdsourcing-based experiments, the recognition system is trained on crowdsourced annotations and tested on clean data (i.e., annotated by experts). For each data set, we perform a 5-fold cross-validation.

We compare our proposed LCSS-based TMMs with three baselines approaches: the Segmented DTW (Ko et al. 2005; Hartmann and Link 2010), Nonsegmented DTW (Stiefmeier et al. 2008) and support vector machines (SVM). For all TMM methods, we use the same strategy to select templates, i.e., the maximum similarity average for our LCSS-based methods and the minimum distance average for DTW based ones. They all have the same quantization preprocessing step as presented in Sect. 18.4.2. The rejection thresholds are selected as discussed in Sect. 18.4.4. For SegmentedLCSS and Segmented DTW, the window length is chosen as the template length.

For SVM, the signals are passed through a sliding window, with 50% overlap. For each window, mean and variance of the signals are calculated and the obtained feature vectors are fed into a SVM classifier. We use RBF kernels and the two RBF parameters are selected by using cross-validation. In this work, we use the LIBSVM library (Chang and Lin 2011) for training SVM.

18.5.3.1 Complexity of Baseline Methods

Segmented DTW belongs, like Segmented LCSS, to the category of sliding window based template matching algorithms. Therefore, roughly, they have the same computational cost. However, unlike SegmentedLCSS, in SegmentedDTW the boundaries of the gestures must be swept exhaustively in the observation window and DTW must be recomputed for each choice to find the best match (Ko et al. 2005; Hartmann and Link 2010). Therefore, when one new sample arrives, the complexity of the SegmentedDTW is $\mathcal{O}(T^3)$ in the worst case. Meanwhile, in SegmentedLCSS the boundary of gesture inside the window can be found easily via matching points and the observation window is shifted to the first matched point in the previous recognition process instead of being shifted forward by only one sample. Thus, SegmentedLCSS has one order of magnitude lower than SegmentedDTW.

Nonsegmented DTW and WarpingLCSS determine gesture occurrences without segmenting the stream. Therefore, they achieve the same computational cost and they are faster than SegmentedLCSS by one order of magnitude.

In the recognition phase, the running time of SVM grows linearly with the length of the window. Hence, SVM has roughly the same computation cost as WarpingLCSS in the recognition phase.

18.5.4 Evaluation Metrics

The distribution of the gesture classes may be highly unbalanced in real-life data sets. Especially, in our data sets, *null class* is predominant. Therefore, we assess the performance of gesture recognition with the weighted average F1 score. The weighted average F1 score is the sum of the F1 scores of all classes, each weighted according to the proportion of samples of that particular class. Specifically,

$$F1score = \sum_c 2 * w_c \frac{precision_c * recall_c}{precision_c + recall_c},$$

where c is the class index and w_c is the proportion of samples of class c; $precision_c$ is the proportion of samples of class c predicted correctly over the total samples predicted as class c; $recall_c$ is the proportion of samples of class c predicted correctly over the total samples of class c.

We present two ways of computing the F1 score, either including (F1-Null) or excluding the *null class* (F1-NoNull). F1-NoNull does not consider the *null class*, but still takes into account false predictions of gesture samples or instances misclassified as *null class*. The recognition system that has high values of both F1-Null and F1-NoNull predicts well both gesture classes and *null* class.

18.6   Results and Discussion

In this section we present and discuss the results of the experiments conducted with synthesized and real crowdsourced annotations.

18.6.1   Results on Synthesized Crowdsourced Annotations

We first present the results with synthesized crowdsourced annotations, sweeping the noise levels as described in Sect. 18.5. The results show that F1-Null and F1-NoNull have a similar trend of performance as the noise levels increase, therefore we report F1-Null score only.

18.6.1.1   Label Noise Simulation

Figure 18.8 shows the results of label noise simulations on the three data sets. WarpingLCSS and SegmentedLCSS are more robust against label noise compared to SVM and DTW-based methods. The performance of LCSS-based methods is stable until a label noise percentage (α) in each class exceeding 70% in Opportunity and HCI data sets and 50% in the Skoda data set. On average, WarpingLCSS outperforms SVM by 22% F1-Null and outperforms DTW-based methods by 36% F1-Null in presence of 60% mislabeled instances. SegmentedLCSS yields similar performance as WarpingLCSS.

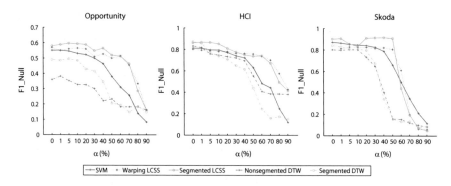

Fig. 18.8 Performance of label noise simulation for the three data sets

SVM performs worse than our LCSS-based methods when α increases. As more label substitutions are added to each class, SVM gets more confused and its performance decreases quickly. The degradation of SVM in performance is expected, since each instance contributes equally to the model building. Hence, wrongly labeled instances can induce the model to choose incorrect support vectors, which severely degrades the performance. Moreover, since the SVM method models *null* class explicitly, it is very sensitive to *delete* noise. Meanwhile, TMMs examine patterns of gesture classes and ignore *null* class in the training phase, thus, TMMs are not influenced with the *delete* noise at all.

The reason why LCSS-based TMMs outperform the ones based on DTW lies in the distance metrics used when selecting the template for each class. Each template is chosen as the one with the highest average similarity to the other instances belonging to the same class. This translates into choosing respectively highest average LCSS and lowest average DTW distance. While LCSS values between a template and an instance of the same class are bounded between 0 and the length of the template, DTW can grow indefinitely. For this reason, when calculating average DTW distances, mislabeled instances bias the average towards high values, regardless whether correctly labeled instances have a low DTW distance. Consequently, DTW-based TMMs are more likely to pick wrong templates, leading to poor performance when α increases.

The difference between LCSS and DTW in choosing templates can be illustrated with a toy-example. Consider three instances A_1, A_2 and B which are all labeled as belonging to class c_A but let B be mislabeled, that is, B actually belongs to class c_B. To simplify matters, let us assume $LCSS(A_1, A_2) = 1$, $LCSS(A_1, B) = 0$ and $LCSS(A_2, B) = 0$. Similarly, let us assume $DTW(A_1, A_2) = 0$, $DTW(A_1, B) = \infty$ and $DTW(A_2, B) = \infty$. With LCSS, A_1 would have an average similarity of 0.5 to A_2 and B; A_2 would have an average similarity of 0.5 to A_1 and B; B would have an average similarity of 0 to A_1 and A_2. Thus, LCSS would pick either A_1 or A_2 as template for the class c_A: both choices would be reasonable. With DTW, A_1 would have an average distance of ∞ to A_2 and B; A_2 would have an average distance of ∞ to A_1 and B; B would have an average distance of ∞ to A_1 and A_2. In this case, the algorithm would not prefer A_1 or A_2 over B, which can lead to choosing as template the mislabeled instance B to represent class c_A. Of course in practice the values of the DTW distance are not infinity, in fact the degradation of DTW-based approaches is not occurring already for a small amount of label noise.

The illustration explains the capability of our LCSS-based methods to pick a good template among noisy instances for a gesture class as long as the number of good instances in a gesture class is still predominant.

By analyzing the starting points of the curves of Fig. 18.8, obtained with $\alpha = 0$ (no noise), we can conclude that our LCSS-based methods have a similar or better performance compared to the baselines also for the case of clean training data sets.

18.6.1.2 Extend Jitter Simulation

When temporal boundaries are extended, data belonging to the *null* class (before and after the gesture) are labeled as belonging to the gesture class. This impacts SVM and TMMs differently. In the case of SVM, the *null class* is modeled explicitly. The noisy feature vectors extracted from extended parts are added into the feature space of each gesture class. Besides that, the data really belonging to the gesture are preserved, thus the models of gesture classes maintain good feature spaces correctly. Therefore, the performance of SVM depends on how much the noisy feature vectors added into the model of each gesture class. Accordingly, it relies on the levels of variability of the signals belonging to the *null* class. If the variability of the signals belong to the *null* class is low, even when the extend level is large, the noisy feature vectors in each gesture class does not grow, leading to the stable of SVM performance. In the converse case, the noisy feature vectors in each gesture class will explode as the extend level increases, causing the decrease in the performance of SVM.

For TMMs instead the *null class* is recognized in the test data by means of the rejection threshold ϵ_c and no template is built for it. Thus, if symbols belonging to the *null class* are present in a test sequence, these will be matched to the symbols present in the extended gesture instances, inducing the TMMs to recognize gestures instead of *null class*.

This is confirmed by an analysis of the results, as shown in Fig. 18.9. TMMs can tolerate up to about 40% *extend level* in the Opportunity and HCI data sets and about 10% *extend level* in the Skoda data set. As the extend level is high, the performance of SVM is stable in HCI and Skoda data sets, but degrades quickly in Opportunity data set. As explained above, the reason of the differences among data sets lie in the different levels of variability of the signals belonging to the *null class* in the different data sets.

18.6.1.3 Shrink Jitter Simulation

When having a *shrink jitter* noise, the effect is that the methods lose information about the gesture data, since only parts of the gestures are labeled. This has a stronger effect in SVM, since the model is corrupted. For TMMs, subsequences are matched, with the

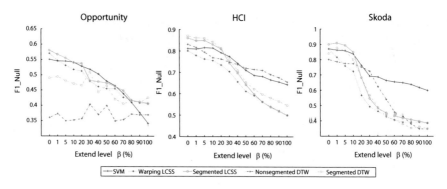

Fig. 18.9 Performance of extend jitter simulation

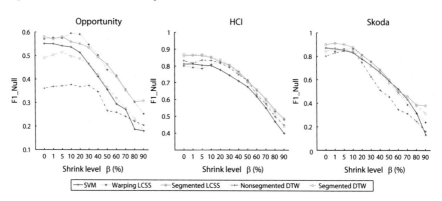

Fig. 18.10 Performance of shrink jitter simulation

effect that shrunk instances still contain information in form of shorter subsequences that can still be matched to the test data. This is confirmed by the results, shown in Fig. 18.10.

Our proposed LCSS-based methods achieve the best performance in the three data sets. All methods can tolerate about 30% shrink level before a degradation compared to training with clean data occurs. The Segmented DTW has a similar results as LCSS-based methods in low-variability data sets (HCI and Skoda). However, Segmented DTW takes a higher computational cost. Moreover, in our experiments, all gesture instances have the same shrink level, i.e., after shrinking, instances of a gesture class are still aligned well and DTW can still achieve a reasonable performance. In a real crowdsourcing annotation setting, different instances may have different shrink levels (see Fig. 18.3b). In that case, DTW will accumulate higher distances due to data misalignment at the beginning and the end of instances (see Nguyen-Dinh et al. 2012 for a more thorough discussion of the weakness of DTW with misalignment in temporal boundaries).

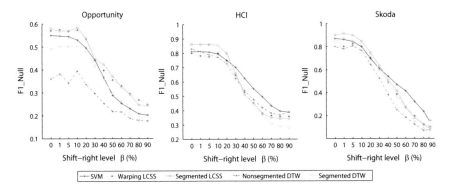

Fig. 18.11   Performance of shift-right jitter simulation

18.6.1.4   Shift-Left and Shift-Right Jitter Simulation

When annotations are shifted, a mixture of the effects described in Sects. 18.6.1.2 and 18.6.1.3 are present. Some samples belonging to gestures are lost and some null class samples are labeled as belonging to a gesture. Figure 18.11 shows the results of *shift-right* jitter simulations (the *shift-left* simulations yield similar results). All methods can sustain about 20% *shift level* before the performance degrades compared to a clean training data set. LCSS-based methods perform often better, or as good as DTW-based methods on the data sets that we examined. TMMs outperform SVM with up to 30% *shift level*.

18.6.2   Results on Real Crowdsourced Annotation

To further validate the outcome of the previous experiments, we use the real crowd-sourced annotations discussed in Sect. 18.3.3. The annotations were performed by AMT workers on the Opportunity data set. We use both the annotations obtained in the one-labeler and in the multiple-labeler scenarios. In these annotations, mixtures of all kinds of the errors listed in the taxonomy (Sect. 18.3.1) are present and jitter levels are varied from one instance to another instance (see Fig. 18.3).

Figure 18.12 reports the performance of the different recognition methods on our real crowdsourced annotation. In the clean annotated Opportunity data set, the performance of SVM is slightly lower than that of LCSS-based TMMs (only lower by 3% for F1-Null and by 7% for F1-NoNull). Two DTW approaches underperform the others. The reason is that DTW is very sensitive to high variation in gesture execution (Nguyen-Dinh et al. 2012) and the Opportunity data set contains large variability in the executions of the daily activities.

In the multiple-labeler annotation, labels of 80% of the data samples match the ground truth. Moreover, only 18% of gesture instances are labeled incorrectly and the remainder are correctly labeled with a *jitter level* of at least 2% (see Fig. 18.3). The

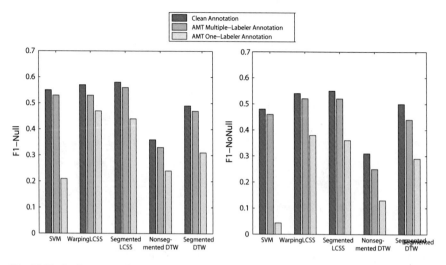

Fig. 18.12 Performance of real crowdsourcing annotation on Opportunity data set

results show that the performances of all recognition methods are slightly decreased by up to 4% for F1-Null and 6% for F1-NoNull compared to the training with clean training sets. Our LCSS-based TMMs yield the best performance. As stated also in Sect. 18.6.1.1, the reason for the robustness of LCSS-based methods lies in their ability to select clean templates also in presence of annotation noise.

In the AMT one-labeler annotation, only 55% samples are annotated correctly. Additionally, about 50% of gesture instances are affected by *label noise*, with many deletions and substitutions. In each gesture class, instances which are labeled correctly are still the majority. The result shows that our LCSS-based TMMs still achieve the best performance. The F1-Null measure decreases by 10% and the F1-NoNull by 16% compared to training with clean annotations.

In the one-labeler annotation, there is a significant difference in performance between TMMs and SVM. The performance of SVM decreases dramatically, down to a F1-NoNull of 5%, which is less than random guessing (which would be around 6% in a 16-class data set like Opportunity). This result confirms what was already measured with the synthetic annotations and discussed in Sect. 18.6.1.1.

Additionally, we conduct a 2-sided hypothesis test at the 0.01 level of significance as in Guyon et al. (1998) among the performance of the methods in the three scenarios. The tests showed that the performance differences among the methods are statistically significant except the comparison of the F1-Null between SVM and WarpingLCSS and the comparison of the F1-NoNull between WarpingLCSS and SegmentedLCSS in the multiple-labeler annotation.

The results on the real crowdsourcing annotation confirm that our proposed WarpingLCSS and SegmentedLCSS are robust to noise and yield better performance on crowdsourcing data set. WarpingLCSS is preferable in online recognition, since it has a lower computational cost.

18.6.3   A LCSS-Based Filtering Component

The results have shown that SVM is very sensitive to the high *label noise* in the training data set. Therefore, a preprocessing component to clean the noisy annotation would be beneficial before using SVM. Given the robustness of our LCSS approaches in selecting templates among noisy instances, as well as in spotting, we further propose a LCSS-based filtering component to filter out noise in crowdsourced annotations before training a SVM. We call this approach FSVM. For each gesture class, the LCSS-based filtering component first computes a LCSS similarity matrix among all pairs of instances in the class. It then keeps only the instances that have an average similarity to other instances of the same class exceeding the average of all the average similarities of all instances in the class. To clean noise inside the *null* instances (e.g., *delete* noise), the filtering component runs the WarpingLCSS on the data annotated as *null* and discards any parts which get classified as any gestures of interest.

For DTW-based TMMs, the performance degrades quickly when the *label noise* percentage in the training data set increases (see Fig. 18.8) because DTW cannot pick a good template among noisy instances. It is interesting to know how templates selected by LCSS perform in the DTW spotting methods. Therefore, we conduct experiments for Segmented DTW and Nonsegmented DTW with templates trained by LCSS. We call these approaches LCSS-SegDTW and LCSS-NonSegDTW respectively. Note that the algorithm running time when the system is deployed remains unchanged: only the training phase is affected.

The performances of FSVM, LCSS-SegDTW and LCSS-NonSegDTW are shown in Fig. 18.13 for the real crowdsourced annotation and in Fig. 18.14 for the synthetic

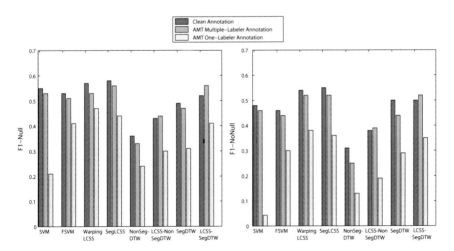

Fig. 18.13 Performance of real crowdsourcing annotation on Opportunity data set for the methods with and without filtering. SegLCSS, NonSegDTW, and SegDTW stand for Segmented LCSS, Nonsegmented DTW and Segmented DTW respectively

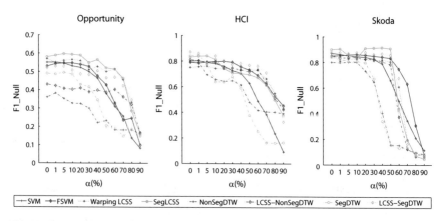

Fig. 18.14 Performance of label noise simulation for the methods with and without filtering

label noise simulation. We present again the performances of the other methods that we discuss above for the sake of comparison.

In the real crowdsourced annotation, the filtering increases the performance of SVM by 20% F1-score and of DTW-based methods by 8% F1-score on average in the one-labeler annotation scenario where high *label noise* exists (see Fig. 18.3). In the clean annotation and multiple-labeler annotation, FSVM performs just slightly worse than SVM (only 2%). This slight decrease can be explained with the fact that the FSVM method decreases the amount training data compared to pure SVM, because the LCSS-based filtering component in the FSVM removes some part of training data, considered noisy. Our proposed LCSS-based methods still outperform FSVM.

The LCSS-NonSegDTW outperforms Nonsegmented DTW in all three scenarios (expert's annotation, AMT multiple-labeler annotation and AMT one-labeler annotation). Similarly, LCSS-SegDTW outperforms SegmentedDTW. The result clarifies that LCSS is capable of picking a better template among noisy instances, compared to DTW. However, LCSS-NonSegDTW and LCSS-SegDTW still underperform compared to our LCSS-based TMMs. The rationale is the same as discussed before. LCSS is more robust to high variation in daily gesture execution, therefore LCSS-based spotting approaches have a better performance than DTW-based ones even with the same templates.

In the synthetic label noise simulation, the FSVM, LCSS-NonSegDTW and LCSS-SegDTW methods outperform SVM, Nonsegmented DTW and Segmented DTW respectively and keep the performance stable much longer when α increases. Our proposed LCSS-based TMMs have similar or better performance than the other methods. Interestingly, with the same templates picked by LCSS, LCSS-SegDTW and LCSS-NonSegDTW have a performance which is similar to our LCSS-based methods in the HCI and Skoda data sets. In the Opportunity data set, the LCSS-NonSegDTW still performs worse than our SegmentedLCSS and WarpingLCSS methods because LCSS is more robust than DTW to high variability in daily gestures (Nguyen-Dinh et al. 2012).

The results show that our LCSS approaches can be used in a preprocessing step for cleaning noisy annotation in the training data for SVM or for selecting templates for DTW-based TMMs.

18.6.4 Wrapping Up

Our LCSS-based TMMs are robust to labeling noise in crowdsourced gesture data sets. Moreover, the LCSS-based TMMs also offer other advantages. (1) They are easy to deploy in online gesture recognition system due to low time complexity. (2) In our systems, signals are converted into symbols, thus SegmentedLCSS lends itself even to embedded implementations. Specifically, string matching in the deployment phase does not involve floating-point operations, thus it can be deployed easily in cheap entry-level microcontroller units. (3) The deployed TMM-based systems are scalable to new gesture classes of interest. After collecting a training data set for a new class, the training phase only works with this class to find a template and the rejection threshold for the class. The template is then integrated directly into the deployed system. Thus, the whole process works smoothly with the new class without interfering with other existing gesture classes.

Our LCSS-based TMMs have been investigated in online gesture recognition with accelerometer data only. Their ability to work with other sensor modalities (e.g., gyroscopes, sound) has been investigated and it has shown promising preliminary results in Nguyen-Dinh et al. (2014).

18.7 Conclusion and Future Work

In this paper, we investigated the robustness of our proposed LCSS-based TMMs for online gesture recognition on crowdsourced annotated data sets. The results show that SegmentedLCSS and WarpingLCSS are robust to crowdsourced annotation noise and yield better performance than DTW-based methods and SVM. We also introduced a taxonomy of annotation noise in crowdsourcing settings and analyzed the distribution of that noise in real crowdsourced scenarios. Our LCSS-based methods are very robust to label noise because they are capable of selecting a good template among noisy instances for a class. In presence of 60% mislabeled instances, LCSS-based methods outperform SVM by 22% F1-score and outperform DTW-based methods by 36% F1-score on average.

With boundary jitter, the performance of the proposed approaches is comparable to that on clean data sets if annotations can keep most of the information indicating gestures (at most 30–40% jitter level). In extreme cases when jitter levels go beyond that limit, our LCSS-based TMMS and the other machine learning techniques fail to recognize the complete segment of gestures. This can be the case for example in real-time labeling, where labelers tend to indicate quickly when a gesture occurs with only one time point, without providing the start and end time of the gesture (e.g., the boundary shrinks to a point). Other techniques (e.g., active learning) are necessary to acquire more labels and improve label quality in such cases.

We showed that our LCSS-based methods can be also used as a preprocessing filtering component to clean crowdsourced training data set with severe label noise before feeding the training sets into other learning techniques such as SVM or select templates for DTW. The filtering increases the performance of SVM by 20% F1-score and DTW-based methods by 8% F1-score on average in the noisy real crowdsourced annotations.

In future work, we plan to deploy the system that crowdsources annotated data to a large number of users who record and contribute gestures. Our methods will then be tested on such real large crowdsourced data sets, with the ultimate goal of having a collaborative database of gestures and associated models with direct applications with wearable sensors.

Acknowledgements The authors would like to thank Dr. Daniel Roggen (University of Sussex) for his useful comments. This work has been supported by the Swiss Hasler Foundation project Smart-DAYS.

References

J. Aggarwal, M. Ryoo, Human activity analysis: a review. ACM Comput. Surv. **43**(3), 16 (2011)

J. Alon, V. Athitsos, Q. Yuan, S. Sclaroff, A unified framework for gesture recognition and spatiotemporal gesture segmentation. IEEE Trans. Pattern Anal. Mach. Intell. **31**(9), 1685–1699 (2009)

R. Amini, P. Gallinari, Semi-supervised learning with an imperfect supervisor. Knowl. Inf. Syst. **8**, 385–413 (2005)

D. Angluin, P. Laird, Learning from noisy examples. Mach. Learn. **2**, 343–370 (1988). April

O. Banos, A. Calatroni, M. Damas, H. Pomares, I. Rojas, H. Sagha, J. del R. Millán, G. Tröster, R. Chavarriaga, D. Roggen, Kinect=imu? learning mimo signal mappings to automatically translate activity recognition systems across sensor modalities, in *Proceedings of the 2012 16th International Symposium on Wearable Computers (ISWC)*, 2012, pp. 92–99

L. Bao, S.S. Intille, Activity recognition from user-annotated acceleration data, in *Proceedings of the 2nd International Conference on Pervasive Computing* 2004

B. Bauer, K. Karl-Friedrich, Towards an automatic sign language recognition system using subunits, in *International Gesture Workshop on Gesture and Sign Languages in, Human-Computer Interaction*, 2002, pp. 64–75

M. Berchtold, M. Budde, D. Gordon, H. Schmidtke, M. Beigl, Actiserv: activity recognition service for mobile phones, in *Proceedings of the 2010 14th International Symposium on Wearable Computers (ISWC)*, 2010, pp. 1–8

R. Bowden, D. Windridge, T. Kadir, A. Zisserman, M. Brady, A linguistic feature vector for the visual interpretation of sign language, in *European Conference on Computer Vision*, ECCV '04. 2004

C.C. Chang, C.J. Lin, LIBSVM: a library for support vector machines. ACM Trans. Intell. Syst. Technol. **2**(27), 27 (2011)

L. Chen, J. Hoey, C.D. Nugent, D.J. Cook, Z. Yu, Sensor-based activity recognition, in *IEEE Transactions on Systems, Man and Cybernetics* 2012

H. Cooper, E.-J. Ong, N. Pugeault, R. Bowden, Sign language recognition using sub-units. J. Mach. Learn. Res. **13**(1), 2205–2231 (2012)

T. H. Cormen, C. Stein, R. L. Rivest, C. E. Leiserson, *Introduction to Algorithms*, 2nd edn, (2001). ISBN 0070131511

A.P. Dawid, A.M. Skene, Maximum likelihood estimation of observer error-rates using the EM algorithm. Appl. Stat. **28**(1), 20–28 (1979)

J. Deng, H. Tsui, An HMM-based approach for gesture segmentation and recognition, in *Proceedings of the International Conference on Pattern Recognition*, ICPR '00 2000

A. Doan, R. Ramakrishnan, A.Y. Halevy, Crowdsourcing systems on the world-wide web. Commun. ACM **54**(4), 89–96 (2011)

M. Elmezain, A. Al-Hamadi, B. Michaelis, Improving hand gesture recognition using 3D combined features, in *Proceedings of the 2nd International Conference on Machine Vision*, ICMV '09, 2009, pp. 128–132

G. Fang, X. Gao, W. Gao, Y. Chen, A novel approach to automatically extracting basic units from chinese sign language, in *Proceedings of the 17th International Conference on Pattern Recognition*, vol. 4, 2004, pp. 454–457

J. Froehlich, M.Y. Chen, S. Consolvo, B. Harrison, J.A. Landay, Myexperience: a system for in situ tracing and capturing of user feedback on mobile phones, in *Proceedings of the 5th International Conference on Mobile Systems, Applications and Services*, MobiSys '07 2007

D. Frolova, H. Stern, S. Berman, Most probable longest common subsequence for recognition of gesture character input. IEEE Trans. Cybern. **43**(3), 871–880 (2013)

T.-C. Fu, A review on time series data mining. Eng. Appl. Artif. Intell. **24**(1), 164–181 (2011)

N. Gayar, F. Schwenker, G. Palm, A study of the robustness of KNN classifiers trained using soft labels, in *Artificial Neural Networks in Pattern Recognition*, vol. 4087, 2006

I. Guyon, J. Makhoul, R. Schwartz, V. Vapnik, What size test set gives good error rate estimates? IEEE Trans. Pattern Anal. Mach. Intell. **20**(1), 52–64 (1998)

J. Hao, T. Shibata, Digit-writing hand gesture recognition by hand-held camera motion analysis, in *Proceedings of the 3rd International Conference on Signal Processing and Communication Systems, ICSPCS '09*, 2009, pp. 1–5

B. Hartmann, N. Link, Gesture recognition with inertial sensors and optimized DTW prototypes, in *Proceedings of the 2010 IEEE International Conference on Systems Man and Cybernetics (SMC)* 2010

Z. He, L. Jin, L. Zhen, and J. Huang. Gesture recognition based on 3D accelerometer for cell phones interaction, in *IEEE Asia Pacific Conference on Circuits and Systems (APCCAS)*, 2008, pp. 217–220

J. Howe, The Rise of Crowdsourcing, June 2006. http://www.wired.com/wired/archive/14.06/crowds.html. Accessed 20 July 2010

P.G. Ipeirotis, F. Provost, J. Wang, Quality management on Amazon Mechanical Turk, in *Proceedings of the ACM SIGKDD Workshop on Human Computation, HCOMP '10* 2010, pp. 64–67

H. Junker, O. Amft, P. Lukowicz, G. Tröster, Gesture spotting with body-worn inertial sensors to detect user activities. Pattern Recognit. **41**(6), 2010–2024 (2008)

C. Keskin, A. Cemgil, L. Akarun. DTW based clustering to improve hand gesture recognition, in *Proceedings of the 2nd International Conference on Human Behavior Unterstanding*, HBU'11, 2011, pp. 72–81

A. Kittur, E. H. Chi, B. Suh, Crowdsourcing user studies with mechanical turk, in *Proceedings of the Twenty-sixth SIGCHI Conference on Human Factors in Computing Systems*, CHI '08, 2008, pp. 453–456

M. H. Ko, G. West, S. Venkatesh, M. Kumar, Online context recognition in multisensor systems using dynamic time warping, in *Proceedings of the Intelligent Sensors, Sensor Networks and Information Processing Conference* 2005

W.S. Lasecki, Y.C. Song, H. Kautz, J. P. Bigham, Real-time crowd labeling for deployable activity recognition, in *Proceedings of the 2013 Conference on Computer Supported Cooperative Work*, CSCW '13, 2013, pp. 1203–1212

N. D. Lawrence, B. Schölkopf, Estimating a kernel fisher discriminant in the presence of label noise, in *Proceedings of the Eighteenth International Conference on Machine Learning*, ICML '01, 2001, pp. 306–313

H.-K. Lee, J.H. Kim, An hmm-based threshold model approach for gesture recognition. IEEE Trans. Pattern Anal. Mach. Intell. **21**(10), 961–973 (1999)

L.V. Nguyen-Dinh, D. Roggen, A. Calatroni, G. Tröster, Improving online gesture recognition with template matching methods in accelerometer data, in *Proceedings of the 12th International Conference on Intelligent Systems Design and Applications (ISDA)* 2012

L.V. Nguyen-Dinh, U. Blanke, and G. Tröster, Towards scalable activity recognition: adapting zero-effort crowdsourced acoustic models, in *Proceedings of the 12th International Conference on Mobile and Ubiquitous Multimedia*, MUM '13 2013a

L.V. Nguyen-Dinh, M. Rossi, U. Blanke, and G. Tröster, Combining crowd-generated media and personal data: Semi-supervised learning for context recognition, in *Proceedings of the 1st ACM International Workshop on Personal Data Meets Distributed Multimedia*, PDM '13 2013b

L.V. Nguyen-Dinh, C. Waldburger, D. Roggen, G. Tröster, Tagging human activities in video by crowdsourcing, in *Proceedings of the ACM International Conference on Multimedia Retrieval*, ICMR '13 2013c

L.V. Nguyen-Dinh, A. Calatroni, G. Tröster, Towards a unified system for multimodal activity spotting: challenges and a proposal, in *Proceedings of the ACM Conference on Pervasive and Ubiquitous Computing Adjunct Publication*, UbiComp '14 Adjunct 2014

N. Ravi, N.D, P. Mysore, M.L. Littman, Activity recognition from accelerometer data, in *Proceedings of the Seventeenth Conference on Innovative Applications of Artificial Intelligence(IAAI)*, AAAI Press 2005, pp. 1541–1546

V.C. Raykar, S. Yu, L.H. Zhao, G.H. Valadez, C. Florin, L. Bogoni, L. Moy, Learning from crowds. J. Mach. Learn. Res. **11**, 1297–1322 (2010)

D. Roggen, A. Calatroni, M. Rossi, T. Holleczek, K. Forster, G. Troster, et al. Collecting complex activity data sets in highly rich networked sensor environments, in *Proceedings of the 7th International Conference on Networked Sensing Systems*. IEEE Press, 2010

M. Rossi, O. Amft, G. Tröster, Recognizing daily life context using web-collected audio data, in *Proceedings of the 16th IEEE International Symposium on Wearable Computers (ISWC)* 2012

T. Schlömer, B. Poppinga, N. Henze, S. Boll, Gesture recognition with a Wii controller, in *Proceedings of the 2nd International Conference on Tangible and Embedded Interaction* 2008

V.S. Sheng, F. Provost, P.G. Ipeirotis, Get another label? improving data quality and data mining using multiple, noisy labelers, in *Proceedings of the 14th ACM SIGKDD International Conference on Knowledge Discovery and Data Mining, KDD '08* 2008

H. Stern, M. Shmueli, S. Berman, Most discriminating segment—longest common subsequence (MDSLCS) algorithm for dynamic hand gesture classification. Pattern Recognit. Lett. **34**(15), 1980–1989 (2013)

T. Stiefmeier, D. Roggen, G. Ogris, P. Lukowicz, G. Tröster, Wearable activity tracking in car manufacturing. IEEE Pervasive Comput. Mag. **7**(2), 1–6 (2008)

M. Stikic, D. Larlus, S. Ebert, B. Schiele, Weakly supervised recognition of daily life activities with wearable sensors. IEEE Trans. Pattern Anal. Mach. Intell. **33**(12), 2521–2537 (2011)

K. Van Laerhoven, D. Kilian, B. Schiele, Using rhythm awareness in long-term activity recognition, in *Proceedings of the IEEE International Symposium on Wearable Computers (ISWC)* 2008

C. Vogler, D.N. Metaxas, Toward scalability in ASL recognition: breaking down signs into phonemes, in *Gesture-Based Communication in Human-Computer Interaction, Lecture Notes in Computer Science* 1999, pp. 211–224

J.A. Ward, P. Lukowicz, H.W. Gellersen, Performance metrics for activity recognition. ACM Trans. Intell. Syst. Technol. **2**(1), 6 (2011)

A. Wilson, A. Bobick, Parametric hidden markov models for gesture recognition. IEEE Trans. Pattern Anal. Mach. Intell. **21**, 884–900 (1999)

J. Wu, G. Pan, D. Zhang, G. Qi, S. Li, Gesture recognition with a 3-D accelerometer, in *Proceedings of the 6th International Conference on Ubiquitous Intelligence and Computing*, UIC '09, 2009, pp. 25–38

H.S. Yoon, J. Soh, Y.J. Bae, H.S. Yang, Hand gesture recognition using combined features of location, angle and velocity. Pattern Recogn. **34**(7), 1491–1501 (2001)

M.C. Yuen, I. King, K.S. Leung, A survey of crowdsourcing systems, in *SocialCom/PASSAT*, 2011, pp. 766–773

P. Zappi, C. Lombriser, T. Stiefmeier, E. Farella, D. Roggen, L. Benini, G. Tröster, Activity recognition from on-body sensors: accuracy-power trade-off by dynamic sensor selection, in *Proceedings of the 5th European Conference on Wireless Sensor Networks*, EWSN'08, 2008, pp. 17–33

Chapter 19
Deep Learning for Action and Gesture Recognition in Image Sequences: A Survey

Maryam Asadi-Aghbolaghi, Albert Clapés, Marco Bellantonio, Hugo Jair Escalante, Víctor Ponce-López, Xavier Baró, Isabelle Guyon, Shohreh Kasaei and Sergio Escalera

Abstract Interest in automatic action and gesture recognition has grown considerably in the last few years. This is due in part to the large number of application domains for this type of technology. As in many other computer vision areas, deep learning based methods have quickly become a reference methodology for obtaining state-of-the-art performance in both tasks. This chapter is a survey of current deep learning based methodologies for action and gesture recognition in sequences of images. The survey reviews both fundamental and cutting edge methodologies reported in the last few years. We introduce a taxonomy that summarizes important aspects of deep learning for approaching both tasks. Details of the proposed architectures, fusion strategies, main datasets, and competitions are reviewed. Also, we summarize and discuss the main works proposed so far with particular interest on how they treat the temporal dimension of data, their highlighting features, and opportunities and challenges for future research. To the best of our knowledge this

A reduced version of this appeared appeared as: M. Asadi-Aghbolaghi et al. A survey on deep learning based approaches for action and gesture recognition in image sequences. In: Proceedings of 12th IEEE International Conference on Automatic Face and Gesture Recognition (FG 2017), 2017.
Editors: Sergio Escalera, Isabelle Guyon, Vassilis Athitsos

M. Asadi-Aghbolaghi (✉) · S. Kasaei
Department of Computer Engineering, Sharif University of Technology, Tehran, Iran
e-mail: masadia@ce.sharif.edu

S. Kasaei
e-mail: skasaei@sharif.edu

M. Asadi-Aghbolaghi · A. Clapés · S. Escalera
Computer Vision Center, Autonomous University of Barcelona, Barcelona, Spain

A. Clapés
e-mail: aclapes@cvc.uab.cat

S. Escalera
e-mail: sergio@maia.ub.es

M. Asadi-Aghbolaghi · A. Clapés · S. Escalera
Department of Mathematics and Informatics, University of Barcelona, Barcelona, Spain

© Springer International Publishing AG 2017
S. Escalera et al. (eds.), *Gesture Recognition*, The Springer Series on Challenges in Machine Learning, DOI 10.1007/978-3-319-57021-1_19

is the first survey in the topic. We foresee this survey will become a reference in this ever dynamic field of research.

Keywords Action recognition · Gesture recognition · Deep learning architectures · Fusion strategies

19.1 Introduction

Automatic human behavior analysis has grown in interest in the last few years. This is due in part to the large number of application domains for this technology, from any kind of human-computer interaction scenario (e.g. affective robotics Wilson and Lewandowska-Tomaszczyk 2014), to security (e.g. video surveillance Vishwakarma and Agrawal 2013), e-Health (e.g. therapy Mousavi Hondori and Khademi 2014 or automatic diagnosis Scharcanski and Celebi 2014), language/communication (e.g. sign language recognition Pigou et al. 2015a), or entertainment (e.g. interactive gaming Marks 2011). Because of this, we can find, in the specialized literature, research works dealing with different aspects of human behavior analysis: action/gesture recognition (Feichtenhofer et al. 2016b; Simonyan and Zisserman 2014), social interaction modeling (Deng et al. 2016; Ibrahim et al. 2016), facial emotion analysis (Araujo and Kamel 2014), and personality traits identification (Joo et al. 2014), just to mention some of them.

Two key tasks for human behavior understanding that have an impact in many application scenarios are action and gesture recognition. The former is focused on recognizing generic human actions (e.g. "walking", "eating", "answering phone", etc.) performed by one or more subjects, whereas the latter is focused on recognizing

M. Bellantonio
Facultat d'Informatica, Polytechnic University of Barcelona, Barcelona, Spain
e-mail: marco.bellantonio@est.fib.upc.edu

H.J. Escalante
Instituto Nacional de Astrofísica, Óptica Y Electrónica, 72840 Puebla, Mexico
e-mail: hugojair@inaoep.mx

V. Ponce-López
Eurecat, Barcelona, Catalonia, Spain
e-mail: victor.ponce@eurecat.org

X. Baró
EIMT, Open University of Catalonia, Barcelona, Spain
e-mail: xbaro@uoc.edu

I. Guyon
UPSud and INRIA, Université Paris-Saclay, Paris, France
e-mail: guyon@chalearn.org

I. Guyon
ChaLearn, Berkeley, CA, USA

more fine-grained upper body movements performed by a user that have a meaning within a particular context (e.g. "come", "hi", "thumbs up", etc.). While both tasks present different complications, they are interrelated in that both are based on analyzing the posture and movement of body across video sequences.

Action and gesture recognition have been studied for a while within the fields of computer vision and pattern recognition. Since the earliest works two decades ago (Kuniyoshi et al. 1990; Yamato et al. 1992), researchers have reported substantial progress for both tasks. As in the case of several computer vision tasks (e.g. object or face recognition), deep learning has also recently irrupted in action/gesture recognition, achieving outstanding results and outperforming "non-deep"state-of-the-art methods (Simonyan and Zisserman 2014; Wang et al. 2015b; Feichtenhofer et al. 2016a).

The extra (temporal) dimension in sequences typically turned action/gesture recognition into a challenging problem in terms of both amounts of data to be processed and model complexity–which in particular are crucial aspects for training large parametric deep learning networks. In this context, authors proposed several strategies, such as frame sub-sampling, aggregation of local frame-level features into mid-level video representations, or temporal sequence modeling, just to name a few. For the latter, researchers tried to exploit recurrent neural networks (RNN) in the past (Waibel et al. 1990). However, these models typically faced some major mathematical difficulties identified by Hochreiter (1991) and Bengio et al. (1994). In 1997, authors' effort led to the development of the long short-term memory (LSTM) (Hochreiter and Schmidhuber 1997) cells for RNNs. Today, LSTMs are an important part of deep models for image sequence modeling for human action/gesture recognition (Singh et al. 2016a; Liu et al. 2016a). These, along with implicit modeling of spatiotemporal features using 3D convolutional nets (Ji et al. 2010; Tran et al. 2015), pre-computed motion-based features (Simonyan and Zisserman 2014; Feichtenhofer et al. 2016a), or the combination of multiple visual (Singh et al. 2016b), resulted in fast and reliable state-of-the-art methods for action/gesture recognition.

Although the application of deep learning to action and gesture recognition is relatively new, the amount of research that has been generated in these topics within the last few years is astounding. Because of this overwhelming amount of work and because of the race for getting the best model/performance in these tasks for which the use of deep learning is still in its infancy, we think it is critical to compile the recent advances and, in general, the historical state of the art on action and gesture recognition with deep learning solutions. In this direction, this chapter aims to collect and review all of the existent work on deep learning for action and gesture recognition. To the best of our knowledge, there is no previous survey that collects and reviews all of the existent work on deep learning for those tasks. This chapter aims at capturing a snapshot of current trends in this direction, including an in depth analysis of different deep models, with special interest on how they treat the temporal dimension of the data.

The remainder of this chapter is organized as follows. Section 19.2 presents a taxonomy in this field of research. Next, Sect. 19.3 reviews the literature on human action/activity recognition with deep learning models. Section 19.4 summarizes the state-of-the-art on deep learning for gesture recognition. Finally, Sect. 19.5 discusses the main features of the reviewed deep learning for the both studied problems.

19.2 Taxonomy

We present a taxonomy that summarizes the main concepts related to deep learning in action and gesture recognition. The taxonomy is shown in Fig. 19.1. The reader should note that with *recognition* we refer to either classification of pre-segmented video segments or localization of actions in long untrimmed videos.

The rest of this section elaborates on the main aspects and findings derived from the taxonomy. We first explain the categorized architectures, and then explore the fusion strategies used in deep learning-based models for action/gesture recognition. We also include a summary of datasets used for such tasks. Finally, we report main challenges have been held for human action and gesture recognition.

19.2.1 Architectures

The most crucial challenge in deep-based human action and gesture recognition is how to deal with the temporal dimension. Based on the way it is dealt with, we categorize approaches into four non-mutually exclusive groups. The first group consists in 2D CNNs, which are basically able to exploit appearance (spatial) information. These approaches (Sun et al. 2015; Wang et al. 2016g) sample one or more frames from the whole video and then apply a pre-trained 2D models on each of these frames, separately. They finally label the actions by averaging the result of the sampled frames. The main advantage of this kind of models is possibility to use pre-trained models on larger image datasets, such as ImageNet (Krizhevsky et al. 2012). Gesture

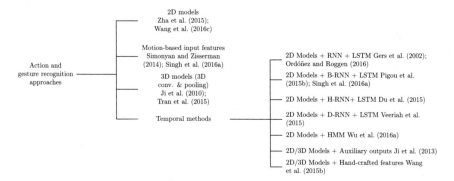

Fig. 19.1 Taxonomy of deep learning approaches for gesture and action recognition

recognition methods mainly fall into this category (Jain et al. 2014a; Li et al. 2015b; Liang et al. 2016).

Methods in the second group, first extract 2D motion features like optical flow and then utilize these features as a different input channel of 2D convolutional networks (Simonyan and Zisserman 2014; Wang et al. 2015b; Gkioxari and Malik 2015; Sun et al. 2015; Weinzaepfel et al. 2015). In other words, these methods take into account the temporal information from the pre-computed motion features. Third group uses 3D filters in the convolutional layers (Baccouche et al. 2011; Ji et al. 2013; Liu et al. 2016b; Varol et al. 2016). The 3D convolution and 3D pooling allow to capture discriminative features along both spatial and temporal dimensions while maintaining the temporal structure in contrast to 2D convolutional layers. The spatiotemoral features extracted by this kind of models proven to surpass 2D models trained on the same video frames. Figure 19.2a–b illustrate these first three groups.

Finally, the fourth group combines 2D (or 3D) convolutional nets, which are applied at individual (or stacks of) frames, with a temporal sequence modeling. Recurrent Neural Network (RNN) (Elman 1990) is one of the most used networks for this task, which can take into account the temporal data using recurrent connections in hidden layers. The drawback of this network is its short memory which is insufficient for real world actions. To solve this problem Long Short-Term Memory (LSTM) networks (Gers et al. 2002) were proposed, and they are usually used as a hidden layer of RNN. Bidirectional RNN (B-RRN) (Pigou et al. 2015b), Hierarchical RNN (H-RNN) (Du et al. 2015), and Differential RNN (D-RNN) (Veeriah et al. 2015) are some successful extensions of RNN in recognizing human actions. Other temporal modeling tools like HMM are also applied (Wu et al. 2016a) in this context. We show an example of this fourth approach on Fig. 19.2c.

For all methods in the four groups, their performance can be boosted by combining its output with auxiliary hand-crafted features (Ji et al. 2013), e.g. improved dense trajectories (iDT) (Wang et al. 2015b).

19.2.2 Fusion Strategies

Information fusion is common in deep learning methods for action and gesture recognition. The goal of the fusion is, in most cases, to exploit information complementariness and redundancy for improving the recognition performance. At times, fusion is used to combine the information from different parts in a segmented video sequence (i.e., temporal dimension) (Wang et al. 2016c). Although, it is more common to fuse information from multiple modalities (e.g. RGB, depth, and/or audio cues), where often, information from the same modality, but processed differently is combined as well. Another variant of information fusion widely used in action and gesture recognition consist of combining models trained with different data samples and learning parameters (Neverova et al. 2014).

In general terms, there are several variants in which information can be fused (see e.g. Escalante et al. 2008). Most notably, early (fusing information before the

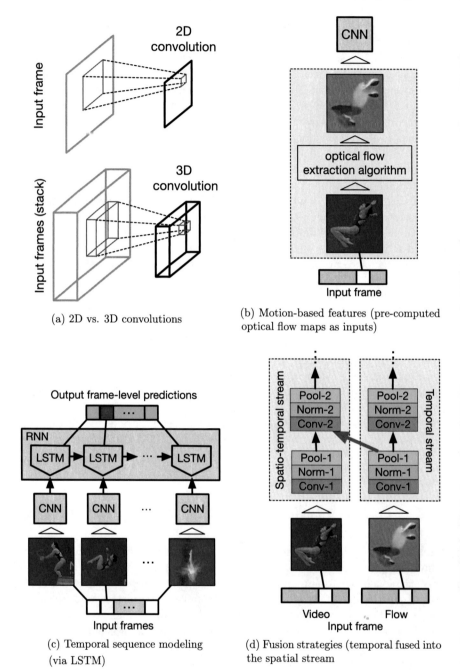

(a) 2D vs. 3D convolutions

(b) Motion-based features (pre-computed optical flow maps as inputs)

(c) Temporal sequence modeling (via LSTM)

(d) Fusion strategies (temporal fused into the spatial stream

Fig. 19.2 Illustrative examples of the different architectures and fusion strategies

data is fed into the model, or the model is used to fuse information directly from multiple sources), late (where the outputs of deep learning models are combined, with another layer of a deep network, a classifier or even by majority voting), and middle (in which intermediate layers fuse information, not directly form the different modalities) fusion. An excellent illustration of the effective use of these three traditional fusion schemes is described by Neverova et al. (2015b). Modifications and variants of these schemes have been proposed as well, for instance, see the variants introduced in Karpathy et al. (2014) for fusing information in the temporal dimension. Ensembles or stacked networks are also common strategies for information fusion in deep learning based approaches for action and gesture recognition (Wang et al. 2016c; Varol et al. 2016; Neverova et al. 2014). In Fig. 19.2d, we illustrate an example of middle fusion of temporal information into a spatiotemporal stream.

19.2.3   Datasets

We list the most relevant datasets according to action/activity and gesture recognition in Tables 19.1 and 19.2, respectively. For each dataset, we specify year of creation; problems for which the dataset was defined action classification (AC), temporal localization (TL), spatio-temporal localization (STL), and gesture recognition (GR); involved body parts (U for upper body, L for lower body, F for full body, and H for hands); data modalities available; number of classes and the state-of-the-art result. The last column provides a hint of how difficult the dataset is.

Figures 19.3 and 19.4 show some frames for each of the aforementioned datasets. From these few examples it is possible to understand the main differences: constrained/controlled environment (IXMAS, KTH, MPII Cooling, Berkeley MHAD, etc.), unconstrained condition of the scene (ActivityNet, CollectiveActivity, Highfive, HMDB51, etc.). Some frames also reveal the high complexity of the dataset, with regard to scene diversity (ActivityNet), low image quality (KTH), to mention few.

Tables 19.3 and 19.4 summarize the most recent approaches that obtained remarkable results against two of the most well-known and challenging datasets in action recognition, UCF-101 and THUMOS-14. Reviewing top ranked methods at UCF-101 dataset, we find that the most significant difference among them is the strategy for splitting video data and combine sub-sequence results. Wang et al. (2016g) encodes the changes in the environment by dividing the input sequence into two parts, precondition and effect states, and then look for a matrix transformation between these two states. Li et al. (2016a) processes the input video as a hierarchical structure over the time in 3 levels, i.e., short-term, medium-range and long-range. Varol et al. (2016) achieve the best performance by using different temporal resolutions of RGB and optical flow.

Looking at the top ranked deep models on the THUMOS 2014 challenge, almost all the winners in 2015 use different combinations of appearance and motion features. For the appearance ones, most of the methods extract frame-level CNN descriptors,

Table 19.1　Action datasets. Notation: In the Modality column: Depth, Skeleton, Audio, grayscale Intensity, InfraRed. In Performance column: Accuracy, mean Average Precision, Intersection over Union

Year	Database	Problem	Body parts	Modality	No. classes	Performance
2004	KTH	AC	F	I	6	98.67% Acc (Zhou et al. 2016)
2006	IXMAS	AC	F	RGB, A	13	98.79% Acc (Turaga et al. 2008)
2007	HDM05	AC	F	S	100	98.17% Acc (Chaudhry et al. 2013)
2008	HOHA (Hollywood 1)	AC, TL	F, U, L	RGB	8	71.90% Acc (Saha et al. 2016), 0.787@0.5 mAP (Mettes et al. 2016)
2008	UCF Sports	AC, STL	F	RGB	10	95.80% Acc (Shao et al. 2016), 0.789@0.5 mAP (Mettes et al. 2016)
2009	Hollywood 2	AC	F, U, L	RGB	12	78.50 mAP (Liu et al. 2017)
2009	UCF11 (YouTube Action)	AC, STL	F	RGB	11	93.77% Acc (Peng et al. 2014), –
2010	Highfive	AC, STL	F,U	RGB	4	69.40 mAP (Wang et al. 2015a), 0.466 IoU (Avgerinakis et al. 2015)
2010	MSRAction3D	AC	F	D, S	20	97.30% Acc (Luo et al. 2013)
2010	MSRAction II	STL	F	RGB	3	85.00@0.125% mAP (Chen and Corso 2015)
2010	Olympic Sports	AC	F	RGB	16	96.60% Acc (Li et al. 2016a)
2011	Collective Activity (Extended)	AC	F	RGB	6	90.23% Acc (Amer et al. 2013)
2011	HMDB51	AC	F, U, L	RGB	51	73.60% Acc (Wang et al. 2016a)
2012	MPII Cooking	AC, TL	F, U	RGB	65	72.40 mAP (Zhou et al. 2015), –
2012	MSRDaily Activity3D	AC	F,U	RGB, D, S	16	97.50% Acc (Shahroudy et al. 2016b)

(continued)

Table 19.1 (continued)

Year	Database	Problem	Body parts	Modality	No. classes	Performance
2012	UCF101	AC,TL	F, U, L	RGB	101	94.20% Acc (Wang et al. 2016c), 46.77@0.2 mAP (split 1) (Weinzaepfel et al. 2015)
2012	UCF50	AC	F, U, L	RGB	50	97.90% Acc (Duta et al. 2017)
2012	UTKinect-Action3D	AC	F	RGB, D, S	10	98.80% Acc (Kerola et al. 2017)
2013	J-HMDB	AC, STL	F, U, L	RGB, S	21	71.08 Acc (Peng and Schmid 2016), 73.1@0.5 mAP (Saha et al. 2016)
2013	Berkeley MHAD	AC	F	RGB, D, S, A	11	100.00% Acc (Chaudhry et al. 2013)
2014	N-UCLA Multiview Action3D	AC	F	RGB, D, S	10	90.80% Acc (Kerola et al. 2017)
2014	Sports 1-Million	AC	F, U, L	RGB	487	73.10% Acc (Yue-Hei Ng et al. 2015)
2014	THUMOS-14	AC, TL	F, U, L	RGB	101, 20 *	71.60 mAP (Jain et al. 2015c), 0.190@0.5 mAP (Shou et al. 2016a)
2015	THUMOS-15	AC, TL	F, U, L	RGB	101, 20 *	80.80 mAP (Li et al. 2016a), 0.183@0.5 mAP (a)
2015	ActivityNet	AC, TL	F, U, L	RGB	200	93.23 mAP (b), 0.594@0.5 mAP (Montes et al. 2016)
2016	NTU RGB+D	AC	F	RGB, D, S, IR	60	{69.20, 77.70}[1] Acc (Liu et al. 2016a)

*A different number of classes is used for different problems. For TL/STL, "@" indicates amount overlap with groundtruth considered for positive localization. For instance, @0.5 indicates a 50% of overlap

(a) Winner method from (http://activity-net.org/challenges/2016/program.html#leaderboard)

(b) Winner method from http://www.thumos.info/results.html

[1] {cross-subject accuracy, cross-view accuracy}

Table 19.2 Gesture datasets. Notation: In the Modality column: Depth, Skeleton. In the Performance column: Accuracy, Intersection over Union

Year	Database	Problem	Body parts	Modality	No. class	Performance
2011	ChaLearn Gesture	GC	F, U	RGB, D	15	–
2012	MSR-Gesture3D	GC	F, H	RGB, D	12	98.50% Acc (Chen et al. 2016)
2014	ChaLearn (Track 3)	GC, TL	U	RGB, D, S	20	98.20 Acc (Molchanov et al. 2016), 0.870 IoU (Neverova et al. 2015b)
2015	VIVA Hand Gesture	GC	H	RGB	19	77.50% Acc (Molchanov et al. 2015)
2016	ChaLearn conGD	TL	U	RGB, D	249	0.315 IoU (Camgoz et al. 2016)
	ChaLearn isoGD	GC				67.19% Acc (Duan et al. 2016)

and video representation is generated using a pooling method over the sequence. The motion-based features used by the top ranked methods can be divided into three groups, FlowNet, 3D CNN, and iDTs. In Qiu et al. (2015), we provide a comparison of those showing 3D CNN achieves the best result.

19.2.4 Challenges

Every year computer vision organizations arrange competitions providing useful datasets with annotations carefully designed according to the problem to face. Table 19.5 shows 5 main challenges in computer vision. For each challenge we report the year in which it took place, the dataset provided to the participant along with the task to be faced, the associated event, the winner of the challenge, and a list of top results obtained against the competition dataset.

19.3 Action Recognition

This section reviews deep methods for action (or activity) recognition according to the way they treat the temporal dimension: using 3D convolutions, pre-computed motion-based features, and temporal sequence models.

Table 19.3 UCF-101 dataset results

Ref.	Year	Features	Architecture	Score (%)
Feichtenhofer et al. (2016a)	2016	ST-ResNet + iDT	2-stream ConvNet and ResNet	94.6
Lev et al. (2016)	2016	RNN Fisher Vector	C3D + VGG-CCA + iDT	94.1
Varol et al. (2016)	2016	Opt. Flow, RGB, iDT	LTC-CNN	92.7
Wang et al. (2016h)	2016	conv5	2-Stream SR-CNN	92.6
Feichtenhofer et al. (2016b)	2016	conv5, 3D pool	VGG-16, VGG-M, 3D CNN	*92.5*
Wang et al. (2016g)	2016	CNN	Siamese VGG-16	92.4
Li et al. (2016a)	2016	CNN fc7	2 CNNs (spatial + temporal)	92.2
Wang et al. (2016b)	2016	3D CNN + RNN hierarchical local	Volumetric R-CNN (DANN)	91.6
Wang et al. (2015b)	2015	CNN, Hog/Hof/Mbh	2-stream CNN	91.5
Mansimov et al. (2015)	2015	CNN feat	3D CNN	89.7
Bilen et al. (2016)	2016	Dynamic feat maps	BVLC CaffeNet	89.1
Jain et al. (2015c)	2015	H/H/M, iDT, FV+PCA+GMM	8-layer CNN	88.5
Sun et al. (2015)	2015	CNN	F_{ST}CN: 2 CNNs (spat + temp)	88.1
Simonyan and Zisserman (2014)	2014	CNN	Two-stream CNN (CNN-M-2048)	88.0
Mahasseni and Todorovic (2016)	2016	eLSTM, DCNN fc7	eLSTM, DCNN+LSTM	86.9
Zhang et al. (2016)	2016	CNN	2 CNNs (spatial + temporal)	86.4
Ye and Tian (2016)	2016	dense trajectory, C3D	RNN, LSTM, 3DCNN	85.4
Peng and Schmid (2015)	2015	CNN fc6, HOG/HOF/MBH	VGG19 Conv5	79.52 ± 1.1 (tr2) 66.64 (tr1)
Karpathy et al. (2014)	2014	CNN features	2 CNN converge to 2 fc layers	65.4, 68 mAP
Jain et al. (2015b)	2015	ImageNet CNN, word2vec GMM	CNN	63.9
Weinzaepfel et al. (2015)	2015	CNN	Spatial + motion CNN	54.28 mAP

Fig. 19.3 Action datasets: sample images

VIVA (2015)

ChaLearn conGD   ChaLearn Montalbano
ChaLearn isoGD   (2014)
      (2016)   MSR-Gesture 3D (2012)

Fig. 19.4   Gesture datasets: sample images

19.3.1   2D Convolutional Neural Networks

In these kind of approaches, action recognition is often performed at frame-level and then somehow aggregated (averaging the class score predictions on individual frames). Some works further explore the possibility of using several frames as input. In particular, Karpathy et al. (2014) studied the different alternatives for considering multiple frames in a 2D model; however they concluded there was not a gain in performance using multiple video frames over averaging single frame predictions. Instead, Wang et al. (2016c) randomly sample video frames from K equal width temporal segments, obtain K class score predictions, compute the consensus scores, and use these in the loss function to learn from video representations directly, instead from one frame or one stack of frames. Zha et al. (2015) convolve each frame of the video sequence to obtain frame-level CNN features. They then perform spatio-temporal pooling on pre-defined spatial regions over the set of randomly sampled frames (50–120 depending on the sequence) in order to construct a video-level representation, which is later l2-normalized and classified using SVM. Wu et al. (2016d) model scene, object, and more generic feature representations using separate convolutional streams. For each frame, the three obtained representations are averaged and input to a three-layer fully connected network which provides the final output. Bilen et al. (2016) collapse the videos into dynamic images, that can be fed into CNNs for image classification, by using *rank pooling* (Fernando et al. 2016). Dynamic images represent are simply the parameters of a ranking function that learned to order the video frames. In Rahmani and Mian (2016), the authors propose a CNN, not to classify actions in depth data directly, but to model poses in a view-invariant high-dimensional space. For this purpose, they generate a synthetic dataset of 3D poses from motion capture data that are later fit with a puppet model and projected to depth maps. The network is first trained to differentiate among hundreds of poses to, then, use the features of the penultimate fully-connected layer for action classification in a non-deep action recognition approach. Ni et al. (2016) exploit the combination of CNNs and LSTM for interactional object parsing on individual frames. Note LSTMs are not used for temporal sequence modeling but for refining object detections. For

Table 19.4 THUMOS-14 dataset results

Ref.	Year	Features	Architecture	Score%
Jain et al. (2015c)	2015	H/H/M, IDT, FV+PCA+GMM.	8-layer CNN	71.6
Zhang et al. (2016)	2016	CNN	2 CNNs (spatial + temporal)	61.5
Jain et al. (2015b)	2015	ImageNet CNN, word2vec GMM	CNN	56.3
Shou et al. (2016b)	2016	CNN fc6, fc7, fc8	3D CNN, Segment-CNN	19 mAP
Yeung et al. (2016)	2015	CNN fc7	VGG-16, 3-layer LSTM	17.1 mAP
Escorcia et al. (2016)	2016	fc7 3D CNN	C3D CNN net	0.084 mAP@50
				0.121 mAP@100
				0.139 mAP@200
				0.125 mAP@500

the action detection task, they then use object detections for pooling improved dense trajectories extracted on temporal segments.

Note that, independently from the discussed method, 2D convolutional filters in 2D CNNs only consider spatial inter-relations of pixels, ignoring their temporal neighborhood. Next we explore the more effective ways of exploiting spatiotemporal information in image sequences, which consist in either using pre-computed motion-based to include implicit temporal information in 2D CNNs or explicitly modeling temporal information with 3D CNNs or temporal sequence modeling methods.

19.3.2 Motion-Based Features

Researchers found that motion based features, such as optical flow, were a rich cue that could be fed directly as a network input. There are accurate and efficient methods to compute these kind of features, some of them by exploiting GPU capabilities (Fortun et al. 2015). The use of optical flow demonstrated to boost the performance of CNNs on action recognition-related tasks (Simonyan and Zisserman 2014; Park et al. 2016; Zhang et al. 2016; Gkioxari and Malik 2015).

Simonyan and Zisserman (2014) presented a two-stream CNN which incorporated both spatial (video frames) and temporal networks (pre-computed optical flow), and showed that the temporal networks trained on dense optical flow are able to obtain very good performance in spite of having limited training data. Along the same lines, Wang and Hoai (2016) propose a two-stream (spatial and temporal) net for non-action classification in temporal action localization. Similarly, Zhu et al. (2016b) use the

Table 19.5 Challenges

Year	Challenge	Database	Task	Event	Winner	Results
2011	Opportunity	Opportunity	AR	–	CSTAR	Sagha et al. (2011b), Chavarriaga et al. (2011), Sagha et al. (2011a)
2012	HARL	LIRIS	AR	ICPR	Ni et al. (2013)	Wolf et al. (2014), Gu et al. (2016)*
2012	VIRAT	VIRAT DB	AR	CVPR	–	Vondrick and Ramanan (2011), Oh (2011)
2012	ChaLearn	CGD	GR	–	Alfnie	Konecny and Hagara (2014)* Escalante et al. (2015)
2013		Montalbano	GR	–	Wu et al. (2013)	Bayer and Silbermann (2013)
2014		HuPBA 8K+	AR	ECCV	Peng et al. (2015)	–
		Montalbano	GR		Neverova et al. (2014)	Pigou et al. (2015b), Neverova et al. (2015b), Shu et al. (2015)
2015		HuPBA 8K+	AR	CVPR	Wang et al. (2015e)	–
2016		isoGD, conGD	GR	ICPR	Chai et al. (2016)	Karpathy et al. (2014), Wang et al. (2017)
2013	Thumos	UCF101	AR	ICCV	Jiang et al. (2013)	Sultani and Shah (2016), Soomro et al. (2015), Peng et al. (2013), Karaman et al. (2013)
2014		Thumos-14	AR	ECCV	Jain et al. (2014b)	Jain et al. (2015c), Shou et al. (2016a), Richard and Gall (2016)
2015		Thumos-15	AR	CVPR	Xu et al. (2015a)	Wang et al. (2015c), Yuan et al. (2016)
2015	VIVA	VIVA	GR	CVPR	Molchanov et al. (2015)	Ohn-Bar and Trivedi (2014)
2016	ROSE	NTU RGB+D	AR	ACCV	SEARCH	Shahroudy et al. (2016a)

*Non-deep learning method

same architecture for key-volume mining and classification in this case for spatio-temporal localization of actions. Chéron et al. (2015) extract both appearance and motion deep features from body part detections instead of whole video frames. They then compute for each body part the min/max aggregation their descriptors over time. The final representation consists of the concatenation of pooled body part descriptors on both appearance and motion cues, which is comparable to the size of a Fisher vector. Park et al. (2016) used the magnitude of optical flow vectors as a multiplicative factor for the features from the last convolutional layer. This reinforces the attention of the network on the moving objects when fine-tuning the fully connected layers. Zhang et al. (2016) explored motion vectors (obtained from video compression) to replace dense optical flow. They adopted a knowledge transfer strategy from optical flow CNN to the motion vector CNN to compensate the lack of detail and noisiness of motion vectors.

Singh et al. (2016a) use a multi-stream network to obtain frame-level features. To the full-frame spatial and motion streams from Simonyan and Zisserman (2014), they add two other actor-centered (spatial and motion) streams that compute the features in the actor's surrounding bounding box obtained by a human detector algorithm. Moreover, motion features are not stacks of optical flow maps between pairs of consecutive frames, but among a central frame and neighboring ones (avoiding object's displacement along the stacked flow maps). Gkioxari and Malik (2015) and Weinzaepfel et al. (2015) propose a similar an approach for action localization. They first generate action region proposals from RGB frames using, respectively, selective search (Uijlings et al. 2013) on and EdgeBoxes (Zitnick and Dollár 2014). Regions are then linked and described with static and motion CNN features. However, high quality proposals can be obtained from motion. Peng and Schmid (2016) show a region proposals generated by a region proposal network (RPN) (Ren et al. 2015) from motion (optical flow) were complementary to the ones generated by an appearance RPN. Note some of the works in Sect. 19.3.3 were using pre-computed motion features, which is not mutually exclusive with using motion features approaches. Varol et al. (2016) uses stacks of 60 pre-computed optical flow maps as inputs for the 3D convolutions, largely improving results obtained using raw video frames. Wang et al. (2016d) compute motion-like image representations from depth data by accumulating absolute depth differences of contiguous frames, namely hierarchical depth motion maps (HDMM).

In the literature there exist several methods which extend the deep-based methods with the popular dense trajectory features. Wang et al. (2015b) introduce a video representation called Trajectory-pooled Deep-convolutional Descriptor (TDD), which consists on extending the state-of-the-art descriptors along the trajectories with deep descriptors pooled from normalized CNN feature maps. Peng and Schmid (2015) propose a method based on a concatenation of iDT feature (HOG, HOF, MBHx, MBHy descriptors) and Fisher vector encoding and CNN features (VGG19). For CNN features they use VGG19 CNN to capture appearance features and VLAD encoding to encore/pool convolutional feature maps. Rahmani et al. (2016) utilize dense trajectories, and hence motion-based features, in order to learn view-invariant representations of actions. In order to model this variance, they generate a synthetic dataset of actions with 3D puppets from MoCap data that are projected to multiple 2D viewpoints from which fisher vectors of dense trajectories are used for learning a CNN model. During its training, an output layer is placed with as many neurons as training sequences so fisher vectors from different 2D viewpoints give same response. Afterwards, the concatenation of responses in intermediate layers (except for last one) provide the view-invariant representation for actions.

Differently from other works, Ng et al. (2016) jointly estimate optical flow and recognize actions in a multi-task learning setup. Their models consists in a residual network based on FlowNet He et al. (2016a) with extra additional classification layers, which learns to do both estimate optical flow and perform the classification task.

19.3.3 3D Convolutional Neural Networks

The early work of Ji et al. (2010) introduced the novelty of inferring temporal information from raw RGB data directly by performing 3D convolutions on stacks of multiple adjacent video frames, namely *3D ConvNets*. Since then, many authors tried to either further improve this kind of models (Tran et al. 2015; Mansimov et al. 2015; Sun et al. 2015; Shou et al. 2016b; Poleg et al. 2016; Liu et al. 2016b) or used them in combination with other hybrid deep-oriented models (Escorcia et al. 2016; Baccouche et al. 2011; Ye and Tian 2016; Feichtenhofer et al. 2016b; Wu et al. 2016c; Li et al. 2016a).

In particular, Tran et al. (2015) proposed 3D convolutions with more modern deep architectures and fixed $3 \times 3 \times 3$ convolution kernel size for all layers, that made 3D convnets more suitable for large-scale video classification. In general, 3D ConvNets can be expensive to train because of the large number of parameters, especially when training with bigger datasets such as 1-M sports dataset (Karpathy et al. 2014) (which can take up to one month). Sun et al. (2015) factorized the 3D convolutional kernel learning into a sequential process of learning 2D spatial convolutions in lower convolutional layers followed by learning 1D temporal convolutions in upper layers. Mansimov et al. (2015) proposed initializing 3D convolutional weights using 2D convolutional weights from spatial CNN trained on ImageNET. This not only speeds up the training but also alleviates the overfitting problem on small datasets. Varol et al. (2016) extended the length of input clips from 16 to 60 frames in order model more long-term temporal information during 3D convolutions, but reduced the input's spatial resolution to maintain the model complexity. Poleg et al. (2016) introduced a more compact 3D ConvNet for egocentric action recognition by applying 3D convolutions and 3D pooling only at the first layer. However, they do not use raw RGB frames, but stacked optical flow. In the context of depth data, Liu et al. (2016b) propose re-scaling depth image sequences to a 3D cuboid and the use of 3D convolutions to extract spatio-temporal features. The network consists of two pairs of convolutional and 3D max-pooling followed by a two-layer fully-connected layer net.

3D convolutions are often used in more cumbersome hybrid deep-based approaches. Shou et al. (2016b) propose a multi-stage CNN, in this case for temporal action localization, consisting of three 3D convnets (Tran et al. 2015): a proposal generation network that learns to differentiate background from action segments, a classification network that aims at discriminating among actions and serves as initialization for a third network, the localization network with a loss function that considers temporal overlap with the ground truth annotations. Wang et al. (2016d) applied 3D ConvNets to action recognition from depth data. The authors train a separate 3D ConvNet for each Cartesian plane each of which fed with a stack of depth images constructed from different 3D rotations and temporal scales. Singh et al. (2016b) prove the combination of both 2D and 3D ConvNet can leverage the performance when performing egocentric action recognition. Li et al. (2016a) uses 3D convolutions from Tran et al. (2015) to model short-term action features on a hierarchical framework in which linear dynamic systems (LDS) and VLAD descriptors are used to, respectively, model/represent medium- and long-range dynamics.

19.3.4 Temporal Deep Learning Models: RNN and LSTM

The application of temporal sequence modeling techniques, such as LSTM, to action recognition showed promising results in the past (Baccouche et al. 2010; Grushin et al. 2013). Earlier works did not try to explicitly model the temporal information, but aggregated the class predictions got from individual frame predictions. For instance, in Simonyan and Zisserman (2014), sample 25 equally spaced frames (and their crops and flips) from each video and then average their predicted scores.

Today, we find the combination of recurrent networks, mostly LSTM, with CNN models for the task of action recognition. Veeriah et al. (2015) propose a new gating scheme for LSTM that takes into account abrupt changes in the internal cell states, namely *differential RNN*. They use different order derivatives to model the potential saliency of observed motion patterns in actions sequences. Singh et al. (2016a) presented a bi-directional LSTM, which demonstrated to improve the simpler unidirectional LSTMs. Yeung et al. (2016) introduce a fully end-to-end approach on a RNN agent which interacts with a video over time. The agent observe a frame and provides a detection decision (confidence and begin-end), to whether or not emit a prediction, and where to look next. While back-propagation is used to train the detection decision outputs, REINFORCE is required to train the other two (non-differentiable) agent policies. Mahasseni and Todorovic (2016) propose a deep architecture which uses 3D skeleton sequences to regularize an LSTM network (LSTM+CNN) on the video. The regularization process is done by using the output of the encoder LSTM (grounded on 3D human-skeleton training data) and by modifying the standard BPTT algorithm in order to address the constraint optimization in the joint learning of LSTM+CNN. In their most recent work, Wang et al. (2016b) explore contexts as early as possible and leverage evolution of hierarchical local features. For this, they introduce a novel architecture called deep alternative neural network (DANN) stacking alternative layers, where each alternative layer consists of a volumetric convolutional layer followed by a recurrent layer. Lev et al. (2016) introduce a novel Fisher Vector representation for sequences derived from RNNs. Features are extracted from input data via VGG/C3D CNN. Then a PCA/CCA dimension reduction and L_2 normalization are applied and sequential feature are extracted via RNN. Finally, another PCA+L_2-norm step is applied before the final classification.

Liu et al. (2016a) extend the traditional LSTM into two concurrent domains, i.e., spatio-temporal long short-term memory (ST-LSTM). In this tree structure each joint of the network receive contextual information from both neighboring joints and previous frame. Shahroudy et al. (2016a) propose a part aware extension of LSTM for action recognition by splitting the memory cell of the LSTM into part-based sub-cells. These sub-cells can yield the models learn the long-term patterns specifically for each part. Finally, the output of each unit is the combination of all sub-cells.

19.3.5 *Deep Learning with Fusion Strategies*

Some methods have used diverse fusion schemes to improve recognition performance of action recognition. In Simonyan and Zisserman (2014), in order to fuse the class-level predictions of two streams (spatial and temporal), the authors train a multi-class linear SVM on stacked L_2-normalized softmax scores, which showed to improve the fusion by simply averaging scores. Wang et al. (2015d), which improves the former work by making the networks deeper and improved data augmentation techniques, simply perform a linear combination of the prediction scores (2 for temporal net and 1 for the spatial net). Similarly, Wang et al. (2016c) combine RGB, RGB difference, flow, and warped flow assigning equal weight to each channel. Feichtenhofer et al. (2016b) fuse a spatial and temporal convnets at the last convolutional layer (after ReLU) to turn it into a spatio-temporal stream by using 3D Conv fusion followed by 3D pooling. The temporal stream is kept and both loss functions are used for training and testing.

Deng et al. (2015) present a deep neural-network-based hierarchical graphical model that recognizes individual and group activity in surveillance scenes. Different CNNs produce action, pose, and scene scores. Then, the model refines the predicted labels for each activity via multi-step Message Passing Neural Network which captures the dependencies between action, poses, and scene predicted labels. Du et al. (2015) propose an end-to-end hierarchical RNN for skeleton based action recognition. The skeleton is divided into five parts, each of which is feed into a different RNN network, the output of which are fused into higher-layer RNNs. The highest level representations are feed into a single-layer perceptron for the final decision. Singh et al. (2016b) face the problem of first person action recognition using a multi-stream CNN (ego-CNN, temporal, and spatial), which are fused by combining weighted classifier scores. The proposed ego-CNN captures hand-crafted cues such as hand poses, head motion, and saliency map. Wang et al. (2016h) incorporate a region-of-interest pooling layer after the standard convolutional and pooling layers that separates CNN features for three semantic cues (scene, person, and objects) into parallel fully connected layers. They propose four different cue fusion schemes at class prediction level (max, sum, and two weighted fusions).

He et al. (2016b) attempt to investigate human action recognition without the human presence in input video frames. They consider whether a background sequence alone can classify human actions.

Peng and Schmid (2016) perform action localization in space and time by linking via dynamic time warping the action bounding box detections on single frames. For bounding box classification, they concatenate the representations of multiple regions derived from the original detection bounding box. Feichtenhofer et al. (2016a) propose a two stream architecture (appearance and motion) based on residual networks. In order to model spatiotemporal information, they inject 4 residual connections (namely "skip-streams") from motion to the appearance stream (i.e., middle fusion) and also transform the dimensionality reduction layers from ResNet's original model to temporal convolution layers. Wang et al. (2016g) train two Siamese networks modeling, respectively, action's precondition and effect on the observed environment. Each net learns a high-dimensional representation of either precondition or effect frames along with the linear transformation per class that transforms precondition to effect. The nets are connected via their outputs and not sharing weights; i.e., late fusion.

19.4 Gesture Recognition

In this section we review recent deep-learning based approaches for gesture recognition in videos, mainly driven by the areas of human computer, machine, and robot interaction.

19.4.1 2D Convolutional Neural Networks

The first method that comes to mind for recognizing a sequence of images, is applying 2D CNNs on individual frames and then averaging the result for classification. Jain et al. (2014a) present a CNN deep learning architecture for human pose estimation and develop a spatial-contextual model that aims at making joint predictions by considering related joints positions. They train multiple convnets to perform independent binary body-part classification (i.e., presence or absence of that body part). These networks are applied as sliding windows to overlapping regions of the input which results in smaller networks and better performance. For human pose estimation, Li et al. (2015a) propose a CNN-based multi-tasking model. The authors use a CNN to extract features from the input image. These features are then used as the input of both joint point regression tasks and body-part detection tasks. Kang et al. (2015)

exploit a CNN to extract features from the fully connected layer for sign language gesture recognition (finger spelling of ASL) from depth images.

Neverova et al. (2015a) propose a deep learning model for hand pose estimation that leverages both unlabeled and synthetically generated data for training. The key of the proposed model is that the authors encode structural information into the training objective by segmenting hands into parts, as opposed to including structure in the model architecture. Oyedotun and Khashman (2016) use CNN and *stacked denoising autoencoder* (SDAE) for recognizing 24 American Sign Language (ASL) hand gestures. Liang et al. (2016) propose a multi-view framework for hand pose recognition from point cloud. They form the view image by projecting hand point cloud to different view planes, and then using CNN to extract features from these views. Lin et al. (2015) propose a CNN that first detect hands using a GMM-skin detector and align them to the main axes. Then they apply a CNN comprising pooling and sampling layers, and on top a standard feed-forward NN that acted as classifier (heuristic rules on top of the output of the NN were defined).

In terms of hand pose estimation, Tompson et al. (2014) propose a CNN that recovers 3D joints based on synthetic training data. On top of the last layer a neural network transforms the outputs of the conv layers into heat maps (one per joint), indicating the probability-position for each joint. Poses are recovered from the set of heatmaps by solving an optimization problem.

19.4.2 Motion-Based Features

Neural networks and CNNs based on hand and body pose estimation as well as motion features have been widely applied for gesture recognition. If one wants to obtain better performance, temporal information rather than spatial data must be included in the models. For gesture *style* recognition in biometrics, Wu et al. (2016b) proposes a two-stream (spatio-temporal) CNN which learns from a set of training gestures. The authors use raw depth data as the input of spatial network and optical flow as the input of temporal one. For articulated human pose estimation in videos Jain et al. (2015a) exploit both color and motion features. The authors propose a Convolutional Network (ConvNet) architecture for estimating the 2D location of human joints in video, with an RGB image and a set of motion features as the input data of this network. The motion features used in this methods are the perspective projection of the 3D velocity-field of moving surfaces.

Wang et al. (2017) use three representations of *dynamic depth image* (DDI), *dynamic depth normal image* (DDNI) and *dynamic depth motion normal image* (DDMNI) as the input data of 2D networks for gesture recognition from depth data. The authors construct these dynamic images by using bidirectional rank pooling from a sequence of depth images. These representations can effectively capture the spatio-temporal information. Wang et al. (2016e) propose a similar formulation for gesture recognition in continuous depth video. They first identify the start and end frames of each gesture based on *quantity of movement* (QOM), and then they construct *Improved Depth Motion Map* (IDMM) by calculating the absolute depth difference between current frame and the start frame for each gesture segment which is a kind of motion features as the input data of deep learning network.

19.4.3   3D Convolutional Neural Networks

Several 3D CNNs have been proposed for gesture recognition, most notably (Molchanov et al. 2016; Huang et al. 2015; Molchanov et al. 2015). Molchanov et al. (2015) proposes a 3D CNN for driver hand gesture recognition from depth and intensity data. The authors combine information from multiple spatial scales for final prediction. It also employs spatio-temporal data augmentation for more effective training and to reduce potential overfitting. Molchanov et al. (2016) extend the 3D CNN with a recurrent mechanism for detection and classification of dynamic hand gestures. The architecture consists of a 3D-CNN for spatio-temporal feature extraction, a recurrent layer for global temporal modeling and a softmax layer for predicting class-conditional gesture probabilities.

Huang et al. (2015) proposes 3D CNN for sign language recognition which extracts discriminative spatio-temporal features from raw video stream. To boost the performances, multi-channels (RGB-D and Skeleton data) of video streams, including color information, depth clue and body joint positions are used as input to the 3D CNN. Li et al. (2016b) proposes a 3D CNN model for large scale gesture recognition by combining depth and RGB video. The proposed architecture is based on the model proposed by Tran et al. (2015). In a similar way, Zhu et al. (2016a) adopted the same architecture, but this time under a pyramidal for the same problem. In the same line, the work by Camgoz et al. (2016) builds an end to end 3D CNN using as basis the model of Tran et al. (2015) and applies it to large scale gesture spotting.

19.4.4   Temporal Deep Learning Models: RNN and LSTM

Interestingly, temporal deep learning models have not been widely used for gesture recognition, despite this is a promising venue for research. We are aware of Neverova et al. (2013), where they propose a multimodal (depth, skeleton, and speech) human gesture recognition system based on RNN. Each modality is first processed separately in short spatio-temporal blocks, where discriminative data-specific features are either manually extracted or learned. Then, RNN is employed for modeling large-scale temporal dependencies, data fusion and ultimately gesture classification. A multi stream RNN is also proposed by Chai et al. (2016) for large scale gesture spotting.

Eleni (2015) propose a Convolutional Long Short-Term Memory Recurrent Neural Network (CNNLSTM) able to successfully learn gesture varying in duration and complexity. Facing the same problem, Nishida and Nakayama (2016) propose a multi-stream model, called MRNN, which extends RNN capabilities with LSTM cells in order to facilitate the handling of variable-length gestures.

Wang et al. (2016f) propose *sequentially supervised long short-term Memory* (SS-LSTM), in which instead of assigning class label to the output layer of RNNs, auxiliary knowledge is used at every time step as sequential supervision. John et al. (2016) uses a deep learning framework to extract the representative frames from the video sequence and classify the gesture. They utilize a tiled image, created by sampling the whole video, as the input of a deconvenet to generates the tiled binary pattern. Then, These representative frames are given as input to the trained long-term recurrent convolution network. Koller et al. (2016) propose an EM-based algorithm integrating CNNs with Hidden-Markov-Models (HMMs) for weak supervision.

19.4.5 *Deep Learning with Fusion Strategies*

Multimodality in deep learning models has been widely exploited for gesture recognition. Wu et al. (2016a) propose a semi-supervised hierarchical dynamic framework by integrating deep neural networks within an HMM temporal framework, for simultaneous gesture segmentation and recognition using skeleton joint information, depth and RGB images. The authors utilize a Gaussian-Bernoulli Deep Belief Network to extract high-level skeletal joint features by, and 3D CNN to extract features from depth and RGB data. Finally, they applied intermediate (middle) and late fusion to get the final result. Neverova et al. (2015b) propose a multimodal multi-stream CNN for gesture spotting. The whole system operates at three temporal scales. Separate CNNs are considered for each modality at the beginning of the model structure with increasingly shared layers and a final prediction layer. Then, they fuse the result of each network by a meta-classifier independently at each scale; i.e., late fusion.

Pigou et al. (2015b) demonstrate that simple temporal feature pooling strategy (to take into account the temporal aspect of video) is not sufficient for gesture recognition, where temporal information is more discriminative compared to general video classification tasks. They explore deep architectures for gesture recognition in video and propose a new end-to-end trainable neural network architecture incorporating temporal convolutions and bidirectional recurrence. The authors test late and different kinds of middle fusions, to combine the result of CNN applied on each frame. Ouyang et al. (2014) present a deep learning model to fuse multiple information sources (i.e., appearance score, deformation and appearance mixture type) for human pose estimation. Three deep models take as input the output the information source from a state-of-the-art human pose estimator. The authors exploited early and middle fusion methods to integrate the models.

Li et al. (2015b) propose a CNN that learns to score pairs of input images and human poses (joints). The model is formed by two sub-networks: a CNN learns a feature embedding for the input images, and a two layer sub-network learns an embedding for the human pose. These two kinds of features are separately fed through fully-connected layers, and then mapped into two embedding spaces. The authors then calculate score function by dot-product between the two embeddings; i.e., late fusion. Similarly, Jain et al. (2015a) propose a CNN for estimating 2D joints location. The CNN incorporates RGB image and motion features. The authors utilize early fusion to integrate these two kinds of features. For gesture recognition from RGB-D data Duan et al. (2016) use two general deep-based network; i.e., convolutional two stream consensus voting network (2SCVN) for modeling the RGB and optical flow and 3d depth-saliency ConvNet stream for processing saliency and depth data. Then, they use late fusion to fuse the result of these networks

19.5 Discussion

In recent years deep learning methods have continued to be a thriving area of research in computer vision. These methods are end-to-end approaches for automatically learning semantic and discriminative feature representations directly from raw observations in many computer vision tasks. Thanks to the massive ImageNet dataset, CNN models overcome other hand-crafted features and achieve the best results on many recognition tasks. These achievements encourage researchers to design deep based models for learning an appropriate representation of image sequences.

In the following sections, the state of the art methods and deep-based platforms are summarized and then compared. We point out some tricks used for improving the result, and also address some limitations for future work.

19.5.1 Summary

As the recent success of deep learning models, many researchers have extended deep-based models representation of the sequences of images for human action recognition. Tables 19.6 and 19.7 list a summary of all methods on human action and gesture recognition respectively. A very simple extension consists in applying the existing 2D networks on individual video frames and then aggregating the predictions over the entire sequence for video classification (hereinafter referred as 2D convolutional models). Since they do not model temporal information of any kind, some methods (the second category) propose utilizing pre-computed motion features as input data for those pre-trained 2D networks. In the third group, different 3D extensions of 2D deep models have been proposed. Methods in the fourth group exploited temporal models (e.g. RNN and LSTM) for processing the temporal dimension.

Table 19.6 Summary of all deep-based action recognition methods. Notations: In the Modality column: Depth, Skeleton. In the Fusion column: Late, Early, Slow, and Middle

Year	Reference	Model				Modality	Fusion
		2D	Motion	3D	Temporal		
2010	Ji et al. (2010)	–	–	✓	–	RGB	–
2011	Baccouche et al. (2011)	–	–	✓	✓	RGB	–
2014	Karpathy et al. (2014)	✓	–	–	–	RGB	E-L-S
2014	Simonyan and Zisserman (2014)	✓	✓	–	–	RGB	L
2015	Chéron et al. (2015)	✓	✓	–	–	RGB	L
2015	Deng et al. (2015)	✓	–	–	–	RGB	L–S
2015	Du et al. (2015)	–	–	–	✓	S	S
2015	Gkioxari and Malik (2015)	✓	✓	–	–	RGB	L
2015	Mansimov et al. (2015)	–	–	✓	–	RGB	–
2015	Peng and Schmid (2015)	✓	–	–	–	RGB	–
2015	Sun et al. (2015)	✓	–	–	–	RGB	–
2015	Tran et al. (2015)	–	–	✓	–	RGB	–
2015	Wang et al. (2015b)	–	✓	–	–	RGB	L
2015	Wang et al. (2015d)	–	✓	–	–	RGB	L
2015	Weinzaepfel et al. (2015)	–	✓	–	–	RGB	L
2015	Zha et al. (2015)	✓	–	–	–	RGB	L
2016	Bilen et al. (2016)	✓	–	–	–	RGB	–
2016	Feichtenhofer et al. (2016b)	✓	✓	-	-	RGB	S
2016	He et al. (2016b)	✓	✓	–	–	RGB	L
2016	Lev et al. (2016)	–	✓	✓	✓	RGB	–
2016	Li et al. (2016a)	✓	–	–	–	RGB	–
2016	Liu et al. (2016b)	–	–	✓	–	D, S	L
2016	Mahasseni and Todorovic (2016)	✓	–	–	–	RGB	–
2016	Ng et al. (2016)	–	✓	–	–	RGB	–
2016	Ni et al. (2016)	✓	–	–	✓	RGB	–
2016	Park et al. (2016)	✓	✓	–	–	RGB	S–L
2016	Peng and Schmid (2016)	✓	✓	–	–	RGB	L
2016	Poleg et al. (2016)	✓	✓	✓	–	RGB	–
2016	Rahmani and Mian (2016)	✓	–	–	–	D	–
2016	Rahmani et al. (2016)	✓	✓	–	–	RGB	E
2016	Shou et al. (2016b)	–	–	✓	–	RGB	–
2016	Singh et al. (2016b)	✓	✓	✓	–	RGB	L
2016	Singh et al. (2016a)	✓	✓	–	✓	RGB	L
2016	Varol et al. (2016)	–	✓	✓	–	RGB	–
2016	Escorcia et al. (2016)	–	–	✓	–	RGB	–

(continued)

Table 19.6 (continued)

Year	Reference	Model				Modality	Fusion
		2D	Motion	3D	Temporal		
2016	Wang et al. (2016d)	–	–	✓	–	D	L
2016	Wang et al. (2016g)	✓	✓	–	–	RGB	L
2016	Wang et al. (2016b)	✓	–	–	✓	RGB	–
2016	Wang and Hoai (2016)	✓	✓	–	–	RGB	L
2016	Wang et al. (2016c)	✓	✓	–	–	RGB	L
2016	Wang et al. (2016h)	✓	✓	–	–	RGB	L
2016	Wu et al. (2016c)	–	–	✓	✓	RGB	–
2016	Wu et al. (2016d)	✓	–	–	–	RGB	L
2016	Yeung et al. (2016)	✓	–	–	✓	RGB	–
2016	Ye and Tian (2016)	–	✓	✓	✓	RGB	–
2016	Zhang et al. (2016)	✓	✓	–	–	RGB	L
2016	Zhu et al. (2016b)	–	✓	–	–	RGB	L

19.5.2 Comparison

The most crucial challenge in deep-based human action and gesture recognition is temporal analysis, for which many architectures have been proposed. These approaches have been classified into four groups; i.e., 2D models, motion-based input model, 3D models, and temporal models. Generally, there are two main issues for comparing the methods; i.e., *how does the method deal with the temporal information?* and *how can such a large network be trained with small datasets?*

As discussed, methods in the first category only use the appearance (spatial) information to extract features. In other words, there is no temporal processing for these methods. However, because of the availability of large annotated datasets (e.g. ImageNet), it is easier for these methods to be fine tuned on pre-trained models. In the second group, motion features such as optical flow, computed from data before their usage, are fed to the deep models. It has been shown that using training networks on pre-computed motion features is an effective way to save them from implicit learning of motion features. Moreover, fine-tuning motion-based networks with spatial data (ImageNet) proved to be effective. Allowing networks which are fine-tuned on stacked optical flow frames to achieve good performance in spite of having limited training data. However, these models can only exploit limited (local) temporal information.

Methods in the third category, learn spatio-temporal features by 3D filters in their 3D convolutional and pooling layers. It has been shown 3D networks over a long sequence are able to learn more complex temporal patterns (Varol et al. 2016). Because of the amount of parameters to learn, training these networks is a challenging task, specially compared to motion-based methods (Simonyan and Zisserman 2014).

Table 19.7 Summary of all deep-based gesture recognition methods. Notations: In the Modality column: Depth, Skeleton, Audio, InfraRed. In the Fusion column: Early, Middle, Late, Slow

Year	Reference	Model				Modality	Fusion
		2D	Motion	3D	Temporal		
2013	Neverova et al. (2013)	–	–	✓	✓	D-S-A	L
2014	Tompson et al. (2014)	✓	–	–	–	RGB-D	–
2014	Jain et al. (2014a)	✓	–	–	–	RGB	–
2014	Ouyang et al. (2014)	✓	–	–	–	RGB	E-M
2015	Molchanov et al. (2015)	–	–	✓	–	RGB-D	L
2015	Huang et al. (2015)	–	–	✓	–	RGB-D-S	L
2015	Lin et al. (2015)	✓	–	–	–	RGB	–
2015	Li et al. (2015a)	✓	–	–	–	RGB	–
2015	Eleni (2015)	✓	–	–	✓	RGB	–
2015	Kang et al. (2015)	✓	–	–	–	D	–
2015	Li et al. (2015b)	✓	–	–	–	RGB-S	L
2015	Jain et al. (2015a)	–	✓	–	–	RGB	E
2015	Neverova et al. (2015a)	✓	–	–	–	D	–
2015	Neverova et al. (2015b)	–	–	✓	–	RGB-S-A	L
2015	Pigou et al. (2015b)	✓	–	–	✓	RGB-D	L-S
2016	Molchanov et al. (2016)	–	✓	✓	✓	RGB-D-IR	L
2016	Wu et al. (2016b)	–	✓	–	–	D	L
2016	Nishida and Nakayama (2016)	✓	–	–	✓	RGB-D	L
2016	Wu et al. (2016a)	–	✓	✓	✓	RGB-D	M-L
2016	Wang et al. (2016f)	✓	–	–	✓	RGB	–
2016	Duan et al. (2016)	✓	✓	✓	–	RGB-D	L
2016	John et al. (2016)	✓	–	–	✓	RGB	–
2016	Oyedotun and Khashman (2016)	✓	–	–	–	RGB	–
2016	Liang et al. (2016)	✓	–	–	–	D	L
2016	Wang et al. (2016e)	–	✓	–	–	D	–
2016	Li et al. (2016b)	–	–	✓	–	RGB-D	L
2016	Zhu et al. (2016a)	–	–	✓	–	RGB-D	E
2016	Camgoz et al. (2016)	–	–	✓	–	RGB	L
2016	Chai et al. (2016)	–	–	–	✓	RGB-D	M
2016	Koller et al. (2016)	✓	–	–	✓	RGB	–
2017	Wang et al. (2017)	–	✓	–	–	D	L

Because of the required amount of data, the problem of weights initialization has been investigated. The transformation of 2D Convolutional Weights into 3D ones yield models to achieve better accuracy than training scratch (Mansimov et al. 2015). The most crucial advantage of approaches in the fourth group (i.e., temporal models like RNN and LSTM) is that they are able to cope with longer-range temporal relations. These models are preferred when dealing with skeletal data. Since skeleton features are low-dimensional, these networks have fewer weights, and thus, can be trained with fewer data.

We find from Tables 19.3 and 19.4, the methods that achieved the best results on two of the most well-known datasets, still using hand-crafted features alongside deep-based features. In other words, action and gesture recognition has not gained a high performance from deep networks compared with other research areas (like image classification). These fields of research still needs to be grown.

Based on the influence of millions of network parameters, in addition to the different strategies for data augmentation, and the current allowed procedure of the usage of pre-trained models, current comparison among method performances for action and gesture recognition is a difficult task. In this sense, we expect in a near future the definition of protocols that will allow for a more accurate comparison of deep-based action and gesture recognition models. More precisely, we refer to Xu et al. (2015b) as the winner of THUMOS 2015 with the best result. This approach used VGG16 to extract frame-level features from the fully connected layers such as fc6 and fc7. Then, using Fisher vector and VLAD, they aggregated all the frames into single video-level representation. They also extracted *latent concept descriptors* (LCD) extracted by a GoogLeNet with Batch Normalization. An enhanced version of improved dense trajectories (iDT), acoustic features MFCC and ASR were also used in this work.

Recently, new deep architectures have started to be used for action/gesture recognition, such as gate-recurrent-unit RNNs (Ballas et al. 2016) (sparse GRU-RNNs that reduce the number of parameters of the network) and siamese architectures (Wang et al. 2016g) (that allow multi-task learning). More insights into these architectures, and, of course, the use of more recent ones (like Radford et al. 2016) are promising venues for research.

19.5.3 Tricks

Regardless of the model, performance is dependent on a large number of parameters that have to be learned from limited data. Strategies for data augmentation and pre-training are common. Likewise, training mechanisms to avoid overfitting (e.g. dropout) and to control the learning rate (e.g. extensions to SGD and Nesterov momentum) have been proposed. Improvements on those strategies are expected in the next few years. The community is nowadays putting efforts on building larger data sets that can cope with huge-parametric deep models (Abu-El-Haija et al. 2016; Heilbron et al. 2015) and on challenge organization (with novel data sets and well defined evaluation protocols) that can advance the state-of-the-art in the field and make easier the comparison among deep learning architectures (Shahroudy et al. 2016a; Escalante et al. 2016b).

Taking into account the full temporal scale, results in a huge amount of weights for learning. To address this problem and decrease the number of weights, a good trick is to decrease the spatial resolution while increasing the temporal length.

Another trick to improve the result of deep-based models is data fusion. There could be separated networks, trained on different kinds of input data, different kinds of primary features, different portions of input data, and so on. It is well-known that ensemble learning is a powerful way to boost the performance of any machine learning approach. It proved to reduce the bias and variance errors of the learning algorithm (Neverova et al. 2014). We find new methodologies that ensemble several deep models for action and gesture recognition, not necessarily combining different data modalities, but with different sampling of the data and learning parameters (Wang et al. 2016c; Varol et al. 2016). This provides complementary information learned by the different deep models, being able to recover from uncorrelated errors of individual models (Neverova et al. 2014). Recently it is common to see this kind of strategies in action/gesture recognition competitions, where a minor improvement of the model can make the difference to achieve the best performance (Varol et al. 2016).

It has been proved that the result of the temporal models (e.g. RNN) on skeletal data can be improved by extending these models to learn two domains, i.e., spatial and temporal, simultaneously (Liu et al. 2016a). In other words, each state of the network receives contextual information from neighboring joints in human skeleton (spatial information) and also from previous frames (temporal information).

Finally, a common way to improve the performance of action or gesture recognition is the combination of deep learning-based features and hand-crafted ones. This combination could be performed in different layers of the deep models.

19.5.4   Platforms

One of the reasons that supports the applicability of deep learning in several areas is code sharing. In fact, there are many open source libraries implementing standard deep learning models. Many authors have published deep-based toolkits that make the research progress easier for the community. Among the most popular ones are Caffe (Jia et al. 2014), CNTK (Yu et al. 2014), Matlab (Rahmani et al. 2016), TensorFlow (Abadi et al. 2015b), Theano (Al-Rfou et al. 2016), and Torch (Liu et al. 2016b).

Caffe (Jia et al. 2014), is the first deep learning toolkit developed by the Berkeley Vision and Learning Center. It is a Python Library primary focused on CNN, with a poor support of RNN. Caffe is useful for performing image analysis and benefits from having a large repository of pre-trained neural network models. It includes state-of-the-art models (mostly 2D networks) that achieve world class results on standard computer vision datasets. Caffe has been also used to implement 3D-CNN for action recognition (Tran et al. 2015; Poleg et al. 2016; Shou et al. 2016b; Wang et al. 2016d; Singh et al. 2016b), and motion-based approaches for both action (Simonyan and Zisserman 2014; Zhang et al. 2016; Singh et al. 2016a; Gkioxari and Malik 2015) and gesture recognition (Wu et al. 2016b; Wang et al. 2017, 2016e). Caffe is preferred to other frameworks for its speed and efficiency, especially in "fused" architectures for action recognition (Singh et al. 2016b; Deng et al. 2015; Diba et al. 2016; Peng and Schmid 2016). Popular network types like FNN, CNN, LSTM, and RNN are fully supported by CNTK (Yu et al. 2014), which was started by speech processing researchers. On the other hand, TensorFlow (Abadi et al. 2015a) is an C++ toolkit in deep learning under an open source Apache 2.0 License by Google. It fully supports 2D CNNs and RNNs implementations, but not 3D CNNs.

Torch (Collobert et al. 2002) is a script language based on the Lua programming language that provides a rich set of RNN functions. For this reason it has been efficiently used for temporal models in action recognition (Liu et al. 2016a; Shahroudy et al. 2016a). Moreover, most of the 3D CNN-based methods utilized Torch to implement their networks. CUDA is a parallel computing platform and application programming interface (API) model created by Nvidia in order to use GPU. Cuda-convnet and CuDNN support all the mainstream softwares such as Caffe, Torch, Theano. Few methods also use MATLAB, e.g. Rahmani et al. (2016); one of the easiest and most productive software environment for engineers and scientists, widely used also in machine learning, signal and image processing, and computer vision.

19.5.5 Future Work

Deep learning methods emerged not so long ago in the fields of human action and gesture recognition. Even when there is already too much work on deep learning in these topics, there are still several directions in which we foresee deep learning can have a broad impact in the forthcoming years. We briefly review these possible line of research that will be fruitful in the short term future.

Regarding applications, deep learning techniques have been successfully used in surveillance (Ahmed et al. 2015), health care (Liang et al. 2014), robotics (Yu et al. 2013), human–computer interaction (Mnih et al. 2015), and so on. We anticipate deep learning will prevail in emerging applications/areas like fine grained action recognition, action description generation, social signal processing, affective computing, and personality analysis, among others.

Another important trend of current deep-based models for action and gesture recognition is the inclusion of contextual cues. While it has been partially considered for gesture recognition (e.g. part-based human-models and scene understanding in combination with depth maps), until recent years very few works considered robust contextual cues for action recognition. We anticipate context information will be critical for developing explanatory deep learning models for action and gesture recognition. Classical action recognition tasks were mainly addressed by the description of spatio-temporal local patches. Nowadays we can find strategies that incorporate environment recognition, and articulated human body (Wang et al. 2016g), places (Zhou et al. 2014), and objects (Jain et al. 2015c). Moreover, we expect novel architectures and fusion schemes to exploit context and enhanced articulated human body pose estimation to keep progressing in the next few years. It is also expected that there will be advances in hybrid models combining handcrafted and learned descriptors (Neverova et al. 2014; Wang et al. 2015b; Ji et al. 2013). Similarly, we think the community will pay attention to deep learning solutions for large scale and real time action and gesture recognition (Han et al. 2016; Zhang et al. 2016). Finally, it is important to mention that most of the surveyed methods targeted merely recognition/classification on already pre-segmented action/gesture clips. Additional effort is expected to advance in the research of methods able to simultaneously perform both detection and recognition tasks in long, realistic videos (Gkioxari and Malik 2015; Shou et al. 2016b). As such, we envision other related problems like early recognition (Escalante et al. 2016a), multi task learning (Xu et al. 2016), captioning, recognition from low resolution sequences (Nasrollahi et al. 2015) and from lifelog devices (Rhinehart and Kitani 2016) will receive special attention within the next few years.

These days, we need to solve the problem of action recognition in more realistic long untrimmed videos. There are some other challenges in human action recognition with deep-based models that have been addressed by few researchers so far, like simultaneous detection and localization (Gkioxari and Malik 2015). Another venue for research is early recognition of actions and gestures (Escalante et al. 2016a). We need to know if the input video contains an action or not and then localizing temporally and spatially the action by finding the frames and regions in those frames, in which action is performed. Then after detection and localization, the action will be classified. It is anticipated that in the near future research will expand on both action detection and localization.

Acknowledgements This work has been partially supported by the Spanish projects TIN2015-66951-C2-2-R and TIN2016-74946-P (MINECO/FEDER, UE) and CERCA Programme / Generalitat de Catalunya. Hugo Jair Escalante was supported by CONACyT under grants CB2014-241306 and PN-215546.

References

M. Abadi, A. Agarwal, P. Barham, E. Brevdo, Z. Chen, C. Citro, G.S. Corrado, A. Davis, J. Dean, M. Devin, S. Ghemawat, I. Goodfellow, A. Harp, G. Irving, M. Isard, Y. Jia, R. Jozefowicz, L. Kaiser, M. Kudlur, J. Levenberg, D. Mané, R. Monga, S. Moore, C. Olah, M. Schuster, J. Shlens, B. Steiner, I. Sutskever, K. Talwar, P. Tucker, V. Vanhoucke, V. Vasudevan, F. Viégas, O. Vinyals, P. Warden, M. Wattenberg, M. Wicke, Y. Yu, X. Zheng, TensorFlow: large-scale machine learning on heterogeneous systems, 2015a, http://tensorflow.org/

M. Abadi, A. Agarwal, P. Barham, E. Brevdo, Z. Chen, C. Citro, G.S. Corrado, A. Davis, J. Dean, M. Devin, et al., Tensorflow: large-scale machine learning on heterogeneous systems, 2015b, http://www.tensorflow.org

S. Abu-El-Haija, N. Kothari, J. Lee, P. Natsev, G. Toderici, B. Varadarajan, S. Vijayanarasimhan, Youtube-8m: a large-scale video classification benchmark. CoRR, abs/1609.08675 (2016)

E. Ahmed, M. Jones, T.K. Marks, An improved deep learning architecture for person re-identification, in *Proceedings of the IEEE Conference on Computer Vision and Pattern Recognition*, 2015, pp. 3908–3916

R. Al-Rfou, G. Alain, A. Almahairi, C. Angermueller, D. Bahdanau, N. Ballas, F. Bastien, J. Bayer, A. Belikov, et al., Theano; a python framework for fast computation of mathematical expressions, 2016, arXiv:1605.02688

M.R. Amer, S. Todorovic, A. Fern, S.-C. Zhu, Monte carlo tree search for scheduling activity recognition, in *Proceedings of the IEEE International Conference on Computer Vision*, 2013, pp. 1353–1360

R. Araujo, M.S. Kamel, A semi-supervised temporal clustering method for facial emotion analysis, in *2014 IEEE International Conference on Multimedia and Expo Workshops (ICMEW)*, IEEE, 2014, pp. 1–6

K. Avgerinakis, K. Adam, A. Briassouli, Y. Kompatsiaris, Moving camera human activity localization and recognition with motionplanes and multiple homographies, in *ICIP*, IEEE, 2015, pp. 2085–2089

M. Baccouche, F. Mamalet, C. Wolf, C. Garcia, A. Baskurt, Action classification in soccer videos with long short-term memory recurrent neural networks, in *International Conference on Artificial Neural Networks* (Springer, Berlin, 2010), pp. 154–159

M. Baccouche, F. Mamalet, C. Wolf, C. Garcia, A. Baskurt, *Sequential deep learning for human action recognition, in International Workshop on Human Behavior Understanding* (Springer, New York, 2011), pp. 29–39

N. Ballas, L. Yao, A. Courville, Delving deeper into convolutional networks for learning video representations, in *Proceedings of International Conference on Learning Representations*, 2016

I. Bayer, T. Silbermann. A multi modal approach to gesture recognition from audio and video data, in *ICMI* (2013), pp. 461–466. ISBN 978-1-4503-2129-7. doi:10.1145/2522848.2532592

Y. Bengio, P. Simard, P. Frasconi, Learning long-term dependencies with gradient descent is difficult. TNN **5**(2), 157–166 (1994)

H. Bilen, B. Fernando, E. Gavves, A. Vedaldi, S. Gould, Dynamic image networks for action recognition, in *Proceedings of the IEEE Conference on Computer Vision and Pattern Recognition*, 2016, pp. 3034–3042

N.C. Camgoz, S. Hadfield, O. Koller, R. Bowden, Using convolutional 3d neural networks for user-independent continuous gesture recognition, in *Proceedings IEEE International Conference of Pattern Recognition (International Conference on Pattern Recognition), ChaLearn Workshop*, 2016

X. Chai, Z. Liu, F. Yin, Z. Liu, X. Chen, Two streams recurrent neural networks for large-scale continuous gesture recognition, in *Proceedings of International Conference on Pattern RecognitionW*, 2016

R. Chaudhry, F. Ofli, G. Kurillo, R. Bajcsy, R. Vidal, Bio-inspired dynamic 3d discriminative skeletal features for human action recognition, in *Proceedings of the IEEE Conference on Computer Vision and Pattern Recognition Workshops*, 2013, pp. 471–478

R. Chavarriaga, H. Sagha, J. del R. Milln, Ensemble creation and reconfiguration for activity recognition: an information theoretic approach, in *SMC*, 2011, pp. 2761–2766. ISBN 978-1-4577-0652-3, http://dblp.uni-trier.de/db/conf/smc/smc2011.html#ChavarriagaSM11

C. Chen, B. Zhang, Z. Hou, J. Jiang, M. Liu, Y. Yang, Action recognition from depth sequences using weighted fusion of 2d and 3d auto-correlation of gradients features, in *Multimedia Tools and Applications*, 2016, pp. 1–19

W. Chen, J.J. Corso, Action detection by implicit intentional motion clustering, in *Proceedings of the IEEE International Conference on Computer Vision*, 2015, pp. 3298–3306

G. Chéron, I. Laptev, C. Schmid, P-cnn: pose-based cnn features for action recognition, in *Proceedings of the IEEE International Conference on Computer Vision*, pp. 3218–3226, 2015

R. Collobert, S. Bengio, J. Marithoz, *Torch: a modular machine learning software library* (Technical Report, IDIAP, 2002)

Z. Deng, M. Zhai, L. Chen, Y. Liu, S. Muralidharan, M.J. Roshtkhari, G. Mori, Deep structured models for group activity recognition, in *Proceedings of the British Machine Vision Conference (BMVC)* ed. by M.W.J. Xianghua Xie, G.K.L. Tam (BMVA Press, Guildford, 2015), pp. 179.1–179.12. ISBN 1-901725-53-7. doi:10.5244/C.29.179

Z. Deng, A. Vahdat, H. Hu, G. Mori, Structure inference machines: recurrent neural networks for analyzing relations in group activity recognition, in *The IEEE Conference on Computer Vision and Pattern Recognition (CVPR)*, June 2016

A. Diba, A. Mohammad Pazandeh, H. Pirsiavash, L. Van Gool, Deepcamp: deep convolutional action and attribute mid-level patterns, in *IEEE CVPR*, 2016

Y. Du, W. Wang, L. Wang, Hierarchical recurrent neural network for skeleton based action recognition, *IEEE Conference on Computer Vision and Pattern Recognition (CVPR)*, June 2015, pp. 1110–1118. doi:10.1109/CVPR.2015.7298714

J. Duan, S. Zhou, J. Wan, X. Guo, S.Z. Li, Multi-modality fusion based on consensus-voting and 3d convolution for isolated gesture recognition, 2016, arXiv:1611.06689

I.C. Duta, B. Ionescu, K. Aizawa, N. Sebe, Spatio-temporal vlad encoding for human action recognition in videos, in *International Conference on Multimedia Modeling* (Springer, New York, 2017), pp. 365–378

T. Eleni, Gesture recognition with a convolutional long short term memory recurrent neural network, in *ESANN*, 2015, https://books.google.cl/books?id=E8qMjwEACAAJ

J.L. Elman, Finding structure in time. Cognitive Sci. **14**(2), 179–211 (1990)

H.J. Escalante, C.A. Hérnadez, L.E. Sucar, M. Montes. Late fusion of heterogeneous methods for multimedia image retrieval, in *Proceedings of the 1st ACM International Conference on Multimedia Information Retrieval*, MIR'08 (ACM, New York, 2008), pp. 172–179. ISBN 978-1-60558-312-9. doi:10.1145/1460096.1460125

H.J. Escalante, I. Guyon, V. Athitsos, P. Jangyodsuk, J. Wan, Principal motion components for gesture recognition using a single example, in *PAA*, 2015

H.J. Escalante, E.F. Morales, L.E. Sucar, A naïve bayes baseline for early gesture recognition. PRL **73**, 91–99 (2016a)

H.J. Escalante, V. Ponce, J. Wan, M. Riegler, A. Clapes, S. Escalera, I. Guyon, X. Baro, P. Halvorsen, H. Müller, M. Larson, Chalearn joint contest on multimedia challenges beyond visual analysis: an overview, in *Proceedings of International Conference on Pattern Recognition*, 2016b

V. Escorcia, F.C. Heilbron, J.C. Niebles, B. Ghanem, DAPs: deep action proposals for action understanding, in *European Conference on Computer Vision*, 2016

C. Feichtenhofer, A. Pinz, R. Wildes, Spatiotemporal residual networks for video action recognition, in *Advances in Neural Information Processing Systems*, 2016a, pp. 3468–3476

C. Feichtenhofer, A. Pinz, A. Zisserman, Convolutional two-stream network fusion for video action recognition. In *Proceedings of the IEEE Conference on Computer Vision and Pattern Recognition*, 2016b, pp. 1933–1941

B. Fernando, E. Gavves, J. Oramas, A. Ghodrati, T. Tuytelaars, Rank pooling for action recognition, in *IEEE Transactions on Pattern Analysis and Machine Intelligence*, 2016

D. Fortun, P. Bouthemy, C. Kervrann, Optical flow modeling and computation: a survey. Comput. Vis. Image Underst. **134**, 1–21 (2015)

F.A. Gers, N.N. Schraudolph, J. Schmidhuber, Learning precise timing with lstm recurrent networks. JMLR **3**, 115–143 (2002)

G. Gkioxari, J. Malik, Finding action tubes, in *Proceedings of the IEEE Conference on Computer Vision and Pattern Recognition*, 2015, pp. 759–768

A. Grushin, D.D. Monner, J.A. Reggia, A. Mishra, Robust human action recognition via long short-term memory, in *The 2013 International Joint Conference on, Neural Networks (IJCNN)*, IEEE, 2013, pp. 1–8

F. Gu, M. Sridhar, A. Cohn, D. Hogg, F. Flrez-Revuelta, D. Monekosso, P. Remagnino, Weakly supervised activity analysis with spatio-temporal localisation, *Neurocomputing*, 2016. ISSN 0925-2312. doi:10.1016/j.neucom.2016.08.032, http://www.sciencedirect.com/science/article/

S. Han, H. Mao, W. Dally, Deep compression: Compressing deep neural networks with pruning, trained quantization and huffman coding, in *Proceedings of International Conference on Learning Representations*, 2016

K. He, X. Zhang, S. Ren, J. Sun, Deep residual learning for image recognition, in *Proceedings of the IEEE Conference on Computer Vision and Pattern Recognition*, 2016a, pp. 770–778

Y. He, S. Shirakabe, Y. Satoh, H. Kataoka, Human action recognition without human, in *Proceedings of European Conference on Computer Vision 2016 Workshops* (Springer, New York, 2016b), pp. 11–17

F.C. Heilbron, V. Escorcia, B. Ghanem, J.C. Niebles, Activitynet: a large-e video benchmark for human activity understanding, in *CVPR*, 2015, pp. 961–970

S. Hochreiter, *Untersuchungen zu dynamischen neuronalen netzen* (Technische Universität München, Diploma, 1991), p. 91

S. Hochreiter, J. Schmidhuber, Long short-term memory. Neural Comput. **9**(8), 1735–1780 (1997)

J. Huang, W. Zhou, H. Li, W. Li, Sign language recognition using 3d convolutional neural networks, in *ICME*, 2015, pp. 1–6

M.S. Ibrahim, S. Muralidharan, Z. Deng, A. Vahdat, G. Mori, A hierarchical deep temporal model for group activity recognition, in *The IEEE Conference on Computer Vision and Pattern Recognition (CVPR)*, June 2016

A. Jain, J. Tompson, M. Andriluka, G.W. Taylor, C. Bregler, Learning human pose estimation features with convolutional networks, in *International Conference on Learning Representations*, Cornell University, 2014a, pp. 1–14

A. Jain, J. Tompson, Y. LeCun, C. Bregler, *MoDeep: a deep learning framework using motion features for human pose estimation*, vol. 9004, 2015a, pp. 302–315

M. Jain, J. van Gemert, C.G.M. Snoek, University of Amsterdam at thumos challenge, in *ECCV THUMOS Challenge 2014* (Zürich, Switzerland, September, 2014), 2014b

M. Jain, J.C. van Gemert, T. Mensink, C.G.M. Snoek. Objects2action: classifying and localizing actions without any video example, in *IEEE ICCV*, 2015b, arXiv.org/abs/1510.06939

M. Jain, J.C. van Gemert, C.G. Snoek, What do 15,000 object categories tell us about classifying and localizing actions? in *CVPR*, 2015c, pp. 46–55

S. Ji, W. Xu, M. Yang, K. Yu. 3d convolutional neural networks for human action recognition, in *Proceedings of the 27th International Conference on Machine Learning (ICML-10)*, 2010, pp. 495–502

S. Ji, W. Xu, M. Yang, K. Yu. 3d convolutional neural networks for human action recognition. *IEEE TPAMI*, vol. 35(1), 2013, pp. 221–231. ISSN 0162-8828. doi:10.1109/TPAMI.2012.59

Y. Jia, E. Shelhamer, J. Donahue, S. Karayev, J. Long, R. Girshick, S. Guadarrama, T. Darrell, *Caffe: convolutional architecture for fast feature embedding, in ACM MM* (ACM, New York, 2014), pp. 675–678

Y.-G. Jiang, J. Liu, A. Roshan Zamir, I. Laptev, M. Piccardi, M. Shah, R. Sukthankar, THUMOS challenge: action recognition with a large number of classes. ICCV13-Action-Workshop, 2013

V. John, A. Boyali, S. Mita, M. Imanishi, N. Sanma. Deep learning-based fast hand gesture recognition using representative frames, in *2016 International Conference on Digital Image Computing: Techniques and Applications (DICTA)*, IEEE, 2016, pp. 1–8

J. Joo, W. Li, F.F. Steen, S.-C. Zhu. Visual persuasion: Inferring communicative intents of images, in *Proceedings of the IEEE Conference on Computer Vision and Pattern Recognition*, 2014, pp. 216–223

B. Kang, S. Tripathi, T.Q. Nguyen, Real-time sign language fingerspelling recognition using convolutional neural networks from depth map, in *ACPR*, 2015, arXiv:abs/1509.03001

S. Karaman, L. Seidenari, A.D. Bagdanov, A.D. Bimbo, L1-regularized logistic regression stacking and transductive crf smoothing for action recognition in video, in *Results of the THUMOS 2013 Action Recognition Challenge with a Large Number of Classes*, 2013

A. Karpathy, G. Toderici, S. Shetty, T. Leung, R. Sukthankar, and L. Fei-Fei. Large-scale video classification with convolutional neural networks, in *Proceedings of the IEEE Conference on Computer Vision and Pattern Recognition*, 2014, pp. 1725–1732

T. Kerola, N. Inoue, K. Shinoda, Cross-view human action recognition from depth maps using spectral graph sequences. Comput. Vis. Image Underst. **154**, 108–126 (2017)

O. Koller, H. Ney, R. Bowden, Deep hand: how to train a cnn on 1 million hand images when your data is continuous and weakly labelled, in *Proceedings of the IEEE Conference on Computer Vision and Pattern Recognition*, 2016, pp. 3793–3802

J. Konecny, M. Hagara, One-shot-learning gesture recognition using hog-hof features, in *JMLR*, vol. 15, 2014, pp. 2513–2532, http://jmlr.org/papers/v15/konecny14a.html

A. Krizhevsky, I. Sutskever, G.E. Hinton, Imagenet classification with deep convolutional neural networks, in *Advances in Neural Information Processing Systems*, 2012, pp. 1097–1105

Y. Kuniyoshi, H. Inoue, M. Inaba, Design and implementation of a system that generates assembly programs from visual recognition of human action sequences, in *IEEE International Workshop on Intelligent Robots and Systems' 90.'Towards a New Frontier of Applications', Proceedings*, IROS'90, IEEE, 1990, pp. 567–574

G. Lev, G. Sadeh, B. Klein, L. Wolf, Rnn fisher vectors for action recognition and image annotation, in *European Conference on Computer Vision* (Springer, New York, 2016), pp. 833–850

S. Li, Z.-Q. Liu, A.B. Chan, Heterogeneous multi-task learning for human pose estimation with deep convolutional neural network. *IJCV*, vol. 113(1), May 2015a, pp. 19–36. ISSN 0920-5691. doi:10.1007/s11263-014-0767-8

S. Li, W. Zhang, A.B. Chan, Maximum-margin structured learning with deep networks for 3d human pose estimation, in *ICCV*, 2015b, pp. 2848–2856

Y. Li, W. Li, V. Mahadevan, N. Vasconcelos, Vlad3: encoding dynamics of deep features for action recognition, in *Proceedings of the IEEE Conference on Computer Vision and Pattern Recognition*, 2016a, pp. 1951–1960

Y. Li, Q. Miao, K. Tian, Y. Fan, X. Xu, R. Li, J. Song, Large-scale gesture recognition with a fusion of rgb-d data based on c3d model, in *Proceedings of International Conference on Pattern RecognitionW*, 2016b

C. Liang, Y. Song, Y. Zhang, Hand gesture recognition using view projection from point cloud, in *2016 IEEE International Conference on Image Processing (ICIP)*, IEEE, 2016, pp. 4413–4417

Z. Liang, G. Zhang, J.X. Huang, Q.V. Hu, Deep learning for healthcare decision making with emrs, in *2014 IEEE International Conference on Bioinformatics and Biomedicine (BIBM)*, IEEE, 2014, pp. 556–559

H.-I. Lin, M.-H. Hsu, W.-K. Chen, Human hand gesture recognition using a convolution neural network, in *CASE*, 2015, pp. 1038–1043

A.-A. Liu, Y.-T. Su, W.-Z. Nie, M. Kankanhalli, Hierarchical clustering multi-task learning for joint human action grouping and recognition. TPAMI **39**(1), 102–114 (2017)

J. Liu, A. Shahroudy, D. Xu, G. Wang, Spatio-temporal lstm with trust gates for 3d human action recognition, in *European Conference on Computer Vision* (Springer, New York, 2016a), pp. 816–833

Z. Liu, C. Zhang, Y. Tian, 3d-based deep convolutional neural network for action recognition with depth sequences. Image Vis. Comput. **55**, 93–100 (2016b)

J. Luo, W. Wang, H. Qi, Group sparsity and geometry constrained dictionary learning for action recognition from depth maps, in *Proceedings of the IEEE International Conference on Computer Vision*, 2013, pp. 1809–1816

B. Mahasseni, S. Todorovic, Regularizing long short term memory with 3d human-skeleton sequences for action recognition, in *Proceedings of the IEEE Conference on Computer Vision and Pattern Recognition*, 2016, pp. 3054–3062

E. Mansimov, N. Srivastava, R. Salakhutdinov, Initialization strategies of spatio-temporal convolutional neural networks, 2015, arXiv:1503.07274

R. Marks, System and method for providing a real-time three-dimensional interactive environment, Dec. 6 2011. US Patent 8,072,470

P. Mettes, J.C. van Gemert, C.G. Snoek, Spot on: action localization from pointly-supervised proposals, in *European Conference on Computer Vision* (Springer, New York, 2016), pp. 437–453

V. Mnih, K. Kavukcuoglu, D. Silver, A.A. Rusu, J. Veness, M.G. Bellemare, A. Graves, M. Riedmiller, A.K. Fidjeland, G. Ostrovski et al., Human-level control through deep reinforcement learning. Nature **518**(7540), 529–533 (2015)

P. Molchanov, S. Gupta, K. Kim, J. Kautz, Hand gesture recognition with 3d convolutional neural networks, in *CVPRW*, June 2015, pp. 1–7. doi:10.1109/CVPRW.2015.7301342

P. Molchanov, X. Yang, S. Gupta, K. Kim, S. Tyree, J. Kautz, Online detection and classification of dynamic hand gestures with recurrent 3d convolutional neural network, in *CVPR*, 2016

A. Montes, A. Salvador, X. Giro-i Nieto, Temporal activity detection in untrimmed videos with recurrent neural networks, 2016, arXiv:1608.08128

H. Mousavi Hondori, M. Khademi, A review on technical and clinical impact of microsoft kinect on physical therapy and rehabilitation. J. Med. Eng. (2014). doi:10.1155/2014/846514

K. Nasrollahi, S. Escalera, P. Rasti, G. Anbarjafari, X. Bar, H.J. Escalante, T.B. Moeslund, Deep learning based super-resolution for improved action recognition, in *IPTA*, 2015, pp. 67–72. ISBN 978-1-4799-8637-8, http://dblp.uni-trier.de/db/conf/ipta/ipta2015.html#NasrollahiERABE15

N. Neverova, C. Wolf, G. Paci, G. Sommavilla, G.W. Taylor, F. Nebout, A multi-scale approach to gesture detection and recognition, in *ICCVW*, 2013, pp. 484–491, http://liris.cnrs.fr/publis/?id=6330

N. Neverova, C. Wolf, G.W. Taylor, F. Nebout, Multi-scale deep learning for gesture detection and localization. ECCVW. LNCS **8925**, 474–490 (2014)

N. Neverova, C. Wolf, G.W. Taylor, F. Nebout, Hand segmentation with structured convolutional learning, in *ACCV. LNCS*, vol. 9005, 2015a, pp. 687–702. ISBN 978-3-319-16811-1. doi:10.1007/978-3-319-16811-1_45

N. Neverova, C. Wolf, G.W. Taylor, F. Nebout, Moddrop: adaptive multi-modal gesture recognition, in *IEEE TPAMI*, 2015b

J.Y.-H. Ng, J. Choi, J. Neumann, L.S. Davis, Actionflownet: learning motion representation for action recognition, 2016, arXiv:1612.03052

B. Ni, Y. Pei, Z. Liang, L. Lin, P. Moulin, Integrating multi-stage depth-induced contextual information for human action recognition and localization, in *FG*, April 2013, pp 1–8. doi:10.1109/FG.2013.6553756

B. Ni, X. Yang, S. Gao, Progressively parsing interactional objects for fine grained action detection, in *Proceedings of the IEEE Conference on Computer Vision and Pattern Recognition*, 2016, pp. 1020–1028

N. Nishida, H. Nakayama, Multimodal gesture recognition using multi-stream recurrent neural network, in *PSIVT*, 2016, pp. 682–694

S. Oh, A large-scale benchmark dataset for event recognition in surveillance video, in *CVPR*, 2011, pp. 3153–3160. ISBN 978-1-4577-0394-2. doi:10.1109/CVPR.2011.5995586

E. Ohn-Bar, M.M. Trivedi, Hand gesture recognition in real time for automotive interfaces: a multimodal vision-based approach and evaluations, in *IEEE-ITS*, vol. 15(6), Dec 2014, pp. 2368–2377. ISSN 1524-9050. doi:10.1109/TITS.2014.2337331

F.J. Ordóñez, D. Roggen, Deep convolutional and lstm recurrent neural networks for multimodal wearable activity recognition. Sensors **16**(1), 115 (2016)

W. Ouyang, X. Chu, X. Wang, Multi-source deep learning for human pose estimation, in *CVPR*, 2014, pp. 2337–2344

O.K. Oyedotun, A. Khashman, Deep learning in vision-based static hand gesture recognition, in *Neural Computing and Applications*, 2016, pp. 1–11

E. Park, X. Han, T.L. Berg, A.C. Berg, Combining multiple sources of knowledge in deep cnns for action recognition, in *2016 IEEE Winter Conference on Applications of Computer Vision (WACV)*, IEEE, 2016, pp. 1–8

X. Peng, C. Schmid, Encoding feature maps of cnns for action recognition, in *CVPR, THUMOS Challenge 2015 Workshop*, 2015

X. Peng, C. Schmid, Multi-region two-stream r-cnn for action detection, in *European Conference on Computer Vision* (Springer, New York, 2016), pp. 744–759

X. Peng, L. Wang, Z. Cai, Y. Qiao, Q. Peng, Hybrid super vector with improved dense trajectories for action recognition, in *ICCV Workshops*, vol. 13, 2013

X. Peng, C. Zou, Y. Qiao, Q. Peng, Action recognition with stacked fisher vectors, in *European Conference on Computer Vision* (Springer, New York, 2014), pp. 581–595

X. Peng, L. Wang, Z. Cai, Y. Qiao, *Action and Gesture Temporal Spotting with Super Vector Representation*, 2015, pp. 518–527. ISBN 978-3-319-16178-5. doi:10.1007/978-3-319-16178-5_36

L. Pigou, S. Dieleman, P.-J. Kindermans, B. Schrauwen, Sign language recognition using convolutional neural networks, in *European Conference on Computer Vision'14*, 2015a, pp. 572–578. ISBN 978-3-319-16178-5. doi:10.1007/978-3-319-16178-5_40

L. Pigou, A.V.D. Oord, S. Dieleman, M.V. Herreweghe, J. Dambre, Beyond temporal pooling: recurrence and temporal convolutions for gesture recognition in video. CoRR, 2015b, arXiv.org/abs/1506.01911

Y. Poleg, A. Ephrat, S. Peleg, C. Arora, Compact cnn for indexing egocentric videos, in *2016 IEEE Winter Conference on Applications of Computer Vision (WACV)*, IEEE, 2016, pp. 1–9

Z. Qiu, Q. Li, T. Yao, T. Mei, Y. Rui, Msr asia msm at thumos challenge 2015, in *CVPR Workshop*, vol. 8 (2015)

A. Radford, L. Metz, S. Chintala, Unsupervised representation learning with deep convolutional generative adversarial networks, in *Proceedings of International Conference on Learning Representations*, 2016

H. Rahmani, A. Mian, 3d action recognition from novel viewpoints, in *Proceedings of the IEEE Conference on Computer Vision and Pattern Recognition*, 2016, pp. 1506–1515

H. Rahmani, A. Mian, and M. Shah. Learning a deep model for human action recognition from novel viewpoints, *arXiv preprint* arXiv:1602.00828

S. Ren, K. He, R. Girshick, J. Sun, Faster r-cnn: towards real-time object detection with region proposal networks, in *Advances in neural information processing systems*, 2015, pp. 91–99

N. Rhinehart, K.M. Kitani, Learning action maps of large environments via first-person vision, in *Proceedings of European Conference on Computer Vision*, 2016

A. Richard, J. Gall, Temporal action detection using a statistical language model, in *CVPR*, 2016

H. Sagha, J. del R. Milln, R. Chavarriaga, Detecting anomalies to improve classification performance in opportunistic sensor networks, in *PERCOM Workshops*, March 2011a, pp. 154–159. doi:10.1109/PERCOMW.2011.5766860

H. Sagha, S.T. Digumarti, J. del R. Millán, R. Chavarriaga, A. Calatroni, D. Roggen, G. Tröster, Benchmarking classification techniques using the opportunity human activity dataset, in *IEEE SMC*, Oct 2011b, pp. 36 –40. doi:10.1109/ICSMC.2011.6083628

S. Saha, G. Singh, M. Sapienza, P.H. Torr, F. Cuzzolin, Deep learning for detecting multiple space-time action tubes in videos, 2016, arXiv:1608.01529

J. Scharcanski, M.E. Celebi, *Computer vision techniques for the diagnosis of skin cancer* (Springer, New York, 2014)

A. Shahroudy, J. Liu, T.-T. Ng, G. Wang, NTU RGB+ D: a large scale dataset for 3d human activity analysis, in *Proceedings of the IEEE Conference on Computer Vision and Pattern Recognition*, 2016a, pp. 1010–1019

A. Shahroudy, T.-T. Ng, Y. Gong, G. Wang, Deep multimodal feature analysis for action recognition in RGB+ D videos, 2016b, arXiv:1603.07120

L. Shao, L. Liu, M. Yu, Kernelized multiview projection for robust action recognition. Int. J. Comput. Vis. **118**(2), 115–129, June 2016, http://nrl.northumbria.ac.uk/24276/

Z. Shou, D. Wang, S.-F. Chang, Temporal action localization in untrimmed videos via multi-stage CNNS, in *CVPR*, 2016a

Z. Shou, D. Wang, S.-F. Chang, Temporal action localization in untrimmed videos via multi-stage CNNS. in *Proceedings of the IEEE Conference on Computer Vision and Pattern Recognition*, 2016b, pp. 1049–1058

Z. Shu, K. Yun, D. Samaras, *Action Detection with Improved Dense Trajectories and Sliding Window*, Cham, 2015, pp. 541–551. ISBN 978-3-319-16178-5. doi:10.1007/978-3-319-16178-5_38

K. Simonyan, A. Zisserman, Two-stream convolutional networks for action recognition in videos, in *NIPS*, 2014, pp. 568–576

B. Singh, T.K. Marks, M. Jones, O. Tuzel, M. Shao, A multi-stream bi-directional recurrent neural network for fine-grained action detection, in *Proceedings of the IEEE Conference on Computer Vision and Pattern Recognition*, 2016a, pp. 1961–1970

S. Singh, C. Arora, C. Jawahar, First person action recognition using deep learned descriptors, in *Proceedings of the IEEE Conference on Computer Vision and Pattern Recognition*, 2016b, pp. 2620–2628

K. Soomro, H. Idrees, M. Shah, Action localization in videos through context walk, in *ICCV*, 2015

W. Sultani, M. Shah, Automatic action annotation in weakly labeled videos. CoRR, 2016, arXiv.org/abs/1605.08125

L. Sun, K. Jia, D.-Y. Yeung, B.E. Shi, Human action recognition using factorized spatio-temporal convolutional networks, in *Proceedings of the IEEE International Conference on Computer Vision*, 2015, pp. 4597–4605

J. Tompson, Y.L. Murphy Stein, K. Perlin, Real-time continuous pose recovery of human hands using convolutional networks. ACM-ToG, **33**(5), 169:1–169:10 (2014). ISSN 0730-0301. doi:10.1145/2629500

D. Tran, L. Bourdev, R. Fergus, L. Torresani, M. Paluri, Learning spatiotemporal features with 3d convolutional networks, in *2015 IEEE International Conference on Computer Vision (ICCV)*, IEEE, 2015, pp. 4489–4497

P. Turaga, A. Veeraraghavan, R. Chellappa, Statistical analysis on Stiefel and Grassmann manifolds with applications in computer vision, in *CVPR*, IEEE, 2008, pp. 1–8

J.R. Uijlings, K.E. Van De Sande, T. Gevers, A.W. Smeulders, Selective search for object recognition. Int. J. Comput. Vis. **104**(2), 154–171 (2013)

G. Varol, I. Laptev, C. Schmid, Long-term temporal convolutions for action recognition, 2016, arXiv:1604.04494

V. Veeriah, N. Zhuang, G.-J. Qi, Differential recurrent neural networks for action recognition, in *Proceedings of the IEEE International Conference on Computer Vision*, 2015, pp. 4041–4049

S. Vishwakarma, A. Agrawal, A survey on activity recognition and behavior understanding in video surveillance. Visual Comput. **29**(10), 983–1009 (2013)

C. Vondrick, D. Ramanan, Video annotation and tracking with active learning, in *NIPS*, 2011

A. Waibel, T. Hanazawa, G. Hinton, K. Shikano, K.J. Lang, Phoneme recognition using time-delay neural networks, in *Readings in Speech Recognition*, 1990, pp. 393–404

H. Wang, D. Oneata, J. Verbeek, C. Schmid, A robust and efficient video representation for action recognition. Int. J. Comput. Vis. **119**, 1–20 (2015a)

H. Wang, W. Wang, L. Wang, How scenes imply actions in realistic videos? in *ICIP* IEEE, 2016a, pp. 1619–1623

J. Wang, W. Wang, R. Wang, W. Gao, et al., Deep alternative neural network: exploring contexts as early as possible for action recognition, in *Advances in Neural Information Processing Systems*, 2016b, pp. 811–819

L. Wang, Y. Qiao, X. Tang, Action recognition with trajectory-pooled deep-convolutional descriptors, in *Proceedings of the IEEE Conference on Computer Vision and Pattern Recognition*, 2015b, pp. 4305–4314

L. Wang, Z. Wang, Y. Xiong, Y. Qiao, CUHK&SIAT submission for THUMOS15 action recognition challenge, in *THUMOS Action Recognition challenge*, 2015c, pp. 1–3

L. Wang, Y. Xiong, Z. Wang, Y. Qiao, Towards good practices for very deep two-stream convnets, 2015d, arXiv:1507.02159

L. Wang, Y. Xiong, Z. Wang, Y. Qiao, D. Lin, X. Tang, L. Van Gool, Temporal segment networks: towards good practices for deep action recognition, in *European Conference on Computer Vision* (Springer, New York, 2016c), pp. 20–36

P. Wang, W. Li, Z. Gao, J. Zhang, C. Tang, P.O. Ogunbona, Action recognition from depth maps using deep convolutional neural networks. IEEE Trans. Hum.-Mach. Syst. **46**(4), 498–509 (2016d)

P. Wang, W. Li, S. Liu, Y. Zhang, Z. Gao, P. Ogunbona, Large-scale continuous gesture recognition using convolutional neural networks, in *Proceedings of International Conference on Pattern RecognitionW*, 2016e

P. Wang, Q. Song, H. Han, J. Cheng, Sequentially supervised long short-term memory for gesture recognition, in *Cognitive Computation*, 2016f, pp. 1–10

P. Wang, W. Li, S. Liu, Z. Gao, C. Tang, P. Ogunbona, Large-scale isolated gesture recognition using convolutional neural networks, 2017, arXiv:1701.01814

X. Wang, A. Farhadi, A. Gupta, Actions˜ transformations, in *Proceedings of the IEEE Conference on Computer Vision and Pattern Recognition*, 2016g, pp. 2658–2667

Y. Wang, M. Hoai, Improving human action recognition by non-action classification, in *Proceedings of the IEEE Conference on Computer Vision and Pattern Recognition*, 2016, pp. 2698–2707

Y. Wang, J. Song, L. Wang, L. Van Gool, O. Hilliges, Two-stream SR-CNNS for action recognition in videos, BMVC, 2016h

Z. Wang, L. Wang, W. Du, Y. Qiao, Exploring fisher vector and deep networks for action spotting, in *CVPRW*, 2015e, pp. 10–14. doi:10.1109/CVPRW.2015.7301330

P. Weinzaepfel, Z. Harchaoui, C. Schmid, Learning to track for spatio-temporal action localization, in *Proceedings of the IEEE International Conference on Computer Vision*, 2015, pp. 3164–3172

P. Weinzaepfel, Z. Harchaoui, C. Schmid, Learning to track for spatio-temporal action localization, in *ICCV*, Santiago, Chile, Dec 2015, arXiv: 1506.01929

P.A. Wilson, B. Lewandowska-Tomaszczyk, Affective robotics: modelling and testing cultural prototypes. Cogn. Comput. **6**(4), 814–840 (2014)

C. Wolf, E. Lombardi, J. Mille, O. Celiktutan, M. Jiu, E. Dogan, G. Eren, M. Baccouche, E. Dellandréa, C.-E. Bichot, C. Garcia, B. Sankur, Evaluation of video activity localizations integrating quality and quantity measurements, in *CVIU*, vol. 127, Oct 2014, pp. 14–30. ISSN 1077-3142. doi:10.1016/j.cviu.2014.06.014

D. Wu, L. Pigou, P.J. Kindermans, N. Le, L. Shao, J. Dambre, J.M. Odobez, Deep dynamic neural networks for multimodal gesture segmentation and recognition, in *IEEE TPAMI*, Feb 2016a

J. Wu, J. Cheng, C. Zhao, H. Lu, Fusing multi-modal features for gesture recognition, in *ICMI*, 2013, pp. 453–460. ISBN 978-1-4503-2129-7. doi:10.1145/2522848.2532589

J. Wu, P. Ishwar, J. Konrad, Two-stream CNNS for gesture-based verification and identification: learning user style, in *CVPRW*, 2016b

J. Wu, G. Wang, W. Yang, X. Ji, Action recognition with joint attention on multi-level deep features, 2016c, arXiv:1607.02556

Z. Wu, Y. Fu, Y.-G. Jiang, L. Sigal, Harnessing object and scene semantics for large-scale video understanding, in *Proceedings of the IEEE Conference on Computer Vision and Pattern Recognition*, 2016d, pp. 3112–3121

X. Xu, T.M. Hospedales, S. Gong, Multi-task zero-shot action recognition with prioritised data augmentation, in *Proceedings of European Conference on Computer Vision*, 2016

Z. Xu, L. Zhu, Y. Yang, A.G. Hauptmann, UTS-CMU at THUMOS 2015, in *CVPR THUMOS Challenge*, 2015a

Z. Xu, L. Zhu, Y. Yang, A.G. Hauptmann, UTS-CMU at THUMOS, 2015b

J. Yamato, J. Ohya, K. Ishii, Recognizing human action in time-sequential images using hidden Markov model, in *1992 IEEE Computer Society Conference on Computer Vision and Pattern Recognition, 1992*. Proceedings CVPR'92, IEEE, 1992, pp. 379–385

Y. Ye, Y. Tian, Embedding sequential information into spatiotemporal features for action recognition, in *CVPRW*, 2016

S. Yeung, O. Russakovsky, G. Mori, L. Fei-Fei, End-to-end learning of action detection from frame glimpses in videos, in *Proceedings of the IEEE Conference on Computer Vision and Pattern Recognition*, 2016, pp. 2678–2687

D. Yu, A. Eversole, M. Seltzer, K. Yao, Z. Huang, B. Guenter, O. Kuchaiev, Y. Zhang, F. Seide, H. Wang et al., *An introduction to computational networks and the computational network toolkit* (Technical Report, TR MSR, 2014)

J. Yu, K. Weng, G. Liang, G. Xie, A vision-based robotic grasping system using deep learning for 3d object recognition and pose estimation, in *2013 IEEE International Conference on Robotics and Biomimetics (ROBIO)*, IEEE, 2013, pp. 1175–1180

J. Yuan, B. Ni, X. Yang, A. Kassim, Temporal action localization with pyramid of score distribution features, in *CVPR*, 2016

J. Yue-Hei Ng, M. Hausknecht, S. Vijayanarasimhan, O. Vinyals, R. Monga, G. Toderici, Beyond short snippets: deep networks for video classification, in *CVPR*, 2015, pp. 4694–4702

S. Zha, F. Luisier, W. Andrews, N. Srivastava, R. Salakhutdinov, Exploiting image-trained cnn architectures for unconstrained video classification, 2015, arXiv:1503.04144

B. Zhang, L. Wang, Z. Wang, Y. Qiao, H. Wang, Real-time action recognition with enhanced motion vector CNNS, in *Proceedings of the IEEE Conference on Computer Vision and Pattern Recognition*, 2016, pp. 2718–2726

B. Zhou, A. Lapedriza, J. Xiao, A. Torralba, A. Oliva, Learning deep features for scene recognition using places database, in *NIPS*, 2014, pp. 487–495

T. Zhou, N. Li, X. Cheng, Q. Xu, L. Zhou, Z. Wu, Learning semantic context feature-tree for action recognition via nearest neighbor fusion. Neurocomputing **201**, 1–11 (2016)

Y. Zhou, B. Ni, R. Hong, M. Wang, Q. Tian, Interaction part mining: a mid-level approach for fine-grained action recognition, in *CVPR*, 2015, pp. 3323–3331

G. Zhu, L. Zhang, L. Mei, J. Shao, J. Song, P. Shen, Large-scale isolated gesture recognition using pyramidal 3d convolutional networks, in *Proceedings of International Conference on Pattern RecognitionW*, 2016a

W. Zhu, J. Hu, G. Sun, X. Cao, Y. Qiao, A key volume mining deep framework for action recognition, in *Proceedings of the IEEE Conference on Computer Vision and Pattern Recognition*, 2016b, pp. 1991–1999

C.L. Zitnick, P. Dollár, Edge boxes: locating object proposals from edges, in *European Conference on Computer Vision* (Springer, New York, 2014), pp. 391–405

Printed in the United States
By Bookmasters